Voyage into Substance

The MIT Press   *Cambridge, Massachusetts, and London, England*

Voyage into Substance

Barbara Maria Stafford

Art, Science, Nature, and the Illustrated Travel Account, 1760–1840

© 1984 by
The Massachusetts Institute of
Technology

This book was set in Palatino
by The MIT Press Computergraphics
Department
and printed and bound by Halliday
Lithograph
in the United States of America.

Library of Congress Cataloging in
Publication Data

Stafford, Barbara Maria, 1941–
Voyage into substance.

Includes bibliography and index.

1. Voyages and travels—Pictorial
works. 2. Landscape in art.
3. Illustration of books. I. Title.
G468.S73
1984   910′.9′033   83–18802
ISBN 0–262–19223–3

The MIT Press wishes to thank the
Publication Program of The J. Paul
Getty Trust for making it possible to
maintain high quality standards in
producing this book.

Publication of this book has been
aided by a grant from The Millard
Meiss Publication Fund of the College
Art Association of America.

MM

Publication has also been aided by a
grant from the National Endowment
for the Humanities.

For Fred
La seconde condition, plus rare à ren-
contrer et plus malaisée à improv-
iser . . . c'est d'avoir pour compagnon
de voyage le compagnon de sa
vie. . . .
Rodolphe Töpffer *renversé*

Contents

List of Illustrations

Preface

In this study I examine the landscape elements that were featured in European illustrated travel accounts published roughly between 1760 and 1840—from their heyday to the advent of photography. I have not hesitated, however, to include pertinent material from earlier and later periods. This holds true also for important nonfiction travel accounts that were not illustrated, such as that of the Lewis and Clark expedition, if they shed light on contemporary attitudes toward the varieties of terrain.

Sifting through the massive publications of travel accounts which the eighteenth and the early nineteenth century produced requires a good deal of selectivity. Nonetheless, I attempt to include all major scientific voyages and expeditions with a natural-history bent that fall within the period of study, especially those that incited great public interest. I have also tried to be catholic in my choice, casting a wide net to embrace representatives of Germany, Sweden, Spain, and Russia as well as England and France. (All translations not otherwise attributed are my own.) For the most part, the relations discussed reach into the more remote regions of the earth and the atmosphere, but I do not neglect unexplored territories closer to home. The unifying factor behind these disparate ventures is the explorers' unblunted appetite for natural phenomena, an enthusiasm expressed both verbally and visually.

The focus of this investigation is thus, of necessity, trained on the strong alliance forged between art and science during the Enlightenment and the subsequent embodiment of this ideal in land, sea, and air explorations carried out "for a purpose." To this end, I am at pains to distinguish and dissect the scientific aesthetic of discovery from that concurrently espoused by the followers of the Grand Tour or the mere seekers after Picturesque scenery. In this regard, the book differs substantially from those previously published on the topic of the imaginary voyage or the travel lie. Further, the masterly studies of Percy G. Adams, Philip Babcock Gove, Hans Joachim Possin, and Paul van Tieghem, who dwell on the fictional incarnations, and those of Clarence J. Glacken, Yi Fu Tuan, and Numa Broc, who ponder the cultural and geographical ramifications, have not been matched by art-historical investigations.

While research on the Picturesque tours and gardens abounds and continues to grow (one thinks of recent works by Dora Wiebenson, Ronald Paulson, John Dixon Hunt, and Gerald Finley), what Angus Fletcher felicitously calls the literature and art of fact has attracted only a handful of scholars. Indeed, even literary historians—with the notable exceptions of Charles L. Batten in his *Pleasurable Instruction: Form and Convention in Eighteenth-Century Travel Literature* (Berkeley: University of California Press, 1978) and Richard B. Schwartz in his *Samuel Johnson and the New Science* (Milwaukee: University of Wisconsin Press, 1971)—have avoided searching for the commonality between the fine arts and the empirical sciences during the second half of the eighteenth century. In various ways, this volume bears on the question of the nature and type of that interrelationship as it manifests itself in nonfiction travel narrations and the accompanying descriptive prints. This work concerns itself, then, with a bivalent genre, one that includes both literature of fact and pictorial statement, both scientific *compte-rendu* and natural history—that is, descriptive word wedded to accurate image. Above all, it is a genre whose very existence and popularity is based on an ardent yearning for facts rather than fictions.

After an introductory discussion that compares and contrasts past and present landscape traditions with those evinced in the texts and illustrations of the scientific voyages, I trace in chapter 1 the rise and development of an empirical attitude toward nature. To accomplish this, I focus first on the radical reforms of language, involving the abolition of varnishing metaphor and the development of a paratactic style, that arose in England and France in the early seventeenth century. I then try to indicate how a "passionate intelligence" and Bacon's inductive "contemplation" came to be thought requisite for the accurate perception of the "real thing" and its "plain" transmission in a "transparent" and "masculine" idiom.

In chapters 2 and 3 I survey the vast repertory of individual obdurate objects and ephemeral effects that the travel account simultaneously revealed and documented as constituting the physiognomy of the earth. During the course of this exposition I examine seventeenth- and eighteenth-century geological, physical, and chemical theories concerning "hard" and "soft" bodies, or, broadly speaking, the widespread apprehension of a universe filled with both enduring robust substances and intermittent or fleeting apparitions and natural powers.

All this leads to a fundamental eighteenth-century assumption: that the infinite metabolism of matter is legible and hence penetrable. In chapter 4

I develop the theme of the secular emancipation of the earth, of singular traces strongly merged with a vital or animate universe—signs that require the lexical gaze of the natural historian rather than the transformational vision of the theologian. The illustrated geological, mineralogical, and biological treatise is shown to be a powerful precursor and ally of the nonfiction travel relation; in both, the investigator functions as a modern Pliny or Empedocles, confronting, probing, and reading natural characters as they actually are rather than skimming over, personifying, or transmuting them into what they are thought to be.

Next, I take up certain identifiable psychological traits that seem to stamp the voyager, regardless of his nationality, and ask how they shaped his perception of the world. Even when part of a group, the scientific explorers perceived their attack on the environment as an escape into freedom, a solitary encounter with a plethora of things resolved into the primal experience of space as vertical or horizontal or as height, depth, and extent. Their overriding goal was to discover the unknown, to see the unseen, to be the first to tread the margins of the world.

In chapter 6 I demonstrate how inquiry made intense produced far-reaching aesthetic repercussions by underscoring novel dimensions of space and also by punctuating particular moments in time. The firsthand and concrete perception of a specific phenomenon, at an identifiable moment, was possible only when observations were "made on the spot." Admiring yet probative scrutiny of the natural object was based on the profound awareness that it was an independent and powerful presence, possessing a history separate from that of man. Further, it fostered a perspective taken from the viewpoint of the object. Such absorption in the chronology and duration of the object is contrasted with the self-absorbed lapse out of time experienced in reverie, meditation, and withdrawal from the world.

In the final chapter I suggest that although the scientific travel account continued to flourish in the nineteenth century, the communicative conventions by which it operated changed significantly. Further, by 1800 a strong reaction had set in, opposing not only the marriage between art and science (the utilitarian premise on which these accounts rested) but also the emphasis on natural facts unaltered by the freewheeling imagination. Despite this caveat, I propose specific ways in which the legacy of the factual travel narrative, forged during the second half of the eighteenth century, shaped nineteenth-century attitudes toward landscape representation. The obsession with a particular, charged site; the isolated, potent natural masterpiece, centrally stationed within the picture plane or commemorated as sculptural and architectural monolith; the "truth to material" dictum discernible in Ruskinian art theory; the attempt to seize the unseizable in a landscape; and even the "romantic" flight into the interior and the reaction against an excess of visibility and external "thingness" are seen as part of the travel narrative's aesthetic bequest.

Acknowledgments

I owe a debt of gratitude to the National Endowment for the Humanities, which awarded a Fellowship for Independent Study (1979–1980) that enabled me to complete the research, and to the Center for Advanced Studies in the Visual Arts of the National Gallery of Art in Washington, D.C., where, as a Senior Fellow, I was privileged to discuss ideas and compose a final draft in truly humanistic surroundings. First and foremost, I should like to thank Dean Henry A. Millon and Assistant Dean Marianna Shreve Simpson of the CASVA for creating a unique environment conducive to scholarly creation and exchange. I am also indebted to the CASVA Fellows for 1981–1982, in particular Irene Bierman, Peter Brunette, Donald Preziosi, and Claire Sherman, for their stimulating presence and their probing questions.

For clarifying the perplexities of Enlightenment philosophy, I am grateful to Professor John W. Yolton, whose seminar on British Eighteenth-Century Materialism, given at the Folger Institute in the fall of 1981, I had the pleasure of attending.

More long-standing debts are owed to Mildred Archer, Keeper of the Department of Prints and Drawings at the India Office Library in London, whose generosity opened those doors to me time after time, and to Roger Quarm, Assistant Keeper of Prints and Drawings at the National Maritime Museum in Greenwich, England. Over the years, the staffs of many libraries have borne partiently with my inquiries, including, most recently, Margo Grier, Tom McGill, and the librarians at the National Gallery of Art. But none assisted me more than the people at the Library of Congress, who, in addition, twice and blessedly assigned me a desk on D Deck.

At all stages of this work, interest and encouragement from friends, colleagues, and fellow scholars has proved invaluable. I think especially of Devin Burnell and Dora Wiebenson, who patiently and openly shared their extensive knowledge and their love of the eighteenth century and inspired me by their example. In addition, I am grateful to Percy Adams for his thoughtful reading of the manuscript, and I thank Dean Karl J. Weintraub of the University of Chicago for helping to defray the cost of photo reproduction rights and other last-minute expenses.

I owe very special thanks to Irene Gallas and Cecilia Gallagher, but it was Deborah Gómez, above all, who took responsibility for the typing of the manuscript. My debt to her is boundless.

Finally, I wish to acknowledge the support of the MIT Press staff.

Voyage into Substance

Introduction: The Taste for Discovery

Things are stubborn and will not be as we fancy them or as the fashion varies, but as they stand in Nature. Shaftesbury

The fundamental assumption of this book is that, at some point near the beginning of the seventeenth century, a profound conviction was coherently voiced that something really is out there and that art and language were to be used to get beyond imitation—that is, beyond a hallowed art and language—in order to grapple with real things. This conscious rejection of certain established mental constructions became part of the larger Enlightenment struggle to avoid the conventionality of verbal and visual languages in pursuit of an unmediated nature.

During the eighteenth century an admirable campaign was waged to get at the truth of the phenomenal world without imprisoning it in self-revelatory idiosyncrasy. The nominalistic impulse will be seen to be most precisely located in the historical context of a modern secularizing movement directed against the falsehoods of ancient imaginings of reality.

The illustrated factual travel account presents an almost pure instance of the possibilities thought inherent in this mode of vision for getting to the bottom of things, precisely because its "art" (or lack thereof) seems to hold itself aloof from any generally available convention of signification. By definition, the explorer's subject is not a known commodity but an alien nature.

It was in the explorers' implementation of a method of discovery based on a willed nonmetamorphic scrutiny of the particulars of this world that truth telling was elevated to aesthetic status. Resisting allegorical or any other nonoptical transformational modes, the traveler in search of fact relied on an exploratory method consonant with that of empirical science as it was defined in the seventeenth century. The explorer's enterprise, like the scientist's, was predicated on the belief that he could discover a tangible (not an illusory) world exuberant with details and alive with individualities that would withstand customary patterning, generalization, or schematization.

One important result was that the particular, under the pressure of intense and original seeing and as it emerged from the humble and "low" descriptions of the travel narrative, gave back the intensities normally linked with traditional "high" genres and "elevated" emotions connected to the heroic and the Sublime. Consequently, the "literature of fact," functioning as an instrument for public knowledge and responding to the serious call for verifiable truth enunciated by the sciences, pointed the way to the salvation of "high" art that had become trivialized through its reliance on too much art and too little matter.

The scientific explorer-artist-writers, in trying to break from the limits of solipsism, custom, and habits of representation, strained to be extra-referential. What emerges from their texts and illustrations is a sense of continuing and demanding alertness to the human desire to inflict oneself on the world. This vigilant resistance to the temptations of illusion and unguided imagination and this denial of self-imposition give these accounts their special flavor of authenticity.

My discussion begins with the fact that much of the later eighteenth century's interest in natural phenomena defined itself against the practices of the Picturesque, in all its historical embodiments. By the same token, the explorers were less interested in the involuntary effect of experience on the individual—the whole psychology-oriented and audience-related strain of eighteenth-century aesthetics—than in the demonstrable nature of the experience itself. Seeking to penetrate a nature conceded to be entirely legible (if sometimes difficult to see), the quester after fact stood at the antipodes from the seeker after sensations who, while wandering over the superficies of this world, capriciously altered them.

Yet it is indicative of the serious challenge posed by an arduous aesthetic that preferred plain transcription of material things to their facile amplification and heightening that the author of a Picturesque journey sometimes felt compelled to emulate his opposite. There are passages to be found, even in the most colored account, in which the traveler, assuming the mantle of the natural philosopher, delivers knowledge with the least possible alteration by a connotative rhetoric. Thus, it is a telling example of historical continuity that, just as in the Renaissance, when a "simple" transcription of natural phenomena crystallized within the heart of a highly mannered and ornate style, so too in the eighteenth century the unvarnished descriptive representation of concrete matter and its documented effects were codified in the midst of a spontaneous and pointedly associative view of landscape.

Willed Seeing

*Every blockhead does that; my
Grand Tour shall be one round the
whole globe.*
Joseph Banks

Among the many "tastes" available in the latter part of the eighteenth century, none was more congenial to the innovative desires of the age than that for discovery. It flourished throughout Europe alongside that for the Picturesque, and indeed was its rival. The frequent identification of the appetite for the *pittoresco* in nature with the writers of travel literature calls for examination of certain salient aspects of this concept: the astonishing, the novel, the unusual, and the extraordinary.[1] Both in the illustrated *voyage pittoresque* or *romantique* and in the landscape garden bearing that designation, nature came to be looked upon pictorially—that is, as a series of pictures created to simulate automatic aesthetic enjoyment. Joseph Hardy's generalized relish for the High Pyrenees is typical of the attitude of such an "enraptured admirer of Nature in all her grand and most interesting features."[2] But it was the Reverend William Gilpin, the assiduous pioneer of Picturesque travel, who bonded its characteristic (and dissonant) visual qualities of roughness of texture, irregularity of outline, and variegated colors to a peculiar kind of beauty that is agreeable in a picture.[3] Sir Uvedale Price and Richard Payne Knight reiterated this position at the close of the century.[4] (However, these two antagonists differ when it comes to the question where this quality is found. Price locates it in the external object; Knight roots it in the beholder's innate modes of perception, in the impulsive energies of the mind.)

In France these same qualities of intricacy and strong, surprising contrast had already manifested themselves around 1730 in the artificial garden, which succeeded the simple, natural *Régence* form.[5] As in the case of the natural objects stumbled across during the English Picturesque tour of some 30 years later, these were "arranged" for the purpose of eliciting unbidden emotions. Thus, judgment was suspended and amusement would be aroused in the beholder rather than any real interest in the particularity of the thing itself. In short, external phenomena existed primarily for the purpose of being provocative.

Similarly, the foliage and turf of Stowe, as in a painted landscape by Claude Lorraine or Nicolas Poussin, subsume raw nature to the transformative energies of the mind. Even the rude boulders and mineral stratifications encountered in Alexander Pope's grotto at Twickenham—despite their geological accuracy—share the underlying philosophy of William Kent's garden, namely the rearrangement of nature's materials in accordance with harmonies already determined by man.[6] A fundamental paradox lodges in all this recasting, since the landscape garden is the only art form that does not seek to evade the physical incursions of matter but actually courts the cooperation of organic growth and decay. At the heart of this irony dwells the central issue of Associationism and the individual's response to a garden's form. The picturesqueness of natural objects depends on the fact that they recall their imitations, that is, their representations

INTRODUCTION: THE TASTE FOR DISCOVERY

in a painting: ". . . Nature's common works, by genius dress'd, with art selected, and with taste express'd. . . ."[7] From this initial and circuitous association sprang a host of others. All were predicated on the heedless arousal of a sequence of ideas that, by definition, flee from the object. In this respect, the tourist, the pursuer of the merely scenic and the Picturesque, differed profoundly from the type of traveler under consideration. The former was interested in the evocation of intuitive reactions, the latter in the deliberate study of external singulars. Thus we can understand the scientifically trained Joseph Banks's fit of pique when some of his more conventional friends said he was a fool to sail with James Cook to the South Seas but should embark upon a European Grand Tour instead, to which he tartly replied "Every blockhead does that; my Grand Tour shall be one round the whole globe."[8]

The serious, scientific traveler was determined to break out of the metaphorical mode of simply "seeing as."[9] The expanded physical universe forced him to focus; he was goaded into observation by so alien a natural scene. Consciously achieving such an underivative and fresh outlook was a Herculean project. Everything seemed to militate against it, particularly the psychological straitjacket of Associationism. By the middle of the eighteenth century, Associationism was so entrenched that its theory had been scrutinized by most English writers on aesthetics, including Thomas Hobbes, John Locke, Joseph Addison, Francis Hutcheson, and Lord Kames. To complicate matters, its arguments shifted constantly. Nevertheless, from Hobbes onward, a central premise holds true: that motion determines all mental activity. That is, single images formed from information gathered by the senses involuntarily generate "trains" of ideas in the mind. The result is serial vision or fancying.[10]

The Picturesque garden does not differ in principle from its supposed antithesis, topiary. In the latter, man dominates, forcing nature and natural substances into inflexible, witty, and highly artificial molds. In the former, unembellished natural form qua natural form is equally disregarded because of the associative faculty's ruthless powers for avoidance of actual contact, untrammeled mental wandering, and selective seeing for the purpose of stimulating the imagination.[11] In both instances what is of interest is the worked-upon, not the working, world.

This enfeebling of material objects was intrinsically inimical to voyagers who believed that distant or strange lands and their marvels existed without the need for human intervention. It proved to be a useless philosophy to explorers of places that, unlike Europe, were not full of recognizable ruins of early civilizations and historical relics fraught with the memory of the myths and legends of the West.

Emptied of their theoretical content, Associationism and its attendant phenomenon, the Picturesque, did nonetheless make a formal contribution to the depiction of foreign landscapes at the close of the eighteenth century.

Specifically, William Gilpin's creation of an "encapsulated" landscape,[12] his use of an individualistic foreground image to prod the imagination, was to be an important (though severely restructured) legacy. In time, the expressive power of the ambient would conflict with the intimation or presence of a human motive or passion that always lurked within the anthropocentrism of the Picturesque.[13]

There was, however, one major designer of landscape gardens who, unlike the creators of Picturesque parks, chose to promote the forms of the terrain itself. Lancelot ("Capability") Brown, in deigning to emphasize the basic materials of the site by studiously eliminating any ostentatious design elements, seems to have heralded the vogue for an artless nature. Brown banished from the garden the groves, temples, inscriptions, and statues that had been placed there to inspire the mind.[14] His attitude was akin to that of the scientific traveler, whose task compelled keen perception, judgment, and loyalty to the given facts of the world to gain knowledge. Although they resembled "common fields," as William Chambers sneered, "naked" Brownian compositions indicated that the garden—freed from encumbrances—might yet be counted among the new localities of empirical philosophy.[15]

Not only was the Picturesque taste doomed to fail among gardenists (it was given the *coup de grace* by Humphry Repton); the garden itself as artificial construct, including the Brownian version, was to be deserted for a wider world. The tourist was pushed out of an ornamental setting into a vast experiential universe. Nor was this revolution limited to England. The French increasingly looked to Switzerland for the dramatic effects found in the later French Picturesque garden, such as the one at Méréville (begun in 1784), and eventually turned to firsthand examination of nature. The important landscape painter and theorist Pierre-Henri Valenciennes speaks for this new attitude when he declares axiomatically, concerning gardens, that "one cannot create nature."[16]

The insufficiency of the decorative garden in the face of the realities of a constantly expanding sensible universe was to become a leitmotif of the travel book. François Le Vaillant, in his 1790 *Voyage dans l'intérieur de l'Afrique*, denigrates the English garden, saying that its streams, artificial hummocks, pretty paths, decaying bridges, and constructed ruins blight the spirit and tire the eye, particularly when one has witnessed the naturally verdant fields of South Africa's Pampoen-kraal.[17] Désiré Raoul-Rochette, in his 1824 *Lettres sur la Suisse*, bitingly satirizes the English garden with its "parasitical ornaments," so methodically created, and its diversities, so miserably monotonous in effect; in short, suggests Raoul-Rochette, man's petty means reveal his insufficiency when contrasted with the surrounding reality of the Swiss mountains.[18] Pervading this criticism is the assumption that such gardens exist only as objects of amusement, as mere stage settings offering scenic variety conducive to a stroll.

A word must be said about the Picturesque's theatrical emphasis, its captious surface play in which art wrestles with nature's intractable and rude materials. Alexander Pope used "scenes" at Twickenham, and Hubert Robert incorporated *"grands tableaux"* at Méréville. In either case, the simple elements of nature were transformed into a series of magnificently conceived and frequently exotic events in which spectators were fully absorbed.[19] The importance of stage design for the representation of natural effects cannot be overemphasized, though I will take up only those aspects of its history that have direct bearing on the problem.

Since the Hellenistic period a kinship had existed between rock painting and landscape. Images of stylized, steep, and ultimately stage-prop boulders wended their way through the mosaics of the Early Christian and Byzantine periods, down to Giotto, Fra Angelico, and Jan and Hubert van Eyck.[20] Italian stage perspective influenced Joachim Patinir's and Henri met de Bles's stone monoliths and helped to ensure that the natural formation established itself as a dominant foreground motif.[21] In turn, the South succumbed to the influence of the North during the second half of the sixteenth century, when Paolo Fiammingo and Lodewijk Toeput (both active in Venice) induced Giacomo Torelli to develop a landscape approach in which figures serve as minor accessories in a vast, dramatic landscape.

An engaging theatrical vocabulary of caves, rocky cliffs, sylvan settings, and inlets—all stressing a wild, untamed environment—was employed more and more. Of course, this "satyric" or rustic mode had been categorized as far back as Vitruvius. Its sinister dens, dark caverns, and dank, fetid places reappeared during the Renaissance. Through the genius of the Florentine stage designer Bernardo Buontalenti, the satyric or landscape setting took on real importance.[22] Filippo Juvarra, in improving upon the *scena per angola* favored by the Galli-Bibiena family, transmitted this rough and mood-filled ambient to the eighteenth century.

It was crucial to the formulation of garden theory that the representation of entangled wilderness depended on the handling of nature in such a way as to produce dramatic, if not spectacular, effects. The belief in the interchangeability of the illusions of theater and the appearances of reality motivated Claude-Henri Watelet, who expounds on the *"spectacle de la nature"* in his 1774 *Essai sur le jardin*, and during the next decade this interest spilled over into Philippe-Jacques de Loutherbourg's phantasmagoric fabrications of nature in flux, created for the *Eidophusikon*.[23]

What concerns us most here is the close affinity between this theatricality, or contrived experience, and exoticism. The invocation of the Chinese garden to justify, among other things, the creation of rockeries and grottos—made known through the writings of seventeenth- and eighteenth-century Jesuit missionaries—suggests the filtering influence of stage design.

The reputedly "pleasing," "enchanted," and "terrible" scenes found in the Imperial Garden in Peking, with their overtones of Burkeian sublimity and their baffling of the spectator's judgment, appear to have left an indelible impression on Sir William Chambers, evident in his influential *Designs for Chinese Buildings* (1757).[24]

Concomitant with this cultivation of deliberate artificiality, which, as in the case of the Picturesque garden, was predicated on a belief that nature is worthwhile only if it astonishes through the intervention of human ingenuity, there emerged the antithetical notion that the interesting could also be completely natural. The same travel accounts that reported on unnatural decoration provided ample evidence of the Far Eastern veneration of living matter. The upholding of the opinion that every locality is individual, unique, and perhaps even numinous expanded the connotation of the exotic.[25] The most important source for both attitudes—and they coexist happily in this narrative—is Johan Nieuhof's *Embassy from the East Indian Company of the United Provinces* (1669),[26] which was published in Dutch, German, and English and in many editions. Nieuhof admiringly and vividly describes the enormous hollowed-out rockeries (*Steinrotzen*) that he saw in several ancient gardens in Peking. In addition to praising these "cliffs made by art," he describes at length the strange mountains and hills of China, unexcelled masterpieces of nature used since time immemorial by geomancers. This passage points to a larger outlook that may be designated the Taoist view of nature. A "philosophy" based on the perception of the earth as a living organism, it affected a variety of eighteenth-century intellectual trends, ranging from Leibniz's dream of a universal religion to the physiocrats' will to return to the land to the travelers' discovery of a sentient earth.[27] What Nieuhof achieved for China, Engelbert Kaempfer accomplished for Japan. His illustrated travel accounts not only discuss Shintoism, replete with its animistic implications, but also stipulate that for the Japanese nature is sacred. Like the Chinese, the Japanese, in creating a garden (except the stone or dry landscape associated with Zen Buddhism), were permitted to modify nature only in order to make it appear more natural.[28]

Enargeia and Energeia

When Catherine saw the pedestal for the first time she asked with an air of displeased surprise "What has been made of the rock!"
Robert Ker Porter

Strivings between nature and art are age-old. In the West, from the time of the Pre-Socratics to the modern era these two concepts were regarded as antinomies; yet an inherent epistemological tension kept them tied together, while separate, so that nature was thought to be that which the artifice of man had not altered.[29] Nonetheless, even in antiquity the word *natura* had many connotations.[30] One that is germane identifies the term with the objective, natural appearance or manifestation of a thing, suggesting a congruence between the natural and the objectively worthy or the general. In an extension of this view, nature could also be understood in a primitivistic vein as the cosmic order, the good or godly in contradistinction to the human, artificial, and civilized society founded on error and circumstance. This thesis implies that the universe is saturated by

INTRODUCTION: THE TASTE FOR DISCOVERY

mind and constituted of ceaseless motion that renders it intelligent and alive. Philostratus's *Life of Apollonius of Tyana* cogently expresses this Pythagorean doctrine of the universe as a great animal, and this panvitalist teaching was perennially vital from the time of Thales down to the Renaissance.[31]

During the Quattrocento the multiple meanings of *natura* were codified, and in subsequent art theory they were identified with two concepts that originated in Greek thought: *natura naturata*, the replication of created nature, and *natura naturans*, the imitation of the processes of creating nature. The latter had been expounded by Democritus, who construed art as the manifestation of nature in action. This position was further developed in the Neo-Platonism of Plotinus (*Enneads* 5.8, 1), who asserted emphatically that the arts do not simply copy visible things but draw on productive principles that constitute the foundations of nature. We may gauge the importance and tenacity of this conception when it is phrased another way: that nature as a power outstrides the individual natural appearances of real things found in the ordinary world surrounding the artist.[32] Out of the complexities of this theory emerged Alberti's idea that nature was perfect as a whole but not necessarily in its parts, that therefore the artist must descry its most beautiful aspects, and that, thanks to judicious selection, a work of art may be more perfect than a work of nature.[33] Countless eighteenth-century critics, chief among them Diderot, warmed to this view that nature's productions are aesthetically imperfect, haphazard, and lacking any real aim or directing force, and that hence natural phenomena are the objects of imitation but it is art that is creative.[34] In a nutshell, this is the attitude of the creators of Picturesque taste. The life-giving power of art by means of its *energeia*—as Plutarch and Horace stipulate—designates the making of the inanimate to "act like things living." Art must wreak kinesis upon dead matter and, for all practical purposes, create something out of nothing. The force of art is so efficacious that its productions appear to "live."[35]

During the eighteenth century these wrestlings of art with nature became more acute. The shift or parting of the ways to be pinpointed is the moment when nature was no longer seen "as" art and, conversely, art was no longer perceived as supplementing and supplanting nature. At the beginning of the century, Addison conveniently set the stage by reiterating the time-honored question: Which is superior, art or nature?[36] He discerns the right of each to primacy, thus preparing the way for the onslaught of testimonials. A characteristic manner in which nature was aesthetically vindicated was through the delight aroused by the disclosure of previously unknown examples of regularity in the cosmic architecture. It was implied that a natural object can acquire the status of an artifact, and that where nature is beautiful it is so because it is like art and unlike itself. The latter disposition spans the century, from the Augustans to Kant. It was not the only one, nor was it always consistently expressed;[37]

nonetheless, its tenacity—like that of Associationism—set the stage for a critical dispute.

That nature is full of works of art and art is full of natural curiosities was, as I have observed, part of the legacy of opposition bequeathed by the Far East and its major contribution to eighteenth-century exoticism. It is also to be found in the recording of "sports of nature" and *ludi* extensively described by Pliny and passed on to the Middle Ages and the Renaissance.[38] The illustrated scientific voyage, regardless of nationality, perfectly corroborates this view while subtly altering the emphasis. Sir William Hamilton, in his *Campi Phlegraei, Observations on the Volcanoes of the Two Sicilies* (1776), minutely observes that "the streams of lava that run down the steep flanks of a volcano [Vesuvius], always cut regular and narrow channels, in fact, so regular as to appear the work of art, and lava is confined to these channels of its own making."[39] Analogously, the "discoverer" of Fingal's Cave, Joseph Banks, declares that its celebrated basaltic pillars are "almost in the shape of those used in architecture." The Swiss biologist Charles Bonnet discourses on the similarity between fossils and marquetry and between salt crystals and obelisks.[40] The French explorer Jean-Baptiste Le Gentil offers an apologia for an impressive rock quarry at Mauritius exhibiting strata so neatly made that one might easily conclude they were "molded" and then laid by art.[41] George Vancouver, in his *Voyage of Discovery to the North Pacific Ocean* (1798), is astounded to find near Monterey "the most extraordinary mountain [he has] ever beheld." "On one side," he continues, "it presented the appearance of a sumptuous edifice fallen into decay; the columns which looked as if they had been raised with much labour and industry were of great magnitude. . . ."[42] The Swiss speleologist Carl Lang, on his journey to examine the world's celebrated natural caverns, notes that at Antiparos the picturesque grouping of stalactites gives the impression of a painting.[43] With the last statement we come full circle, back to those critics who for centuries were more interested in art than in nature.

Yet an alternative view coexisted with the one just indicated, sometimes inhabiting the identical text. This view gives the particular—the mere appearance, *natura naturata*—superiority over the artistic production on the basis of the presumption that God is the supreme artist and the world is a great work created by him. This theme, like its antithesis, was enunciated powerfully at the beginning of the eighteenth century. For Shaftesbury, the recognition of nature's distinctive wonders is predicated neither on their resemblance to human efforts nor on an obligation to conform to a generalized amalgamation of the world's contents. No, glorious nature is supremely fair precisely because its "every single work affords an ampler scene, and is a nobler spectacle than all which ever art presented." Shaftesbury's emphasis on "things of a natural kind, where neither art nor the conceit nor caprice of man has spoiled them" is based not on the perception of their regularity but rather on the fact of their being individual "rude" rocks, "mossy caverns," grottos, uncouth forms—the conspicuously unwrought embodiments of the teeming chaos of natural life.[44]

A major factor in nature's regaining some of its former magical properties was the confirmation of the sentience of matter. Not art but nature is alive.[45] By the middle of the eighteenth century one finds amazing reversals. The Abbé Laugier's interpretation of the primitive hut no longer has it mimicking the first, tentative steps of human craft hypothesized by Vitruvius, but rather has it incarnating the inventiveness of nature.[46] Giovanni Battista Piranesi's etchings visually metamorphose remnants of Roman architecture into dynamic natural forms; the cryptoporticus of a villa becomes an *arco naturale*, and the wreckage of the Colosseum is a fractured volcanic crater.[47] Travel literature of all sorts contributed substantially to this conversion. Jean Houel's *Voyage pittoresque* (1782) offers the transformation of the ruins of the Temple of the Olympian Jupiter at Agrigentum into a "sea" or "ocean" of debris.[48] Not only does Houel copy it as such, he also states that this was his intention. Of the *View of the Remains of the Largest Temple at Selinunte* he writes that "the columns become visible from such a great distance, that it is as if one were at sea, and they offered guidance to the ship's pilot."[49]

Inextricably bound to the taste for ruins is the fact of their having been rooted for ages in the soil, assimilated with it, and thus behaving more like works of nature than like works of art. J. H. Bernardin de Saint-Pierre addresses both the question of archaeological debris, mired in matter, in which art becomes obscured by losing the battle to an encroaching nature, and the natural fragment itself. Upon the sight of unpolished and unsquared rocks, natural monuments, and masterpieces, he exclaims how futile and useless appear the magnificent piles that man erects.[50]

Georg Forster, a crucial figure in Anglo-German relations and a scientist and world traveler who accompanied Cook on his second voyage, expresses an analogous fashionable primitivism. In his *Ansichten vom Niederrhein* (1791–1794) he comments that the high, slender columns in the nave of Cologne Cathedral stand "like the trees of a primeval forest."[51] Similarly, Goethe and Johann Jakob Wilhelm Heinse descriptively dissolved the entirety of Strassburg Minster into plant forms in accordance with the belief that artistic energy had become merely one manifestation of organic nature.[52] Not until 1789, however, was this premise carried to its inevitable conclusion. In that year the German scholar Samuel Witte published his treatise on the origin of the pyramids. With an outburst of rapture appropriate to one who has undergone an epiphany—and basing his findings on the sober writings of the French vulcanologists Nicolas Demarest and Barthélemy Faujas de Saint-Fond—he joyously proclaims the Egyptian pyramids, the Palace of Darius at Persepolis, the temples of the Incas in Peru, and the rock caverns at Ellora to be basalt eruptions. In sum, he naturalizes all the archaeological remains of ancient civilizations.[53]

How did art sink so low? Science was culpable. For the moment, consider the opinion of George Adams. In his 1787 *Essays on the Microscope*, this British author discusses the consternation to be experienced in examining microscopically certain objects usually considered triumphs of art and artifice: "What a humiliating contrast shall we meet with!" Deformity and imperfection are everywhere in evidence in the work of man. Even more astounding than nature's superior regularity (which had impressed earlier thinkers) is its immense and seemingly inexhaustible variety.[54] Nature creates directly, exuberantly, lavishly; it requires no intermediary. Witte's notion that earthquakes, volcanic eruptions, and other physical calamities had created the colossal masterpieces of antiquity does not differ at bottom from the straightforward proclamations of toiling botanists; the practice of engraving actual plant skeletons, that is, printing the anatomy of the leaf and thus achieving an immediate impression also renders art super-fluous.[55] Even evanescent atmospheric phenomena were not considered void of artistic potential; it was claimed that the sun daily "paints" itself in watery reflections, in parhelias and rainbows, making such perfect portraits that it is exceedingly difficult to distinguish the likeness from the original.[56] The entire environment was ready to become a work of art independent of any human interference. The circumnavigator Bruny d'Entrecasteaux best sums up this attitude in *Voyage à la récherche de La Pérouse* (1792) by saying that vigorous nature is always old and perpetually new.[57]

If nature is creative, embodying its energies in individual manifestations, the argument ran, then art is mechanical, a mere machine. The French vitalist Jean-Baptiste-René Robinet states this explicitly: "Man has discovered the laws of mechanics, but of a completely artificial and external mechanism. . . . all his machines are inorganic, & the vast buildings in which he roams as if lost are but lifeless heaps, without motion. On the contrary, everything lives in nature, all the beings which it produces are essentially organic. . . ."[58] It is notable that the simile of painting functioning like a *"grande machine"* surfaces in the midcentury treatises of the Abbé Jean-Bernard LeBlanc, La Font de Saint-Yenne, and Antoine-Joseph Dézallier d'Argenville.[59] It is just this lifeless, conventionalized, and generalizing machinery of art, attempting to construct a coherent whole from an assemblage of parts, that Robinet attacks. Precisely at the heart of the definition of *machine* is that it consists more of craft and manipulation of the beholder than in the free power and sturdiness of matter.[60]

A concrete instance of the preference for nature's processes over the automata of art is made salient by their juxtaposition in Etienne Falconet's equestrian statue of Peter the Great. The critical furor over the pedestal for this monument is a case in point. Faujas de Saint-Fond deems the immense and indestructible block of granite, hauled at great expense from the Karelian swamps, worthy of inclusion in his *Essai de géologie* (1803–1809). He intimates that it, not Falconet's potentially friable bronze sculpture, will attest eternally to the greatness of the monarch.[61] A decade later, Robert Ker Porter, traveling in Russia, laments that Falconet tampered with this now enormous "but formerly most astonishing" mass. The French sculptor's none too restrained chiseling of the base "by fine curves and studied shapes soon robbed it of all sublimity" and "left nothing of nature but the matter of which it was composed." According to Porter (a former student of Benjamin West), Catherine the Great showed no sympathy for this attempted subjugation of powerful and animate substance to the listless rules of art and the spirit of decoration.[62] She irately demanded of Falconet, "What has been made of the rock!"[63]

Equivocal Artifice, Characteristic Nature

Et quant aux termes qui seront assis sur le rocher des fontaines, il y en auroit un qui seroit comme une veille estatue mangée de l'ayr ou dissoutte à cause des gelées, pour demonstrer plus grande antiquité. Et après cestuy-là il y en auroit un aultre qui seroit taillé en forme de rocher rustique, au long duquel il y auroit plusieurs mousses et petites herbes, et un nombre de branches de lierre, qui ramperoient à l'entour d'iceluy pour denotter une grande antiquité. . . .
Bernard Palissy

The Augustan habit of seeing a thing in different ways at the same time, which gave rise to the polysemous forms[64] of the Picturesque garden and the multiple perspectives of the Grand Tour, was being countered simultaneously by the scientific and vitalist realization that the natural object possesses an innate character in its own right. Where, in the history of art rather than in the history of ideas, did this notion of expressive particularity arise? Paradoxically, it can be identified within that most deliberately artificial of styles, Mannerism. The ambiguous attitude toward nature so typical of the late sixteenth century is nowhere more in evidence than in the architectural nymphaeum or *baignerie*.[65] Most influential of all, however, for the eighteenth-century garden, and for eighteenth-century science as practiced by Bernard de Fontenelle, Georges-Louis-Leclerc, Comte de Buffon, and Georges Cuvier, were the ceramic grottos at the Tuileries and the Palais Ecouen designed by Bernard Palissy. Executed in Palissy's ingenious *style rustique*,[66] they appeared untouched by man. Their creator was constantly spurred by the desire to present art not as equivalent but as identical with a segment of nature. Palissy was not only interested in the energies of *natura naturans*; he was also genuinely smitten by naturalia, that is, the individual expressions of a humble *natura naturata*. His geological and paleontological researches, discussed in *Recepte véritable* (1563), *Architecture*, and *Discours admirables* (1577), found concrete outlet in the creation of wonderful pottery. The fabrication of *rustique figulines* involved taking molds of rocks, plants, and reptiles, then glazing them with realistically colored enamels for the purpose of not only expediting the process but also ensuring complete verisimilitude.[67]

This difficult technique was seamlessly conjoined with Palissy's wish to conform to the weatherbeaten ruggedness and primeval antiquity of his models. In his grottos destined for the Duc de Monmorency and Catherine de Medici, natural forces seemed to slowly transform the features of matter.[68]

It is Palissy's "science" that distinguishes him from other practitioners of the *stilo nonfinito*.[69] His confidence in induction and empiricism caused him to discover purpose and perfection where his contemporaries discerned only chance, *scherzo*, caprice. With him, Mannerist *stupore* or the stunning of judgment when encountering "freaks of nature" changes into lucid awareness for everything robustly phenomenal. On the other hand, in the famed grottos of Pratolino, Castello, and Boboli, and in Francesco Primaticcio's Grotte de Pin at Fontainebleau, a playful tension always exists between morphous and amorphous, between art and nature—a *difficultà* predicated on maintaining the observer in a state of irresolvable ambiguity. Although in these gardens human and animal figures tend to merge with their surroundings, the forms left purposively uninterpreted (for example Gian da Bologna's colossal Apennines at Pratolino, Bartolommeo Ammanati's identical subject at Castello, and Michelangelo's Slaves at Boboli) are intended to breed deception and unclarity, not perspicuous awe for the real thing.[70]

The same love of paradox crops up in the *Weltlandschaft* of the North, which, in trying to embrace the earth in its totality, shows, not accidentally, the influence of the progressive exploration of the cosmos.[71] Joachim Patinir and Jan Mostaert, in particular, created landscapes exhibiting fantastic and disquieting earth formations that do not merge with, but crush, all staffage figures. The hostile wastes depicted seem to express an intuition of primeval slime (also found in the wild surroundings painted by Albrecht Altdorfer), and the high chalk cliffs appear on the verge of becoming menacingly animate.[72]

The anthropomorphic and zoomorphic picture puzzle, or rotatable *Vexierbild*, shared the Mannerist property of polysemousness; the human or animal head amalgamated with a rocky, water-ringed landscape represented only a single point of departure for multiple interpretations of changing shapes and thus accentuated the composition's inherent lack of clarity.[73] The Arcimboldesque recipe of composed heads—based on the assumption that man is a *mixtum compositum* of all creation—was given continued prominence in the early seventeenth century. At this time it must be related, however, to the Islamic and Far Eastern custom of recognizing in the configuration of the terrain the traces of gigantic demiurges, dragons, and tigers, thereby capturing in tangible form the hidden transformative forces of the universe.[74]

Among the most significant formal contributions made by the late Mannerist landscape, and a tenet that resurfaced in the Picturesque, was the activated foreground of the picture plane in which impressive singular landscape elements were grouped ornamentally.[75] As Heinrich Franz has convincingly demonstrated in the landscapes stemming from the 1590s by Peter Stevens, Cornelis van Dalem, Lucas van Valckenborch, and Gilles van Coninxloo, a dominating rock mass was singled out from the fantastic multiplicity that constituted the mature Mannerist landscape. In cartouche fashion, the now autonomous formation was abruptly juxtaposed with a distant view that it dialectically served to both "confront" and "screen."[76] These large isolated fragments, which in Patinir and his followers functioned only as contributing motifs in a wide panoramic *Weltlandschaft*, now became the main pictorial theme, detached from the meaning of the rest of the composition.

At the same time, a generation of artists was hard at work opposing such discontinuities. The growth of pure "view" painting, in which landscape becomes the image of a section of nature rather than embracing a visionary global space, was basically subversive of Mannerist aesthetics.[77] Nevertheless, late Mannerism's focus on sublime particulars and its eschewal of the placid domesticity of the quotidian was to be revived in the illustrated voyages of the eighteenth and the early nineteenth century. Similarly, its cultivation of linear abstraction, optical restlessness, and ornamental framing devices would recur during the Rococo period.

A process of clarification ensued during the Baroque period that had objects behaving unambivalently: either as art or as nature, not "as if" one or the other.[78] The precipitating out of various landscape categories tended to eradicate ambiguity. For example, Roger de Piles in his *Cours de peinture* (1708) institutionalizes this separatist view by confining himself to a discussion of two kinds of landscape: the heroic and the pastoral or rural. He does this despite the reiteration of Renaissance assurances that "landscape is a type of painting that represents the countryside and all the objects in it" and that "of all the productions of art and nature there is none that cannot be admitted into the composition of these paintings."[79] In other words, as a genre it is not inferior or subordinate to any other.

The heroic use of landscape—at the farthest remove from the fanciful caprice, and embodied in certain paintings by Poussin—implies that nature possesses a determinable physiognomy. It literally echoes or corresponds with human action and human history, not in accordance with the older language of allegory (as in the *paysage moralisé*) but in a newly expressive manner.[80] Like the otherwise totally dissimilar late Mannerist work, nature no longer functions simply as background or mood setting for human activity. Nonetheless, in the epic vein, art's powers are concentrated on producing a general effect of grandeur in nature as a whole enunciated in a particular mode.

Although it is in striking counterpoint to Poussin and Claude, Salvator Rosa's employment of hyperbole in summoning up scenes of pendant rocks is also imbued with a generalized, not a particularized, expression. Sir Joshua Reynolds in his *Lives* states, concerning the Neapolitan artist, "Everything is of a piece: his Rocks, Trees, Sky, even to his handling, have the same rude and wild character which animated his figures."[81] Reynolds makes perfectly clear that, whether we are dealing with the loftiness of the elevated style or the idiosyncrasy of the characteristical (not to mention the ornamental), these designations do not imply that each and every thing in nature possesses a distinctive physiognomy. Quite the opposite. In either style, natural objects are given a unified cast that imposes on them this or that general character but certainly not highly individualized traits. Thus, despite the growing ascendancy of Rosa's fame in the second half of the eighteenth century, he was not praised by the advocates of particularity, although, as expected, he figures prominently in the reports of the Picturesque travelers.[82]

A more fruitful avenue of exploration in the search for aesthetic origins leads directly from the prophetic Mannerist union of colossal architecture and sculpture with nature to the Baroque. The Austrian architect Johann Bernhard Fischer von Erlach, through his influential *Historische Architektur* (1721), played a decisive role in disseminating the taste for immense scale, dynamic power, and spectacular siting of buildings that seemed to vie with nature's sublimity. Indeed, Fischer's Baroque categories—shaped by seventeenth-century travel narratives—were remarkably prescient of Burke's emphasis on vastness, gloom, opacity, and the elemental massiveness of matter.[83]

Fischer has been singled out precisely because of the cosmopolitan nature of his style. It is rooted in a vivid awareness of Dutch and Portuguese trade, in the recognition of an internationalism fostered by missionaries to China, and in the hermetic investigations into strange and exotic cultures undertaken by such unorthodox scholars as Athanasius Kircher.[84] Instead of concentrating on Greece and Rome, he juxtaposes gigantic structures found in the ancient Near and Far East. Fischer surveyed for the first time all the famous monuments that were then known and placed each in its historical and geographical context. Not only did he graphically indicate the natural character of the countries in which these constructed marvels were situated, he also included representations of several natural or ambiguous wonders.[85] It is impossible to overemphasize the importance for the eighteenth century of Fischer's illustrations of enormous artificial and natural forms preserved in their existing state and maintaining their natural integrity. In short, Fischer adopted the means of the factual travel account and made them serve a useful aesthetic end.

Among Fischer's most powerful images is the realization of Deinocrates's Hellenistic project, the transforming of Mount Athos into the figure of Alexander the Great (figure 1).[86] This reconstruction is particularly apt because it forces the beholder to gaze determinedly upon the landscape configuration. Such focus must not be confused with the ambiguous, playful Mannerist *Vexierbild* and its instantaneous provocation of phantasia as if by chance. Fischer does not show Alexander's body indistinguishably bonded to stone; rather, he emphasizes the different composition of their individual substances. This separation of man from nature's matter and the visual implication that the earth—like the hero—leads an epic life of its own was to become a leitmotif of eighteenth-century writings on natural history. It also represents part of the evolution that catapulted nature into a position of superiority over art. In the last analysis, Fischer is not interested in the outer world as the mere random setting and occasion for the display of human ingenuity or a theater where the thing in itself can be pried apart from its appearance in the work of art.

Fischer's undertaking to depict accurately the sites in which the architectural masterpieces of antiquity were embedded raises the far-reaching issue of scientific naturalism and the quest for topographical verisimilitude.[87] That the formulation of a "zero degree" style—based on the perception of a real model and on a visual analysis of the natural world— was connected to scientific interest is amply illustrated by certain Renaissance masters. Andrea Mantegna's legendary "geological relish" is a recurrent feature of his work, most conspicuously evident in the basaltic crystallizations of the Uffizi Madonna of the Quarry.[88] Similarly, immense natural rock formations, scrupulously observed, crop up frequently in the paintings and drawings of Leonardo da Vinci and Albrecht Dürer.[89] In the North, the mineralizations of Hieronymus Bosch and Pieter Brueghel the elder, the dramatic landmarks along the River Meuse of Patinir, and the craggy embankments of Gerard David all testify to a new and intimate knowledge of the composition of matter.[90] At this time, alchemy was in many respects one of the experimental sciences, and it involved a practical acquaintance with the behaviors of various substances.[91]

But the roots of the Renaissance's sympathetic and investigatory attitude toward nature go back to the Hellenistic age. Appositely, Hellenistic science, in the person of Ptolemy, developed a form of illustration based on using maps to reproduce the specific contours of countries rather than presenting large undefined areas of the world. These cartographic *chorographies* included "topography," that is, the representation of typical, characteristic sites or settings.[92] (Apelles reputedly also possessed that magical ability to reproduce what lay before his eyes.) The rendering of a specific aspect and an identifiable place rather than a *Wunderkammer ludus* is at the heart of what, in the seventeenth century, particularly in the Low Countries, was codified into view painting.[93] Unlike the *vedute ideata, capriccio,* or fanciful scene of such eighteenth-century Venetians as Francesco and Giovanni Antonio Guardi and Giovanni Paolo Pannini, the topographical view stressed precision. From the 1760s on it was sustained on a magnificent scale by the efflorescence of sumptuously illustrated travel books, published in the wake of scientific voyages, that flooded all the major capitals of Europe.[94] The popularity of topography seemed to lend credence to Giovanni Paolo Lomazzo's assertion that with *paesi* one might image the universe.[95]

At the beginning of the eighteenth century the distinction between landscape painting (as the imaginary construction of an ideal of scenery, whether epic, Arcadian, or wildly rustic) and topographical painting (as the factual portrait of an actual place outdoors) began to crumble. The dictates of science urged a move away from the formulas of view hunting in the manner of Claude or Jacob von Ruisdael toward the naturalistic depiction of scenery that was worthy in itself. The topographer ascended to, if he did not transcend, the level of the landscape painter precisely insofar as he emulated the penetrating, retentive habit of obervation instilled in the scientist.[96] The process recapitulated the transference of aesthetic values from the artifact to the natural object.

There are two major modes of perception inherent in the topographical approach. The first represents a fondness for wide—either shallow or deep—panoramas. These ignore the foreground, leaping over its relative emptiness to give an impression of distance and remoteness to the landscape and the objects it contains.[97] The second mode embodies a passion for minuteness and contracted sight that is consubstantial with the meticulous recording of the "look" of strange localities. This foreground focus owes to the tradition of naturalist-artists who carefully absorbed the appearance of the particularity situated before them.[98] Both visual methods, by their very connection to a field of interest outside of art (the world of natural objects), connect with other disciplines similarly inclined to explore the appearance of physical things. This relation, in turn, points toward a novel solution for a vitiating criticism: the impossibility of proving topographical accuracy.

Increasingly, during the course of the eighteenth century, artists discovered the multiple faces of landscape as specifically understood and experienced at first hand by geologists, mineralogists, and botanists, the promulgators of new and experimentally verifiable ideas about the earth.

Running like Ariadne's thread through thematic and stylistic considerations alike, and spanning the gamut from Mannerism to the Baroque, is the artistic struggle either to subvert or to capture the sensuous physicality of nature's matter. By contrast, the Rococo style as created by Jacques La Joue, Juste-Aurèle Meissonnier, and Nicolas Pineau seems to dematerialize the world.[99] What could be more remote from the fastening of a keen mind on its object than fleeting reverie? Yet Rococo paintings of mist and vapor are the altered precedents for the metamorphosis of poetic evanescence into scientifically inspired ephemera—specifically, into the nebulous and the *grisâtre* also found within the pages of the factual travel book. Consequently the latter spurred interest not only in enduring natural masterpieces, the earth's monumental features, but also in fugitive atmospheric effects and intangible physical forces that pervade the universe. Admittedly, the predilection of the creators of the *fête galante* for decorative fantasies, artificial settings, and blurred visions of a golden age *locus amoenus* is far removed from the straightforwardness of topographical reality.[100] Nonetheless, at a deeper level, with the Rococo style's development of a sixteenth-century materialistic vocabulary—an instance of Mannerism *redivivus*—these discussions come full circle.

The use of *rocaille* (an amalgam of pumice, stalactites, and rocks cleverly heaped up in paradoxical refashioning of nature) in eighteenth-century garden grottos was a lighthearted reprise of Palissy's technique of taking castings directly from life. Once again we find that fascination for artful rupestral particularities, for those multiple lithic fragments, ruins, and specimens that constituted the components of the original *style rustique*, but now they function wholly as divertissements. These playful and illusory ornaments were perceived to exist in a seamless margin between art and nature and to be formed by both.[101]

Both stylistically and materially, the Rococo contributes to our topic on at least two levels. The display of expressive energy incarnated by the dynamic and organic arabesque of the ornamental print, which harks back to the vitalist *Knorpelstil* of the sixteenth century, provides a visual correlative in an artificial medium to the scientific valorization of the concrete powers of nature.[102] At the same time, the interest of Rococo artists in capturing "unpaintable beauties"—those physical substances whose very essence it is to vanish—finds corroboration in the existence of an actual atmosphere that vivifies the inorganic world. Further, the monolithic earth *rocaille*—whether in the ambient of the world or that of art—gives itself (or is given) over to the forces of time and decay. Thus, it reasserts the power inhering in any material medium, natural or artistic.[103]

Although the scientific spirit was hostile to the fragile and idyllic creations of the Rococo, the period was rife with cabinets of natural history founded by avid collectors and artists.[104] These were brimming with samples that showed nature complexly manifesting itself in picturesque forms of wood and stone. It is ironic that this playful view of science as a source of delectation helped, in the end, to impel ornament out of the aesthetic sphere into the living, growing world.

Abandoning the Ornamental Garter

Le gôut des découvertes dans tous les genres est la marque caractéristique des siècles éclairés. . . .
Raymond de Saugnier

In the eighteenth century, as during the Renaissance, great explorations abruptly widened the cultural and geographic horizon. The world of realities in which men lived changed, growing broader, richer in possibilities, and ultimately limitless. The eighteenth century undertook and largely achieved a heroically vast description of the sensible universe that moved from discovery to discovery. It is against this background that the expression "the taste for discovery" becomes comprehensible.[105]

Already in the seventeenth century the word *infinity*, which had been associated with God, had begun to be applied to an expanded cosmos. The New Science, especially Newton's astronomical physics, permitted a view of the whole of a detranscendentalized nature.[106] By extension, it was left to the remainder of the eighteenth century to conquer the physical universe down to its minute particulars. The triumphant note of discovery was sounded, not quite simultaneously, in France and in England. Pierre-Louis Moreau de Maupertuis, in his *Lettre sur le progrès des sciences* (1750), addressed to Frederick the Great, focuses on what he considers to be the three burning issues of his day: the locating of a Northwest Passage to Asia, the ascertaining of the real stature of the enigmatic Patagonians, and the discovery of the Great Southern Land or Continent.[107] He urges that an enlightened prince should launch two or three ships each year for the sole purpose of resolving these perplexing matters, reasoning optimistically that even if the stipulated purpose of the expedition is not met "it scarcely would seem possible, considering all the things which remain unknown on the face of the globe, that one could not achieve some great discovery."[108] This reflection leads Maupertuis to a lengthy disquisition on the investigation of "new marvels," both curious and important, which ought to be encouraged by the government. The list adds up to an impressive summary of the leading scientific concerns of the day, from electricity to dreams, but it is the conclusion that is momentous. In a utopian prophecy, Maupertuis pronounces that the scientist's time has come and that shortly he will replace the philosopher, as abstract or theoretical divigations have flourished for many centuries but in all that time metaphysics has not progressed one iota.[109] As many were to conclude after Maupertuis, speculative (that is, cabinet) philosophy would never subjugate the physical world.

Denis Diderot, in particular, voiced his support for scientific progress. Five years after the publication of Maupertuis's treatise, he glowingly described the great revolution taking place "at this moment" in the sciences. In the *Pensées sur l'interprétation de la nature* Diderot formulates the axiom that an era in which society esteems inventors is an era in which the sciences are burgeoning, and like his predecessors he marvels that all his contemporaries share the hope of distinguishing themselves in the eyes of posterity by some illustrious discovery.[110] Simultaneously, Diderot's *Encyclopédie* stated that, although the word *discovery* had been bestowed upon everything new appearing in the arts and sciences, this lax usage imparted an erroneous connotation to the term. The author claims that its sense is not simply one of novelty but that it also denotes knowledge, usefulness, and difficulty.[111]

That the aims of scientific discovery and of the research voyage were completely compatible had already been made plain by Maupertuis (a traveler of note himself), but it was Charles de Brosses who canonized the objective of disinterested scientific exploration within the framework of a factual travel narrative. He is, if not the earliest writer to formulate what might be called a psychology of discovery, one of the earliest. The preface to de Brosses's monumental *Histoire des navigations aux terres australes* (1756) sets forth what must surely have appeared a shocking program. He bluntly states that an expedition must have no other goal than that of being successful, and that not until the voyage is a total success should anyone be occupied with gainful activities. He assures the reader that these practical exigencies will present themselves after the fact of discovery and in due course. Then follows the crucial passage: "Too much haste in enjoying the fruit of one's projects often leads only to their failure. In the beginning let us think of nothing but geography, of the pure desire to discover, of the acquiring of new lands and novel inhabitants for the universe. . . ." In this undertaking the serious traveler must emulate the profound mathematician who, after attempting to fathom abstractions that initially have no aim other than pure knowledge, witnesses them becoming the objects of applied science.[112]

Somewhat later than the French, and in a different genre, the English debated the merits of scientific discovery. Edward Young, in his not unique but highly influential *Conjectures on Original Composition* (1759), laments the famine of poetic invention and asserts that, in order to repopulate this wasteland of the unattached imagination, writers should incorporate scientific findings into their compositions. This assertion gains additional force in our context when Young claims that at the moment man has larger prospects of enriching his imagination because physical, mathematical, and scientific knowledge is on the increase, and "these are new food to the Genius of a polite writer."[113] In other words, poetry should avail itself of scientific genius and scientific discoveries in order to extricate itself from its dearth of inventiveness. Henceforth, and to the close of the eighteenth century, the primacy of scientific genius was ensured. The researchers' inventions and constant discoveries were, as William Duff expressed it in his 1767 *Essay on Original Genius*, the result of a dominant, vivid, plastic "imagination" that illuminates like the "collected, concentrated, piercing rays of vision" rather than the "diffused" light of poetry. Moreover, original genius (the highest form) is identified with a radical power of the mind capable of "discovering something new and uncommon in every subject on which it employs its faculties."[114]

But it is John Hawkesworth, the much-maligned compiler of the voyages of Commodores Byron, Wallis, and Carteret and Captain Cook, who reminds us that the most comprehensive and meaningful definition of discovery is one that incorporates travel. In 1764, George III, shortly after he ascended the throne, began a campaign to search out untrodden lands. His navigators were given the same general and deliberately open-ended instructions outlined by de Brosses some 10 years earlier. Quite simply, their task was to make discoveries in the southern hemisphere.[115]

The entire age was dominated by travelers. Hence the aptness of Michel Foucault's comment that the two fundamental perceptual structures of the eighteenth century were a child's being born blind and later receiving sight and a foreign observer's shock at being thrust into an unknown country.[116] These primal experiences alter the processes of vision in a way that is possible only when a fundamental discovery is made.

The contemporaries of Captain James Cook and Jean-François de Galaup, Comte de La Pérouse, unlike those of Charles Darwin, lived in a period in which nature seemed new and many landscapes remained to be discovered, far from the Victorian conviction that the extremities of the earth had been penetrated and the limits of knowledge reached. Andrew Sparrman, the Swedish naturalist who accompanied Cook on his first tour of the South Seas, affirms this taste for great scientific voyages when he claims their accounts had never been more popular than in 1777. Sparrman's acknowledgment of the "avidity" with which these relations were bought up and the "eagerness" with which they were read furnish undeniable proof of the era's "turn for experiment" and its "disposition to enquire."[117]

But it is time to let the travelers speak for themselves.

As early as Cornelius Le Bruyn's *Travels to Muscovy and Persia* (1737) a sense of urgency was being voiced in the matter of producing discoveries. Upon returning to The Hague after 19 years of uninterrupted journeying, Le Bruyn was again anxious to wander despite infirmity and old age. As he proudly informs the reader, scholars have persuaded him that he might still make discoveries of greater importance "than he had been able to make in former days."[118] Like so many gentlemen of the seventeenth and the early eighteenth centuries, Le Bruyn intended mainly to search into and meditate upon the antiquities of the countries he encountered. However, in the next generation the purposes of the travelers changed. Here is Cook glancing back at the achievements of his initial expedition to observe the transit of Venus: ". . . although discovery was not the first object of that voyage I could venture to traverse a far greater space of sea, till then unnavigated, to discover greater tracks of country in high and low South latitudes, and to persevere longer in exploring and surveying more correctly the extensive coasts of these new discovered countries, than any former Navigator, perhaps, had done during one voyage."[119] Still more emphatic is George Vancouver's profession of faith: "In contemplating the rapid progress of improvement in the sciences, and the general diffusion of knowledge since the commencement of the eighteenth century, we are unavoidably led to observe, with admiration, that active spirit of discovery, by means of which the remotest regions of the earth have been explored. . . ."[120]

It seemed as if there was nothing that could not be embraced by "the spirit of traveling and investigation."[121] The Estonian Adam Johann von Krusenstern, in the record of his circumnavigation (1813), states unambiguously that in the narration of a voyage "not undertaken professedly with the view of making discoveries" his curiosity is "less excited than in one where discovery is the primary object."[122] The growing premium placed on witnessing the new, on a purity of perception, gave rise in the nineteenth century—when novelty's horizon was shrinking—to the rep-

INTRODUCTION: THE TASTE FOR DISCOVERY

resentation of the act of finding. A paradigmatic case is that of Lieutenant Hood, who accompanied the first of the Franklin expeditions to the Polar Sea and commemorated the moment of "the Expedition discovering the Copper Mine River"[123] (figure 2).

There is abundant testimony that the taste for discovery functioned as an antidote to the triviality thought to have been rampant in the pre-Enlightenment era. The indictment of triviality was never stronger than when it issued from the French. Reporting on the invention of the hot air balloon and the stunning possibility of "space" travel, the *Journal de Monsieur* contrasts the marvelous decade of the 1780s with the century's "ignoble past." The anonymous author declares unreservedly that few epochs in the annals of mankind can vie with the years 1777–1783 in superb events and singular discoveries.[124]

The balloon promenade escaped the onus of superficiality by appealing to the Baconian criterion of practicality that was applied to other scientific ventures. De Brosses chose to begin his polemic passage on the need for discovery with an exhortation from the *Instauratio Magna de Augmentis Scientarum*. He reminds a war-embroiled Europe that, unfortunately, *la gloire* is the passion of kings and it has been their persistent error to seek it on the battlefield. But, he says, Francis Bacon knew better. Only in discovery is the grandeur of the objective matched by usefulness. De Brosses concludes that "to augment the earth with a new world, to enrich the old world with all the natural productions and serviceable customs of the New; this would be the effect of such a discovery."[125] Bacon had proclaimed the advancement of knowledge for the benefit of mankind as the goal of the scientist, and his affirmation that the purpose of such research was neither to acquire fame nor to produce miracles but to improve the condition of mankind was absorbed by all the explorer-scientists.[126]

Jacques-Etienne and Joseph-Michel Montgolfier's fateful realization of lighter-than-air flight at Annonay in 1782 led to more and more "instructive voyages" in aerostatic craft. The popular periodicals of the day warned that the hardy aeronauts would achieve immortality only if their discovery were to be "put to scientific service."[127] The meteorologists were the first scientists to perceive the enormous significance of this radical expansion of nature. The French meteorologist Pierre Bertholon, in his impassioned apologia for "aerostats," ranks them with diving bells and sees no end to the illuminating investigations that can be carried out in the upper reaches of the atmosphere and in the depths of the sea.[128] Indeed, the word used for balloon flight—*expérience*—was synonymous with experiment.

Primarily, it was hoped that the balloon would provide answers to age-old questions concerning the secrets of different climatic conditions, thereby opening up entirely new fields of knowledge.[129] Among other things, the aerial traveler was expected to take hygrometric and barometric measurements like his maritime counterpart. He was also expected to perform

Figure 1
J. B. Fischer von Erlach, *Mount Athos
Transformed into Alexander the Great*, from
Historische Architektur, 1721, I, pl. 18.
Engraving.

Figure 2
John Franklin, *The Expedition Discovering
the Coppermine River*, from *The Polar Sea*,
1823, pl. p. 237. Drawing by Lt. Hood,
engraving by Edward Finden. Photo
courtesy British Library, London.

a variety of acoustical and electrical experiments in mid-flight. But his supreme task was to examine and record attentively everything that could be learned about the behavior of meteors. Consequently, Bertholon urges that a camera obscura be carried along during flights. Bertholon transcribes a ravishing vision in which he is transported into cloudy regions where weather and wind conditions change before his very eyes. Here water vapors freeze and coalesce into snow, the moon's corona and the sun's parhelion become distinct, and the rainbow appears at last as a perfect circle rather than an imperfect arc.[130] Further, the naturalists Tiberius Cavallo and Faujas de Saint-Fond point out that by the use of these marvelous flying machines the shape of certain seas and lands may be better ascertained than by conventional overland or water exploration. And with what ease! The balloonist soars over mephitic swamps, untraversable mountain ranges, dangerous plains, and barren ice caps while his earthbound brethren toil and tire below.[131] To the inventor of the hydrogen *charlière*, J. A. C. Charles, goes the honor of being the first aeronaut to carry instruments to measure atmospheric pressure and temperature. In 1803, another physicist, the colorful Belgian "Professor" E. G. Robertson, leaving from Hamburg, proposed the first truly scientific flight; this attracted scholarly attention the world over. Less flamboyantly, astronomers and chemists, among them Pierre-Simon de LaPlace, Claude-Louis Berthollet, Jean-Baptiste Biot, and Jean-Louis Gay-Lussac, were pressed into service to create new experiments for the laboratory in the stratosphere.[132] In 1804 Gay-Lussac himself took to the air.

Despite Charles de Brosses's valiant attempt to deflect royal attention away from warmongering to the arena of disinterested discovery, the military use of the balloon began in 1793 with the siege of the city of Condé. The National Convention wanted to organize a troop of military aeronauts and succeeded in establishing a school of aerostatics at Meudon. After his return from the Egyptian campaign, Napoleon closed that institution because he knew only too well the zeal for liberty of its founder, Nicolas-Jacques Conté. However, the problem at the heart of balloon invasions (Bonaparte contemplated crossing the Channel in a surprise attack) remained that of guidance.[133] This problem also affected scientific excursions. Difficulties with steering may have squelched the use of the balloon as a spy instrument or a tool of war, but did not dampen the ardor of travelers.

That balloon flights were considered a valid if not superior method for scientific exploration was made plain by Bertholon:

If voyages made to other climes and under other skies, if these circumnavigations are so strange, so interesting, so practical in pushing back the frontiers of science through the comparison of exotic objects which they reveal, is it possible for us to believe that those undertaken above our earth, and in the vast stretches of the atmosphere, could be any less instructive and capable of piquing curiosity? Yes, soon we shall witness bold aerial navigators, the Columbuses, the Vascos de Gama, the Bougainvilles, the Cooks, the Pagès, animated by a noble ardor, thrusting themselves into the plains of the air, and embarking under the auspices of physics and of the Montgolfiers on aerostatic voyages into regions that seem prohibited to man. . . .[134]

Whether on land, in the air, or upon the sea, from 1760 until the 1830s, we are unavoidably enmeshed in an epoch in which spatial discoveries loom large. And what is appealing about these innumerable and dangerous adventures is the intensity of pleasure they convey. The enjoyment and evident relish mirrored in these narrations is based on the idea that the scientific traveler is usefully, not trivially, engaged. No one could speak more to the point of *utile et dulce* than Cook: "Was it not for the pleasure which naturly results to a Man from being the first discoverer even was it nothing more than sands and Shoals, this service would be insuportable especially in far distant parts, like this [Australia], short of Provisions and almost every other necessary. The world will hardly admit of an excuse for a man leaving a Coast unexplored he had once discover'd. . . ."[135] La Pérouse lends his voice to the chorus: In the past, expeditions were undertaken out of ambition and self-interest. These motives cannot be confused with the pleasure produced by "voyages of discovery whose object is to carry beneficences to human kind, and to swell the field of science." Public pressure was so great that even business enterprises, hardly known for their philanthropic largesse, were at pains to change their purely commercial image. Thus, Samuel Hearne assures the reader of his *Hudson's Bay to the Northern Ocean* (1796) that the Company is not "averse to making discoveries of every kind."[136]

The scientific or predominantly factual voyage, then, differed decidedly from all other forms of wandering. James Bruce, in his *Travels to discover the source of the Nile* (1790), meditates that this new golden age that finally saw humanitarian interests united with those of science exempted men of liberal minds and education, "employed in the noblest of all occupations, that of exploring the distant parts of the Globe," from "being any longer degraded, and rated as little better than the Bucaneer or pirate."[137] In contrast with the situation among privateers, gentleman antiquarians, or seekers solely after the Picturesque, international collaboration was a powerful motivation for the scientific explorers, even in a period of strong European rivalry.

Science, as a transcendent interest, often was set above narrowly commercial, military, or colonial exploitation. Its ascendance is particularly apparent in the multinational assortment of expeditions mounted to observe the transits of Venus in 1761 and 1769.[138] The "veil of secrecy" that in former times had been drawn over the results of these enterprises had thwarted the propagation of useful information "to every European nation; and indeed, to every nation however remote," as Cook noted.[139]

Figure 3
Nicolas-Jacques Conté, *A Balloon at a Military Camp*, ca. 1794. Watercolor. Photo courtesy Musée de l'Air, Paris.

Figure 4
Nicolas-Jacques Conté, *Preparation of the Varnish*, ca. 1794. Watercolor. Photo courtesy Musée de l'Air.

Figure 5
Nicolas-Jacques Conté, *Varnishing the Balloon*, ca. 1794. Watercolor. Photo courtesy Musée de l'Air.

Bataille de Fleurus gagnée par l'Armée Française le 8 Messidor de l'An

Even the French frequently adhered to this enlarged and benevolent spirit (except when it touched upon the question of who invented the balloon). The French astronomer Jean-Sylvain Bailly movingly eulogized Cook as an archetypal great man after his sudden death in Hawaii: "His memory will not die. . . . England mourns a great man; France demands his panegyric. One weeps for him in Tahiti, in that asylum of innocent mores; one weeps for him on that unfortunate isle where he met his fate; and this sadness, common to savage and civilized nations alike, is the most beautiful encomium that virtue and genius has ever received. . . ."[140]

A further consequence of the scientific (that is, factually motivated) travel description is its favoring of a plain, rhetorically unornamented, and seemingly artless style. The goal of telling an unvarnished tale meant that the writer with scientific pretensions could not rely wholly on such classical models as Herodotus, Xenophon, Pausanius, Strabo, or Horace.[141] The struggle to find an innocent mode of literary and visual expression that would convincingly do justice to the novelty of the material circumstances encountered is discussed in the preface to every notable relation of a voyage of discovery published between the middle of the eighteenth century and the middle of the nineteenth. This wrestling with the problem of clear and meticulous articulation, and with the narrative ordering of details (particularly in the description of natural phenomena), finds nothing truly precursory in such variations on the genre as the "imaginary" or extraordinary voyage and the "travel lie."[142] Equally unhelpful in the matter of veracity or the equation of matter with adequate expression was the pastoral legend of an earthly paradise that continued to tinge the utopias sought by the *philosophes* in the voyages to the South Seas which they incited. The constructed *bon sauvage* of Defoe, Pope, Rousseau, and Chateaubriand and the *sage chinois*, Turk, or Persian of Montesquieu and the Abbé Raynal, and their descendents, provided only negative models when it came to setting down geographical and physical truths.[143]

Despite the attention it seemed to pay to nature, the ornamented *style touriste* or Picturesque style, whose latest florescence came in the 1770s, was inadequate for an art whose purpose was instrumentality and the duplication of material existence. These collections of unfocused evocations, stressing the poetic qualities of mountains, rivers, forests, and lakes, served for the most part as private sources of amusement. What could be more disconcerting to the pursuer of the scenic than the demanding procedure of gathering facts?[144]

What, however, of the archaeological expedition to the Levant, which was on the rise from 1750 on and which clearly sprang from the atmosphere of the Grand Tour and its more intellectually demanding extension? Private gentlemen adventurers such as Richard Pococke, Robert Wood, Louis LeRoy, and (earlier) Jacob Spon and Sir George Wheler may, in their obvious desire to return to the primitive sources of architecture, have spurred a similar quest in the realm of nature.[145] Pococke, in the preface to his *Description of the East* (1743–1745), comments that, having seen several parts of Europe that had been visited by few and that "either were formerly very remarkable in ancient history, or are curious at present with regard to natural history," he "thought it might be agreeable to give a succinct account of them in these lights particularly."[146] Accuracy in describing antique monuments, regarded as mandatory from mid-century on, tallies with that thought to be requisite in the investigation of natural history.

The proliferating voyages into past civilizations were also coincident with the appetite for the elegiac ruin and its concomitant dark sense of sublime eternal mutability. Consider the following, from Adam Neale: "Not a rock or precipice, not a grove or ruined temple, but recalls the recollection of some hero of antiquity, chaunted by the poet, or celebrated by the historian. . . ."[147] It is specifically out of the perpetually colliding traditions of a detailed and detached account of ruins as recent objects of scientific study and as symbols of cultural decay and natural cataclysm that the archaeological publication forges a link with our topic. But the most decisive influence emanates from the handsomely illustrated mineralogical or geological treatise. The scientific travel account is the continuator and consummator of this serviceable repository of fresh knowledge, forcibly directing the observer's attention away from himself to the individualities of a dynamic world.

It is important to remember that Humanism was not yet dead. One of the essential traits held in common by the voyagers of this period was that they were never narrowly specialized. For them, and for their audience, art and science were not at the antipodes. What entered the realm of science soon expanded the domain of art. More to the point, it was the duty and vocation of an expedition party to make discoveries about the external world; the travel writer, in this capacity, was first and foremost a researcher. It is this will to experience directly natural, not merely human, phenomena, this acquired knowledge of places, this gleaning of information from sea, air, and soil, that forms the subject of our quest. It made artists out of seamen and scholars out of wanderers, forcing them not to speculate about but to penetrate and disclose the present landscape in order to discover those features still unaltered by the hand of man. As La Pérouse declared, "savants and artists form an essential part of these expeditions."[148] For the votaries of the descriptive, how intoxicating the scene on which they gazed; what a widened and deepened perspective they created. For the moment, art could again serve a practical purpose; it could be a vehicle for knowledge without stigma. Indeed, it was nothing short of heroic for the artist to voluntarily expose himself to perils when following the examples of an explorer like La Pérouse or a scientist like Saussure.[149] Travel added to landscape perception the irreplaceable component of lived experience and engaged contact with material substances recorded by those shadowy figures who rarely emerged from the obscurity in which their transcriptive role cast them.

The Scientific Gaze

Human knowledge may be carried much farther than it has hitherto been, if men would sincerely, and with freedom of mind, employ all that industry and labour of thought, in improving the means of discovering truth which they do for the colouring or support of falsehood, to maintain a system, interest, or party, they are once engaged in. . . .
John Locke

I let everything come to meet me and do not force myself to find this or that in the object. As I have contemplated nature, so I now contemplate art . . . and from this aspect too my mind develops and acquires a more untrammeled perspective. . . .
Johann Wolfgang von Goethe

The struggle to find a way to "re-present" reality without the intervention of habit was a part of the larger preoccupation with the nature of truth that engaged seventeenth-century thinkers. As Lawrence Manley has shown, Descartes, Malebranche, Hobbes, and Locke searched diligently for the grounds of certainty and concluded that the norms previously thought to lodge in nature as an atemporal guiding principle were engendered by the mind. The crisis that this important shift produced led to an emphasis on subjective tests for truth. Thus, the traditional body of rationalist thought (handed down from Plato and Aristotle), with its stress on the *a priori*, was challenged by empiricism. The latter underscored the participatory role of individuals in shaping the world and focused on the origins and development of knowledge and all social institutions, including the arts and the sciences. In this era, which saw the birth of modern subjectivity, the aim of the burgeoning "objective" sciences was the progressive search for certain truth based on the ideal of unanimous consent. Though the Royal Society recognized that experimenters would not always achieve identical apprehensions of reality, its official stance was one of "probabilism"—that is, its members (and those of other scientific academies) would assent to what, upon common deliberation, seemed most probable. Hence, findings were to be expressed as part of an upward-spiraling series of hypotheses depending on firsthand report, observation, confirmation, and ever-renewed discoveries.

Whereas the Greek post-Socratic view was that natural philosophy contemplates an immutable nature, a forward-looking Baconian science undermined this notion of nature's permanent and abiding status. Lord Verulam's scientific method set the restrictive norms of ancient tradition and authority against a modern, ongoing study based on the "consents of the senses with their objects" (*Novum organum*, IV). Thus, the task of science was to seek truth in the minute elements of the phenomenal world.

The tolerant and nondogmatic implications of the Baconian approach married the subjective test of truth (based on judicious individual viewing) to a firm belief in the existence of a universal order at the end of the investigation.

On the other hand, Continental science, inspired by Descartes's equation of thought and existence (*Méditation*, III), was less modulated by the spirit of common sense espoused by the "father of experimental science" (as Voltaire named Bacon). While English theorists at the close of the seventeenth century tended to articulate the particular in terms of a more general principle, modified by an appeal to human psychology and shifting social values, the French were more interested in bringing the contingent firmly under the thumb of unchanging rules. In this spirit, Charles Perrault in the *Paralèlle* of 1688—basing his views on the radical Cartesian distinction between knowledge founded on universal reason and that bound to a blind subjectivity—instanced art as an example of the latter and the natural sciences as an embodiment of the former. Modern scientific progress, according to this view and Fontenelle's subsequent view, ensured that people would hold different conceptions of nature than the ancients, and truer ones as well.

It was at this profound epistemological level that British and French philosophers, however different in other respects, came together. From opposing perspectives they bequeathed to eighteenth-century discourse an awareness of the personal component of vision complemented by the recognition that nature had been redefined as composed of equally individual and mutable particulars.

It was Locke, however, who codified for England and the Continent the modern view of nature as the object of ongoing scientific research. This "new" nature was not the alien, bare intellectual principle that since antiquity had governed the normative approach to human practice and production, nor (in its Newtonian incarnation) was it the mere dull "naked matter" of Ralph Cudworth (*True Intellectual System of the Universe*, 1678). This novel investigation of the world was based on "a person's," not on "man's," individual scrutiny of lively phenomena.

Locke, in his *Essay Concerning Human Understanding* (1690), took pains to distinguish the primary and real qualities of bodies (solidity, extension, figure, number, motion or rest), which are always in them and which are sometimes perceived by us, from secondary and imputed qualities. The epistemological conundrum Locke set for all subsequent philosophers up to and including Kant was that, if knowledge is limited to our ideas, which in turn are images derived from our senses, then the extent of our knowledge must fall short of the reality of external things. The only possible path to salvation out of inevitable skepticism is that foreseen by the seventeenth-century scientific academics: One must continually labor to see in order to know what lies outside the mind. The scientific gaze was thus defined as a tireless and unrelenting visual exploration, the determined effort to "prove" the existence of the external. This program, elevated to an aesthetic, was bodied forth in the assertion of the primacy of primary pleasures. As Addison put it (*Spec.* 416), the impact of experience was proportionate to the individual's will to perceive nature directly, in contrast with the modulated effect of secondary pleasures arising from recombinative mental efforts (*Spec.* 447). It was in the scientist's resolution to be present to things themselves—witness the testimony of Newton and Goethe—that a fruitful bond between art and science could at last be cemented. The belief in the possibility of such nontransformative vision, a consciously analytical study of physical data, was to enrage Blake and Wordsworth, who were devoted to the belief in the transparency of self-expression in the media of painting and poetry.

Seventeenth-Century "Plain" Styles

... car j'entends icy par ce terme voyageur, non ceux qui voyagent simplement, mais ceux en qui se trouve & une curiosité fort étendue, qui est assez rare, & un certain don de bien voir, plus rare encore....
Joseph Pitton de Tournefort

So far from prescribing rules for his conduct, they [the British legislature] conceived that the man whom they had chosen, prompted by his natural love of science, would endeavour to derive the greatest possible advantages from his voyage. He was only therefore directed to exercise all his talents, and to extend his observations to every remarkable object....
Georg Forster

William Blake, in the *Four Zoas*, leveled his criticism of a "narrowed" mode of "single vision" (with the physical eye alone) against the then-ascendant empirical sciences. Blake's advocacy of inspired prophetic vision was hostile to what Michel Foucault terms the panoptic "observing gaze," a habit of conscious perception in which the beholder wills to refrain from intervening in order to see things as they are. The control over the associating powers of the mind that results from the latter kind of seeing is expressed in a rhetoric determined largely by the sensible immediate, by the powerful language of the visible, before which the activity of the transfiguring imagination is, if not stilled, reduced. According to Roland Barthes, the "myth" of such sober and unromantic discernment belongs peculiarly to the classical mode; I would argue that, by extension, it also belongs to the accomplished scientific researcher who looks patiently at individual phenomena, thus gaining access to their truth.[1] Underlying these dual attitudes is the fundamental realization that man lives in a world he constructs in order to come to terms with it: the world he inhabits in fact and the mental one he desires to actualize.

The estimation of the physical sciences as instruments for getting at truth and the concomitant demand for close and faithful observation of natural objects during the period of (roughly) 1600–1800 are among the causes of Blake's and Coleridge's outbursts against the hegemony of the external. Their doctrines of a constructive or redemptive imagination posited that the duplication of discrete material things weakened, deadened, and obliterated the internal inventive faculties of the mind: " ... though Reason is feasted, Imagination is starved; whilst Reason is luxuriating in its proper Paradise, Imagination is wearily travelling on a dreary desert. ... " Quite different is Andrew Sparrman's expression of a pure delight to know. The 1785 journal of this Swedish naturalist, whom Forster engaged as an assistant at the Cape of Good Hope, documents that he was "fired with the love of science and of truth." In the company of Cook's shore party, Sparrman intrepidly set out "for the desert wilds of Africa," prepared "to sacrifice fortune, ease and health" in the cause of science. Claiming "never to rely" on the relations of others, he "sees everything with his own eyes, and trusts only to the report of his own senses."[2]

Sparrman's asserted readiness to perceive the environment at first hand is clearly founded on an awareness of scientific method in which each concrete item is made to expose its material qualities and made to contribute to the knowledge of objective reality. The process of exploration is thus necessarily involved with the work of establishing things as visually accessible.[3] Far from skimming superficially, as Blake would have it, the instrumental vision of the scientist directs a penetrating, if at first isolating, look at the world. As Sparrman's enthusiasm makes plain, natural pursuits can, in time, exalt while they deepen understanding; they postpone but do not weaken genuine feeling, and they do not repress meditation. Only after the habits of accuracy oblige the mind to attend to facts and make it conversant with the particular forms of things will it attain its ultimate aim: the systematic and organic knowledge of the universe. The naturalist must be open to fine distinctions, attentive to all modulations; in short, he must be capable of laying bare the language of the object in the presence of the object.[4] Sparrman speaks for all scientifically trained travelers when he firmly asserts that he will brook no secondhand vision.

The public or minimal style of discourse operating to communicate a rich variety of matter and shaping the utterances of the voyager in quest of natural occurrences is based on the long-established ideal of a "classical" and transparent language. The demand for clarity and readability that marks the contiguous or paratactic aesthetic of Gotthold Ephraim Lessing, Johann Joachim Winckelmann, and the mature Goethe similarly stresses composition by juxtaposition. Yet in the case of the traveler-scientist this method of classification in apposition is related not to furthering the tranquil contemplation of ancient sculpture but to actively revealing the method by which the components of nature are acquired. This descriptive device belongs to a mimetic tradition originating in the Homeric epic. As Auerbach demonstrated, Homer presents a nonpsychological, externalized reality, noting carefully the separate existence and the coterminous operation of things in accordance with their natures. Stylistically this means that visible phenomena, palpable in all their parts, are not merged but brought into spatial and temporal proximity; they operate as neighbors in the foreground and in the present.[5]

In its more immediate historical context, the development of modern scientific vision goes hand in hand with the development of a utilitarian prose style. The latter can be traced to the scientific academies of the seventeenth century and to their linguistic reforms. The focusing light of science and reason—an important image that would continue well into the eighteenth century—was intended to illuminate the accounts sanctioned by these academies.

Rhetorical innovations concerned with establishing a purposive prose consonant with recording corporeal things emerged from an anti-Ciceronian doctrine stipulating that words must be adequate to objective physical reality. The radical restriction of figured language was central to the ideology of the Royal Society, founded by Charles II in 1660. The eradication of verbal and mental imprecision, obscurity, and mystification in the description of the universe is at the core of the scientific humanism fostered by the Royal Society, which was dedicated to the improvement of natural knowledge through the accumulation of large stocks of data. Significantly, the society's journal, *Philosophical Transactions*, founded in 1665, ensured an internationalism and a spirit of collaboration that went far beyond the bounds of British science.[6]

The increase in raw sense data gathered by proponents of the "New Philosophy" or the "Scientific Movement" generated a linguistic revolution. Bishop Thomas Sprat, the historian of the Royal Society, proposes to survey ancient and modern sources of imagery in order to determine which are depleted and which are still viable for modern usage. While history, the manners and mores of different countries and climes, and the Bible are supposedly alive and well, classical mythology and philosophy are deemed no longer fertile. Sprat upholds the view that literary images must be concrete and based on direct sense experience. Thus, both mechanical arts and works of nature are rich mines for contemporary authors. In contrast with the experimental keenness of the moderns, the ancients are exposed as deficient in physical knowledge, and this is judged to impair considerably their creative imagination. A small store of information provided them with only a few, tired images, and these had to be repeated constantly. Sprat stresses that the incorporation of exciting new data into prose and poetry would make them comprehensible to all and that hence they would constitute a universal characteristic or scientific language. Further, he defines the ideal of an aphoristic language without residue. He excoriates "the luxury and redundance of speech," the "trick of *Metaphors*," that produce beautiful deceit, the "mists" brought on knowledge by the use of tropes and figures invented by the ancients. To his mind the Royal Society has been rigorous in formulating "the only remedy possible for such verbal extravagance: . . . a constant Resolution, to reject all the amplifications, digressions, and swellings of style: to return back to the primitive purity, and shortness, when men deliver'd so many *things*, almost in an equal number of *words*." Sprat continues: "They have extracted from all numbers, a close naked, natural way of speaking; positive expressions; clear senses; a native easiness: bringing all those things as near the Mathematical plainness, as they can: and preferring the language of Artizans, Countrymen, and Merchants, before that, of Wits or Scholars. . . . " In short, it is the genius of the English to be more concerned with the matter than with the finesse of what they say. To that end, Sprat suggests that the Royal Society employ some of its fellows to converse with seamen and travelers about foreign countries and their natural history.

Sprat makes clear that visual and linguistic tasks are identical. The experimental philosophers' goal is, "in short, to make faithful *Records*, of all the works of *Nature*, or Art, which can come within their reach; that so the present Age, and posterity, may be able to put a mark on the Errors, which have been strengthened by long prescriptions; to restore the Truths, that have lain neglected: to push on those which are already known, to more various uses: and to make the way more passable, to what remains unreveal'd. . . . " He notes further that "the Genius of *Experimenting* has endeavored to separate the knowledge of nature from the colours of rhetoric, the devices of fancy, and the delightful deceits of fables." These investigators wish to create "a steddy, a lasting, a popular, and uninterrupted work." Some 20 years later in France, Charles Perrault, in the *Parelèlle des anciens et des modernes* (1688), trod in Sprat's footsteps by praising the experimenter, the observant *philosophe*, who had given the world an accurate history of progress in "the knowledge of natural things." The moderns, with the aid of the telescope and the microscope, had discovered "a kind of immensity in large and small bodies which imparts an almost infinite extension to the Science which has them for objects."[7]

In foreseeing a perpetual garnering of information deliberately couched in a style that did not draw attention to the writer's personality or feelings, the *History of the Royal Society of London, For the Improving of Natural Knowledge* (1667) also served to legitimize the quest for novel subjects or for matter asserting its particularity. Scientific and pseudo-scientific works of the seventeenth century show a further consequence of this emphasis on untarnished or plainly presented experience in their frequent use of the adjectives *new* and *unheard of*.

In France the *Journal des sçavans* rather than the Academy's *Mémoires* reflected the struggle between the vigorous and growing knowledge of a vital century and the largely futile assumptions of the ancients. The multiplication of scientific works based on *expérience* (experiment) and largely inspired by Descartes's "New Method" prepared for this constant feeling of excitement in the face of innovators. The literary implications of "useless Truths" were not lost on Voltaire, whose *Letters Concerning the English Nation* (1733) poke fun at the set of "compliments" published annually by the French Academy, comparing them unfavorably with the *Transactions*. Infused by the cross-Channel spirit of language purification and showing himself in this to be a disciple of Charles Perrault, Voltaire urges his compatriots to set about publishing the works of the great moderns, that is, authors from the age of Louis XIV. The texts of Thomas Corneille, Molière, and Jean de La Fontaine are to be "purged from the several Errors of Diction which are crept into them" and are to be transformed into models in order to teach language "in its utmost purity."[8]

The concept of the progress of knowledge that informed Sprat's *History* and Perrault's *Paralèlle* had, of course, been proclaimed by Bacon, first in *Advancement of Learning* (1605) and then in *Novum Organum* (1620) and *De Augmentis Scientiarum* (1623). In these treatises and in *New Atlantis* (1628) Bacon announces a philosophical program to revolutionize the whole of science, one that influenced the founders of the Royal Society and Diderot's *Encyclopédie*. The systematic search for the novel and the refusal to accept pre-established meaning was inherent in his call for the collaborative progress of science through cooperation—the modern, non-individualistic ideal of research. Searchers and discoverers, no matter what their nationality, were all believed to contribute to a common goal of describing the world.[9]

Verulam's ideal of scientific progress is a process that can never be completed. His insight, owed to Hugh of Saint Victor, is that scientific knowledge is brought about step by step through contributions made by generations of explorers who build and amend; it is not a luxury based on self-revelation or a vague aspiration toward truth. From this utilitarian point of view, art involves mere subjective play and fosters the creation of illusion. The Baconian legacy of adherence to a narrowed instrumental function of language as illustration and its devotion to copying data relegates the fine arts, as traditionally conceived, to being slight creatures of fancy rather than Promethean expressions of science's "bold excursions of the human mind."[10]

The humanistic critics of the experimental sciences in the Augustan Age thought they spied still another danger lying beneath the Chancellor's praise of the progressive experimental sciences. The emphasis placed in the new logic on sense observation and the absorbing study of the environment seemed to portend that the world of man would soon be sunk in the realm of nature.[11] This fear of deanthropomorphization, of a phenomenological purity in competition with civilized man, proved prescient. The image of the vast and generative laboratory of nature was constantly pressed into service both by English and French writers of factual travel accounts. Thus, the Baconian view of science as providing a rich storehouse for human improvement helped to dispel the old theological suspicion of anything in its natural state. By the outset of the eighteenth century, the perception of the world as full of self-sustaining, estimable physical objects challenged any lingering simplistic conviction of anthropocentricity.[12]

What is at issue is nothing less than the rise of empiricism. John Locke's *Essay Concerning Human Understanding* (1690) is strongly laced with reminiscences of both Descartes's "New Philosophy" and Bacon's and the Royal Society's "New Science." Like them, Locke acknowledged the primacy of vision and experience in thinking only to arrive, in the end, at a marked skepticism about the limitations of cognition. Locke is of interest

THE SCIENTIFIC GAZE

to our argument not because of his avowed pessimism, but because of his insistence that what one knows must somehow be made present to the mind, and that these objects are not fictions but ideas of something. In this respect Locke resembles Bacon, whose aesthetic pronouncements he seems to echo. In "Some Thoughts Concerning Education" (section 174), Locke groups poets with thieves and gamblers as liars. The poet's preoccupation with what is unreal, judged in the light of perception and understanding, becomes contemptible. The creator of such figments, thus beset and not wishing to be taken as merely fanciful, must operate within the framework of a mirroring form of representation and a "simple" rhetoric.[13]

Although Locke argued that we could not know the nature of material substance but could only form ideas of it (apart from such abstract qualities as solidity, extension, and figure), he felt that the corpuscular theory at hand offered at least a probable hypothesis for its nature. Advancing what Voltaire called a narrow theory of human knowledge, Locke nonetheless took a pragmatic stand on the issue. He undercut his own skepticism by admonishing us to investigate nature in order to push out the balance of knowledge as far as possible—ideally, beyond mere subjectivity. In this light, his question as to whether mental images resemble the things of which they are ideas is to be seen as closely connected with the objective of scientific discovery and with the methodologies predicated on the achievement of accurate correspondences between words and things developed by the Latitudinarians and the Royal Society.

The undeniable relativism of Locke's thought, its keen eighteenth-century awareness of the contextuality of all knowledge, must also be interpreted as a necessary corollary to his and the New Science's perception of the exhaustion of the ancient normative order. His epistemology is wholly dependent not upon the authority of an ancient pattern of viewing, but upon progressive individual research that continuously alters the perception of the world and its contents. As Voltaire comments while comparing the systems of Descartes and Newton: "the very Essence of Things is totally chang'd. You neither are agreed upon the Definition of the Soul, nor on that of Matter."

There is a profound difference, however, between Locke's hard-working view that perception is the passive "inlet of knowledge" from which the mind wills to form ideas and the automatic mental motions of later Associationists. Locke does not fall prey to the radical representative theory of perception espoused by his contemporary Nicolas Malebranche in *De la recherche de la vérité* (1674, 3.2.1, section 1), which holds that we can know only what is intimately and constantly connected to the soul. Although Locke would agree that we do not see physical objects directly, each person's study of individual appearances—providing it receives corroboration—may yet lead beyond the person, out of the mind, to say

VOYAGE INTO SUBSTANCE

something truthful about the composition of the world. Thus his attitude constitutes a fundamental methodological principle of empiricism: that no opinion is to be accepted as an instance of knowledge until it is proved to be established through undeviating observation.[14]

Yet the problem of cognition that bedeviled eighteenth-century thinkers needs to be rephrased. How does the mind adequately grasp in images or ideas corporeal things, objects different in kind from, and lying outside, itself? Despite his ambivalence, Locke stands apart from philosophers, such as Berkeley or Spinoza, for whom ideas were either signs of other ideas or actions of the mind. Locke subscribed firmly to the analogy between knowing and ocular vision.[15]

The empiricist model of the mind and its working is derived in a variety of ways from a nonmental nature. Hence, "impression" is a favorite figure of speech in the eighteenth century, implying as it does the "pressing in" of the outer world, the insistent clamor raised by virtual matter. The exploratory activity of the scientific gaze appears consonant with a major tenet of Lockean psychology: that thought is inseparable from sense perception.[16] Further, Locke divides matter into primary and secondary qualities—the former proceeding entirely from such objects as are before the eyes, the latter flowing from sequences of ideas stimulated by the sight of visible objects. The essayist Joseph Addison, in developing this point, notes that primary pleasures arise from the sight of what is great, uncommon, or novel in nature, whereas secondary pleasures stem from objects once seen but now absent and only recalled to mind. Consequently, intervening memory, dimly outlining a remote but recollected image, is prejudicial to the spirit of on-the-spot scientific examination.[17]

In France empiricism developed differently, although in a way connected to the scheme just outlined. By the middle of the eighteenth century the philosophy of Locke had become authoritative not only in England but on the Continent (in Sensualist philosophy) as well. Etienne Bonnot de Condillac, Jean D'Alembert, and Montesquieu specifically adapted Locke's and Newton's method of attentive observation to their special field of inquiry, welcoming conscious perception that led to a rational, not a theological, explanation of the universe. Their concern, too, was not purely scientific but was part of a wider intellectual and political movement.[18] The English and French devotees of the empirical veer away from one another most notably, however, in that the former appealed to sensations rather than to *sensibilités*. In both instances psychology and physiology pass into each other, primacy is given to the sensory experience of reality, a new aesthetic reservoir of natural objects is recognized, and matter resonates with a vital rather than a mechanical movement. Yet the French seem more attuned to the biological forces than to the spiritual agencies existing within the universe.[19]

THE SCIENTIFIC GAZE

The *Essai sur l'origine des connaissances humains* (1746) is as central to French empiricism as is Locke's *Essay* to that of the British. Like Locke, Condillac wanted to shed Aristotelian metaphysics (which proposed to treat of everything in general without having observed anything in particular) and believed that scientific language assisted in the discovery of truth. Indeed, his first project was to replace the rationalist metaphysics of the seventeenth century with the empirical philosophy of Locke. Condillac even shared Locke's ambiguities, treating sensations sometimes as produced by external reality and sometimes only as responses to an interior state of being.[20] Further, Condillac's Sensualist psychology, outlined in the *Traité des sensations* (1754), is steeped in the Newtonian ideas about matter that were so important to the development of a French vitalistic materialism.[21] The members of Condillac's extended circle, including La Mettrie and Diderot, were pondering a dynamic and aggresive world of atoms and the representational problem of its translation into a counterpart, an inner world of mobile sensory images.[22]

ক

An insistent empiricism underlay the explorers' method of perception and saved them from complete bewilderment and inarticulateness in the face of an unedited nature. Armed with a sense-oriented and lucid idiom derived from the burgeoning sciences, they could situate themselves in the world and reason about it. The manifest intention behind descriptions and illustrations was not to transform the visible but to be nonstereotypical, to reproduce for the uninitiated eye the earth's novel, unknown, or undepicted realities.[23]

The structure of a specifically scientific way of seeing—as defined by its practitioners—can be distinguished from other eighteenth-century visual modes. The scientific observer looks at, not over, that which he explores. The eye is intently engaged by the aggressive identity of a particular object with respect to which the beholder takes up a position.[24] Viewers seize things differently when they focus on objects than when they automatically glide over them; in fact, they pursue their researches in different worlds. This thesis helps to explain the traveler's reaction of "scales falling from the eyes," "lightning bolts," or "inundation" before the epiphany of a "new" nature that he himself had only just discovered.

The scientific gaze entails a purposive curiosity that goes hand in hand with the utilitarian ideal of "spreading knowledge."[25] In the words of H. W. Beechey, "the advancement of science and general knowledge" offers the only justification for a traveler's appearing before the public.[26] Both the French and the English allude obliquely to the progressivist assumptions implicit in this method of observation. In a series of *Journal de Trévoux* articles examining the "nature" of the aurora borealis (beginning in 1732) it is proposed that "the sky has become more fecund in magnificent spectacles insofar as we are more assiduous in observing it." The author concludes that in unenlightened epochs men scarcely realized that the northern lights existed, whereas in the experimental age not a year went by without a minimum of several sightings. This led R. P. du Fesc to hypothesize not that these lights appear only intermittently but that the frequency of modern observations contributed to, or structured, the perception of the regular nature of their appearances.[27] Fifty years later, one of the founders of the new science offered a reprise of this theme. Père Cotte, in his *Mémoires sur la météorologie* (1788), marvels at the uncustomary spate of physical observations rolling in year after year. He touches on a major issue: "When it comes to a question of observation, never has the science of meteorology been more blessed with heedful observers, good instruments, and accurate records than it is at present; nevertheless, unfortunately, the possession of these diverse advantages is only of a recent date, and this is why theory is so little advanced. . . . "[28] These authors were committed to the inductive view that the more the beholder observed the more he saw, and the more was seen the greater was the need for systematization. What lies behind Cotte's text is the presupposition that the scientist fastens his mind on things that are intrinsically worthy of inquiry and that progressively increase in worth. Such perspicuity is taken on by the explorer, who must test conflicting views through observations and experiments carried out on location. Both the Académie des Sciences (in the early instance of Louis-Antoine de Bougainville and La Pérouse) and the Royal Society (beginning with Cook's dramatic first voyage, in 1768) organized expeditions to settle debates arising from a multiplicity of reports. The issues ranged from the transit of Venus to the location of a Northwest Passage. Like the "pure" researcher toiling in his laboratory, the discoverer of new lands or the rediscoverer of old, intellectually unincorporated worlds wrestled with undigested material.[29] In writing of their experiences, the travelers undertook to give visible shape to the chaos of existence, since, as Locke argued, only form could enter consciousness. The puzzling and the marvelous were reckoned to be amenable to explanation and hence to reproduction. By this standard of intellectual conquest, illustration or description must not fall short of the thing it resembles.[30]

In England the contrariety between perspicuous gaze and "literary" vision emerged from Baconianism and added its special flavor to the treatises on the poetic imagination that proliferated around the middle of the eighteenth century. William Duff's *Essay on Original Genius* (1767) is representative of the genre. Duff characterizes the imagination of the inventive philosophical genius as marked by regularity, clarity, and accuracy—properties required of scientific observation. The mind of the natural philosopher gathers the "rays" of fancy and concentrates them in a point, conceiving a design from the scrutiny of details. On the other hand, the intellect of the original poetic genius is stamped by irregularity, energy, and enthusiasm; the rays of fancy are concomitantly diffused and scattered, and their brilliance is less piercing.[31] In stressing the dichotomous operations of these two sorts of imagination, Duff points the way to a needed merger within the hierarchy of experiential values—one that binds the poetic obscurity of "I feel" to the scientific luminosity of "I see." The Abbé Jean-Baptiste Du Bos, in his 1719 *Réflexions critiques sur la poésie et sur la peinture,* had already rendered prominent the idea that the fine arts belong to a realm of personal taste and affective perception rather than to one governed by an immutable reason. The work of art was to be judged by sentiment rather than rules; that is, by an individual beholder. Caprice could be avoided by positing a universal human nature according to which all men held in common a certain way of feeling responsive to changing circumstances. A constantly susceptible perception thus seems more directly in contact with the processes of the world than any form of conventionalized sight. The Abbé Charles Batteux, taking a different tack, arrived at a science of informed sensation, not of sensation as the whole of information. In contrast with the Abbé Du Bos, he urged artists to imitate natural philosophers who gathered data. He further stipulated that, like Newton, they should then formulate a coherent pictorial system subsuming these aggregates under an overriding coalescent principle. Despite their obvious differences, Du Bos and Batteux both struggled with the complex role played by the emotions in adequately seeing and judging the individual components of the world.[32]

Batteux voices the conviction that judicious science and discriminating "sentiment," when submitted to the checks and balances of nature, do not follow divergent paths. It is precisely on this score that the scientific traveler's vision differs subtly from that of his enraptured, sensation-seeking peers. The explorer would have agreed with Leibniz that the unguided emotions represent the lowest rung of true perception. Long before Ruskin's astute analysis of the "pathetic fallacy" in *Modern Painters,* the attentive traveler recognized that the superior optic was practiced by the person who apprehended rightly, in spite of his immediate emotions.[33] Merely opening one's eyes and idly (though sensitively) avoiding the time-consuming labor of focusing was unbefitting the discoverer. In view of this caveat, the factual travel account exhibits a language recording forceful action wholly in keeping with the explorer-scientists's joyous plunge into conquest of the earth. This lively curiosity was monitored, however, by the greater task of, and "will to," judicious observation.[34] Thus, William Thorn, in his *Memoir of Java* (1815), chastises the Dutch, who for two centuries fixed the seat of their eastern empire and yet did so little "in satisfying the natural desire of men to acquire a knowledge of regions, the productions of which have been sought with avidity." He derides this sign of their "frigid insensibility for the concerns of science, and the progress of the human mind."[35] In different corners of the world, Horace Bénédict de Saussure (in the monumental *Voyages dans les Alpes* of 1786–1796) and Georg Forster (on Cook's second exploration of the

South Pacific in 1772) brought an intent but critically observant eye to bear on unfamiliar regions. This "passionate intelligence" embodying the harmonization of scientific goals with serious feeling is distinct, as Doctor Samuel Johnson reminds us, from "petty inquisitiveness" expended on "trivial employments and minute studies."[36] It demands as its objective correlative nothing less than the committed and discerning examination of the total material world, from the nebular stars to the mosses growing on granitic rocks. Every great sparkling idea, every vivid sensation, must be carefully noted, side by side with the attendant facts.

Bernardin de Saint-Pierre was the first major writer to address the inherent contrarieties implicit in such desiderata. In his *Voyage à l'Ile de France* (1773) he ruminates on the difficulty of tackling this interesting yet trying genre. The composition of travel books, he insists, requires of its author a universal knowledge, a conspicuous sense of order evident in the design, and a warmth of style; sincerity must be coupled with intellectual probity, since the conscientious writer ought to speak of everything. With refreshing candor, Bernardin admits the impediments to such an undertaking: If a topic is omitted, then the account is imperfect; if all is discussed, then it appears disordered and interest flags.[37]

Bernardin was a key figure in a movement threading its way from the seventeenth century into the nineteenth—one that upheld the conviction that science provides a firmer basis for aesthetic response and, conversely, that art is not inimical to science. The sciences stressed the expressive power and significance of the natural world. They perceived beauty lodged in unmanipulated objects and the possibility of perfection lying outside the bounds of culture. The seeming paradox of a passionate intelligence becomes historically situated when we realize that the inheritors of Baconian science forged disinterested delight into a perceptual method uniquely suited to the appreciation of external nature. Otherwise stated: They coupled the willed control of the emotions in observation with the warmth and enthusiasm transmitted in a work. The scientist's aim was to make enthusiasts without being one himself. Alexander von Humboldt disagreed with Edmund Burke on this point, taking issue with the writer's claim that it is only our ignorance of nature that arouses admiration and excites emotion.[38] But one does not have to scour nineteenth-century texts. Georg Forster speaks of "the rage of hunting after facts."[39] Mungo Park, indicating the motives behind his grueling exploration of the River Niger, baldly asserts "I had a passionate desire to examine into the productions of a country so little known; and to become experimentally acquainted with the modes of life and character of the natives. . . . "[40]

A "hunger for knowledge," a "*curiosité dévorante*," an openness to everything, and an intellectual boldness—in the best tradition of the Baconians, the empiricists, and the progenitors of the *Encyclopédie*—brand these published ventures.[41] An international (and in some ways deliberately supranational) rhetoric characterizes Daniel Solander's, H. D. Spöring's, and Sparrman's zeal for more accurate "investigations of nature" and stamps Philibert Commerson's "rage to see."[42] Whether on bleak Easter Island, in the midst of Brazil's opulent vegetation, or clambering over active volcanos, the naturalist could readily echo Faujas de Saint-Fond's exclamation "je désirois ardemment . . . y retourner."[43] Le Vaillant's *Voyage dans l'intérieur de l'Afrique* (1790) raises scientific ardor to the acme of passion: "Little by little, the genius of discovery has spread its wings; arts and letters have ceded their place to the sciences; the passion for voyages awakened an even more insatiable desire to know and to compare; these have become enlarged in proportion to the miracles which they have wrought; one no longer knows any bounds. . . ."[44] With an uncharacteristically French spurning of *la gloire*, the ornithologist François Le Vaillant confesses that he was capable of moderating the "violence" of his appetite to explore only by giving himself up wholly to a voyage of discovery: "I buried myself in several unknown African deserts: I conquered a small portion of the earth. . . . I did not dream about my reputation. . . ."[45]

In sum: The victor's palm of an informed, eager visualism was borne away by "men of greater penetration"[46] whose most profound insights were achieved by working through, while simultaneously formulating, empiricist procedures in the field, applying and creating as the occasion arose. Implicitly at work was the assumption that by vigilant circumspection conducted according to a scientific plan nothing intrinsically worthy would be found to lie beyond the scope or ken of the investigation of the visible world.

It is customary to think of the search for an objective standard of truth and the attempt to see the object as it really is as a distinctively Victorian preoccupation. The writings of John Ruskin, Matthew Arnold, Thomas Carlyle, John Stuart Mill, and even Thomas Hardy, and the paintings of the Pre-Raphaelite Brotherhood, constantly cultivate a "finer optic," stemming from the assumption that subjectivity distorts.[47] These Victorians, like the earlier empiricists, emulate scientific standards of truth, but their desperate (if extraordinary) sensitivity to minutiae is antithetical to the eighteenth-century delight in the concrete particular. This statement requires some justification. It has often been noted that the aesthetic prejudice against particularity was a sturdy one.[48] From his synoptic vantage, Sir Joshua Reynolds, in his third Discourse, cautions that the effect of beauty and grandeur consists in selectivity and getting "above all singular forms." In this matter he must be seen as a highly influential continuator and consummator of the Augustan tradition that distrusted particularity because of its identification with the accidental. Reynolds addresses this point in the fourth Discourse: "I am very ready to allow that some circumstances of minuteness and particularity frequently tend to give an air of truth to a piece, and to interest the spectator in an extraordinary manner . . . yet the usual and most dangerous error is on the side of minuteness. . . ."

So that there might be no mistake concerning his momentary leniency toward the actual, he exhorts the artist to remember that "the general idea constitutes real excellence." Again, "as in Invention, so likewise in Expression, care must be taken not to run into particularities. . . ."[49] Alexander Cozens, in his pamphlet *A New Method for assisting the Invention* (1785), similarly takes to task those students of landscape painting who pay too much heed to copying natural details, thereby losing the main features of the composition. His "blottesque" system reasserts the importance of presenting a general idea.[50]

Not surprisingly, the nonscientific travel account frequently reflects such a bias. Pococke, in the preface to his *Description of the East* (1743–1745), indicates his prepossession when he states (concerning the illustrations) that on occasion he has "*descended* to several particulars."[51] The distaste for the circumstantial for its own sake is also apparent in the Picturesque voyage in which specifics function as surrogate symbols or stimulants to mental wanderings. George Heriot, roaming in the Pyrenees, exhibits a basically rambling and unriveted approach to what he perceives as the random contingencies of life, those "most interesting as well as romantic" parts of the continent of Europe.[52]

Nonetheless, by the second half of the eighteenth century an emerging climate of realism also existed throughout Europe which called into question the conventional understanding of mimesis.[53] Doctor Johnson's *Rasselas* (1751), the critical and rhetorical writings of the Scotsmen Lord Kames, the works of John Ogilivie, George Campbell, and Hugh Blair, and the articles of the *Encyclopédie* place a clear emphasis on the value of quantitative chunks of reality. Although, as Reynolds affirmed, too many trivial parts detract from a composition (literary or artistic), these influential authors recognized that generality could be equally vitiating.[54] The distinction is an Aristotelian one. In the *Poetics*, Aristotle differentiates between the respective tasks of poet and historian: The first expresses what is universal and excludes all accident, the second what is particular. Aristotle was absorbed in various ways by systems of aesthetics urging the poet and the painter to fear the pitfall of fantastical singularity.[55] During the Enlightenment, a counterrevolution in the making since the seventeenth century and spurred by the sciences opposed the Aristotelian dictum and promoted the view that the more general the terms the fainter the picture, and the more special the brighter or sharper. Conjoined with this conviction was the suggestion that the distant (or memory-based) image was the more superficial one and the closer (or experience-based) representation was the more meaningful and "real" one.[56]

Emphatically individual units of matter seemingly propelled by their own peculiar energy into the human consciousness are eminently congruent with new attitudes toward landscape that were surfacing. Scientific sensitivity to the physiognomy of a tract of land, the terrain, or a specific geographic region helps to expose its intense and incontestable personality. Descriptive poetry, as early as Thomson's *Seasons* (1730), lauded sections of country for their natural features and configurations. The unmistakable aspect of a given area—its natural signs and marks—no longer seemed to require mediation or the superimposition of a human mentality. The land demanded to be thought of as itself, as an imperious visual presence.[57] Goethe testifies that such fundamental perceptual reorientation does not come easily. During his trip to Switzerland in 1786 with Graf Stolberg, the poet commemorated his struggle not to see the Alps as a picture, that is, within the framework of a preexisting, generalized pictorial tradition. What finally permitted him to grapple with and to sketch faithfully the peculiarities of the milieu was his searching determination to investigate and fix them.[58]

Only by observing Goethe's empiricist stratagem can the artist or writer hope to do justice to the scene before him. As the French Neoclassical landscape painter and theorist P. H. Valenciennes has it, the artist's sensibility "does not prevent him from studying sublime scenes." Even when disconcertingly near a volcano, the true student of scenery must *"examine that sublime spectacle."*[59]

The factual travel reports appear to be structured according to an empirical construct of knowledge in which cognitive processes move in accordance with the sequential accumulation of particulars in pursuit of a verifiable image of reality. Lockean psychology, uneasily committed to the proposition that there is a world outside the mind, seemed to find its keenest perceptual tool in the "piercing" eye of the sailor, forced to see both near and far, and in the "penetrating" eye of the subterranean explorer, the discoverer of marginless lands, and the balloonist, compelled to strain in order to see well.[60] As Richard Walter grasped when discussing the advisability of sailors being taught to draw, "those who are habituated to delineating objects, perceive them more distinctly than those who are not similarly accustomed."[61]

Embarking upon the empiricist program, discoverers probed the actualities of real environments: Michel Adanson in Senegal "renders himself up solely to the study of nature."[62] Banks in Tahiti hopes to find "something worthy of observation."[63] Joseph Acerbi in Finland and Sweden plunges into "an unconfined survey of nature."[64] Jacques-Gérard Milbert, a student of Valenciennes laboring on Mauritius, determines to present nothing that falls short of the "exact and truthful."[65] Jacques-Etienne-Victor Arago, on the Freycinet expedition, commits himself to producing "faithful representations" and "accurate views."[66]

The Quest for Transparency

In his short story *The Real Thing*, Henry James succinctly sums up a problem that had been fundamental to the fine arts since their inception.[67] He pointedly alludes to a basic criterion of Aristotle's literary theory, namely the distinction between two major divisions of discourse: rhetoric

Combined with this was another perversity—an innate preference for the represented subject over the real one; the defect of the real one was so apt to be a lack of representation. I liked things that appeared; then I was sure. . . . She was the real thing [Mrs. Monarch] but always the same thing. . . .
Henry James

Now every authentic and well-written book of voyages and travels is, in fact, a treatise of experimental philosophy. . . .
Andrew Sparrman

and dialectic and poetics (that is, political and philosophical writing versus drama, epic, and lyric poetry). The branch of dialectic, consisting of questions and answers, is of special interest because it was considered by the ancients to embody what today would be called the model or theory of formal scientific writing. As a class it constituted what Thomas De Quincey, in 1823, termed a "literature of knowledge" (whose function is to teach) in contradistinction to a "literature of power" (whose function is to move).[68] The first category (the lesser one, in the critic's eye) involves the transcription of real rather than invented subjects, and therefore embraces dictionaries, encyclopedias, grammars, histories, biographies, travels, and scientific treatises. In contrast with De Quincey, Coleridge, Blake, and other nineteenth-century writers who praised a higher creative faculty, Aristotle did not draw a hard and fast line between these two families of verbal expression. He did not posit a simplified antithetical formula to imply a severe insulation of, or a repulsion between, the theories and techniques operating in the two systems. In the *Topics,* Aristotle recognized the propriety of conveying truth in scientific writing by means of a feeling persuasiveness in oratory.[69] In view of this, he provides still another paradigm for the formation of an apodictical "literature of statement." He implies that the proper and effective mode of persuading one's readers is to render one's own experience in the encounter with reality as exactly and vividly as possible. The issue of a verbal (and pictorial) scientific style revolves around investigation of the connections between statements (or images) as verbal and pictorial phenomena and the facts to which the words and pictures refer.

An especially vexing question is that of the degrees and kinds of correspondences that must exist between verbal and visual descriptions of reality and reality itself if those descriptions are to be convincing to a large public. Two available stylistic responses to this troublesome query were made in the factual travel accounts: the abolition of metaphorical extravagance and the cultivation of a masculine, "plain" language. One of the chief advantages of this clear style of "vivid illustration" or "representation" is that it seems not so much to narrate as to exhibit the natural scene. The style appears transparent and does not call attention to itself, nor do similes thrust themselves upon our notice.[70] Scientific discourse, in contrast with poetry, must build up to probabilities by arranging particular details. The reader of a scientific work and the viewer of a scientific illustration were conscious not only of new thoughts but also of the form they took; the discovery of truth was assisted by the style.[71] Although the matter to be communicated is paramount in an aesthetic of information, the seemingly unmediated, "artless" form of its transmission is instrumental in producing the effect of verisimilitude. Such a probative style necessarily avoids connotative associations and conspicuous metaphors, since its terms imply an isomorphic relationship between the phenomenal world and the representation.[72] To wit: It contends with "the real thing."

THE SCIENTIFIC GAZE

Aristotle's doctrine of metaphor endows the rhetor with the ability to bind distant figures.[73] The speaker makes invisible things visible, brings them into novel conjunctions, and fills with liveliness and motion images that possess no intrinsic life or worth. The alacrity with which the imagination manipulates allusive and figured language differs radically from the "plain" light of reason and from the nominalistic attitude of science that wills to name things. The difference may be summed up as one between energeia (forceful writing) and enargeia (vivid description). The former relates to the metaphoric habit of ensouling nature through the power of the imagination, that is, the projection of psychic dynamism that supplements what the external signs indicate only in part; the latter relates to the creation of illusion.[74]

Parataxis (setting things side by side), as a weapon of eloquence, functions in opposition to the obtrusive flourishes of poetic color. Notwithstanding an "unliterary" directness of expression, it is capable of supporting a radical content; hence, it is eminently suitable to the "truthful" declaration of the external world's plenitude. Nor do its replicating and self-concealing devices exclude it from ever being incorporated as a rudiment of the elevated style. Parataxis and a "simple" style are employed when one is overwhelmingly interested in being understood by a large and broad-based audience. To this end, its utilitarian power depends on bringing forward juxtaposed, isolated, and independent pictorial or verbal blocks, thus producing the effect of nearness and brevity. Such controlled compression acts as a foil to the immense content. The "naked" statement, bereft of the *tertium comparationes*, achieves intense presence and immediacy.[75]

The paratactic composition, based on the ideal of linguistic or representational transparency and primitive terseness, is the preferred mode for itemizing the findings of the natural sciences. Similarly, it answers the need for achieving an impression of directness and clarity in the description or "demonstration" of landscape features expected from the factual travel narrative. That it was a deliberately chosen technique, eliminating ambiguous, inadequate, and misleading tropes removed from the testimony of the senses, is made clear by numerous voyagers. Georg Forster, in the preface to his *Voyage round the World*, states that he did not aim at being "curiously elegant" but, rather, struggled for "perspicuity," paying the strictest attention to this particular of style so indispensable to the "philosophical" recital of facts. Bougainville, in the *Discours préliminaire* to his *Voyage autour du monde* (1772), reminds the reader that he had spent his youth as a disciple of the mathematician D'Alembert. This experience, however, did not arm Bougainville with a "literary" style. On the contrary, his writing is stamped with the mark of a "roving and savage" life spent for the most part during the past twelve years either in the forests of Canada or on the high seas. Bougainville proudly affirms that he is "a voyager and a sailor, that is to say, a liar and an imbecile in the eyes of that class of slothful and arrogant writers, who speculate the livelong day about the world and its inhabitants in the penumbra of their study, thus imperiously submitting nature to their imaginations. . . . "

James Morier, in Persia, testifies that the report of what he saw and heard there "will be found unadulterated by partiality to any system and un-biassed by writings and dissertations of other men." George Landmann, in his *Observations on Portugal* (1818), dispels the notion that his book might be filled with personal adventures. He refuses to "please the eye without conveying any solid information," and this labor is to be discharged by means of "plain description, and correct representation of striking objects." Alexander von Humboldt, surveying the history of Latin American narratives of discovery, contrasts the conquistadores' "candid language" and exact description with the overblown didactic prolixity and specious erudition of later clerical authors.[76]

A style larded with conspicuous metaphors, giving things names that by rights belong to other things, is also inconsistent with a taste for partic-ularity. Although situations are never perceivable without the application of conceptual structures, the recognition of difference—of the alien—entails a refutatory concentration on single objects while others are tem-porarily held in abeyance.[77] It comes as no surprise, then, that the rhetorical use of parataxis and the affecting of a distinguishing or nominal stance before the world has a bearing on the fine arts. Eighteenth-century linguistic theory identified a visual equivalent of the purely reflective crystallization of substantives in the archaic system of "word-painting." Pictograms were thought to embody the acme of intense presence, imaging not individual sounds but things themselves. Eighteenth-century formulators of spec-ulative etymologies (among them William Warburton, Jean-Jacques Rous-seau, Johann Heinrich Lambert, and Antoine Court de Gebelin) believed that at the earliest stages of their history the Mexicans and Egyptians had proceeded directly, creating roots or proper picture concepts for each object that doubled nature without metaphoric displacement.[78] In modern times, they believed, the reverse of this development had occurred: Fig-urative expressions had been succeeded by exact and precise ones. With the stricter and more rigorous demands inaugurated by the "philosophic spirit" of inquiry, as Diderot was to observe, the reign of figures passed and that of things unfurled.[79]

An attendant and long-standing aspect of "plain" description was the assumption that it was emphatically masculine, in contrast with the fem-inine fancies of the beautiful fine and literary arts. Rational *acumen ingenii* or sharpness of discernment was part of "that chastity and masculine vigour of expression, as well as justness and propriety of sentiment, which are only compatible with maturer age."[80] A hardy virility thus became a peculiar prerogative of the traveler's scientifically educated eye. This par-tiality helps to explain the writer's often-expressed desire to maintain the vigorous "candor" of the sailor's laconic and uncolored tale. Both de Brosses and La Pérouse revel in "the rough, rude, but concise style of the mariner."[81] Matthew Flinders, in his *Voyage to Terra Australis* (1814), notes that "a polished style was therefore not attempted, but some pains have been taken to render it clearly intelligible." "Matter, rather than manner," was "the object of [his] anxiety."[82] The translator of Otto von Kotzebue's *Voyage of Discovery into the South Seas* (1821) captures this attitude best, stating that he composed in a "natural and manly language as it would become an English naval officer to write."[83]

The rhetorical model of a masculine, undecorated style finds its visual complement in a panhistoric phenomenological Naturalism. This much-debated term characterizes a mode of representation devoted to the truthful, unenlivened depiction of natural phenomena. In the fine arts, at least since the Renaissance, it has been identified specifically with nature studies founded on a keen observation and the unadorned communication of items making up the world. Yet naturalistic traits certainly can be found in European post-Classical art since the High Middle Ages, particularly in the arabesques surrounding illuminated manuscripts and in the plant forms ornamenting the architectural members of the Rheims or the Naumburg cathedral. A similar, seemingly neutral or value-free conception (that is, one without obvious connection to any literary or historical milieu) exists in botanical or technical illustrations that seek answers to how phenomena function by visually questioning them. An analogous technique came to the fore in the fine arts just before 1800. Dürer, Leonardo, Fabien G. Dagoty, J. R. Cozens, and C. D. Friedrich are united, despite their temperamental and intellectual differences, in their ability to suppress a demonstrative manner in order to better attend to the matter of nature.[84] All could be engaged; all could, by the act of plain copying, respond to the call issuing from the landscape itself.

The traveler-illustrators not only drew attention to this attitude but also did much to shape it. Dominique Vivant-Denon, the artist savant who accompanied Bonaparte's expedition to Egypt, remarks that, because he "traversed a country that Europe scarcely knew by name," it "became imperative to describe everything." He affirms—as did so many others before and after him—that he drew only those objects that "stood before the eyes," and laments the realization that, upon his return to France, circumstances would grant him neither the time nor the facilities to render what he had seen. He then provides a picture of the artist in hot pursuit of novel images, riding across an unexplored desert. Mounted on horseback and following the always unpredictable maneuvers of Napoleon's army, Vivant-Denon strove nevertheless to capture at least "the first glimpse of great things before rendering them in detail." In addition, he makes an excellent case for the artist-traveler's laying aside of all the egotism normally associated with his profession. Vivant-Denon cautions that when setting forth the artist should be concerned only with the aspect of the spot he proposes to depict.[85] In the words of his contemporary G. A. Oliver in the *Voyage dans l'Empire Othoman* (1804), it is expected that the artist "transport himself to all regions where observations may be made, facts collected. . . ."[86] In sum, "nothing is beautiful but the real."[87]

To place these observations in context, it should be remarked that travelers wrestled with both *realitas* and *actualitas*. While the latter implies human intervention, the altering and shaping of reality to conform with circumstance, the former denotes reality as pure phenomenonalism. The belief in the "standing on its own" of any object, independent of and prior to the cognitive activities of a perceiving subject, represents a mentality crucial to the naturalistic assumption that everything physical occupies its own time and place in the fabric of the world.[88] This premise binds artistic activity to the Platonic notion of simulation; hence, imitation of deceptive appearances is at an equal remove from Ideas and from the doctrine *arte et supra res.* The low position that landscape in general and the topographically true *vedute* in particular held in the normative Idealistic aesthetics of seventeenth- and eighteenth-century academic theory can be accounted for by this antimaterialistic bias. The farther we proceed toward the end of the eighteenth century, however, the oftener we encounter the assertion that an optically and haptically experienced reality serves as a needed corrective to the artifice of invented beauty.[89] The factual travel account, by exhibiting incontrovertibly the phenomenological "thereness" of the external world, contributed to the formulation of that *realitas.*[90] And it did so not only through description but also through illustration.

By the end of the eighteenth century, the word *illustration* had become identified largely with engravings. Its meaning had been extended to embrace "embellishment" as well as "explanation" or "intellectual illumination."[91] The merely decorative (Picturesque) implications of the term are not of interest to us, but its continuing expository and visually propositional overtones are. The Baconian notion that a language stocked with the proper word for each object gives us information that could not have been obtained without that language was the overt motive behind the rise of the illustrated travel account, in which text and image were integral to the process of learning. The writer alone, no matter how indefatigable his powers of perception, could not hope to give a complete representation of all the facets of a scene. An illustration, therefore, is a picture of the thing world inserted into a verbal text, and represents a gesture towards semiotic wholeness.

The above discussions of scientific language suggested that it is, by definition, a resolutely descriptive or inherently pictured idiom. Hence, it was uniquely suited to the depiction of landscape forms in their phenomenal or concrete individuality. Since the empiricists postulated that knowledge was conveyed in the form of sensible images, painting could help to dispel any lingering obscurity still clinging to words.[92] Positively, it could make present to mind the material energy of the phenomenal world. The instinct of thoroughness, whether preserved in prose or fixed in illustration, is germane to immediate observation rather than to mediate reflection. To phrase it differently: The sequential disclosing of what is seen during travels is substantially and temporally unlike the unifying philosophical, moral, or political broodings that these sights subsequently occasion.[93] In this spirit, J. R. Forster, the truculent father of the long-suffering Georg, compiled his own scientific observations of Cook's second voyage to compete with the official account sanctioned by the Admiralty.[94] His course was followed by many travelers let loose on life. New data "demanded" to be presented in the contexts in which they were met, thus making the new reality assimilable. The technique for attaining this goal was an art of observation that distinguished and defined. Just as writers learned to individualize objects by "transparently" noting their characteristics, artists relied on modern techniques such as aquatint (utilized in England from about 1775) and optical instruments such as the camera obscura to aid them in rapid transcription.[95] This happy conjunction was again confirmed by Georg Forster. While outlining the background for Cook's voyages, he noted that the modern era, which had witnessed the triumph of scientific exploration, had been graced by three such expeditions of discovery before George III decided that "the greatest navigator of his time" was to be accompanied "by a man of science [J. R. Forster] to study nature in all her recesses and a painter [William Hodges] to copy some of her most curious productions."[96]

Implicit in the discussion of the birth of a scientific language, the influence of empiricism, and the rise of naturalism—all of which contributed to the fashioning of a "scientific gaze," or the ability to see in order to acquire knowledge—is the assumption that the study of natural history was immensely popular. Since the seventeenth century the scientific revolution had made it possible for the public to be reached by the same ideas far more quickly than before. Pujoulx's paean (1801) embodies the fruition of a long-standing desire to make science the common property of the educated and uneducated masses alike, a wish that Diderot had enunciated 50 years earlier: "Let us hasten to make science popular."[97]

At the fringes of this argument is the notion that science promised shortcuts to truth, new possibilities for the control of cosmic powers and for the expansion of the mind. Science's frank, "manly" pursuits dispelled at one blow the tyranny of antiquity and the "feminine" beguilements that seemed to color the "frivolous" activities of the first half of the eighteenth century.[98] However, a remarkable idiosyncrasy of the late eighteenth century, which at once characterizes it and divides it from the Baconian era, is that the science that was taught, was popularized, and was available was the science that was actually being done. The most novel discoveries and the most recent theories diffused immediately into the public domain and gave rise to lively discussion.

Learning the World

The magnificence and beauty, the regularity, convenience, and utility of the works of creation, cannot fail to afford man the highest degree of pleasure, so that he who has seen and examined most of these, must the more perfectly admire and love the world as the work of the great Creator. . . .
Linnaeus

Quoi de plus merveilleux que les sciences physiques et l'étude de l'histoire naturelle? Quoi de plus intéressant, de plus attachant, de plus étonnant que les phénomènes que nous présentent la physiologie animale, la fécondation des plantes, la formation des cristaux. . . .
J. B. Pujoulx

One had only to be intelligent, rather than competent in a specific discipline. From Fontenelle to the Abbé La Pluche, from Benjamin Franklin to Joseph Priestley, from Abraham Werner to Goethe, the accessibility of science separated it from the mendacity and covertness of magic.[99] From the establishment of "scientific museums" (on the rise from the late seventeenth century, and housing natural rarities)[100] to the entertaining and highly favored balloon ascents of the late eighteenth century, everyone shared in the progressive pleasures of experimentation.[101]

This wide-eyed fascination growing in the subsoil of popular fantasy adapted itself elastically to the conception that the natural sciences constituted a new mythology.[102] Just as the languages of obstructing metaphor and ancient allegory were defunct for the proponents of the moderns, the fictitious prodigies of obsolete legends were countered by believable wonders. It was realized at the time that the very process of observation would provide an obvious source for a new history of matter and, ultimately, of landscape painting. Unlike the artificial tales of the Greeks and Romans, which had ceased to evoke the direct experience of nature that had originally inspired them, scientific scrutiny recaptured the innocent eye of the archetypal encounter with the earth. The traveler, searching in virgin forests or remote poles far from civilized nations, provided an image of the naked world in its youth that was commensurate with the scientist's search for a primal involvement with the universe.[103]

It may be objected that the aim of science, by definition, is the nonmythical explanation of the cosmos; that, in contrast with alchemy or religion, it invents the world through rational explanation.[104] Nonetheless, during the course of the eighteenth century this goal took on heroic if not fabulous dimensions. The indisputable reality of competitive biological forces and cataclysmic geological powers unseated spurious fabrications and sham teachings. And, of all the burgeoning sciences, it was natural history that incarnated the verity of the new mythology. The "archaeological" methodology of natural history enjoined piercing analysis of the anatomy, form, or habitat of a certain being or object until its individual identity was laid bare. This procedure was uniquely suited to a new estimation of the instrumental rigors of sight, the application of a studied and exploratory visualism in the observation of nature.[105]

Before we turn to Linnaeus and Buffon, who established the perimeters of the profession within which eighteenth-century practitioners operated, it is important to realize that the term *history* changed its meaning during this period (or, as Michel Foucault comments, returned to its primitive signification). Until the middle of the seventeenth century, the task of the historian was to establish a large collection of documents, which were then rearranged and reiterated. Thereafter, and until the outset of the nineteenth century, an entirely new function was imposed on the genre. For the first time the student of human affairs was expected to level a scrupulous gaze at things themselves and to transcribe what was gleaned in a neutral, limpid prose.[106] Conversely, this pure picture of things depended on belief in the existence of a transparent language that did not distort the data. As an extension of these exigencies, the historical idiom was peculiarly suited to the description of natural phenomena whose particular traits had been left unseen and unsaid. Simultaneously, the image of creatural events, as developed in the hands of Montesquieu, Voltaire, Gibbon, and Hume, emerged as that of a stage full of deceptions and vagaries without moment. What a distance separates such despicable or risible human occurrences from the grandeur of nature as recorded by its historians! What a contrast obtains between Buffon's or Erasmus Darwin's fundamental attitude of deepest awe for natural structures—down to their meanest detail—and Montesquieu's or Gibbon's jaundiced panorama of mankind's past![107] In sum: A physical, topographical, material sublimity is a consequence of the scientific representation of nature as a historical and tangible process coextensive with, if not surpassing, that of man.

Not only could the human condition appear petty and circumscribed in comparison with the endlessly changing face of the earth, but the lesson taught by Smyrna, Pompeii, Herculaneum, Lima, and Lisbon seemed to indicate that it might be necessary for the ordering of the universe to include upheavals unfavorable to man.[108] The Genevan geologist Saussure gives poignant articulation to this dramatic shift away from vainglorious anthropocentricity. Standing atop Mont Blanc and gazing at the majestic disorder of the surrounding peaks, he glimpses the pathos of earth's illimitable history.[109] Saussure's perilous assault on one of the colossi of the Alps was living proof of the dissimilarity between the modern natural historian and the old-fashioned speculative philosopher. The former successfully dislodged the baleful influence of the latter, of the "indoor readers," the dreamers who spend their lives "forging specious systems" and whose every effort resulted only in "the creation of a house of cards."[110]

Glorification and knowledgeable love of the earth grew out of the taste for natural history. The quest for specimens (animal, vegetable, or mineral) joined with the growing tradition of the life sciences. Lavoisier, Maupertuis, Diderot, and Rousseau were influenced by this approach, which rejected the use of mathematics as the basic experimental tool and tended toward nominalism. Biology, like botany and mineralogy, studied discernible physical properties and stressed the influence of the environment in the formation of organic and inorganic substances. Both disciplines posited that life had emerged from a teeming earth, and thus saw the earth as a repository of great historical interest.[111]

The antagonists Linneaus and Buffon epitomized the great age of classification. Controversies raged over the divisions of species and genera and how they might be arranged. Linnaeus's system appeared reactionary to the French because of its apparent concentration on the simplicity of identification. On the other hand, Buffon, who was suspicius of all methods, called in his practical approach to the problem of natural character for the complete description of things before any attempt at establishing a formal nomenclature.[112] In either case, a technique of careful description was emphasized—one capable of dealing with the complexities of natural phenomena.

Linneaus, in his *Reflections on the Study of Nature* (1754), announces that his science is founded on observation and dedicated to the investigation of the "intricacy" of nature. In the decade immediately preceding the mounting of the first great scientific expeditions, he presciently mentioned that even the earth, made up of innumerable wonders, might be considered a museum furnished with the works of the Creator and disposed in three classes. Speaking of the nobility intrinsic to the study of natural history, he declares: "Among the luxuries . . . of the present age, the most pure and unmixed is that afforded by collections of natural productions. In them we behold offerings as it were from all the inhabitants of the earth; and the productions of the most distant shores of the world are presented to our sight and consideration. . . . can anything afford us a more innocent pleasure, a more noble or refined luxury, or one that charms us with greater variety . . . ?"[113]

In Linnaeus's system of biological classification, plants, animals, and even humans are described not so much according to their particular features as according to the features common to them as a class. This organization of the unfamiliar into clear concepts as classes or types contributes to the ease in comprehension of a great mass of disparate data. Buffon's approach, by contrast, avoids the instantaneous crystallization of individual traits into their essence, and instead plunges into the less tidy realm of complete description:

Natural history, taken in its widest sense, is an immense history, it embraces all the objects that the universe presents. This prodigious multitude of quadrupeds, birds, fish, insects, plants, minerals, etc., offers to the inquiring brain a vast spectacle. . . . There is a characteristic strength of mind and of intellectual courage in being able to look, without being astonished, upon nature in the innumerable multiplicity of its productions and to believe oneself capable of understanding and comparing them; there is a species of taste for loving them, greater than the taste that has as its aim only particular objects; and one could say that the love of the study of nature presupposes two qualities of intellect that seem contrary: the broad survey of an ardent genius who embraces all in one glance and the narrow attention of a laborious instinct that attaches itself only to a single point. . . . [114]

The study of natural history, then, helped to undermine the strict Baconian tradition that established an antithesis between science and poetry, thinking and feeling. This revolution was brought about largely by followers of Linnaeus and Buffon. In England, France, and Germany, a unique and fruitful relationship was forged between the creative and the empirical adventure of scientific investigation.[115] The visual documentation of the terrain could begin.[116] On the assumption that the scientific component renders the genre meaningful, the naturalist Sparrman vindicates an age not infrequently accused of frivolity and indolence: "Its turn for experiment . . . and disposition to inquire into fact is universally acknowledged. . . . Now every authentic and well-written book of voyages and travels is, in fact, a treatise of experimental philosophy. . . . it is therefore in the original writers of itineraries and journals, that the philosopher looks for genuine truth and real observation. . . . "[117]

VOYAGE INTO SUBSTANCE

2 *The Natural Masterpiece*

Nor ... is there any reason to be alarmed at the subtlety of the investigation, as if it could not be disentangled; on the contrary, the nearer it approaches to simple natures, the easier and plainer will everything become; the business being transferred from the complicated to the simple; from the incommensurable to the commensurable; from surds to rational quantities; from the infinite and vague to the finite and certain; as in the case of the letters of the alphabet....
Francis Bacon

The aim of the factual travel account was to spread graphically before the reader and viewer a great range of exact information about the world. This alliance between science and art suggested that accurate text wedded to precise image would offer a progressivist paradigm for understanding the physical processes at work in the universe. The act of observing, recording, or charting nature's operations, however, was predicated on the larger eighteenth-century interest in the structure of matter. To gain meaningful access to the physiognomy of the nonhuman environment—to comprehend particular formations and landmarks on their terms, not man's—required admiration for, and penetration of, their individual corporeal composition. The rise of visual consciousness and descriptive configuration of the natural masterpiece (that is, of the wholly physical and untampered creation of earth) hinged on the perspicuous examination of its medium as medium, a procedure underway at least since the opening years of the century.

The eighteenth-century viewer's informed regard for extraordinary stone formations may be fruitfully compared to the late Hellenistic tradition of the wonders of the world. The ancients' notion of marvel or *mirabilia*, usually associated with architecture or sculpture on a colossal scale, embraced those works that were thought to rival the great creations of the physical universe. By the sixteenth and seventeenth centuries a close connection existed between the concepts of *mirabilia* and masterpiece, although distinctions were still drawn between fabricated wonders and those of an artless kind. It was in England, however, rather than in France (where the modern notion of a consciously crafted "masterpiece" seems to have originated) that the distinction became blurred. Stonehenge occupied a special place, straddling the line between the artificial and the natural, and produced a progeny of ambiguous monuments. Walter Cahn's study of the idea of the masterpiece traces the history of that elusive word and its hallowing of human effort and skill. Clearly, the obverse of such an inquiry should be how the matchless wonder of art becomes supplanted by the prodigy of nature—whether in its most minute or its most grandiose incarnation—located in the Linnaean "museum" of the world.

From differing but not mutually exclusive perspectives, this chapter and the next one bear on the question. Although in the seventeenth century science had begun to redefine the state of nature from a condition of utopian stasis to one of changefulness, as reflected in matter's mutability and variety, eighteenth-century Newtonianism and materialistic philosophies focused more sharply on the dynamism lurking in even the most seemingly stable objects, down to their constituent particles. By dint of this redefinition, natural phenomena were recognized both as records of and as memorials to the passage of time. The perception of their temporal and historical dimensions—part of the intense eighteenth-century concern for historiography—not only imparted to them a prehistoric past and primitive status as abiding objects, but also exposed them as heroic substances that had suffered the vicissitudes of the earth's evolution and now nobly wore the marks and traces of terrestrial "passions." The unearthing of matter's history was thus based on the voyaging natural historian's ability to detect its embodiments in landmarks freed of human intervention, on the willingness to dissect faithfully the literal deeds of nature.

Vital Elements

[I have] anatomized so considerable a tract of land, and given the most exact representation of each minute part of which it is composed. . . .
Sir William Hamilton

A vast deal of matter. . . .
Thomas and William Daniell

The definition of matter as eternal and self-perpetuating represents a long-standing conundrum for philosophy. The Pre-Socratics and the Stoics conceived of the earth as alive in all its parts; minerals, metals, stones, were thought to possess a vital force and to grow like the cosmos. Generally, the world was regarded as animate until the Renaissance; thereafter, during the seventeenth century, the old hylozoistic fallacy gradually gave way before the construct of the universe as a mechanism devoid of intelligence and life.[1]

Despite the incursion of Cartesianism, however, with its formulation of a cosmic clockwork and its radical distinction between bodies that think and those that do not, the notion of life in matter still required extirpation. It was most ably excoriated in 1678 by the British clergyman Ralph Cudworth, one of the Cambridge Platonists, who classified the four varieties of materialism bequeathed by antiquity to the modern era and judged them all equally reprehensible. According to his compendium, matter is either "dead and stupid"; or, as for Democritus, all things in nature are fortuitously "concreted" out of certain rough, smooth, "hookey," and crooked atoms; or, as for Epicurus and the Stoical atheists, matter is sensible and recurring; or, as for Strato Lampsacenus, an inward plastic life exists in the several parts of all physical stuff whereby they could "artificially" frame themselves to the best advantage without any conscious knowledge. The latter unreflecting, not quite animal, yet "plastick," hylozoic life exists in all the several parts of matter without sense. For

Cudworth—only too keenly aware of the possible threats to religious orthodoxy posed by materialism in all its guises—hylozoism is "nothing but a Dull and Drowsie, *Plastick* and *Spermatick* Life, devoid of all *Consciousness* and *Self-Enjoyment*." Cudworth heaps opprobrium on the hylozoic corporealist who multiplies the "lives of Matter in its infinite atoms" and whose god is "a certain blind *shee-god* or Goddess," a "perfect Non-sence."

Somewhat later, in France, the Huguenot critic Pierre Bayle, in his *Dictionnaire* (1697), similarly recorded the disturbing claims of the ancient geographer-philosopher Dicaearchus, who argued that the soul is a "Power equally common to all living Things, and which forms but one single being with the Bodies called living." Bayle astutely perceives this position's threat to anthropocentrism and man's traditional superiority in the hierarchy of the universe; whoever reasons that a collection of bones and nerves feels and cogitates ought, by that very same logic, to maintain that every other system of matter thinks.[2] We are not far from Diderot's conjecture that even the stone must feel.

Several ingredients from this philosophical controversy, then, were important for eighteenth-century developments. Certain pre-Socratic hylozoist ideas had already been revived—in art, for example, with the *Knorpelstil* of the late Renaissance. This decorative system of patterning vivified inorganic forms (which were interpreted as an expression of panpsychism) and exerted a strong influence on the Rococo ornamental print.[3] At the same time, in cosmography, Benoît de Maillet returned to the doctrine of Thales that everything was born from the ocean's flux. The *philosophe* Jean-Claude-Izouard de l'Isle de Sales expounded the Pythagorean idea of the world as a dynamic *"colosse organisé."*[4] At the close of the century, the mysterious Antoine Fabre d'Olivet, influenced by narratives produced by travelers to India, discoursed about metempsychosis and related it to the ancient dogma of universal animism.[5]

But the French were not alone in thinking that nature no longer resembled the Platonists' dull and inert matter. The German poet Christoph Martin Wieland and the critic Johann Gottfried von Herder—grounding themselves in Spinozistic thought—found the universe to be a sentient, living, moving organism. Erasmus Darwin's *Loves of the Plants* (1789) again filled the cosmos with quasi-sexual forces reminiscent of Empedocles's war between love and strife.

The mention of Erasmus Darwin reminds us that it was in England, at the outset of the eighteenth century, that dangerous speculations concerning matter's potentially "animated" states were bruited about. Locke set the controversy ablaze with his hypothesis that God could, if he desired, "superadd" thought to a sophisticated bit of matter. Writing in opposition to Berkeley, he claimed that there was no contradiction in the notion that the first eternal thinking being could, if he pleased, "give to certain systems of created senseless matter, put together as he thinks fit, some degrees of sense, perception, and thought." Though Locke's statement clearly emerged against the background of the Cartesian man-versus-machine controversy, and though he was at pains to deny the possibility that matter is the creator, the debate was on.

Locke was as opposed as Cudworth and Bayle to the hylozoist "fallacy." It is evident from the objections to materialism listed in the *Essay Concerning Human Understanding* (4. 10. 14–17) that he does not espouse an *animus mundi*. Locke counters this "absurdity" with the hypothesis that an eternal thinking in substance is plausible as long as we realize that, whatever "excellency, not contained in its essence" be superadded to matter, it "does not destroy the essence of matter, if it leaves it an extended solid substance." This final caveat demonstrates that Locke, despite his detractors, was still speaking of matter as a bare and naked substratum. In England, the shift from this view of a solid and "dead" corporeal stuff, endowed in some parts with motion, to the vision of a lively, force-riddled, and quite unmechanistic ether did not occur until the 1740s, with the Newtonians. Therefore, a discussion of the role of the theory of gravitation stated in terms of action at a distance and its supposed revival of "occult" powers properly belongs to the following chapter.[6] Suffice it to say for now that the rankling aspect of Locke's position was immediately perceived: If one can augment matter by one property (thought) that is not part of its essence without destroying its nature, can one not augment it by others? Further, where does the process stop?

Half a century later, Diderot, in his ambivalent struggle to break with Descartes and the mechanistic tradition in France, developed the argument that matter is in constant transformation. He constructed a material monism, a transformistic vitalism, that opposed the metaphysical pantheism of Spinoza, who claimed there was no being outside the one substance of the universe.[7] For Diderot there is only one substance—matter—and sensibility is an essential quality of that matter: "the stone must feel."[8]

Diderot, looking not to Locke but to Shaftesbury, Leibniz, and the French biological vitalists, developed a concept of self-motion residing in physical stuff. Leibniz had emphasized the dynamic community of all monads, from the human soul down through the vegetable kingdom to the monads of apparently inorganic substances.[9] Diderot came to see the universe as process, an organic unity of evolving particulars responding and interrelating in a way no longer mechanistic. He followed up on the ambiguity inherent in Leibniz's monadology which suggested that the three traditionally distinct realms of nature are not easily kept separate but flow together. In fact, D'Alembert is made to say: "Every animal is more or less human; every mineral is more or less animal; every plant is more or less animal. There is nothing precisely demarcated in nature. . . ."[10]

Like Diderot, the Swiss biologist Charles Bonnet envisaged a great chain of being, an uninterrupted succession of grades descending from the highest to the lowest forms and mobilized by imperishable germs. Bonnet, despite himself, immortalized the difficulty of distinguishing among the three kingdoms of nature by focusing on the polyp controversy. The polyp aroused perplexity because scientists were uncertain as to whether it was plant or animal: "Polyps are situated on the frontiers of another universe that one day will have its Columbuses and Vespuccis. . . ."[11] If such ambiguity is found at the border between animals and plants, Bonnet reasons, what enigmas await us at the zone between vegetables and minerals?

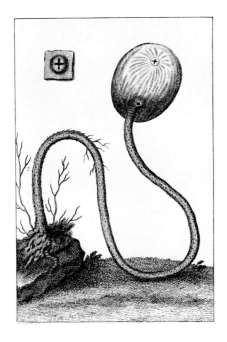

Thus, "science" contributed to the conjectures on the innermost constituent particles of matter. Its investigations were hurried along by the constantly shifting picture of nature that emerged from the microscope: It was superabundant, lavish, prolific; it "swarmed," "heaved" with life.[12] This delightful instrument demonstrated how apparently dead motes were, in reality, animate entities: " . . . a world reveals itself to our eyes, nature, become transparent, will not slow down its progress: its studios and laboratories shall be opened. . . ."[13] Bonnet and Robinet were writing of their lively discoveries—extending the topography of vision, in effect—at the time (1761–1768) when major scientific expeditions were getting underway: those of Samuel Wallis, Philip Carteret, Bougainville, Bruce, and Cook. It is no wonder that such "research" produced vitalist ruminations and led to the spectacle of travelers watching rocks grow, clams spout, and the earth secrete many hybrid forms. Louis-Sebastien Mercier, praising the physicians Gerolamo Cardano and Paracelsus to the detriment of Newton, exclaims: "Minerals are engendering themselves, stones grow . . . a generative power insinuates itself into the hardest rock: a mine has its own organization just like the oak swaying atop the mountain summit. . . ."[14] Early-eighteenth-century mineralogists often attributed the formation of fossils to "*semina*" and crystals to "germs," thus assuming they possessed sexuality.[15] Still-life painters portrayed how shells and corals mimic flowers. The sober Jesuit Frézier, citing Palissy for support, insisted that silver and copper were daily renewed underground.[16] Conversely, just as islands and metals could be born, Robinet declared that rocks could die.[17]

These materialistic convictions—whether grounded in the recrudesence of ancient "sensible matter" philosophies, in misinterpretation of Locke, or in scientific speculations—were all in some way based on an axiomatic belief in the potency of the earth's core. This faith simultaneously denied the existence of the inanimate and affirmed that expression or "force" was intrinsic to all natural forms.[18] Of course, such a thesis ran counter to much of Western aesthetics, which since Greek antiquity had put forward the infusion of life as a fundamental task of art and posited the impossibility of a self-generated beauty residing in inorganic objects such as the earth forms and the "singularities" of this chapter.[19] This attitude is best summed

THE NATURAL MASTERPIECE

up by the French Academy's dictum that the artist's task was to "give life to inanimate things"; to imprint life "upon insensible matter."[20]

In the eighteenth century, on the other hand, estimation of the inorganic was founded squarely on the denial of its inanimateness, not on the "pathetic fallacy" or the imposition (via association) of human liveliness onto rigid, cold, and in themselves unlovely things.[21] This alternate aesthetic development, which went against the grain of the Picturesque, found support in the natural symbolism employed by pre-Classical art. Eighteenth-century thinkers were cognizant that, in pre-Classical art, landscape features were approached as "living stones," the recognizable images of organic creatures—a primitive custom that did not escape the attention of William Borlase or Antoine-Chrysostôme Quatremère de Quincy.[22] Similar ideas could be found in non-Western cultures and were fostered by seventeenth- and eighteenth-century travelers to the Far East. As noted, Johan Nieuhof, through his *Embassy to China* (1669), disseminated the topographic, geomantic system of Fong Chouei, which purported to reveal the inner, hidden essence of nature on the basis of the assumption that everything living possesses an individual sign; through this terrestrial scheme the Chinese interpret the configuration and position of hills and mountains as if they were moving planets.[23] By means of these accounts Nieuhof and Kircher communicated to the West the Taoist vision of nature as an organism whose living materials man regarded with awe.[24]

Irrespective of the form it takes, the belief that matter is self-sufficient melds with certain aesthetic tenets that preoccupied philosophers of the Enlightenment. Both primitive and non-Western art appear unconventional precisely insofar as they respect the integrity of a nonhumanized earth articulating itself in specific vital forms.[25] Paralleling this estimation of non-Classical and foreign cultures, scientific and pseudo-scientific discoveries made by perspicuous travelers showed the earth to be a *plenum formarum* full of strange material things.[26] This emphasis on the study of a world now revealed to be nothing short of profanely miraculous is, as we saw, related to the empiricist model of the mind, in which no ideas are innate but all arise from sensation and visual exploration.

Eighteenth-century materialists argued that matter, once set in motion, could have resulted in the actual organization of the universe without the aid of a divine blueprint. Such an assertion was tantamount to claiming that all matter in action produces regular, organized, sensitive bodies— in short, truly natural masterpieces. The logical outcome of this dictum on self-systematization was a concerted Anglo-French formulation of the concept of active matter reflected in diverse ways in Maillet's *Telliamed* (1748), Buffon's *Théorie de la terre* (1770–1781), Robinet's *Considérations philosophiques* (1768), and Priestley's *Disquisitions Relating to Matter and Spirit* (1777).

By contrast, in the Platonic or Idealistic view of substance the fundamental task of the work of art was to lighten and sublimate matter, or at best to treat it as a negligible entity to be overcome. Ovid makes this abundantly clear in his tale of Vulcan's forging costly metal doors for the palace of Apollo; only by artistic metamorphosis will the lowly material be transcended. Plato, Aristotle, the Abbot Suger, Nicholas of Cusa, the Scholastics, and the Neo-Platonists agree that the Idea of all things in its perfect state is completely immaterial. By an extension of this thought, the mastery of the artist is demonstrated by the fact that he makes matter submissive to an abstracting mental form—hence the importance in art theory bestowed on the *concetto* indifferent to its clothing, the almost impalpable *disegno*, and the simple, bodiless circumscription.[27]

This chapter is concerned not with those transparent materials that occasionally found favor in the Idealistic system because they seemed to deny their own phenomenality, but rather with the self-assertive varieties of primitive, brute, and opaque matter: the natural masterpiece of rude, unregenerated stone, uninhabited mountains, uncultivated deserts, primeval forests, and impassable rivers.

For the expedition artists the traditional elements—earth, air, fire, and water—seemed to possess unequal value. Earth appears to have appealed most readily largely because of its unrefined, unpurified physicality. This most primary and chthonic of all the elements ranges in expressive potential from dust, to chunk, to mud. The eloquent multiformity of ostensibly solid, massive, hard, impenetrable bodies was especially suited to the exemplification of what eighteenth-century natural historians confirmed as the individual acting out of the universal metabolism of matter.[28] Consequently, the most striking physiognomy of a place derived from the rocks underlying it. Such robust features, more than any others, were governed by geological conditions and physical processes operating on and within stones rather than by the intervention of man.[29] Traditionally they embodied both the opaqueness of the world and its recalcitrant autonomy, yet, by virtue of the characters of rocks they also suggested a way of getting at the world.

Rude boulders, *pierres brutes*, and colossal crags, mountains, ravines, and chasms had been looked on favorably since the close of the seventeenth century. Roger de Piles (1708) admitted that such enormous specimens, by their diversity, possessed *"certains caractères"* that could not be captured by the artist unless he examined them *"sur le naturel."* Rock banks, stratified beds, salient or recessed blocks, connected or isolated masses—each geological species enjoyed its proper character. Nor, de Piles cautioned, could the superficial effects of erosion be ignored. Fractures, fissures, holes, crevices, the incidental covering of brush and moss, and spots that time imprints all contributed to the idea of verisimilitude when well executed

Figure 8
W. Borlase, *King Arthur's Bed*, from
Antiquities . . . of the County of Cornwall,
1769, pl. 20. Engraving. Photo courtesy
Library of Congress.

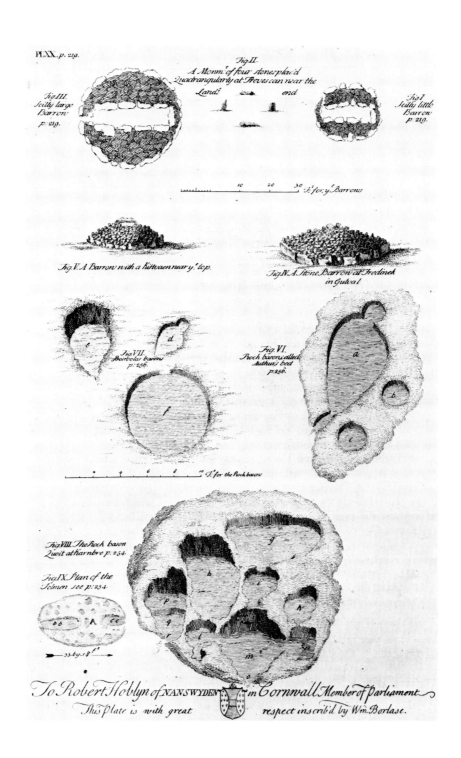

VOYAGE INTO SUBSTANCE

Figure 9
J. Nieuhof, *Suytjeen: The Mountain of the Five Horses' Heads*, from *Embassy . . . to China*, 1669, pl. p. 55. Engraving. Photo courtesy India Office Library, London.

Figure 10
A. Kircher, *Fe of Fokien Province*, from *China Monumentis*, 1667, pl. p. 172. Engraving. Photo courtesy Newberry Library, Chicago.

by the artist.[30] According to de Piles, boulders, mountains, and other extraordinary sites belong to the milieu of the heroic rather than the pastoral landscape, particularly when they evoke melancholy. But de Piles does not linger in the wilderness of the rude sublime. He sees water as mollifying these asperities, imparting to them a soul that ''in a certain sense renders them domestic.''[31]

In the East, sensitive awareness for the individual wild traits of stones long predates any such aesthetic recognition in the West.[32] As early as the twelfth century the amateur Chinese petrologist Tu Wan drew up a descriptive list of 114 stones gathered in a single private collection. Most were strictly utilitarian (usually medicinal) in function, but the place of honor was awarded to those samples, of whatever size, that were admired for their apparently purposed yet uncultivated shape, color, and texture. The *Mustard Seed Garden* (1688)—a celebrated treatise on Chinese painting, marked by the Taoist doctrine that things possess a vitality, a spirit, the *ki-yun* that must be made to resound—was transported to Germany in 1692 by Dr. Kaempfer, who accompanied the Dutch embassy to Peking.[33] The Japanese haiku master and wanderer Bashō, in his travel diary *The Narrow Road to the Far North* (1689), shows a similar affection for the rupestral, whether it be the noxious Slaughter Stone at Kurobane or the naturally patterned Shinobu Mottling Stone.[34]

Figure 11
Cornelius Le Bruyn, *Singular Rocks*, from *Travels to Muscovy, Persia...*, 1737, I, pl. p. 62. Engraving. Photo courtesy Library of Congress.

The Dutch physician Cornelius Le Bruyn (and Norden after him), traveling by caravan in Persia in 1703, was struck by the convoluted rocks rife with animal and human faces emerging from the surrounding desert. The identical ferine landscape exists in Islamic miniatures that transpose the bestiaries of the Sung and Yuan dynasties.

''It happened,'' writes Le Bruyn ''that we had unwarily got into a sandy plain, between some downs of moving sand where it is impossible to travel without danger. Behind these downs there are lofty mountains, between which is the road to *Sawa* and to *Com*.... About *eleven* we reached a stony mountain, whose rocks represented all sorts of objects, a surprizing thing to behold: I drew them at distance, together with the mountain on the right hand of the town.... The first is like the head and neck of an animal, and the rest are to the full as remarkable....''[35]

Le Bruyn's commentary seems to indicate that the interest in expressive, nonzoomorphic monuments and monoliths arose in the later eighteenth century. The same period grew to value (although not exclusively) a rock's inherent and nonmimetic spirit. Thus, William Marsden in Sumatra singles out a view of Padre's Rock.[36] John Barrow, in *A Voyage to Cochin China in the Years 1792 and 1793*, reproduces Samuel Daniell's aquatint of the Ilheo or Loo Rock at Funchall. Although Barrow seizes the effect of a storm blowing up, his gaze is largely concentrated on ''a huge insulated mass of black lava, surmounted with batteries, [which] constitute a foreground that is well-suited to the grandeur of the scenery on shore.''[37] On a subsequent journey from the Cape of Good Hope to the Karoo or Arid Desert (1801), Barrow speaks of the Paarlberg, a hill of moderate size that he feels to be worthy of debate in the *Philosophical Transactions* because of a distinctive "chain of large round stones that pass over the summit, like the pearls of a necklace."[38] These blocks of South African granite share the property of visual, even heroic, isolation with paratactically grouped boulders in other scenes, such as John Webber's rockbound Harbor of Taloo (figure 12). Precipitous vertical insularity is an often-remarked characteristic of figured and nonfigured outcroppings. Consider William Daniell's and George Bellasis's descriptions and sketches of the saliency of Friar Rock. Bellasis writes: "Entering Friar's valley from the east, the central object is an immense pile of rocks rising perpendicularly eight hundred feet above the level of the sea. On the right is seen a fine opening to the Atlantic Ocean; and on the left, another in the centre of which appears a very curious and interesting object composed of five rocks, firmly cemented by nature, affording a fanciful resemblance of Friar, in the habit of his Order. . . ." Similarly, but with greater geological astuteness, Clarke Abel, in the *Narrative of a Voyage in China* (1815), is struck by the "singularity" of the scenery, whose total effect is constituted by the perception of unique particulars. Prominent in this mountain environment is "a marbled rock on the right bank, rising perpendicularly from the surface of the water to the height of two or three hundred feet, [which] particularly arrested [Abel's] attention." "The breccia," he continues, "rose only a few feet above the water. The principal mass of rock resting upon it exhibited no stratification, but appeared to be one entire mass of fine-grained flesh-red granules of limestone. . . ."[39]

Thomas and William Daniell, in their compilation *Oriental Scenery*, show themselves susceptible to the material presence of "insulated" masses. As Benjamin West told Joseph Farington, the Daniells (uncle and nephew) were known for their faithful portraits of remarkable places. One of the most exceptional was that of Fakeer Rock, in the Ganges near Sutangunge (figure 15). The imposing mass of gray granite was assigned to a "very remote" antiquity, not only because of its primary substance but also because of the archaic relief sculpture evident on many of its faces.[40] En route to India in 1785, the Daniells paid a visit to China. Entering Macao past the Ass's Ears, they again noted a gigantic, but this time, unadorned, pillar of granite. In the Straits of Malacca they encountered a high white rock, Pedro Branca, that had provoked comment on its artlessness from Richard Chambers during Anson's circumnavigation some 40 years earlier.[41]

Obtrusive, free-standing stone—often "naked," heterogeneous in composition, and ungoverned in appearance—crops up all over the world. Adam Neale, traveling along the Elbe, is galvanized by the "living rock" that surrounds him; the fortress of Königstein, located 16 miles upriver from Dresden, has its buildings "placed on the summit of an enormous

THE NATURAL MASTERPIECE

Figure 12
John Webber, *View of the Harbour of Taloo,
in the Island of Eimee* (October 1777), for
Views in the South Seas . . . , 1808, pl. 7.
Watercolor. Photo courtesy National
Maritime Museum, Greenwich, England.

VOYAGE INTO SUBSTANCE

Figure 13
William Daniell, *Rocks at Sandy Bay, Saint Helena* (June 1794). Watercolor W.D. 240. Photo courtesy India Office Library.

Figure 14
G. H. Bellasis, *The Friar Rock in Friars Valley*, from *Views of Saint Helena*, 1815, pl. 5. Color aquatint. Photo courtesy India Office Library.

mass of free-stone, insulated like that of Dumbarton, and hanging over the Elbe, as the latter does over the Clyde."[42] Lieutenant Tuckey, in *Expedition to Zaire* (1818), reveals that he visited the Fetiche Rock, a conglomerate of granite mixed with quartz and mica that stands perpendicular to the water and in isolation, "completely command[ing] the river."[43] Such startling and literally unavoidable tangible apparitions share with the Sacred Rock of Djebel el Berbel in Ethiopia, the "solitary stones of immense size" towering in isolation atop the summits of many Norwegian mountains, and the "almost insulated" boulders of "vast size" scattered throughout Ceylon and India an underlying brute and irreducible existence.[44]

No formation was deemed more worthy of apprehension as a natural monument or considered more controversial, however, than those framed from basalt—the true rival to the earth's unmetamorphic and granitic rocks. Unlike primary strata, which underwent slow transformations and hence were symbolic of lastingness, basalt (depending on one's scientific prejudices) was thought to be the result of volcanic activity. Prismatic basalt, in particular, was believed to be a consequence of submarine eruptions. The French and German geologists Nicolas Demarest and Rudolf Erich Raspe came to the latter far-reaching conclusion at the outset of the 1770s.[45] Diversely contoured aggregations of prismatic columns were noted to clump together in conspicuous single crags or dramatic promontories. The crater or source of this molten matter, in the words of the British geologist John Whitehurst, must "have been absolutely sunk and swallowed up into the earth, at some remote period of time, and become the bottom of the Atlantic Ocean" during "a period indeed much beyond the reach of any historical monument, or even of tradition itself." Whitehurst was stirred to these meditations not only by Fingal's Cave and the regular pillars of the Giant's Causeway (figure 19) but also by other "magnificent works of nature" described by travelers. Specifically, he alludes to Hodges's account (composed during his Indian tour of 1781) of a basaltic cliff called Matagena.[46] There is a strong impulse evident in these illustrations to copy the formations as if they were physical units rooted in the structure and contour of the terrain and thus mirroring the very processes of their creation.

Jean-Benjamin de Laborde, in his *Description de la France* (1781–1796), momentarily departs from his scenic intent in his depiction of the Chateau de Rochemaure, which is shown jutting above, yet physiognomically integral with, the black banks of the Rhone (figure 22). He states that it is the bold prisms that form the subject of his representation, not the seemingly tiny man-made edifice surmounting it. The union of these tightly linked basalt pillars and the natural system prevailing in their arrangement and multiple positions is of predominant concern to Laborde, who notes that "one sees either bold vaults of basaltic stone, sculpted by nature with all the geometry of vaults built by an enlightened architect; or orbicular basalt formed from diverse concentric beds."[47] Jean Houel, in the Midi and in Sicily, draws analogous attention to the multitudinous morphological expressions possible to this igneous rock. He asserts that on his voyage he delineated and described at least five or six different types of "these marvels," ranging from domes to spheroids.[48] Humboldt, atop the Mexican plateau at Regla, is moved to reflect on the ubiquity of natural stone masterpieces in the presence of solitary masses of basalt: "In all climates, the lithic crust of the globe presents the same aspect to the voyager. . . . Everywhere the same monuments attest to the same results in the revolutions which have progressively changed the surface of the earth. . . . "Animal and plant life may be different in far-flung regions, but not rock masses.[49]

Other uncompounded specimens were admired, ranging from curved veins of gneiss originating in the Western Isles of Scotland to intricate coral emerging from the floor of the South Pacific and established on shore at Tonga, "projecting above the surface, and perforated and cut into all those inequalities which are usually seen in rocks that lie within the wash of the tide."[50] Because most scientists believed these marine "plants" to be living and growing organisms, a discussion of their pictorial fate belongs properly to the section on forests. Nevertheless, as established "petrifications" they constitute a staple ingredient of the treatises composed by polemically inclined naturalists and travelers. The Abbé La Pluche says of this marine phenomenon that "such an arrangement [of juxtaposed tartar and salt layers with their heads always directed toward the bottom] makes one suspect even more that these types of bushes are only petrifications analogous to those attached to the ceilings of certain caves."[51]

Of the extraordinary rock formations, doubtless the natural arch is the most frequently described and portrayed. It was a common element in Mannerist landscape painting and in theatrical sets of the period and beyond.[52] In the factual travel account, however, the perforated rock loses the whimsical and paradoxical aura of a piece of art masquerading as nature to approximate the robustness of the real thing. Joseph Banks describes such an unwrought arch discovered in Tolaga Bay, New Zealand, and H. D. Spöring illustrates it (figure 23). Banks writes: "We saw . . . an extraordinary natural curiosity. . . . It was certainly the most magnificent surprise I have ever met with, so much is pure nature superior to art in these cases. I have seen such places made by art, where from an inland view you were led through an arch six feet wide, and seven feet high, to a prospect of the sea, but here was an arch twenty five yards in length, nine in breadth, and at least fifteen in height. . . . " About a fortnight later Banks came upon a related wonder. He writes in his journal that what made it truly "romantic" was that much the greater part of the stone was "hollowed out into an arch, which penetrated quite through it." Sidney Parkinson, the official artist on that same voyage, took similar note of "a most grand natural arch" upon which was perched a Maori *hippa*, or place

THE NATURAL MASTERPIECE

Figure 15
Thomas and William Daniell, *S.W. View of the Fakeer's Rock,* from *Antiquities of India,* 1799, pl. 9. Color aquatint. Photo courtesy India Office Library.

Figure 16
D. Vivant-Denon, *Djebelein, or the Two Mountains,* from *Voyage dans la Haute et la Basse Egypte,* 1801, II, pl. 52. Engraving. Photo courtesy British Library.

Figure 17
John Edy, *A Remarkable Stone,* from *Boydell's Scenery of Norway,* 1820, II, pl. 68. Color aquatint. Photo courtesy British Library.

VOYAGE INTO SUBSTANCE

Figure 18
William Daniell, *Hindu Temple near Madanpur, Bihar* (February 1790). Watercolor. Photo courtesy India Office Library.

THE NATURAL MASTERPIECE

Figure 20
T. Black, *Singular Rocks at Doobrajpoor,*
from Sir Charles D'Oyly's *Scrapbook,* 1829,
fol. 121. Lithograph. Photo courtesy India
Office Library.

THE NATURAL MASTERPIECE

Figure 21
Thomas Postans, *Rock Inscriptions near
Girnar*, 1838, fol. 99. Wash drawing W.D.
485. Photo courtesy India Office Library.

Figure 22
J.-B. de Laborde, *Basaltic Rocks* (Château
de Rochemaure), from *Description de la
France*, 1781, II, pl. 3. Engraving by Née
after drawing by Le May. Photo courtesy
Bibliothèque Nationale.

THE NATURAL MASTERPIECE

Figure 23
H. D. Spöring, *A Fortified Town or Village, Called a Hippah, Built on a Perforated Rock at Tolaga in New Zealand,* from John Hawkesworth's *Voyages,* 1768, pl. 18. Engraving. Photo courtesy National Maritime Museum.

Figure 24
A. de Cappell Brooke, *Mountain and Caverns of Torghatten,* from *Travels through Sweden . . . ,* 1822, pl. p. 208. Engraving.

of retreat. He was intrigued by the visual tension between the man-made and the natural and by the fact that one side of this eminence was still connected to land while the other freely "rose out of the sea."[53]

Further, John Henry Grose, on his voyage to the East Indies, sighted a "crevice" in Malabar Hill at Bombay that communicated with "a hollow that terminates at an opening outwards towards the sea." Cook, at Christmas Harbour (1776), met with a remarkable "high rock which is perforated quite through so as to appear as the arch of a bridge." Cordiner, in Scotland, was smitten by "Caledonian obelisks," that is, a rugged and "vast mass of rock [which] has an open vault that passes wholly through it." William Alexander, in China, copies a "great cliff with a keyhole-shaped opening.[54] Whether the artist calls the marvel a "tunnel" (as Cassas does in Syria and Brooke in Sweden) or an "arched chasm" (as Owens does in Madagascar), what is judged noteworthy is the combination of a void—through which the sun occasionally shines—and the simultaneous exposure of the solidity of the mass. This visual effect is enhanced by the actual activity of a distinctive eminence's thrusting abruptly out of the waves or springing vertically from the land.[55] (See figures 24–26.) Pierced rocks are perceptually and essentially connected to other environmentally worked-upon phenomena, among them beetling scarps molded into bleak domes. Kerguelen-Trémarec (1771) discovered just such a "Hangcliff or Hanglip"—shaped by the ocean—in the Shetland Isles.[56]

After the hollowed rock, the natural bridge received the most concerted attention. Laborde found the *département* of the Rhône fascinating for the naturalist desirous of contemplating the earth's singularities; he cites in particular the rustic span located above the parish of Engin.[57] That fabrication, the Pont du diable in Switzerland (dating from the twelfth century), was made by Caspar Wolf to duplicate the character of the natural setting in which it manifested itself (figure 27). Alexander von Humboldt attests to the phenomenon's continuing popularity when he records that the quartzose bridge of Iconozo, situated some 2,500–3,000 meters above sea level, manages to weaken in some measure the effect of the colossi of Chimborazo, Cotopaxi, and Antisana.[58]

A further consequence of this quickness to respond to the lithic was the simultaneous rise of interest in assemblages of rocks pictorially constituting a collective, if restricted, totality. In Anson's *Voyage round the World* (1744), Chambers is drawn to five isolated rocks, white with the guano of tropical birds and surging from the bay immediately beneath the Mexican hill of Pataplan. He unites them perceptually into a precise figure: "Four of these rocks are high and large, and, together with several smaller ones, are, by the help of a little imagination, pretended to resemble the form of a cross, and are called the White Friars. . . ."[59] William Alexander, accompanying Lord Macartney's embassy to the Emperor of China, left numerous watercolors of rocks strewn along the Canton River which he apprehended

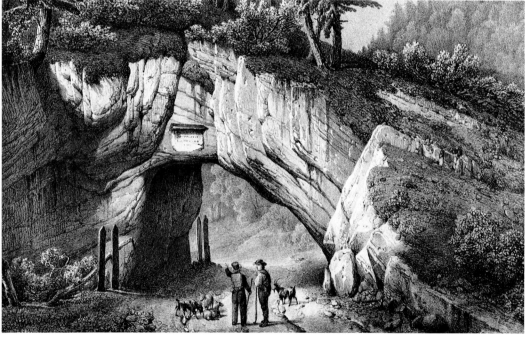

Figure 25
John Ross, *A Remarkable Iceberg,* from
Voyage of Discovery, 1819, pl. 58. Aquatint
by Havell and Son. Photo courtesy British
Library.

Figure 26
D. Raoul-Rochette, *Pierre Pertuis,* from
Lettres sur la Suisse, 1824, I, part II, pl. 15.
Lithograph by Villeneuve and Engelmann.
Photo courtesy Cabinet des Estampes,
Bibliothèque Nationale.

THE NATURAL MASTERPIECE

VICTORI PACIFICO

Carolo Guill: Ferdinando Duci Brunsuicensi Regn:

Pontis Diaboli Delineationem

D. D. D. R. Hentzi, Prævocatus Nobilianus in arte Principiis Auriaci Gubec:

Figure 27
Caspar Wolf, *Pont du Diable*, from *Vues
remarquables de la Suisse*, second edition,
1785, pl. 7. Color aquatint by J. F. Janinet
and C.-M. Descourtis. Photo courtesy
Cabinet des Estampes, Bibliothèque
Nationale.

as tightly juxtaposed monoliths. (See figure 28.) On Teneriffe in the Canaries, George Staunton enumerated the "craggy heaps" and "singular combinations" adjacent to the huge cone of the Peak.[60] Louis-François Cassas, in Dalmatia, scrutinized vertical "rocs" whose summits were gigantic walls forming a solitary and invincible rampart.[61] Laborde, in the Dauphiné, saw banks composed of calcareous schist adding up to a "singular form." And Mungo Park, writing on his last mission to Africa, concedes that the apparent uniformity of the terrain is, in fact, compound; he traveled "for more than two miles over white quartz large lumps of which were lying all round; no other stone to be seen."[62] The Daniells in Africa and Tuckey sailing up the Congo cite contiguous anthills (figure 29) as organic examples.[63]

Forbidding obstructions and austere crags or precipices represent variations on the theme of compact land masses existing in proximate relationships and brought close up. Captain Robert Smith, on Prince of Wales' Island in 1821, took sketches that did not minimize the dorsal stones contouring Mount Erskine (figure 30), and James Wales captured the solidity of blocks strewn in apposition over Elephanta (figure 83). John Davy, in the interior of Ceylon in 1821, avers that solitary hills that are nothing but "immense masses of rock" punctuate extensive and arid plains. Robert Ker Porter, trekking across Persia in 1822, acknowledges it to be "a region of naked rocks" connected by their fragmented and severed aspects. Major Cockburn, conjuring up a vicinal image of the region around Mount Cenis and the Simplon Pass in Switzerland in 1822, vaunts two neighboring outcrops rearing from the bottom of an abyss (figure 32). And Lieutenant-Colonel Forrest, in Bengal, praises the majestic boulders of Colgong and notes that the place is rendered anomalous by "three singular masses of rock" standing in the body of the Ganges.[64]

Salient and abutting shapes were not restricted to soaring, seemingly self-propelled, from the depths of a rugged valley or a dusty plain. The frozen sea, in the chill reaches of the far north—at first smooth and unbroken—could suddenly become rougher, assuming an undulating appearance mirroring the choppy waves by which it had once been agitated. Joseph Acerbi, traveling on the ice over the Gulf of Bothnia to Finland in 1802, anticipated a monotonous journey. As his sleds advanced mile after mile, he was astonished to meet with "masses of ice heaped one upon the other, and some of them seeming as if they were suspended in air, while others were raised in the form of pyramids." "On the whole," he continues, "they exhibited a picture of the wildest and most savage confusion, that surprised the eye by the novelty of its appearance. It was an immense chaos of icy ruins, presented to view under every possible form, and embellished by superb stalactites of a blue green colour. . . ."[65]

THE NATURAL MASTERPIECE

Figure 28
William Alexander, *Rocks by the Canton River*, for *Lord Macartney's Embassy* . . . , 1797, pl. p. 79. Watercolor no. 252. Photo courtesy India Office Library.

Figure 29
Thomas and William Daniell, *White Ants Nest*, from *Animated Nature*, 1807–1812, pl. 29. Aquatint. Photo courtesy Newberry Library.

Figure 30
R. Smith, *View of Mount Erskine and Pulo Ticoose Bay*, from *Views of Prince of Wales Island*, 1821, pl. 1. Color aquatint by William Daniell. Photo courtesy India Office Library.

Figure 31
R. K. Porter, *Views of the Akarkouff*, from
Travels in Georgia . . ., 1822, II, pl. 68.
Aquatint by J. Clark.

VOYAGE INTO SUBSTANCE

Figure 32
J. P. Cockburn, *View Taken in the Valley of
the Grande Chartreuse*, from *Views to
Illustrate the Route of Mont Cenis*, 1822, pl.
7. Lithograph by C. Hullmandel. Photo
courtesy British Library.

"Acts" of Matter

*C'est un affreux désert, que celui où
je me trouvois [the Brèche de
Roland]. Point de végétation; des
neiges, accumulées du côté de la
France, à une hauteur considérable,
plus rares du côté de l'Espagne, &
moins durables, mais qui
découvrent, en cédant aux ardeurs
du Midi, de longs ravins & des
vastes éboulemens . . . des rochers,
de toutes parts, plus âpres & plus
herisées du côté de la France, plus
dégradés du côté de l'Espagne . . . la
forme & la blancheur des sommets,
rappelle l'idée de vagues
courroucées. . . . La, s'ouvre une
perspective immense. . . .*
Ramond de Carbonnières*

*In other hill fortresses, the scarp or
perpendicular part of the height, is
usually at or near the summit,
while at Dowlutabad it is at the
foot of the elevation. . . . [It is]
formed out of an insulated hill and
as it stands alone on the plain, it
looks as though, in the convulsions
of the deluge, it might have been
separated from the High Land. . . .*
Robert Elliott*

The recognition and the reporting of "singular figures of earth" opened a new path leading between actuality and art. Embedded in the travelers' descriptions is the growing sense of the natural object's existence as a dynamic event in its own right. No singularity was more prone to being perceived as self-productive drama than the mountain. During the second half of the eighteenth century, cosmopolitan wanderers and explorers traversed the Alps of the four cantons, the Valais, the Tessin, and the Grisons. But the crowning achievement of such forays remained the Bernese Oberland, systematically explored by the "tireless" Marc-Théodore Bourrit and that pioneer of Mont Blanc, Horace-Bénédict de Saussure. William Coxe toured this region in 1779. Two years earlier, Ramond de Carbonnières—by then already famous—left his imprint on Swiss soil. Concurrently, the *fermier-général* Laborde was preparing his sumptuous *Tableaux topographiques de la Suisse* (1777) and, while readying it, sent the naturalist Hippolyte Bisson into the Valais.[66] What binds their endeavors with those of students of bold outcrops is a continual search for the varied faces of phenomena and for tangible encounters with phenomenality that is one of the paths of true science.

It was mountain scenery (as a variation of the perception for rude idiosyncratic rocks), rather than the sea or remote lands, that first seriously engaged knowledgeable beholders.[67] The abstract depiction of desolate wastes (as, for example, in the Mannerist landscapes of Joos II de Momper) is characterized by pronounced flattened silhouettes, steep declivities, and deep ravines, from which vegetation is swept away. Strongly charged curves and abrupt contrasts indicate the orbit of this ludic and deliberately artificial style.[68] Although in an earlier chapter I established certain affinities between the eighteenth century's attitudes toward landscape and those of Mannerism, it seems appropriate now to point out a major distinction. Diderot makes explicit what has been implicit in the exposition concerning the material diversity of the natural masterpiece. In the *Salon* of 1765 he remarks that, after variety, what startles most in nature is mass. Foremost among his paradigms—including the pyramids, the elephant, the whale, the marginless ocean, and the depths of the forest—are the Alps and the Pyrenees.[69] Diderot probes a leading eighteenth-century preoccupation with the earth viewed in relief, that is, the seemingly instantaneous reaction elicited by significant, simple, and tangible mass. As he recognized, this sturdy amplitude was archetypally embodied in colossal granite blocks. By its sheer scale and its insistent verticality, simultaneously hinting at an enormous load-bearing horizontal foundation, the mountain forces a response.

Coeval with and dependent on the revitalization of matter during the later seventeenth century was the recognition that mountains were not deformed but "solid and substantial blessings." In the 1680s and 1690s, Henry More and the Cambridge Platonists, along with the English divine Ralph Cudworth and the noted naturalist John Ray, refocused attention on the idea of a plastic nature, a dynamic principle functioning as an

VOYAGE INTO SUBSTANCE

antonym to the concept of a mechanical universe. Although they took the field against mechanism—by upholding the Stoic idea of the *logos spermatikos*—they inadvertently managed to dislodge the disdain fomented by Thomas Burnet for the lumpish imperfections of the earth.[70]

Still more decisive was the publication in 1708 in London of Johann Jacob Scheuchzer's *Itinera Helvetica*, with its strange plates of towering mountains. There followed Abraham Stanyon's *Account of Switzerland* (1714), Albrecht Haller's "Les Alpes" (1732), and Rousseau's *Julie, ou la Nouvelle Héloïse* (1761), but for our purposes nothing enhanced interest more than the attractive, handsomely illustrated *Vues remarquables des montagnes de la Suisse* (1785), with aquatints by Descourtis and Janinet made after oil paintings by the Swiss artist Caspar Wolf. Wolf displays a discriminating sensitivity for the particularity of the terrain, rendering boulders and peaks with sculptural clarity. He shares with the learned beholder the almost nearsighted scrutiny of natural objects, observed as animate matter rather than dead detail. Thus, these cockscomb mountains belong to the modern naturalism born of scientific exactitude that was endemic to the period.[71]

Although the *Vues* were accompanied by extensive natural-history observations, the voyages conducted by geologists into the region of the high Alps were overtly scientific yet no less aesthetic. In 1776, Jean-André Deluc published anonymously the *Relation de différentes voyages dans les Alpes du Faucigny*. Shortly prior to this technical work, the painter and ecclesiastic Bourrit composed his series of *Descriptions des glacières* (1773–1785), following in the hallowed footsteps of Johann Georg Altmann and Gottlieb Siegmund Gruner.

Most significant of all to the particular evolution of ideas under study is the work of the Genevan Saussure, who for twenty years, from 1760 on, assiduously mounted campaigns against Mont Blanc. Saussure's *Voyages dans les Alpes* (1779, 1786, 1796) outstrode their forebears and were widely read. The French critic Sainte-Beuve, convinced of the *Voyages'* literary merit, devoted one of his *causeries de lundi* to them.[72] With Saussure's monumental study, orography entered its initial scientific stage. On the heels of his ascent of Mont Blanc came the revelation of the total organization of the Alps, based on the knowledge of their individual aspects. In a celebrated passage, Saussure destroys the illusion that the Alps were arranged in orderly fashion along a line. Instead of presenting a picturesque prospect, he revealed that they were distributed either in great triangles or in bizarre clumps isolated from one another. Stimulated by this discovery, Saussure drew a distinction (which was of utmost importance for future morphological studies) between primary mountains strewn by chance and secondary mountains disposed according to regular alignments. Not content with examining the external shapes of such ranges, Saussure, along with his colleague Déodat de Dolomieu, was among the first to comprehend that various chains possess different mineral structures.[73]

VUE DE L'HOSPICE & DE LA   CHAPELLE DES CAPUCINS,
au haut du   Mont S. Gothard.

Summo Pontifici   *Summum Templum*

Humillime   *Vovebat*

Figure 33
Caspar Wolf, *View of Hospice and Chapel of
Capucins, Mont Saint-Gothard*, from *Vues
remarquables de la Suisse*, second edition,
1785, pl. 11. Color aquatint by J. F. Janinet
and C.-M. Descourtis. Photo courtesy
Cabinet des Estampes, Bibliothèque
Nationale.

This acumen in sounding the depths of a formation's character is reflected to a minor extent in Bourrit's accompanying diagrams.

The journeys of such geologists suggested to perceptive readers a heroic and primal dimension in the stony wilderness. The physiognomy of the Alps was laid bare in image and in prose. Their scabrous summits emerged as bony, skeletal, beetle-browed. Their snow-capped peaks arrogated the root form of Newtonian prisms. Their asperities—analogously formed—mimicked a petrified sea.[74]

Two leading interpretations of morphology took on aesthetic significance with respect to the world's major mountains. The first was the continuity of mountain chains. (The Vivarais commences again on the other side of the Rhone, the Appennines ascend once more in Sicily, and the African Atlas Mountains resume in Arabia.) The second was the law of manifest singularity, which recognized the existence of certain monolithic, solitary, and independent mountains that seem to spring from the plains. (Mount Etna, Vesuvius, Adam's Peak, the Peak of the Teneriffe, and the Pic du Midi are models of such isolation.)[75]

Although Switzerland seriously entered the European consciousness around 1760, the assimilation of the Pyrenees occurred only during the 1780s. The young Ramond de Carbonnières, as secretary to the Cardinal de Rohan (whom he followed into exile), translated William Coxe's *Letters on Switzerland* and augmented them with his own *Observations faites dans les Pyrénées* (1789). From these scientific ponderings to the publication of his masterpiece, *Voyage au Mont-Perdu* in 1801, Ramond accomplished for the limestone chain of the Pyrenees what William Brockedon and Major Cockburn in the fullness of time achieved for the granitic Alps. His description of the Pic du Midi as viewed from Bagnères deserves quotation because it succinctly demonstrates why such colossi seized the imagination:

One cannot take a step in this place over which I am roaming without all things forcing one back to the Pic du Midi. Ruler over the best-known section of this terrain, it forms everywhere the most imposing object of the scene. Its situation from the plains presents the extraordinary spectacle of an elevation that one rarely beholds from so close up, and its apparent dimensions, coupled with its relative height, seem to subjugate the higher mountains that are grouped behind it. Inaccessible from the side where it presents itself most majestically, it has twisting avenues that lead gently to the summit. . . .[76]

Ramond's persuasive and enthusiastic praise of towering natural monuments, including the semicircular amphitheater of Gavarnie, the legendary Brèche de Roland, and the formidable and supposedly inaccessible Maladetta viewed from atop the marble boulder Penna Blanca proved memorable. Moving easily between the domain of cascades and frost and the region environing the colossus La Maudite, the Alsatian engraver, writer, and naturalist Ramond evoked the magic of the Pyrenees and claimed

THE NATURAL MASTERPIECE

them for art and science.[77] Ramond's *Observations* and *Carnets pyrénéens* (1789) belong within the province of this study because his numerous climbs (he scaled Mont-Perdu 35 times between 1787 and 1810) were not mere touristic adventures. He explored the Pyrenees in order to study their geology, to determine the climatological elements, to ascertain mean temperatures and barometric pressures, to gauge prevailing winds and the system by which clouds were formed, to witness atmospheric phenomena, and to catalog the varieties of vegetation. This information was conveyed in a warm and informative style worthy of his Alpine rival Saussure. Like the Genevan, Ramond was no dilettante, having studied botany with Antoine-Laurent de Jussieu. Before the revolution of 1789, Ramond laid the groundwork for the critical reception of Baron Taylor's expansive *Voyage pittoresque*. (Taylor's volume on the Pyrenees did not appear until 1843.) Influenced by Ramond's magisterial formula for a voyage of discovery, Chapuy's work for Taylor seeks to emulate his predecessor's observational rigor in the examination of natural sites and monuments.[78]

Naturalists were equally important in the exploration of the globe's more remote mountain chains and monoliths. Pierre Bouguer, on the voyage of Charles-Marie de la Condamine (who accomplished the first scientific exploration of the Amazon River), produced one of the earliest profiles of the Cordilleras (figure 34). Following the route taken in the sixteenth century by Pizarro and Dom Pedro Alvarado, Bouguer offers a vivid account of a tortuous climb in a drenching rainstorm. From Guayaquil he ascended Chimborazo on foot to capture the lateral unfolding of the western and eastern sections of the Peruvian range. "The Cordillera," he writes, "are nothing less than a long series of mountains whose infinity of sharp points lose themselves in clouds; it is impossible to traverse them except through the gorges...."[79]

The Genoese navigator Alejandro Malaspina, in the only major scientific expedition launched by Spain during the eighteenth century (1790–1794), pursued the trail blazed by his *conquistador* ancestors. His exploration took him to the lovely Pass of Santiago de Chile at Mendozo, which was commemorated by the ships' artists. As leader, he reviews the purpose of the voyage in a letter posted from Callao: "It can be seen that we ought to sacrifice to the perfection of the work undertaken, and the brilliance of our nation's renown, not only the fulfillment of a voyage round the globe, but also the exploration of the Straits of Malacca, and, above all, that limit to our voyage which we predetermined for 1793...." Typically, Malaspina assures the Spanish Admiralty of his "desire for accuracy," particularly in the views and astronomical observations taken at the summit of Chimborazo.[80]

But it is chiefly with the German scholar Alexander von Humboldt that we associate the pampas and craters that leap to mind at the mention of the Andes. In 1799, Humboldt—friend to an international coterie of princes and academicians—set forth on a five-year expedition to South America and Mexico with the French botanist Aimé Bonpland. Humboldt's knowledge of graphic techniques and his close supervision of the approximately 50 artists who transcribed field sketches ensured both the scientific accuracy and the aesthetic appeal of the resulting work.[81]

The introduction to Humboldt's *Relation historique* (1810) asserts his intention to examine the geological structure of South America. Humboldt visually decomposes the new continent, perceiving a succession of rocks identical with that existing elsewhere in the western hemisphere. Since the granites, mica schists, and gypsum of the Peruvian chain originated in the same epoch and are compositionally identical with those of the Swiss Alps, he concludes that "the whole globe appears to have undergone the same catastrophes."[82] With this discovery, Humboldt confirms and caps the notion of significant matter underpinning the concept of ubiquitous and enduring terrestrial monuments. His speculations cut an even wider swath. Concerning the geological theory of the formation of the Andes, he adds: "In all climates, it is not so much the absolute elevation of mountains but their aspect, their form, and their arrangement that bequeath a particular character to the landscape. It is this physiognomy of mountains that I attempted to represent in a series of drawings. . . ."

In presenting the disparate faces of the three chains, Humboldt notes a profound paradox: While advancing across the Cordillera, one is persuaded that it is part of a boundless plain covered with prickly mimosa and ringed by remote mountains. From this perspective one can be lured into thinking that the uneven crests are isolated peaks—Pichincha, Cayambe, Cotopaxi. Hence, the Andes appear to be a chain only when glimpsed from a distance. When seen from the central plateau, far from obscuring one another, they give the illusion of distinctness, with their "true form" freely projected against the sky.[83] After Humboldt, it became imperative for any serious seeker traveling to Chile or Bogotá to tackle the great Cordillera. Among the most sensitive of these travelers were Alexander Caldcleugh, Charles Stuart Cochrane, and Charles Darwin, who shipped with the artist Conrad Martens aboard the *Beugle*.[84]

In the seventeenth century, the Jesuit Jerome Lobo, in his dissertation "Upon Aethiopia or Abyssinia," spoke of the "steep rocks" of the Kingdom of Ambara, "many of which appear to the Sight like great cities; and one is scarcely convinced even upon a near View that one doth not see Walls, Towers and Bastions. . . ."[85] Lobo's urban similes exhibit an architectural vocabulary typical in descriptions of rugged mountains. This constructional idiom marks the inception of a tradition that develops completely only in a later era's ideal of a caricatural *beauté horrible*. From Sebastien Mercier to Victor Hugo, bald excrescences and naked asperities are viewed as grotesque collections of Gothic towers, menacing columns, and barbaric

Figure 34
P. Bouguer, *Section and View of the
Cordillera in Peru*, from *La figure de la
terre*, 1749, pl. p. 110. Engraving. Photo
courtesy British Library.

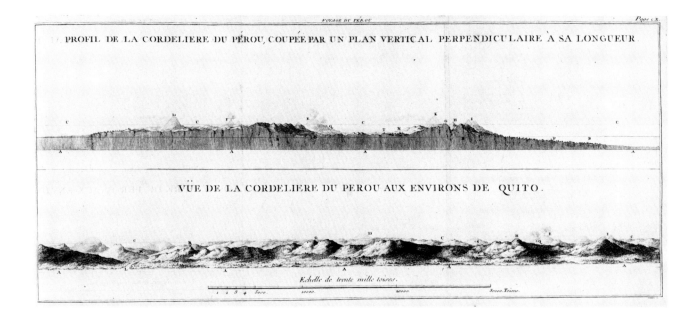

Figure 35
A. von Humboldt, *Chimborazo from the Plateau of Tapua*, from *Vues des Cordillères*, 1814, pl. 25. Color aquatint by Boguet. Photo courtesy British Library.

THE NATURAL MASTERPIECE

temples constituting the fabric of some fantastic town.[86] For a concrete, relatively metaphor-free narration on these mountains, one must progress to the relation of James Bruce:

> The mountains of Abyssinia have a singular aspect from this [Laberbey], as they appear in three ridges, the first is of no considerable height, but full of gullies and broken ground, thinly covered with shrubs; the second, higher and steeper, still more rugged and bare; the third is a row of sharp, uneven-edged mountains, which would be counted high in any country in Europe. Far above the tops of all, towers that stupendous mass, the mountain of Taranta, I suppose one of the highest in the world, the point of which is buried in the clouds, and very rarely seen but in the clearest weather. . . . It is not the extreme height of the mountains in Abyssinia that occasions surprise, but the number of them, and the extraordinary forms they present to the eye. Some of them are flat, thin, and square. . . . Some are like pyramids, others like obelisks or prisms, and some, the most extraordinary of all the rest, pyramids pitched upon their points, with their base uppermost. . . .[87]

To comprehend the character of these upheaved peaks, one must consult Henry Salt's deliberately inurbane renderings (figures 36 and 37).[88]

The British, in pursuit of empire and acquisition, also best captured the ghauts and droogs of India. A ghaut is any difficult mountain pass or range crossing from the northern to the southern section of the Peninsula and forming the barrier of the Mysore country. These formidable masses divide the occurrences of the monsoons of the Coromandel and Malabar coasts. Droogs are hill or rock fortresses especially conspicuous in the Carnatic and Mysorean territories. As Captain Charles Gold puts it, they may be considered as "so many Gibralters in miniature."[89] William Westall on an 1803 expedition to China, Lord Valentia during his 1809 travels, and Robert Grindlay engaged in his 1826 tour of western India were among the foremost draftsmen of the ghauts.[90] The views of the principal droogs were published by William Hodges (best known as the official draftsman on Cook's second voyage), Majors Allan and Colebrooke of the India Company's Service, and Robert Home, an artist who accompanied Lord Cornwallis's army to Seringapatam in 1792. Hodges's *Select Views in India* (1786) underscore how coarse cliff and rustic fortification mold themselves into a compact, homogeneous mass.[91] Less strong are Sir Alexander Allan's sketches of Anchittidrug (Mysore), which depicts a desolate, rock-strewn hill.[92] Robert Home, a specialist in Indian scenes, evidently savored savage wastes of "barren rocks" and tiger-infested thickets. His *Select Views in Mysore* (1794) record the "stupendous fortress" of Savendroog, some two days' march from Bangalore. Home manages to capture the bleak rock mounds rising about a half-mile perpendicularly from a base 8 or 10 miles in circumference. (Savendroog is also known as the Rock of Death, because of its pestilential atmosphere.) The Daniells were among the most notable investigators to fall under the spell of these forbidding military fortifications that function visually as artless tumuli.[93]

Figure 36
Henry Salt, *View near the Village of Asceriah in Abyssinia*, from George Annesley's (Viscount Valentia's) *Voyages and Travels to . . . Abyssinia and Egypt*, 1809, pl. 17. Engraving. Photo courtesy India Office Library.

Figure 37
Henry Salt, *Town of Abha in Abyssinia*, from *Twenty-Four Views taken in Saint Helena, the Cape, India, Ceylon, and Abyssinia*, 1809, pl. 16. Color aquatint by R. Havell. Photo courtesy India Office Library.

THE NATURAL MASTERPIECE

Figure 38
R. H. Colebrooke, *Prospect of the Country
near Mooty Tallaow*, from *Twelve Views of
Places in the Kingdom of Mysore*, second
edition, 1805, pl. 3. Color aquatint by
J. Harding. Photo courtesy India Office
Library.

View of
Dindigul (reformed?).
1700

Figure 40
Alexander Allen, *View of Anchittidrug
(Mysore)*, for *Views*, 1794, pl. 4. Pen and
wash W.D. 107. Photo courtesy India
Office Library.

Figure 41
Anonymous, *View of Dindigul*, from *Colin
MacKenzie Collection*, 1790. Watercolor
W.D. 640. Photo courtesy India Office
Library.

VOYAGE INTO SUBSTANCE

Notwithstanding their hostile and impregnable mien, the ambiguous Indian ghauts and droogs did not compare in size, complexity, and austerity to the Tibetan mountains, which were just beginning to be explored in the early nineteenth century. William Orme, in his *Twenty-Four Views in Hindostan* (1805), vouches for the accuracy of William Daniell's representations of the Himalayas. They are "some of the most extraordinary irregularities on the face of the globe." "In the distance of the perspective [figure 42] are seen vast mountains of ice. . . . In the foreground, on the right, is a Hindo temple, formed of large stones; it is evidently the rude work of nature, but is held in great veneration by the inhabitants, particularly the Brahmins, who relate traditions from time immemorial: It is something of the same nature as Stonehenge, near Salisbury. . . ." Orme was preceded in this inhospitable domain by Captain Turner, who in 1783 was on his way to visit the Teshoo Lama.[94]

The scientific exploration of Tibet was due largely to the persistent efforts of the British military. In 1793 the ruling power of Nepal asked the Bengal government (under the aegis of the English) for assistance in repulsing Chinese forces. Colonel Kirkpatrick (then a captain) was appointed to defend one of the East India Company's richest possessions. In the historic *Account of Nepaul* (1811), Kirkpatrick chronicled the effort required to dispatch a large army across the "dreary and elevated regions of Tibet." Although the mission was aborted, he left an illustrated memoir of the "amazing ramparts of snow," "this magnificent object" that soars into the sky above Katmandu. Although Kirkpatrick's visit commenced under circumstances unfavorable to free research, "which alone can lead to accurate information," and although its duration did not exceed 7 weeks, he was able to observe the geography of the area. His panoramic views of the valley encompass a 9-mile extent "bounded on the north and south by very stupendous mountains."[95]

In 1814 the English launched an attack against the Gurkas, the warlike Brahmins of Nepal. With the Scottish reserves came a painter, James Baillie Fraser, who was able to move with ease between the plains and the Gartzwal. There, enticed by the beauties of Nepal, Fraser left the army, climbed the valley of Soutledji, and advanced toward the unexplored peaks of the Himalayas. Upon his return to Europe in 1820 he published twenty labyrinthine landscape views in folio, aquatinted by Robert Havell. Far exceeding the military prints of Kirkpatrick, Fraser's close-up images of convoluted and upward-surging ridges were supplemented with scientific gleanings. In the same year he also brought out the *Journal of a Voyage into the Snows of the Himalaya*, containing both notes on the military campaign and geographical observations.[96] Following in Fraser's footsteps came James Manson, who was attached to the superintendent of the geographical survey of the Himalayas and who published mountainscapes of ice-sheathed Almorah.[97]

　　　　THE NATURAL MASTERPIECE

Figure 42
William Orme, *Thebet Mountains*, from *Twenty-Four Views in Hindostan*, 1805, pl. 10. Color aquatint by William Daniell. Photo courtesy India Office Library.

Figure 43
J. B. Fraser, *The Ridge and Fort of Jytock*, from *Views in the Himala Mountains*, 1820, pl. 7. Color aquatint by Robert Havell & Son. Photo courtesy India Office Library.

Figure 44
J. B. Fraser, *Bheem Ke Udar,* from *Views in the Himala Mountains,* 1820, pl. 12. Color aquatint by Robert Havell and Son. Photo courtesy India Office Library.

Figure 45
J. B. Fraser, *Fort of Raeengurh,* from *Views in the Himala Mountains,* 1820, pl. 9. Color aquatint by Robert Havell and Son. Photo courtesy India Office Library.

Figure 46
James Manson, *View of Part of the Himalya at Snowy Range from Kalee-Mundee Pass,* from *Twelve Drawings of Almorah,* 1826, pl. 12. Color aquatint. Photo courtesy India Office Library.

Figure 47
James Manson, *Village of Ghour,* from *Twelve Views of Almorah,* 1826, pl. 6. Color aquatint. Photo courtesy India Office Library.

VOYAGE INTO SUBSTANCE

"Judgment and love of science" marked those artists in the employ of Colonel Crawford, the surveyor-general in Bengal who extended his interest to the frontiers of Sikkim. Kirkpatrick, Fraser, and Hamilton spurred the discovery of "a country previously unknown"; they approached a ridge of "snowy Alps" that was "totally insuperable."[98]

In comparison with these mammoth and intricate chains, other ranges played a secondary role. The Castravan mountains,[99] the Mountains of the Moon (celebrated since antiquity),[100] the Atlas range of West and South Barbary,[101] the Azores,[102] the Mei-ling ridge of China,[103] and the Western Chain or Rik mountains of South Africa[104] made only intermittent appearances in the literature. Nonetheless, their explorers fostered a perceptiveness for "rugged precipices," "immensely high" "enormous piles," "innumerable rocks," and "uninhabited barriers." In short, by a firsthand encounter with "singular geological phenomen[a],"[105] they shaped the taste for discovery.

Consonant with the formal interest in accurate panoramic views of distant, heterogeneously contoured mountain chains was the myopic scrutiny of individual peaks. By definition, these were more approachable than continuous ridges. The "solitary, insulated mountain" is a persistent fixture of the factual travel account, functioning equally well as a landmark or a seamark.[106] The most expressively heteroclite were volcanic in origin and therefore belong to the discussion of intermittent phenomena undertaken in the next chapter. Nonetheless, they enter into the present considerations when perceived as enduring monuments. In that perception, the paradigmatic pictorial incarnation takes the form of a "famous peak." Early on, Pococke extolled Mount Tabor, near Nazareth, for its lone impressiveness and easy accessibility.

Yet for the eighteenth century perhaps the most typical lone mountain was the Peak of the Teneriffe, discovered by Vasco de Gama on his initial voyage of 1497 and subsequently arrogated by the French. The French presence in the Indian Ocean (highly evident between 1750 and 1770) was due largely to the efforts of Pierre Poivre. Poivre's *Voyages d'un philosophe* (1768) records his trials and tribulations on behalf of the Compagnie des Indes, which dispatched him on numerous missions to the Philippines, Indochina, and Madagascar, where he established and fostered scientific centers.[107] The volcanic Peak of the Teneriffe, a "maritime marvel," falls within the construct of the enduring natural masterpiece when it is termed a *colosse immobile*. Jacques-Gérard Milbert, who invoked that phrase to capture its dominance over the sea, also noted the interest that the monolith's "particular beauties" held for the attentive observer.[108]

William Alexander, the student of the watercolorists William Pars and Julius Caesar Ibbetson, was especially sensitive to the power exerted by

THE NATURAL MASTERPIECE

Figure 48
E. Brenton, *Apes Hill, Atlas Mountains,*
from *Voyage of Captain Edward Pelham,*
1796. Watercolor. Photo courtesy National
Maritime Museum.

Figure 49
Anonymous, *Ice Islands.* Engraving. Photo
courtesy National Maritime Museum.

Figure 52
Anonymous, *The Peak Mountain upon the
Island Teneriffe*, 1670. Engraving. Photo
courtesy National Maritime Museum.

VOYAGE INTO SUBSTANCE

the natural monument of Santa Cruz. On his 1792 journey to China while attached to Lord Macartney's embassy, he sketched that "famous Peak [which] may in clear Weather be seen at an immense distance/apparently riding on the Clouds/and is about two miles and a half from the surface of the Sea."[109]

The Ile de France, made famous by Poivre and Bernardin de Saint-Pierre, could be approached easily by sailing from the Canaries. After one has crossed a becalmed sea, its tufa-littered coast loomed harshly into view. Le Gentil revoices in his *Voyages dans les mers de l'Inde* (1779) the age's preoccupation with trenchant summits and rugged cockscomb crests.[110]

Lion or Table Mountain on the Cape of Good Hope also entered the literature because of its natural monumentality. Bernardin de Saint-Pierre, in his *Voyage à l'Isle de France*, comments: "Its head is detached and composed of a crude boulder, whose strata represent the mane. The body is molded of the croups of various hills. . . ." Georg Forster, undertaking the arduous ascent, provides an account that shows his intimate acquaintance with the terrain. From the seaside (Bernardin's point of view), the land has a "parched and dreary appearance." While botanizing, Forster gradually becomes aware of the myriad faces of the mountain—especially the "bold, grand chasm, whose walls are perpendicular and often impending rocks, piled up in strata"—that become apparent at midclimb. Although the Daniells and John Webber focus on the distinctively arid "flat summit" of this "bare, enormous rock," they do not overlook the fact that there are actually three mountains in sequence. These are composed of a multitude of rocky strata "piled on each other in large tabular masses," adding up to the single image of a lion.[111] A few, select samples of many similar statements follow, illustrating the perceptual dominion wielded by diverse monoliths over the observer and the environment in which they disclose themselves.

Jacques-Julien, Houton de Labillardière, during the course of his futile search for La Pérouse (1799), took time in the Port of d'Entrecasteaux to linger near a mountain made unparalleled by "a small peak in the form of a cone which terminates its summit." George Vancouver, in his *Voyage of Discovery in the North Pacific Ocean* (1798), confirms the intrusive abruptness of Mount Rainier. Cassas, while taking a view of Spalatro, pauses to comment that it is nestled at the foot of a springing "enormous mountain." Laborde, in Catalonia, delineates the polymorphic cones encroaching upon the monastery of Saint Benoît. James Cordiner, surveying Ceylon, explains—as did so many others—the eye's attraction to the cubic "stupendous mountain of stone" christened Adam's Berg by the Dutch. Nor was Lord Valentia immune to its energetic "acute point." In Mexico, Humboldt focuses on the obtrusive porphyritic mountain of Actopan, famous under the name *los Organos*. And what of the Andean giants— Chimborazo (considered the world's highest peak until the discovery of

THE NATURAL MASTERPIECE

Figure 53
William Hodges, *Table Mountain, Cape of Good Hope* (November 1772). Oil, 38 × 49 inches. Photo courtesy National Maritime Museum, on loan from Ministry of Defence (Navy).

VOYAGE INTO SUBSTANCE

Figure 55
A. de Laborde, *View of the Hermitage of Saint Benedict,* from *Voyage pittoresque en Espagne,* 1806, I, pl. 34. Etching by Guyot. Photo courtesy British Library.

the Himalayas), the Ylimani, and the singular Cotopaxi? In Peru, Mount Potosi, renowned for its silver mines, raised its reddish crest. Gibraltar's upheaved topography circumscribed in a jutting black rock, placed it at the forefront of maritime monuments.[112]

Last, but not least, there are the Swiss colossi with which this discussion began: the Wetterhorn, the Eiger, the Jungfrau, and the Monk. During the late eighteenth century and first third of the nineteenth, giants such as Mont Blanc, the Rigi, and Mont Pilatus ruled the travel accounts. The latter in particular was thought to be an "extraordinary curiosity," a heroic *lusus naturae.*[113] Like Mount Snowdon in Wales, it attracted from an early date a host of observers drawn by its solitary position.[114]

An extension of the fresh, vitalist approach to physical data exists in the exploration of caves. These hollows in mountainsides were now seen to expose the universal matrix of matter, while themselves embodying yet another individualized expression of the potency of the earth's core.[115] From Palissy's untamed, *crotte rustique* to the more ambivalent garden grottos of the Renaissance, the protean dynamism of nature was thought to preside over their creation.[116] With this scientifically updated awareness in hand, Alexander Pope—relying on the assistance of the Reverend William Borlase, an antiquarian, natural philosopher, and painter—"finished" his grotto at Twickenham. Pope constructed the rustic chamber—suppressing the more traditional edificial aspects—as a cavern place much like an actual mine or quarry. Thus, the real elements of nature (its rock strata, crystals, and stalactites), rather than art, became his models.[117]

By the late eighteenth century, the architectonic grottos of the Renaissance and Baroque periods were actively being divested of art—with which they were often placed in ironic juxtaposition—and "deconstructed" into their primitive state as natural hollow or pierced boulders. (See figure 60.) Behind this inversion and this effort at barbarization surely lay the travelers' descriptions of the caverns of Greece and other, more alien outposts.[118] The most celebrated of these artless enclaves was one situated on the otherwise uninspiring island of Antiparos. A French botanist, expedited by Louis XIV to the Near East, used it to test an old hypothesis on the "vegetation" of stones. Crawling down the "horrible precipice" of the opening, Pitton de Tournefort at last entered the subterranean region. The cavern's interior is discussed in chapter 4; here, we are concerned solely with its material autonomy and its coherent structure. This cavern was later investigated by Choiseul-Gouffier and the Abbé de Saint-Non.[119] No doubt the hidden logic implicit in the operations of this separate and autonomous world beneath the world intrigued the explorers. Thus, the individual morphology of dim vaults began to be noted and mapped. In the spirit of the discovery of yet another universe, the Swiss speleologist Carl Lang, in his *Gallerie der unterirdischen Wunder* (1806–1807), draws

VOYAGE INTO SUBSTANCE

Figure 56
A. von Humboldt, *Volcano of Cotopaxi*,
from *Vues des Cordillères*, 1814, pl. 10.
Color aquatint by Arnold. Photo courtesy
British Library.

Figure 57
Paul Decker, *The Fortress of Gibraltar*,
1705. Engraving by John August Cervinus.
Photo courtesy National Maritime
Museum.

THE NATURAL MASTERPIECE

Figure 58
H. A. West, *Gibraltar*, from *Six Views of Gibraltar*, 1828, II, pl. 2. Hand-colored lithograph by T. M. Baynes. Photo courtesy Yale Center for British Art, Paul Mellon Collection, New Haven, Conn.

VOYAGE INTO SUBSTANCE

Figure 59
P. Benucci, *View in Gibraltar taken near the
Naval Hospital,* from *Six Views of Gibraltar
and its Neighbourhood,* 1825, pl. 6. Hand-
colored lithograph. Photo courtesy Yale
Center for British Art, Paul Mellon
Collection.

THE NATURAL MASTERPIECE

a cosmic analogy between the effect of sparkling expansiveness produced by the high-ceilinged stone chamber and the glittering, uncompounded, and equally natural spaciousness of the starry heavens.[120]

The late-eighteenth-century discovery of Indian rock-cut temples was similarly rich in aesthetic promise, precisely because the elemental grandeur and the rugged shape of the temples were in large measure produced by, and conjoined with, nature. The uncertainty about the age and origin of Elephanta and Ellora, and their great dimensions, linked them to such absolute chthonic expressions as the Grotto of Antiparos. William Hodges, Thomas and William Daniell, James Wales, Henry Salt, and Robert Grindlay grasped the overwhelmingly material aura of these Hindu sanctuaries.[121] In Hodges's *Travels in India* (1794), the caverns retain their ancient numinous yet intensely corporeal quality. However, now the intimation of the sacred is—according to the dictates of eighteenth-century materialism—melded with the bald assertion of robust physicality. These narratives, in the manner of the accompanying prints, abound in defiantly tangible terms and substantial images of unregenerated rudeness, maleness, ponderousness, density, heavy gloom, weighty haunts.[122] James Forbes, while stationed in Bombay, frequently visited the decaying catacombs on the islands of Salsetta and Elephanta and saw an unfabricated and brute nature at work within "those sculptured mountains of Canara."[123] If these, and the sacred caverns of Benares, intrigued because they so closely approximated nature, cavities that were wholly the result of the "devouring" forces of the globe proved to be even more beguiling. Thomas Anburey was drawn to the holes gaping darkly near the northern entrance to the Gundecotta Pass, and Thomas Postans rendered the "very fine natural cave on the sands of Kurrachi."[124]

Humboldt, on another continent, visited the cave of Caripe in Venezuela, with its entrance over 70 feet high and its echoing halls resounding with the shrieks of guachero birds. Boisgelin de Kerdu, roaming the island of Malta in 1804, came upon the Grotto of Calypso.[125] Jan Knops, the Dutch surveyor of the south coast of the principalities of Java, published a multilayered section of the seemingly pulsing stalactite corridors at Musigid Selo in the island of Nooso Cambagan (figure 69).[126] William Westall, long after his epoch-making voyage with Flinders to Australia, explored the "deep gloom" of Yordas Cave, in Yorkshire. Admiring its grooved and ropy walls, he compares this cave's calcareous formations to those of Derbyshire. Variations on the theme of a primeval and anciently configured antrum include the submerged cavern sighted by William Mariner whose floor was the bottom of the Pacific Ocean.[127]

Descending into a cave was not unrelated to being lowered into a mine. Rock quarries, salt works, and metal mines were commercial adjuncts to the natural and equivocal grotto. Many years before the establishment of the renowned mining academy in Freiburg in 1766—the first school of

Figure 60
A. de Laborde, *The Chateau of Plessis-Chamand,* from *Nouveaux jardins de la France,* 1808, pl. 67. Engraving by Niquet after drawing by Constant Bourgeoisie. Photo courtesy Cabinet des Estampes, Bibliothèque Nationale.

GROTTE
D'ANTIPAROS.

+ Passage pour aller
derriere l'Autel

Autel ou Pyramide

ç Trou par ou
l'on descend
de la Caverne
dans la Grotte

Tom. I. Pag. 190.

DETAILS
Géométriques de la Grotte
D'ANTIPAROS.

PLAN DE LA GROTTE D'ANTIPAROS.

COUPE PRISE SUR LA LIGNE A B. DU PLAN

COUPE PRISE SUR LA LIGNE B C.

Figure 61
J. Pitton de Tournefort, *Grotto of Antiparos,*
from *Voyage du Levant,* 1717, pl. p. 190.
Engraving. Photo courtesy British Library.

Figure 62
M. G. A. Choiseul-Gouffier, *Plan and
Section of the Grotto of Antiparos,* from
Voyages pittoresques de la Grèce, 1782, I, pl.
37. Engraving by J. B. Tilliard.

Figure 63
M. G. A. Choiseul-Gouffier, *Entrance to Grotto of Antiparos*, from *Voyages pittoresques de la Grèce*, 1782, I, pl. 36. Engraving by J. B. Tilliard.

Figure 64
Thomas and William Daniell, *Caves 10 and 12, Kanheri, Salsette (Bombay)*, 1793. Watercolor W.D. 547. Photo courtesy India Office Library.

Figure 65
James Wales, *Deemar Leyna*, from *Hindoo Excavations in the Mountains of Ellora . . .*, 1816, pl. 9. Color aquatint by Thomas Daniell. Photo courtesy India Office Library.

VOYAGE INTO SUBSTANCE

Figure 66
Henry Salt, *Rock Temple, Carli (Bombay)*,
from *Twenty-Four Views Taken in Saint
Helena, the Cape, India . . .*, 1809, pl. 14.
Color aquatint by R. Havell. Photo
courtesy India Office Library.

Figure 67
R. N. Grindlay, *Hermitage at Currungale in
Ceylon*, from *Scenery . . . Chiefly on the
Western Side of India*, 1826, I, pl. 15.
Sketch by Capt. Charles Auber, drawing
by William Westall, color aquatint by R. G.
Reeve. Photo courtesy India Office Library.

Figure 68
Thomas Anburey, *Northern Entrance of Gundecotta Pass*, from *Hindoostan Scenery*, 1799, pl. 7. Color aquatint. Photo courtesy India Office Library.

Figure 69
Jan Knops, *Stalactite Cavern at Manchigan (Java)*, from *Raffles Drawings*, no. 23. Watercolor W.D. 2991. Photo courtesy India Office Library.

Figure 70
William Westall, *Stalactites in Yordas Cave*,
from *Views of the Caves near Ingleton,
Gordale Scar, and Malham Cove in
Yorkshire*, 1818, pl. 6. Aquatint. Photo
courtesy British Library.

THE NATURAL MASTERPIECE

its kind in the world and the foremost scientific institution in Europe[128]—travelers were plunging headlong into the earth's entrails.[129] The founding of the Freiburg School of Mines provided a special impetus to investigate the physiognomy of the subterranean world as it was both revealed and shaped by the miner. This is not to deny that views of collieries had been popular in the landscapes of Henri met de Bles and other Flemish Mannerists, but these had fallen from favor during the seventeenth century as artists had concentrated on prospects.[130] A resurgence of interest in the topic occurred during the second half of the eighteenth century, when Jean Houel studied the salt mines near Rouen, Pehr Hilleström recorded the iron mines of Falum, Léonard Defrance illustrated underground sites and subterranean feasts, and Paul Sandby and Joseph Wright of Derby painted coal and slate pits.[131] Nevertheless, the most extensive exploration of these nether regions was carried out by travelers in search of the varieties of matter's expressiveness. The Daniells, in *Animated Nature* (1807–1812), depict an arcuated high-roofed salt mine at White Haven (figure 71). Boisgelin de Kerdu, in his *Travels in Denmark and Sweden* (1810), systematically plumbs the recesses blasted open at Sahla, Afnestad, Soeter, and, of course, Falum (so dear to E. T. A. Hoffmann and the German Romantics); he also comments on the "very curious porphyry quarries" of Elfdal. R. K. Porter, journeying across Sweden (1813), was encouraged to make the by now obligatory descent at Falum in order to view the "vast masses of rock." John Edy, traversing Norway (1820), reconnoitered among the Königsberg silver mines and the cobalt mine at Fossum, but was most taken by the "exquisite mine of quartz" lying nearby. Lieutenant Beechey, coasting off the northern shores of Africa in 1828, halted to probe the "singular pits" and quarries that had once served to build the ancient city of Berenice.[132]

In sum: The exploration of mines and caverns helped to form a widespread taste for rupestral localities and monuments of earth. Along with rock monoliths, mountain chains, and colossal peaks, grottos, collieries, and caves exhibited evidence of the shaping and structuring energy lodged within matter.

An "Ocean" of Ruins

Alors la plaine [of Siberia], vue d'un endroit élevé, offre une nouvelle mer formée tout-à-coup au milieu du Continent. . . .
Jean Chappe d'Auteroche

The purpose of the long-standing practice of having naval draftsmen take coastal profiles was to provide as clear an indication of the shape of unmapped land—not neglecting its geological structure, contour, and vegetative cover—as the distance from the ship would permit. This method for accurate observation was specifically associated with running traverse. On the contrary, panoramic views drawn from high points of land were connected with triangulation surveys that sighted on important landmarks from the interior. Thus, William Hodges was actively engaged in making watercolor studies of both littoral and inland scenes. Continuing this procedure, the landscape painter William Westall transmitted the novelty of Australia's inshore rock formations. In 1809 he secured an order from the Admiralty to paint pictures from which the plates illustrating the official account of Flinders's expedition would be engraved. Upon their exhibition at the Royal Academy in 1812, these paintings aroused considerable interest. Such commissions were also behind the production of drawings and engravings from sketches taken by officers involved in Captain W. E. Parry's voyage for the discovery of a northwest passage (1821).[133] Inherent in the vast cartographic enterprise—to which these artists contributed— is the clear notation of the varying heights of banks and the tracing of the terrain's changing margins. Refinements of this process for painstaking observation include the registration of meteorological changes, cloud formations, and atmospheric conditions.

The image of a dramatic coast pierced by openings and compounded of rugged cliffs and promontories originated, as did so many elements of landscape painting, in the Hellenistic period. While admirers of the Vatican's Ulysses Frieze are reminded of the edges of southern Italy or Sicily when gazing upon its rough ground, fantasy surely outweighs nature in the setting created for the hero's adventures.[134] A turn for the precise is coterminous only with the long, exacting reality of "coasting." Again it is Cook, on his first voyage to record the transit of Venus (1768), who indelibly establishes this practical optic by the sheer scale and heroic proportion of his endeavor. Two thousand miles of shore were exactly placed on the chart when he skirted New South Wales. As he advanced past promontories and bays on this and subsequent explorations, the names and delineations of natural monuments advanced with him. These were complexly derived from lived experience, actual characteristics, and later Cook's own emotions. There were few resources for nomenclature his log did not illustrate in the end: Ram Head, Cape Home, Mount Dromedary, Bateman Bay, Point Upright, the Pigeon House, Long Nose, Red Point, Point Desolation, Christmas Harbour.[135]

Although Cook serves as a paradigm, many mariners—both earlier and later—contributed to the recording of lithic forms witnessed from the sea. Michel Adanson, in his *Histoire naturelle du Sénégale et voyage* (1757), describes the sensation of finding himself directly across from Cape Verde. After 4 months in the arid interior of Africa, Adanson was unaccustomed to seeing a coast. He was particularly drawn to the rocky shore, with its countless shells and its flying fish. Constantine Phipps (trained in mathematics and astronomy, and Banks's closest friend on board the *Niger* during their excursion to Newfoundland) embarked on only one voyage of discovery. This attempt to locate a passage to the North Pole in 1773, though unsuccessful, earned him the nickname Ursa Major. While adrift on frigid waters, Phipps copied the remarkable features that came his way. Hakluyt's Headland and a bare rock ("so called from the top of it resembling a cloven-hoof,—which appearance it has always worn, having been named by some of the first Dutch navigators who frequented these seas") are detached from the other mountains joined to the rest of the islands by a long isthmus. Their visual uniqueness and navigational usefulness, as Phipps is at pains to prove, stem from the fact that they preserve in all situations the same form, never disguised by snow.[136]

THE NATURAL MASTERPIECE

Figure 71
Thomas and William Daniell, *Interior of a Salt Mine*, from *Animated Nature*, 1807–1812, pl. 18. Aquatint. Photo courtesy Newberry Library

Figure 72
William Alexander, *Profiles of Hey-san Islands on the Coast of China*, for *Lord Macartney's Embassy to . . . China*, 1797, pl. p. 42. Watercolor W.D. 960. Photo courtesy India Office Library.

VOYAGE INTO SUBSTANCE

Figure 73
William Hodges, *Christmas Sound, Tierra del Fuego* (December 1774), from *Plates to Cook's Voyages, 1777*, II, pl. 32. Engraving by William Watts. Photo courtesy National Maritime Museum.

Figure 74
John Ross, *Coburg Bay, Cape Leopold & Princess Charlottes Monument*, from *Voyage of Discovery*, 1819, pl. p. 161. Aquatint by R. Havell and Son. Photo courtesy British Library.

The unfortunate Kerguelen-Trémarec imposed his name on one of the most distinctive promontories of the Antarctic. Although the journal of his voyage was suppressed in France, it is known that he and Allouarn sailed from Mauritius in 1771 with the ships *La Fortune* and *Le Gros Ventre*. In mid January of the following year, he sighted the two Isles of Fortune and the Round Island (or Isle Ronde). Almost immediately thereafter he spotted land. The two ships suddenly became separated, and Kerguelen was driven back to the Ile de France. When he returned to Europe he was hurriedly dispatched once more to the Antarctic in the 64-gun vessel *Roland* and the frigate *l'Oiseau*. After barely glimpsing the forbidding land he had discovered previously (aptly renamed Desolation Point by Cook), Kerguelen set sail for home, infamy, and imprisonment at Saumur without making any additional discoveries.

Equally unfortunate, but not correspondingly ignoble, was the destiny of the scientist-*philosophe* La Pérouse. He should have entered Brest in triumph on the eve of the revolution of 1789 after having explored vast stretches of the Pacific. Instead, *La Boussole* foundered one stormy night on a coral reef off Vanikoro, without a single survivor. Nonetheless, the fame of La Pérouse's expedition spread with the publication of the voyage, and his name was affixed to a pinnacle west of Hawaii and to the strait north of Hokkaido. The variety of observations, the quality of analyses, and the scope of perspectives found in La Pérouse's narrative exceed those of Bougainville, Kerguelen-Trémarec, and even Cook. Consistent with the manly style of the navigator, and wholly in agreement with an empirical mode of viewing things, La Pérouse's journal falls within the tradition of the scientific travel account. Soberly, yet memorably, he describes the fog-shrouded coast of Japan: "It is only in these regions of mist that one perceives, and rarely at that, horizons of a very large extent; as if nature desired in some way to compensate by instants of the most intense clarity, the profound and almost perpetual darkness that overspreads these seas. . . ."[137] Under more benign skies, the Daniells and William Alexander patrolled the edges of Cochin China: "It is a bold but barren coast, and bears few traces of vegetation, with none of culture. No high forest trees are seen sheltering the rocky summits, which the approaching tempest often overshadows, with dark recumbant clouds, No rice plantations are discovered on the shore; the land, like the ocean, wears a rude but sublime aspect of desolation. . . ."[138]

George Vancouver, making a serene passage from Cook's Inlet to Prince William's Sound, was—like John Webber—struck by Port Dick, a projecting promontory whose west end terminates in "an abrupt cliff." Bleaker yet to Vancouver, and to La Pérouse's crew before him, was Mount Saint Elias. A "gloomy atmosphere," a "dreary obscurity," and the blowing of a fresh squall accentuate the "high abrupt cliffy point" of Alaska that soars above the fractured shore. It is ringed by an uninterrupted sheath of ice, and eastward, from the steep scarps, ascend a chain of mountains "whose summits are but the base from whence Mount Saint Elias towers, majestically conspicuous in regions of perpetual frost." Krusenstern, in his *Voyage round the World* (1813), recounts how he steered among the Washington Islands and thought the coast of Nukahiwa to be similarly "very wild but beautiful," yet Franklin, in his *Journey to the Polar Sea* (1823), is less enthusiastic about Cape Barrow's rocky and forbidding coast.[139]

Nor were parched areas bereft of remarkable headlands. James Morier, on his journey from Bombay to Bushire, felt the intense presence of an entire continent, punctuated by notable capes on which he spotted camels grazing. Lycett and Péron studied the seamarks of Cape Pillar and Mount Dromedary ascending from the baked surface of Van Diemen's Land. Lieutenant Beechey, threading his way from Tripoli to Bengazi, stopped to draw the "formidable appearance of the coast of Zoffran," with its "heaps of sand and seaweed . . . thrown up with these blocks of stone, and the roar and confusion which a moderate gale of wind occasions." J. B. Debret, during his historic stay in Brazil (1816–1831), reproduced "the groups of mountains that compose the shoreline of Rio de Janeiro, and among which several are known by bizarre names like Sugar Loaf, the Recumbent Giant. . . ."[140]

The apprehension of sandy or stony atolls suddenly rising from an otherwise empty ocean is fundamentally related to the perspicuous study of strongly configured coasts. Unlike the sixteenth century, which was obsessed with the finding of new continents, the eighteenth century was fascinated by the apparition of islands. Among the era's most sensational "discoveries" was Bougainville's revelation of Tahiti, bruited about Paris during the summer of 1769. Here, at last, was a prestigious achievement by the French in an age when such accomplishments seemed to have become the exclusive prerogative of the English. The tale of the visit to "New Cythera" gripped Diderot and the *philosophes* largely because of the interpretation of Philibert Commerson, the naturalist on the expedition. The reasons behind the creation of a Rousseauian utopia in the midst of the South Seas lie outside our concern; what is pertinent, however, is the physical aspect of that Edenic island as it emerged from Bougainville's more sober account. As a former prize pupil of D'Alembert, Bougainville described prudently the agreeable aspect of the steep and rough land, the outlines of whose shore consolidated into an ampitheater. "Although the mountains are of a great height," he notes, "the rocks nowhere exhibit a sterile nudity, everything is wooded over. . . ." Weary sailors scarcely believed their eyes when they discerned crests covered with trees up to the summits. At their feet spread the plantations of the beach.[141] With greater terseness, Sidney Parkinson declares that "the land appeared as uneven as a piece of crumpled paper, being divided irregularly into hills and valleys; but a beautiful verdure covered both, even to the tops of the highest peaks."[142]

THE NATURAL MASTERPIECE

Figure 75
John Webber, *Kerguelen's Land* (December 1776), from *Sketchbook*, B.M. Add. MS 15, 513, fol. 3. Watercolor. Photo courtesy British Library.

Figure 76
John Webber, *A View of Snug Corner Cove in Prince Williams Sound* (May 1778), from *Sketchbook*, B.M. Add. MS 23, 901, fol. 88. Watercolor. Photo courtesy British Library.

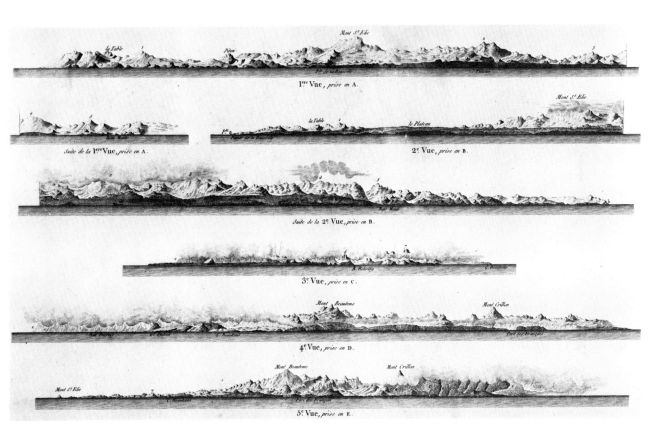

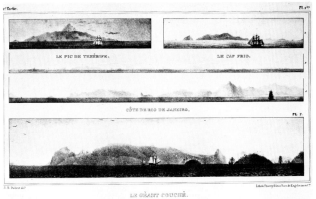

And Johann Reinhold Forster ruminated at length on the multiformity of islands in general. In his important *Observations made during a Voyage* (1778), Forster carefully categorized many islets according to physical appearance. He stipulates whether they are situated in the Tropics or in the Temperate Zone; in the former instance, they may be divided into high and low relief. Jutting tropical islands, including Tahiti, the Society Islands, the elevated Friendly Islands, Tonga-tabu, and New Caledonia, are surrounded by reefs and have flats near the seashore. However, some tropical islands, such as the Marquesas and the New Hebrides, do not have reefs. This process of classification, born of careful observation, stimulates Forster to formulate an overview of nature: "O'Taheitee and all the high islands, are in general more happy and more fertile, than the low islands, and those of a moderate height. The high hills in the middle of the first, attract by their situation, all the vapours and clouds that pass near them; there are but few days, on which their summits are not involved in fogs and clouds. . . ." Forster, like Humboldt later on the subject of mountains, is interested in fathoming the prominent physiognomy of the earth: "The high islands of both kinds appear at a distance like large hills in the midst of the ocean, and some are greatly elevated, so that their summits are seldom free from clouds. Those which are surrounded by a reef and by a fertile plain, along the sea-shores, have commonly a more gentle slope; whereas the others are suddenly steep. . . ." By means of this system he made feasible the categorization of islands according to their material traits: high, reefless Easter Island; the volcanic Sandwich Islands; craggy, clustered Juan Fernandez Island; and Tierra del Fuego.[143]

Intersected by deep bights or channels and forming the lonely habitations of numerous sea fowl, who "stunned our ears with their discordant screams," these heteroclite islands—assimilated to an intellectual order—are part of the mariner's topographical legacy. Thomas Pennant, in a *Tour in Scotland and Voyage to the Hebrides* (1772), asserts that the Island of Booshala near Fingal's Cave is composed of pillars without any visible signs of stratification. James Wales sketches the celebrated sanctuary of Elephanta, depicting the colossal statue from whence it received its name while simultaneously including the low-lying finger of Butcher Isle on the right and the humped island of The Cross in the background; in the left distance lies the faint prospect of Bombay Harbor and of Old Woman's Island, terminated by its lighthouse. William Westall, in the Pellews with Flinders, ventured on a boating excursion among this group to study their distinctively hard, close-grained sandstone features. Henry Salt, during his voyage to Abyssinia in 1809, copied conglomerated marine alluvials forming the compact masses of the islands of Amphila. Iceland emerges from the accounts of Eggert Ólafsson and Edy as an island superficially dotted with beautiful plains but composed, in reality, of mounds of fallen rock and uncultivated mountains with summits perpetually enveloped in snow and ice. Correspondingly, the Faroe and Stappen Islands arrange themselves into deterrent barriers when spied from the sea. More fetching is the aspect of Ceylon, exhibiting a nearly heart-shaped figure when optically conjoined with the adjacent island of Jaffnapata. And "Owhyee," at least to the eye of Kotzebue, outstripped all rivals. It "rises majestically, in grand unbroken lines, from the waves, and forms, in an enormous mass, three different mountain summits."[144]

Viewed in another light, however, coasts and islands had serious limitations. Jacques Arago, who accompanied the Freycinet expedition, censures the strictures imposed upon the circumnavigator in a report presented to the French Academy of Sciences: "A circumnavigation of the globe, during which nothing is seen but islands or coasts of small extent, can present no geological series, calculated to exhibit the nature of the soil, or notions of the antiquity and superposition of the strata. Our navigators were necessarily confined to insulated observations, to specimens of rocks, detached from the strata, which appeared by their quantity to predominate and to characterize the different countries. . . ."[145]

It remains to be seen how the desire to penetrate the land horizontally was given concrete expression. From the standpoint of the investigator of mountains, the plains do not display their constitutive layers except through the chance effect of erosion. Saussure voices this prejudice against uniform, flat sections of the earth when he pits them against high ridges, so infinitely varied in their substance and form. From the heights of Mont Blanc or Mount Etna, he notes, one can see clearly and grasp immediately the extent rolled out under foot; icy ramparts, subterranean fires, and borderless oceans engage the natural philosopher standing on top of the world.[146]

The advent of the attraction for the level is attributable to the fact that the charge of monotony could be mitigated, if not entirely dispelled, by the virtue of immensity. As I remarked in the introduction, the archaeological publications of the eighteenth century increasingly popularized the visual integration of ruins with their natural surroundings, drowning the productions of mind in the engulfing energy of matter. The factual travel account enhanced and extended these illustrations, authenticating the intimate relation that bonded gigantic man-made remains with a horizontal barren stretch. Cornelius Le Bruyn, in his 1711 *Travels to Persia*— far exceeding the pallid 1686 journey of the Frenchman Chardin—shows himself to be a precursory figure in this development. His accurate views of the ruins of the Palace of Darius verify that these stony relics become disemburdened of the vestiges of culture as they merge with the immense plain over which they are strewn and which stretches toward the distant horizon: "With respect to the city of Persepolis, there are not any traces of it now remaining, only the rocks that appear on each side, incline one to believe that there were buildings formerly, beyond the enclosure of

VOYAGE INTO SUBSTANCE

Figure 79
William Hodges, *Oparee (Tahiti)*. Oil, 30¹/²
× 48¹/² inches. Photo courtesy National
Maritime Museum.

Figure 80
William Hodges, *Huahine (Society Islands)*.
Oil, 13 × 20 inches. Photo courtesy
National Maritime Museum.

THE NATURAL MASTERPIECE

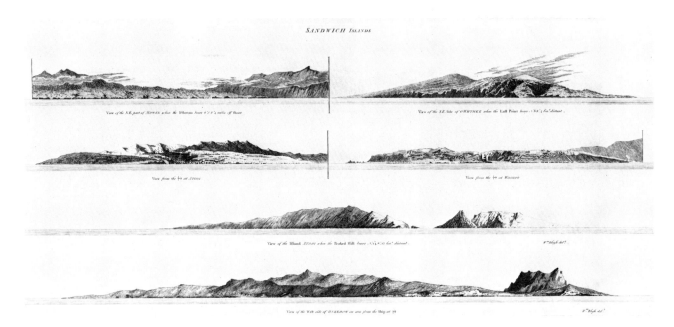

Figure 81
William Bligh, *Sandwich Islands* (November
1778), from James Cook's *Voyage to the
Pacific Ocean*, 1784, II, pl. 83. Engraving.
Photo courtesy Library of Congress.

Figure 82
Piercy Brett, *Juan Fernandez, Chile: East
View*, from *Anson's Voyage*, 1761 edition,
pl. p. 94. Engraving by F. de Bakker.
Photo courtesy National Maritime
Museum.

Figure 83
James Wales, *View from the Island of
Elephanta*, from *Twelve Views of the Island
of Bombay*, 1804, pl. 12. Color aquatint.
Photo courtesy India Office Library.

Figure 84
William Westall, *View in Sir Edward
Pellew's Group—Gulph of Carpentaria*, from
Matthew Flinders's *Voyage to Terra-
Australis*, 1814, II, pl. p. 172. Engraving by
John Pye. Photo courtesy British Library.

THE NATURAL MASTERPIECE

the edifice which has been described [the Palace of Darius]. The Persians say, and it likewise appears by their writings, that this city was one of great extent, situated in a plain. . . ." Le Bruyn is perhaps the first traveler to accentuate the fact that the colossal masses of decaying sculpture and fragments of architecture are sunken, rooted in the environs, "overthrown, and half-buried in the ground."[147]

The longevity of this motif is easily established. William Browne and Luigi Mayer, writing of Cyprus and Egypt, pinpoint its persistent fascination for the West. According to Browne, "it is unquestionable, from the stupendous masses of architecture, and gigantic works of art which at this day lie scattered on its plains, or from their solidity [, which] still braves the efforts of Time, that there was a period, when its population must have been immense." Plaintively, Mayer observes that the torso of the colossal sphinx, carved out of live rock, "is now buried in the sand and moldering away."[148] Such boundless tracts produce the sensation of being preeminently material. They function as a concrete locus where art can be disembroiled from its servitude to idea or form. With the demise of the edifice, the wide plain regains its virtual power and the lateral site assumes paramount visual interest.

The savage beauty of such deserted, silent landscapes could be found all over the world. John Lewis Burckhardt, in the summer of 1812, explored the ruins of Petra in Arabia. Writing of the impact made by the debris of this necropolis, he declared that the effect of somber magnificence was due in large part to the "admirable marriage" between barren environment and perishing tombs.[149]

Similar attitudes toward the enigmatic remains of ancient Europe can be documented. "Druidic" monuments—"pillar" and "rocking" stones, menhirs and cromlechs, baituilia, terms, and tolmens—littered the primeval downs of Cornwall, Wiltshire, and Brittany. Rowlands in *Mona antiqua restaurata* (1766), Borlase in *Antiquities of Cornwall* (1769), d'Hancarville in *Recherches sur l'origine, l'esprit, et le progrès des arts de la Grèce* (1785), Knight in *Symbolical Language of Ancient Art* (1818), and Grimm in *Teutonic Mythology* (1835–1836) all discuss unfabricated or scarcely touched rock memorials and earth tumuli as if they are inseparable from the life of the desolate districts on which they are planted.[150]

Neolithic mounds are created by heaping the actual materials of the region over the body, creating hillocks that become eroded and depressed with time. These unwrought hollows and sepulchral cavities commingle with rustic grooved basins and stately pillar stones to form ruins more "natural," more intimately melded with the real substance of the land—undergoing and being shaped by its vicissitudes—than even the illustrious, if decaying, sanctuaries of ancient Near Eastern civilizations.[151] (See figures 8 and 91.)

From such a composite and enriched soil sprang the aesthetic vindication of the plains. The mysterious survivors of Druidism, such as Stonehenge and Avebury, were conceived to have "sprouted up in their places, like mushrooms," in the evocative phrase of William Stukeley. Unobstructed by intrusive or adjacent configurations, the *chorea gigantum* imparted an air of primal openness to the monotonous terrain around Salisbury. Unencumbered from competing visual relationships, Carnac, with its massive and regularly aligned menhirs, suggested uninterrupted spaciousness to Cambry. Godfrey Higgins adds the following: "These stones have the most extraordinary appearances. They are isolated in a great plain without trees or bushes—not a flint or fragment of stone is to be seen on the sand which supports them; they are poised without foundations, several of them are moveable. . . . they bring to our minds a period not to be reached by history or calculation. . . ."[152] It became apparent that throughout Europe, Asia, and the Pacific multitudes of protean and austere monoliths stretched majestically toward countless horizons in the midst of otherwise abandoned plains. Cordiner was conscious of their presence in Ceylon, and Porter saw them assembled in Swedish fields.[153]

The emphasis placed on the primitive or phenomenal order, rather than on the civilized or human, established a needed link between sandy flats on which venerable rock fragments of equivocal origin were grouped and a forthrightly undomesticated countryside. A single telling case exemplifies the new attitude. The wracked area surrounding Sicily's violent volcanos offers a prime instance of a previously disdained natural form in which the earth's history was now understood to receive aesthetic expression. The clearings lying at the bases of Vesuvius and Etna mirrored the pitched battle between fertility and sure destruction in the seemingly mild South Italian district. Hamilton, Brydone, Goethe, and Humboldt pondered the heroic dimensions of this worldwide struggle. Consequently, the capacious plain—gradually evolving from being a mere receptacle of artful ruins, to generating grandiose outcrops, to embodying the seat of cataclysms— developed perceptually and ontologically into a worthy geological opponent of the dramatic and enduring mountain.[154]

The varied manifestations of the denuded plain may be summarized under several major headings. Jean Chappe d'Auteroche is an early spokesman for the unimpeded tundra of Siberia: "This vast plain is furrowed in all directions and wears everywhere [the signs] of disorder and desolation. Thus the plain observed from a high point, furnishes a new ocean formed suddenly in the midst of the Continent. . . ." Adam Neale, in Moldavia, characterizes "the immense, undulating" steppes as being "of great beauty and vast extent, covered with the most luxuriant crops of grass." Their "primeval character" seemed to lessen the aspect of monotony "only interrupted from time to time by small round lakes."

THE NATURAL MASTERPIECE

Figure 85
Cornelius Le Bruyn, *Stairway Leading to the
North Facade*, Palace of Darius, Persepolis,
from *Travels in Muscovy, Persia . . .* , 1737,
II, pls. 124, 125. Engraving.

Figure 86
Cornelius Le Bruyn, *Second View of
Persepolis*, from *Travels in Muscovy,
Persia . . .* , 1737, II, pl. 118. Engraving.

Figure 87
Cornelius Le Bruyn, *Pilaster from a Portico,*
from *Travels in Muscovy, Persia . . . ,* 1737,
II, pls. 148, 149.

THE NATURAL MASTERPIECE

Figure 88
Luigi Mayer, *A Colossal Vase near Limisso
in Cyprus*, from *Views in the Ottoman
Empire*, 1803, pl. 23. Color aquatint by
T. Milton. Photo courtesy British Library.

Figure 89
Luigi Mayer, *Head of the Colossal Sphinx*,
from *Views in Egypt*, 1801, pl. 22. Color
aquatint by T. Milton. Photo courtesy
British Library.

Fig I. The Wringcheese pa.173.

Fig V

The Altar stone in Wendron pa.200.

Fig IV

The Altar stone in Trescan Scilly pa.200.

Fig II

Fig III

The Tolmen in St Mary Scilly p.174.

The Tolmen in Northvethel Scilly p174.

To Smart Lethieullier of Aldersbrook in Essex Esqr. F.R.S.
This plate engrav'd at his expence is with great respect inscrib'd by Wm. Borlase.

Figure 90
William Borlase, *The Wringcheese; The Altar
Stone in Wendron; The Altar Stone in
Trescan Scilly; The Tolmen in St. Mary's
Scilly; The Tolmen in Northnethel Scilly.*
From *Antiquities of Cornwall*, 1769, p. 12.
Engraving. Photo courtesy Library of
Congress.

Figure 91
A. de Laborde, *Ancient Sepulchral Remains
in the Town of Olderdola,* from *Voyage
pittoresque en Espagne*, 1806, I, pl. 41.
Etching by Reveille. Photo courtesy British
Library.

Figure 92
Godfrey Higgins, *Entrance to Stonehenge from the Northeast*, from *Celtic Druids*, 1829, pl. 5. Lithograph by W. Day.

Figure 93
Godfrey Higgins, *Monuments of Carnac*, from *Celtic Druids*, 1829, pl. 42. Lithograph by W. Day.

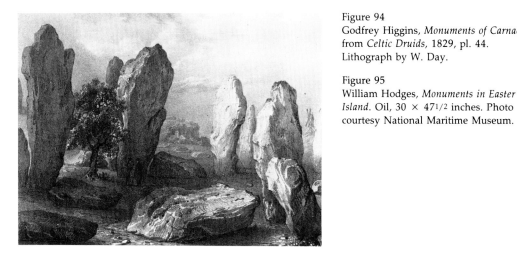

Figure 94
Godfrey Higgins, *Monuments of Carnac*,
from *Celtic Druids*, 1829, pl. 44.
Lithograph by W. Day.

Figure 95
William Hodges, *Monuments in Easter
Island*. Oil, 30 × 47½ inches. Photo
courtesy National Maritime Museum.

Figure 96
William Hamilton, *Mount Etna and Environs*, from *Campi Phlegraei*, 1776, II, pl. 12. Color aquatint by Peter Fabris. Photo courtesy British Library.

Figure 97
Joseph Acerbi, *Travelling on the Ice over the Gulf of Bothnia to Iceland*, from *Travels through Sweden, Finland . . .* , 1802, I, pl. p. 183. Engraving by John Pye. Photo courtesy British Library.

The interpreter Jean-Baptiste-Barthélemy Lesseps, put ashore at Kamtschatka and dispatched by La Pérouse and Langle to alert Paris of the progress of the expedition, presents a harrowing picture of Eurasia in the dead of winter. On a grueling crossing by dogsled, beset by starvation and ringed by death, he describes once-verdant stretches now transformed into frozen wastes. Orientation, not tedium, became an overriding concern: "But how to situate oneself in a plain so measureless, covered with snow, and where one perceives neither forests nor mountains nor rivers? . . . The most insignificant butte, the tiniest shrub, is sufficient to guide one back to the trail. . . ." Cook records an analogous experience, punctuated only by the "melancholy howling" of dogs, that took place during his third voyage, and Acerbi captures Scandinavia's marginless fields of ice, where all trails vanish.[155]

The United States presented images of "vast tract[s] of land" nearly competitive with the far-reaching barrens of Russia. Jonathan Carver, in his *Travels in North America* (1778), heralds the "immense space" connecting Lake Champlain with Lakes George and Ontario. The Midwestern prairies, extending from Ohio to Mississippi, obliged Volney to christen the area an "American Tartary" since it possessed the wide-open characteristics of its Asiatic counterpart. Lewis and Clark, engaged in making a survey of the territory along the banks of the Missouri, confirmed the uninterrupted expansiveness of the prairies in their typically laconic style; notwithstanding the annoyance of mosquitos, the stampede of buffalo, and the threat of the Mandan tribe, they succumbed to its "smooth and extensive" space.[156]

The South American savannah, below Jorullo or on the plateau of Bogotà, was given its classic incarnation in the relation of Humboldt. As part of the same filiation, the pampas lying beyond Buenos Aires and Montevideo gained aesthetic currency. The traditional home of wandering Argentinian Indians, they constitute "an immense plain" located between the 36th and 39th degrees of south latitude. The traveler to these haunts of the armidillo, the ostrich, and the wild horse finds no signs of cultivation; "as far as the eye can reach, nothing but plain is to be seen." Travelers crossed the pampas from Buenos Aires to Mendozo at night because of the scorching sun. Vidal conveys a lasting image of an intransigent and level land:

. . . nothing is to be seen but here and there a flock, or rather, a herd of guanacos. . . . there are also beautiful large birds and partridges in vast numbers, as also hares, and wild cattle and horses, who reign supreme lords of these immeasurable wilds, where there is nothing to impede the sight but one vast boundless horizon. The Spaniards might well term it *Escambradas*, for the sun, as it is rising, appears as if emerging from the earth, and without rays, till it is some way above the horizon. It is the same at its setting, for its beams disappear before the body of the sun is covered. . . .

Figure 98
E. E. Vidal, *A Country Public House &
Travellers*, from *Buenos Ayres and Monte
Video*..., 1820, pl. p. 67. Color aquatint
by T. Sutherland. Photo courtesy British
Library.

Figure 99
E. E. Vidal, *Balling Ostriches*, from *Buenos
Ayres and Monte Video*..., 1820, pl. p. 85.
Color aquatint by T. Sutherland. Photo
courtesy British Library.

Captain Robert Fitzroy, commander of the *Beagle* expedition, vividly recalls the treelessness of "those immense plains, called pampas":

... over the wide desolation of the stony barren waste not a tree—not even a solitary "ombu" [a kind of elder]—can be discerned. Scattered herds of ever wary guanacoes, startled at man's approach, neighing, stamping, and tossing their elegant heads; a few ostriches striding along in the distant horizon, and here and there a solitary condor soaring in the sky, are the only objects which attract the eye. Certainly, upon looking closely, some withered shrubs and a yellow kind of herbage may be discerned; and, in walking, thorns and prickles assure one painfully that the plain is not actually a desert: but I am quite sure that the general impression upon the mind is that of utter hopeless sterility. Is it not remarkable that water-worn shingle stones and diluvial accumulations compose the greater portion of these plains? On how vast a scale, and of what duration must have been the action of those waters which smoothed the shingle stones, now buried in the deserts of Patagonia. . . .

Darwin, by contrast, trains the objective and practiced eye of the geologist (not the would-be theologian) on the great calcareo-argillaceous deposit forming the wide extent of this parallel plain:

From the Strait of Magellan to the Colorado, a distance of about 800 miles, the face of the country is everywhere composed of shingle: the pebbles are chiefly of porphyry, and probably owe their origin to the rocks of the Cordillera. North of the Colorado the bed thins out, and the pebbles become exceedingly small, and here the characteristic vegetation of Patagonia ceases. . . .[157]

Martens captures this dead level playa, these unbroken South American "steppes," stretching away on both sides of the River Santa Cruz.

Nor were the fields of earth forgotten when travelers drifted over them in the expanse of heaven. One of the most important aftermaths of the balloon ascents was the growing perception of land as an all-embracing champaign when observed from above. Vincent Lunardi, the first aeronaut to launch himself from English soil, was struck that "the earth appeared as before, like an extensive plain, with the same variegated surface; but the objects rather less distinguishable." Monck Mason, in his 1837 *History of Aerostation*, explains this optical phenomenon by noting that the balloonist floats along atmospheric currents. From the zenith all known fixed and stable objects rapidly retrogress "upon the plain beneath." This experience was verified by Thomas Baldwin.[158] Consequently, the balloon voyage was instrumental in shaping the perception of an uninterrupted surface below.

Upon abandoning the perspective of dizzying heights, the earth's constricted plains appear more muted. As noted, Polynesia was riddled with alluring islands whose roads, leading from sacred maraes to rocky shores, cut through green plantations that were quite flat. When sailing up the Nile shortly after its flooding, John Ledyard unexpectedly witnessed "an unbounded plain of excellent land."[159] These fertile areas constitute a

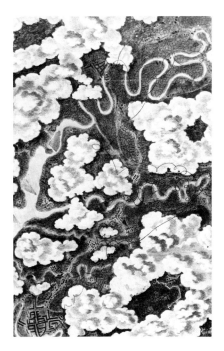

Figure 100
Thomas Baldwin, *A Balloon Prospect from Above the Clouds*, from *Airopaidia*, 1786, pl. p. 154. Color engraving by Angus. Photo courtesy Smithsonian Institution, Washington, D.C.

THE NATURAL MASTERPIECE

visual foil to rock fields, devoid of human presence, shooting undeviatingly into the distance. J. C. Hobhouse, whose journey to Albania inspired Lord Byron, brooded over the somber and compacted soil at Marathon. R. H. Colebrooke, in Mysore, executed a prospect showing the interminable and untenanted rock-strewn vacancy of Mooty Tallaow (figure 38). Francis Hamilton, in Nepal, managed to tear his gaze away from the distant panorama of "one mountain heaped on another" to concentrate on being situated within the great plain of Hindustan. More refractory yet were the "hard and rocky" lowlands encountered by Browne en route to the Sinai and by Lichtenstein on the lion-infested flats of South Africa. Humboldt, scaling the slopes of Chimborazo, and Maria Graham, exploring Chile, stared down upon an "arid plain" whose stony aspect was barely mollified by a scant covering of schimus molle cactus, agave, and molina. (See figures 35 and 102.) On the trail to La Paz, Edmond Temple remembers traversing an unyielding tableland covered with loose gravel on which "a tree [was] rarely to be seen for a distance of five hundred miles."

The perennial dryness of New South Wales did not savor of humanity to Ferdinand Bauer or Barron Field, Australia's first native poet and author of the important *Geographical Memoirs* (1825). John Oxley speaks to the same point when he records his progress down the Lachlau River; apart from deep bights formed by its course, the country passed through was "extremely low" and "broad." Belzoni, landing at Abusimebel, found an "extensive plain" on the west bank of the Nile, charged with black, smooth stones. Unlike John Ledyard's experience of alluvial richness, the land near the second cataract presented "nothing to the eye but bare stone and sand" and an occasional sycamore.[160]

Scarified volcanic regions, noted by Hamilton, MacKenzie, and Porter, likewise presented large dismal tracts whose topsoil was concealed under black cinders eradicating any trace of vegetation. The netherworld is visually related to this terrene obliteration and blight of a once-verdant ground. Beneath the disfigured earth, accessible only through mine shafts, arch splendid galleries that open out upon "subterranean plains washed by rivers that had never known the sun's rays; and now lay not only congealed but glittering with ten thousand brilliant pyramids shaped by their formerly dashing waters, frozen to crystal, and reflecting every beam from our numerous torches."[161]

Bleaker still flow the unconfined and "immense field[s]" of ice covering the oceans in the far north and south. When Cook lost his bearings amid Polar fog, Forster could still discern enormous translucent sheets glinting and stretching as far as the eye could see. The vacancy of the Antarctic Circle, which Cook crossed three times during his second voyage, was interrupted by pack ice, in a state of either impregnable uniformity or dangerous disintegration. During the 1820s, Captains Parry, Franklin, and Ross substantiated the early navigator's assessment of this bitter solitude where frozen rafts and radiant flotillas menacingly drifted by.[162]

A variant of this involvement with ocean-borne phenomena is the promotion of the investigation of shoals and reefs. These barely submerged obstructions, fringing high islands or mainland coasts, culminate in the Great Barrier Reef. Composed of flats growing on the continental shelf common to Western Papua and Queensland, and over 1,000 miles long, they consist of myriads of separate cays, mainly dry or slightly awash at low tide. Each is compounded of a mass of calcereous detritus and the skeletons of countless marine organisms: corals, mollusks, coralline algae, echinoderms, crustaceans, polyzoa. The Great Barrier Reef is only one of many such provinces native to the southwestern Pacific. Matthew Flinders, on his circumnavigation of the Australian coast, was one of the earliest scientific explorers to leave an accurate account of these banks and their formation. He comments perceptively that they are in different stages of progress: ". . . some, like this [Half-Way Island], are become islands, but not yet habitable; some are above the high-water mark, but destitute of vegetation; whilst others are overflowed with every returning tide. It seems to me that when the animalcules which form the corals at the bottom of the ocean, cease to live, their structures adhere to each other . . . and a mass of rock is at length formed. . . ." The same unitary bond between earth and ocean was seen by Adelbert von Chamisso, the naturalist on Kotzebue's voyage of discovery, who noted that in the lee of Assumption Island (an inhospitable volcano to the north of the Ladrones) "numerous sandbanks of considerable extent, shine, white and bare, above the surface of the waves." An appreciative recognition of the adamantinely level encountered within a marine setting is also reflected in the language and imagery used to describe the Giant's Causeway: "a vast mass of basaltic pillars [that] forms a sort of promontory on the coast of Antrim, in Ireland. It stretches out towards the sea, and terminates in a point over which the breakers dash with violence. . . ."[163] (See figure 19.)

The travelers' investigation of all manner of permutations on the theme of tundra, steppe, savannah, veldt, maquis, ice cap, or even prospect reached its acme in the exploration of the desert. By definition, absence of refuge or shelter characterizes any radically exposed and desolate environment. None appears more bereft of the amenities of life or more hostile to anything organic, let alone human, than the lonely wasteland. If a certain invariability and lateral magnitude is implicit in all level districts, an extreme degree is evident in the supreme incarnation of horizontality.[164]

It is a mistake to suppose, however, that these reaches exist only under the burning sun. "Wastes" and "uniformities" were identified by Cook in New Caledonia: "Everything conspired here to make us look upon the country as a solitude . . . without a single habitation. . . . [It] is for the greater part very barren and desert. . . ." Cordiner in Ceylon—at first impression an equally unlikely candidate—finds "captivating" the "uncultivated wilds" near Penacratchy. John Davy, a visitor to that same island, utters incongruous praises of its "charming deserts." In a weightier tone, Humboldt speaks of the mountain fastness of the Andes as "desert

THE NATURAL MASTERPIECE

Figure 101
Heinrich Lichtenstein, *View of a Group of the Karree Mountains,* from *Reisen im Südlichen Afrika,* 1811, II, pl. p. 338. Engraving. Photo courtesy British Museum, London.

VOYAGE INTO SUBSTANCE

Figure 102
Maria Graham, *From the Foot of the Cuesta de Prado*, from *Journal of a Residence in Chile*, 1824, pl. p. 196. Aquatint by Edward Finden. Photo courtesy British Library.

Figure 103
J. C. Ross, *Part of the South Polar Barrier . . . 2 February, 1841*, from *Voyages*, 1847, I, pl. p. 17. Lithograph by J. Murray. Photo courtesy National Maritime Museum.

solitudes," and Easter Island, at least since the days of Roggeveen, Cook, and La Pérouse, was recognized by its "iron bound shore" and drought-stricken surface.[165]

This nomenclature, rooted in the language of the Old and New Testaments, had in more recent times been affiliated with gardens. Rousseau's ideal of an untilled ground formed part of the literary tradition of idyllic rural imagery. Addison, in the *Spectator* (412), tabulates its many connotations: "By greatness I do not only mean the bulk of any single object, but the largeness of a whole view, considered as one entire piece. Such are the prospects of an open champaign country, a vast uncultivated desert of huge heaps of mountains, high rocks and precipices. . . ."[166] The emulation of natural wildness insinuated itself into the French Picturesque garden, specifically the projects of Georges-Louis Le Rouge. Geographer to the Comte de Clermont, Le Rouge was, in addition, the composer of voluminous notebooks on the topic of the "Anglo-Chinese garden" (1774–1789). Following the Mannerist conceit of paradoxical antithesis, he reproduces startling or theatrical "natural" effects, noting the importance of passing abruptly from a "delicious garden" into a "horrible desert." Le Rouge does not intend by this phrase that the viewer should be confronted by a sterile or inartificial scene. What primarily defines such an area as forlorn is the fact of its being untended and uninhabited; secondarily, it is the presence of scattered debris, burnt-out or ruined houses, blasted trees, caves occupied by monsters, and "the illusion of Vesuvius."

Jean-Benjamin de Laborde, in an account of the "desert" at Ermenonville, describes it as a "vast" terrain containing novel objects deliberately placed in unique juxtaposition: ancient gorse, cedar, juniper, firs of varying heights strewn irregularly over an arid soil, enormous rocks, and streams (some of which roll negligently in clay or sandstone beds while others, collected and stagnating, form marshes and lakes exhibiting a virtual image of the absence of agriculture). Laborde writes that "one wanders here with trepidation and contemplates in silence the disorder of nature left to its own devices."[167] As might be expected, only the hut of Rousseau was thought suitable to ornament this place.

In light of this strange mixture, it is apparent that within the Picturesque aesthetic the term *desert* simply indicates the absence of husbandry or conspicuous management. The *Geography* of the Greek author Strabo should be cited as countering such fictitious *folie*. Worlds apart from the mentality of the gardenist who defines as desert any land left unploughed, Strabo first articulates the reality of a fiery wilderness. Libya, resembling the leopard's skin, is dotted with unpopulated places and desert land. Its interior, which "produces silphium," affords "only a wretched sustenance," being for the most part a "rocky and sandy desert." Strabo used analogous words to portray the region extending from Carthage to the Pillars of Hercules ("full of wild beasts") and the territories of Arabia and Ethiopia ("without water and habitable only in spots").[168]

Figure 104
William Hodges, *Monuments in Easter Island*, from James Cook, *Voyage towards the South Pole*, I, 1777, pl. 49. Engraved by William Woollett. Photo courtesy Newberry Library.

Figure 105
J.-B. de Laborde, *View of the Desert at Ermenonville*, from *Description de la France*, 1789, V, pl. 25. Engraving by Fessard l'aîné after a drawing by Tavernier. Photo courtesy Cabinet des Estampes, Bibliothèque Nationale.

As a modern spokesman for the actual desert, Cornelius Le Bruyn again exemplifies the early will to verisimilitude. Traveling by caravan across Persia, he reached what formerly must have been a fine plain but now was "all parched up by the heat of the sun and the great droughts." The meager amenities of the country include a "bitter and lofty herb, jassian" and sands "as hard as gravel." As part of his cosmogonical speculations, the influential French writer Maillet develops a powerful image of the Syrian and Egyptian deserts. His *Telliamed* sets itself the task of outlining the natural process by which the earth in its present state, together with various organic species, was generated. Although the *Telliamed* is questionable as a strictly scientific document, for travelers it served to explain the crystallized features of Near Eastern topography. Maillet attributed the formation of these countries to the evaporation of a primitive ocean that had left behind saline deposits.[169]

Such ruminations prompted Eyles Irwin to exclaim in the midst of the naked retreats of the "desarts of Thebais" that "chaos [was] come again." James Bruce, ferreting out the source of the Nile, paid fresh homage to "the vast expanse of the Desert," filled with some of "the most magnificent sights in the world," including artless pillars of salt and shifting sands. In the dedication to his work, Bruce reflects movingly on the nature of his accomplishment:

From Egypt I penetrated into this country, through Arabia on one side, passing through melancholy and dreary deserts, ventilated with poisonous winds, and glowingly eternal sunbeams, whose names are as unknown in geography as are those of the antediluvian world. In the six years employed in this survey, I described a circumference whose greatest axis comprehended twenty-two degrees of the meridian, in which dreadful circle was contained all that is terrible to the feelings, prejudicial to the health, or fatal to the life of man. . . .

Mungo Park, less eloquently, recorded the fractured and unfarmed areas of the principality of Senegal.[170]

Figure 106
Mungo Park, *A View of a Bridge over the Ba-Fing or Black River,* from *Travels in Africa,* 1799, I, pl. p. 338. Engraving by W. C. Wilson. Photo courtesy British Library.

Egypt is two-faced. At the heliacal rising of the dog star, the rainy season commences in the tropics; then the Nile becomes swollen and floods its banks. Without this annual inundation, the whole of the land is "parched with almost perpetual drought." Vivant-Denon, riding toward Assouan with Bonaparte, accompanied a small detachment ordered to engage Mourad-Bey in diversionary skirmishes. For 24 memorable days after leaving Syene the French artist subsisted in these wilds, "extending his exploration to Nubia, above Philae." Largely because of the Napoleonic conquests and Vivant-Denon's efforts (he edited the text of the monumental scientific report resulting from the campaign and directed the work of a pleiad of artists), the meticulous depiction of the spacious Egyptian wastes could be claimed as a Gallic achievement. The characteristics of the wide-spanned wilderness—adequately seized for the first time in the pictorial format of compressive narrowness coupled with unfurling extent—emerge from Vivant-Denon's illustrated narrative. Thebes is a razed sanctuary,

VOYAGE INTO SUBSTANCE

and its ruined granite denizens are "abandoned," "isolated," and "going down into the desert that vanquished them." The small band, their thirst unslakeable, trekked across "sand formed only from the primitive and constitutive stuff of granite." From a high plateau, the immensity of the desert through which the Nile slowly snaked its way finally stood revealed. Vivant-Denon also speaks of the multiformity of the terrain, of scoriated inflexible surfaces brittle with the dregs of decomposing primary rock, and of resilient elasticities easily sustaining the tracks of a gazelle or the slight furrows raised by the wind.[171]

Travelers made the public tangibly aware that the Ottoman Empire, particularly Arabia Petrea and the Holy Land, was far removed from its biblical incarnation as a paradise of lush hills and fertile vales. Another French explorer, G. A. Olivier, added a new dimension to the perception of the Babylonian wilderness. Instead of an unmitigated wasteland, he perceived subtle and unobtrusive signs of life. This revelation comes to Olivier in Egypt. He declares that if one penetrates far enough in this harsh land one discovers plants that seem to defy observation. Tiny, covered with dust, and white in color, they blend with and submit to the severities of the soil. The sight of these valiant and frail survivors leads Olivier to a larger realization that the common, uninformed conception of broad, uninhabitable sections of the globe (the deserts of Africa, Asia, and Egypt) is exaggerated and false. In imagining this absolute nakedness one conjures up a sea of sand and thinks no plant or animal life can survive. In fact, this vision of an eternal sterility is destroyed by the traveler's firsthand experience of vegetation and the spotting of numerous insects, reptiles, and birds.[172]

Despite Olivier's meliorating assurances about the Near East, the image of its North African counterpart was untouched. The Sahara long remained the Himalaya of deserts; in fact, the Arabic word was synonymous with the latter. James Jackson, in his *Empire of Marocco*, states that, with the exception of occasional oases, throughout vast stretches of North Africa "the scorpion delights in stony places." Immense hills of loose and moveable sand are "from time to time driven by the wind into various forms" and "so impregnate the air with particles of sand for many miles out to sea, as to give the atmosphere an appearance of hazy weather." Saugnier's *Côte d'Afrique* presages this view of the "Saara," riddled with buttes, incessantly displaced hillocks, and sparsely interspersed with refreshing oases. The *Proceedings of the British Africa Association* corroborate this evidence, filled as they are with accounts of "dreary wastes of sand" whose endless barrens are smothered by suffocating heat. Lucas en route to Fez in 1788, Browne traveling with a Sudanese caravan in 1799, and Leyden making the hazardous journey in the same year all had as their destination "the Great Desert." Common to their descriptions is an awareness of intense prospect where vegetative and even atmospheric impediments to visibility (with certain telling exceptions) are nonexistent.

1. *Couvent dans le Désert.* 2. *Village de Nagadi dans le Désert.* 3. *Couvent dans le Désert.*

Figure 107
D. Vivant-Denon, *Desert Scenes*, from
Voyage dans la Haute et la Basse Egypte,
1801, II, pl. 73. Engraving by J. Garreau.
Photo courtesy British Library.

Figure 108
D. Vivant-Denon, *Statues of Memnon*, from
Voyage dans la Haute et la Basse Egypte,
1801, II, pl. 44. Engraving by L. Petit.
Photo courtesy British Library.

Figure 109
Richard Pococke, *The Statue of Memnon*,
from *Description of the East*, 1745–1747, I,
pl. 37. Engraving. Photo courtesy Library
of Congress.

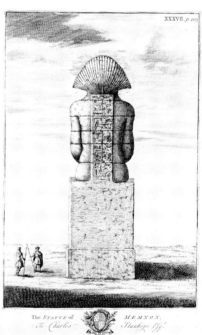

THE NATURAL MASTERPIECE

Attention is focused on a remorseless plain on whose back the traveler remains pitilessly exposed.[173]

The Sahara embraces the extent of land lying between the narrow strip termed Barbary and that more felicitous tract south of Cape Verde running to the Red Sea. The Africans call it the Sudan. Its surface comprises an area equal to half that of Europe and contains islands of great fertility with some population. During the eighteenth and early nineteenth centuries, the western division between Fez and the Atlantic was reckoned as being approximately 50 caravan journeys (that is, some 800 miles) in breadth from north to south, and double that extent in length. Lyon, in his *Travels in North Africa*, and (most especially) Jackson, in his vivid *Account of Timbuctoo*, disclose what one could expect when taking the Mecca caravan from Fez in early March. For the first 20 days, the travelers are immersed in a dusty plain resembling the ocean. After pitching tents at night they are obliged to shake the sand from the tops; otherwise they would be engulfed before morning. The approaching horrors, transmitted in the terse, unemotional speech of the Arab Shabeeny quoted by Jackson, become more ominous. For the following 20 days the caravan passes into a wilderness wholly without water; not a drop is to be found even by digging. On the borders of this country the Bedouin roam. Here, too, the fierce Esshume, the hottest wind imaginable, blasts from east to west. After 20 more days, the exhausted party enters a country that finally varies in aspect, graced by an occasional fertile spot and the token of wild myrtle.[174]

The scientific exploration of the world's deserts was not limited to the French and the English. Friedrich Hornemann, a student at Göttingen whose mentor was Blumenbach, the professor of natural history, set out for the heart of Africa in 1797. Hornemann was unusual in that he recognized the need to know Arabic, a facility he acquired in Egypt. When Bonaparte landed in Alexandria, he sent for Hornemann (with that characteristic magnanimity he extended to scholars) and supplied him with passports and money enabling him to join a caravan leaving from Cairo. On September 8, 1799, Hornemann entered the Libyan desert—dreaded since Strabo's day. Echoing the theories of Maillet, he relates that "the surface of the sandy waste over which [he] traveled, precisely resembled a shore from which the waters have retired after a storm." John Lewis Burckhardt (similarly, if not superiorly, trained in Arabic, and with a rigorous background in chemistry, astronomy, mineralogy, and medicine) followed in Hornemann's footsteps in 1809. Burckhardt's death delayed the penetration of the countries of the Niger (leaving them for Sir Richard Burton and John Speke), although he managed to reach the Red Desert.

The idiosyncratic Italian excavator of Nubian temples, Giovanni Battista Belzoni, contributed significantly to the increasing literature on the desert. He left a sympathetic account of the Bedouin pitching camp on the bleak path between Siout and Tahta, having left behind in the surrounding

Figure 110
James Jackson, *West View of the City of Marocco with the Mountains of Atlas*, from *History of Marocco*, 1811 edition, pl. p. 116. Engraving by J. C. Sadler. Photo courtesy British Library.

Figure 111
G. F. Lyon, *A Slave Kaffle*, from *Travels in North Africa*, 1821, pl. p. 325. Lithograph by J. Lighton. Photo courtesy British Library.

desert the tribe's old men and women. Immersed in a wilderness of sand dunes; these nomads allow the desert to hide their tents in case of surprise attack—as Belzoni's sketch shows.[175]

In summary: By the 1820s, tenantless or marginally inhabited wastes are encountered with rising frequency in the factual travel accounts. Lieutenant Beechey toiled across the barren Great Syrtis, Lycett struggled through the "desert" that made up Australia's outback, and Robert Mignan, in his *Travels in Chaldea*, affirms that once one abandons the banks of the Tigris and heads north only lonely "pathless deserts"—reminiscent of Diodorus Siculus's account and the Book of Joel—can be awaited.[176]

If plains and deserts were notorious for their unyielding horizontality, valleys—although to a lesser extent—entered the observer's consciousness because they shattered the integrity of the absolutely level. Depressions and declivities pierced the surface of the earth to create geologically revealing cuts and hollows. Again, archaeological publications established an important precedent for the depiction of gaping natural cavities. Pococke represents a case in point. In the *Description of the East* (1743–1745) he shows "a very narrow valley" leading undeviatingly to sepulchres for the kings of Thebes. Similarly, the surveys carried out by the British during the 1780s in India often included views of rock-cut temples hewn into the Barabar (Bihar) and other hills. Traveling in search of these wonders, troops, artists, naturalists, and surveyors crossed many a valley.[177]

William Hodges drew the steep ravines at Etawa in the Doaab slicing openings between the Rivers Jumna and Ganges (figure 39). These abysses "are formed by the Rains washing away the loosest Part of the Soil leaving vast chasms of great length and depth"; the country on the western bank of the river is "likewise full of these Ravines." Nor were the Daniells oblivious to the pictorial potential of valleys. In many of their river scenes—like that of the Koah Mullah—the real subject is the sudden interval created by the gorge formed of steep inclined and uplifted rocks, on the left, and great slabs piled up, on the right, through which the stream flows.[178]

The valley as topographical rift suffers in comparison with other imposing figures of earth because the traveler's gaze is, more often than not, arrested by what it contains rather than by the hiatus it intrinsically is. For example, George Annesley, in his *Voyages and Travels* (1801), admires the "singular" valley of Sandy Bay at Saint Helena because it houses "a conspicuous object": the artless column of Lot, surrounded by his "family" (figures 13 and 14). There are, of course, exceptions to this perceptual rule. Humboldt observes that the canyon is among the most majestic and multiformed phenomena visible in the region of the Cordillera. Unlike mountains whose peaks can be grasped only from a considerable distance because the plateau from which they are visible is itself at an elevation of 2,500–3,000 meters, the amplitude of such rents does not suffer from a corresponding impression of diminution. These breaches are deeper and narrower than their crevasse counterparts in the Alps and the Pyrenees; some fissures are so profound that Vesuvius and the Puy-de-Dôme could be lodged safely within their depths without the crests exceeding the neighboring summits.

In an analogous vein and traveling over an equally marginless area, Martin Heinrich Lichtenstein, accompanied only by a loyal band of Hottentots, explored the defiles that disrupt the terrain of South Africa. He reports in *Reisen im Südlichen Afrika* (1811) how they wandered from valley to valley without finding any trace of human life.[179] In these trailless haunts of the shy ostrich and the invisible wild horse, Lichtenstein understandably remarks upon any caesura that ruptures the monotony of the earth's crust. (See figure 101.) Allen Gardiner reacted similarly to arroyos discovered in the Zulu country. Belzoni, seeking relief from the arid mountains curtaining Thebes, gazed down upon the broad valley of Beban el Malook and from thence upon the entire valley of Egypt. Lyon, as keenly perceptive, looked from the vantage of the Gharian Mountains upon the road from Tripoli over which he had just traveled as it wended its way through a "barren, but beautiful and romantic" pass.[180]

Discrete Particulars

The Ficus Indica, *or Banyan Tree, famed for its eccentric growth, and held sacred by the Hindoos . . . rises high in the air, then drops its boughs which take root, and successively create new stems, till a vast extent is covered with the arched shade. It is even said to form of itself a forest of arched avenues, and a labyrinth of alleys impenetrable by the rays of the vertical sun. . . .*
Captain Charles Gold

The charged vocabulary of the Bible and the astringent idiom of Strabo mark the hallowed beginnings of wilderness imagery. Lucan, in a highly wrought passage, describes a Celtic forest sanctuary near Massalia violated and eventually destroyed by Caesar, and in the process formulates another descriptive prototype: ". . . there were many / dark springs running there, and grim-faced figures of gods uncouthly / hewn by the axe from the untrimmed tree-trunk rotted to whiteness." The nemeton or holy place in the gloomy, frightening wood occupies the visual antipodes from the many-faceted clearings just examined. Greek and Roman writers were struck not only by these ceremonial enclosures but also by the dense forests that cloaked them.[181] The dim barbaric grove, like the trackless desert, contrasts pointedly with the rural and agrarian continental world. Uncleared, chaotic woodland is also antithetical to a defined, urban pattern of life. By its very essence it stands in opposition to anything open, whether it be town, plain, or coast. Thus, since aboriginal times the secluded thicket—like the grotto and the sacred spring or pool, and unlike the flatland—has materially "housed" the numinous. The secret powers of this organic seat of the godhead emerge from its tangled depths, not its superficies. Further, the history of its more modern aesthetic appreciation is rooted in the recondite "Druidic" cult of the Gauls.[182]

The theme of this chapter—the artless masterpiece created by a nature unmanipulated by man—attains its apogee in the virgin forest. The memory of the vast stands of unfelled timber that had once covered Britain and Germany was vividly brought to mind during the pre-Revolutionary

Figure 112
G. Belzoni, *Bedouins Camp*, from *Plates Illustrative of the Researches of . . . in Egypt and Nubia*, 1820, pl. 25. Hand-colored lithograph by A. Aglio. Photo courtesy British Library.

Figure 113
Richard Pococke, *The Sepulchres of the Kings of Thebes*, from *Description of the East*, 1745–1747, I, pl. 30. Etching. Photo courtesy Library of Congress.

Figure 114
Thomas and William Daniell, *View in the Koah Mullah*, from *Oriental Scenery*, 1797, II, pl. 15. Color aquatint. Photo courtesy India Office Library.

Figure 115
A. von Humboldt, *Volcano of Torullo*, from *Vues des Cordillères*, 1814, pl. 43. Color aquatint by Boguet. Photo courtesy British Library.

Figure 116
G. Belzoni, *General View of the Scite of Thebes*, from *Six New Plates Illustrative of the Researches and Operations of . . . in Egypt and Nubia*, 1822, pl. 1. Hand-colored lithograph by A. Aglio. Photo courtesy British Library.

THE NATURAL MASTERPIECE

era by the developing interest in Northern mythologies. The critical reception of a power-filled primitive universe as it emerged from the pages of the *Eddas* or MacPherson's *Ossian* is connected with the contemporary scientific belief in the animate life of all organic substance. Linnaeus's and Bernardin de Saint-Pierre's asseverations concerning the heightened existence of plants imparted a new dignity to the overgrown and teeming wood.[183]

Geographically, North America formed the principal locus for the forest primeval. Isaac Weld, in his *Travels*, declares that the first objects to meet the eye on approaching the coast south of New York are treetops. As one draws nearer, these unite into a "tall forest rising gradually out of the ocean," which, at last, presents itself majestically in luxuriant splendor. Weld, in the manner of every thoughtful European who alighted on these shores (like Alexander MacKenzie), notes the Americans' "unconquerable aversion to trees." He deduces from the double evidence that they are "cut away without mercy" and that the face of the land is "entirely overspread with them" that the inhabitants must be satiated by their relentless presence. Constantin-François de Chasseboeuf, Comte de Volney, echoes his contemporary's judgment but develops it against the background of his own wider perspective. From the standpoint of a French voyager accustomed to the denuded countries of Egypt, Asia, and the coasts of the Mediterranean, he affirms that the overriding physical trait of America is the monolithic thickness of its forests, stretching almost uninterruptedly from coast to coast and becoming more compact as one advances into the interior. His initial impression is shattered, however, by the sight of massive deforestation in the states of Delaware, Pennsylvania, Maryland, Virginia, and Kentucky. During his tour he constantly encounters paths bordered by overturned trees and rotting stumps. Silence, monotony, and aridity reign, not the charming solitude envisioned by novelists safely dreaming in the bosom of some European city. Indeed, he points out that the "vast deserts," called savannahs by the Spaniards and prairies by the North Americans, resulted largely from fires set by the "Red Skin" and the pioneer. By 1828, Volney's muted elegy had become a lament. Milbert, following an itinerary along the Hudson, composed a threnody on the "ancient and universal forests" that in less than a century had been ruthlessly destroyed.[184]

Nevertheless, "intricate and impenetrable" forests could be experienced in their pristine state in remoter regions of the world. Georg Forster recorded their grave presence in Queen Charlotte's Sound and Dusky Bay, New Zealand.[185] Further, Cook contributed substantially to the conception of verdant tropical paradises by describing the abundant groves of Tahiti, New Ireland, Amsterdam, and Duke of York Islands, and the French explorer Crozet immersed himself in the thickets of Guam, where no signs of man's intervention were yet visible. The organic insistency seemed to exclude, or at least undermine, any human incursion. Somewhat paradoxically, trees abounded in regions commonly held to be wastes of snow and ice or of blazing sun and sand. The French naval geographer O'Hier de Grandpré praised the flourishing forests of the Congo. Burckhardt, making his way along the Sinai Peninsula, suddenly came upon a dense wood teeming with evergreen tamarisk and the occasional camel feeding on thorny shoots.[186]

The solid impenetrability implicit in the experience of a vast stand of trees is most cogently embodied in the tropical rain forests, which exceed all others in conveying a sense of being hostile and alien to man. Inimical to stasis, they incarnate on a magnificent scale the apotheosis and final triumph of vegetative energy. More than any other, the name of the German naturalist, painter, and explorer Johann Moritz Rugendas is linked with the pictorial propagation of the primitive forests of Brazil. Arriving at Rio in 1821, Rugendas spent the next four years gathering data on the natives and their land. Upon his return to Europe he met Humboldt (then in Paris), who wanted to involve the young artist in illustrating a new edition of *Geographie der Pflanzen* (1807). Drawings made by Rugendas in the Brazilian forests were to have been part of this great work. Despite the failure of Humboldt's revised text to materialize, the fruits of Rugendas's first expedition—100 prints lithographed at Engelmann's—were published in *Voyage pittoresque dans Brésil* (1835). In addition to the depiction of native customs, Rugendas demonstrated a sensitivity for capturing the luxuriant tropical landscape. In Rugendas's wake followed Ferdinand Bellerman, who set a course for Venezuela, and Eduard Hildebrandt, who retraced Rugendas's steps to Brazil. Alexander Caldcleugh was lured into a "dark wilderness" of arborescent ferns, siliquous plants, and fallen trees in inaccessible forests of green mangroves and towering palms. He reminds us in his *Travels to South America* (1825) that he, too, harkened to the call of Humboldt. No matter how soured the Europeans might become by the want of comfort or the intolerable heat and humidity, they were not immune to tropical scenery.[187]

It is but a short leap from the wet and lavish green stretches of Brazil to the dank, dark jungles of Siam and India. The Dutch explorer Kaempfer traces a picture of rampant ferns, several species of matted cypress grasses, and prevailing floodlands that immobilize anyone who would wander in Java and Laos. The Burman Empire and Ceylon presented to the eyes of the British, accustomed to more temperate climes, a sea of "lush trees," rivers glutted with lily pads, and an exuberant greenery fed by perpetual downpours. The inhabitant of Rangoon, inspecting the city from the anchorage, sees golden spires of countless temples rising abruptly from the impenetrable jungle just as the Buddhist pilgrim must seek out within it his sacred monuments. Java "abounds with elephants," trapped in the "vast wildernesses" of Munmipoor, Asam, and the Arracan mountains. Wild herds of elephants, jackal, deer, and antelope dwell in inundated regions of penumbrous foliage. William Hodges paints a moonlit evening in the Jungle Ferry of Bengal and also aquatints a heavily chiaroscuroed

Figure 117
John Webber, *A Morai in Atooi*, B.M. Add.
MS 23, 921, 1778, fol. 73. Engraving by
Lerpernere. Photo courtesy British Library.

Figure 118
John Webber, *A View in Otaheite* (1777),
from *Sketchbook*, B.M. Add. MS 15, 513,
fol. 13. Watercolor. Photo courtesy British
Library.

VOYAGE INTO SUBSTANCE

Figure 119
J. B. Fraser, *Gungotree, The Holy Shrine of Mahadeo,* from *Views in the Himala Mountains,* 1820, pl. 11. Color aquatint by R. Havell and Son. Photo courtesy India Office Library.

Figure 120
A. Cappell Brooke, *Scene in the Forests of Russian Lapland,* from *Winter Sketches in Lapland,* 1827, pl. 22. Hand-colored lithograph by J. D. Harding. Photo courtesy British Library.

THE NATURAL MASTERPIECE

VOYAGE INTO SUBSTANCE

Figure 121
François Le Vaillant, *Camp at Pampoen-kraal*, from *Voyage de . . . dans l'intérieur de l'Afrique*, 1790, I, pl. p. 166. Engraving. Photo courtesy British Library.

Figure 122
A. von Humboldt, *Air Volcanoes of Turbaco*, from *Vues des Cordillères*, 1814, pl. 41. Color aquatint by Boguet. Photo courtesy British Library.

THE NATURAL MASTERPIECE

daylight version for the *Select Views of India* (1786): "Situated on the hills that seem evidently thrown up by some violent convulsion of nature, the shapes of these hills have more the appearance of large single stones, with trees growing from them, giving them an unusual singularity. . . ." Thomas Williamson, in his colorful *Oriental Field Sports* of 1807 (which surely influenced the naive jungle scenes of the Douanier Rousseau) shows a tiger being slain within the same district. Similarly, Robert Elliott depicts the identical area made fertile by the muddy water of the Ganges.[188] The ever-blooming groves and thickets of India, "inhabited by tygers and other animals," form a leitmotif of the factual travel account. Colebrooke stumbles through them in Ramgherry, and Johnson fears the "tyger haunts" at the center of the island of Salsetta.[189]

The drenching humidity of the jungle was exceeded only by the unrelieved wetness of the swamp. Daniel Beeckman, in his *Voyage to Borneo* (1718), describes the land of the orangutan lying north of Java and east of Sumatra as full of "vast swamps of mud." John Byron, lying off the coast of Chile, notes the "uncouth" aspects of the area. A "deep swamp" is the reigning soil of this country in which woods float rather than grow.[190] The North possessed a desolate counterpart in the morass. Joseph Banks, in the journal of his exploration of Newfoundland and Labrador (1766), notes the heat and closeness enveloping the little town of Croque, surrounded by a morass engendering "mosketos and gadflies in Prodigious abundance." Adam Neale conjures up the unique aspect of the Moldavian territory, which still retains the remains of oak forests intersected by marshes. These observations shed valuable light on what Mecklenburg and the French Vendée must have looked like before cultivation. Georg Forster's *Blick in das Ganze der Natur* includes a survey of overgrown areas filled with rotting wood where, instead of blooming plants, one encounters only mosses, fungi, and the like. Stagnant water and slime render the water undrinkable and the air foul-smelling. Poisonous insects and noxious plants fill these morasses. In penning this passage, Forster must have recalled exploring the mangrove-covered shores of Caledonia and the fetid lagoons of the Society Islands. Isaac Weld did not shun the Great Dismal Swamp, which takes up some 150,000 acres from Virginia to North Carolina. This tract, ladened with enormous cypress and ancient juniper, is so crowded with brushwood that in many parts it is absolutely "impervious," and in the interior wild cattle, bears, wolves, deer, and "wild men" are rumored to live. Milbert paid an equally "miry" visit to this "unfordable labyrinth" snared with reeds, ivy, vines and ferns of all kinds, brambles, and a multiplicity of mosses, among which live repellant snakes, rats, toads, and crocodiles.[191] The blind, instinctual life of the swamp, more so even than that of the jungle or virgin forest, was utterly removed from the refinements of civilization.

A more exquisite but nonetheless related world is that of the aquatic plants visible to the observer stationed on dry land or immersed in a stream.

Pococke swam twice in the Red Sea, idly drifting over "groves of coral or madreporae." The Abbé La Pluche assures the reader of the *Spectacle de la nature* that the bottom of the ocean is "covered by vegetation that differs entirely from ours" and "possesses its forest and prairies in which the inhabitants of these waters find the nourishment they require, and the retreats in which they might repose." Le Gentil, gazing into the limpid transparency of the Indian Ocean, offers an elegant reprise of the motif of the submerged, not the reflected, wood: "There is nothing more agreeable than those pastimes [undertaken] when the sea is tranquil and the weather is fine; one sails in the midst of a forest of variegated coral, whose stems break the surface; there are times when one can observe polyps leaving their domiciles. . . . One meets with the most beautiful, multicolored fish, with sea mushrooms, etc. In addition, the sand is carpeted with sea urchins of different types. . . ."[192]

The appreciation of specific underwater vegetation recalls us to the point that the tree—independent of its manifestation in a crowd—is also upon occasion an individual, valued for its lone appearance. Traditionally one of the ornaments of landscape painting, as Roger de Piles reminds us, this genre was expanded by the late eighteenth century to embrace the numerous exotic species classified in factual travel narratives. In the Orient, long accustomed to the sensitive and deferential observation of nature, distinctive specimens were singled out at an early date. Bashō's pen name was the Japanese term for an exotic plant originating in China. It was during his haiku journey to Honshu's remote province—a difficult and perilous undertaking—that Bashō composed his travel diaries, in which trees play an important role. A profound underlying mysticism is evident in his reverential attitude toward the Takekuma pine that "just as in olden times . . . rose from the earth divided into twin trunks." Matsushima, "the most beautiful place in all Japan," is an area of countless islands, some tall like fingers pointing to heaven, some lying prostrate on the waves. Their visual character resides in the dark green pines whose branches are bent by the salty sea winds into graceful and idiosyncratic shapes.

Travelers to the Far East commented profusely on the grave elegance of the indigenous flora. Lord Macartney dwells at length on the old dwarf trees of the Chu-san Islands, which bear the marks of venerable ruins.[193] But by far the most frequently cited tropical tree is the Banyan. Known in antiquity, it was described by Pliny. Alexander the Great admired it, and upon this authority Milton placed it in paradise. Cornelius Le Bruyn reintroduced it into the modern consciousness. On the southern coast of Arabia Felix, not far from Ispahan, he met with a "most remarkable" tree whose massive trunk was 52 spans in circumference. Also known as the Dragtoe, it was sacred throughout the Near East. William Hodges captured its towering stature and the intricacy of its form. Captain Gold, in his *Oriental Drawings* (1806), and Sir Charles D'Oyly, in his *Scrapbook*

THE NATURAL MASTERPIECE

Figure 123
Captain J. Kershaw, *View from Pagoda,
Rangoon, Burma*, from *Description of a
Series of Views in the Burman Empire*, 1831?
Color aquatint by William Daniell. Photo
courtesy National Maritime Museum.

VOYAGE INTO SUBSTANCE

Figure 124
Samuel Daniell, *View between Galle and
Mattura*, from *Ceylon*, 1808, pl. 4. Color
aquatint. Photo courtesy India Office
Library.

Figure 125
William Hodges, *A View in the Jungle
Ferry*, from *Views in India*, 1786, pl. 2.
Color aquatint. Photo courtesy India Office
Library.

THE NATURAL MASTERPIECE

Figure 126
Cornelius Le Bruyn, *Banyan Tree*, from
Travels to Muscovy, Persia . . . , 1737, II, pl.
233. Engraving. Photo courtesy Library of
Congress.

(1823–1825), state that it is famous for its eccentric growth and that under its snaky boughs yogis practice their austerities. Maria Graham, in the journal of her residence in India (1812), reports that she was moved in the sacred presence of this expansive tree from whose main trunk tentacular tendrils and branches descend to lodge in the ground, thus invading a vast space. During the course of a later voyage to Brazil she hastened to examine one of the wonders of Teneriffe celebrated by Alexander von Humboldt; alas, the Dragon Tree was by 1819 a "noble ruin."

The banyan's only rival in intricacy was the mangrove, whose roots locked together in every direction, mired in "an endless labyrinth of creeks and lagoons.[194] A more grandiose rival to this "venerable vegetable," as Maria Graham piquantly termed it, was the cedar of Lebanon. But its monolithic compactness was remote from the banyan's mazelike complexity. To the eyes of Pococke it looked "like very large spreading oaks." Unlike deciduous trees, however, the cedars—like the tall firs of Finland and the redwoods of California—were surrounded by a sense of eternity and exuded a memorable fragrance.[195]

A word remains to be said about the perception of giant bodies of water, from the lakes of North America to the rivers of India and China to the oceans. Since their aspect was usually determined by some form of motion, they did not exhibit the face of lasting, albeit vital, matter that dominates the features of phenomena discussed in the present chapter. Yet, upon occasion, quiescence was perceived as essential even within those things most apparently characterized by fluidity. Isaac Weld, in discussing Lakes Erie and Huron, focuses not only on their waves but on the totality of the surface, the immensity of the waters. George Heriot, another topographical traveler, wandered through most of Quebec and Ontario before returning to England in 1816. Some of his North American watercolors were exhibited in London as early as 1787. In *Travels through the Canadas* (1807), he observes that the country's lakes and rivers are "the vast and principal objects which are calculated to inspire wonder and gratification." Specifically, their "immense volumes" can recompense the researches of the naturalist, as can the "gigantic flood" of the Saint Lawrence.

The habit of gazing into still waters was inaugurated by Jonathan Carver in the region of the great North American lakes. He calls attention not only to the "many acres" constituting the surface of Lake Erie but to its great depth. La Rochefoucauld-Liancourt, during his visit to the United States in the 1790s, proclaimed this lake a sea with no end in sight. A similar experience is recorded by Houel as he looks into the water filling the crater of volcanic Lipari Island. In spite of its juxtaposition with a gaping caldera, he is impressed by the water's "vast precinct."[196]

Pure, tranquil waters also form the subject of Landmann's *Observations on Portugal* (1818). Traveling toward Silves, the ancient capital of Algarve,

VOYAGE INTO SUBSTANCE

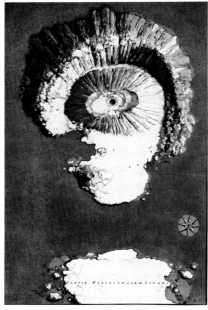

Figure 127
Sir Charles D'Oyly, *Sculptures under a Great Pipal Tree*, from *Sketchbook*, 1823–1825, fol. 72. Lithograph. Photo courtesy India Office Library.

Figure 128
J. Houel, *Plan of the Island of the Volcano* (Lipari Islands), from *Voyage pittoresque des isles de Sicile, de Malte et de Lipari*, 1782, I, pl. 63. Aquatint. Photo courtesy British Library.

THE NATURAL MASTERPIECE

Figure 129
G. Landman, *Silves, The Ancient Capital of Algarve*, from *Historical . . . Observations on Portugal*, 1818, II, pl. 124. Color aquatint by J. C. Stadler. Photo courtesy British Library.

Figure 130
R. M. Grindlay, *The Mountains of Abon in Guzerat, with the Source of the River Suruswutee*, from *Scenery . . . Chiefly on the Western Side of India*, 1826, I, pl. 6. Drawing by William Westall, color aquatint by T. Fielding. Photo courtesy India Office Library.

Figure 131
J. Lycett, *Scene of the River Huon, Van Diemens Land*, from *Views in Australia*, 1824, II, pl. 12. Color aquatint. Photo courtesy India Office Library.

Figure 132
D. Vivant-Denon, *Views of the Nile*, from
Voyage dans la Haute et la Basse Egypte,
1801, II, pl. 64. Engraving by Paris. Photo
courtesy British Library.

VOYAGE INTO SUBSTANCE

Figure 133
G. Belzoni, *Exterior View of the Two Temples at Ybsambul*, from *Plates Illustrative of the Researches & Operations of . . . in Egypt and Nubia*, 1820, pl. 42. Hand-colored lithograph by A. Aglio. Photo courtesy British Library.

THE NATURAL MASTERPIECE

he glided over an untroubled "wide sheet." The Swiss lakes, in contrast with the empty shores of their American counterparts, were generally surrounded by villages that drew attention away from their still depths and clarity. A singular exception was the Lake of Waldstetten, whose majestic aspect worked irresistibly on the soul.[197] This was certainly also true of the "deep hollows" of the Congo as well as the aquaeous "great plain" of the Ganges and the Suruswtee. In South America, the true rival of the Andes was the vast province of the Rio de la Plata, formed from the mingled streams of the Parana, the Paraguay, the Uraguay, and other less considerable tributaries. Together, these constituted "such a mass of fresh water not to be paralleled in the rest of the globe for width and magnificence." The Rio Magdalena, "among the wonders" of Colombia and often cited by Humboldt, could not hope to challenge this unbroken volume of liquid energy *in potentia*. Nor could the river Bogotà, with its enormous breadth and depth quickly wroiled by the cleft through which it was impelled to pass.

In Russia, the Don offers an impressive image of a great accumulation of water. Crossing the Precopian or Little Tartary, it wends its way eastward for a long way and then takes "a vast sweep toward the Volga."[198] The language used to describe the world's monumental rivers, more often than not, was composed of dynamic images. Nevertheless, as with lakes, a sense of serenity could occasionally rise to the surface. Browne witnessed the Nile in such a quieter mood. Sailing to Assiut on its wide bosom, just after the annual inundation, he marvels at the greatness of that body of water, "perfectly calm and unruffled." Vivant-Denon, observing the Nile's point of entry into Egypt, watches the slow spreading of its flood as it insinuates itself between granitic needles. Whether stationed at the fountainhead or with Burckhardt, Legh, Smelt, and Belzoni just above the second cataract, Vivant-Denon can detect its timeless uniformity. Even the "impetuous Niger," in Lucas's communication to the Africa Association—because of its considerable width at the point of passage, 100 miles south of the city of Cashna—hints at harmonious and unbroken duration.[199] Hence, all these rivers, whose rises and terminations remained mysterious until well into the nineteenth century, could assume an air of impenetrability which even the chance movement of waves and falls did not perturb.

The subject matter of the sea, never more popular in France and England than between 1760 and 1800, was of course spurred by the voyages launched by Bougainville and Cook. The world's oceans, like its rivers, enter our present considerations only when perceived as an "immense expanse." Cook on occasion can speak in this manner about the Pacific. Crozet denominates it "an immense space" that bounds our entire planet to its easternmost horizon. Lewis and Clark, although inured to the fury of the Columbia River's "boisterous scene," comment how the river serves to "widen" and stretch its marginless waters. The Dead Sea was perhaps

VOYAGE INTO SUBSTANCE

best suited to yield the impression of an immobile expanse, and yet its slow encroachment and gradual gaining on the land over the years was attested to as early as Pococke's visit to its shores.[200] These bodies of quiet water, then, were but part of that greater cosmic process in which—sometimes perceptibly, sometimes imperceptibly—all the elements worked continuously in determining the physiognomy of the earth.

THE NATURAL MASTERPIECE

3   *The Fugitive Effect*

I am induced by many reasons that they (the motions) may all depend upon certain forces by which the particles of bodies, by some causes hitherto unknown, are . . . mutually impelled towards one another. . . . These forces being unknown, philosophers have hitherto attempted the search of Nature in vain.
Isaac Newton

In Newton this island may boast of having produced the greatest and rarest genius that ever arose for the ornament and instruction of the species. Cautious in admitting no principles but such as were founded on experiment; but resolute to adopt every such principle, however new or unusual. . . . While Newton seemed to draw off the veil from some of the mysteries of nature, he showed at the same time the imperfections of the mechanical philosophy; and thereby restored her secrets to that obscurity, in which they ever did and ever will remain.
David Hume

It was Newton who, in the *Principia* [*Mathematical Principles of Natural Philosophy* (1687) and *Opticks* (1706)], most cogently defined for the eighteenth century the heretofore antithetically conceived nature of matter as belonging to the same level or status of being. Because of the enormous impact of his natural philosophy and its attendant metaphysics, the premise that empirical science does not exclude transmaterial forces from the fabric of the world and the furniture of heaven became wedded to his equally insistent espousal of the reality of hard, corpuscular particles. Thus, Newton's picture of a tangible as well as intangible structure of nature was to prove prophetic, as Alexandre Koyré has shown.

According to Newton, matter had an essentially granular organization. Composed of small, gritty motes interspersed with vacuum, it was endowed with attributes already discerned by Hobbes, Locke, and other modern empiricist philosophers (extension, hardness, impenetrability, and mobility)—with the highly significant addition of inertia. It is notable in light of the description of and the emergent sensitivity to the natural masterpiece that Newton wanted to admit as essential properties of matter only those that are empirically given to us—that is to say, qualities of bodies are known only by experiments, by discoveries made through our senses. (Newton's program, therefore, marks the fulfillment of the Advancement of Learning movement and the logical outcome of the Baconian Great Instauration.) That an abundance—one might even say an indefinite number—of bodies are hard and speak the language of tactile surfaces we learn from a direct probing of the environment. It is this understanding of the world, fostered by the heralds of the New Science in the century capped by Newton and brought to fruition by him, that emerges in the aesthetic estimation and physical description of the monuments discussed in the foregoing chapter.

THE FUGITIVE EFFECT

It is to the second component of this new scientific world view that we must now turn. The conception of an indefinite (and probably infinite) number of material phenomena existing and somehow connecting in an infinite space pervaded by "spiritual" agencies (as Newton's theory was uniformly misstated) hinged upon Newton's formula of universal gravitation. It is a well-known fact that he did not believe in attraction as a real, physical force but rather as a "mathematical" law, i.e., that matter virtually acts at a distance or is animated by a spontaneous, quasi-hylozoistic impulsiveness. Nonetheless, Newton's ambiguity on this point encouraged some readers to infer that the "agent" that "causes" gravity was not operating simply according to strict mathematical laws but was immaterial—perhaps even God, or more plausibly the "spirit of nature" as posited by Ralph Cudworth, Henry More, and the Cambridge Platonists.

In the *Principia* (translated into English in 1729) Newton distinguishes between the *vis insita* or *inertiae*, that innate force of matter equivalent to a power of resisting by which every body endeavors to preserve itself in its present state, and the *vis centripea* or centripetal force—exemplified by gravity, magnetism, and electricity—by which all bodies tend to the center of the earth as iron "tends to" the lodestone. Thus, gravity, and its related physical manifestations of attraction and repulsion, could be hypothesized to act throughout the universe; moreover, even "hard" bodies could not exist without its agency, since it prevents particles from flying apart and dispersing into space. The General Scholium addresses the question of the structure and system of indivisible space. Newton declares that we cannot perceive absolute space, only those things in it and their motions in respect to each other; that is, we can know only relative space, relative motion, and relative place. Only motion's material effects, or the activity of matter, visible in the very thin, elastic substance or rarefied ether that fills the space of our solar system, are accessible to empirical knowledge. Yet this attraction, operating throughout all extension—this "great Spring by which all Nature is mov'd," as Voltaire put it—was almost immediately upon publication removed from the "Laws of Mechanics," where Newton had endeavored to situate it, and placed among the dynamic energies of an unknown pneumatological principle supposedly operating in nature.

What the *Mathematical Principles* and *Opticks* confirmed, Newton's *New Theory About Light and Colors* (1672) adumbrated. According to Voltaire's *Letters Concerning the English Nation* (1733), the reason that colors arise in nature is nothing but a "secret disposition" of bodies to reflect rays of a certain order and to absorb the rest. Analogously, light reflects on our eyes from the very "bosom" of the "pores" of opaque bodies. According to Voltaire, Newton demonstrates that "we are not certain that there is a cubic Inch of solid Matter in the Universe, so far are we from conceiving of what Matter is." The "Vibrations or Fits of Light, which come and go incessantly" are only one of many such effects hovering on the verge of the immaterial and the invisible that were made comprehensible by Newton. In sum: Whether we focus on matter's being "hard" or irreducible to arrive at individual monuments or whether we discover the animating forces inhering in and constitutive of bodies intermittently exhibited, Newton and the Newtonians make it plain that the only doors open to the interpretation of the universe are observation and controlled imagination.

What lies at the heart of Newtonian corpuscular physics, then, is a hypothesis that even the tenuous aspects of reality may be experienced. Hence the importance of the traveler and his process of penetration. In the face of the attacks on his theory by Leibniz and Berkeley, Newton explains that he does not introduce "occult qualities" and magical causes, but, on the contrary, restricts his investigation to the study and analysis of observable phenomena, to the probable characters of "real things" evinced in another physical mode. This pronouncement binds his system to the central issue at hand: the existence of a nature suddenly unconventionalized because previously unknown without the benefit of the Newtonian hermeneutic. Not only is this nature eminently worthy of study, but it operates independently without the intervention of man.

Absolutes Dissolved

Matter however rarify'd or dense
In watery globules or in sparkling
gems,
In flux emissive and absorptive
flows;
Hence the cement of all cohesive
mode
The plastic life of man or brute or
stone,
But for this gen'ral renovating flux
Tenacity must fail, and form decay
And matter sink to chaos
monotone. . . .
John ("Walking") Stewart

Heaven opens on all sides her
Golden Gates; her windows are not
obstructed by vapours; voices of
celestial inhabitants are more
distinctly heard, and their forms are
more distinctly seen, and my
cottage is also a shadow of their
houses. . . .
William Blake

Nothing differs more from the method of isolating an object from the accidental conditions and circumstances in which it is found at a particular moment in order to arrive at its abiding character than the habit of seizing evanescent effects—the topic of our present inquiry. We observed how eighteenth-century science, literature, and fine arts attest the rise of interest in material substances that affect the senses. The close analysis of the environment—examined in the previous chapter in connection with the artless masterpiece, the enduring monument of nature—will be extended to embrace its visual corollary: the interpretable expressive acts of matter. The multiple metamorphic statements articulated by air, water, fire, and light, the gestures traced by intangible forces pervading the cosmos, are intimately tied to the deciphering of highly individualized matter.

The scientific problem of "incorporeals" versus "corporeals" was a crucial issue during the Enlightenment that had ramifications for theories of matter and theories of cognition or perception. For centuries natural philosophers had possessed a working acquaintance with solids and liquids, but all less palpable agencies remained shrouded in confusion and ambiguity. Acute difficulties arose over "effluvia" (an ambiguous category comprising rainbows, magnetic influences, force fields, and gases) and such perplexing prescences as flame, heat, and cold. By the 1780s these "elastic aeriform fluids" were pretty well mastered and were considered as so many material, if intangible, substances with distinct properties. This conclusion was the result of a long and momentous struggle. Traditionally, any theory of matter was required to distinguish between those things that are genuine bodies and those that are not, between "material substances" and "immaterial agents," between "corporeals" and "incorporeals," "ponderables" and "imponderables." In 1700 everyone agreed that solids and liquids were corporeal, but beyond them all was incoherence. Through the course of the century three criteria were hammered out to distinguish "matter" from other phenomena: All agents capable of producing physical effects were deemed corporeal, generally only impenetrable objects qualified (although vapors such as steam were allowed), and only those things subject to gravity and therefore possessing mass were considered bodies.[1]

Especially bitter hostilities raged in the 1750s between proponents of "hard" and "soft" bodies. The Swiss mathematician Daniel Bernoulli and the Leibnizians waged war against Moreau de Maupertuis and Leonhard Euler, denying the existence of an unyielding stuff and claiming that masses taken for irreducible are, in reality, flexible—that only great rigidity renders the ductility of their parts imperceptible. This combat served to reawaken an earlier battle, since it reflected the legacy of Newtonian ideas about space, mass, and gravitation.

Newton—himself the creator of "light-corpuscles" and ether particles—would have hesitated to rule out all possibilities for soft or "imponderable" bodies. Specifically, in 1717, when Newton brought out a second edition of the *Opticks*, he conceived the universe in a new manner that veered away from the Lucretian or Epicurean world view of the 1706 version, in which material atoms move in an empty space and interact by means of short-range forces. Now he described the cosmos as filled with an ethereal medium "exceedingly more rare and subtile than Air, and exceedingly more elastick and active." It represents a qualitative or substantial unity that precedes and makes possible all relations that can be discovered within it, not a mere abstract lattice of quantitative relations.[2] Consequently, the doctrine of the ether revealed and unmasked the conceptual limitations surrounding the very notion of an obdurately independent thing. The awareness of and the polemic about this tenuous kind of matter and its "environment" or setting infiltrated scientific theory and also shaped philosophic and aesthetic thinking.

On a scientific plane, the debate challenged Plato's attack on the Sophists and vindicated their "confusion" of matter with form. In the world of appearances, all those objects of which we are directly aware are changeable. A certain blurring and mobility is intrinsic to them and is termed potency, in contradistinction to the absolute invariability ascribed to the world of Ideas. Hence, the material thing varies—flows—without ceasing to be that particular thing. Newtonian science demonstrated that both definiteness and indefiniteness are formally constitutive of physical substance.[3] Moreover, Newton's hypothesis about the ether and his terminology involving enigmatic forces helped to impel thinking away from Democritean and Lucretian models of separate and hard atoms to a Heraclitean participation of all things in all things. Newton provided scientific validation for matter's actual fluctuating vagueness or potency. Thus, the theory of intrinsically unrelated, corpuscular motes was subverted more and more by that of connective essences or bonding germs (caloric, electricity, and magnetism) streaming in waves or rays from the most distant stars. Indeed, Newton, by asserting the existence in bodies of forces by which they act upon each other in spite of the distance separating them, affirms the corpuscular structure of matter while denying it.[4]

The difference in attitude between the beginning and the end of the eighteenth century—and the ambiguity characterizing post-Newtonian materialism, which had bodies shot through with forces—is shown by the following two passages. Shaftesbury, in the guise of Theocles in his Platonizing *Moralists*, asks

if [matter] can present us with so many innumerable instances of particular forms, who share the simple principle by which they are really one, live, act, and have a nature of genius peculiar to themselves and provident for their own welfare, how shall we at the same time overlook this in the whole, and deny the great and general ONE of the world?

By contrast, the perambulating eccentric John Stewart, espousing a quasi-scientific, pneumatological view and proposing a fraternity of "homo-ousiasts" or children of nature in his *Revelation of Nature*, perceives the bipolar visage of matter:

however rarified or dense,
In watery globules or in sparkling gems. . . .[5]

Light, magnetic force, gravity, and ether all seem to belong to, or constitute, the "atmosphere" of material beings. As a beneficiary of Newton's cosmic vision, Stewart perceives the inherence of a more-than-mechanical agency—a "spirit"—in nature that acts in and on bodies.

Inseparable from the discussion of imponderables is the larger realization that man is surrounded by invisible but not imperceptible agents. Post-Newtonian physics and chemistry, with their models of melding powers and weightless corpuscles, rallied to provide connections between tangible matter and apparently impalpable energy. The heavy and the fixed was inextricably bound with the buoyant and the fleeting, the apparent with the nonapparent. Taking their cue from the sciences (and the pseudo-sciences of Mesmer and Cagliostro), the Masonic dreamers and Illuminati who flourished prior to the French Revolution propounded the existence of universal fluids and currents exerting control over soul and organism as well as over celestial and terrestrial bodies. These effluvia were believed to penetrate all solid flesh, so that nothing could withstand their incursion. In the popular press and in serious publications, the hard and the soft became intertwined, the material was divinized, and the intangible was corporealized. On one level, this very popularization owed to the breakdown underway in all disciplines during the eighteenth century of the Cartesian dualism between mind and body, between spirit and matter. Newton, perhaps better than anyone, reconciled the divided self of substance. The world might not possess a soul, as the hylozoists both ancient and modern would have it—it was not an "animal"—yet Newtonian physics demonstrated irrevocably that it could not be reduced to Descartes's clock.[6]

Tangible energies laving the earth are frequently alluded to in accounts of balloon excursions. An almost carnal sense of their presence was thought to be most perceptible in this method of travel, since the aerostat drifted within the ether. The Montgolfiers in their taffeta hot-air *montgolfière*, the physicist Charles in his hydrogen-gas *charlière*, and the Marquis d'Arlande and Pilâtre de Rozier in their fragile cloth envelope were all exposed to the enigma of the "initial spectacle of an immense globe rising into the atmosphere and seeming to be maintained there by an invisible power."[7] The balloonist's perspective enhanced the view that nothing is stable or settled. Objects and the amorphous medium that bathes them are ever in motion, sliding away from beneath the eye, evading the pursuing mind. Early aeronauts contributed decisively to the controversy raging in science and cosmology over the physical composition of the universe. Champions of a "charged" space, balloonists dramatically vindicated the Newtonian world view by vividly reporting the aerial sea of matter as residium for a congeries of transmaterial forces.

Congruent with an energized perception of the world containing mutating particles and palpable "spirits" reduced to the point of inobservability is the broader implication of a want of calm in nature. The new-found "finer optic" that saw life trembling in stones was also capable of sensing dim exhalations and faint perturbations. The balloonists' experiential documentation of a corporeous space represents an antiphonal response to the archives of earth that abide. Protean physiognomic variety couched in rock, desert, and jungle is matched by an unsettled atmosphere seen as a vast laboratory of transformations; a characterology of ponderousness is matched by a phenomenological aesthetic of subtlety.[8] Nevertheless, a positive view of the nebulous (that is, of atmospheric reality) was long restrained by medical opinion that looked upon the primitive purity of the air as constantly besmirched by mephitic currents of organic life and decomposition. The saturation with lethal materials of this once-crystalline liquid, based on the assumption that the atmosphere is continually invaded by insalubrious exhalations, was corroborated by the oppressive presence of fetid air in cities. During the quarter-century preceding 1789, Antoine Laurent Lavoisier and the Abbé Bertholon were particularly assiduous in drawing attention to the emission of dangerous gases from the cesspools and privies of Paris. Vitiated air emanating from theaters, hospitals, and charnel houses, decaying animal and vegetable substances, putrid odors, and stagnant and polluted waters were all thought to poison the ambient.[9]

These ideas were by no means novel. John Evelyn's *Fumifugium* (1661) speaks of the burning of English sea coal, whose smurry clouds lie "perpetually imminent." In Evelyn's words, London resembles Mount Etna, the court of Vulcan, Stromboli, or the suburbs of Hell. "Horrid smoake" and impure vapors thus gave all manner of exhalations a bad reputation. Equally prejudicial was the nascent environmentalist theory that fog, wind, rain, hail, snow, heat, cold, and drought were accidental, introduced into the mechanism of nature by the soiling hand of man. Altering the course of a river, draining a swamp, driving a mine shaft, piercing a mountain, or digging a harbor troubled the serenity of the climate, and the pernicious effects of human intervention and commerce were global. This thesis, clearly also mirroring a radical theological point of view, held that every being, by eating, digesting, and breathing, mixes his perspiration and wastes with the great reservoir of the atmosphere and thus disturbs its original rarefaction. There was, however, another scientific school of thought active in the second half of the eighteenth century that managed to discover a providential mechanism of order maintaining the healthiness of the atmosphere. Joseph Priestley, Carl Wilhelm Scheele, and Jan Ingen-Housz were of this persuasion. In this view, such activities of matter as plant transpiration and "reverberation" purify and revitalize air by absorbing septic particles; far from befouling or disfiguring our environment, these pervasive vapors regenerate it.[10] This exception aside, it was not easy to dislodge the value that, since antiquity, had been attached to transparent air without even the ghost of a vapor. Hippocrates's thesis articulated in *Airs, Water, Places* was coupled to climatic theories by later thinkers such as Alberti, who claimed (looking back to Vitruvius) that the dry air lapping the Athenians had sharpened their wits whereas the thick damps surrounding the Thebans had dulled theirs.

By the late seventeenth century the appreciation of the air of a specific place, the recognition of the varieties of air, and the benefits of a change of air hinted at the study of the aspects of nature to come.[11] In this respect, the Abbé La Pluche's opinion is characteristic of the prescientific era. In his *Spectacle de la nature* (1740–1748) La Pluche acknowledges that, although air ideally is an immaculate whole, its composite qualities constantly manifest themselves. Enormously versatile, this fluid is light, ductile, and able to sustain both compression and dilation, and its very elasticity and spring impart to it an aura of primordial energy.[12] This was never more apparent than in the phlogiston debate, which began around 1700 with Georg Ernst Stahl, a professor of medicine at Halle, and involved the entire scientific world before its turbulent climax at the close of the 1780s. Lavoisier and Priestley, who had been assiduously anatomizing the "element" of air, were the chief contenders in the fray. My purpose here is not to retrace the distinct phases of this historic squabble but to note how the discovery of oxygen (phlogiston, or the "fire substance"), like the precursory dissection of ether into prototypical energies such as electricity, drew further attention to the multiple and dynamic properties of a tangible nature.[13] The designation of air as a vital force, augmented by the discovery of its gaseous components and assisted by the research of meteorologists

Figure 134
Le Noir, *To the Honor of Messrs. Charles
and Robert*, 1783. Ibl, fol. 82. Etching.
Photo courtesy Cabinet des Estampes,
Bibliothèque Nationale.

Figure 135
Etienne, Chevalier de Lorimier, *First Aerial Voyage made in the Presence of the Dauphin*, 1783, from B. Faujas de Saint-Fond, *Description des expériences de la machine aérostatique*, 1783, I, frontispiece. Engraving by N. de Launay. Photo courtesy Library of Congress.

Figure 136
J. F. Janinet, Entrance ticket to Luxembourg "experiment" of July 11, 1784. Collection Hennin, CXV, fol. 9. Etching. Photo courtesy Cabinet des Estampes, Bibliothèque Nationale.

THE FUGITIVE EFFECT

like Bertholon and Cotte, helped to rescue it from being the mere cistern of deleterious and impure toxins. Indeed, it recaptured some of its ancient numinous status.

A Newtonian vision of indwelling energy and a Heraclitean pursuit of eternal flux—tied to the larger conquest of the interstices of space—aesthetically and epistemologically retrieved the immemorial pneuma, which scientists and explorers demonstrated to be lodged within even the most obdurate matter. The earth, visibly surrounded by a belt of aqueous vapors approaching its surface from the stratosphere or ascending from its soil and clotting into clouds or meteors, presented a modern, secularized scene of cosmic respiration.[14] The venerable doctrine of a world soul, reiterated afresh in eighteenth-century materialism, dwells at the heart of Enlightenment theories about substance. These theories were rooted in the belief that a physical and a spiritual current not only interpenetrates or coexists with but incorporates the two faces of an identical entity. Thus, modern scientific "powers" and ancient dynamism blended.

The idea of the universe as a growing, breathing being had many supporters in antiquity. Moschus, whom Strabo identifies as living before the Trojan War, claimed that the cosmos existed by itself and was composed of indivisible particles endowed with shape and motion, ceaselessly generating, self-destroying and self-renewing. Leucippus, Democritus, Epicurus, Lucretius (who adopted Moschus's system), Spinoza, Leibniz, and Diderot all attribute to atoms an animate, sensitive nature. Whereas ancient and modern materialists banish every trace of divine providence from inhering forces that move bodies, monists welcome a single immaterial substance, the One, that fills the universe with its various modifications and is conclusively responsible for every phenomenon. Parmenides, Zeno of Elea, Plato, Pythagoras, the Neo-Platonists, Malebranche, Berkeley, and Hemsterhuis hold the view that matter is pure illusion, body mere appearance. Even the Timaean *hyle*, lurking behind the four elements, seems to point to the existence of a basic activating agent imperceptible to the senses.[15]

In succeeding epochs, the life force of the ancient materialists continued to have vociferous apologists. The hermeticism endemic to the Italian and German Renaissance, exemplified in the treatises of Cornelius Agrippa, Nicolas Cusanus, and Giordano Bruno, affirmed that the universe is an organic being inhabited by spirit. From this conviction, underlying the operations of benevolent magic and alchemy, emerged the doctrine of correspondences, the belief in the existence of a pervasive accord knitting individuals together by connecting them with the rhythm and harmony of the cosmos. During the seventeenth century the alchemists carried the suppositions of the ether theorists to their logical conclusion: From the Pre-Socratic and Neo-Platonic admission that a life force subsists in some matter they went on to posit vitality in all matter. Although the mathematical approach of Newton and Descartes nominally resulted in the defeat of such necromancers, they were never completely silenced. Paracelsus more than anyone kept this tradition alive during the ascendancy of mechanism. His creed influenced Lavoisier, insinuating itself into the great French chemist's trust in the living reality of physical stuff just as Henry More's pneumatology had been reflected in Newton's theory of force.[16]

The psychology of Leibniz, so influential in Germany and France during the second half of the eighteenth century, furthered this view of a material plenum in which there are no discrete intervals by relating it to perceptual theory. Leibniz emphasized the interdependent community of all monads, from the human soul down through the vegetable kingdom to apparently inorganic substances. Leibniz's thought, despite its stringent anti-Newtonianism, followed the evolutionary course of Enlightenment reasoning in general with regard to the meaning of an energy-laden power. In his 1694 essay "On the Reform of Metaphysics and on the Notion of Substance," Leibniz uses the term to designate a mechanical mode of operation. By the time of the 1705 "Considerations on the Principles of Life, and on Plastic Natures," it has become a law upholding an almost pantheistic physical (not spiritual) and kinetic energy joining the evolving, perceptive soul with the changing universe. Addressing the issue of preestablished harmony, Leibniz states: ". . . there is no portion of matter in which there are not numberless organic and animated bodies; under which I include not only animals and plants, but perhaps also other kinds which are entirely unknown to us. But for all this, it must not be said that each portion of matter is animated. . . ." The timorousness of the closing qualification made no impression on Leibniz's successors. Herder, in his "Vom Erkennen und Empfinden" (1778), not only incorporates David Hartley's psychology based on "vibrations" occurring in an ethereal medium (here interpreted as a system of biologically sensitive fibers), but also follows Leibniz's antimechanistic suggestion that bodies are merely the palpable concrete effects of *Geist* just as the haze of the Milky Way is the result of starlight and clouds the product of raindrops.[17]

In England a less physical concept of subtle fluids was put forward by Berkeley, whose treatise *Siris* (1744) exercised a notable influence on later speculations about electricity. Berkeley, who was among the most virulent opponents of Newton, declares that forces are "abstract, spiritual, incorporeal" and prescind from gravity and matter. God, as the soul of the universe, deploys a subtle fire throughout space; by comparison, Newton's ether is judged too coarse. Like all the modern thinkers mentioned so far, Berkeley perpetuated pre-Newtonian ideas—ideas also rooted in the hylarchic principles of Henry More and the Cambridge Platonists.[18]

Berkeley's "Immaterialism" and Leibniz's dynamism are crucial to an understanding of the period's conception of what constitutes the matter

THE FUGITIVE EFFECT

of nature and how it might be known. They also represent a reaction against the theological implications of the corpuscular half of Newton's theory and the Hobbesian notion that God is physical substance. Berkeley, in particular, counters Newton's belief in the divisibility of mass and the identification of body with solidity by banishing from his metaphysics the concept of prime matter. The substratum of corporeals, at last, becomes either nothing—existing only in the mind of the perceiver—or nothing but the Deity acting in a special manner in those parts of space he thinks fit. It is notable that these philosophers, divergent in so many ways, were united by their preoccupation with ductile spirits, pneumatic fluids, and dynamic exhalations of one sort or another. Thus, from the webwork of a long cosmological tradition of animism and sensitive matter, which gradually became interwoven in the middle of the eighteenth century with the new chemical science of the ether theorists and decomposers of air, the powerful image of a universe in dissolution was disengaged. Just as bodies were no longer perceived as necessarily or intransigently hard, the entire corporeal world could be unmade, its "hard" substance effaced and dispelled into mutable effects. These overt "acts of matter" were consonant with the workings of a hidden agent lodged within substance itself. It is of central importance to the eighteenth-century apprehension of nature that the concept of matter as ponderous blocklike entity or atomlike sturdy continuum coexists with, while being subverted or even "ruined" by, the affirmation of its heterogeneity, "porosity," and fluidity. In short, matter becomes as subtly complex in composition as the perceiving mind (Berkeley) or as changeable as the apperceptive individual (Leibniz). This more intricate way of seeing an energized material universe, dissolved by the active observer into fluid and therefore mentally digestible effects which simultaneously are sensuously experienceable, must be distinguished from the passive pictorial convention of representing vaporous aerial perspective. There is a marked rupture—evident in the travel accounts—between the long-standing artistic custom of enveloping objects within a landscape in an attractive, superimposed haze (the aesthetic of effortless illusion) and the knowing late-eighteenth-century representation of the virtual processes of matter bodied forth in dim exhalations, startling ephemerides, and atmospheric meteors.

It is a commonplace of Picturesque practice that in temperate climes and vernal months, at dawn or dusk, exhalations ascending from the ground lose their density. In Italy, particularly in scenes of the Roman Campagna invented by Claude, a visible rarefaction transfigures and dematerializes objects bathed in pleasing vapors. The *Encyclopédie* essay states: "When aerial perspective is properly exercised in a picture, & when a very faint mist renders objects delicate and mellow, one says that a beautiful vapor dominates this painting: its contents are soft & delicate. Wouwerman & Claude excell in this genre. . . ." Thirty-five years later, P. H. Valenciennes ignored the established pattern and turned to the scientific sections of the *Encyclopédie*. His *Eléments de perspective* reflects the new materialism and the tangible language of self-activation encouraged by the burgeoning discipline of meteorology. Vapors, Valenciennes declares, are aqueous emanations mounting from soil and sheets of water to form a fog. Propelled still higher, their drops are converted into clouds, whose ultimate source is the emanations continually given off by the land. Because they climb only to a certain height, they disturb the purity of the atmosphere, refracting light diversely in a manner totally different than when the air is limpid or invisible and does not alter separate hues. Valenciennes admonishes the novice landscape painter to "bethink himself as to the effects that nature presents." That is, in contemplating his composition he must take into account the time of day and the color and appearance of the vapors. Further, he must be aware of environmental modifications; for example, vapors are more abundant in humid and marshy spots than on mountain summits, where they rapidly condense into clouds.

Valenciennes's informed attitude, involved with trying to see things as completely as possible, does not shrink from the inclusion of foggy or inclement weather and feebly visible moonlight. His visual stance is part of the scientific delight in facts about the world's aspect, in "natural principles"—in short, for those material agencies that, as the *Encyclopédie* notes, originate by "insensible degrees" but in time "palpably trouble the air."[19]

The French meteorologist Jérôme Richard astutely observes in his *Histoire naturelle de l'air et des météores* (1770) that "the first rays of the dawning sun cause an agitation in the body of air, at the moment when it becomes luminous and tinted, it rises and dissipates leaving nothing behind but delicious coolness, wet pearls, and glittering furrows that reflect the light." Richard stresses the electrically charged nature of such nebulosity, thereby alluding to the principle of superfine physical forces in constant competition. Yet, for Richard, condensation and evaporation offer only a fragment of the total cosmic picture. These "acts" are fleshed out by the precipitous startings and stoppings reported as characterizing the larger vital behavior of our planet. The astronomer Alexandre-Guy Pingré aptly notes in the *Journal Encyclopédique* that "the globe which we inhabit is subject to continual vicissitudes."[20] Even the sterner aspects of the earth newly analyzed by science were shown to possess ingrained mercurial properties, evinced in the birth of islands and the activity of volcanos, avalanches, and glaciers.

Thus, the Newtonian redefinition of a self-sufficient porous matter—complexly married with the generically Heraclitean recognition of flux or energy in potency—generated from ca. 1740 on a corresponding growth in perceptual acuity for matter's effects played off against an intervening (even intrusive) space, and, further, led to the volatilization of more compact entities. Newton's discoveries assured that objects could no longer be locked firmly and atemporally into a monolithic void or studied as immutable, unrelated sets of appearances.

THE FUGITIVE EFFECT

Substantial Visions

As a reprise of the discussion about "hard" and "soft" bodies, let me now assert that the material individuality of enduring media—characterized by opacity, density, and solidity—is paralleled by a growing apprehension for optical evidence that testifies to the indefiniteness possible to physical substances caught on the run. The gleam, the glimmer, the *lueur* spreads throughout and transforms vacancy; it diffuses and suffuses beyond the perimeters of the visible. Instead of changeless boulders, there is blunted light; in lieu of stable mountains, smoky tendrils; in place of absolute contours, filmy space.[21]

If the early-eighteenth-century poets adored the "Newtonian sun" (especially when it shone in full meridian splendor, its light streaming in straight lines, diverted as little as possible by cloud or mist), later writers and artists were less enthralled by the atmosphere's tonic blue. The landscapist—like Poussin—who turns his back to the sun sees objects illuminated directly, sculpted in all their solid massiveness by clear light and crisp shadows. The landscapist—like Claude—who gazes toward the remote horizon succeeds in volatalizing objects. James Dalloway in Constantinople (1797) speaks to this point when he describes an evening view of Brusa brilliantly lit by the setting sun: "The horizon was intirely of the most transparent azure and the skirting clouds were light and fleecy, suspended considerably below the bare cliffs. Nothing could exceed the clearness of tint which pervaded every part of this lively landscape. From the extreme thinness of the air very distant objects are brought so much more forward than in England, that they appear with lustre; and the haziness with which even a confined view is frequently obstructed, is almost unknown here. . . ."[22]

Although "pure marble air" was valued in antiquity for its salubrious qualities, so was its antithesis for the aesthetic reason that it reduced the direct visual impact of material things. Ptolemy in the *Opticks* speaks of a luster or gleam applied to mural paintings in order to make the colors of objects appear distant or veiled. Pliny describes a well-known artifice of Apelles, the laying of a dark coating—a *tramentum*—over his finished work. A chief purpose of this glaze was to prevent the brilliance of the colors from offending the eye; it gave the dimmed impression that the spectator was seeing them through a window of talc.[23] Although recent scholarship has demonstrated that the Odyssey frieze (probably modeled after a Hellenistic prototype) was not blurred initially, the background rocks and figures are lighter and less distinct than the foreground figures. It was a ninteenth-century restorer who created the visionary fading away of concrete elements into a sea of vapor. Immeasurability, infinity, and dreamlike mirage, however, can be found in the contemporaneous poetic sacro-idyllic landscapes at Boscotrecase, which were adapted on several occasions by eighteenth-century Venetian painters.[24]

The use of mist to obliterate any sense of corporeality and measureable depth can also be discovered in Sung through Ching mountain and water paintings, known to the West through seventeenth- and eighteenth-century Jesuit missionaries. A famous case in point is that of Father Castiglione, who was not only a member of the Jesuit order but an accomplished painter as well. In 1765, he prepared drawings for the *Conquêtes de l'empereur Kien-long*; the emperor had decreed that sixteen copper engravings were to be prepared in Europe after drawings made by Western artists at his court. Although every precaution was taken that no exemplar of the 200 printed remained in the hands of engravers, some certainly escaped into the public domain and circulated outside the confines of the royal library.[25] Significantly appropriating the "selfless" style of the Chinese masters, Castiglione captured the intricate relationship between mountain peaks and enveloping mist.

Mention of the representation of the vaporous in Hellenistic and Roman murals and Chinese scroll and silk paintings raises the aesthetic issue of the distinction between a contrived and a natural (embodied in physical fact) effect.[26] During the eighteenth century the concept of effect or *effet* as it functioned in the fine arts included a complex of meanings. The *Encyclopédie* article on painting states that the final composition is made up of several parts, each of which contributes to the impact of the whole. Thus, the sensations aroused sequentially by each segment, when blended together through the artist's mastery, create the general effect communicated to the beholder. Roger de Piles had noted earlier—and this definition was taken up by the *Encyclopédie*—that the effect of a painting is directly linked to its preestablished compositional unity, an overlaid harmony that imposes an artificial connection on individual objects through the manipulation of light and shade: "Indeed, nature is neither gilded nor silvered, it has no general color: its nuances are made up of a mixture of broken hues, reflected, variegated. . . ."[27]

If one seeks a more immediate artistic precedent for nature perceived not as actual unstable sketch but as painterly rough draft, surely no style is more pertinent than the Rococo. This period delighted in unseizable perfumes, in mobile appearances scattered by mirrors, lights, and fragile media—sensuous artifice that eluded rational coalescence.[28] Specifically, the heightened luminous effects endemic to the art of Antoine Watteau, François Boucher, and particularly Jean-Honoré Fragonard are pertinent for establishing an opposition between the autonomous acts of matter and the equally independent activity of the artist. In Fragonard's park scenes of the 1770s or the *Roland furieux* project of the 1780s, an increasing density of pale, bright illumination and billowing masses of vapor occlude any sense of depth. Of course, Watteau had already painted the distance-shrouding muted envelope of air bathing objects in his *fête galantes*; consequently, in these garden scenes individual phenomena are uniformly mellowed by the created atmosphere and exist intangibly on the picture's surface.[29] But it is Fragonard, the young friend and touring companion of the Abbé de Saint-Non, who seems to cloak forms in an irradiated sunny mist that casts everything in terms of dematerialized fantasy.

Fragonard's tonal subtlety is adumbrated in the *Rymbranesques* of Bernard Picart. His brush, which "animates" pigment, corresponds to the blonde, magical *sprezzatura* of Giovanni Battista Tiepolo and the nervous calligraphy of the Guardi. It is prepared for by the steam—possessing both substance and color—that often rises from teapots and cups in Jean-Baptiste Chardin's still-life paintings.[30]

Contrived indistinction is to be found especially in the medium of soft-ground etching, as practiced by Giovanni Battista Castiglione, since the technique softly blurs lines. But in the area of printmaking, the Venetian architect Piranesi excelled in producing images of drifting smoke tangibly hovering above cauldrons or issuing from urns. In his *Grotteschi*, from the *Opere Varie* (1750), however, a materialist aesthetic more overt than the subtly paraphrastic one furnished by the Rococo painters of mist and vapor seems to be heralded. Six years before Burke's epoch-making *Essay on the Sublime and the Beautiful*, Piranesi realized that a corporeous darkness, not just a vagueness, could be a structural property of the pictorial universe. With the substantial films inundating the *Capricci* (1743) and the *Carceri* (1741–1750) and settling on walls of vast, incomprehensible subterranean worlds of stone, water, and silence, Rococo light as metaphor for intangible spirit is effectively dimmed.[31] A thickening nebulosity consonant with and parallel to the pathos of matter's existence, and a monochromatic somberness, separate Piranesi's achievements from the insubstantial opacities of Fragonard.

This chthonic reaction to the sublimation of the densities of the world by the poetic imagination that has fantasy deepening into concrete mystery and ornament into lithic sublimity has a counterpart in literature. Bernardin de Saint-Pierre, in *Harmonies de la nature* (ca. 1794), shows a sensitivity for the actualities of floating chiaroscuro, calm dawns, vaporous twilights, "stellar whiteness," fugitive clouds, and muted tints. Goethe, during a winter trip to the Brocken and subsequently at Chamonix, carefully examined subtle vapors and gray seas of fog. Considerably earlier even, the English poet James Thomson, in describing the Carter Fell region in the "Autumn" section of *Seasons* (1730), evokes a land steeped in stealthy mists, rolling fogs, copious exhalations, and a "dim-seen river." Like the French and German authors, Thomson shows reluctance to present the independent outlines of objects, preferring the modulated connective luminosity of atmospheric effects. Here, and again in the "Winter" segment, vapors tangibly impinge upon the senses and turbid air provides an authentic flavor of actual weather conditions.[32] Hugh Blair makes plain in his *Critical Dissertation on Ossian* (1763) how the gray shades of northern heroes were celebrated in song. These semi-material ghosts of the dead were forced to "wander in thick mists beside the reedy lake."[33] Such a predilection for giving atmospheric body to an abstraction may be seen to form part of a larger materialist aesthetic preoccupied with the visual specificity of the imprecise and the obscure.

The Piranesian and Ersian incarnation of the palpably vague is communicated directly. This tangible pictorial and verbal language declares the sensory attraction exerted by an elemental landscape clothed in penetrable fog. Intense focus on actual effects, on moonlit exhalations, strange meteoric apparitions, bluish glints and gleams, and spirits and phantoms, illuminates how caprice was transformed into science. Paradoxically, the operative word is *ghost*. As was mentioned above, medical theory had long asserted that air exerts an influence over man. Unmentioned, however, was its ability to affect the brain and those parts of the body governed by the intellect and the will. More complex and susceptible to outside influences than the rest of the organism, the mind is the seat of dreams and fancies. Contingent on the quality of the atmosphere, which in turn was dependent on climate, perceptions of external things, it was believed, could become clouded, dissipated in imaginings.[34] This hypothesis was worked out further in the eighteenth century. Among the Viennese physician Anton Franz Mesmer's adepts were the three Puysegur brothers, who discovered somnambulism in 1784. They declared that by means of intensely willed vision or the force of hypnotic gaze a "magnetic" sleep could be engendered. In this trance, induced by physical "fluxions" transmitted through space, man was transported into that universal corporeal dream dreamt more or less knowingly by all life forms, including the lesser animals and even plants and minerals. The Puysegurs' investigations into the correspondences between "matters" are only a single spectacular example of Enlightenment interest in the intimate linkage of soul and body, between spirit and matter, seemingly adverted in sleep. By the "scientific" examination of such an acute kind of mental vision, the materialists, in particular, hoped to show that it approaches physical actuality. Thus, enhanced vision could be reduced to a manageable natural phenomenon.[35]

The dissection of nocturnal visions into their corporeal components represents a transformation of the earlier English analysis of "the vapors." This affectation of the splenetic arose at the court of William and Mary in imitation of *"les vapeurs,"* the French fashion for *ennui*, which was based on Greek humoral pathology. According to the ancients, melancholy occurs when atrabilious vapors originating under the breastbone ascend through hollow fibers and cloud the clear white animal spirits of the brain, thus bringing forth phantasms. Consequently, the hypochondriac's fabrication of shapes out of nothing or merely out of a vivid imagination was linked to the history of environmental theories and also closely allied to the history of medicine. Stagnant waters, dark and humid places, and frosty and foggy climates were thought from Hippocrates down to Robert Burton to breed (but not to embody) sour melancholia, with its distemper of "curst illusion."[36]

The question of the substance of visions plays an important role in eighteenth-century aesthetic theory. Thomas Hobbes asserts that all material data are supplied to the imagination by the sense of sight—an argument taken up by Locke, Addison (*Spec.* 419), and Diderot. According to empiricist psychology, a secondary process is required to reproduce objects in memory, where they are "formed into agreeable Visions of Things . . . either Absent or Fictitious." Addison, later to be echoed by Duff, proudly notes that the gloominess and the temperamental eccentricities of the fogbound British result in correspondingly vivid poetic representations of fairies, demons, and sprites. Diderot, in his article "Fantômes" in the *Encyclopédie*, subtly opposes this traditional humoral theory by citing Hobbes's alleged fear of ghosts and claiming that such oppressive shades can be dissipated by means of direct experience and natural philosophy.[37] These considerations ultimately devolve upon the question of the concrete pictorial representation of unreal figures. In the *Salon* of 1761, Diderot praises Edmé Bouchardon's drawing of Ulysses invoking the shade of Tiresias, noting that the sculptor's composition is far more dramatic than its antique prototype; moreover, the ancients did not render "*ces figures aériennes*" attracted by the odor rising from the sacrificial altar. Like Johann Kaspar Lavater, Tobias Sergel, and Johann Heinrich Fuseli a decade later, Diderot is interested in their material diaphanousness, fluidity, and projected energy. These *daimons* or demiurges possess an intense physical presence whose self-sufficient coherence is not to be ignored.[38]

Diderot's remarks are pertinent because they display a scientific and materialistic bias in the interpretation of onirocritic phenomena. In 1751, the Abbé Lenglet-Dufresnoy published a comprehensive collection of ancient and modern treatises dedicated to the exploration of "apparitions, visions, & dreams." Diderot could not have been unaware that he provides ample documentation "proving" that "natural apparitions" were continuously being voided into the air. Rotting bodies, improperly disposed, perpetually emit mephitic vapors that can, according to this theory, take the form of the cadavers from which they came, and these "real" phantoms can be transported into remote regions by faint breezes that do not decompose them into their constituent particles. Thus, Lenglet-Dufresnoy concludes, there is nothing miraculous about such specters; they, too, are but an instance of the activities of matter. Indeed, their formation helps to shed light on the morphological processes behind cloud images of men, animals, and trees.[39]

This hypothesis concerning the reality or materiality of a supposedly spiritual effect appears less strange when we remember that the chemists Claude-Louis Berthollet, Antoine-François Fourcroy, Pierre-Joseph Macquer, Lavoisier, and Priestley analyzed the air and showed it to be a compound of gases. The materialists Jean D'Alembert, Charles Bossut, and Jean-Jacques Lalande pointed out that the natural history of the soul coincided with that of bodies; the word *gaz*, defined as the volatilization of a material substance, or matter revealing itself in another guise, derived from the Dutch *ghoast*, meaning spirit, *esprit*. Thus, Newton used the term *spectrum* in the 1704 Latin edition of the *Opticks* to denote any ghostlike optical image emanating from a material form, not a band of pure colors produced by an unclouded prism. Indeed, as Roux's *Journal de Monsieur* article of 1781 reminds us, there are fashions in the sciences as well as in the fine arts: "Today, chemistry seems to be preponderant. One converses only about gas, phlogiston, absorbent earth, phosphoric acid, volatile alkalis, dephlogisticated air, etc. This science has become so fashionable that, with the aid of its jargon, a frivolous science has been created making use of repartee, *bon mots*, equivocations. Such is the taste of the French. . . ." In a less dyspeptic mood, Roux enumerates the carnal operations possible to matter: Nothing is more charming than chemistry; it makes alliances, then precipitates divorces; it creates mixtures, then causes separations, "ultimately creating beings, rendering them visible, to make them subsequently disappear at will." More seriously, these witty transformations remind us that, since Newton, gases and ghosts belonged to that expanded class of incorporeals that could never be bubbled through water and bottled neatly. Gravity, ether, vital spirits, and even the human soul were impossible to see in themselves but could be physically experienced. It would have been unreasonable to demand a handful of phlogiston, magnetism, or electricity, yet they palpably existed. Richard Watson in his *Chemical Essays* of 1781 neatly phrases the underlying premise: "There are powers in Nature, which cannot otherwise become the objects of sense than by the effects they produce. . . ."[40]

It is instructive to compare and contrast the rising tide of interest in evanescent phenomena (whether artificially created or naturally present) with the aesthetic tradition of unpaintable beauty descending from antiquity. Although traditionally art embraces only visible, optical facts, representational painting does not necessarily coincide with the literal, raw data of objects. Indeed, since antiquity the conception that a painter can depict everything has coexisted with the notion that there are things that remain undepictable.

Pliny states that Apelles "painted things that cannot be painted [such as] thunder and lightning." "It may seeme, then," he continues, "that Theophylactus Simpcatus did cast his eye upon some such relation when he maintaineth that Painters undertake to express such things as Nature is not able to doe. . . ." Junius, in his *Painting of the Ancients*, comments in connection with this passage that there are thus two kinds of imitation available to the artificer. Junius censors the daring painter who, by eschewing mere imitation, is emboldened to meddle "with such things as doe not offer themselves to the eyes of man." It is noteworthy that this sixteenth-century compiler of time-honored theories quotes Ausonius's 17th epistle as a warning against total reliance on inward imagination or invention. Although it is clearly admirable for the artist to follow his

THE FUGITIVE EFFECT

"phantasie" and not just to ape external nature, he must be guided by common sense: "A painted fogge . . . delighteth us no longer than it is scene. Except it be such a painted miste as is described by the same Ausonius in another place (*Eydillio* 6) where the painter doth represent the dimme shade of hellish blacknesse by a painted mist, and designeth in it how the ancient Ladies torment the crucified Cupid in hell for having dishonoured them in the times of the Worthies. . . ."[41]

Ausonius absolves the artificer from the counterfeiting of mere meaningless blots or self-sufficient mists and clouds upon the wall if they contribute to a narrative event. During the Renaissance, however, the realization of a nonpresence or of an insubstantial appearance was an important subject for Dürer and Leonardo independent of any discursive intent. The persistence of the desire to mimic the unmimickable, to conjure with the pictorial paradoxes of *sfumato* and the *mezzo confuso,* to vie with the effects of nature through art, can be traced through the great clouded domes of Parma, to the "fire paintings" of Alessio de Marchis and Francesco Guardi, to the volcanos of Joseph Vernet and Pierre-Jacques Volaire.[42] In this connection André Felibien praises Poussin's painting of a gathering storm in which the sky suddenly changes, clouds collect, and a howling wind raises swirls of dust. He relates Poussin's pendants to Apelles "because in the one (*L'Orage*) and the other (*Le Temps calme*), by having captured these kinds of subjects, one might state that he perfectly imitated things which are inimitable." Time and again Poussin turns his hand to natural effects that seem unportrayable. In the beautiful *Echo and Narcissus* (Louvre), not only does he capture the watery image of the dying youth; he also achieves something nature cannot: He metamorphoses the pining woodland nymph into an acoustic reflection.[43]

Roger de Piles, in the section devoted to "l'Etude du paysage" in his *Cours de peinture* (1708), discusses the class of transitory moments occasionally occurring in nature. In contrast to the precisionist approach of the various eighteenth-century sciences of matter, de Piles states that it is useless for the painter to try to fix what he admires. He counsels that it would be more profitable for the artist to sketch quickly what strikes him as extraordinary, that is, to capture the general effect rather than to hope for accuracy in the "impossible" particular. De Piles's obvious pleasure in these "effets merveilleux" (tempered by caution when it came to the question of translating nature's mutability into paint) was characteristic of the neoclassical tendencies of the eighteenth century. The Abbé Jean-Bernard LeBlanc in his *Lettre sur l'exposition de . . . 1747* firmly declares "one cannot imitate exactly inimitable things" and therefore advocates the pursuit of a state of repose, in a manner prescient of Lessing and Winckelmann.[44] Two points need to be made in this connection. First, the warning issued to artists by classical theorists to avoid the imitation of "such things as doe not offer themselves to the eyes of man" had become thoroughly outmoded because of Newtonian revelations concerning the complex composition of matter and space. The virtual animation and states of substance exceeded what *phantasia* might conjure up. Second, an important mechanical development occurred in the late eighteenth century—one revelatory of this new attitude. The seemingly authorless activities of a machine that concealed its art challenged both painterly facture and the powers of the imagination. The conviction that the phantomlike in nature might be materially "realized" underlies the Eidophusikon of Philippe-Jacques de Loutherbourg (1781). This moving panorama projected an animate image by means of transparent scenery that bathed an entire stage in atmospheric effects. Paradoxically, the Alsatian painter and set designer's invention is wholly dependent on the technological capacity for utilizing light and its multiple appearances. As a result, the production of natural effects becomes the result of an exaggerated scenography, that is, an artificial replication of sunrise, sunset, hail, storms, conflagrations, celestial portents.[45]

Although de Loutherbourg's summoning of phantasmagoria seemed to portend that painting (conceived as vying with nature through the agency of the reproductive imagination) might be superfluous or at best outmoded in its ability to simulate an apparitional model, a wide range of atmospheric studies came to its rescue. Hence, Valenciennes could overcome the conventionalized aesthetic vocabulary of distant vaporousness to base his exhortations to the landscapist on a scientific scrutiny of nature. He identifies a new category of painter-experimentalist, the "artist-observer," ready to tackle every variety of meteor. When he takes up the rubric of aerial perspective, Valenciennes defines air after the fashion of the physicist as "an odorless, buoyant, transparent, elastic fluid, without color, which is diffused throughout nature, and which extends in all directions." But, as he hastens to qualify, an empty stratosphere is an ideal, an absolute conception, since in fact it is usually more or less charged with terrestrial vapors. Further, he is aware of the Newtonian hypothesis that has light streaming in waves from the sun, penetrating all corporeal bodies and, by means of transmaterial modifications experienced by the aerial ocean, producing "admirable effects."[46]

Consequently, not until the rise of meteorology[47] and the atmospheric sciences[48] during the eighteenth century and their efflorescence at its close did all the unseizable particularities of climate and weather—now recognized as material realities—enter landscape portrayal. These researches were fostered and in large measure carried out by travelers in the process of discovering nature. In this sense, the traveler, better than any other type of direct observer, managed to involve simultaneously his whole bodily and mental being in the process of exploring physical actuality.

Representing the Impalpable

A nexus of interrelated scientific, philosophic, and aesthetic concerns—Newtonian bivalent substance, materialism, ghostly gases, unpaintable qualities, and burgeoning atmospheric studies—bears on the creation of

*Dans plusieurs de mes voyages,
entrepris pour des observations
particulières sur l'histoire naturelle,
& pour mieux connoître les grands
phénomènes de la nature relatifs
aux météores . . . (j'ai observé) des
grands brouillards, plus élevés que
ceux qui sont près de la terre. . . .*
P. Bertholon

*I found the day breaking, the
balloon at a prodigious height over
a wilderness of ocean, and not a
trace of land to be discovered far
and wide within the limits of the
vast horizon. . . .*
Edgar Allan Poe

the factual travel account. All contributed to the enterprise of "realizing"—adequately getting at the world of appearances, which is in continual transformation. Such investigations worked by different means to draw attention to a wide range of phenomena possessing only transitory or seemingly insubstantial existence. It was as an aspect of this larger movement involving the pictorialization of the fugitive that meteors (atmospheric phenomena or appearances) entered public consciousness.

Aristotle succinctly defined those natural occurrences whose forms are not limited, circumscribed, or otherwise determined. He read vague signs, surging and dissolving in the sky, as indices of imminent fluctuation or perturbation.[49] Of these, haze was the most difficult phenomenon to characterize. In the eighteenth century the Abbé Richard amplified and refined Aristotelian meteorological classification through close observation of subtle episodes in the life of matter, of "humid smoke" tenuously rising in wisps to float in the evening air. By dint of being on the spot, travelers contributed to the recording of nature's "impossible" effects. Arthur Brooke, crossing the Polar Circle, provides a detailed description of the crepuscular, light-shot atmosphere prevalent during the days immediately preceding the winter solstice. The moon no longer reigns: "Her orb, at this time rendered more indistinct by a faint haze, diffused a soft light over the wide extent of distant mountains and pine forests buried in snow. I could just discern the frozen stream of the Tornea. . . ." The Far North also offered another gauzy peculiarity. Both the elder and the younger Forster, and William Wales, the astronomer accompanying Cook on his second expedition, discussed the "blink of the ice" created by light reflected from floes. Constantine Phipps, on his journey to the North Pole, noted that pilots could always sense when they were approaching glacial sheets "by a bright appearance near the horizon."[50]

Fog, often associated with chronically cold areas or seasons, received careful analysis in many travel accounts. However, its most dramatic revelation to a wide audience as a potent, material phenomenon came in 1783. As Bertholon and writers in the leading journals of the day report, a "singular" fog veiled all Europe for several months. It was so dense that one could gaze directly at the sun without wearing spectacles. The obscured sun took on shifting colors, mutating from blood red to yellow. This arresting incident achieved what no amount of proselytizing could: the recognition by even the simplest person of an atmospheric meteor's potent physical force. The implication of material energy made visible and the intimation of natural revolution rather than religious retribution were adduced in the reasons mustered to explain this strange, but not unique, apparition. A series of purely natural causes were put forth by the scientific community. The preceding fall had been unusually cool and damp; simultaneously, a terrible earthquake had jolted Calabria, its tremors lasting for 5 months. In its wake an island had emerged near the coast of Iceland, its birth linked to the concurrent eruption of Vesuvius. The upheaval in Southern Italy was interpreted as the source for this "electric" and "sulphurous" curtain whose charged vapors, borne on the prevailing winds, generated storms.[51] Violent tempests of all kinds draw attention to a visually dense air. The historiographer on La Pérouse's expedition, Jean-Baptiste-Barthélemy Lesseps, exposed to a severe snowstorm in Russia in the winter of 1788, notes that not only was the sky thick with flakes, but also the accumulation on the ground, incessantly buffeted by powerful gusts, created such turbulence that a thick fog was formed, which made it impossible to see ahead for more than six paces. Brooke remarks on a similar event he experienced in Lapland: After his sledges had slipped down the Solivara Mountains, the small band became hidden in "the dense volume of mist that floated slowly along, and completely concealed those who entered it from those in the rear." The whole surface of the snow "seemed at once raised by the storm"; assuming the form of minute crystals, it constituted a thick "snee-fog." William Scoresby's 1820 account of the Arctic region visually conjoins "hard" and "soft" matter. On John Mayen Island, Scoresby climbed to the summit of a crater and, looking toward "a stupendous mass of lava," simultaneously witnessed to the north "a thick fog . . . which, as it advanced in stately grandeur towards us, gradually shrouded the distant scenery, until the nearest mountains were wrapped in distant gloom." During his second journey to the Polar Sea (1828), John Franklin camped on the Foggy Islands, so called because of the engulfing presence of wet films, "opaque," and dreary weather.[52]

La Pérouse, off the coast of California, speaks of the "eternal fog" enveloping Monterey and admires it as the source of the fertility of the surrounding countryside. On the same voyage in May 1787, while skirting the shores of Japan and China, he thinks he glimpses Tartary's mountains and ravines: ". . . a bank of mist, the most unusual that I have ever witnessed occasioned this hallucination: we observed it dissipate; its forms, its tints rose to lose themselves in the region of clouds, and we passed several additional days before no vestige of doubt remained concerning the existence of this chimerical land. . . ." Mist presaging change was deemed especially worthy of remark. (In the tropics, claps of thunder announce the arrival of periodic rains.) George Mollien, in his *Travels in the Interior of Africa* (1820), testifies to the swiftness with which a storm gathers in the east "like a thick fog, enveloping the highest mountains from our sight." Maria Graham evokes the existence of this phenomenon in commensurately warm climes; whereas Humboldt remarks on the bracing blue firmament against which the Cordillera are sharply etched, she notes the rolling fog that clears gradually by sinking into valleys, thus opening the Andean summits to view. Traveling in Colombia, Charles Cochrane singles out the fog peculiar to the La Guayra, not the Caracas, side of the Silla Mountain. Like Graham, who trained herself in scientific observation, he offers a knowledgeable explanation for this occurrence: The sun's heat, beating down on rocks and amplified through reflection, activates the humid air of the lower level, which then ascends into the atmosphere until it condenses and precipitates.[53]

THE FUGITIVE EFFECT

Figure 137
A. Cappell Brooke, *Preparations for Passing
a Night in a Fishing Hut . . . with the Effect
of the Aurora Borealis*, from *Winter Sketches
in Lapland*, 1827, pl. 18. Lithograph by
C. Hullmandel. Photo courtesy British
Library.

Figure 138
A. Cappell Brooke, *Laplanders Encountering the Snow Drift*, from *Winter Sketches in Lapland*, 1827, pl. 11. Lithograph by J. D. Harding. Photo courtesy British Library.

Figure 139
George Back, *Expedition Doubling Cape Barrow, July 25, 1821*, from John Franklin, *Polar Sea*, 1823, pl. p. 366. Engraving by Edward Finden. Photo courtesy British Library.

The conjunction of mountain and mist, of hard and soft, operating in these accounts occasionally is reminiscent of Far Eastern vaporous silk or paper and ink painting. This Taoist persuasion can be located in narratives dealing with those regions. Kaempfer, in the *History of Japan* (1717), describes "burning" yet enduring Mount Fuji, whose beauty is exceeded by none: "The top of it is cover'd with everlasting Snow, which, being, as it frequently is, blown up into flocks by the violence of the wind, and dispers'd about, represents as it were, a smoking hat. . . ."

The Daniells, in *Oriental Scenery*, comment from a differing perspective on the mountain ridges of Hindustan, alternatingly sunlit or shadowed and crowned by great puffs of mist; the granular texture of aquatint lends itself beautifully to capturing the soft gray haze that habitually collects within a moisture-laden sky. Grindlay's drawing of a morning view taken from Caliann near Bombay (and painted by William Daniell) shows the thrusting mass of mountains drifting in an ocean of white fog. Enlarging upon this theme, James Wales, exploring the rock temples of Dehr Warra, fastens on the material effect of elusive transparent smoke as it clots into nebular patterns on darkened and stained walls. According to an analogous dialectic, Henry Salt captures the floating tendrils that touch the Mountain of Samayut in Abyssinia or insinuate themselves into the Vale of Calaat.[54]

The Newtonian redefinition of space-filled matter led to the volatilization of more compact entities. The propensity of eighteenth-century travelers for interpreting the fume of waterfalls as barely visible yet acutely sensible signs of matter's physical powers stimulated a mode of *plein-air* immersion that was given scientific blessing by Jérôme Richard. This meteorologist-traveler cites the cataract at Terni as a chief example of the economy of nature. It plunges from the Mountain del Marmore to founder some 200 feet below. There, its stream is broken violently by rocks, causing a small cloud or electrically-charged *"polverino d'aqua"* to remain suspended in air. Neither the charm nor the environmental lesson of this mist is lost on Richard; because of the action at a distance wrought by this powdery fluid, the environs are constantly enveloped in a light but thick fog penetrating but not drenching the soil, and "a gentle coolness, a palpable moistness" insinuates itself into the entire region. Witnessed from the opposite bank, the cascade presents a "marvelous sight of matter's mutability in process"—particularly when cut by the sun's rays and fractured into multiple rainbows, which ascend or descend depending on the hydraulic pressure and the direction of the breeze.

The Swiss landscape painter and Alpine traveler Caspar Wolf was especially attentive to the indefiniteness possible to physical substance observed on the spot. In numerous field sketches and paintings he depicts the Staubbach undergoing metamorphoses consonant with its plural material essence. Every hour reveals a different effect in "that prodigious quantity of particles which the spectator standing near the large maple

Figure 140
Thomas and William Daniell, *Between Taka
Ca Munda and Sirinagur,* from *Oriental
Scenery,* 1797, II, pl. 22. Color aquatint.
Photo courtesy India Office Library.

Figure 141
Thomas and William Daniell, *Cape
Comorin, Taken near Calcad,* from *Oriental
Scenery,* 1797, II, pl. 1. Color aquatint.
Photo courtesy India Office Library.

Figure 142
R. M. Grindlay, *Morning View from Calliann near Bombay,* from *Scenery . . . Chiefly on the Western Side of India,* 1826, I, pl. 18. Painted by William Daniell, color aquatint by R. G. Reeve. Photo courtesy India Office Library.

Figure 143
James Wales, *Dehr Warra,* from *Hindoo Excavations in the Mountains of Ellora,* 1816, pl. 24. Color aquatint by Thomas Daniell. Photo courtesy India Office Library.

Figure 144
Caspar Wolf, *Second Fall of the Staubbach,*
from *Vues remarquables de la Suisse,* 1776,
pl. 6. Color aquatint by M. Pfenninger.
Photo courtesy Cabinet des Estampes,
Bibliothèque Nationale.

Figure 145
Caspar Wolf, *Second Fall of the Staubbach
in Winter,* from *Vues remarquables de la
Suisse,* second edition, 1785, pl. 6. Color
aquatint by J. F. Janinet and C.-M.
Descourtis. Photo courtesy Cabinet des
Estampes, Bibliothèque Nationale.

sees represented." A "silvery curtain" rises above the Monk and the glaciers at the bottom of the valley. Those who contemplate this sight see "numerous small transparent clouds jostled about by the impetuous descent of the waters." Wolf exhibits his training in natural history and his visual acuity for a relative and pervaded space by seizing that most unpaintable moment when the south wind blows and no perceptible drop falls for at least two minutes; only "a white thread," a thin "line traced in the air" is faintly visible.

The Staubbach waterfall had numerous admirers throughout the eighteenth and nineteenth centuries. Like Wolf, Raoul-Rochette focuses on the non-authorial and self-propelling agencies at work (the italics are mine):

Soon, borne away by winds, the two rivulets ceaselessly change direction and shape; they heave in the air. . . . decomposing at last and reduced to a humid and subtle dust, they reunite at the base of the boulder and together hurl themselves into the Lutschine. These waters, like a buoyant gauze, sketch their undulations during their aerial flight. The circular rainbows, which sway alongside the columns of water and which simultaneously present the most varied colors and combinations; these waves of dust and pearls . . . *hanging in the air by an invisible force*, settle upon the earth as a gentle dew. . . .

This torrent does not lose its fascination during the winter, when nature's creative powers mold it into crystalline shafts, bizarre stalactites, and heaps of azure lacquer—a subtle chemical transformation from gas to liquid to solid already captured by Wolf.[55]

The self-activating manifestations of a no-longer-recalcitrant matter depending neither on the maintenance of man nor on the vigilance of God also surface in narratives about remoter regions. James Bruce, progressing toward the elusive source of the Nile, records the visual process of coming upon a sudden new sight, the cataract of Alata. The river, swollen by recent rains, falls in a single sheet without interval. "A thick fume or haze, covered the fall all round, and hung over the course of the stream both above and below, marking its track, though the water was not seen. . . ." Equally palpable was the juncture of the River Bogotà with the River Magdalene at Tequendama. When this enormous body of water issues from a dark chasm, it "forms an arch, broad and brilliant in appearance." A little farther down it "resembles a white fleece," and as it descends still lower it "darts forth myriads of fanciful shapes, more like fireworks than anything else." The evaporation is "excessively great and rapid," and the changes "beautiful and various," as this vast body of water "sends up its dense vapours, which ascending and mingling with the atmosphere, form beautiful rainbows."[56]

According to the bivalent view of matter, aqueous fumes could also be connected to groups of material phenomena behaving immaterially. The perception of their insubstantiality is relative; that is, it is founded on establishing a visual correspondence to something more solid—indeed, to itself in another, antithetical physical incarnation. For example, Grose, sighting a waterspout in the Indian Ocean, commented that at its advent it resembled "a black smoak" rising from the water's compact surface. Le Gentil, sailing across the same seas, observed off the coast of Java the identical instance of nature in process. Delicate, faintly perceptible streamers collapsed almost instantaneously upon sighting into extreme rarefaction, "manifesting themselves only as a thin, concentratedly dark, & intensely subtle contour that touched the sea."[57]

Volcanos similarly revealed the conflict of matter conducted at the level of its constituent parts—as was the case with the dialectical tension established between the representation of the sea as infinite surface, as relative solid, and as momentary apparition, prototypical power. In fact, their character (both virtual and pictorial) as "hard" bodies or mountainous monuments was undercut by travelers confirming, as did Chappe d'Auteroche and Houel, that a "thick smoke" persistently emerges before, during, and after their activity. When Vesuvius erupted in 1767, the Neapolitan volcanologist Giovanni Maria della Torre studied the formation of those exhalations remaining on the summit after the initial disgorgement. He was able to trace the evolution of the crater's perturbations by analyzing the electrically charged fumes launched with scoriae—ranging in composition from foam to sparks to ashy vitrifications resembling chemical sublimations to dense black plumes. Richard comments perceptively on the delicate clouds formed from the abundant exhalations streaming from Vesuvius' mouth. Suspended on vapors of differing widths; like flexible cords, they glide from the bottom to the top of the mountain to mingle with the smoke billowing from the crater and finally to dissipate "dans le vague de l'air." Analogously, Captain Cook at Tanna and Patrick Brydone atop Mount Etna—both peering into a "hellish gulf"—focused not on its intransigent physiognomy but on contours made tractable by volumes of "sulphureous smoke" much heavier than the circumambient air. Rolling (not rising) "down the side of the mountain like a torrent, till coming to that part of the atmosphere of the same specific gravity with itself," it "shoots off horizontally, and forms a large track in the air, according to the direction of the wind."[58]

Fumigatory substances, or "sulfuric smoke," were conspicuous not only amid an ocean of molten matter but also in the depths of a mine. The pits of Falum described by Ernst Moritz Arndt in his *Reise durch Schweden* (1806) and by Johann Friedrich Ludwig Hausmann in his *Skandinavische Reise* (1818) were infamous for acrid vapors that mysteriously appeared and disappeared at the behest of a sudden draft. Above ground they became less lethal and took on a magically luminous quality when irradiated by the sun. Not surprisingly, Boisgelin de Kerdu began to smell sulfur long before reaching Falun: "[When] we arrived in the night, the atmosphere appeared on fire, as did the town, owing to the great number of furnaces lighted in the open air for calcining the ore. The mine was

THE FUGITIVE EFFECT

Figure 146
P. Bertholon, *Erupting Volcano*, from *De l'électricité des météores*, 1787, II, pl. 2. Engraving by L. LeGrand. Photo courtesy Smithsonian Institution.

Figure 147
J. Houel, *View of the Upper Crater of Etna*, from *Voyage pittoresque des isles de Sicile, de Malte et de Lipari*, 1787, I, pl. 123. Aquatint. Photo courtesy British Library.

Figure 148
William Hamilton, *Interior View of the Crater of Mount Vesuvius*, from *Campi Phlegraei*, 1776, II, pl. 10. Color aquatint by Peter Fabris. Photo courtesy British Library.

Figure 149
J. Houel, *View of the Crater of Stromboli*, from *Voyage pittoresque des îles de Sicile, de Malte et de Lipari*, 1782, I, pl. 72. Aquatint. Photo courtesy British Library.

THE FUGITIVE EFFECT

overspread by a thick fog. . . ." Much earlier, Borlase had noted similar inflammable mineral damps hovering in and above the pits and collieries of Cornwall; they "cannot but affect the air with their steams . . . and the facility with which their parts separate and ascend."[59]

It is only a matter of time until drifting haze and fog consolidate into nebulosity. This inevitability arrested the travelers, who discerned a perceptual similarity between mounded vapors and mountains. Both optical attractions are predicated on the renunciation of some (not all, as in the case of exhalations) sense of order; both (as in the instance of volcanos) are simultaneously solid and ephemeral. Like the earth monument, the cloud formation tempts the observer to see anthropomorphic and zoomorphic shapes in its disposition. This visual provocation is based on the interchangeability of different forms—all inherently dynamic—that participate in the plural powers of physical substance. Like rocks or ruins, clouds crumble and dissolve noiselessly, losing their surface and reentering the realm of the fluctuating and the inchoate. Although without contour, they possess greater volume than do mists; consequently, they exert a more tangible power while visibly firming up or tearing apart in the atmosphere.[60] Thus the cloud is the perfect natural pictogram of a vital universe, simultaneously incorporating emergence and eradication, immutability and mutability, openness and closure, matter and spirit.

Not only Richard but English meteorologists as well relied heavily on travel accounts to provide close observation of the particulars of cloud formation. J. F. Daniell, in his *Meteorological Essays*, claims that the polar narratives of Captains Scoresby and Parry shed light on the fluctuations of wind and weather endemic to those regions, constructive perturbations that shape the higher reaches of the atmosphere. Similarly, the mountain "observatories" of Switzerland proffered nebular effects made easier to examine by the presence of rarefied air.[61]

British travelers to temperate areas also recorded the formative processes of nubilative matter. Lord Macartney, scaling the Peak of the Teneriffe, could not glimpse the base of that monolithic cone. Rapidly whirling "hillocks," like an "immense sea," hid its foundations from view. They rolled into valleys far below, at last reaching the ocean, over which some continued to hang while others incorporated with its waves. In the long run, Table Mountain proved to be the more telling locus for the student of clouds interested in the combat waged between hard and soft substance. John Webber, the artist on Cook's third expedition, is interested in this natural monument dominating the Cape, that is, as looming, imposing, and solidly arid in appearance. He focuses on it to the exclusion of the other two mountains present by maintaining a low viewpoint and gazing toward it over Capetown. Yet all scientifically trained voyagers, including Webber and Hodges, took note—in addition to such impalpabilities as aromatic scents and gentle breezes—of the "Table Cloth" overspreading the massive outcrop while every other part of the hemisphere showed a clear blue sky undisturbed by a single vapor. (See figures 52 and 53.) Barrow, perched on the ridge, also perceives the mountain as an exercise in matter's antiphonal expressiveness. He looks upon the myriad "skeletons" of quartz rock, once resistant but now moldering away into sand, while overhead a more rapid metamorphosis takes place. Fleecy clouds produced by the evaporation of sea water during the summer heat rest on the plateau. (Saussure, in his ruminations on the birth and development of clouds, dating from 1788, spoke of similar "parasites" attached to Swiss peaks.) James Johnson, in the *Oriental Voyager* (1807), adds that the Capetown phenomenon occurs during the monsoon. Water absorbed by evaporation is transported to the continental shelf, where, having condensed, it rests like a thick blanket. As suddenly as it floats over the isthmus, as quickly it "vanishes into air—thin air."[62]

Certainly, mornings and evenings experienced between the tropical parallels of 10° north and 5° south present an "assemblage of fantastic clouds" hovering near, and tinged by, the sun. But these were more than matched by the nimbous effects endemic to the poles. Bernard O'Reilly, accompanying a whaler to Greenland in 1818 in order to rectify "the absolute want of scientific information on the subject of northern climates," took accurate drawings of "phenomena of the atmosphere, new to men of science." Among his views sketched on the spot is a weather gall, dreaded by sailors because a severe wind generally comes from the place where it originates. A "remarkable cloud of singular hue, being of a deep blue, with a dash of yellow, which gives it a greenish cast," it "generally appears embosomed in other clouds, occupying a very small space."[63]

Along with disclosures concerning nebular singularities characteristic of the far north and south, balloon ascents made the most significant contribution to the steadily advancing literature on clouds. As Faujas de Saint-Fond observes in *La machine aérostatique* (1783), not only does this instrument for discovery float at the whim of the winds but by its very essence it replicates one of the most majestic operations of nature. The bold conception of filling a vast, thin-skinned shell with a buoyant vapor succeeded in creating "a kind of artificial cloud." Thus, the aerostat, operating on the principle of the ascension of lighter-than-air gases and skimming through Lavoisier's "elastic fluid" to confront Newton's "electric spirit" at its source, becomes one cloud among many, climbing into regions where storms and meteors brew.

The public fetes at which these "experiments" were launched received wide coverage in the press. The exuberance associated with these events is captured in the multitudinous prints that were issued on such occasions. The *Journal Encyclopédique* reports that at the time of the Montgolfier ascension from La Muette on November 21, 1783, "all Paris" came to watch one of the greatest inventions of mankind: "Not a person was

Luminous Arch

Figure 150
B. O'Reilly, *Luminous Arch and Weather
Gall,* from *Greenland . . . ,* 1818, pl. p. 196.
Aquatint by F. C. Lewis after S. Koenig.
Photo courtesy British Library.

VOYAGE INTO SUBSTANCE

Figure 151
B. Faujas de Saint-Fond, *Inflation of the Balloon*, from *Description des expériences de la machine aérostatique*, 1783, I, pl. 3. Engraving by Bertault. Photo courtesy Library of Congress.

Figure 152
J. Houel, *Aerostatic Balloon*, 1783. Aquatint. Photo courtesy Cabinet des Estampes, Bibliothèque Nationale.

present who did not tremble to see two men, in the prime of manhood, and distinguished by their love of the sciences, navigating at three or four thousand feet in the air, stationed next to a fiery furnace from which they were separated only by a simple cloth to which was attached a fragile basket, itself filled with the most combustible of substances. The imagination is terrified by this sight; but they were well recompensed for their intrepidness by the admiration and applause of the onlookers. . . ."

Wonder could readily be transformed into passion. The French physicist and balloonist Jacques Charles, after his memorable flight of December 1, 1783, received, along with the charming pencil sketch shown as figure 153, the following anonymous letter: "You have become the object of all my thoughts, the hero of my heart, the genius that has transfixed it; I experience an innocent and tangible pleasure in telling you that I have forever imposed upon myself the command of remaining unknown to you. If, in a crowd, you should cast your eyes on the women assembled there, inquire of the one who strikes you most: were you at the experiment of the Tuileries? If you should reascend in this chariot that my tear-filled eyes have followed for so long, my soul will be there. . . ."[64]

Apart from their diverting or military purpose, frequent invocation of the names of Columbus, Vespucci, Newton, Lavoisier, and the students of meteorology indicates that these flights were not regarded as merely amusing episodes. Physicists such as Charles, Pilâtre de Rozier, Biot, and Gay-Lussac took to the air for a scientific intention. The admission tickets printed for these expeditions invariably show the aeronauts in the atmosphere's waves; even the torn stub for the aborted and much-ridiculed flight of Miolan and Janinet depicts the would-be explorers avidly examining turbulent clouds. (See figures 154 and 136.)

Across the Channel, Thomas Baldwin expatiated on the view above the clouds, where nature could be observed in the act of self-creation: "The imperceptibly Slow yet perpetual Changes they underwent, strongly called to Remembrance, the Opinion of the great Berkeley, as well as of ancient Philosophers, that AIR GIVES FORM TO THINGS; scarcely a Breath of which seemed, however, to disturb their general Order. . . ." Riding in Vincent Lunardi's balloon, and speeding over the city of Chester, Baldwin seized a circular panorama taken at the greatest point of elevation. His wondering gaze met with "the perspective of a vast Series of Thunderclouds of a sulphureous and metallic Tinge, placing themselves in Ranks, each beyond the Other in bright and tremendous Order, and a sort of Battle-Array, beyond Conception grand yet beautiful; coud [sic] not pass under him without Notice." "The immense circular and visible Distance of the NEBULOUS Horizon." Baldwin goes on, "extended Now 102 Miles at THE LEAST round the Eye . . . was a grand Source of the Sublime. . . ." Not only did Baldwin pass over these magnificent thundercaps, whose semitransparent colors ranged from blue to violet-purple; like his French contemporary Blanchard, he passed through them, being penetrated by, and penetrating to, the core of a "soft" matter in a way not possible by any other mode of travel.[65]

The pleasurable yet serious exploits of the practitioners of the nascent technology of aerostatics specifically recall the late eighteenth century's enlarged classification of meteors. Père Cotte, in the important treatise already cited, categorizes them into four groups. Aquaeous (by far the largest class) includes mists, fogs, clouds, dew, snow, and hail; aerial comprises winds and waterspouts; igneous embraces thunder, will-o'-the-wisp, Saint Elmo's fire, and other flaming apparitions; and luminous denotes rainbows, parhelia, and northern lights. While useful, neither the grouping nor the nomenclature is hard and fast. Bearing this in mind, we turn next to those brilliant "emphatic" meteors that share a certain whiteness and volatility with clouds and fleetingly streak across their domain.

The search for a more technical and exact idiom and image congruent with actuality—prevalent in the observation of land forms—extended to the firmament. Although Newtonian light as "monolithic" and protracted purity was everywhere present in the prose and poetry of the early part of the eighteenth century, the aesthetic recognition of extreme fluctuating lambency, expressed in violent, abrupt effects, belongs to its last quarter.[66]

Unlike mists drifting loosely or composed into clouds, and intimately if tenuously attached to more evidently corporeal phenomena (waterfalls, oceans, volcanos, dense atmosphere), halos, coronas, and auroras seemingly possess no ground or "substratum" whatsoever. They are the acme of an invisible energy's transitory effect, uniquely defined by their momentary visibility, by their staining of a relative space. Benjamin Franklin's discovery of atmospheric electricity in 1752 inspired speculation that all such luminous phenomena expressed the activity of its hidden springs.

Halos, and other meteors specifically connected with the sun or the moon, are perceptible only when moisture is present in the air. The parhelion depends on humidity and results from the image of the solar disk being impressed on a passing cloud that at once receives and transmits its beams like a mirror. Such a charged atmosphere was present in Peru where La Condamine and Bouguer caught "a rare spectacle": two distinct suns setting simultaneously. William Thorne in Java witnessed a related effect at sunrise when the orb shot out of the gray mist "like an immense fiery balloon." O'Reilly, bound for Greenland, offers the most precise description:

. . . dark vapory cirrostratus and others in profile, pointing northward: larus maximus seen: at 10 P.M., a beautiful pahelion appeared above Disko. This phenomenon, which is commonly named a mock sun, exhibited two distinct portions of an iridescent circle surrounding that luminary, and parallel to the line of the horizon: no portion of such light as the sun affords, but the brilliant colours of the rainbow, were re-

cette 2ème lettre.

Figure 153
Anonymous, *Young Woman gazing at a
Charlière*, 1784. Pencil drawing. Photo
courtesy Library of Congress, Tissandier
Collection.

Figure 154
Anonymous, *Entrance ticket for "experiment" of Messrs. Charles and Robert,* 1783. Ibz, fol. 102. Etching. Photo courtesy Cabinet des Estampes, Bibliothèque Nationale.

Figure 156
Balsset fils, *Sic Itur ad Astra*. Entrance ticket for Blanchard's "experiment" of February 28, 1784. Ibz, fol. 15. Etching by Dery. Photo courtesy Cabinet des Estampes, Bibliothèque Nationale.

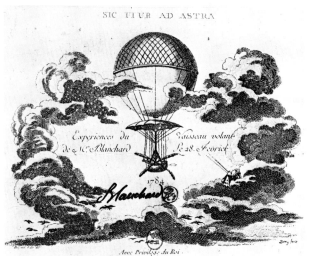

Figure 155
Thomas Baldwin, *A View from the Balloon at Its Greatest Elevation,* from *Airopaidia,* 1786, pl. p. 58. Color aquatint by C. Heath. Photo courtesy Smithsonian Institution.

flected from the sun's light upon a deep brown bed of cirrostratus, through which the sunlight broke. . . .[67]

In the course of this lengthy account, O'Reilly repudiates the traditional designation of "mock sun" and insists that what he saw is most closely allied to the radiant insubstantialities of the rainbow. The rainbow, glorified since Biblical times, was too well known to offer anything radically new to the travelers; indeed, it had to share its former singularity with other luminous meteors. Two of its incarnations, however, received a modern focus. The first has already been met with: the tenuous colored arc arising from the electrified fume of a waterfall. The second is the Brocken Specter, described as long ago as La Condamine's and Bouguer's accounts of Peru (1737) and subsequently glimpsed in mountainous areas from the Alps to the Hartz. As with coronas and parhelia, this airy "sketch" manifests itself at a temporal turning point when matter's eventual form is still ambiguous: Usually at sunrise, when mounting vapors have not yet coalesced, the voyager perceives a ghostly human figure of monstrous proportions; it is his shadow projected onto a cloud. At one instant this phantom colossus is feebly visible; at another, he is strongly outlined and makes his dim presence substantially felt.

The reflection of light from remote (and therefore effectively impalpable) bodies, combined with atmospheric interference experienced as mists, hazes, and clouds, became an absorbing scientific problem for those embarked on expeditions of discovery. William Wales had numerous opportunities when he sailed with Cook to observe, under the most divergent skies, phenomena in which heavenly bodies were partly obscured by exhalations. Not only the shifting aspects of the sun (viewed with special sharpness through Herschel's telescope in 1785–1789), but also the contemplation of distant stars and the "faces" of the moon under nebulous conditions were getting underway.[68] Bernardin de Saint-Pierre remonstrates with peripatetic artists who undertake long voyages to the Indies in search of exotic naturalia but fail to go to London in order to "paint the sun as it looks through a telescope." Bernardin—anxious to make the journey himself—underscores the fact that this supposedly stable fulcrum of our solar system (and, indeed, any "fixed" stellar body viewed in such a penetrating manner) will reveal "a multiplicity of effects" contributing to a deeper knowledge of their basic structure.

The sea voyagers were particularly susceptible to blunted light. Both the Abbé de La Caille and John Barrow note that, in the midst of raging storms, the appearance of heavenly bodies becomes strange and terrible. "The stars look larger, and seem to dance," writes Barrow; "the moon has an undulating tremor; and the planets possess a sort of beard like comets. . . ."[69] Nothing seemed more wonderfully uncommon, however, than the appearance of the northern and southern lights (the aurora borealis and aurora australis) in the lower and higher latitudes. Since the days of James Cook, John and James Clark Ross, George Back, Edward Parry,

VOYAGE INTO SUBSTANCE

and John Franklin, the public was kept informed of an exotic region filled with strange "loomings." Intent on giving a rational, scientific description of the Arctic and Antarctic environment, these navigators searching for the Northwest Passage were acutely aware of the quality of light. Weird phenomena and odd visual effects, ranging from the dazzling to the murky, produced an acute sense of the triumph of an inorganic universe. Vast emptiness and eerie sounds, such as the thin cry of a bird, the roar of a glacier, the boom of a pack splitting, and the movement of floes, confirmed the image of an unstable, protean cosmos.[70]

Auroras especially (although by no means exclusively) were attributed in Joseph Priestley's *History of Electricity* (1767) to the atmosphere's constant state of electrification. Indeed, as Giovanni Battista Beccaria demonstrated, even in serene weather the atmosphere is a residium of small electrical charges, operating unseen. In the many descriptions of auroras, each phase of their evolution is scrutinized. According to R. P. du Fesc, the first appearance is often in the form of a "luminous smoke, like a subtle mist." Occasionally the screen of vapor is so fine one can see the stars twinkling behind it. At times the apparition appears absolutely stationary, and at other moments it is pulsating, a rolling and whirling dense fog darting about in an infinity of arcs, bands, patches, veils, or rays. Columns of light spring from the midst of this seething vapor. Black turbidity may also shape itself into arcs spanning the horizon, with a whitish bow vaulting over it. Gradually, the plasmic spectacle dilates; it divides into delicate clouds almost completely covering the sky, finally to disappear entirely. At the instant that the "smoke" dies down, multicolored rays shoot out perpendicularly from its nucleus. Beyond these probing beams lies yet another bright light, as if separated from the rest, and after the luminous shafts ebb this illumination persists for several hours in a muted display of energy.

The German physicist Friedrich Daniel Behn, who devoted a dissertation to the subject of the northern lights, declares that the beautiful and perpetually shifting light play, refraction, and mutable vapor can never be seized by art. It is as if the entire atmosphere behaved like a colossal mirror beaming back shining and intangible images.[71] Or, to draw an analogy with the "acts" of moonlight whose rays often "paint" the inchoate surface of rarefied clouds, the sun's beams pierce and color the exhalations present in the sky, staining them with red or blue brilliance while molding them into arcs through reflection. In this regard Bertholon, in his *De l'électricité des météores* (1787), speaks admiringly of the aurora borealis as "a veritable Proteus," metamorphosing, pulsing, and assuming various centrifugal forms as if to trick the most attentive observer. The physicist Jean-Louis Carra, friend to Marat and self-styled scientific successor to Newton, also focuses on the volatile qualities of this elusive radiance.[72]

The eighteenth century was familiar with the correlation between sunspots and northern lights. Dortous de Mairan, whose treatise on auroras was

Figure 157
B. O'Reilly, *Disco near Lievely with Parhelion*, from *Greenland* . . . , 1818, pl. p. 44. Aquatint by F. C. Lewis after S. Koenig. Photo courtesy British Library.

Figure 158
George Back, *Boats in a Swell amongst Ice*, from John Franklin's *Second Journey to the Polar Sea*, 1828, pl. p. 171. Engraving by Edward Finden. Photo courtesy British Library.

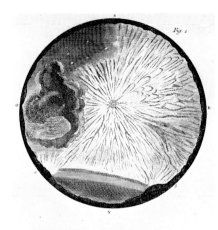

Figure 159
(After Dortous de Mairan), *Aurora Borealis and Northern Lights*, from *Encyclopédie*, 1767, IV, "Physique," pl. 1, figs. 1 and 2. Engraving by Bernard after drawing by Goussier. Photo courtesy Library of Congress.

Figure 160
P. Bertholon, *Aurora Borealis and Northern Lights*, from *De l'électricité des météores*, 1787, II, pl. 3. Engraving by L. LeGrand. Photo courtesy Smithsonian Institution.

THE FUGITIVE EFFECT

the first textbook devoted to the subject, noticed that since 1688, when the flashes had become weaker, no more sunspots had been evident. This situation had prevailed until 1720, bracketing the so-called Little Ice Age. However, beginning around 1730, Mairan witnessed an upsurge in auroras and coronas and a resumption of sunspot activity. Thermal curves compiled by scientists during the eighteenth century indicate that in certain seasons, winter in particular, temperatures were clearly lower than in the twentieth century. This circumstance was of utmost importance for the rising awareness of phenomena typically associated with cold weather or frigid regions.[73] The scientific travelers provided both additional vindication and new data to bolster this fact. Georg Forster, in the Antarctic, corroborates the reborn splendor of this "beautiful phaenomenon," which "consisted of long columns of clear white light, shooting up from the horizon to the eastward, almost to the zenith; and gradually spreading on the whole southern part of the sky." Kerguelen, in the Arctic, minutely recorded the atmospheric "explosion" of fiery particles exhibiting variegated shapes and colors. Franklin was instructed specifically to observe what kind or degree of influence the aurora borealis might exert on the magnetic needle at the Pole and "whether that phenomenon was attended with any noise," and "to make any other observations that might be likely to tend to the further development of its cause, and the laws by which it is governed. . . ." This is in marked concurrence with an established naval practice dedicated to accurate registering of unusual atmospheric disturbances: The Royal Society's *Directions for Seamen, Bound for Far Voyages* (1666) enjoined mariners "to observe and record all extraordinary *Meteors*, Lightnings, Thunders, *Ignis fatui*, Comets, etc. marking still the places and times of their appearing, continuance, etc."

Arthur Brooke, in Lapland, further confirmed that, since winter was rapidly approaching, this corruscation could be expected to make regular appearances. Anxious to catch sight of the "singular phenomenon," he ventured forth one clear and frosty midnight; the heavens, to his astonishment, "were perfectly illuminated with this wonderful light, which flitted along with inconceivable velocity, in large patches of a pale hue, without assuming any defined form." (See figure 137.) No sound accompanied this flicker, which in the course of the following month considerably "increased in brilliancy." During the first decade of the nineteenth century, Jacques Garnerin, the inventor of the parachute and a specialist in nocturnal flights, recreated aloft for a rapt Parisian audience the effect of crystalline columns aflame with a mysterious nebular fire.[74]

As Père Cotte argues in the *Traité de météorologie* (1774), the brightness of the northern lights is analogous to the lambency of the Milky Way, similarly observed to occur periodically just after sunset or sunrise. The misty gleam of this boundless belt of stars shares the aurora's disposition for mutability. Not only are both phenomena classified as luminous meteors, resulting from the combination of tenuous vapors with fluid light, but both also seem to undergo incessant transformations, palely animating the obscurity of the night. Perceived as a celestial river coursing across the firmament, not as a static aggregate of fixed bodies, this teeming mass shared in the diffuseness and optical gauziness of other corruscations. Thomas Wright, in *An Original Theory and New Hypothesis of the Universe* (1750), perceptively inquired into the nature of the filmy starlight girding the heavens. The British astronomer William Herschel substantially advanced these initial researches and published his findings in *Observations Tending to Investigate the Construction of the Heavens* (1784). The chief revelation of the reflecting telescope—equal to that of the microscope in the seventeenth century—was that it increased the range of vision. In this instance, it disclosed an intensity of light not visible to the naked eye. The powerful instrument, radically improved by Herschel, divulged that this watery swath consisted of a suspension of innumerable separate and distinct stars, strewn (in the phrase of the Abbé La Pluche) like sand upon the borders of the sea. D'Alembert probed into the essence of this measureless "whiteness" and distinguished it from other weak radiances—held, as it were, in emulsion—located in distant parts of the sky. Both D'Alembert and Mairan saw a fundamental visual and structural analogy between charged nebulas and northern lights.

Diminutive and large radiances alike were attributed to atmospheric effects supposedly surrounding individual tiny stars. The travelers, following suit, often conjoined the two manifestations. Anders Skjöldebrand, in his *Journey to the North Cape*, asserts that "those who have not witnessed the fine winter-nights of a northern climate cannot believe the description of them." "Here," he continues, "the skill of the painter is baffled: who can represent that sky, clear and serene, which seems to have doubled the number of its stars? That snow, which by the rays of the moon, looks as if it were composed of precious stones, whose brilliancy is a thousand times more resplendent than that of diamonds . . . ? The horizon was illuminated by moving masses of coloured light, sometimes forming radiated circles, sometimes irregular figures. . . ."[75]

The foregoing discussion of nebulous and nebular scintillations leads to a consideration of their complementaries, sharp igneous meteors. The northern lights and the Milky Way—chief among subtle luminous effects—were rivaled by a fiery species pointedly playing out its brief but memorable role against the nocturnal sky. As Bertholon remarks, man never becomes accustomed to the deep impression these radiances make, since they possess, at one and the same time, the penetrating brilliance of reality wedded to the ephemerality of illusion. All meteors, but especially the first two classes, emphasize by their trajectories the immensity of the ether in which they swim or dart. Coexisting unstably with stars, planets, and other gleaming bodies, they compel man to look up. The sky itself seemed to define the entirety of a force-filled nature.[76]

THE FUGITIVE EFFECT

Figure 161
Edward Hawke Locker, *Garnerin, . . . from a Sketch made on [the] Aerial Voyage, July 5, 1802.* Engraving. Photo courtesy Library of Congress, Tissandier Collection.

VOYAGE INTO SUBSTANCE

Figure 162
Thomas Wright, *The Via Lactea*, from *An Original Theory or New Hypothesis of the Universe*, 1750, pl. 12. Mezzotint. Photo courtesy Library of Congress.

Figure 163
Thomas Wright, *The Via Lactea*, from *An Original Theory or New Hypothesis of the Universe*, 1750, pl. 14. Mezzotint. Photo courtesy Library of Congress.

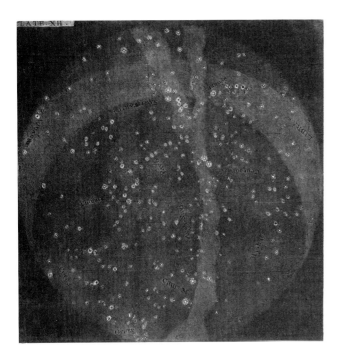

Cotte helps to account for such ephemera as Saint Elmo's or Castor and Pollux's fire, will-o'-the-wisps, and jack-o'-lanterns. Unlike the grander trails traced across the heavens by comets and meteorites, such flickers are perceptible closer to earth during storms at sea, when masts, riggings, decks seem aflame. On land, they behave enigmatically (and, countryfolk say, malevolently) as tiny, wandering sparks hovering above swamps and cemeteries in the autumnal gloom. These glittering motes were interpreted as the initial particulate link in that grand burning chain of electricity that clamped "burning" atoms together with lightning and thunder.[77] These minute, flashing, puzzling, and occasionally nameless meteors only sporadically engaged the attention of the travelers. Belzoni sighted one at Denderah; "it first appeared of a bluish colour, then became white, and lastly red; leaving apparently many sparks on the way it had passed. . . ." Kaempfer, departing from Bangkok and sailing down the Menam River, was astounded by myriads of glowworms "which settle on some trees, like a fiery Cloud, with this surprizing circumstance, that a whole swarm of these Insects, having taken possession of one Tree, and spread themselves over its branches, sometimes hide their Light all at once, and a moment after make it appear again with the utmost regularity and exactness, as if they were in a perpetual Systole and Diastole. . . ."[78]

Intense scholarly interest was expended instead on a more grandiose ramifiction of the study of light emission: During the second half of the eighteenth century, phosphorescence became the most hotly debated igneous meteor, and sea voyagers played a central role in the polemic. Bioluminescence, as it is now called, is considered one of the major discoveries made by François Péron and Charles-Alexandre Lesueur during their expedition to austral lands in 1800–1804. Péron notes that this illumination exists in all oceans, in the midst of equatorial waves as well as in the seas skirting Norway, Siberia, and the Antarctic. His weightiest conclusion, however, is that all phosphorescent waters, no matter how different in appearance or how widely separated in location, may be attributed to the action of small marine animals, particularly mollusks and zoophytes. Cook's journal corroborates Péron's generalizations; the *Resolution* experienced little wind and hot weather in March and April of 1774. J. R. Forster, in this connection, discusses at length the "wonder" of an immense "rotting sea," becoming stinking and highly putrid, in which a great many dying animal substances "cause the luminous appearance we so much admire." Like Cotte, and unlike Péron, he attributes this phenomenon to the effects of electricity. Banks, in his *Endeavour* journal, remarks that on the evening of October 29, 1768, "the sea appeared uncommonly beautifull, flashes of light coming from it perfectly resembling small flashes of lightning, and these so frequent that sometimes 8 or ten were visible at the same moment. . . ."[79]

Bernardin de Saint-Pierre, heading for the Ile de France in 1768, comments how the melancholy of being at sea is alleviated by interesting scenes, occurring especially in warmer latitudes, like the glitter observed in the ship's wake either during tempests or calms. Many years later, in *Harmonies de la nature* (1794), he returns to the theme; this time, not just animals but plants—bathed by waves of sun and moonlight—exude a bluish phosphorescent glimmer.[80]

In full confidence of the interest noctiluca elicited, other voyagers soon followed suit. Macartney in Sumatra, stationed under dark storm clouds, vivid flashes of lightning, and the low growl of thunder, watched how phosphoric light scudded across the surface of the sea. Brooke, hastening home just before midnight, saw Lapland at sunset:

I now, for the first time, had an opportunity of witnessing the extraordinary luminous appearance of the waters of the Northern Ocean, and in how very high degree they are phosphorescent. There are few who have been much at sea who have not observed this beautiful appearance: but it is in the high latitudes that it is seen in its greatest brilliancy, from the greater number of medusae, and other extremely minute marine animals, which the water contains, and which are supposed to be the principal cause of this phosphoric light. Our boat appeared frequently cleaving a sea of fire; and after each stroke of the oar a pale lambent flame would suddenly blaze forth from the place whence it emerged, burning for several seconds. In this manner our track would be marked for some distance, presenting altogether so singular and beautiful a spectacle, that I did not regret the loss of the sun, which, by its disappearance, had enabled me to enjoy it. . . .[81]

The origin of aerial meteors was long held to be equally problematical and ascribed to the universal agency of electricity. Cotte deems this "agitated air" as belonging to that refreshing and purifying portion of the atmosphere moving like a current with a certain velocity and in a certain direction. The naturalists Pieter van Musschenbroek, Georges Buffon, and Jérôme Richard believed they arose from a lack of equilibrium within the ethereal "ocean," and D'Alembert spoke of the flux and reflux of its "tides." These theories were predicated on a belief in the manifold perturbations occurring within an electric fluid—controlled by the force of gravity—cycling between the earth and its ambient.[82]

What the factual travel accounts contributed to the study of winds was the anatomization of casual variety into a scientifically ordered taxonomy of elements. These ranged from the "faint breeze" that enveloped Georg Forster his first morning within sight of Tahiti and wafted "a delicious perfume from the land" to the monsoon that threatened Kaempfer on the China Sea. The fury of "la mousson," its immense force accompanied by huge hollow waves, struck Grandpré off the coast of Yemen. It arrives at the end of November and lasts until June, blowing hard from the south to the southeast. En route it becomes laden with vapors exhaled by Abyssinia, whose very sand it robs; consequently, the air appears inflamed

　　THE FUGITIVE EFFECT

and the sky red upon its arrival. William Westall grasps the engulfing wetness of the forbidding harbinger in his views of *Malay Bay from Pobassos Island* and of *Wreck-Reef*. The Daniells were sensitive to its destructive energy, depicting the incursion of storm-driven waters infiltrating even the great rock caverns at Elephanta. And Grindlay, gazing over the northern section of Bombay Harbor, watches its palpable buildup and subsequent dispersion while fishermen repair stakes and tackle injured by "the violence of the weather during the monsoon, or rainy season."[83]

It is instructive to compare the wet ravages with the dry ravages wrought by the sirocco, the southeast wind that blows in South Italy and Malta during July, bringing along, in the words of Patrick Brydone, "a violence of heat." The scorching blast, "like the burning steam from the mouth of an oven," is the "same wind that is so dreadful in the sandy deserts of Africa." Mercifully, as suddenly as it sweeps down, as quickly is it succeeded by the tramontane, a bracing north wind. James Jackson, in his *Account of the Empire of Marocco* (1809), crossed the "trackless" Sahara, pursued by the "hot and impetuous winds denominated Shume, [that] convert the Desert into a moveable sea . . . a sea without water, more dangerous than the perfidious waves of the ocean." Belzoni, in Egypt and Nubia, experienced the parching camseen wind that commences in April and blows for 50 days, raising the sand "to a great height" and forming "a general cloud, so thick that it is impossible to keep the eyes open, if not under cover."

India was notorious for the bladelike wind that blew westward of the River Jumna. Major William Thorn recalls how the British army suffered indescribable misery from this burning blast, which "after passing over the great sandy desert, imparts to the atmosphere in these regions an intensity of heat scarcely to be conceived even by those who have been seasoned to the fury of a vertical sun." The closest analogy to this "pestiferous current" is the "extreme glow of an iron foundry in the height of summer," though "even that is but a feeble comparison, since no idea can be formed of the causticity of the sandy particles which are borne along with the wind like hot embers, peeling off the skin, and raising blisters wherever they chance to fall." Similarly, Captain Fitzroy describes the "furious *pamperos*" that sweep along the drought-stricken Patagonian soil, which is capable of producing only scanty grasses and gigantic thistles.[84]

The mass of the darting waterspout is not unrelated to the form of a buffeting tower assumed by withering whirlwinds. The *Encyclopédie* groups it among aerial meteors imperiling ships especially during warm, dry weather. This sea typhoon, not to be confused with a land hurricane, is a condensed cloud part of which is in circular motion owing to the collision of two winds blowing at cross purposes. Eventually, because of its weight, it drops to the surface, taking the form of a serpentine conical or cylindrical funnel with its base buried in the clouds and its apex sunk in the ocean.

Bertholon, in his quest for an electrical explanation of the phenomenon, turns to the descriptions of Cook and those of Dampier, who recorded spotting a "tornado" near the Celebes. One of the most exciting of the many natural effects experienced during Cook's second voyage was the meeting (on May 17, 1773) with waterspouts in Cook's Straits, New Zealand. Cook, Forster, and Wales recorded every detail of their materialization and dissolution. Forster's observations confirmed his belief in Benjamin Franklin's hypothesis that whirlwinds and waterspouts have a common origin in electricity.

French interest did not lag. Le Gentil's *Voyage dans les mers de l'Inde* (1779) minutely describes and illustrates snakelike clouds uncoiling from a dense bank to join the roiled surface of the water just off the Malabar coast. Johnson's *Oriental Voyager* (1807) praises this "curious phenomenon"— "a liquid column," a "fluid vortex" towering above its "foaming base." Peter Schmidtmeyer, sailing to Chile during squally weather, sighted a waterspout whose existence he clocked at 12–15 minutes. After bursting, it left only a "faint form" to remind the beholder of the passing of one of Coleridge's "tremendities" of nature.[85]

The manifestation of nature's shooting energy made explicit in these operations was paralleled by the upsurge of hot springs. Martin Sauer, secretary on Commodore Billings's geological and astronomical expedition to northern Russia (1785), duplicated William Alexander's *View of the Ozernoi Hot Springs near Kamtschatka*. Pillars of smoke, boiling water and muffled sounds announce the imminent arrival of this impulsive phenomenon. George MacKenzie similarly was attracted by the fitful outpourings of Iceland's geysers. He provides a beautifully precise recital of the physical circumstances attending an eruption of the Great Geyser: "Such a midnight as was now before us, can seldom be witnessed. Here description fails us altogether. . . . It raged furiously and threw up a succession of magnificent jets, the highest of which was at least ninety feet. At this time I took the sketch from which the engraving was made: but no drawing, no engraving can possibly convey any idea of the noise and velocity of the jets, nor of the swift rolling of the clouds of vapour, which were hurled, one over the other, with amazing rapidity. . . ." The operations of the New Geyser were just as fugitive and as unpaintable. MacKenzie dwells upon the gigantic "force of the steam, that although a brisk gale of wind was blowing against it, the column of vapour remained as perpendicular as it is represented in the engraving." He continues: "It proceeded in this magnificent play for more than half an hour, during which time I had an opportunity of taking a correct sketch of this beautiful Geyser. A light shower fell from the Vapour, which has been attempted to be expressed; but the imitation is very far short of the fine effect it produced. . . ."

On several occasions during the 1820s the *Journal des Voyages de Découvertes* garnered descriptions from contemporary narratives on the per-

Figure 164
William Westall, *View of Wreck-Reef Bank, Taken at Low Water*, from Matthew Flinders's *Voyage to Terra-Australis*, 1814, II, pl. p. 312. Aquatint by John Pye. Photo courtesy British Library.

Figure 165
R. M. Grindlay, *Approach of the Monsoon, Bombay Harbor*, from *Scenery . . . Chiefly on the Western Side of India*, 1826, I, pl. 2. Drawing by William Westall, engraving by T. Fielding, color by J. B. Hogarth. Photo courtesy India Office Library.

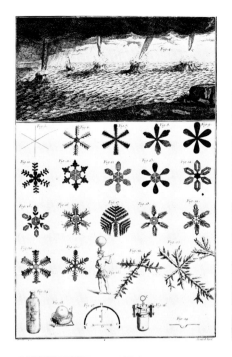

Figure 166
Anonymous, *Waterspouts and Snow Crystals*, from *Encyclopédie*, 1767, IV, "Physique," pl. 2, figs. 2 and 3. Engraving by Bernard after drawing by Goussier. Photo courtesy Library of Congress.

Figure 167
F. W. Beechey, Waterspouts and eclipse of the sun, from *Narrative of a Voyage to the Pacific . . .* , 1831, pl. p. 149. Engraving by Edward Finden. Photo courtesy British Library.

Figure 168
G. MacKenzie, *Eruption of the Great Geyser*, from *Travels in the Island of Iceland*, 1811, pl. p. 224. Engraving by J. Clark. Photo courtesy Yale Center for British Art, Paul Mellon Collection.

ceptual impact exerted by watery colossi caught in the act of pulverization. Clearly, what impressed the English and the French alike was their tremendous vertical surging, their fluctuating motion ranging from violent monolithic spurts to fine rain or mist, and their sudden exhaustion as they sank spent beneath the earth.[86] Most tellingly, these observers relished immersing themselves within the phenomenon at the very instant that its erstwhile solidity was being unmade.

Flux and reflux stand at the heart of the ephemeral effect. Flowing water—the traditional domain of waves, and the font of aqueous meteors—had from earliest times entranced man with its rhythmic motion. This agitation, ranging from faint to fierce, was encountered again in spheres of reality lying far beyond the visible, obdurately material world in phenomena that behaved immaterially. Late-eighteenth-century and early-nineteenth-century scientists, including Cotte, Herschel, and Johann Wilhelm Ritter, demonstrated that all palpable and impalpable appearances obeyed the same laws of reflection, refraction, and diffraction.

From Saint Augustine to Dominique Bouhours, the ocean's swell and ebb symbolized not only the immensity of God and the hidden abyss of his wisdom but also the plenitude and purity of his being. The reverse was also true; by virtue of its instability it was emblematic of inconstancy and the vanity of human effort.[87] This latter incarnation, newly interpreted as an instrument for real change, moved the French naval geographer Grandpré. Standing above the flats of Moka, he watched how the sea "visibly withdrew." Indeed, the base on which the mountains of Arabia repose daily liberated itself from the yoke of the ocean: "The sea appears to have abandoned it [the plain] only yesterday. In several places one might say one was on a beach deserted by the reflux. . . ." In typical late-eighteenth-century fashion, Grandpré places these ruminations within an historical perspective. The mind becomes confused when calculating how many centuries must yet pass before the ocean entirely forsakes the coast across from Aden: "The islands and reefs with which it is riddled are so obviously the summits of hills which it slowly vacates; its gradual retreat is so evident, that one cannot fail to impute in advance . . . to whatever epoch, that this vast gulf shall yet be converted into a valley. . . ."

For the benefit of the landscape painter, Valenciennes minutely anatomizes the disorderly energy of breaking water, offering the eye multiple planes that reflect unequally the sky and surrounding objects. The visual confusion and the obvious combative friction of the waves are indicative of "the penetrating power of the surge." This language of nature's self-articulation marks Cordiner's view that the Atlantic "excavated these romantic caverns, and formed the insulated rocks at Caussie" during winter storms unleashed off the coast of Moray. Forrest, contemplating the strange rocks of Colgong in Bengal, notes a similar "singular occurrence" in connection with these boulders, namely, the change in their position with respect to the Ganges:

VOYAGE INTO SUBSTANCE

Some 40 or 50 years earlier, not only were they perched on *terra firma* but they were located considerably inland and remote from the water. The river, having its source in the Himalyas, is subject to periodic vernal and autumnal floods. Therefore its bed, composed of rich alluvial soil, is constantly shifting because of the drive of the current and its soft and yielding banks are incessantly undermined, so that "the work of destruction then is most wonderfully rapid." The rocks of Colgong "owe their present situation to a gradual change of this nature." Though "formerly they were high inland," now they are "in the bosom of the Ganges."[88]

By an extension of vitalist thought, the eighteenth century made of this element the storehouse of tempests, the primal moving force present at the genesis of the world. Through flood and catastrophe, as Maillet propounded in his pseudo-scientific cosmology, water is gradually converted into land. The dramatic and fugitive activities accompanying this turbulence, such as winds, clouds, spouts, and phosphorescence, have been enumerated. Occasionally, however, the storm, taken in its pervasive or overarching totality, manages to emancipate itself in some degree from being either a repository for meteors or the stereotypical embodiment of deluge and cataclysm. Chappe d'Auteroche, in Siberia, captured the first intimations of an imminent perturbation, announced unmistakably despite the apparent serenity of the atmosphere. Suddenly, it became difficult to breathe; the reigning calm grew heavy into a physical oppressiveness. Toward noon "an exceedingly dark cloud appeared on the horizon"; "insensibly it rose," followed by rumblings, strong winds, dust devils, and lightning, until finally the sun grew wan. William Hodges's illustrations prominently feature turbid, squally conditions, whether occurring inland on Easter Island or off the Cape of Good Hope. (See figures 52 and 95.) Bernardin de Saint-Pierre chronicles the history of a gale experienced at sea in June of 1768. At daybreak, from the bridge, he observed several white and copper-colored clouds speeding across the sky. The wind blew hard from the west, where the horizon gleamed fiery red as if the sun were about to rise; perversely, the east remained stubbornly black. "The sea formed monstrous crests resembling peaked mountains composed of several ranges of hills. From their summits shot large jets of foam tinted in rainbow hues. . . . The wind made such a roar in the rigging that it was impossible to hear oneself speak. . . ." At sunrise, the gusts redoubled their efforts and "clouds of foam" inundated the decks. Analogously, Basil Hall, during a stopover on volcanic Sulphur Island en route to Korea, encountered sullen weather, high wind, and pounding surf, whose lowering quality William Havell captured in aquatint for the frontispiece to Hall's account. Krusenstern, upon leaving Alaska and sailing for Japan, ran afoul of "a great typhoon": "The waves ran mountain high from the southeast; the sun was of a dead pale colour, and was soon concealed behind the clouds which flew with rapidity from the same quarter, and the wind. . . . Nothing could equal the violence of the gale. Much as I had heard of the typhons [sic] on the Chinese and Japanese coasts, this exceeded all my expectations. . . ."[89]

THE FUGITIVE EFFECT

The Universe in Process

Vesuvius itself, in the background of the scene, discharging volumes of fire and smoak, and forming a broad track in the air over our heads, extending without being broken or dissipated to the utmost verge of the horizon. . . .
Patrick Brydone

. . . ses glaces d'une blancheur éblouissante, dressées en forme de hautes pyramides, sont un effet étonnant au milieu des forêts de Sapins qu'elles traversent & qu'elles surpassent. On voit enfin de loin le grand glacier des Bois, qui en descendant se recourbe contre la vallée de Chamouni . . . Les glaciers majestueux, séparés par des grandes forêts, couronnés par des rocs de Granit d'une hauteur étonnante, qui sont taillés en forme de grands obélisques, & entremêlés de neiges & de glaces, présentent un des plus grands & des plus singuliers spectacles qu'il soit possible d'imaginer. . . .
Horace-Bénédict de Saussure

From a consideration of the sea not merely as an arena or background where aqueous meteors combat but as the seat of epochal change, it follows that the cataract can also function visually as an active agent, if not independent of then at least apart from the "everlasting incense" of its haze. The role of erosion in "sculpting" the globe was realized as early as Leonardo, who noted the importance of running water in modifying the earth's surface. However, eighteenth-century theorists—whether espousing fluvialism or catastrophism—were most cognizant of this powerful activity in its destructive, rapid, and grandiose manifestations: torrents, rivers, and avalanches.

In this spirit, continental travelers (one thinks primarily but not exclusively of Goethe and Etienne Pivert de Senancour) were always remarking on waterfalls. Caspar Wolf, a student of Aberli's who received part of his training in Paris under de Loutherbourg, produced his artistic masterpiece in 1775. Wolf's "Gallery" of views taken in the Bernese Alps, the *Merkwürdige Prospekte aus den Schweizer Gebürgen und Derselben Beschreibung*, reproduced the mountain world. Like his compatriot Albrecht von Haller, who contributed a preface, Wolf climbed the high peaks in order to sketch on the spot. Wolf invented a direct and elegantly intricate pictorial language to correspond to the multifarious "unpaintable" effects of cascades and avalanches. Avoiding the establishment of distance through one-point perspective, he brought the structural properties of the Staubbach at Lauterbrunnen close up. He seized the metamorphic nature of water, portraying it as flowing, trickling, spraying, falling, and even murmuring within stone hollows. The Pisse-Vache near Saint Moritz continued to lure a host of voyagers during the following century. Major Cockburn dwells not upon its palpable spray, as did so many others, but on its recurring plunge, "precipitating perpendicularly from the summit of a stupendous mountain"—an attribute also noted by Webber at Sallanche.[90]

The torrents of Scandinavia vied with those of Switzerland, receiving precise and enthusiastic study by William Coxe, John Boydell, and Boisgelin de Kerdu. Even earlier, Skjöldebrand devoted his attention to the cataracts and canal of Trollhätta (1804). Of special interest is Skjöldebrand's description of the fall at Toppö. Its furious headlong pitch is caused by the disruptive obstacle of an abrupt and folded rock, forcibly compressing the stream's flow and squeezing it downward into a precipice. The optical analysis of the sluice of Polhem presents the moment after, when, freed of all obstruction, its luminous surface unified into a transparent green sheet mingled with tendrils of foam, it strikes the chasm's boulders and shatters into an ascending billow of snow. Boisgelin de Kerdu corroborates the accuracy of Skjöldebrand's observations and transcribes almost verbatim his perceptive remarks on naturally induced effects that "appear and disappear in the twinkling of an eye."[91] Another example may be taken from Louis-François Cassas's 1802 voyage to Istria and Dalmatia. This artist, explorer, architect, and archeologist had his career intimately

Figure 169
D. Vivant-Denon, *Luxor at Dawn* and *Luxor in a Hurricane*, from *Voyage dans la Haute et la Basse Egypte*, 1801, II, pl. 47. Engraving by Baltart. Photo courtesy British Library.

Figure 171
John Webber, *The Nan Darpenaz Waterfall*, from *Sketchbook*, B.M. Add. MS 17, 277, fol. 59. Watercolor. Photo courtesy British Library.

Figure 170
Caspar Wolf, *First Fall of the Staubbach*, from *Vues remarquables de la Suisse*, second edition, 1785. Color aquatint by J. F. Janinet. Photo courtesy Cabinet des Estampes, Bibliothèque Nationale.

bound up with the popularity of the illustrated travel book. His tour of the Dalmatian coast, financed by a group of connoisseurs headed by the Emperor Joseph II, resulted in the sketching of many singularities, both natural and artificial. Chief among the former were the "violent" Kerka River and the Falls of Scardona. Like the previously cited travelers, he discusses in fluidly sculptured terms both the falls and the abyss where the Ruecca is disgorged. The "mobile surface of the waves" acquires a "polish" deriving from its velocity and thus rivals the purest crystal. From a distance, all harsh angles appear rounded and the beholder believes he is gazing at translucent cylinders.[92]

Such observations were revoiced by explorers to more remote and exotic regions. On the island of New Britain, Bougainville and his crew intentionally made an expedition to view a "marvelous cascade" which "art would struggle in vain to reproduce for the palace of a king," although "nature has discarded [it] here in an uninhabited corner of the world." He particularly admired the ropy clusters rending and splitting the monolithic aspect of the fall. These liquid "massifs" dug a hundred multiform basins brimming with a transparent fluid tinged by the color of surrounding trees. The implication of an inherent shaping force also informs Cook's account of a visit paid in the company of Hodges to a springing cascade on Dusky Bay: "Huge heaps of stones lay at the foot of this cascade, which had been broken off and brought by the stream from the adjacent mountains. . . . I brought away specimens of every sort, as the whole country, that is, the rocky part of it, seemed to consist of those stones and no other. . . ." Georg Forster remarks that the falls at Cascade Cove "gushed" from lofty heights to coalesce "in a clear column" emerging from the penumbra of a shaggy, overhanging wood.[93]

But North America contained the most spectacular and massive hieroglyph of a perennially active flood. Father Hennepin in the 1680s, and Jonathan Carver a century later, recorded many amazing bodies of water hurtling down countless precipices. None exceeded Niagara in terms of dynamic character. The French diplomat and author François-Auguste-René de Chateaubriand faithfully chronicles every stage of his journey toward that phenomenon: camping in forests primeval and subsisting in solitudes, finally to behold the majesty that "effaces all others." George Heriot, traveling through the Canadas, probes the "extent and depth of the precipitating waters," the "ceaseless intumescence and swift agitation of the dashing waves below," and the "solemn and tremendous noise." Jacques Milbert, a student of Valenciennes who visited the United States in 1815, fell under the spell of many of its falls, but he, like Isaac Weld, found words and brush hopelessly inadequate to render this vitalistic marvel of nature. Milbert pinpoints the difficulty intrinsic to portraying such unpaintable ephemera: the impossibility of "securing its effects." This moving tableau shifts continuously before one's eyes. The passage of a cloud, the intrusion of a more brilliant ray of sunlight, the advent of dawn or dusk, calm or wind—all these natural phenomena, in themselves fugacious, produce "modifications in the [waterfall's equally natural and multiple] effects." Hence, even the best description or illustration of the color and shape of this fluid giant appears false after a few moments.[94]

This lament of art's insufficiency in unrolling a panorama or focusing on an aspect threads its way like a leitmotif through various narratives. When the weather suddenly cleared, Viscount Valentia confronted the waterfall at French Hoek on the Cape of Good Hope and watched its waters heave through a cleft in the mountains. At first, he was vexed by the Fall of the Cauvery, so praised at Madras by persons who had seen it in the rainy season. Yet, even in the absence of water, the impressive dry channels stimulated him to reflect upon the "tremendous force" necessary to tear out huge chunks of earth. If falls could exceed the traveler's expectations, they could also disappoint, as we have just seen. This was never more the case than with legendary cataracts of the Nile. One might justifiably anticipate that, after cutting a swath through Abyssinia and Nubia with its magnitude increased by various tributary streams, the Nile's descent would be powerfully accelerated. Indeed, at different places and to some extent it is. However, when its course becomes confined to a narrow valley wedged between two mountain ridges in the neighborhood of Assouan, the fabled last cataract is no more than a rapid. Pococke did little to disguise his frustration: "I ask'd [the inhabitants] when we should come to the cataract, and to my great surprize they told me, that *was* the cataract. . . ." Mayer and Vivant-Denon found its reputation to be equally out of proportion with reality. Tumbling over the same granite rocks that constituted the famed quarries of Thebes from which its colossi were hewn, the great Nile's fall is only several inches. Vivant-Denon complains that the trickle is barely visible and difficult to draw. However, he was moved by the black mountains somberly reflected in that constricted portion of the river, and he assures the reader that a beautiful painting might well result from this subject—captured in its characteristic colors— because it "would provide the singular advantage of offering at one and the same time a true and novel image of nature."[95]

Such, in brief, was the empirical orientation toward the imperishable, if mutable, current. This perspicuity was not limited to water. William Hamilton depicts a lava stream issuing from Mount Vesuvius and running toward Resina as "a beautiful cascade of fire more than fifty feet perpendicular falling and escaping pure and in its fluid state from under the Scoriae"; it "fell into the hollow way, and produced the finest effect, that can possibly be imagined." This stream was no less lovely when its former liveliness hardened into prismatic basalt or fractured obsidian gashing the hillside. Subterranean flowstone creeping down grotto walls was described in an idiom that similarly coincided with its instability. Countless congelations, varied to infinity and seemingly on the verge of yet another transformation, intrigued the scientific travelers. Since the publication of

Figure 172
A. F. Skjöldebrand, *Fall at Toppö*, from
*Description des cataractes et du canal
Trollhätta en Suède*, 1804, pl. 3. Aquatint.
Photo courtesy British Library.

Figure 173
A. F. Skjöldebrand, *The Cascade at the
Sluice of Polhem*, from *Description des
cataractes et du canal de Trollhätta en
Suède*, 1804, pl. 4. Aquatint. Photo
courtesy British Library.

VOYAGE INTO SUBSTANCE

Figure 174
Thomas Fraser, *The Great Falls of the Cauvery River, Sivasamudram (Madras)*, ca. 1800. Watercolor W.D. 365. Photo courtesy India Office Library.

Figure 175
James Manson, *View of the Road from Namik to the Village of Sune*, from *Twelve Drawings of Almorah*, 1826, pl. 9. Color aquatint. Photo courtesy British Library.

THE FUGITIVE EFFECT

Figure 176
D. Vivant-Denon, *Cataracts of the Nile*,
from *Voyage dans la Haute et la Basse
Egypte*, 1801, II, pl. 69. Engraving by Paris.
Photo courtesy British Library.

Romé de l'Isle's *Cristallographie* in 1783, stalactite drapery, coagulating into pendant shapes and undulating masses, was interpreted as the confused and stammering first utterance in the long evolutionary process of mineralization, in matter's painful growth toward articulateness. In short, these concretions actively struggling against the encroaching forces of petrification hourly continue to enact the battle waged originally within the primordial waters of chaos.[96]

If falls, by definition and irrespective of their substance, invariably trace an insistently downward trajectory, volcanos perpetually consume themselves in an innate and unpredictable upward motion. As in the case of so many eighteenth-century scientific interpretations of ephemera, including fireballs, auroras, earthquakes, whirlwinds, and phosphorescences, electricity was hypothesized as the vital force stoking this deadly furnace. Never was a phenomenon simultaneously more duplicitous and seductive. If extinct, it left behind a rich and fertile soil; if active, it constantly menaced destruction. In either instance, its transitory visible signs hint at a hidden order, a cosmic energy lodged deep within the earth. This interpretation existed in essence in Athanasius Kircher's *Mundus subterraneus* (1655). The Jesuit polymath speculated on a wide range of recondite subjects, including the deep-seated formation of volcanos and the eruptive physiognomy of the sun, to which he devoted splendid portraits in section. Eighteenth-century thinkers, however, were particularly intrigued by the fact that, unlike mountain chains, volcanos had not always existed. In the words of Valenciennes (who relied on the expertise of Faujas de Saint-Fond), they are born, develop, and disappear when no longer nourished by an underground fire.

Ancient ravages and continuing convulsions were notably evident in Sicily. By the middle of the eighteenth century, southern Italy had developed into a laboratory for travelers like Patrick Brydone, William Hamilton, Henry Swinburne, the Marquis de Foresta, and the Comte de Forbin, who earnestly sought matter's deeds recorded as cataclysm.[97] The proliferating studies produced by professional or amateur volcanologists must be distinguished from the genre of volcano painting that flourished at Naples and elsewhere during the eighteenth and nineteenth centuries. These artificial displays of light, more reminiscent of fireworks than of nature's operations, led a hearty aesthetic life from the days of de Marchis, Vernet, and Volaire. Akin to the "burning cities" motif of Mannerist set designs and to the infernal landscapes of Bosch and Brueghel, their purpose is ostentatious display of artistic effects rather than probing scrutiny.[98]

Prime instances of the latter are William Hamilton's trenchant descriptions and Peter Fabris's studied aquatints, prepared under the British Consul's watchful direction, of the eruptions of Vesuvius observed daily at close

THE FUGITIVE EFFECT

Figure 177
William Hamilton, *Part of the View inside the Mountain of Somma,* from *Campi Phlegraei,* 1776, II, pl. 35. Color aquatint by Peter Fabris. Photo courtesy British Library.

Figure 180
A. Kircher, *The Volcanic Face of the Sun,*
from *Mundus Subterraneus,* 1664–65, pl. p.
64. Engraving. Photo courtesy Library of
Congress.

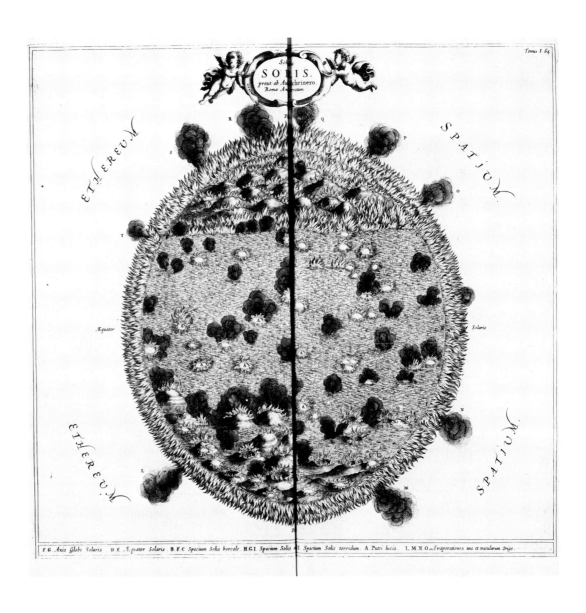

Figure 181
A. Kircher, *Mount Vesuvius*, from *Mundus Subterraneus*, 1664–65, pl. 1. Engraving. Photo courtesy Library of Congress.

　　　　THE FUGITIVE EFFECT

hand or from a distance in 1767, 1776, 1777, and 1779. None of the electric and catapulting aspects eluded Hamilton. These became especially evident at night. When an eruption is imminent, "the smoke often comes out in a circular form . . . and this ring enlarges till it is lost." Taking a sketch from the ocean of the towering promontory called Capo dell'Arco in the Island of Ventotiene, some 30 miles from Ischia, Hamilton remarks on the likelihood that all these islands represent only the ruins of the cone of the parent caldera, the greater part of which has been worn away by the sea. Hamilton also clambered into the dormant crater of the mountain of Somma, "to give a more precise idea of those very curious horizontal and perpendicular strata of lava."

Patrick Brydone's *Tour through Sicily and Malta* (1770) echoed the British Consul's triumphant espousal of willed seeing and sublimity, thus forcibly substantiating the aesthetic component of science and the scientific complement of art. And again, it is the volcano that most profoundly stimulates the "truly philosophic eye." Brydone marvels that, although Etna and Vesuvius often lie dormant for many months, even years, without the least appearance of fire, "Stromboli is ever at work, and for ages past has been looked upon as the great light-house of these seas." "It is truly wonderful," he goes on, "how such a constant and immense fire is maintained for thousands of years, in the midst of the ocean. That of the Lipari islands seems now almost extinct, and the source of the whole seems concentrated in Stromboli; which acts as one great vent to them all. . . ." Jean-Pierre Houel devoted numerous gouaches, destined for the monumental *Voyage pittoresque des isles de Sicile* (1782), to these Aeolian Islands of antiquity. (See figure 128.) His oculuslike view peels back the successive structural layers, revealing them to be the visible result of subterranean fire. Houel was equally arrested by transitory environmental effects, all that "the winds might bring about . . . the accidents of light and shade, the reflection of the waters [these are necessary] if one desires a complete idea of the admirable tableau one enjoys on this shore. . . ."[99] Despite the title of his work, he voices the intent of plumbing the real foundations of the world, thus sharing in Hamilton's natural-history venture.

Inseparable from the volcanic researches conducted in Sicily were the concurrent forays being made into the Auvergne. As early as 1768 the French geologist Nicolas Desmarest introduced his epoch-making ideas on the volcanic origin of basalt, soon transmitted to Germany via Raspe and Goethe. This momentous conclusion, which challenged the notion that basalt was a sedimentary rock, spurred numerous explorations of regions hitherto left unassessed. Faujas de Saint-Fond, by the publication of *Les volcans éteints* (1778), singlehandedly converted the Auvergne into a volcanologist's laboratory. Through materially dense and highly particularized illustrations by (among others) Fabien Gautier Dagoty and De Veyrene, idiosyncratic crags, pitted scoriae, burnt crevices, and fissures, glassy streams of lava and tilted hexagonal prisms became France's rejoinder to Southern Italy's adamantine effects. Faujas depicts the *Roche-Rouge* or the *Chateau de Rochemaure*, towering above the Rhone, as basaltic buttes suddenly and vehemently extruded—not as resting upon the formidable granite bands through which they had to pass.[100]

The basalt controversy infiltrated other types of scientific voyage literature as well. Alexander von Humboldt, contemplating the serene regularity of the cone of Cotopaxi, was struck all the more by the presence to the southwest of a disjunctive rock mass bristling with needles. A popular tradition insisted that this isolated "Head of the Incas" had once been part of the Andean giant's summit, but that in the first eruption this fragment had been ejected to its present position. (See figure 56.) Humboldt carefully documents further the visible effects of Cotopaxi's choleric temperament: its surface, everywhere littered with conspicuous piles of broken stones; its ominous rumbles; its intermittent spewing of ash.

Besides gaping craters vomiting lava, or some equally violent effect,[101] the image of the jutting, raggedly contoured volcanic island was frequently pressed into visual service. The eighteenth-century voyagers were especially prone to studying nature in the act of giving birth to land. Indeed, it was such narratives that bolstered Desmarest's argument that basalt was an igneous rock. Georg Forster, on Huahine (part of the Society Islands group) and on Tanna in the New Hebrides, recognized battered slopes as the former seats of volcanos. In fact, when he landed at Tanna in August 1774, he "saw the flame of the volcano in the evening blazing up, with an explosion once in five minutes or thereabouts." "The transactions of the day," writes Forster, "prevented my speaking of this wonderful phaenomenon, though it was in continual agitation. . . ." Sparrman adds that throughout Cook's stay the volcano showered ash on the crew. Yet he exults in total immersion: "The smoke, flame, and loud thunder proceeding from this mountain, afforded a beautiful and sublime spectacle. . . ." Langle (the commander of the *Etoile* on the La Pérouse expedition), like the British before him, was convinced that Easter Island was of volcanic origin and discerned the remnants of an ancient cone at its southernmost tip.

These relations promulgated the even grander judgment that all the Edenic islands of the Pacific Ocean were but the eroding summits of once active craters and periodically emerged from or subsided into the sea. Not only here but elsewhere we hear the reverberating echo of the myth of Atlantis. Bernardin de Saint-Pierre cites the commonly held opinion that the Canaries, with their valiant relic, the Peak of the Teneriffe, are the debris of Plato's drowned continent. Le Gentil, steeped in the geological writings of Buffon, examined the blackened terrain of the Ile de France; he concluded that it had suffered some concussive shock and that at some remote date all the stones chaotically strewn over its surface had been flung by a volcano.[102]

Figure 182
William Hamilton, *Eruption of Mount
Vesuvius on Monday Morning, August 9,
1779*, from *Campi Phlegraei, Supplement,*
1779, pl. 3. Color aquatint by Peter Fabris.
Photo courtesy British Museum.

Figure 183
William Hamilton, *View of the Great
Eruption of Vesuvius Sunday Night, August
8, 1779*, from *Campi Phlegraei, Supplement,*
1779, pl. 2. Color aquatint by Peter Fabris.
Photo courtesy British Library.

Figure 184
William Hamilton, *The Promontory called Capo dell'Arco*, from *Campi Phlegraei*, 1776, II, pl. 34. Color aquatint by Peter Fabris. Photo courtesy British Library.

THE FUGITIVE EFFECT

Figure 185
B. Faujas de Saint-Fond, *Basaltic Crag of
Roche-Rouge*, from *Recherches sur les
volcans éteints*, 1783, pl. 19. Engraving by
Claude Fessard after a drawing by De
Veyrene. Photo courtesy British Library.

Figure 186
B. Faujas de Saint-Fond, *Chateau de
Rochemaure*, from *Recherches sur les volcans
éteints*, 1783, pl. 2. Engraving by P. C. Le
Bas after drawing by A. F. Gautier-Dagoty.
Photo courtesy British Library.

Fig.1 *Vue de l'Isle de Baziluzzo* A. *et de l'Ecueil de Dattalo* B.

Dessiné et gravé par J. Houel.

Fig. 2   *Ecueil de Strombolino.*

Figure 187
J. Houel, *Baziluzzo, Dattalo, and Strombolino,* from *Voyage pittoresque des isles de Sicile, de Malte et de Lipari,* 1782, I, pl. 69. Aquatint. Photo courtesy British Library.

Figure 188.
John Webber, *Three Views of Arched Point
on Kerguelen's Land [Island of Desolation]*
(December 1776), from James Cook's
Voyage to the Pacific Ocean, 1784, I, pl. 82.
Engraving. Photo courtesy Library of
Congress.

Figure 189
William Hodges, *Oaetepha Bay, Tahiti*, Oil.
36 1/2 × 54 1/2 inches. Photo courtesy
National Maritime Museum.

Figure 190
G. Tobin, *Santa Cruz, in the Island of
Teneriffe*, 1791. Engraving by Wells. Photo
courtesy National Maritime Museum.

Nor was the far north neglected. One reason Banks sailed for Iceland in 1772 although it could not possibly rival the utopian expectations elicited by the South Seas was that its volcano beckoned. George MacKenzie and Eugène Robert, similarly bound, report on the first sight of a stream of lava near Thingvellir:

The melted mass had been heaved up in every direction, and had assumed all sorts of fantastic forms; on every side chasms and caverns presented themselves. . . . Beyond this spot we saw the most dreadful effects of subterraneous heat all around us; and as far as the eye could reach over a wide extended plain nothing appeared to relieve it from the black rugged lava, which had destroyed the whole of the district. The surface was swelled into knobs from a few feet in diameter to forty or fifty, many of which had burst, and disclosed caverns lined with melted matter in the form of stalactites. . . .

John Edy records Norway's towering, unheaved terrain, punctuated by talus slides, and analogously, he comments on the numerous occasions when volcanic eruptions in the surrounding sea result in islands. The Danish government was so keenly interested in this phenomonen that when one suddenly appeared in the spring of 1783, all ships bound for Iceland were given the order to "examine the newly formed island." However, "so entirely had it vanished, that none of them either saw, or could discover the slightest trace of it. . . ."[103]

A disconcerting aftereffect of eruptions, producing greater consternation than smoke and flame, was the earthquake. As Lisbon demonstrated in 1755 and Caracas in 1812, its tremendous energy was indiscriminately murderous. And yet two decades later the catastrophes that wrecked Messina, burned Calabria, and activated the craters of Iceland were classified among the scientific marvels of the age.

Although the transitory movements of the earthquake defy illustration, its accompanying conditions of desolation, dust, and ruin were rendered. It was supposed by geologists that, apart from God's wrath, there was a physical cause behind the destruction of Lisbon. Subterranean grottos defying the age-old conception of a *terra firma* lurked beneath its soil, ready to cave in. The mineralogist Déodat de Dolomieu, speaking of Etna, lucidly outlines the manner in which lava forms underground galleries: When the molten matter that pushed its way upward from the earth's core to lodge just below the crust sinks once more, it leaves behind extensive vacant chambers. These were recognized to exist the world over. In time, as part of nature's perpetual transformations, the hollows slowly fill with calcareous deposits until that unpredictable moment when the terrible process repeats itself.[104]

Bourrit recalled that on the occasion of the Lisbon disaster the Swiss Alps near Simplon had tottered on their foundations and the entire valley had shaken from north to south, yawning wide at several locations. A decade earlier, Chambers had surveyed the inaccessible and needle-like boulders

Figure 191
John Edy, *View in Torredal River*, from
Boydell's Scenery of Norway, 1820, I, pl. 11.
Color aquatint. Photo courtesy British
Library.

Figure 192
Anonymous, *Lisbon Earthquake*. Engraving.
Photo courtesy National Maritime
Museum.

THE FUGITIVE EFFECT

of Tierra del Fuego, whose bedrock was cleaved by crevices. Not surprisingly, he had judged that they must have been formed by earthquakes, since their flanks were almost perpendicular and they seemed to have cracked the primitive core supporting them. Dom Pernety, on the Malouine Islands in 1769, actually survived such a cataclysm; despite the experience, he admired "nature's prodigious effects" and wondered how all those rocks of varying sizes, tumbling helter-skelter, had managed to arrange themselves in a negligent semblance of order. William Hodges, during the course of his travels in India, had many occasions to observe fissures, broken strata, and shattered granite resulting from "the horrid crush and downfall of mountains." Alexander Laborde remarked that just such a monolith, rived from its parent by an earthquake, was set up in the garden at Morfontaine. This rock was deemed worthy of having a strophe, taken from "Les jardins" of the Abbé Delille, carved on its face: "Its indestructible mass has wearied time."[105]

From the vantage of the preceding discussion, it is instructive to analyze the fascination the glacier held for the eighteenth-century explorers. Like the volcano and the earthquake, the glacier—by the sheer variety of its activities—had the capacity to elicit a sentiment that lies at the heart of scientific curiosity: astonishment. Like them, it could be a potent, though intermittent, instrument of havoc. In contrast with the previously mentioned catastrophes, however, detailed descriptions of glaciers are rather rare before our period. Peter Martel, in 1749, published an early account of the great Savoyan colossi. In the 1760s Gottlieb Siegmund Gruner compiled what others had written earlier, producing the first great theory of glaciology, and from 1775 on Bourrit was primarily a discoverer of new glaciers. But of overriding importance were the ascents, which multiplied after 1780, spurred by Saussure's continuing researches into the mysteries of Mont Blanc. Early frontal illustrations of the Mer de Glace, the Glacier des Bossons, the Bernina, and the Grindelwald accentuated their appearance as encroaching, turreted seas of ice, frozen agglomerations resembling a petrified hurricane or a creeping saurian monster.

The natural-history notes accompanying Caspar Wolf's *Vues remarquables des montagnes de la Suisse* shed important light on the growing recognition of various types of glacier morphology. When snow is congealed in a valley, it forms a monolithic, level mass, much like a flattened ridge. On the other hand, when the highest summits themselves are linked by an icy crust or *Firn* containing dangerous vaults and bridges, it imitates a stormy ocean that suddenly froze with all the waves in a crest position. Ice thus constantly building up finally shatters and cascades into even lower valleys, impelled by a precipitating torrent.

Glaciers must also be placed within the context of climatic history. At the beginning of the eighteenth century, alpine glacier retreat was limited to

500 meters per year, in comparison with the twentieth-century rate of 1–2 kilometers. Furthermore, in 1700 there was no worldwide universal regression, such as exists today; only a modest regional reflux. Strong glacial activity took place in the period between 1550 and 1760; in fact, this was its maximal age. In general, it may be asserted that the epoch before 1850 witnessed majestic dimensions and immense masses that were lost later. A case in point is that of the Mer de Glace at Chamonix. From the eighteenth century up to and including the time when John Ruskin gazed upon its choppy splendor, this glacier was not, as it is now, hidden behind the somber rocks of Mottet. Instead, it persistently spread, intruding upon the hamlet of Bois and remaining clearly visible from the plain of the Arve. The Glacier des Bossons, the Glacier d'Argentière, and the Grindelwald also extended menacingly into the countryside.[106]

These growing, agitated, and steadily advancing giants were captured in numerous travel studies. Caspar Wolf focuses not only on the effect of this imposing progression but also on the surging subglacial torrents of the Arveyron, forcing its way between the glaciers of Argenière and Rosière, and the Lutschine, pushing from beneath the Grindelwald. Nor does he neglect the by-product of this coursing stream; he depicts the ancient yet continuously waxing moraine formed of enormous boulders chaotically heaped on the shore. The conjoined image of desolation and dissolution also crops up in Bourrit's *Nouvelles description des vallées de la Suisse* (1778) and in his *Description des aspects du Mont Blanc* (1783) precisely in conjunction with these accumulating mounds of shattered stone: "What is most striking is the aspect of these piles or beds of ice that descend from on high to the bottom. . . . Their curious debris [adds] to the rich productions of the valley. The most conspicuous of these conglomerations imitates a city laid waste: one glimpses towers, pyramids, obelisks. . . . The most magnificent part of this representation remains the dazzling shimmer, the whiteness and transparency of these objects when the sun darts its rays. . . ."

An evanescent consequence of glacial energy was the ice cavern filled with massive hummocks and greenly glinting stalactites. The Grotte de Glace at Chamonix, with its diamond walls and incessantly changing "rooms," impressed beholders such as Martel, Aberli, Wolf, and Laborde with the powerful drama of nature.[107]

Although glaciers existed not only in Switzerland, Austria, and Dalmatia but were part of the general scenery of the far north, the calamitous view of them as agents of demolition was firmly attached to the Savoyan in-carnations.[108] Glacier catastrophes as well as volcanic eruptions continued throughout the eighteenth century and enhanced the view of a world in ceaseless upheaval. Without the intervention of man, they changed the face of the land by means of inundations and avalanches. Travelers to other portions of the globe, such as Bashō in the seventeenth century and

Figure 194
G. S. Gruner, *The Mer de Glace*, from *Die Eisgebirge des Schweizerlandes*, 1760, pl. 12. Engraving by A. Zingg after drawing by F. Meyer. Photo courtesy British Library.

Figure 195
G. S. Gruner, *The Bernina Glacier*, from *Die Eisgebirge des Schweizerlandes*, 1760, pl. 17. Engraving by A. Zingg after drawing by G. Walser. Photo courtesy British Library.

THE FUGITIVE EFFECT

Figure 196
Caspar Wolf, *Lauteraar Glacier*, from *Vues remarquables de la Suisse*, second edition, 1785, pl. 19. Color aquatint by J. F. Janinet. Photo courtesy Library of Congress.

GLACIER DE   LAUTERAAR;
Canton de Berne   Province d'Oberhasli.

Dédié à Madame la   Baronne d'Erlach de Spietz.

LA LUTSCHINEN SORTANT DU GLACIER INFÉRIEUR DU GRINDELWALD.

Canton de Berne, Province d'Interlaken.

Figure 197
Caspar Wolf, *Grindelwald Glacier with the
Lutschine,* from *Vues remarquables de la
Suisse,* second edition, 1785. Color aquatint
by C.-M. Descourtis. Photo courtesy
Library of Congress.

Figure 199
Anonymous, *Ice Grotto in the Glacier des Bossons*. Eighteenth century. Etching. Photo courtesy Cabinet des Estampes, Bibliothèque Nationale.

THE FUGITIVE EFFECT

the Marquis de Chastellux in the eighteenth century, drew attention to the power of landslides. Whether occurring in Japan or North America, it was evident they could alter the course of rivers, obliterate roads, and bury human handiwork. They left behind immense rocks as historic and vivid monuments to an unstable past and as potential crucibles for a refashioned future. In the Swiss Alps, rockfalls and avalanches were complementary phenomena.[109]

Sebastien Mercier brooded over the apparently stable beauty of the mountains above Neufchâtel, from whence he predicted would issue the decimation of the seemingly peaceful countryside. The subversionary theme of toppled rocks, of "rude, resistless ruins," in the words of Major Cockburn, Raoul-Rochette, and Hilaire Sazerac, recalls the pictorial contrast frequently evoked by volcanologists between Sicily's perishable fertility and its annihilating lava streams. Gruner, in the *Histoire naturelle des glaciers de Suisse* (1760), gives an eyewitness account of such a radical and instantaneous razing. One summer day in 1756, he heard an ominous thunderclap;

As I looked around with surprize, from the highest peak of the Wetterhorn covered with perpetual ice, I saw a chunk of snow detach itself and fall from on high down to the scarped slope of the first summit. One portion rose like dust; the other dashed like a swift torrent against a rock projecting from the center of the mountain: Again, this concussion caused a kind of mist to ascend, & the remainder of this enormous mass tumbled to the foot of the mountain. . . .

Caspar Wolf, on the Eiger, also to the accompaniment of noisy peals, witnessed obliterating snowfalls or *Schneelavinen* career from the highest rocks and spring over crevices until they finally crashed into the valley below where, in a twinkling, they burst into foaming water. Johann Georg Sulzer sounds the note of abrupt erasure and resurgence so prevalent in accounts of volcanic islands; yet the talus on which the traveler to Switzerland is forced to walk reminds him more of the Biblical flood, for what is this cultivatable land but the result of the caducity of mountains?[110]

The broader conception of an energized nature, firmly grounded in Newtonianism and the related contributions of eighteenth-century geology, physics, chemistry, natural history, and astronomy, provided the underpinnings for the rational, not merely fearful, fathoming of glaciers and avalanches. Glaciers too were made to fit within the sometimes violent but always force-filled order of the universe. As with all the ephemera dealt with in this chapter, travelers strained to be present at every phase of their evolution, but most particularly at their inception. This holds true when we examine the related event of iceberg formation (that is, the fragmentation of glaciers) in the Antarctic and the Arctic. Vaster and more desolate than the Alpine world, the harsh polar environment nevertheless attracted passionate exploration. We have seen how its luminous meteors

LA GROSSE PIERRE SUR LE   GLACIER DE VORDERAAR
Canton de Berne   Province d'Oberhaßi.

Dediée à M.le Comte de Meuron   *Chambellan de S. M.e Prussienne.*
Colonel proprietaire d'un Regiment   *Suisse au Service de Hollande.*

Par son tres humble Serviteur et Ami B. hentzi.

Figure 200
Caspar Wolf, *The Great Rock on the
Vorderaar Glacier*, from *Vues remarquables
de la Suisse*, second edition, 1785. Color
aquatint by J. F. Janinet and C.-M.
Descourtis. Photo courtesy Library of
Congress.

could assume strange, almost supernatural forms, at once stunning and terrifying. Now we revert to it as a land of silence or fearful sounds, purged of any living thing. The inhumanly infinite was made concrete through the multifarious manifestations of ice. William Hodges, on board the *Resolution* in the Antarctic, produced a series of startling watercolors which were subsequently engraved. He profited from the presence of scientists in recording these floating mountains wrecked by the sea. Georg Forster, who on the same voyage counted 186 icebergs from the masthead during a single day, speculates that the cold of the circumambient air was due partly to these large frozen masses. Further, he acutely notes the inherent polyvalency of such bodies that are both stable and yet perpetually eroded by the spray, pounding density into mist. The elder Forster elaborates on this image of drift and change: "Stupendous large and high ice islands, likewise solid but formed in the most strange manner into points, spires, and broken rocks . . . extended as far as the eye could see. However, it is likewise remarkable, that in different years, seasons, and places of the sea, we found the ice differently situated. . . ." A host of British navigators, including Phipps and Chappell, reproduced these "remarkable icebergs." John Laing, en route to the Spitzbergen, noted how frost sports with crumbling chunks shaping them constantly afresh into "singular forms."[111]

The great classifier of these phenomena, however, was John Ross, who on his voyage of 1818 carried along as lieutenants such celebrated seamen of the future as William Edwin Parry, James Clark Ross, and Edward Sabine. He meticulously distinguished among a pleiad of specific characters possible to frozen matter: bergs, fields, patches, streams, loose ice, sailing ice, brash ice, cakes, and hummocks. From such vivid description emerges a clear picture of felled mountains, sheets without visible boundaries, impassable barriers, projecting tongues, mangled pieces, lumps calved or nipped, decaying or honeycombed ice, ice whose depth is enormous, and (most terrible of all) ice that besets and strands. This incredible variety, immured within a boundless ocean, is captured by Parry amid an "extensive chain" in Baffin's Bay, by Scoresby in search of the elusive Beluga whale on the banks of Newfoundland, "crowded with these wonderful productions of the Frigid Zone . . . ," and by Buchanan nipped in the ice off the Spitzbergen or immobilized in a swell near Flaxman's Island.[112] Ross and his distinguished precursors and followers also shed light on a more delicate fugacity: Crimson snow stained the face of a rugged cliff and "presented an appearance both novel and interesting," and frozen rain created vanishing tubes of crystal.[113]

The chill, paradoxical world of mountains that flow and sheets that drift has a fiery counterpart in the region of moving sands. The botanist Michel Adanson, in his *Histoire naturelle du Sénégale* (1757), vividly conjures up

VOYAGE INTO SUBSTANCE

Figure 201
D. Raoul-Rochette, *Rock Slide*, from *Lettres sur la Suisse*, 1826, II, part III, pl. 11. Lithograph by G. Engelmann after Villeneuve. Photo courtesy Cabinet des Estampes, Bibliothèque Nationale.

Figure 202
William Hodges, *The Ice Islands*, from James Cook's *Voyage towards the South Pole, 1772–1775*, 1777, I, pl. 30. Engraving by B. T. Pouncey. Photo courtesy Newberry Library.

Figure 203
John Ross, *A Remarkable Iceberg*, from *Voyage of Discovery*, 1819, pl. p. 46. Aquatint by R. Havell and Son. Photo courtesy British Library.

Figure 204
John Ross, *Passage through the Ice*, from *Voyage of Discovery*, 1819, pl. p. 46. Aquatint by R. Havell and Son. Photo courtesy British Library.

VOYAGE INTO SUBSTANCE

Figure 205
W. Scoresby, *Beluga or White Whale,* from
An Account of the Arctic Regions . . . , 1820,
II, pl. 14. Engraving by W. and D. Lizars
after drawing by P. Syme. Photo courtesy
British Library.

THE FUGITIVE EFFECT

the scorched and dusty countryside on the left bank of the Niger. Similarly, James Jackson, exploring Morocco, describes "moveable sand impelled by the wind into waves continuously changing their position, resembling the billows of the ocean, and hence aptly denominated a sea of sand," and George Lyon, traveling in North Africa, portrays swirling particles flying about in blinding quantities. Thus, just as volcanos engulf, avalanches encroach, and icebergs beset, these seemingly solid motes dissolve into corporeous energy. Dust storms, urged on by hot winds, spasmodically cancel the contours of such mounds, decomposing them into smoke that darkens the air. James Bruce often braved the *simoon* in the Nubian desert: "I saw from the southeast a haze come, in colour like the purple part of the rainbow, but not so compressed or thick. It did not occupy twenty yards in breadth and was about twelve feet high from the ground. It was a kind of blush upon the air, and it moved very rapidly, for I scarce could turn to fall upon the ground with my head to the northward, when I felt the heat of its current plainly upon my face. . . ." Attendant upon the apparition of the "blue meteor" were translucent pillars of sand. Since the swiftest horse could not carry the caravan out of danger, its members stood riveted to the spot. The effect of this "stupendous sight" was that of a thick wood almost darkening the sun. When the solar rays succeeded in penetrating the gigantic shafts, they transformed them into pillars of fire spangled with stars of gold.

Kotzebue encountered a similar obscuring phenomenon amid the heat and barrenness of Persia's plains, on which not a blade of grass grows to relieve the uniformity. The provoking sameness, in which for weeks on end not a breath of air is felt, was jolted by the continuous and violent blowing of the wind. Enveloping dust, remaining suspended in the air, and whirlwinds, forming dense cylinders nearly reaching to the clouds, rolled over the camp. "It was singular enough that when one of these columns encountered an object offering resistance, it divided into two parts, which again closed after passing the object, and pursued its course. . . ." Clouds of pulverized soil, stirred up by mule convoys making the long summer trek from Mendoza to Buenos Aires, are also typical of the South American pampas.[114]

Such shifting environments are the perfect locus for mirages and optical illusions. Our investigations have now come full circle, since humid vapors and metallic haze are the atmospheric screen on which these impalpabilities are projected. Belzoni, craving water in the Nubian desert, was convinced he saw a still, deep, clear lake, totally unruffled by the wind so that everything rising above it was distinctly reflected. As he approached the pool it became shallow and mobile as a field of grain, and dissolved before the thirsty traveler's eyes.

However, the most "extraordinary phenomenon in the world," as Patrick Brydone unequivocally asserts, is one that has often been observed near

VOYAGE INTO SUBSTANCE

Figure 206
G. F. Lyon, *A Sand Wind on the Desert*, from *Travels in North Africa*, 1821, pl. p. 70. Lithograph by D. Dighton. Photo courtesy British Library.

Figure 207
E. E. Vidal, *Convoy of Wine Mules*, from *Buenos Ayres and Monte Video*, 1820, pl. p. 91. Color aquatint by T. Sutherland. Photo courtesy British Library.

THE FUGITIVE EFFECT

Messina. Only recently investigated with a "philosophical" eye, its true cause was finally assigned in the eighteenth century, although it had been surmised earlier. Ancients and moderns alike often remarked that in the heat of summer, after the sea and air had been disturbed by winds and a perfect calm had followed, there appeared around dawn over the Straits of Messina "a vast variety of singular forms, some at rest, some moving about with great velocity." These shapes gradually became more transparent until just before sunrise they disappeared entirely. This fata morgana was the subject of a learned treatise by the Jesuit Domenico Giardina. In the *Discorso* (1643), Giardina declares that the heavens appear like a kaleidoscopic theater, crowded with a protean host of oscillating things: palaces, woods, gardens, men, and animals. One hypothesis suggested that its cause was some uncommon refraction or reflection of the sun's rays from the water of the straits as it was roiled by various eddies and tides. Brydone, in a more advanced and sophicated age, suspected that its plastic nature was akin to that of the aurora borealis and, like many mercurial natural phenomena, depended on electrical energy. In the Torrid Zone, Bernardin de Saint-Pierre admired an equally unpaintable beauty. At dawn or dusk on Mauritius, he observed the fluctuating spectacle of airy landscapes forming and reforming in the sky. There he encountered by chance dematerialized promontories and steep rocks dissassembled into their constituent prismatic hues.[115]

Watery illusions were a nautical peril. Cook reflects on this danger and the observant role of the mariner who depends on ocular demonstration; how many times had he sailed through seas where lands had been thought to exist and found none? "Though supposed to have been seen by former navigators, at the approach of his ships, [they] sunk into the bosom of the ocean, and like the baseless fabric of a vision left not a rock behind. . . ." Commodore Byron recorded such a shifting "land of fog," sighted on November 12, 1764, lying just beyond Rio de Janeiro. The crew was convinced they perceived an island of great extent covered with blue mountains. Soon, several among them imagined they saw waves crashing on its sandy beach; all of a sudden, what they had taken to be solid ground sank without a trace.

Illusory phenomena took many forms. Le Gentil, skirting the Indian Ocean, was certain he spotted two ghostly sailing vessels. Aeronauts, actually floating along a cloud stream, experienced at first hand how "the sun's rays were reflected amidst these enormous masses of vapour, and caused singular mirages far exceeding the liveliest fancy. . . ." "Nothing on earth [could] be compared to the sublime magnificence of the scene. . . ."[116] The mirage, then, stands at the antipodes from the enduring natural masterpiece. To the beholder of such atmospheric "play" it seems as if the chameleonlike illusion creates itself against the backdrop of a more constant and substantial reality.

VOYAGE INTO SUBSTANCE

In sum: Experiment in science, like discovery of the particulars of this world, offers the best hope for arriving at primary characteristics wedded to their secondary manifestations. Nature's effects exhibit the very activity and structure of matter. The quest for certainty lies at the heart of research and travel after fact. Steering between the uncritical dogmatism of the Scholastics and the modern skepticism of the empiricists, the voyagers labored to see and corporealize the powers of nature as they encountered them. Their search was sanctioned by a premise—increasingly unavoidable since the middle of the seventeenth century—that one must attempt to learn, and to impart (since there is a social component to knowledge), all that is open to human scrutiny.[117]

THE FUGITIVE EFFECT

4   *Landscape Freed of Culture*

*If [the ancients] could gather to-
gether some extraordinary Qualities
of Stones, or Minerals, some Rarities of the Age, the food, the Colour the shapes of Beasts, or some
vertues of Fountains, or Rivers:
They thought, they had perform'd
the chiefest part of Natural Historians . . . [but the Royal Society's work
is] rather a painful digging and toiling in Nature. . . .*
Thomas Sprat

*En admirant tout autant ces grands
et superbes monumens de la nature,
dont les formes, ainsi que les dégra-
dations, sont les époques et les hiér-
oglyphs des temps . . . l'histoire
naturelle, le physique des montagnes, et des vallées, leurs configurations, leur composition, leurs
variétés, leurs accidens, étoient mon
objet, et je ramassois des pierres. . . .*
François Pasumot

This chapter will address two major and interconnected concerns: the eighteenth-century invention of the voyage into phenomena and the si-multaneous discovery of a landscape freed of culture. These exploratory ventures are connected to the attempts to paint an accurate picture of material reality.

Recall that Bacon's reformation of learning involved the injunction to purge the mind of established systems and opinions sanctioned by the ancients. The observer was to return to a sensuous knowledge of natural things based on direct contact with concrete facts and material objects in all incarnations. To that end, Bacon defined irrevocably for the pre-Dar-winian era a program for carrying out a "Natural and Experimental His-tory." Bacon's ideal natural historian, his interpreter of the primary materials of the universe, was to dwell constantly among the data of nature, to be in continual conversancy with the external world. The noble purposes of such a natural history were, as R. F. Jones has indicated, to furnish philosophy with the stuff of true and lawful induction and to eradicate specious metaphysical schemes.

Bacon's democratic conception of this vast undertaking entailed two other ideas that were crucial for the explorers: that no rare intellectual ability was required, and that there was a need for selfless cooperation to advance knowledge. These mutually reaffirming conditions suggested that natural history might be practiced by anyone who was suitably trained in seeing the world's aspects; further, they inspired in a wide range of observers, collecting from the widest sources, a profound desire to contribute tangibly to this far-ranging enterprise.

Bacon's view of the process of gathering information was not entirely sanguine, however. The "Idols" of the Tribe, the Den, and the Marketplace—those mental characteristics, common to all men, by which they conceive of the mind as the measure and truth of reality—tended to bend things into conformity with themselves. Thus the germ of skepticism—which bore much fruit in the thought of Locke, Newton, Voltaire, and Hume—was planted. The "Idols," then, were impediments to certainty based on the recognition that the mind and its faculties are inherently destructive of any drive to find out what is self-sufficiently real in nature.

Notwithstanding that serious epistemological problem, it is significant for our present purpose that Bacon suggested a remedy for these obfuscating psychological factors qualifying perception in the very procedure to be followed by the natural historian: He was to trust the evidence of the senses, not that of precodified meaning provided by reason, thereby guiding and controlling the mind viscerally through observations and experiments. The Baconian imperative to get to the bottom of physical things, made all the more pressing by the awareness of the shallowness of the understanding in the face of the complexity of nature, is mirrored in a leitmotif of the travel account: the profoundly expressed need to penetrate the inward substance of natural particulars, to disclose the history and struggles of an active matter. Stated optimistically, it was thought that the method of inductive discovery—implemented through the process of voyaging *into* matter—would, in the fullness of time, unmask nature.

Inextricably conjoined with the visual archaeology of penetration was the momentous finding—which must be fully credited to the eighteenth century—that the individual components of matter are eloquent of their own history. During the Enlightenment it was no longer simply a question of divinely allegorizing nature, as had been customary from Saint Augustine to Hugh of Saint Victor or as would become typical for the Victorians and the Transcendentalists. Rather, there was the recognition that the myriad particularities of this world constitute a concrete text laying bare to the eye of the natural historian a physical language embedded in marks, traces, images, imprints, and impressions that articulates their innermost substance. In short, they frame a real character, a real allegory of the actual physical formation and evolution of the real world. The natural hieroglyph, from its tersest, most primitive embodiment in the facture of the meanest mineral to its sublimely singular incarnation as aged rock and primeval tree, contains plastic clues lodged within its very medium not only to its own material history but also to the creative manner and method of a detranscendentalized, nonauthorial nature at work.

The freshly discovered value of a "naked," unmetaphoric landscape, disencumbered of human trammels or divine trappings, presents yet another reprise of the nature-versus-art controversy. It was on the threshold of the eighteenth century, at the very moment when empiricist psychology declared the difficulty of ever distinguishing between ourselves and the external world, that the changing shapes of experience were perceived also to lodge contextually within, not outside, matter.

Articulate Phenomena

While the Particles continue entire, they may compose Bodies of one and the same Nature and Texture in all Ages: But should they wear away, or break in pieces, the Nature of Things depending on them, would be changed. Water and Earth, composed of old worn Particles and Fragments of Particles, would not be of the same Nature and Texture now, with Water and Earth composed of entire Particles in the Beginning. And therefore that Nature may be lasting, the Changes of Corporeal Things are to be placed only in the various Separations and new Associations and Motions of these permanent Particles. . . .
Isaac Newton

Pythagore à qui la Nature entière a paru animée, veut graver sur un rocher les scènes dont il vient d'être témoin; le rocher s'anime encore sous le burin qui le mutile, & le philosophe recule de surprise— Quoi! tout est sensible. . . .
De l'Isle de Sales

Behind the discussion of the foregoing chapters are two as yet unarticulated assumptions: that matter is legible and that it is penetrable. Underlying the apprehension of a natural masterpiece is the recognition of it as an archive writ in stone. Complementary to this visual experience of tangible object as pictured text is the acknowledgment of the universe as pervaded by matter's actions or effects.

In the eighteenth century's modifications of or deflections from the traditional ways of looking at nature, the sacred book or manuscript of creation became a secularized text through the findings of geology, chiromantic Signatures were transformed into a system of lithic writing, the Renaissance's valorization of artificial ruins was inverted into an esteem for wholly natural relics, the negative Biblical "chaos" (matter before the infusion of spirit) was redefined positively in scientific theory, and the ancient *topos* of nature sporting was recast such that the ambiguity between art and nature on which the concept pivots was metamorphosed into unequivocal statements made by fossils articulating the virtual history of matter. Further, late-eighteenth-century theories of matter and aesthetics converged in a common point of reference, namely the discourse concerning technique and facture; i.e., the physical "blots" manipulated antithetically by art and nature. These strands will be bound together in the overriding construct of semantic hieroglyph or material character—mineralogic, linguistic, physiognomic, or aesthetic—that structured the eighteenth century's perception of the world.

The metaphor of nature as a book originated with Plotinus, who compares the stars to letters perpetually being inscribed on the heavens or inscribed once and for all and yet moving. The image crops up notably in Dante, Alan of Lille, Francis Bacon, and Shakespeare. During the unfolding of the eighteenth century, however, the meaning of the figure was broadened and laicized to frame a literal geological or mineralogical language. Maillet observes in the *Telliamed* (1784) that the thorough physical investigation of many countries proves the ocean's level was once much higher. He effectively counters the prevailing belief in a universal flood with the declaration that "everything in our earth speaks of the imperceptible fabrication of land, & of the diverse materials which the sea employs." Similarly, Niebuhr, while studying the shores of the Red Sea, notes that there and all along the Arabian coast one encounters telltale "indices," natural signs of the water's withdrawal over the course of centuries. The geologist John Whitehurst, in his *Original State and Formation of the Earth* (1778), makes the case for self-modeling more emphatically. His mind fastens on the forces responsible for shaping the Giant's Causeway. Although no human record has been handed down concerning such a tremendous event, writes Whitehurst, "the history of that fatal catastrophe is faithfully recorded in the book of nature, and in language and characters equally intelligible to all nations, [and] therefore will not admit of a misinterpretation; I mean those stupendous cliffs which environ a part of the Atlantic Ocean. . . . "[1] (See figure 19.)

LANDSCAPE FREED OF CULTURE

That nature as dictionary also "speaks" audibly through its sounding rivers, murmuring springs, and rustling trees represents a traditional phonetic corollary to its being an open book: "To the eyes of the geologist, the earth is animated like a great book, recounting the miracles of past creations; each rock has become a page, sometimes calm or majestic, and sometimes reverberating and terrible . . . [recording] either the slow and tranquil deposits of the ocean . . . or the revolutions and upheavals of mountains."[2]

By the close of the eighteenth century two trends predominated in geology. A theological, "creationist" theory taught how things devolved "vertically" from the moment of their emanation from God and testified to his continuing power. A profane, history-conditioned hypothesis posited that things developed sequentially from and by themselves. A salient feature of the latter system is the interpretation of the earth's history as one of perpetual metamorphosis. From this perspective it is instructive to compare again Whitehurst's view of the Flood with Maillet's cosmic speculations in the *Telliamed*. Whitehurst paints the picture of a remote time when subterranean fire and water first came together. What ensued was "an explosion beyond all human conception," in which "the terraqueous globe being thus burst into millions of fragments . . . must certainly have been thrown into strange heaps of ruins: for the fragments of the strata thus blown up, could not possibly fall together again into their primitive order and regularity." In contrast with this "big bang" theory, Maillet portrays a process of ongoing cosmic dissolution. He claims that if we could but sound the depths of all planets we would uncover evidence of numerous inundations. Our earth, he says, corroborates this hypothesis. Hidden within its flanks are "vestiges of several worlds ranged one on top of the other; entire cities, enduring monuments, & everything that can be found today [existing] on the surface." Successive deluges, not a single Biblical flood, annihilated old worlds and gave birth to new ones; the present globe is not merely the ruin of a destroyed past but the result of an inexorable march forward.[3]

Inseparable from any consideration of eighteenth-century geologic constructs is Buffon's internationally influential *Epoques de la nature* (1778), which presents a relentless view of the earth's evolution from a fiery inception to a frozen extinction, from the first shock of a comet striking the sun to the precisely dated instant when our globe is destined to die. Buffon underlines the linear and irreversible (not the cyclical) nature of this historic trajectory: As the earth gradually cools, heat is constantly discharged into the atmosphere, . . . these factors are responsible for the unleashing of chiliastic havoc.

Not until James Hutton's 1795 *Theory of the Earth* was a fatal blow dealt this vulcanist picture of waning global energy and declining temperature. Hutton, a Scottish geologist, discovers neither beginning nor end to the earth's material continuum, only interdependent events operating within an infinitely stretching horizontality. In describing what befalls minerals in the earth's interior as they rise through volcanic activity, Hutton notes that the "system of universal decay and degradation" does not cease with their elevation above sea level. "It assumes, however, a new direction, and from the moment that they are raised up to the surface, is constantly exerted in reducing them again under the dominion of the ocean. The solidity is now destroyed which was acquired in the bowels of the earth; and as the bottom of the sea is the great laboratory where loose materials are mineralized and formed into stone, the atmosphere is the region where stones are decomposed, and again resolved into earth. . . ." Through the agency of water, then, as "the most active enemy of hard and solid bodies, "all terrestrial formations speak a language easy to be interpreted." Hence, the footsteps of time stamp the works of nature "usually deemed the most permanent, . . . those on which the characters of vicissitudes are most deeply imprinted." Bold and rocky coasts, abrupt contours, deep gulfs, and salient promontories all "mark" the action of the sea. Though he follows a Neptunist tack, Hutton, like Buffon, traces back to prehistory the progress of indefatigable physical agents working together with Newtonian gravity to tear down the resisting fabric of this world. He reads the individual fragments of the present land until he comes into sight of "that original structure, of which the remains are still so vast," an "immense mass of solid rock, naked and unshapely, as it first emerged from the deep" and "incomparably greater" than all that is now before him. The massive, endless, and wholly artless transportation of materials is incontrovertible, since "the granite of Mont Blanc is seen in the plains of Lombardy, or on the sides of the Jura; and the ruins of the Carpathian Mountains lie scattered over the shores of the Baltic."[4]

A related instance of this new-found confidence in reading the world aright (that is, according to its own language) is the corollary trust placed in the piercing powers of vision. The assumption that no material physiognomy long resists the penetrating eye or the inquisitive mind—clearly operative in the studies of Buffon and Hutton—differs markedly from the time-honored view of a nature whose most profound identity lies hidden or is located outside its bounds. Traditionally, both anamorphic perspective games and chiromantic or geomantic practices are founded on the assumed existence of a dissimulated or concealed image to be extracted from ambiguous visual signs.

Chiromancy, the art of recovering the essence of a thing from its external characteristics, is associated in the West particularly with Paracelsus. This sixteenth-century physician and advocate of natural magic elucidated lines traced on physical objects just as one might interpret marks scrolled on the palm of a hand. He declared that there was a chiromancy of herbs, leaves, woods, rocks, mines, and of landscapes veined by roads and rivers. On a grander scale, even the face of the land, marred by cracks opened in its crust by earthquakes, could similarly be probed. The chiromantic diviner is bent on revealing covert occult forces emanating from on high but lurking under natural forms. According to Paracelsus, the bodies of all things function as signs of spiritual properties other than those constitutive of their gross material selves.[5] Thus, even his doctrine of Signatures, on the face of it consonant with the paradigm of matter as truly "speaking," differs from it in a fundamental respect. In this difference also lies the distinction between the Renaissance's (Cornelius Agrippa's) conception and the modern scientific or Newtonian view of matter. For Paracelsus, the astral Signature or *Zeichen* aids the observer in penetrating the corporeal envelope of the body to arrive at a spiritualized essence whose source lies elsewhere. In short, chiromancy represents yet another method for getting beyond the physicality of phenomena by redeeming—repossessing—matter through a system of transcendental correspondences.[6]

On the contrary, the natural historian's joy in fossils, the geologist's delight in petrifactions, "medals of creation," consist precisely in the perception that they are not evasive signs eluding the facticity of their medium. The discovery that the earth is literally in ruins, compounded of artless fragments providing visual entry into a time past conception, exposed a real history latent in the simplest features of the landscape. Exploratory perception thus became akin to a natural archaeology. In lieu of an ambivalent artificial sign, an immaterial Signature pointing either beyond itself toward Paracelsus's Archeius and the "superior stars" or mingling with the cultural traces of humanity, the voyager as naturalist retrieved the wild imprint merged with an uncivilized nature.

Moreover, the notion of lithic writing is inseparable from the eighteenth-century struggle to hammer out distinctions between "hard" and "soft" bodies. Obdurate matter, taken absolutely, involved attributes of resistance, toughness, and impenetrable rigidity. By definition, hardness is synonymous with a principle of visual and corporeal exclusion. From this perspective one comprehends a new, and deeper reason why the period, prepared by the Newtonian ontology of the *Principia* and of the *Opticks* and its Queries, warmed to the view of a dense matter in ruins. The condition of ruination is expressive of the virtual character of a particulate substance, fragmented, porous, and in thrall to transmaterial energies.

Further, the "ruining" of solidity that Newton imagined at the "atomic" level was mirrored in the more visible dynamic actions of wind, weather, cataclysm, and evolution that geologists revealed was taking place topographically.[7] By exhibiting themselves as fragments of a larger, wholly material reality, the natural *macchia* (the physical object still in the state of becoming, still existing in the condition of the *non-finito*) and the natural ruin reveal the metamorphic strata lodged within the most seemingly monolithic of elements. These wild sketches and indicators of a primordial morphology are silent signifiers documenting what they once were or could yet become.[8]

The eighteenth-century appreciation of the ruin in all its guises further illustrates the new-found apprehension of a dynamic matter interpreted within a historical, not allegorical, framework. Descriptions of natural stubs and torsos reflect the confidence that in any random fragment plucked from the face of the earth the totality of its destiny can be discerned. These contracted models of the structural complexity of the entire material world are closely connected to two major theories: the senescence of the earth and mutability as the root of all things.[9]

The first idea, that of the decay of nature, originated with Hesiod and was reiterated by Seneca, Ovid, Varro, and Virgil. The present era, so the argument runs, requires active toil to achieve that which in the Golden Age was spontaneously bestowed by the earth. Obtrusive marks everywhere testify to the globe's extreme age: stones vanquished by time, high towers toppled, rocks destroyed. Natural objects and artifacts betray signs of mortality. The Enlightenment version of this philosophy differs, however, in a significant way from that of antiquity and from its subsequent embodiment in the seventeenth-century quarrel between the ancients and the moderns. Diderot's concept of universal process is revealing. He holds that potential energy inhering in matter can become kinetic, that motion is virtually omnipresent in immobile bodies. Within the immense sea of physical stuff, liveliness and change are universally manifest. Praising the ruin paintings of Hubert Robert in the *Salon* of 1767, Diderot muses: "The objects which surround me announce an end and I resign myself to what awaits me." "What," he asks, "is my ephemeral existence in comparison to the cliff that wears away and the boulder that totters?" Diderot is not convinced that nature has run its course and is crumbling to a final dissolution. Material ruins, for him, are not signs of the weariness of matter and of unalterable decay but rather indices that the infinite treasure of nature is constantly changing—a fact documented by the history of its individual parts. What had been implicit in the classic formulation of the theory, namely that the universe and mankind evinced signs of corruption, has now been radically dislocated by Diderot. Man is vicious and corrupt in every stage of life, as his history proves; however, nature's history shows it to be burgeoning, vital, and self-renewing. This inversion was made clear and expanded to denigrate the entire artifactual world by Sebastien Mercier, who in *Mon bonnet de nuit* (1784–85) opposes the lesser ruins of art, which stem "merely from yesterday," to the greater remnants of nature, which antedate human history. Erasmus Darwin, in the *Temple of Nature* (1803), insists equally on the great age and the continuing vitality of the earth, and is spurred to this conclusion by evidence suggesting that all animals and plants now existing—but not man—are survivors deriving from microscopic motes once drifting in a primeval ocean.[10]

The second supposition (which may be characterized as the Diderotian one without its modern natural-history component) is epitomized in the doctrines of the Pythagoreans, the Stoics, and Lucretius, whose ideas were so significant for eighteenth-century thought. It is that "change, not death, is the essence of the universe, and life and evolution are the eternal order of all things." Nothing in the cosmos keeps its frame. All things are in a state of flux; hence, matter is indestructible. This philosophy permeates the accounts of eighteenth-century voyagers contemplating cities and mountains going down into the immensities of the desert. Not only do these represent a wreckage of perfection; more underivatively, the perception of them exposes an Empedoclean desire to be embedded or submerged in a substance that destroys but is itself imperishable. Le Bruyn succumbs to this dual vision in his depiction of the staircases at Persepolis. Many are "half buried under the earth," owing in part to the "rising ground." Indeed, "figures are sunk up to the knees in the earth," and "the other portals are likewise sunk."[11]

The historical context in which the eighteenth century viewed natural ruins as monuments of the world before culture now in the process of dissolution and rebirth in another material avatar, or artificial ruins as tangible evidence of matter's propensity to engulf form, was conjoined with a new valuing of particulate chaos. Not only were both types of ruins conventionally "shapeless," but their loosened configuration was perceived as redolent of catastrophes actually experienced by the totality of physical substance. The once-teeming prehistoric landscape, empty of man, was thought to be dimly glimpsed and aesthetically recoverable in those regions that still participated in the undifferentiation that preceded creation. Humboldt, traveling in the tropics, was overwhelmed by a virginal territory in which so little of humanity was apparent. Similarly, Bourrit, Saussure, Goethe, and Ramond appreciatively employed the word *chaos* when looking at high mountainous regions displaying an unsorted accumulation of upheaved masses and ruptured planes alien to any vision of containment or stability. Charles Darwin saw through the tangled forest of Brazil to the untamed physical exuberance of nature, in comparison with which the hedged existence of man pales.[12]

In the eighteenth century, then, chaos—secularly defined as proceeding form, not merely as matter bereft of superadded shape—came to be valued because it was realized that the vitality of substance exceeded any formal molds or restraints the mind might wish to impose. As noted, the view of a "lively" or empowered nature posited in the writings of the Pre-Socratics, the Cambridge Platonists, Shaftesbury, Leibniz, Diderot, Robinet, and Buffon became wedded to Lockean "powers" and Newtonian "occult" qualities. If every mote in the universe is dynamic, then the new hermeneutics of natural phenomena must depend on the fact of a thing's process, its activity, contained in the history of its continuing evolution.

VOYAGE INTO SUBSTANCE

Figure 208
J. Houel, *General View of Ruins of Temple at Selinunte,* from *Voyage pittoresque des isles de Sicile, de Malte et de Lipari,* 1782, I, pl. 20. Aquatint. Photo courtesy British Library.

Figure 209
Cornelius Le Bruyn, *Two Porticos and Two Columns, Persepolis,* from *Travels in Muscovy, Persia,* 1737, II, pl. 121. Engraving.

More emphatically: If all particles of matter are legible because they are effectively historical, no form is impenetrable.[13]

To sum up our course thus far: Just as the progressive divorce of geology from theology in the eighteenth century transformed the sacred book of nature into a lexicon, relocated the "charge" of signs from the transcendental sphere to make them inherent in matter rather than "above" or "underneath" it, and metamorphosed the "ruins" of nature into readable and not Biblically "chaotic" documents of matter's dynamic history, so too an alteration occurred in the *topos* of nature sporting. On the surface, both the ancient conception of the *ludus* or sport and the modern view that the earth generates itself derive from the conviction that matter is alive, striving, and transformational. Generally speaking, a power appears lodged in the object that is not imposed by the beholder.[14]

That nature is a "most fertile artificer" was recognized by the Stoics. Seneca states in the *Quaestiones naturales* that "nature is still a great deal better able to paint, especially when shee meaneth to make her selfe some sport in the midst of her jollie fertilitie." Apuleius in the *Apologia* speaks of the checkerwork of oyster shells and the designs of the peacock's tail. Pliny is astounded by the pattern on the tiger, the leopard, and other "painted" creatures. In the *Natural History*, Pliny also devotes attention to "the manifold picture of gemmes, the partie-coloured spots of pretious stones." Curious rarities resulting from "a casual painting of Nature" are seen to fall out by "mere chance." However, Junius who provides a fascinating summary of these ideas, doubts that these "marvels" and "miracles" are merely a "casuall" kind of picture.[15]

Skepticism about the validity of the view that had a brute and insensitive matter mindlessly churning out aberrations by happenstance attained fever pitch in the second half of the eighteenth century. Louis Bourget's *Traité des pétrifications* (1742) outlines two major and opposing opinions on the subject of figured stones or fossils. Before midcentury, it was commonly held that petrifactions resembling animals or plants were indebted for both their shape and their surface traits to simple fortuity. As tokens of nature's capacity to "sport" or caricature, the distinctive decorations etched along contours and visible amid matter's "formal chaos" were interpreted as accidents. On the other hand, mineralogists increasingly put forward a more plausible hypothesis. They speculated that imaged gems are remains of marine flora and fauna, opening tantalizing vistas onto the dawn of history.

Johann Georg Sulzer, in his natural-history commentary to the revised edition of Scheuchzer's *Natur-Geschichte des Schweizerlandes* (1746), interprets the abundance of "imaged stones" or plant and animal fossils as "new proofs of the former condition of the earth far different from that of today!" Sulzer continues: "India, the opposite hemisphere, appears to have been here [in Switzerland] in ancient times. Many snails, shells and

VOYAGE INTO SUBSTANCE

also plants that are met with alive only in the remotest lands and seas lie here in their true form but petrified. . . . " At this juncture Sulzer stresses the importance of alpine voyages by naturalists. Travelers, not similarly versed in science, might traverse Switzerland a hundred times and not see the "workings of nature"; they would be oblivious to the fact that fossils are tokens (*Zeuge*) of conditions obtaining at the beginning of the world.

Johann Friedrich Henckel's *Flora Saturnis* (1722) displays an intermediary stage in the development of the fossil's articulate self-sufficiency. Henckel is at pains to distinguish between the figured stone's character as *lusibus* and as *petrefactis*, emphasizing that only its shape, not its substance (which belongs either to the plant or the animal kingdom), is playful.[16] This ambiguity of expressiveness and this false dichotomization between form and content would be rectified by a new natural history that regarded fossils neither as whimsies nor as the results of astral influence.

Just as the bible or sacred manuscript of creation was laicized into a dictionary, the old language of immanent numinousness merged with the fossil's newly discovered secular speech. The chief of Jesuit science in Rome occupied an intervening position between the traditional macrocosm-microcosm analogy, initiated by Thales and advanced by Aristotle, and the Enlightenment versions of entropic materialism. Of course, during the Renaissance Leonardo had perceived living organisms couched within seemingly inert masses of earth, and Palissy had explained mineral concretions by hypothesizing the existence of a "congealing force" promoting mutual powers of attraction among salts.[17] But it was Athanasius Kircher (among the most quoted authors of the middle of the seventeenth century) who presented, in *Mundus subterraneus* (1665), the visually compelling picture of a stationary earth generating substances underground which in turn give rise to physiographic alterations. This volume is rife with illustrations of sprouting clumps of crystal and rude pictograms stamped on stones.[18] Kircher repeated a theory that was only gradually becoming obsolete and that could have found authority among reputable eighteenth-century scientists, namely that metals floresce in fissures. He believed that mines, if covered over, would "bear" once more. The image of a plastic earth as a gigantic alembic or distilling furnace proved persistent and enthralled geologists like John Woodward, philosophers like Leibniz, chemists like Robert Boyle, and physicians like the Sieur de La Colonna. The latter, a Roman living in Paris and thus an important transmitter of ideas between the two capitals, even posits in the monumental *Les principes de la nature, ou la génération des choses* (1731) that mountains possess roots like trees and that metals and crystals mature from "seeds" deposited by rivers flowing overland.[19]

Travelers were enlisted in the cause and asked to determine whether the regrowth of metals and minerals in the bowels of the earth was true.

Frézier, in his *Relation du voyage* (1716)—citing Theophrastus and Palissy—declares that the rebirth of copper, gold, or silver, whether in the mines of Hungary or Peru, is no fiction. He cites as proof an "experiment" performed in a quarry at Potosi: Foreign bodies were introduced into it, and in the fullness of time these were found to be overgown with and penetrated by filaments that looked just as if they had originated within a shaft. Cornelius Le Bruyn mentions he was given a curious "melon stone" by Father Abdella in Palestine. When he split open one of these geodes found "germinating" near Mount Carmel he discovered a petrified, yet paradoxically evolving, geocosm. Similarly, basing his mineralogical theories on the assumption of the universal metabolism of matter, Joseph Pitton de Tournefort describes "one of the most beautiful items in nature." He sees the Grotto of Antiparos as verifying a great law of physics, namely the growth of stones. The French botanist (sent to the Levant by Louis XIV) and his successors attempted to confirm this "principle" by traveling to the actual site in order to philosophize with greater certitude. Jean-Baptiste Robinet, reiterating his celebrated predecessor's views a half-century later, designates such caverns "hidden laboratories" for the clandestine growth of fossils revealed only to the chosen few who are admitted to nature's shrine. Alexandre de Laborde, inspecting the imposing cascade of Saint Michel in Spain, notes that a strange hollow pierces the center of this mountain. What specifically attracted him here and at Mont Serrat was the sight of singularities wrought by the earth in its "interior." With similar intent, the Swiss speleologist Carl Lang descended into innumerable dens, seeking to witness how "nature builds in hiding." Vast artless chambers disclosed to Lang perpendicular vistas and diagonal vaults where mountain spirits might easily dwell. At the Petersburg in Maastricht, Lang peered through a torchlit labyrinth; what moved him was not the toiling miners but the sense of being surrounded by a cemetery housing an infinite succession of organisms.[20]

Consequently, the *philosophe* De l'Isle de Sales is not unique in his position when he imagines in "The Twelve Surprises of Pythagoras" that the philosopher dare not repose on a rock, for the substance on which he reclines is not dead or inorganic but a sentient fossil. Indeed, in a stentorian voice and objecting to the mutilating stylus inscribing this aperçu, the boulder announces that it is not only composed of a mixture of conglomerate and coral but "internally carpeted with nerves & membranes." Diderot, in *Rêve de D'Alembert* (1769), similarly looks out upon a dynamic world incorporating "an immense reservoir of multiple elements existing scattered in the entrails of the earth, on its surface, in the bosom of the oceans, in the waves of the atmosphere. . . . " Mercier, in *Mon bonnet de nuit*, pronounces that "minerals are engendered and stones grow." Robinet, the intellectual successor to Diderot, denies in the vitalist *Considérations philosophique de la gradation naturelle des formes de l'être* (1768) that such petrified organisms displaying nature's facture are mere "sports." Nature's "sketches," its first thoughts, even its dead ends expressed in a concrete medium are "a source of instruction." By pondering its rough drafts one may surmise how the earth experimented with lower organisms, casting trial samples in stone of hearts, brains, jawbones, kidneys, ears, eyes, and even of sexual organs, thereby proclaiming in a most unambiguous fashion the subsequent evolution of all material beings.

Of still greater importance is Robinet's discussion of the prototype denoting an abbreviated paradigm and a compact biological hieroglyph in which the diversity of physical reality is embedded in embryo. A shell, a rock, a cavern, an oak, an ape, and a man all are graduated variations spun out of an elemental substance. These preformational and evolutionary suppositions are predicated on the premise that an innate life force resides in all epiphanies of matter, from rock to plant to man. Hence, the picture of a constantly changing universe was fleshed out not merely by a recycling of ancient ferment theories but by a biological vitalism as well. In the words of Bernardin de Saint-Pierre's *Voyage à l'Ile de France* (1773), "everything is related in all directions, and each species forms the great spokes of a cosmic wheel, and is, at the same time, the center of a subordinate sphere. . . . "[21]

Tracts such as Antoine van Leeuwenhoek's *Sendbrieven* (1685–1718) received enthusiastic receptions precisely because they focused on the remarkable restorative powers of organisms. If the microscope helped to establish the stature of the minute and the existence of yet another infinity, it also abetted the understanding of the laws of matter's metamorphosis and reproduction. Leeuwenhoek writes: "For my own part, I will not scruple to assert, that I can clearly place before my eye the smallest species of those animalcules concerning which I now write, and can as plainly see them endued with life, as with the naked eye we behold small flies, or gnats sporting in the open air, though these animalcules are more than a million of degrees less than a large grain of sand. For I should not only behold their motions in all directions but I also see them turn about, remain still, and sometimes expire. . . ." The microscopist Jan Swammerdam, Leeuwenhoek's precursor, expressed a fondness for, and lovingly described, commonly detested vermin that made all dissecting knives appear crude when pitted against the delicacy of their internal organs. The Dutch botanist and physician Hermann Boerhave, in *Biblia natura* (1737–38), paid tribute to the scientist who, with the aid of the microscope, penetrated the secret of metamorphosis, discerning the gradual, almost imperceptible change that the caterpillar undergoes before turning into a moth or a butterfly. Aided by that miraculous instrument, he comes to the stunning conclusion that all characteristics of the future moth are "hidden in the caterpillar, or rather, under its skin in the same manner that a tender flower that begins to grow is enclosed in its bud." Thus, the moth or the flower, like the fossil script, exists nowhere else but in the concrete form, envelope, or carapace of its matter.

LANDSCAPE FREED OF CULTURE

Figure 210
M. G. A. Choiseul-Gouffier, *Interior View
of the Grotto of Antiparos*, from *Voyage
pittoresque de la Grèce*, 1782, I, pl. 38.
Engraving by J. B. Hilair.

Figure 211
Thomas and William Daniell, *Grotto of
Antiparos*, from *Animated Nature*,
1807–1812, II, pl. 6. Aquatint. Photo
courtesy Newberry Library.

Figure 212
A. de Laborde, *Interior View of Stalactite Grotto of Mont-Serrat,* from *Voyage pittoresque en Espagne,* 1806, I, pl. 36. Etching by L. LeGrand. Photo courtesy British Library.

Figure 213
Carl Lang, *Interior View of Petersberg at Mastricht,* from *Gallerie der Unterirdischen Wunder,* 1806–1807, I, pl. p. 76. Color aquatint. Photo courtesy Bibliothèque Nationale.

Figure 214
J. C. I. de l'Isle de Sales, *Pythagoras*
("What! Everything is animate."), from *De la*
philosophie de la nature, 1777, II, pl. p.
389. Engraving by F. D. Née. Photo
courtesy Cabinet des Estampes,
Bibliothèque Nationale.

Figure 215
E.-M. Patrin, *Florentine Stone*, from *Histoire*
naturelle des minéraux, 1800–1801, III, pl.
p. 280. Engraving by Le Villain after
drawing by Desene. Photo courtesy
Cabinet des Estampes, Bibliothèque
Nationale.

Perhaps the most momentous microscopic revelation for the eighteenth century, however, was not that of the insect world but that of the life of a freshwater hydra. In 1740, Abraham Trembley communicated to the foremost entomologist of the early eighteenth century, René-Antoine Ferchault de Réaumur, facts surrounding the willful recuperative strengths of the polyp. Charles Bonnet, in developing the typically eighteenth-century theory of ontogenesis, declared unequivocally that the polyp was located "on the frontiers of another Universe" that one day would have "its Columbuses and Vespuccis." The materialist philosophers La Mettrie and Diderot cited its gnomic behavior as proof that there were no absolute borders dividing the three kingdoms. Resembling otherwise dissimilar shells and corals in its activity, this otherwise humble invertebrate mimicked the generative properties of beings inhabiting entirely different dimensions.[22] (See figure 7.) The mutable polyp, then, like its microscopic brethren, communicated the infinite "speaking" individuality of matter and thus was no more considered a mere sport or *ludus* than was the growing mineral.

Both these instances exhibit that what stands starkly apart from conventional ancient and Renaissance panpsychic musings is the later eighteenth century's sensuous plummeting of natural phenomena as if they were archives of matter, not indicators of spirit. This empirical and multilayered probing opened up visual perspectives onto the environment in which they arose and the one in which they now subsided. By piercing the exterior of substance, the natural historians ranged freely, concretely, through the depths of time. Their capacity to read deeply both spatially and temporally illuminates the voyagers' visceral experience of nature as matter which one pushes across and through. This totally involving corporeal methodology—parallel to the immersion of an archaeological dig—is intimately bound up with the Enlightenment's desire to recover tangibly lost realities.

It is specifically from the vantage of a material and graphic record—now demonstrated to be an exemplary one among many—that we return to the case of the figured stone at mid-century. In its most epigrammatic expression as a sample of ruined particulate matter, a dynamic fragment torn from the life of the earth, it offers a nuggetory model of the documentary potential inherent in all concrete substances. Moreover, it suggests a new, unconventionalized method for seeing the data presented by this world.

Consistent with this repeated visual effort to return to the source is Eugène-Mélchior Patrin's discussion of Florentine Stones and their literal images of antediluvian forests and crumbling cities. What the Abbé La Pluche judged to be accidental figures akin to those imagined in clouds the mineralogist Patrin interpreted as records mirroring the physical revolutions that had produced them.[23] In the words of an anonymous French poem of 1763, metals reveal your exhortative structure and shells speak through your patterns; these

LANDSCAPE FREED OF CULTURE

demonstrate the [occurrence of a] great deluge to our descendents
Such that that [your] masses of debris, relocation
[coupled with [your] marine traits constitute the entire argument.

The poem goes on to say

Petrifications! How that word speaks volumes!
Infinity confounds us within its transformations. . . . [24]

The fossil as legible monument receives it most convincing apology, how-ever, from Linnaeus. In *Reflections on the Study of Nature* (1754) he praises the petrifactions, lying submerged under the Alps, embedded in strata constituting the remains of an ancient world, "and which reach far beyond the memory of any history whatever." The Swedish botanist and explorer goes on to say that the maker of all things has furnished the globe "like a museum," and this splendid theater requires a probing investigator to study it.[25]

A code to Linnaeus's paean to mountains and to the petrified relics of an ancient world which they house is Romé de l'Isle's hypothesis that crystals are authoritative memorials. In the epoch-making *Cristallographie* (1783), he argues one must study all the varieties of geometric form to which a particular crystal is susceptible. This modern directive contributed to the awareness that an uninterrupted chain of being also was operative within the confines of the mineral kingdom. One gem, distinguished by a definite and highly individualized composition, could manifest itself in a wide range of expressions running the gamut from shapeless matrices to superbly faceted polyhedrons. Hence, by inspecting the evolution of a single mineral type, the astute observer was presented with a completely exteriorized formal continuum in which certain historic moments of its past stood out, frozen as it were, in the stone. These charged instants could also be read vertically. Romé de l'Isle notes how rock crystal and selenite frequently encloses a foreign body of a completely different chemical composition than its parent. Probing the limpidity of its transparent depths, he discovers feldspar prisms, schorl needles, and mica flakes. Each inclusion is an indicator of some geological disturbance experienced by matter.[26] La Métherie and Patrin develop this point, suggesting that the entire history of the organic and inorganic earth exists in this microcosmic physical abridgement.[27]

Dolomieu, following a different tack (exclusively that of the student of internal chemistry) was also a seeker after every crystal's individual and primitive incarnation. This student of the Alps and the Pyrenees, after whom the mineral dolomite was named, states that, in reality, what the mineralogist confronts in the field is a sea of fragments. He discovers masses that are but the fractured, eroded, or imperfectly formed portions of an aboriginal whole. By penetrating the secrets of a crystal's chemical composition one discovers that some minerals resemble one another—not because of apparent shared surface properties—but fundamentally and in depth, because of the mutual possession of certain "integrating molecules" bonded together by elective affinities. Dolomieu concludes that every mineral leads two lives in matter, one hidden and the other visible. The former constitutes its primordial "chemical" existence, the latter its current physical embodiment. Between the two stretch the vicissitudes of history.

Dolomieu's thesis represents the triumph of international Newtonianism. As Joseph Priestley makes plain in his *Disquisitions Relating to Matter and Spirit* (1777), matter is not that inert substance it had long been supposed to be, since powers of attraction and repulsion are necessary to its very being. These powers are not distinct from matter, as had been thought before Newton. Consequently, the shape of any figured thing is due to the mutual attraction of its parts—a truism that affects equally the smallest atoms and the largest bodies. Again, the fundamental principle underlying such a proposition is that no material thing is chaotic; nothing haphazard occurs in nature. Crystals simply bear witness more absolutely than compounded substances to the law of matter's intrinsic communicability, to the fact that every being possesses an individual, decipherable, and characteristic physiognomy. Similarly, Abraham Werner, in his influential *Von den aüsserlichen Kennzeichen der Fossilien* (1774), brilliantly renovated the study of mineralogy by focusing exclusively (unlike Dolomieu and, to a lesser extent, Romé de l'Isle) on their external characters. As director of the mining school at Freiburg, Werner taught that a significant connection exists between the linguistic science of grammar and the syntactical structure of the earth bodied forth in the lapidary language of minerals.[28]

Thus, the new mineralogy, too, moves us far afield from Pliny's conception of *ludi* or Albert's view of *mirabilia*. It is now evident that, for the late eighteenth century, minerals were not tokens of Fortuna's strange powers but carriers of a wholly material script. Patrin, in his *Histoire naturelle des minéraux* (1800), and Faujas de Saint-Fond, in his *Essai de géologie* (1803–1809), elaborate on the idiosyncratic behavior of graphic granite. This natural hieroglyph, compounded of quartz crystals and occasionally feldspar, "presents a certain kinship with Hebrew or Arabic letters." In laying bare the rudimentary alphabet of these inscribed stones, James Hutton compared them to runic writing. Related phenomena are the orderly compartments and cloisons created by quartz and other crystals when injected into veins of a dissimilar substance. These rectangular and pentagonal cells resemble columnar basalt. Both catalog the retreat of a fluid which, after its gradual withdrawal, leaves behind an inventory of its passage. William Borlase, the explorer of Cornwall's tin mines, touches equally upon the issue of semipellucid pyrites or "mundics" offering "testimonies" of matter shaped into colored fretwork or scrolled into asterisks. George Wolfgang Knorr's handsome four-volume *Recueil de monumens des catastrophes que le globe de la terre a essuiées* (1768–1775) reproduces rare arborescent and marbled dendritic "pictograms" resembling hoarfrost crystals. Knorr argues effectively against the theory that figures arise in stones through the agency of an "idea" or an Archeius.[29]

LANDSCAPE FREED OF CULTURE

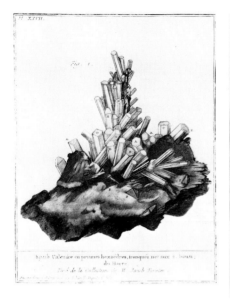

Figure 216
Fabien G. Dagoty, *Hexagonal Calcareous Spar Crystals*, from *Le règne minéral*, 1783, pl. 27. Hand-colored engraving. Photo courtesy British Library.

Figure 217
Fabien G. Dagoty, *Solitary and Clustered Selenite Crystals*, from *Le règne minéral*, 1783, pl. 11. Hand-colored engraving. Photo courtesy British Library.

Figure 218
E.-M. Patrin, *Graphic Granite of Siberia*, from *Histoire naturelle des minéraux*, 1800–1801, I, pl. p. 101. Engraving by Caquet after drawing by Desene. Photo courtesy British Library.

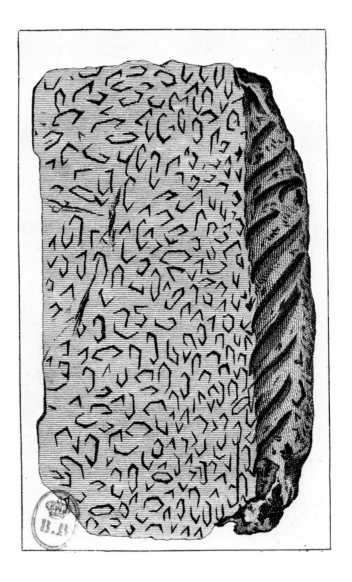

Figure 219
Fabien G. Dagoty, *Quartzose and Cellular Ludus*, from *Le règne minéral*, 1783, pl. 30. Hand-colored engraving. Photo courtesy British Library.

Figure 220
Fabien G. Dagoty, *Clay Ludus with Calcareous Veins*, from *Le règne minéral*, 1783, pl. 29. Hand-colored engraving. Photo courtesy British Library.

Figure 221
W. Borlase, *Cornish Crystals*, from *Natural History of Cornwall*, 1758, p. 13. Engraving. Photo courtesy British Library.

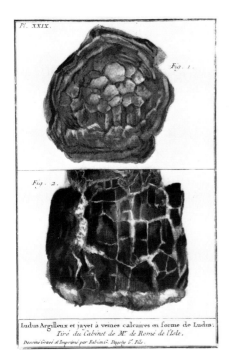

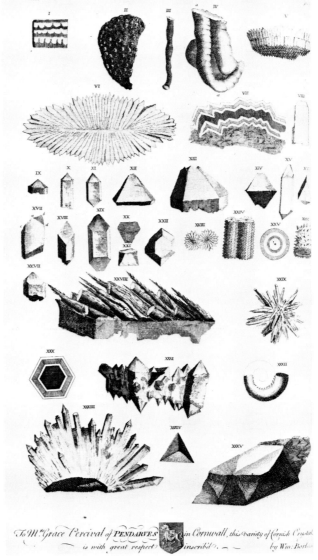

Figure 222
G. W. Knorr, *Dendritic Agate*, from *Recueil
de monumens des catastrophes,* 1768–1785,
I, pl. 5. Hand-colored engraving.

The power accorded the mineralogical text attained its acme in the theories of the German scholar Samuel Witte, which were sufficiently influential to arouse the ire of the young Alexander von Humboldt. According to Witte, all the major monuments of antiquity are naturally derived. He upholds the opinion that the inscriptions discovered by the explorers Jean Chardin and Le Bruyn at Persepolis are, in reality, traces left by volcanic scoriae. No wonder, he declares, archaeologists routinely dismissed them as illegible; only a natural historian could spell out a narrative composed by metamorphic basalt. With calm objectivity, by contrast, William Hamilton, in the handsome *Campi Phlegraei*, levels careful scrutiny upon samples of volcanic matter taken from the mouth of Vesuvius. He proffers "readings" of strangely ramified lava tinged with sulfur and vitriol.[30]

Natural Hieroglyphics

You will no more be able to penetrate the moral of the next marbled page (motly emblem of my work!) than the world with all its sagacity has been able to unravel the many opinions, transactions and truths which still lie mystically hid under the dark veil of the black one. . . .
Lawrence Sterne

These mineralogical schemes concerning the meaningfulness and historical richness of natural markings can be closely correlated with aesthetic theory. Alexander Cozens's contemporaneous conjectures on landscape composition (1785) and the role of the black mark or "blot" in its creation may fruitfully be contrasted with such graphic stones punctuated by natural imprints spatially deployed over a tangible surface. Indeed, the polemical reason behind Cozens's formulation of an aesthetic of artifice seems to be precisely the popularity and universality of recognition allotted to an unmanipulated, "naked" hieroglyphic of nature.

In contrast with Leonardo's organic stains soiling ancient walls, which fire the artistic imagination because of their accidental mimicry of natural forms, Cozens posits the existence of an artificial spot that is not legible in and of itself (before matter is worked upon or buffered by art). Again, key issues are the locus of signification and the separate expressive media of nature and of art. In contradistinction to the natural mineral marking that must be peered at closely and in depth in order for its real shapes to be made out, the man-made "blot" becomes perceptually comprehensible only at a distance, at which it loses its aura of raw facticity and its material rudeness and, through an optical illusion, comes to resemble that even more artificial and dematerialized construct, a drawing. Cozens's ruminations highlight the distinctions between the naturalist's intimate (almost carnal) scrutiny of the individual and particular object out in the "real" world—discerned to be intrinsically representational by and through itself—and the artist's generalized, abstract, invented, distant view, consigned to white paper, which seems to turn its back on both the real thing as *factum* and nature. The sketch, as Cozens envisages it, removes itself from the sphere of the concrete to evoke a wholly mental pleasure stimulated through and overlaid by the free-wheeling association of ideas.

The location of meaning, for Cozens, is solely within the imagination of the observer. In short, the "blot" becomes a description of the viewer's mind, lacking the "body" contributed by the outside world. This dislocation of feeling from external things allows the observer to fill in the blank

LANDSCAPE FREED OF CULTURE

spaces and to "construct" at will the inky marks traced on the paper. In contrast with the direct and immediate physicality of the wild sketch's or the natural hieroglyph's language, only the large masses of the blot, those eliminating all tangible detail, are expressive, and in this sense they approach the abstracted translations of the Ideal.[31] Quite the reverse holds true for lapidary writing, which relies on nature's literal skill and on matter's virtual process or facture.

Cozens's theory is prescient because, henceforth, the natural trace and the artificial spot, *macchia*, or *tache* stand in opposition, unlike the ambivalent *ludus* conventionally partaking both of art and of nature. Bearing in mind this very nineteenth-century antithesis between the dictionary of nature and the fabricated, parallel language of art, we may look ahead to the conclusion of Edgar Allan Poe's *Narrative of A. Gordon Pym*. Poe provides a remarkable description and illustration of "singular stratifications" and "natural figures" supposedly found by the narrator in a black granite chasm on the island of Tsalal in the Antarctic. In a tale redolent with the memory of eighteenth-century scientific voyages, it is only appropriate that the nineteenth-century writer pay tribute to the Enlightenment belief in the legibility and historicity of matter. Exploring a spur shooting off from a black granite chasm, Peters draws Pym's attention to a range of enigmatic indentures. Although the former is willing to adopt the "idle opinion" that the traces were alphabetical characters (i.e., manmade), Pym "convinced him of his error, finally, by directing his attention to the floor of the fissure, where, among the powder [, they] picked up piece by piece, several large flakes of the marl, which had evidently been broken off by some convulsion from the surface where the indentures were found, and which had projecting points exactly fitting the indentures; thus proving them to have been the work of nature. . . ."[32] Pym's hypothesis concerning artlessness is in line with eighteenth-century mineralogical theories and not with Cozens's aesthetic of artifice. The main point for him is that even a fragment, a small tangible piece of the work of nature, has the power to open up a new universe, to give concrete form to a whole material world that would otherwise be lost. Through the act of voyaging into matter, both Pym and the crystallographer recover nature's process mark by mark. Their stony characters function as transparent portraits, as natural signs, not symbols; they dispense with the mediation of art. To state it otherwise: According to the proto-Kantian philosopher Johann Heinrich Lambert, the natural sign is merely the abbreviated and concentrated expression of the thing itself, the brute fact compacted and intensified. In contrast with the mentality of the Baroque era, in which signs constantly pointed toward something beyond or below (a supernatural "more" or a supranatural "higher" and "deeper"), the late eighteenth century was not permeated by similar ideals of transcendence. Instead, the analogs, metaphors, symbols, personifications, and abstract emblems of the preceding period became localized in a real thing, whether it was the work of art or of nature. When the image of the aphoristic hieroglyph arose again as a miracle of pervasiveness—as it did during the Enlightenment—it was not merely as the traditional abstruse, sacred rebus, but also as a primitive material relic of its own secular history.[33]

The ubiquity of the term *character* or *caractère* in eighteenth-century discourse has recently received extended study. It often denoted "essential quality," but when botanists or mineralogists spoke it could connote physical grafts or incisions essential to orderly classification. In addition, in a century captivated by universal alphabets, pictograms, and hieroglyphics, the word was singularly appropriate to a form of writing that, in its broadest designation, included the distinctive "marks" of the natural world.[34]

Moreover, eighteenth-century speculation on the origin of languages, touching as it does upon a nexus of distinctive intellectual problems, affords a revealing entry into the temper of Enlightenment thought. Among these problems were the search for the primitive in art and nature and their initial relationship—the bond between image and letter, the role of convention in human development and the process of freeing oneself from its bondage, the quest for a ground or meaning in which to "root" knowledge, and the growth of a multivalent historical consciousness. Against the backdrop of this overriding construct of semantic form, it should be reiterated that an important manner in which the eighteenth century habitually apprehended the world was to perceive figures in all things, including stones, metals, minerals, and crystals. Thus, to the natural-history contribution to a perception of physical things as transparent may now be added the linguistic component, namely the multiple attempts to create a literal characteristic representing the real universe with an economy of statement.[35]

The mention of the formulation of a real character recalls to mind seventeenth-century efforts to construct a sensible mirroring language. Bacon, in the *Advancement of Learning*, noted as especially worthy of inquiry not only "characters real, which express neither letters nor words in gross," but also "things or motions." Further, he urged the creation of a philosophical grammar examining the analogy between words and things. Bacon's interest in a universal language grew out of the conviction that knowledge should be delivered in aphorisms; i.e., real invention implies terseness, producing an addition to matter, not to manner. According to Bacon, and significant for what was to follow, writing in aphorisms, which concentrates or crystallizes content, is one and the same with the inductive method of the acquiring and inquiring sciences. It is a "plain" discourse predicated on transmitting knowledge drawn freshly from concrete particulars and in direct sight of particulars. Verulam's injunction was heeded by the Royal Society; it received its most complete expression in Thomas Sprat's *History* of that institution and in John Wilkins's *Essay towards a Real Character and Philosophical Language* (1668). Inspired by the idea that

Figure 223
William Hamilton, *Specimens of Volcanic Matter Found in the Crater of Vesuvius,* from *Campi Phlegraei,* 1776, II, pl. 46. Color aquatint by Peter Fabris. Photo courtesy British Library.

Figure 224
William Hamilton, *Fragment of New Lava Pores filled with Vitrified Matter,* from *Campi Phlegraei, Supplement,* 1779, pl. 5. Color aquatint by Peter Fabris. Photo courtesy British Library.

Figure 225
Edgar Allan Poe, *"Natural Figures" from the Island of Tsalal,* from *Narrative of A. Gordon Pym* (Vintage Books Edition, 1975, p. 873). Photo courtesy Kevin Donovan.

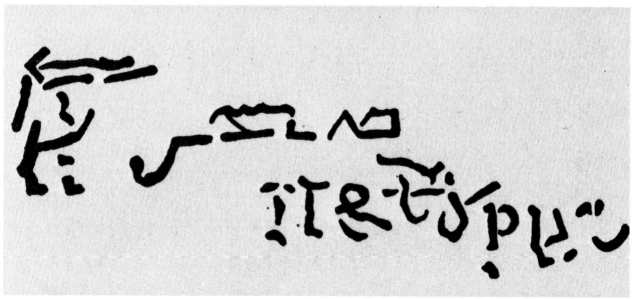

in mathematics and chemistry there is a symbolism that is universally understood, Wilkins proposed to create an artificial language that would enable scientists the world over to communicate their discoveries. Leibniz, too, became involved. While in England in 1673, he criticized the projects of Wilkins and of the pasigrapher George Dalgarno and set out himself to discover "the real character which would be the best instrument of the human mind, and extremely assist both the reason and the memory, and the invention of things."[36]

While seventeenth-century schemes like those of Wilkins and Leibniz generally were founded on mathematical or algebraic models for the manufacture of a simple, unequivocal character, one line of eighteenth-century linguistic theory develops the notion Bacon adumbrated, namely that of a concise idiom in which marks can be natural and not artificial.

What ensues is by way of indicating a graphic prototype for a material language—composed of contracted figure and "real" character—through which phenomena might portray their "actions" without paraphrase or evident art. William Warburton, in the second book of *The Divine Legation of Moses Demonstrated* (1741), develops an important and influential theory concerning the origin of writing in which hieroglyphics are interpreted as the original, abridged, and public form of communication. Challenging the theories of Porphyry and Clement of Alexandria—in short, the entire school of Christian apologetics, and, in more modern times, of Kircher— he denies that hieroglyphics were invented by a priestly caste for the purpose of concealing wisdom.

Certain arguments emerging from Warburton's analysis underscore that a material medium is capable of "expression," that a physical object can exist simultaneously as an articulating image and text, and that nature recognizes the value of brevity in its creation of material aphorisms and epigrams. Warburton declares that there are two ways of transmitting ideas to others: through sounds and through pictures. Of these, the most "natural" method in either category is by means of marks and figures. He views the Egyptians as unique among ancient civilizations—unfavorably comparing the Mexicans and Chinese with them—precisely on the grounds of the supposed concreteness of their language, marrying real picture to real character in the primal hieroglyphic. However, he notes that, as the years passed, along with an increase in contraction, an artificiality and refinement set in, and with it the habit of making one thing stand for or represent another. Even this "metaphoric" hieroglyphic was still based on the observation of natural forms, but these were now combined through the agency of "wit."

The Egyptians carried the aboriginal picture through all stages of improvement up to and including an artificial alphabet of letters constituting a compendious abridgement of former multiplicity. Warburton stresses that the early mode of writing did not fall out of use but coexisted alongside more abstract developments. He sees a perfect consonance between the Eastern or Oriental need to embody material things (instead of demater-ializing them into abstractions) and the reliance on expressing thoughts by apologue or physical acts—a mental habit that coincides perfectly with recording them by virtual images.

Warburton also sets in a new light the tradition of "speaking" creation. For him, the fable codifies the legend of the "articulate" beast or tree, believed to have flourished during the first ages of the world. He hastens to add, however, that for the Greeks this brutish speech was enunciated in a human tongue. It was only among the Arabs and the Goths that animals and plants were first perceived to possess a language of their own. Warburton attributes this deanthropomorphized development to the nomadic existence lived by "barbarians" roaming a savage and uncultivated environment. Implicit in this line of argument, of course, is the notion that it requires someone conventionally uncivilized, living in wastes and deserts, to heed the inhuman vocables of the "other."

As speech improved into art, apologue and fable evolved into simile and then metaphor, or into a "similitude in little." Yet the common foundation for these refinements remained the quintessential picture conveying in-formation directly to the eyes. Warburton's careful dissection of the four types of Egyptian writing is especially pertinent. The first, or hieroglyphic, is of two sorts: rude and curiologic, and more artificial and topical. The second, or symbolic, is double also, either simple or mysterious. Signif-icantly, the first two categories are composed of marks (not letters) con-substantial with material things, not relayed by obtrusive and intrusive words. In contradistinction to the interpretations of Clement and Porphyry, Warburton stresses the unmetaphoric, unsymbolic nature of the curiologic hieroglyph: a "plain and simple imitation of the figure of the thing intended to be represented, which is directly contrary to the very nature of a symbol, which is the representation of one thing by the Figure of another." In other words, the curiologic mode involves the smallest possible gap or displacement between an object and its imitation, not departing from or transforming the real thing. Further, Warburton indicates that this simple hieroglyphic functioned metonymically, not metaphorically like the topical hieroglyphic, by putting the principal part of a thing for the whole. Al-though Warburton does not declare this explicitly, he implies that the return to metonymy, to the concrete fragment of nature, or (in the frame-work of eighteenth-century aesthetic theory) to the material "ruin" or remnant of the totality of matter is a return to tangible simplicity, to the convention-free, to the inartificial that once was nature existing without the interval contributed by man.

This hypothesis appears validated when Warburton suggests that the fate of speech parallels the development of written hieroglyphics, moving from clarity to darkness; from apologue to fable, parable, riddle. As speech or writing evolved, the original "close expression" (that is, close to or at one with matter, and physically occupying a constricted space)—characteristic of the Egyptians, the Chinese, and the Iroquois—became adorned with cosmetic flourishes of art or wit. Warburton concludes that the Asiatic style of rhetoric, epedeictic in its ostentation, and the prophetic or "dark" sayings of the Bible were fashioned to the model of this symbolic hieroglyphic, whereas the Attic Style was constructed to emulate the curiologic expression of conceptions not in lengthy, mediating words but in shortened things.

Warburton's exegesis provides an additional demonstration of how to get back to a "plain-speaking" matter and away from the endless glosses of human interpretation. He establishes a connection between hieroglyphic writing of a symbolic sort and the true onirocritic, or interpretation of dreams. Basing his arguments on the treatises of Artemidorus and Macrobius, he concludes that there are two kinds of dreams: the speculative and the allegorical. The first kind (mirroring dreams) picture events directly; the second paint an oblique and vaporous image. Only the latter vision requires interpretation. Just as the Egyptians supposed that the gods were inventors of hieroglyphic learning so, likewise they supposed that they sent dreams, thus employing the same manner of expression in both revelations. Warburton refocuses the dialectic between a primary, scarcely mediated agency of expression located within substance and that overlaying it when he elucidates the technical term used by the onirocritics for the phantasms or "elements" witnessed in dreams. He explains the oddity of this usage by arguing that it was derived from symbolic hieroglyphics. That is, symbolic marks were denominated elements. In using symbols to decipher dreams, the onirocritics bequeathed the identical names upon the same significative image whether it was inscribed on the stone or impressed in the fancy. Warburton surmises that the Egyptians called their symbolic and hieroglyphic marks *elements* because this method of writing employed all sorts of beings, spread throughout the entire extent of nature, to denote their ideas or mental specters. If the elements of the onirocritics equal the first principles of things out of which everything arises and of which they are compounded (that is, the *philosophia prima*), then the phantasms operate as tangible symbols of all animal, vegetable, and mineral creation—now transposed to another level of being. The creation of a separate, self-contained pictorial world reconstituting the universe through artistic materials (remember Cozens) stands at the antipodes from the curiologic hieroglyphic bodying forth matter's naturally framed articulations couched in marks seemingly traced by that matter.

The Bishop of Gloucester's theory made strong inroads in France, where its genetic perspective and principle of language as an instrument for the analysis of ideas infiltrated Condillac's 1746 *Essai sur l'origine des connoissances humaines*. Further, its subtle distinctions among kinds of hieroglyphics structured Antoine Court de Gebelin's monumental repository of primitive customs originating in nature, *Le monde primitif* (1773–1784).[37]

The aim of this nine-volume encyclopedia was to resuscitate a vivid image of the structure of the past by interpreting the material debris (natural and artificial) surviving from a former world. Court's ideas, disseminated among the distinguished membership of the masonic *Loge de Neuf Soeurs*, spurred scientists and travelers to set about recovering the speaking likeness of an untarnished earth. He maintains that the most elevated abstractions hark back to primal sensible perceptions of actual, physical conditions once existing in the cosmos. That is, the grammatical structure of languages displays each concept in a genetic relation to the structure of human reason or of the world. Among the advantages of etymological studies Court cites their ability to assist humanity in approaching things that are both distant and remote or obscured by conventionalized signification. Under the guidance of a figured language, not only do we perceive man's first mental and psychological steps, the intellectual evolution of humankind, but each root word is a vivid, terse "painting" of the thing it originally designated—much like Warburton's curiologic hieroglyphic. Etymology "conducts us back to the origin of each word, thus returning us to the primitive state existing in the period of its inventors." Since the components of words are taken from physical elements then existing in nature, each word becomes a forcible and exact material image of primeval traits which we can come to seize again.[38]

Consequently, the origin of all myths lies in the crystallized vocabulary of a handful of objects that existed from the beginning. These were transmitted first through the natural phenomena themselves, later in the barely transmuted sublimely naive representations of pictograms, and finally in the dimly imaged, compressed messages contrived for those who could divine their hidden meaning. As mineralogists, Illuminati, etymologists, and mythographers knew, in the beginning the hieroglyph did not exist as mystery or gnomic statement but as an eminently physical presence intimately conjoined with other concrete objects making up the totality of creation. It sent the "reader" and perceiver into nature.

Court's theory is reminiscent of Giambattista Vico's position that modern man is capable of recovering the mentality of his ancestors. According to Vico's *New Science* (1725), primitive man in his ignorance grafted anthropomorphic figures onto original speech, and these still faintly glimmer within the prerational archetypal patterns of thought transmitted by myths and fables. Thus manipulated, nature becomes nothing but the process of naming or interpreting the external world through poetic characters or metaphors.[39] The endeavors of late-eighteenth-century natural historians (whose efforts are now being placed within a linguistic and cultural perspective) differ, however, from Vico's aims. They felt compelled to proceed back through the cycle of evolution of the human consciousness not only to arrive at man's initial thought processes, but also to discover a palpable picture of the primitive earth and its landscape.

LANDSCAPE FREED OF CULTURE

The pictorial and epistemological stratagem of anatomizing and piercing[40] is nowhere more minutely employed than in the peculiar amalgam of fable and science that determines a strain of late-eighteenth-century landscape painting. The mutable effects or intermittent life of the earth materialized in its individual signs—explored in the two foregoing chapters—become the characters of a documentary mythology.

After 1769 the German artist P. J. F. Weitsch devoted himself to capturing one of the most primeval and ambiguous monuments of the Harz mountains: the colossal gorge of the Bodetal, which is featured in local legends that attempt to explain its horseshoe configuration. According to folklore, a beautiful giantess, pursued by a malevolent river spirit, fell into the chasm. Her tormentor absconded into upper air, leaving behind the hoof print of his demonic steed. The notion that the present character or real physiognomy of a specific region is revelatory of an abstract past—the epiphany of an act of nature, metaphorically expressed through personification—continued in the art of C. D. Friedrich and Carl Gustav Carus and in the writings of Friedrich Gottlieb Klopstock, Goethe, A. W. Schlegel, and Gotthilf Heinrich Schubert.[41]

The uncertainty as to whether the abyss of the Bodetal was natural or artificial, indeed, its Druidic implications, permit us to repair once more to the Celtic remains. Discussed previously within the context of lonely plains charged with enigmatic fragments, these outcrops native to Germany, France, and England may now be seen to possess an additional archival value. The eccentrically weathered Wringcheese in Cornwall and the natural rock stack of Brimham Crag near Harrowgate were taken for material hieroglyphs as old as the world. The dolmens at Carnac and the alignments of standing stones scattered throughout Brittany were interpreted as repositories of ancient wisdom, condensing a fragmentary utterance that had yet to be fully deciphered. (See figure 93.) Borlase, in the *Antiquities of Cornwall* (1769), speculates on how these rocks were first singled out by the original inhabitants of this area precisely because they seemed untouched, because of "the firmness of their substance, continuing still the same, neither disappearing soon, as Fire; not ruffled, and by drought dissipated, like Water; not wasting away like Earth; and therefore proper emblems of Strength, Shelter, Shade, and Defence." His description makes clear that in the beginning they functioned as pure presence, as the thing itself, as natural sign, and only afterward did they become "symbols," when the rocks were shaped. Bernard de Montfauçon perceived these rude stone monuments, when unmanipulated by man, to be surer guides to truth than all the deceptive texts of ancient history put together.[42]

At last disemburdened of human authorship or divine trammels, dolmen and rock stack, forest and cliff, mountain and river, rough wall and slope, volcano and ocean exist as historical "acts" testifying to earth's former behavior. They assert their character directly as culture-free embodiments of natural catastrophe, wilderness, change, and endurance. They form the natural characteristic of the "naked" landscape recorded in the factual travel account. We may now judge why, broadly speaking, the pivotal construct at work is that of physiognomics and the principal discourse is that of penetration. Not a thinker under discussion—neither Linnaeus nor Court de Gebelin—believed that anything lay hidden within the osteology of the earth that could not be read by the trained eye. The methodology of structural exposition that bonds Lavater and Werner, Hogarth and Borlase, Warburton and Faujas de Saint-Fond, Romé de l'Isle and Saussure, is a central one. Each of these men, in his own discipline, attempted to make the external figure correspond with the internal substance, the visible shape with the invisible process or with empowered matter, the surface with depth—all localized within a concrete, historically rooted object.[43]

Composed in this spirit of penetration, Bourrit's *Description des aspects du Mont Blanc* (1776) imposes admiration for the evolution of lithic forms occurring on a monumental scale. As he apprehends them, surrounded by enormous colossi of ice, "the image of cataclysm & of chaos, ideas of eternity & of nothingness, of revolutions & order crowd to mind; the imagination is silenced." Bourrit continues: "What can it conceive to exceed such effects? In contemplating these mighty monuments [bearing witness] to the age of the universe, thought remounts for several centuries, & fixes upon the impressive and well-attested antiquity of these places. . . . " In an analogous way Laborde muses, in the *Tableaux de la Suisse* (1780), on the marks of passage left by the Grindelwald Glacier: " . . . what are historical eras in comparison to the immense changes disclosed by the study & examination of high mountains?" Forty years later, Raoul-Rochette fastened his mind on the deep structure revealed in the heart of the Jura: "At every step, one encounters boulders whose layers, convulsed in a horrible fashion, still betray the imprint of the upheavals of a primitive world. . . . " Tokens of powerful and prehuman surging, these boulders are the root letters, the building blocks of an undomesticated and temperamental landscape undergoing perpetual, if currently less visible, movement. By extension, Raoul-Rochette salutes those solitary monoliths washed down into Alpine meadows. These "solid," "abiding," and "eternal" giants are "witnesses" to the formative operations of the earth. Their size, internal confusion, and insistent verticality are signs spelling out the beginning and end of the world. Wetzel similarly comments on the "monstrous blocks of granite" punctuating the shores of Lake Zug—"venerable remains of the hoary [natural] monuments of our globe." At the antipodes of Asiatic Tartary, Lord Macartney read a huge inverted stone as if it were a reliable text. Unhesitatingly, he declared it "a monument [indicating] the height of the ancient surface . . . [betokening] a greater change upon the globe than any mentioned in the records of mankind." Bernardin de

Figure 226
G. Higgins, *Cheese Wring near Liskeard,
Cornwall,* from *Celtic Druids,* 1829, pl. 32.
Lithograph by W. Day.

To the Revd Charles Lyttelton LL.D. Dean of Exeter &c.   This Tolmen in Constantine Parish in Cornwall
                    is most gratefully   inscrib'd by W.^m: Borlase.

Figure 227
W. Borlase, *Tolmen in Constantine Parish in Cornwall*, from *Antiquities . . . of Cornwall*, 1769, pl. 13. Engraving. Photo courtesy Library of Congress.

Figure 228
B. Faujas de Saint-Fond, *Orbicular Granite of Corsica*, from *Essai de géologie*, 1803–1809, II, pl. 20. Engraving. Photo courtesy Bibliothèque Nationale.

Saint-Pierre stooped to hear the quieter utterance of "a tiny pebble from one of our rivers [that] is more ancient than the pyramids of Egypt."[44]

Georg Forster, on Tonga, was equally expert at deciphering the overhanging and indented coral cliffs, which communicated to him "a strong proof of some great change on our globe, as this rock can only be formed under water." Corals and madrepores are among the most conspicuous marks deposited by the sea. According to the *Reise durch Russland* (1774), Samuel Georg Gmelins perused Bogda Mountain abruptly rising from the plains and asserted that its "remarkable petrifactions" documented the former existence of a boundless stretch of salt water where now there were only measureless steppes. Morier describes the richly veined marble of Tauris, whose banded morphology gives impeccable evidence for the gradual drying up of the lakes and marshes of ancient Persia. With ease, the piercing eye recapitulates the historical process legible in the stone. Analogously, Cook discerned the faint and wavy tracks of the ocean's transit on Norton Sound Peninsula; he points out that it must once have flowed over the isthmus. According to such "physiognomic" investigations we may also comprehend the senior Forster's observations that Easter Island reveals "the appearance of a land that has lately undergone a great alteration by fire."[45] Decoding the coast of Norway, Edy determines that it "bears an exact resemblance to the fragments of a world in ruins, or to the elements of one about to be created." Otto von Kotzebue concludes from his study of the South Seas that man is "very young on this old earth." He extends the content of the vast archives of the Pacific to include the strata of mountains in which "the ruins of a more ancient world lie buried."[46]

The characterizing message in code is evident primarily in the tendency to speak in a pruned idiom of spatial vectors. Burke, by his discussion of power in the *Essay on the Sublime and the Beautiful* (1756–57), primed the reader that "a perpendicular has more force in forming the sublime than an inclined plane." This apperception gained currency through the research in depth conducted by geognosts and mineralogists. By examining the vertical structure of mountains they recognized the signs of sudden upheaval, and by perusing horizontal strata they discerned the serenity of infinite duration. Schubert, in *Ansichten von der Nachtseite der Naturwissenschaft* (1808), senses in the crooked, jutting layers of primary granite mountains a "surging, bold spirit" striving from within the mass. Literally, the weight of resistant matter is uplifted by an inhering power. Romé de l'Isle's Neptunian vision of widespread primitive crystallization suggests plunging deeps in which an aboriginal substance precipitates out.[47]

Analogously, mines, grottos, hollows, and hidden or submerged landscapes elicit an idiom of fathoming consonant with entering the matrix of the earth. Conversely, valleys, deserts, defiles, and rivers evoke lateral sundering, the piercing of barriers, the skimming of a plane surface. Hence,

Figure 229
D. Raoul-Rochette, *The Roche Ohistein*,
from *Lettres sur la Suisse*, 1823, I, part I,
pl. 21. Lithograph by Villeneuve and
Engelmann. Photo courtesy Cabinet des
Estampes, Bibliothèque Nationale.

LANDSCAPE FREED OF CULTURE

the vertical, the horizontal, and the diagonal form an abbreviated physical vocabulary of the forces operative in the world at its advent and still at work, covertly or overtly. The nineteenth-century French sculptor David d'Angers best sums up this persistent scheme to recover a lost visage and thereby to understand better the present face of the land: "Mountains are passions, the signs of global revolutions. . . . " Differently stated, when the world experiences one of its catastrophes, perforce its "physiognomy" is altered.[48]

"Naked" Precincts

O! que le spectacle séroient intéressant; O! que notre curiosité séroit agréablement flattée, s'il nous étoit permis de pénétrer jusques à ces Principes. Un nouveau Monde se dévoileroit à nos yeux; la Nature devenue transparente ne céléroit plus sa marche: ses ateliers & ses laboratoires séroient overts. . . .
Charles Bonnet

They [modern chemists] penetrate into the recesses of nature and show how she works in her hiding places. They ascend into the heavens: they have discovered how blood circulates, and the nature of the air we breathe; they have acquired new and almost unlimited powers; they can command the thunders of heaven, mimic the earthquake, and even mock the invisible world with its own shadows. . . .
Mary Shelley

Fundamental to the progress of scientific exploration in the eighteenth century is the Ruskinian truism that insight into the operations of nature is gained only through a sensitive nonegotistical penetration of its vital and individual parts. The foregoing discussion adapts itself elastically to the idea that the complement to the informed enjoyment of scenery is the intellectual pleasure that arises from the perception of a bond between the terrain and its rudest mineral constituents. In short, the entire surface becomes augmented by an infinitely stratified sense of history. Place becomes archive whose buried geology must be paleontologically exhumed through the powers of scientific piercing to the root and record of every substance. Hence, an old landscape plays a role in the present one; its enigmatic survivals function as vestiges of an ongoing process.[49]

The close-up, nontransformative scrutiny of the mineralogist probing a crystal core offers an important, if not the decisive, perceptual prototype for the appreciative penetration of the real and concrete substances of the world, an aesthetic on the ascendant during the first half of the nineteenth century. Creating an experimental *ars combinatoria*—a new and elemental Universal Characteristic—that relied on linguistic and physiognomic skills to interpret physical traces, the natural historians indicated how future travelers and serious observers might confidently prospect for imprints and correctly view earth formations, small and large.

Recently, Michel Foucault has unfolded the development of a visual science that moved from the great systems of classification launched in the second half of the seventeenth century to the clinical gaze of the early nineteeth century and was bent on the investigation of deep structures. He distinguishes between the "look" of the physician, endowed with the power of decision and intervention, and that of the earlier natural historian, gifted with the ability to read horizontally. The isolation of a specifically "medical" vision —which Foucault firmly identifies with the figure of Xavier Bichat—is defined by its ability to travel along a new path, plunging vertically from symptomatic surface to the core of tissue.[50] As we have seen, this downward optical voyage through strata, beds, and layers— attempting to render the hidden or remote manifest and near—occurred first not in the nineteenth century or in the annals of medicine, but in the eighteenth century and especially in the pages of mineralogical treatises and nonfiction voyages.

VOYAGE INTO SUBSTANCE

The objective correlative corresponding to this method of deep inquiry may be denominated the natural hieroglyph. The mineralogical sign—unlike the human glyph—constituted a living language, one that was intelligible, decipherable, and spoken by the individual manifestations of nature. Whereas the latter, according to Court de Gebelin, discloses to the initiate the secret behind the mythic origins of culture and society, the former makes known to the adept of natural history the earth's revolutionary past, present and future. In both the cultured and the wild instance, pictographic revelation of the distant and the remote occurs close up and within the narrow "framed" confines of a lithic fragment. The chunk or sample of earth (whether delicate quartz crystal or rude basalt lump), depending on whether it is scanned horizontally or vertically, functions simultaneously as a material relic of the geologic past transported to the present and as a tangible sign of collapsed spatial and temporal perspectives. The natural imprint permits penetration to the fabled time of "the beginning," and, unlike the obscurantism of the human construct, it also manifests the course of the terrain's evolution.

Such recasting of perception imparts an entirely new signification to the word *discovery*, which now takes on a richer meaning. The scientific discoverer, like the mineralogist, "pushes back" frontiers and delves beneath the obvious; he explores across while thrusting through obstacles. In a nutshell, his aim is to reveal directly what he sees clearly, to express concisely what he lucidly "reads" in and under all natural appearances.

In light of what has been said, the physical and intellectual penetration of nature—though clearly endemic to the second half of the eighteenth century—was not so late an occurrence as Foucault would suggest. Nor was it limited to natural history. In Germany, in the field of aesthetics, Winckelmann and Herder were attracted to a sensuous plenitude lurking under the ocean and in the human nervous system. In France, in the area of poetics, André Chenier apostrophized Buffon for peering into the earth's entrails and ignoring any false barrier or obstruction. He had similar high praise for the astronomers Jean-Sylvain Bailly and Sir William Herschel, who, by means of the telescope, pierced the clouds.[51] Following a different tack, the British writers Gerard and Duff specifically commented that a genius for science is formed by honing one's powers of sagacious penetration whereas a genius for the arts depends on the cultivation of a shallow "brightness." By this epistemological opposition they established a tension between searching knowledge and surface brilliance.[52]

These ideas attached themselves to the poetics of absorption. Scottish moralists of the stamp of Francis Hutcheson, Hugh Blair, and Lord Kames suggested that moral judgment involves a sympathetic participation with those other than the agent himself, that to be engrossed in something results in the obliteration of one's identity. Such sympathetic engulfment by the activities of man—characteristic of the early eighteenth century—was transmuted by the century's close into the scrutiny of alien terrain.[53]

By the same token, the pursuers of basic morphologies, from Saussure to Goethe, fathomed the ancient history of singular forms. This exacting and directed mode of vision differed fundamentally from that of Rousseau, who dreamed of existing unconsciously within nature.[54] Rousseau's *Reveries du promeneur solitaire* (1782), which epitomized the undemanding quality of sensations, found a spiritual kinship with certain rites and primitive devotions. To capture this attitude of passive admiration, the Daniells sketched the waterfall at Papanasam, recording intent and unquestioning worshipers prostrate before rock carvings. The text of *Oriental Scenery* (which contains this illustration) extols the swift stream noisily carving its way through a gorge. The authors muse how these sights effortlessly stimulate piety and operate with great effect "upon the minds of the Hindoos, who attach ideas of a religious nature to these objects."[55]

The absence of distance or recognition of separate identity of beholder from observed phenomenon, implicit in Rousseau and in the world's nature cults, had to be rectified by dint of hard looking. The fluid continuum between man and nature characteristic of the former modes of perception became a substantial interval traversed by a vertical act of penetration in the latter.

Georg Forster takes up the naturalists' will to see in *Ein Blick in das Ganze der Natur* (1781). From the perspective of his world travels, he asks a momentous question: What is nature? What is this amazing plasticity that mutates, transforms, dissolves, and renews itself? Is it what Plato and his followers claimed: an Intelligence, a World Soul, the immediate act of God, a living force that enlivens everything and reconstitutes matter? As a scientist, Forster refuses to enter into the quagmire of metaphysical speculation. Instead, he voices a modern attitude: Truth is dependent on observation. Like the British materialists and the French vitalists, Forster sees perpendicularly at the same instant that he sees broadly. Everything in the universe is infused with a living energy. Indeed, like so many of his contemporaries, he returns to the Pre-Socratic philosophy of the four elements: "There is no lifeless, infertile element. . . ." Entering the interstices of matter, discovering the interior of things—differs, therefore, from a Rousseauian passive curiosity and from an Oriental worshipful acceptance. Aggressive and admiring inspection responds to the individuality of substance.[56]

The scientific and totally Western compulsion to overcome a resisting world implies a struggle foreign to the Picturesque. The case of James Hakewell will serve as both reprise and brief reminder. In the introduction to his *Picturesque Tour of Jamaica* (1825), Hakewell remarks that the ad-

Figure 230
J. B. Fraser, *Bhyramaghattee*, from *Views in the Himala Mountains*, 1820, pl. 19. Color aquatint by R. Havell and Son. Photo courtesy India Office Library.

Figure 231
Thomas and William Daniell, *The Water-Fall at Puppanassum*, from *Oriental Scenery*, 1797, II, pl. 2. Color aquatint. Photo courtesy India Office Library.

jective *picturesque* is bestowed on any work "intended to convey a general idea of the surfaces and external appearance of a country."

On the contrary, the sudden access opened to the material reality of nature by the willed gaze of the natural historian represents a move toward a vertical perception penetrative rather than a horizontal imagination associative.[57] The new vision recognizes that nature is both envelope and ensemble of hidden operations. Thus, Maupertuis laments the colossal inutility of the Egyptian pyramids and of all such monuments riddled with underground cavities. He, like De l'Isle de Sales, voices the criticism that the pharaohs would have done better to excavate the interior of the earth to the same depth as the height of their gigantic tombs: "We know nothing of the netherworld; our deepest mines barely dent its outer crust; if we could but first arrive at its core, it is easy to conceive that one would find substances very different from those we know & very singular phenomena. . . ." Mercier adds his regrets: "Empires fall, generations are annihilated, seas change their beds, continents larger than Europe are overwhelmed, mountains are opened by subterranean fires, but the substance of the globe does not seem to feel it; it is but a puncture on an orange; the form, the grandeur, are unaltered, and it is the surface only that is lightly scratched. . . ."[58]

How different are the vituperations of Rousseau; how antipathetic to Enlightenment trends are his moralistic dislike of the Mineral Kingdom and his preference for botany conducted on the level! In the *septième promenade* of the *Rêveries du promeneur solitaire* (1782), Rousseau spurns the depths of the earth with its buried treasures constantly tempting man's cupidity. He interprets these riches as a reservoir, serving as a supplement to surface wealth that one day will contribute beneficences more properly within human reach. Man "mines the earth"; he "seeks imaginary goods instead of real ones within its center at the risk of his life, at the expense of his health." He "flees the sun and daylight, which he is no longer worthy to behold"; he "buries himself alive and no longer merits living in the open." "Quarries, gulfs, forges, furnaces, an apparatus of engines, hammers, smoke, and fire" replace "the gentle image of pastoral labor." Where Rousseau perceives only degradation, Christoph Traugott Delius, in his *Bergbaukunst* (1773), marvels at "the subterranean geography." Since it remains unknown in its greatest depth, he declares that it would be of greatest interest to scientists to fathom the internal matrix of mountains—which surely exceeds either the horizon or the ocean's extent.[59]

As these authors suggest, the eighteenth century's paradigm for a landscape in depth was the natural cavern, grotto, cavern, or cave. Since antiquity— and this was confirmed by architectural practice during the Renaissance— these hollows had symbolized entry into the earth, descent into a Plutonian zone bereft of light but laden with darkness and density.[60]

VOYAGE INTO SUBSTANCE

Yet the multifaceted veneration of the grotto is only a single, salient example of a pervasive trend. In fact, beginning with the second half of the eighteenth century, the explorer's total effort may be characterized as one of penetrating nature in all its facets—and not only vertically.

At this juncture, certain firsthand reflections on what might be termed the psychology of exploration are pertinent. John Leyden, a student of Africa, remarks in his *Discoveries and Travels* (1799) on the necessity for thoroughness on the part of just such an investigator. Nevertheless, he urges caution in the examination of objects that seem obvious to the senses. In addition to the bane of exaggeration and poetic license, perceptual mistakes may arise. One such ingrained behavioral mechanism impels the mind to fill a painful void even when its survey of the scene is admittedly imperfect. He warns that the law of *horror vacuity*, so important in the earlier stages of progress, has become in the nineteenth century a principle "pregnant with perceptual error"; "To relieve the uneasy feeling which it occasions, the geographer seeks, with the most imperfect means, to fill up the wholes of that space, of which he conceives the habitable world to consist. . . ." What Leyden pinpoints as the geographer's characteristic fear of emptiness—his belief in complete penetrability—may be extended to include explorers of all stamps.

Fontenelle, in a eulogy of Pitton de Tournefort delivered before the French Academy of Sciences, praises his colleague for having realized that botany is not a sedentary pursuit. This discipline cannot be acquired through repose, while one is sequestered in the comfortable penumbra of one's study. Like the practicing geographer, the student of plants must cross mountains and forests, clamber over steep rocks, and expose himself to dangers. "The only Books [i.e., plants] which can profoundly instruct us in this matter are randomly scattered over the face of the earth and must be gathered. . . ." Fontenelle then muses on the rarity of Pitton's gifts: "The degree of passion [for completeness] which suffices to make a different kind of scientist, does not suffice to produce a great Botanist. . . ."[61]

At midcentury, Charles Bonnet took up this refrain, speaking on behalf of biological and mineralogical explorers, who were only then "beginning to traverse the rich & vast collections of nature." Bonnet continues: ". . . amid this innumerable multiplicity of diverse productions which it has assembled, how many exist which we have not even imagined, & of which we do not even suspect the existence?" Saussure states this more succinctly: "The sole aim of the majority of voyagers who call themselves naturalists, is to collect curiosities; they walk, or rather, stride, eyes fixed on the ground gathering tiny bits and pieces here and there without countenancing any general observations. . . ." Disdainfully, Saussure likens these practitioners to antiquarians who scratch away at the Roman soil, ignoring the glories of a Pantheon or Colosseum. He hastens to add that he is not advocating negligence in the observation of detail. On the contrary,

LANDSCAPE FREED OF CULTURE

such precision forms the unique basis for solid knowledge. Saussure's words evoke the distant memory of Pitton de Tournefort. The serious observer of mountains must depart from broad, well-worn valley roads and clamber among high summits. The reward for difficult excursions where horse and carriage is renounced, where enormous fatigue is endured, and where one is exposed to great dangers is a comprehensive view of the world below.[62]

It is exactly this language desirous of completeness that emanates from the pages of the factual travel accounts and permeates their illustrations. In April 1786, when La Pérouse left Easter Island bound for Hawaii, he quite naturally reflected on the enormous contributions made by Cook: "Chance allows the most ignorant to discover islands; but only great men are capable of leaving nothing wanting concerning the countries which they have seen. . . ." D'Entrecasteaux, in the preface to his *Voyage à la recherche de La Pérouse* (1808), takes up this theme of filling in gaps. He shows no desire to halt at the threshold of the unknown. While visiting the southern tip of Van Diemen's Land, he hugged the coast in order to chart its every sinuosity. Martin Sauer, who accompanied Joseph Billings on his *Expedition to North Russia* (1802), was enraged when his commander abandoned all thoughts of revisiting the American coast to the south of Cook's River because the season was too far advanced: "Nothing in the world could have afforded me less satisfaction than this resolution, which I regarded as the conclusion of an expedition that was set on foot with unbounded liberality by the most magnanimous sovereign in the world; which had raised the expectations of all nations to the highest pitch, and induced mankind to anticipate the satisfaction of obtaining the most complete knowledge of geography of this unknown part of the globe. . . ."[63]

Both the desire and the possibility for more penetrative exploration are grounded in certain historical factors that distinguish eighteenth-century endeavors from earlier ventures. Bailly, in eulogizing Cook, remarks that, in spite of the achievements of Columbus and Magellan, the globe remains unknown at its extremities. This situation held true until the 1760s. Without chronometers and scientific personnel, voyagers could carry out only superficial geographical exploration; they were unable to study in any profound manner the lands they discovered. Among the English, John Byron quickly crossed the Pacific to the Marianas, only touching upon some insignificant islands. Samuel Wallis, his successor, rediscovered Tahiti, first sighted in 1606 by Pedro de Quiros and named Sagitarea. Philip Carteret became separated from Wallis after emerging from the Strait of Magellan. He discovered Pitcairn Island, sailed to the outposts of Polynesia, provided a more accurate chart indicating the profile of the Solomons, and revealed the existence of the Saint George Canal between New Britain and New Ireland.[64]

The Frenchman Louis-Antoine de Bougainville did more for science and the goal of discovery in depth than the three Englishmen who preceded him. His expedition was not just another crossing of the Pacific. He remained for lengthy periods in South America, Indonesia, and South Africa. Moreover, he left an unforgettable image of the Bay of Rio before departing for the South Seas. His description of the natural beauty of the Moluccas and the Celebes, though somewhat conventional, represented a novel effort to enter into the individual presence of a place. Like Cook (whose first voyage coincided with his own) and La Pérouse, Bougainville helped to disclose the immensity and the relative emptiness of the Pacific.

On his second voyage, to avoid the "westerlies," Cook sailed west to east across the Pacific, following a course never before attempted. Using several chronometers to navigate in totally unknown waters, he entered areas and saw lands which were not only unexplored but whose existence had not even been suspected. In sum, the glory of modern (as opposed to ancient) geography, and that of the latter part of the eighteenth century in particular, was its penetrating maritime ventures.

However, one cannot ignore the progress in overland travel. At the beginning of the eighteenth century many continents were vast cartographic blanks. To be sure, the Cordillera of the Andes and the volcanos of the Canaries had been known since the sixteenth century, but neither they nor any other of the major land masses discussed in chapter 2 had actually been probed. In 1749, Buffon declared that the heart of Africa was almost as unknown in his era as it had been in antiquity. Japan and China, which had been mapped by the Jesuits in the seventeenth century, became partially closed to foreigners in the eighteenth century. On the other hand, Persia, where Tournefort had herborized in 1701, was thoroughly crisscrossed by Le Bruyn.

Geographers also made significant progress on more far-flung frontiers. In one of the first scientific expeditions organized by a learned academy and protected by a government, Bouguer and La Condamine headed for the Andes in 1736 to carry out geological tests. After 1750, as was the case with maritime voyages, terrestrial expeditions multiplied. In 1786, Catherine the Great invited the German naturalist Peter Simon Pallas to explore the Urals and Siberia. James Bruce discovered the source of the Blue Nile and delineated the massif of Abyssinia. George MacKenzie trekked across the Canadian Rockies, and Constantin-François de Volney visited the mountain chains of Lebanon in 1783 before revealing the Appalachians to the French public in 1803. Bernardin de Saint-Pierre and Le Gentil provided some sense of the terrain endemic to Madagascar and of the forbidding, stormy reefs and barriers of the Indian Ocean.[65] Generally speaking, however, it was not until the nineteenth century, with the monumental efforts of Humboldt and Rugendas, that the interior of tropical lands became better understood.

The Montgolfiers' invention of 1783 embodied the acme of extension into the limitless. Flight, as the inverse of confinement, resulted in a penetrating

LANDSCAPE FREED OF CULTURE

Giovanni Luder fece asceso in Aria per mezzo di un Globo
Aerostatico diretto dal Sig.: D.r Gael: Cioni Dalla Piazza d.
Carraine di Firenze il dì 16. Luglio 1795. a ore 7½ pomerid.
e discese alle 9. nella Piev.e di Lemole distante 8. Mig: da Firen·
cino al Pontassieve.

and panoramic view of any country or situation. The excursion upward or across the landscape meant that the aeronaut was wholly immersed in the atmosphere while visually embracing areas still inaccessible to more conventional forms of travel.[66] Not land or sea but virgin space became the object of the balloon voyage.

Indeed, manned flight indicated the conquest of a new element. The ascending gods of modern scientific mythology floated at the behest of air currents, recently analyzed by French and British meteorologists. According to a contemporary account, in contrast with a ship, which is partially immersed in water, an aerostatic vessel is completely submerged; it "forms a whole [*un tout*] with the fluid in which it swims."[67] Rouland, in his *Tableau historique des propriétés et des phénomènes de l'air* (1784), reiterates this theme of immanence. Balloons offer man the opportunity "to penetrate to the center of the atmosphere, & and to traverse immense distances in a very short time, while voyaging at the whim of the winds."[68]

In this specific connection it is important to underscore that balloon flights, in contradistinction to all other modes of travel, by definition avoided surfaces. This point was clearly recognized at the time, and Faujas de Saint-Fond's astute observations may stand for a host of others. Bereft of the solid support of the earth or the flexible undulations of the ocean, the balloonist flies *in* the air. The French scientist remarks in *La machine aérostatique* (1783) that the word *navigation* connotes a hard body sustained on a level plane. Hence, the use of this word is inappropriate for a soft, ethereal medium of clouds, mists, and exhalations. One cannot be on the surface of the atmosphere, he asserts, but must be immersed "even to the very depths of this liquid."[69] The *European Magazine*, in its report of André-Jacques Garnerin's descent by parachute on September 21, 1802, enlarges on this theme of spatial intrusion by quoting from the French balloonist's journal: "I rose amidst the most express silence, and launching into infinite space. . . . I quickened my ascending impulse, and rose through light and thin vapors, where the cold informed me that I was entering into the upper region. . . ." In fact, this first regular user of the parachute actually increased his sensation of vertiginous euphoria at being where man was not by plummeting downward through the nebular domain of aerial meteors.[70]

The foregoing overview prepares us for the conclusion that an aggressive Plinean impulse was at work in the factual travel accounts. Not only balloonists but all manner of travelers from the late eighteenth century on comment on the snares and delights of being enmeshed in cloud and mist. Otto von Kotzebue, near the Aleutian Islands and in the Bering Strait, declares: "We penetrate through the gloomy veil, which eternally hovers over these seas, and shores not shaded by a tree inhospitably frown upon us with their snow-covered summits. We shudder to find

VOYAGE INTO SUBSTANCE

man also settled here!" A no less active approach is indicated by visitants to falls and geysers; recall that the artist depicting the Pisse-Vache or the Staubbach stationed himself "in the fume." (See figure 144.) During his *Travels in Iceland* (1811), MacKenzie, while standing on a feeble support overhanging an abyss, became "enveloped in thick vapours; his ears stunned by thundering noises."[71]

More generally, it may be said that the fervor for studies involving intrepidness seems to belong inherently to the students of the natural sciences. The Abbé de Saint-Non proffers an assessment. While meditating on the death of the Elder Pliny, he was moved to reflect upon the modern breed of investigator: "One cannot perhaps admire enough the kind of audacity sparked by curiosity when it has developed into a passion.... Such it seems to me was [that possessed by] Pliny tranquilly and leisurely strolling under a burning atmosphere, marching in cold-blood towards danger, & observing, his tablets in hand, the most terrible spectacle that could strike the eyes...." Pliny's fiery fate, well known through the letters of his son, was foreshadowed by the leap into the gulf of Etna made in the fifth century B.C. by the Sicilian philosopher and mystagogue Empedocles.[72] Nevertheless, that fanatical act of immolation, motivated by the ambition to be declared a god, differs pronouncedly from Pliny's serene study of the eruption of Vesuvius. The Greek's mysterious disappearance relates more to the Rousseauian desire to lose oneself in the immensity and even the violence of nature than to the knowing penetration of matter. His impulse, unlike Pliny's methodical act, was not a deliberate sacrifice on the altar of science. It is just this distinction that sets the eighteenth-century scientific explorer apart from his more picturesquely and subjectively inclined colleagues.

William Hamilton, according to the documentation provided in the *Supplement to the Campi Phlegraei* (1779), invoked comparison to the shade of the ancient naturalist by his bold action and his fearless attitude:

After an Eruption, I have walked in some of those subterraneous, or cover'd galleries, which were exceedingly curious; the sides, top, and bottom being worn perfectly smooth, and even in most parts, by the violence of the current's of the red hot Lava's, which they had convey'd for many weeks successively; in others the Lava had incrusted the sides of those Channels with some very extraordinary Scoriae beautifully ramified. White salts, in the form of dropping stalactites were also attached to many parts of the ceiling of those cover'd galleries. . . .

The eagerness of Hamilton's pursuit of this branch of natural history was demonstrated again by a hair-raising walk along a red-hot, bubbling "river" of lava loaded with scoriae. At one point, he forded the newly toughened crust, some 50–60 feet wide, coasting through heat and smoke along "its Channels up to its very source, within a quarter mile of the Crater," where loud explosions and the smell of sulfur greeted him. (See figure 148.)

In the *Campi Phlegraei* (1776), Hamilton provides numerous descriptions and illustrations of the shifting interiors of craters. He justifies this procedure by noting that they perpetually change their form with every eruption, "so that Travellers' accounts of this part of the Volcano can seldom agree." The specimenlike closeup of the entrails of Mount Vesuvius is consonant with the dictates of scientific scrutiny. Houel, despite the title of his work, was correspondingly committed to the view that one must narrowly examine magma, smoke, and crevices in order to correctly capture Etna's gaping mouth.[73] (See figure 147.)

This wholehearted giving oneself up to ardent perusal has a watery counterpart. Georg Forster, in his description of a spout sighted off Cape Stephens in May 1773, minutely records how the ship approached and finally became established "directly over the whirl-pool." The crew was terrified at being in a boiling sea from which arose gradually tapering funnel clouds that seemed to descend to meet a rising spiral of liquid. The Forsters, however, as befits men of science, did not flinch even when pelted by hail: "Our situation during all this time was very dangerous and alarming; a phaenomenon which carried so much terrific majesty in it; and connecting as it were the sea with the clouds, made our oldest mariners uneasy and at a loss how to behave; for most of them, though they had viewed waterspouts at a distance, yet had never been so beset with them as we were. . . ." Lesseps underwent a congruous experience inland in October 1787. A violent hurricane ("*l'ouragan*") suddenly blew up in the small Russian hamlet of Tchekafki. Although the sight of the tremendous gust at first made Lesseps fling himself on the ground, he writes, "it struck my fancy to wander in the environs; I scarcely took several steps, when, seized by the wind, I felt myself totter: I remained firm and wanted to pursue my notion & my chase. . . ." Arriving at a river bank, he soon repented of this folly.[74]

A case quite unlike that of the self-induced experiences of Hamilton, Houel, the Forsters, and Lesseps was that of the corvette *Atrevida*, which during the Malaspina expedition found itself surrounded by icebergs. This occurrence, on the night of January 28, 1794, took place just west of Cadiz and was commemorated in a view taken by the ship's artist, Fernando Brambila. The sketch accentuates the height of the icebergs in relation to the beset vessel, conveying the impression that it is totally lodged within a dynamic nature. Kotzebue, during his expedition made to the South Seas, noted that after a tremendous storm the voyagers suddenly discovered they were ringed by ice. Just as in the cases of Hamilton and Forster, this novel situation of looking out from within an active matter caused Kotzebue to see what remained concealed when viewed from afar. With astonishment the crew perceived that "the interior of the berg was fabricated of pure ice." Based on this information, they "all went—armed with swings and crowbars—in order to examine more narrowly this wonder." The scientific party soon became convinced that the towering hundred-foot mass was

330   VOYAGE INTO SUBSTANCE

"*Ur-Eis*," not only because of the purity and homogeneity of the core lodged beneath a superficial covering of moss and grass but also because of the many mammoth bones and teeth revealed as it melted in the sun.

Captain Back, the artist on Franklin's first and second journeys to the Polar Sea, captured the predicament of boats in a swell amongst ice. (See figure 158.) The account makes perfectly plain that this outing was voluntary and was embarked upon for the purpose of close observation. The party set forth at daybreak on August 24, 1826, advancing a few miles between heavy floes. Aiming for Mount Conybear, which was directly in sight, they were unexpectedly exposed to a long swell that drove the sheet of bay ice formed the night before onto the reefs. "It therefore became necessary to penetrate into the pack, and keep by the side of the reefs; but in doing so, the boats were exposed to no little danger of being broken in passing through the narrow channels between the masses of ice which were tossing up the swell, and from which large pieces frequently fell. . . ."[75]

Thus, running like Ariadne's thread through various narratives is an expressive vocabulary of piercing, predicated on the craving to be "*au milieu*," to witness "*das Innere*," to "walk across." A logical extension of this longing to penetrate led to the ultimate in deep exploration. Strangely, as noted, balloon accounts usually did not stress height or verticality as much as they focused on submersion within the atmosphere. On the contrary, a particular aspect of voyage literature concerning the exploration of the ocean accentuated a plunging gaze. The diving bell (experimented with by the astronomer Edmond Halley in the seventeenth century but perfected by the Swede Triedwald at the close of the eighteenth century) ensured that no part of nature would be wholly secluded from human entry. Typically, a diver might sit comfortably for 90 minutes at a depth of 52 feet. George Adams writes that "by the glass at the top of the bell, so much light was transmitted when the sun shone, and the sea undisturbed, that [the diver] could see perfectly well to read and write, or to find anything that lay at the bottom; but in dark weather, and when the sea was rough, he found it as dark as night at the bottom."[76]

Although the sea (unlike the air) possesses surface, its soft density and swell suggest a comparable richness contained within, lurking under the waves. It is in this incarnation that Bernardin de Saint-Pierre apostrophizes the ocean and urges its exploration by diving bell. Open waters are a "cradle," a "tomb," but above all a liquid repository in whose bosom slumbers the debris of the earth: the heaps of rocks washed down by torrents and rivers. Within them float dissolved oils, bitumins, and nitrates that contribute to the fabrication of onshore volcanos. Here, too, over the course of centuries cities were buried and human ambition overrun— behold the example of Rome, the better part of whose empire no longer reposes above ground but slumbers on the bed of the Tiber.

To spot ruins trapped beneath the waves (indeed, to probe the deeps at all), the eye must avoid looking at surface reflections. The gaze cannot skim if it means to discern the mosses, corals, submarine grottos, fish, and even inundated civilizations inhabiting these fluid regions. It was the reports of the existence of submerged relics that first drew attention to natural phenomena dwelling below the tides. Richard Pococke tells of sunken remains at Alexandria. Forbes, in the *Oriental Memoirs* (1813), reports that the archives of the Jains at Kurkul mention a golden colossus swallowed long ago by the sea, which they believe "can still be sometimes seen at low water."[77]

What is most telling in this connection is the perception and recognition of an independent undersea world possessing its own logic and coherence. Pococke, in the *Description of the East* (1743–1745), describes how he "looked on" the Dead Sea, how he tasted and tested its brackish liquid, and that he "was much pleased with what [he] observed of this extraordinary water." Furthermore, he "swam" in it and "dipped several times." Though he did not immerse himself in the Atlantic, Chappe d'Auteroche reflected on the alien power that relentlessly drew the inquiring mind to examine the face of the ocean. Life aboard ship, he suggests, is tedious and uniform only to those who cast an indifferent look at nature. "The calm of a beautiful day is in some measure less interesting than those agitated moments, when the waves, raised by the winds, seem to become confounded with the sky. Profound abysses gape at every instant. . . ." He concludes that man, "through his genius and audacity," is "worthy of embracing the extent [of nature] & of penetrating its marvels."

Phosphorescence typically induced prolonged plummeting of the ocean's recesses. Andrew Sparrman states that, in addition to the usual glimmers found sparkling on the surface, "there was seen in the night a strong gleam of light called by sailors *maarsken*, or sea-shine." "This," he goes on, "opened to me a door, if I may be allowed the expression, to nature's copious storehouse in the deep; so that at one hasty overview I could get a glimpse of that amazing superfluity, which feeds millions of fish, and at the same time lines the inside of the whale, that great colossus of the deep. . . ."

Examples are so numerous that one more will stand for the entire class. Bioluminescence was especially characteristic of tropical waters. Jacques Milbert, on his voyage made to the Ile de France, noted that it was customary for naturalists and artists to station themselves each evening at portholes of the corvette's main cabin:

We passed hours at a time gazing at the golden and silver masses moving in all directions at the bottom of the waters: their brilliance is all the more vivid when the sea is agitated and the night especially dark. . . . by the effulgence of these mobile phosphorescences one can distinguish other animals, particularly swordfish, others, more dim, deprived of this luminous property display [their] enormous silhouettes by swimming in the midst of this apparently encircling sea. . . .[78]

Clearly, such vertical perception was not limited to the oceans. Jonathan Carver, traveling in North America, admired that extensive river, the "Ouisconsin." "The water of it is exceedingly clear, and through it you may perceive a fine and sandy bottom, tolerably free from rocks. . . ." Perhaps most beautiful is Carver's Winckelmannian portrayal of the remarkable depth and immaculate pellucidity of Lake Superior:

The water in general appeared to lie on a bed of rocks. When it was calm, and the sun shone bright, I could sit in my canoe, where the depth was upwards of six fathoms, and plainly see huge piles of stone at the bottom, of different shapes, some of which appeared as if they were hewn. The water at this time was as pure and transparent as air; and my canoe seemed as if it hung suspended in that element. It was impossible to look attentively through this limpid medium at the rocks below, without finding, before many minutes were elapsed, your head swim, and your eyes no longer able to behold the dazzling scene. . . .

Many years later, Jacques Milbert jotted down a similar experience on Lake George that compelled him to look deeply. Jean Houel, on the road to Catania, peered into the Channel of La Brucca, whose untroubled and translucent flow allowed the traveler "to see the moss and sand that carpets its floor." Houel continues:

This sand is enameled, it sparkles with all sorts of colors reflected by tiny shards of variegated stones of which it is composed. In this humid and serene region one takes a boat ride [simply] for pleasure. One quickly identifies the fish that play in this limpid water, water so perfectly transparent that it vanishes, such that the fish seem to fly rather than to swim; & occasionally one is tempted to believe that the boat is suspended in space, & touching nothing. These fish from time to time are lost to sight under forests of flowering moss, & in rocaille palaces that nature herself built for them. . . .[79]

Henry Salt's description of the banks of the River Tacazze in Abyssinia is more robust. As his party progressed upstream, he found its passage interrupted by numerous fords containing deep holes or pits. These "present a similar appearance to the small lochs or tarns found amoung our own mountains in the north," and "it is in these depths that the hippo chiefly delights." When shot, the animals dropped quietly to the bottom; "the water being very clear," Salt could "distinctly see them so low as twenty feet beneath the surface."[80]

A visual corollary to watery observation in depth is land perception in breadth. Forceful lateral movement across a terrain carries with it analogous overtones of penetration. The attack on the interior of a region is best epitomized by the florescing exploration of Africa. James Jackson, in the introductions to his *Accounts* of Marocco (1809) and of Timbuctu (1820), recapitulates the tale of more than half a century of struggles to conquer the dark continent, which "has baffled the enterprise of Europe (unlike every other part of the habitable world)" and which "still remains, as it were, a sealed book, at least if the book has been opened, we have scarcely got beyond the title page." Jackson calls for an end to solitary travel (here

Figure 234
Henry Salt, *View on the Banks of the*
Tacazze, from *Voyage to Abyssinia . . . ,*
1814, pl. p. 357. Engraving by C. Heath.
Photo courtesy British Library.

he is thinking of explorers ranging from James Bruce and Mungo Park to Captains Peddie and Tuckey) and heralds the dawning age of group effort. Prime mover for the latter approach was the African Association, formed in 1788 and counting among its founders Sir Joseph Banks. The society was expressly constituted "for the purpose of Promoting the Discovery of the Inland Districts of Africa." The published plan of this assembly, however, is more universal in significance, since it sheds light on the state of exploration in general at the close of the eighteenth century. Its underlying premise is that nothing excites the learned and the unlearned so equally as "the nature and history of those parts of the world which have not, to our knowledge, been hitherto explored." The plan continues: "To this desire the Voyages of the late Captain Cook have so far afforded gratification, that nothing worthy of research by Sea, the Poles themselves excepted, remains to be examined; but by Land, the objects of Discovery are still so vast, as to include at least one third of the habitable surface of the earth: for much of Asia, a still large proportion of America, and almost the whole of Africa, are unvisited and unknown. . . ." The exhortative language of the *Proceedings* is unmistakable: "Notwithstanding the progress of discovery on the coasts and borders of that vast continent, the map of its interior is still but a wide extended blank, on which the Geographer, on the authority of Leo Africanus, and the Xeriff Edriffi the Nubian Author, has traced, with a hesitating hand, a few names of unexplored rivers and of uncertain nations. . . ."[81]

The English were not alone in their appetite for exact information about an unbounded area assaulted successively by Savery, Le Vaillant, Volney, and Grandpré. The *Relations de plusieurs voyages à la côte d'Afrique, à Maroc, au Sénégal, à Gorée, à Galam, etc.*, compiled by Raymond Saugnier in 1791, attests to the fact that, despite suffering endured by Gallic visitors to equatorial climes, they were constantly "devoured by the desire to return to the interior" in order to make discoveries they believed would be "very useful for commerce and natural history."

Despite these heroic French efforts, the specific incursion into West Africa was undertaken most stunningly, and was executed with fearlessness and perseverence, by Mungo Park, following the scheme outlined by the Association. Simultaneously, a private traveler, W. G. Browne, urged on by curiosity and the spirit of adventure, attempted unsuccessfully to traverse the area from east to west. He managed to penetrate into Dafur (Egypt), believing it would be relatively easy to enter Abyssinia by Kordofan. In May 1793, Browne finally joined the Sudan caravan making its way over a sterile mountainous track to Gebel Ramlie, "a valley of unbounded extent, covered with rocks and sand, diversified with scattered date trees, and stunted bushes." Captain Philip Beaver of the Royal Navy explains in his *African Memoranda* (1805) how he established a settlement on the western coast and the government's resulting interest in the best mode of opening a communication inland. By 1820, George Mollien could confidently, if misleadingly, entitle his narrative *Travels in the Interior of Africa*. Originally intent on retracing Mungo Park's steps, Mollien soon became resolved that it was more important to "strike out a new track." "The regions which I had to traverse in pursuing this direction were almost unknown," he went on, "and afforded scope for observations equally numerous and interesting." Benefiting from the geographical expertise of the French naturalist Eyries, who had been aboard the frigate *Medusa* in 1816 when she was wrecked south of Cape Blanco on the west coast of Africa, Mollien's journey through Senegal demonstrates a spirit of international cooperation novel for overland travel but long connected with ocean voyages.[82]

East and South Africa experienced attacks markedly different from those unleashed on the western part. Henry Salt, who roamed Abyssinia, left the only modern description of this part of Africa since Captain Hamilton had sailed there in 1720. Captain Beaver wandered through Quiloa, the ancient capital of East Africa, and Lord Valentia navigated along its margins from Guardafui to the Straits of Babelmandel. The shores of South Africa, by contrast, had been well known since the early seventeenth century, when the Dutch established a settlement at Cape Town. The first detailed narrative of this outpost was written in 1718 by Peter Kolbe. Regarded as authentic for nearly half a century, it was cast into disrepute for its inaccuracies by the Abbé de La Caille, an eminent French astronomer, who headed for the Cape in 1760. Most significant from the viewpoint of penetration were the several natural-history excursions performed by Andrew Sparrman. Both Le Vaillant in 1780 and Barrow in 1797 were influenced by the eminent Swedish scientist's intimate acquaintance with the different kingdoms of nature. The latter even traversed the territory belonging to the colony as far as the Orange River. Jackson's epochal documentation of the north coast of Africa has already been noted. As late as 1828, however, Beechey could still assert that "the country through which we have passed is, even in the present day, little known to the general reader." Egypt, which only began to be seriously delved into at the time of the Napoleonic campaigns, continued to offer fertile fields for research in the first two decades of the nineteenth century. Thomas Legh and Smelt, as recounted in the *Journey in Egypt* (1816), were unexpectedly permitted "to penetrate into the interior of Nubia [, where] every object assumed an additional importance." Johann Ludwig Burckhardt, who commenced traveling in that sector in 1812, interpreted his two Nubian explorations as forwarding his main objective: "penetrating into the interior of Africa."[83]

The Plinean drive to arrive at the unfamiliar center of any territory is inseparable from the provocative presence of an unknown land mass, especially if it is epically measureless. John Byron, who was a member of Lord Anson's squadron until cast away on a desolate island in the South Seas, explains how a small fraction of the *Wager*'s crew made its way back to England. The men were obliged to march over a naked tract lying between the western mouth of the Magellanic Strait and the capital of Chile. Though this desert contained nothing to sustain life, Byron noted that "it must be allowed there can be no other way of ascertaining the geography and natural history of a country which is altogether morass and rock, incapable of products or culture than by setting down every minute circumstance which was observed in traversing it." Philibert Commerson, in the contemporaneous *Supplément* (1772) to the voyage of Bougainville, reflects on all those countries he has not as yet penetrated. In keeping with the tenor of the period, he longs to see, not speculate about, "the interior of the vast empires of China, of Asiatic Tartary, Japan, Formosa, the Philippines, and an infinity of other places in the immense Polynesia of the South Seas."[84]

However, as Georg Forster perceptively descried, there was perhaps no portion of the world that was thought a more likely candidate for investigation—next to Africa—than the gigantic stretch of New Holland. Apart from the fact that no one had traced its contours, there was the unresolved question of its "vast interior space of ground," which was "equal to the continent of Europe, and in great measure situated between the Tropics, entirely unknown, and perhaps uninhabited." John Oxley chronicles the continuing saga of the "invasion" of Australia's hinterland. The *Journal of Two Expeditions* (1820) commemorates, in addition to Oxley's own trials, earlier nineteenth-century attempts to "penetrate into the interior of the country, by crossing the range of hills known to the colonialists as the Blue Mountains." Explorers who ventured far afield in New South Wales soon found themselves "entangled among gullies and deep ravines for a considerable time, insomuch that they began to despair of ultimate success." Lycett's *View in Australia* (1824) states the case more strongly: "The epidermis of the country has . . . hardly yet been scratched."[85]

The challenge of the broad was often coupled with the slighter affront of the enigmatically narrow. Tiny Easter Island, a mere speck in the wide Pacific, awakened the longing in Georg Forster to "walk into the country." Far from verdant or beckoning, the whole of its confined space was "covered with rocks and stones of all sizes which seemed to have been exposed to a great fire, where they had acquired a black colour and porous appearance." Yet even on less severely circumscribed South Sea atolls, graced with more than two or three shriveled species of grasses, Cook's party refused to linger. Just as the explorer and his skilled geographers were able to diversify the "vacant uniformity of former charts of this ocean" by the "insertion of some new islands," they visited the interiors in order to gratify "philosophical inquiry." At Tahiti, their first care was to "leave the dry sandy beach," which "could afford . . . no discoveries in [their] science," and to "examine the plantations." In short, the beaten path was profitable neither to the scientific mind nor to mankind. The discoverer must carry out "bold Researches through all the immensity of space, where world beyond world rises to the view of the astonished observer."[86]

To fill the void, Samuel Hearne was motivated to walk "over the immense continent" of North America, and MacKenzie contemplated the practicability of "penetrating across" that forbidding unknown land. Milbert ensconced himself "in the bosom" of pathless primeval forests and "in the midst" of pestilential marshes. As he defiantly declares, all these explorations along the Hudson River were undertaken "*à travers*" a completely new country. Captain Turner, in his account of a mission to Bootan (1800), proudly asserts that he "penetrated" where no European had gone before. Correspondingly, the scientific expedition mounted by the Dutch scholar Reinwardt in 1819 had as its objective the revelation of the interior of Java.

These voyagers hold in common the opinion that only when one plumbs the depths or moves into or across substance does one encounter anything worthwhile. Arago writes that at Tinian he saw "nothing but a wild and barren land, which Anson's residence has alone rendered famous," but that "when you penetrate amid the brambles, and find yourself in front of those colossal remains, called *Houses of the Ancients*, you ask involuntarily what is become of the people who raised these pillars." Even Johnson, in the West Indies, is enchanted by "the wild and desolate appearance which the interior of the country for the most part presents."[87]

We may conclude that for the scientific explorer the act of penetration of that which is at a remove, foreign, "other," from man is one and the same as the discovery of a naked reality in all its facets. It is only appropriate that Cook should have the last word:

While we direct our studies to distant worlds, which, after all our exertions, we must content ourselves with having barely discovered to exist, it would be a strange neglect, indeed, and would argue a most culpable want of rational curiosity, if we did not use our best endeavors to arrive at a full acquaintance with the contents of our own planet, of that little spot in the universe, on which we have been placed, and the utmost limits of which, at least its habitable parts, we possess the means of ascertaining, and describing, by actual examination. . . .[88]

Structure Penetrated

Ce sont des milliers de rochers rompus, brisés, écroulés, dispersés; ce sont d'affreuses aiguilles qui s'élevent menaçantes à travers les eaux. . . .
Louis-François Cassas

Implicit in the physical terminology of penetration that looms from the pages of the factual travel accounts is the firsthand discovery of uncivilized struggles at work in nature. Not only does the material world present a certain obduracy and opacity to the explorer that demands to be conquered physically and intellectually, but, as we saw at the beginning of this chapter, it is itself prone to the clash of opposing forces that leave behind traces and imprints. The dissection of this natural text, in the idiom of combat, also forms a fitting coda to the discussion in chapter 1 of the scientific voyagers' masculine language of action or dominion, and their plain and paratactic style.

By the second half of the eighteenth century, the persistent incursions of Newtonian and other soft "powers" into a corpuscular system of the

VOYAGE INTO SUBSTANCE

The whole Missouri is suddenly stopped by one shelving rock, which without a single niche and with an edge as straight and regular as if formed by art, stretches itself from one side of the river to the other for at least a quarter of a mile. Over this it precipitates itself. . . .
Lewis and Clark

universe formerly thought to be composed of unrelievedly "hard" bodies, the increasing testimony provided by mineralogists to the historical changes of matter, and the valorization of physical process over mentally super-added form—whether expressed as a hylozoism redivivus or as a modern materialism—all served to illuminate the independent life of nature re-corded in its active phenomena. The challenge issued to the natural his-torians to penetrate their individuality was one and the same with the challenge to read aright the text recording their mutability. It is according to this physiognomics of change that we must interpret the late eighteenth century's rebarbarizing of speech and art, wherein words and images correspond to an uncultivated attack on the unknown and simultaneously mirror the internally warring constituents of natural phenomena.[89]

The perceptive traveler reinforced the Lucretian view of corporeal creation as a sensual, fierce, and continuous process. George Forster, in *Ein Blick in das Ganze der Natur* (1781), succinctly states the case for ceaseless strife. The primordial stuff composing the earth is in constant motion; thus, nature undergoes repeated metamorphoses, absorbing old forms and bearing new ones. This belief that an ideal natural wholeness is in actuality divided or "ruined," varied by environmental vicissitudes, is evinced in countless narratives. Cassas's depictions of the Falls of the Kerka in Dal-matia and of the Nahr Qâdes flowing by the cedar forests of Syria breathes of contravention. The rocks over which the furious flood hurls itself are "fractured, broken, eroded, scattered." Their "menacing" aspect is con-tested by a tumultuous "ocean" that "roars," "stirs," and violently "casts" itself over shapeless giants; i.e., those impassable boulders that dispute its right of way: "Their struggle dawned with the world; their days of battle are centuries and their vanquisher, always terrible, always fleeting, strikes them, subdues them, flees them, hides in the seas, thickens the clouds with its vapors, forms the storms that returns them to earth, and reconstitutes itself afresh in the entrails of the globe, finally to reappear and reconfront one another, still unwearied after a thousand years. . . ."

Less overtly impassioned, Lewis and Clark's description of the Falls of the Missouri is nonetheless redolent with implied opposition. A laconic vocabulary informs the reader that the mighty stream has been halted suddenly in its course. Similarly, Vidal's *Buenos Ayres and Monte Video* (1820) portrays the River Mendoza and its five "tributary" hot springs as benevolent assailants: "The combat of these opposite waters on the hu-midity of the air above, produces the most beautiful crystallizations in almost every kind of figure that the imagination can possibly conceive. . . ."[90]

Violent language often quickens even the most analytical account of vol-canic activity. When Patrick Brydone climbed Mount Etna, he was as-tonished to behold (like Humboldt on Cotopaxi), in "perpetual union," the "two elements that are at perpetual war": an "immense gulph of fire

LANDSCAPE FREED OF CULTURE

Figure 235
L. F. Cassas, *Nahr Qâdes*, from *Voyages
pittoresque de l'Istrie . . .* , 1802, pl. 62.
Engraving.

for ever existing in the midst of snow that it has not power to melt" and "immense fields of snow and ice for ever surrounding this gulph of fire, which they have not power to extinguish." (See figure 56.) Houel, atop the same summit, is less paradoxical. Gazing about, he itemizes the differing degrees of transformation endured by every substance: ". . . all is change: that solid and sterile ice ceases to be such through the fluctuations of temperature in the atmosphere; it even transforms itself into a beneficial liquid that revitalizes . . . before surrendering itself to an immense reservoir, itself containing many animate beings, & from whence it soon emerges as an invisible vapor, to clot into cloud, produce tempests, wander in the air at the behest of winds, and return to mold compact and diaphanous bodies which can be seen on the crest of high mountains. . . ." (See figure 147.) In another context, speaking of the volcanic Lipari Isles, Houel observes that crater walls frequently shatter, and that "the mouth alters its position; that is to say, the fire of the volcano lays bare another egress; from whence it pours forth." "Hence," he continues, "this shifting opening vomits its terrifying issue in all directions, which forms in the end, after having relocated several times, mountainous heaps greatly varied as to shape and size, & all the more diverse because the energy that produces them on one side destroys them on the other. . . ."[91] (See figure 128.)

Faujas de Saint-Fond offers further documentation of the earth's passionately unsettled condition. Focusing on the basaltic pavements and cliffs of the Auvergne, he discovers spheres and prisms of lava that have been extruded forcibly "at a single throw." William Borlase, in his *Natural History of Cornwall* (1758), employs congruous expressions to evoke dynamic protrusions and precipitous fusions.[92]

Indeed, we can now see from another vantage the kinship between the natural hieroglyph in mineral, metal, or stone as a pictorial document of secular change—the topic with which this chapter began—and the vehement script employed by every particle of matter existing in everlasting fermentation. As Borlase and Henckel explain, it is the procreative "plastick power" of nature that "throws the flexile liquid materials of the fossil kingdom into various figures." In the vitalist language of Louis Bourguet's *Traité de pétrifications* (1742), the multiformity of stones is caused by the rotation of our planet, the circulation of water, and the variable resistance and tug of surrounding stuff. More emphatically still, Romé de l'Isle sets down as a fundamental law of nature an intrinsic will to form operating throughout matter. According to this axiom, related crystalline substances, although dissolved in a liquid, are "determined" to become reunited through mutual attraction or elective affinity, emerging in the guise of a geometric solid.

The treatises of Demarest and Ferber, but particularly those of Raspe (quoted in the *Illustrations of the Island of Staffa*), dwell on the intentional consolidation of the hot current, which forces it to "rise up" from the

Figure 236
B. Faujas de Saint-Fond, *Spherical Lava amid Irregular Prisms*, from *Essai de géologie*, 1803–1809, III, pl. 25. Engraving by P. Magne after drawing by A. E. G. Dagoty. Photo courtesy Bibliothèque Nationale.

Figure 237
B. Faujas de Saint-Fond, *View of a Portion of the Crag of Mallias*, from *Recherches sur les volcans éteints*, 1783, pl. 4. Engraving by P. Boulland after drawing by De Veyrene. Photo courtesy British Library.

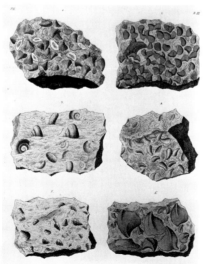

Figure 238
Thomas and William Daniell, *Cave of Fingal,* from *Animated Nature,* 1807–1812, pl. 24. Aquatint. Photo courtesy Newberry Library.

Figure 239
G. W. Knorr, *"Plaques" of Pectonculites,* from *Recueil de monumens des catastrophes,* 1768–1775, II, part I, pl. B-III. Hand-colored engraving.

LANDSCAPE FREED OF CULTURE

bottom of the sea as the result of a "mighty convulsion." In the earlier *Animated Nature* (1807/1812), the Daniells rely upon the testimony of Joseph Banks to pit the apparent stability of Fingal's Cave against the "furiously agitated" sea, whose breakers "dash with violence over the fallen fragments."[93]

The tough and sinewy discourse of the factual travel accounts, corresponding to the actual depredations of time and the blunting agency of the elements, also hinges on a combative physical dialectic between the rudely intractable and the malleable, or, more subtly, between a male and a female nature. This is evident in William Daniell's illustration of Staffa, in which smooth, soaring basaltic pillars are contravened by a pliant sea. The reverse could also hold true, as John Edy demonstrates, in Norway, where the great North Sea "rolls its vast watery mountains on the craggy shores, dashing and foaming over the sheer and desolate rocky islands, until it meets a proud defiance from the majestic frowning bulwarks of granite which form the barrier of the country." It is a rare perspective, however, that has rocks batter and shred the spraying sea. Suffice it to say that the destructive action of the ocean, its deforming of the formed, its incursion into the resistless, implies an optical as well as a virtual tension between the turbulent and the finished, between the wild and the tame. This primitive battle was also tangibly evident inland in nature's weatherbeaten monuments. John Barrow's reminiscences should bring to mind a host of others discussed in chapter 2. In *Travels into the Interior of South Africa* (1801), Barrow harshly juxtaposes Devil's Mountain, "broken into irregular points," with the Lion's Head, a "rounded" and solid mass of stone.[94] (See figure 53.)

Souvenirs of ancient cataclysm and heralds of future revolution were thus sensuously embodied in a language of almost libidinal antagonism. New scientific concepts of catastrophism grew in the last quarter of the eighteenth century and came to a head in the years around 1800. Nothing contributed more, however, to the vision of a ferocious and uncivilized universe in which man is weak, helpless, and incapable of shaping his destiny than the Lisbon earthquake. The impact on Voltaire and his contemporaries of this irrational upheaval, which seemed to expose the fragility and even perishability of the cultivated, artifactual world, has often been remarked. The disaster's importance for our purposes is that it lent credence, along with everything else in nature, to a vision of particulate war. Man could trust in nothing, not even the solid earth.[95]

In conclusion: Both the surviving imprinted stone object of nature and the concrete text object of early civilization function as tangible tableaux, pictorially demonstrating an intrinsic inseparability of fractured form from variable content. (See figures 109 and 239.) The naturally "framed" lithic script of fossil, mineral, or crystal—like the curiologic hieroglyph with its material "surround," bearing a condensed image plainly mirroring things—

offers a "real" picture of layers of time pinned out in space. As a metonymic part or fragment wrested from the material continuum of the planet, it aphoristically opens visual access in depth to the convulsive prehistoric landscape without obliterating the surface traces of its present configuration.[96] This small or large earth relic is an individual and rebarbative work of nature's art. When scanned by the sapient explorer or held in the hand, it is both concrete tablet and tablature "speaking" of nature's power to create in unparaphrasable acts, not a Lockean tabula rasa on which personal impressions are heaped. It is, then, specifically the probing journey into substance that emerges as the eighteenth century's distinctive contribution to the venerable genre of travel literature.

The natural historian as Plinean traveler was instrumental in fashioning that aspect of eighteenth-century vision seeking to recover a world purified of the human component.[97] By dint of a penetrative seeing (in lieu of a transformative one)—with the eyes of matter, not those of man—the discoverers approached and reconstituted both the structure of actuality and that of the fabled time of the beginning.

5   *Sectarians of the Unknown*

Let us fix our attention out of our-
selves as much as possible: Let us
chace our imagination to the heav-
ens, or to the utmost limits of the
universe; we never really advance a
step beyond ourselves, nor can con-
ceive any kind of existence but
these perceptions, which have ap-
pear'd in that narrow compass; this
is the universe of the imagination,
nor have we any idea but what is
there produc'd. . . .
David Hume

There is a love for the marvellous, a
belief in the marvellous, intertwined
in all my projects, which hurries me
out of the common pathways of
men, even to the wild and unvisited
regions I am about to explore. . . .
Mary Shelley

If it is agreed that travel for a purpose entails the desire to communicate unadulterated news from the real world, it is also undeniable that the process of gathering information involves its passage into and its being reported out of a single consciousness. As the observer journeys through to penetrate an ever-new environment, he is constantly forced to absorb the idiosyncracies of scenery and to turn them into inclusive reflections on the run—in short, to make sense of the unknown. As we have seen, exploration is conducive to the abandonment of conventionalized opinions. The traveler, perpetually invading phenomenal reality, is forced by experience to discard his view of nature as predetermined Nature. That is, he can no longer look upon it as a mere abstract intellectual principle or norm that since antiquity was thought to govern human action and production. Continually encroaching on the minute facts of material existence, the discoverer is constrained to commune intimately with phenomenal works. The psychological and bodily hardship attendant on such a deliberate and intent gaze is described by the Dutch physician Bernard de Mandeville: "It is with our Thoughts as with our Eyes." We can keep the latter open all day looking about without hurting or wearying them, but "when we contract the Sight, and directing it to a particular place, keep it employ'd in examining some very minute Points" the difficulty sets in. Mandeville's observation concerning this painstaking optic is not unrelated to the perceptual and mental exaction involved in formulating a standard of depersonalized vision then being hammered out by voyagers. Georg Forster, praising the British Parliament for not having sent himself and his father round the world merely to collect butterflies and dried plants, asserts: "They conceived that the man whom they had chosen, prompted by his natural love of science, would endeavor to derive the greatest possible advantages from his voyage. He was only therefore directed to exercise all his talents, and to extend his observation to every remarkable object." Yet, as Forster recognized, to see analytically and well implied in the end the synthetic construction of a comprehensive natural philosophy, one that would coherently order nature's inexhaustible storehouse for the understanding. In light of that recognition, this chapter will investigate some of the deeper perceptual structures invented to cope with a territory not witnessed before.

A corollary of the effort to master the world is the realization that knowledge is in some sense individual, even when it is not intentionally so willed. The preliminary and fundamental distinction made between a Picturesque and an anti-Picturesque attitude toward the land, however, continues to hold. Not only does the objectively oriented traveler struggle to get at truth by actually experiencing the universe part by part; he also submits his findings to the checks and balances of future discoveries before constructing a picture of the whole. Consequently, he does not hold with Hume's *Treatise on Human Understanding* (1740), in which the great skeptic posits his relativistic view: "Whatever other objects may be comprehended by the mind, they are always consider'd with a view to ourselves; otherwise they wou'd never be able either to excite these passions, or produce the smallest encrease or diminution of them." Indeed, the spectator versed in natural history proves bodily that perceptions do in some verifiable measure correspond to things and that there is a distinction between ourselves and external objects.

Nonetheless, the establishing of two such autonomous realms becomes most controversial when the subjective language of the Sublime and the marvelous is invoked to describe a novel reality, i.e., one that sidesteps or otherwise circumvents the habitual and the daily. Tzvetan Todorov's exhaustive analysis of the fantastic illuminates a way out of this epistemological quandary. If the fantastic represents the hesitation of the beholder before a reality controlled by laws unknown to him, and if the uncanny indicates his decision that the laws of nature remain intact and permit a rational explanation of the phenomena described, then the marvelous (especially in its exotic and scientific incarnations) corresponds to the goal of total exploration of universal reality, to an examination of the virtual presence in the world's frame of natural yet seemingly supernatural effects. The brutal or sudden intrusion into the continuum of everyday life of tangible mystery (that which has not yet been explained) does not necessarily mean that the event is imagined or imaginary. Interpretation is simply held in abeyance until further proof is provided, until a more elegant hypothesis can be shaped to embrace yet another new fact.

Shaping the Plenum

The considerations of the preceding chapter, particularly the discussion of penetration, logically raise the larger question of the predilections and mentality of scientific travelers. As noted, the laboratory of these formulators and disclosers of an ever-enlarging world is physical nature, *natura rerum*. But how, specifically, does the human eye toil to see, and

I went in quest of the manifold objects which nature had scattered throughout the land. . . . But above all, it is to be observed, that the same objects may have been seen in different points of view, and that the same fact may often have given rise to different ideas. . . .
Georg Forster

how does the mind make contact with the unfamiliar? How are visual order and truthfulness simultaneously achieved when one confronts a previously unexperienced, baffling force or site?[1] Michel Foucault's aperçu is that the two fundamental experiences of the eighteenth century are the person blind from birth who becomes enlightened (Réaumur's operation) and the foreign observer who is thrust into a strange land (the discoverer's situation). In addition there is Gombrich's Popperian admonition that there is no innocent beholder. Although the stated aim of the scientific voyager is to heed all messages his eye receives from the external world with neutral impartiality, because to be selective introduces a bias and therefore a distortion of truth, distinctive corporeous qualities were attended to. Along with the nominalistic desire to embrace "the manifold of objects," a sensationalistic selective process takes place (as Forster, for one, realized). Gombrich states the case for the prison of perceptual conventionality:

. . . just as there is a physical focusing at the moment of intake, there is something like a mental focusing in the mysterious process of attention which psychology has not yet quite unriddled. Without this final selection we would be flooded by messages to the point of distraction. We could not find our way through the world if we could not, at any moment in time, take very much as read. . . .[2]

Yet, as has been argued, it is precisely in the combination of willed seeing with total saturation in physical abundance that the traveler breaks out of the fatalistic impasse of schematization that Gombrich defines. Further, determined sight and penetration are inimical to the maintenance of illusion. Emerging from the accounts of the natural masterpiece and the fugitive effect are certain clues to how the actual landscape was experienced. Scientific method permits neither the personification of phenomena in order to make them the mere accomplice of our emotions nor their allegorization to articulate a moral content. Both habits represent the draining away of meaning to leave behind the insignificant husk of the world. Thus, the arduously attained individual vision of a new universe is congruous with comprehending and respectful emotion. Authors and artists alike exulted in finding out phases of the earth that had never become hackneyed, that had never been reduced and, indeed, were irreducible.[3]

For the coupling of a "passionate intelligence" with an aspect of nature, again it is Forster's unerring appraisal that serves as guide. In the preface to *Voyage Round the World* (1777) he notes that there are many circumstances "familiar to the navigator, who has been bred on the rough element, [that] strike the landman with novelty, and furnish entertainment to his readers." "The seaman views many objects on shore with a retrospect to maritime affairs, whilst the other attends to their oeconomical uses. In short, the different branches of science, which we have studied, our turns of mind, our heads and hearts have made a difference in our sensations, reflections, and expressions. . . ." At the first joyful sighting of Dusky Bay's antediluvian forests after a journey of 122 days and 3,500 leagues,

SECTARIANS OF THE UNKNOWN

Forster lapses into reflection: ". . . so apt is mankind, after a long absence from land, to be prejudiced in favour of the wildest shore, that we looked upon the country at that time as one of the most beautiful which nature unassisted by art could produce. . . ." He notes that the strain of physical debility undeniably affects vision. Navigating from New Zealand to Tahiti, Cook's crew discovered, on August 11, 1773, a small, low island lying to the south. "It appeared to be almost level with the sea, only some groups of trees rose above the horizon, and among them a few cocoa-nut palms out-topped the rest. To people in our situation, exhausted with a tedious passage, the bare sight of land was sufficient to give some consolation, though we could not expect to reap any benefit from its productions; and therefore this island, though divested of everything strikingly beautiful, yet pleased the eye by the simplicity of its form. . . ." In point of fact, however, dragging boredom could often dim perspicuity instead of sharpening it. In the Antarctic, Forster writes, Cook lamented that "the tediousness of our cruize, which the sight of birds, porpoises, seals and whales, now too familiar to our eyes, could not prevent from falling heavily upon us." Birds such as the albatross "afforded momentary relief from the gloomy uniformity with which [they] slowly passed dull hours, days, and months, in this desolate part of the world." They were "almost perpetually wrapt in thick fogs, beaten with showers of rain, sleet, hail, and snow . . . surrounded with innumerable islands of ice against which [they] daily ran the risk of being shipwrecked." It is no wonder, then, that after protracted bouts with inclement weather, illness, and death Cook's men feasted their eyes on Tahiti, "an object, of which they were taught to form the highest expectations."[4]

Such experiences were not limited to the eighteenth-century voyagers. Jacques Arago writes

Continually in view of the same objects, and having nothing to amuse us but the sound of thunder, the rapid flashes of lightning that deaden the fires kindled on the slopes of the mountains. How monotonous is such a life: How tiresome the view of those heaps of lava! The most active seamen are disheartened; a scorching sun exhausts the strength of the most intrepid; serious diseases prevail on board. . . .

Porter, traveling among the fjords in Finland, found that in the end even sublimities lose their luster. "The eye and the imagination, fatigued with a too-prolonged gaze on gigantic nature, turn with delight to the little green valley, where some cottage lurks. . . ." On the contrary, Landmann, clambering over the wild declivities flanking Portugal's Oeiras River, claimed that this mountainous region offered "fresh delight" to anyone who has just crossed "that tiresome, level, and uninteresting sameness of country, which nearly fills the whole of the space between Alcazar de Sol and the Sierra de Mertela." Belzoni summarizes well the experiential tension between tedious monotony and surfeit of novelty, and the two extremes in travelers: "The one who is just arrived, has never before been in the country, and of course, has no knowledge of customs and things, cannot see one quarter of what he should see: the other is so thoroughly initiated into their customs, manners, [natural history, landscape,] that those which shock at first lose their effect on him; he almost forgets his own ways, and does not reckon anything he beholds extraordinary or worth attention, though perhaps even of the greatest consequence. . . ."[5]

Doubtless these writers reflect, at particular instants of their narratives, the psychological power of scenery over the emotions. They offer glimpses of the consciousness in which external phenomena are no longer deployed for their own sake but are constrained to correspond with a private mood. Certain settings, such as the eternally gray and socially neutral wilderness of the Antarctic that was described by Forster and that so moved Coleridge, were conducive to solipsistic meditation. In personal moments when landscape as experienced is assimilated into a flowing and imaginative (not an interrogative and perceptual) process, it fuses with a state of mind and thus is only partially itself. Stated otherwise, at that moment nature belongs more to the realm of feelings than to that of things, more to the thinking subject than to the encountered object.[6] The completion of scenery by unfiltered spectator response implies resistless Empedoclean immersion of man within nature, not vigilant Plinean penetration of man into nature. The latter stance, by definition, keeps the characters or identities of the two domains separate and distinct.

It is well to remember in this connection certain contributing medical factors. Melancholy (under various names) was the reigning distemper from the middle of the sixteenth century on—the same period when Europeans, but particularly the British and the French, were consumed by scurvy. This enigmatic psychological ailment was accompanied by bodily infirmities that sapped the mind while often imparting to it heightened brilliance. The alternatingly enervating and stimulating blight that settled upon the scorbutic, malarial, or plague-stricken voyager, whether the poles or in the tropics, is mirrored in the dyspepsia or euphoria of the passages just quoted. Both condition and disease, it rampaged through all social classes but was especially prevalent among seamen. The findings of Dr. John Lind's *Treatise on the Scurvy* (1753) were completely confirmed by Cook's experiences on the second voyage (1772–1775). Nonetheless, the doling out of lime juice aboard ship was not officially adopted as a prophylactic until 1795.

French urban planners, spurred by Lavoisier's chemical discoveries of the 1770s, were deeply concerned about mephitic exhalations endemic to crowded cities or vessels and also localized above marshy or swampy land. Rouland asserts in *Tableau historique des propriétés et des phénomènes de l'air* (1784) that

there is no one who has not been affected by atmospheric changes: it is known that when the weather is rainy & the air charged with vapors, one experiences a kind of *mal-aise* & uneasiness that makes us heavy, ponderous, & almost incapable of executing the functions of our position. . . . But when the atmosphere, always preserving the same mass, becomes serene, & when the equilibrium between interior & exterior air is re-established, our bodies assume their natural condition; we exhibit greater gaiety, greater vivacity, and greater activity; our functions are freely carried out, everything returns to its natural order. . . .[7]

Forster, exhibiting his scientific scruples, does not shrink from letting the reader know "the colour of the glass through which [he] looked." Indeed, he informs us that he battled with himself in order to be both comprehensive and objective: "I have always endeavoured in this narrative to connect the ideas arising from different occurrences, in order, if possible, to throw more light upon the nature of the human mind, and to lift the soul into that exalted station, from whence the extensive view must justify the ways of God to man. . . ."[8] Although we may rightly disallow his asserveration that "a gloomy, livid tinge hath never clouded [his] sight," Forster's double-barreled attempt at achieving the universal in the particular, at welding moving survey and detached focus, is significant. The dilemma of Forster and of all travelers in search of concrete realities rather than mental fictions was that they lived in an age in which the ideal of the nonspecialized man came into conflict with the isolating tendencies of the new disciplines surfacing: the physical sciences that pushed man into the world and a mechanistic associational psychology that pulled him back into the mind. Renaissance humanism had bequeathed both by theory and by example the model of an all-around and uniformly perfected personality. Conformable emotion balanced by an empirically well-stocked mind was in diametric contrast with progressive specialization. In essence, specialization itself arose because of the overwhelming actualities of the era. Quite simply, to orient oneself narrowly through particularization, through the riveting of one's gaze, became mandatory in the face of a disconcerting abundance of phenomena that ceaselessly clamored for attention. Both the outer and the inner world seemed immense, boundless, richer. The concomitant rise of an Olympian "perspective consciousness"—which Erich Auerbach locates first in the sixteenth century, the period of the initial circumnavigations—had a corresponding influence on observation at a distance. The image of life absolutely embodied in a discrete example no longer became the only one possible. The awareness of the manifold conditions of the natural world required adding up its facets into a totality. Whereas in the sixteenth century Shakespeare could not isolate man from his setting, because this was out of keeping with the religious concept of a magical and polyphonic cosmos, in the late eighteenth century Forster was compelled for secular reasons to bring individual experience into a mutually adequate relationship with the manifold of things.[9]

The travelers discovered a restricted number of spatial signs naturally inhering within most landscapes. These provide a point of entry into the realities of a variegated environment and into the reconstitutive powers of the mind. Limited directional or positional signs provide an interpretive key to the active reading of natural phenomena. These immanent vectors, which recur in both written and painted descriptions, constitute a substructure underpinning the surface traces found in a given area as well as a cognitive stratum undergirding perception. Thus, the similarities among late-eighteenth-century and early-nineteenth-century narratives stemming from entirely different countries and composed by persons of opposing temperaments though all of scientific disposition, support the thesis of a shared modality of vision.[10]

Energetic spatial metaphors—tearing, crossing, immersing, penetrating—structure the images of the factual relations. All mirror the explorers' Promethean endeavor to conquer space by duplicating the fluid processes of the universe revealed by eighteenth-century entropic materialism. The issue of an individual consciousness locating itself outside itself bears on the varieties of the Sublime (rhetorical, natural, religious) enumerated in antiquity and compellingly recast by Edmund Burke. In Longinus's definition of *hypsos*, or height, the reader is "uplifted" as though he physically undergoes what he merely hears. That is, the encounter with artistic excellence (the "rhetorical Sublime") is structurally cognate with the lived transcendence excited in the observer during the meeting with landscape (the "natural Sublime"). Recently, critics have noted the collapse of polarities operating within the eighteenth-century version of the Sublime, which brought the high and the low into dangerous proximity. In Longinus, *bathos* is more or less the equivalent of *hypsos*. Pope, however, persuasively reconstitutes the notion such that the aspirant to the profound operates in an antinatural and antithetical way, proliferating metaphors into unruly sequences by mingling bits and pieces of the most varied and discordant kinds as it pleases his fancy. A sense of charm arises from such counterpositions and contraries. Eventually, truth and fiction mingle; the credible and the incredible blend, forming the category of *peri bathous*, or the marvelous.

Burke, with a different intention, contributes to this erosion of hierarchy by favoring "an easy observation of the most common, sometimes of the meanest things in nature." Especially revelatory from this point of view is the explicit enlargement of personal perspective made congruent with flux. Thus, the older book of nature swelled with new phenomena recognized as heightening, deepening, or broadening the mind.[11]

The emphasis placed in the factual travel accounts on descent into mines or caverns tallies with the psychological desire to plumb sublimely dangerous depths. As early as Pitton de Tournefort's *Voyage du Levant* (1717), vertical intrusion into the tenebrous was accentuated by "slithering" down a series of steep passageways. From the bottom of the first passageway gapes a second, more terrible still, and so on. To reach the inmost chamber of the Grotto of Antiparos, the explorer has to slide and, in the end, to crawl. When he emerges from the impossibly narrow corridors, a spacious sight greets him: A lofty dome reveals large rounded masses, grooved towers, cascading draperies of flowstone, and others riddled with jagged, lightninglike spikes or hung in long festoons and grape clusters. (See figure 61.) A century later, Boisgelin de Kerdu relentlessly lowered himself into the mines of Sahla, Afvestad, Soeter, Ornoes, Mora, and Elfdal. The plunge into the pit at Fahlum, as elsewhere, was contrived by means of buckets. The confined motion downward is accentuated in the narrative by periodic marginal interruptions. Flickering torches carried by the traveler permit him to see in passing the galleries hewn in the stone, against whose edges he is sometimes violently thrown by the rope. The sudden experiential contrast of up and down, narrow and broad, is amplified by lateral considerations, just as total darkness is mitigated by occasional flashes of illumination: "Nothing can be more superb than the effect of the lighted fires in different parts of the mine. The vaulted roofs are extremely noble. The communications very wide, and the greatest neatness prevails throughout the whole. . . ."

The headlong dive, pitching the traveler underground, finds a perceptual equivalent in the mineralogist's gaze beneath a material surface. The mental activity of laying bare the prototype hidden underneath the confusing miscellany of available types, as practiced by Bonnet and Robinet, is closely allied with the crystallographer's precipitate pursuit into the chasm of matrices and root structures of metals and minerals.[12] An active optic that dips or discloses demystifies the secretive and unbars the shut; in short, it explores. Hence the visual attraction of an "apparently bottomless abyss," one that might equally be embodied in downpouring cascades. Lycett can serve as a paradigm. He praises Beckett's Falls on the River Apsley in Australia and traces the attempt of the eye to follow the roaring torrent in its descent only to be "arrested by the immense mass of rocks, with which the sides of the Glen is almost covered." Monck Mason, in the appendix to his *History of Aerostation* (1837), records that the balloonist's eye "insensibly assumes a downward course," and that "he becomes at once assailed with a mass of observations and reflections, among which astonishment at the unusual tranquillity that accompanied alterations so rapid and so remarkable, is one of the most prominant." "Without an effort," Mason continues, ". . . the whole face of nature seems to be undergoing some violent and inexplicable transformation." As the balloonist pursues fast-retreating forms and the rapidly diminishing size of all those objects lately by his side, it "seems as if the earth has suddenly been precipitated into the murky recesses of some unfathomable abyss below."[13] (See figure 155.)

The soaring vertical implications of flight are countered by crushing and claustrophobic images and sensations of heaviness. The mental desire to re-erect or redress matter is contravened by figures of density and weight. Thus the dynamic impression made by hills and peaks may, at other times, be opposed by a sense of prostration. Belzoni, standing at the foot of towering Libyan mountains and gazing at the rock-cut burial places of Thebes, finds them incomparable, both as astonishing sepulchres and as inducers of oppressiveness. Creeping through interminable passages, he finally reached a spot high enough for him to sit—

But what a place to rest! Surrounded by bodies, by heaps of mummies in all directions which previous to my being accustomed to the sight, impressed me with horror. The blackness of the wall, the faint light given by the torches for want of air, the different objects that surrounded me, seeming to converse with each other, and the Arabs with candles or torches in their hands, naked and covered with dust, themselves resembling living mummies, absolutely formed a scene that cannot be described. . . .

Belzoni's consciousness of being buried—here made to stand for an entire class of experience underground—hinges on the psychological dialectic between open and closed sites. This dialectic was identified in the seventeenth century by Roger de Piles. Belzoni's description, however, implies a certain baffling of judgment that is alien to the clarity of de Piles's distinction.[14] While clearings and level stretches provoke feelings of being uncovered, Belzoni's harrowing journey into the decaying opacity of matter activates the sensation of being concealed. From this ghoulish excavation he can see without being seen, meditate without being threatened.

Bougainville's account of discovering refuge at New Cythera is equally informative. After months of radical exposure on the back of a seemingly illimitable ocean, he and his crew embraced Tahiti as a haven incarnating the vision of a succoring paradise. Even its mountainous aspect was far from appearing melancholy and savage; it served, by comparison, to enhance the face of the countryside—"*les champs élisées*"—richly stocked with sugar cane and coconut, banana, and breadfruit trees.[15]

In the uncharted vastness of space, greater even than the unmapped flats of the Pacific, the traveler might yet find refuge. Pilâtre de Rozier, chronicling his first experiment in a *montgolfière*, remembers how, when the balloon first burst out of the clouds, an immense terrain suddenly unfurled in which all objects were confounded. (See figure 100.) Seeing what even the most fertile imagination could not conceive, and "enjoying reality rather than illusion born of a lie," his spirits were buoyed and his thoughts exalted. He terms the balloon a lofty *bâtiment*, an enveloping building or shelter imperceptibly carried along by winds and protecting him from them.[16] (See figure 6.)

The balloonists' conception of naked immensity has terrestrial equivalents. The desert or wilderness and the sea are two radically empty places that compete with the sky. The traveler scanning such absolute prospects rarely encounters objects, only more and ever-wider horizons. Both are indifferent to human time and are characterized by an absence of limi-

SECTARIANS OF THE UNKNOWN

tations. Visibly possessing neither beginning nor end, the desert functions as a surface continuum which one rides or walks over but does not enter as into the fabric of the earth. Conversely, the ocean may be penetrated; it teems with life glimpsed below the waves.

Vivant-Denon memorably captures the extreme prospect of Egypt at Assouan. After his detachment left him at the abandoned convent of Saint Lawrence, in the middle of nowhere, he was overwhelmed by "the gigantic expanse of heaven, of such a measureless horizon of sand, of a widespread light as sad and pallid as that of night." On another occasion, he remarks that in this "tranquil nothingness" the wind roams the vast horizon "without finding any other objects except ourselves." "Silent," he goes on, "we recollect still in the midst of darkness, the enormous and melancholy space by which we were surrounded. . . ." (See figure 107.)

If the ends of the earth have their terrors, they also have their peculiar pleasures. Beechey, exploring the desolate and sandy tracts of North Africa, admits that "there is something imposing, we may say sublime, in the very idea of unbounded space which it occasionally presents; and every trifling object which appears above its untenanted surface, assumes an interest which we should not on other occasions attribute to objects of much greater importance. . . ." From Bruce's account of Abyssinia to Oxley's and Lycett's journals composed in Australia, the theme of a jolting vertical interruption of an otherwise uniform plain is sounded. They recorded that "anything like an eminence was grateful to our sight" in regions where land was perfectly level or boundless, or the territory "immense."[17]

Life at sea, perpetually out-of-doors, is also conducive to panoramic perception; the sailor constantly gauges the "fetch" of open water surrounding him. While contemplating the horizon, the observer's attention is quickly directed beyond the element over which, simultaneously, he is slowly moving. In a fashion more intricate than that experienced by the overland traveler, he has conflicting sensations of distance, surface, and depth, of which only surface seems to offer any tangibility. As in the desert, the ocean's extent provides multiple and shifting points of view from which the summits of hills, mountains, crags, steep coasts, abrupt islands, overhanging cliffs, and trees appear strikingly erect.

Most nearly akin to this fluctuating visual complexity is the unusual vantage of the aeronaut. Faujas de Saint-Fond enumerates the peculiarities of a filmy milieu comprising differing thicknesses, "through," "in," and "across" which one floats. During the course of the *"expérience"* conducted at the Champ de Mars on August 27, 1783, the balloon rose so precipitously that, after just two minutes of flight, it was "lost" in a dark cloud. Shortly thereafter it "pierced" the cover, reappearing briefly, before being swallowed by yet another fog bank. Matters were complicated by a rainstorm that struck at the moment of ascent, pelting the fragile frame as it "voyaged in space."

As noted in the popular reviews and prints of the day, the Montgolfiers were credited with having invented an artificial cloud, a cumuliform vehicle that refuses to stay and thus is identical with nature's processes. Buoyant, with its capacious "sail" enclosing an invisible gas, and meteorlike in submitting only to the directives of atmospheric conditions, it is impelled along tidal waves and visible to other worlds. In the words of Antoine de Parcieux's *Dissertation sur les globes aérostatiques* (1783), this "natural" machine "swims" in the air so that its occupant is submerged "the way fish are in water." Moreover, the new argonaut is only too palpably aware that, because the atmosphere is composed of "an infinity of layers whose densities diminish according as one distances oneself from the surface of the earth," the rising balloon "encounters an ever lighter air, & finally must achieve equilibrium, swimming between two airs the way one observes bodies swimming between two fluids."[18]

Sexual imagery also played a significant role in the ordering of the landscape. Since antiquity, a panvitalist cosmology had posited the universe as a plenum of opposed yet mutually attracted forces. This opinion, as has been remarked, was discredited and displaced by Cartesian mechanism and then revived during the Enlightenment in a refined form as a compound of entropic materialism, Newtonian dynamism, and empirical hylozoism. Seneca, in *Quaestiones naturales*, makes the case for the existence of a stronger "male" earth couched in such firm, abiding substances as stones and rocks and a floating "female" element lurking in changeable waters and fit to be manipulated.

Again, the reminder that we are dealing with animistic theories not literary personifications seems warranted. The often facile use of the latter by eighteenth-century poets meant the attribution of anthropomorphized life, emotion, and physiognomy to physical objects. Despite his gender-dominated idiom, Seneca does not assign humanity to nature; he does not have the morning "smile," the mountain "nod," or the field be "cheerful." Rather, natural phenomena individually express a certain character that is intrinsically allied with the dual cosmic properties of form and chaos, hard and soft, solid and liquid. This materialist view of immanence is thus remote from the poet's desire to graft his human life and passion onto what he judges to be inanimate things.[19]

The pagan assumption of a virile earth incarnate in durable, raw, and artless landmarks was revoiced by archaeological and scientific travelers. William Borlase, in describing the unwrought memorials of Cornwall (figure 90), suggests that their selection was probably determined by "something expressive either in the number of the Stones of which the Monument did consist, or in the Shape of the Stones themselves, or in the Order and figure in which they were disposed." Thomas Pennant, in *Journey to Snowdon* (1781), speaks analogously of colossal, coarse cromlechs whose

SECTARIANS OF THE UNKNOWN

Figure 240
L. Boisgelin de Kerdu, *Mine at Fahlum,*
from *Travels in Denmark, Sweden . . .* , 1810,
II, pl. p. 221. Aquatint by J. Merigot.
Photo courtesy British Library.

Figure 241
J. Lycett, *Mount Wellington near Hobart
Town, Van Diemen's Land*, from *Views in
Australia*, 1824, II, pl. 7. Lithograph. Photo
courtesy British Library.

Figure 242
Le Vachez, *Monde lunaire*, eighteenth
century. Engraving. Photo courtesy
Cabinet des Estampes, Bibliothèque
Nationale.

"Druidical" austerity conjures up the shadowy magician Merlin. The brutality (or lack of polished surface articulation) implicit in such gigantic forms is consonant with their unrelieved and inelegant uprightness. A congruent implication of primitive and crude vigor dwelling within an unyielding pile of rock dating from time immemorial has often been encountered in the foregoing discussions. One example should suffice. According to Bellasis, Friar's Rock on Saint Helena (figure 14) bears the uncivilized appearance of ruthless perpendicularity, having been forced up "a distance of 800 feet by subterranean fire."[20]

Not only blunt, dominating outcrops, but entire unadorned regions as well, could qualify as relentlessly male precincts if they were suitably intractable and resistant to society's incursions. Acerbi, traveling in Sweden and Finland, commented that expeditions to the far north—highly favored in his day (1802)—"will be undertaken by those only who have a just and masculine taste for nature." Surely these "hardy" quarters are remote from the insinuating blandishments (i.e., the "effeminacy") of southern Europe, for this adamantine region "does not by any means hold out the same luxuries, the same allurements of climate, and the same temptations to pleasure that are presented by a more genial and inviting soil."

The late-eighteenth-century controversy over which was the more Sublime, the Pyrenees or the Alps, also fits within this scheme. The Comte de Guibert claimed that the Swiss colossi are superior because they are higher, more majestic, and possess greater character than their Franco-Iberian counterparts. Atop those icy ramparts one discovers only the most august phenomena: magnificent effects of light, shadow, color, and prodigious glaciers that give rise to the mighty rivers of Europe. By contrast, in the punier French range rarely does one's hair stand on end. Guibert concludes disdainfully that a voyage to the Pyrenees may suffice to give women some idea of the essence of mountains, but "a man, a man who desires to know, a man who ought to prefer great masses to details & superb horrors to the charms of a landscape . . . must prefer to go observe and study nature in the Alps." Fully comparable are Goethe's musings on granitic mountains (1783). Goethe maintains that these mountains' inmost cores and loftiest crests are stamped by an unshatterable masculine presence, and he apostrophizes this primary rock as "the oldest, firmest, securest, most indestructible son of nature."[21]

Montesquieu, one of the foremost political philosophers of the eighteenth century, based his theories on climatological considerations. He maintains in *L'esprit des lois* (1743) that climate is the principal cause of a nation's peculiar genius. Like his Renaissance forebears Jean Bodin and Pierre Charron, Montesquieu admits only three great divisions of the world, each corresponding to 30 degrees of latitude: the North, the South, and the Temperate Zones. He posits a physiognomical identity between specific locations and their inhabitants. Alpine dwellers are inflexible, truculent, and bellicose, like the heavily shadowed ridges of the Alps, whereas natives of France, Italy, and Spain are easygoing, colorful, and affable, mirroring the undulating terrain and the mild weather.[22]

A case can be made for aquatic and related meteorological imagery as the accommodating sexual antitheses to nature's flinty petrifactions and aggressive heights. Empedocles, Plato, and Cicero discuss the feminine nature of the air. Medieval alchemists created "marriages" between contrasting hot, dry and cold, wet substances. More specifically, during the eighteenth century the indefinable, undifferentiated, and amorphous faces of the landscape were seen as possessing a womanly cast. Burke's *Essay on the Sublime and the Beautiful* (1756–57) prepared the way for the aesthetic identification of the fluctuating with the feminine or the infinitely adjustable. The farther we proceed to the end of the eighteenth century, the more often we encounter this coupling. The German dramatist and poet Friedrich von Schiller, in his youthful prose writings, undermines Lessing's absolute distinctions between masculine time and feminine space by conjoining the two under a single rubric. He designates the Sublime as energetic and the Beautiful as melting (*schmelzende*) loveliness—only another way of stating that the first incorporates a masculine, vigorous, empowered articulation of the universe and the second a feminine, adaptable, ductile one. Gone for the moment is Winckelmann's option of an equivocal sensuous androgyny embodied in a slightly swollen contour and identified with unblemished, tasteless, and softly running water. It is within such a physical context that the exploits of the aeronauts must be placed. The balloonist breaks away from the solid earth and is compliantly borne aloft into an incomparably fluid region of mists and vapors. Unable to steer his craft, he must "submit" to the vagaries of evanescent meteors.[23]

Environmental Incursions

Isolés & séparés de la nature entière, nous n'apperçevions plus sous nos pas que ces énormes masses de neiges, qui, réfléchissat la lumière du soleil, éclairoient alors infiniment l'espace que nous occupions. . . .
Pilâtre de Rozier

Their situation in a small four-oared boat, on an immense ocean, far from any inhabitable shore, surrounded with ice, and utterly destitute of provisions, was truly terrifying and horrible in all its

The affecting and intangible sensations of solitude and silence augment the primal experience of rudimentary directions. Shaftesbury, an early apologist for the joys of isolation, has his spokesman Theocles extol the entirety of nature, down to its nethermost regions: ". . . all ghastly and hideous as they appear, they want not their peculiar beauties. The wildness pleases. We seem to live alone with Nature. We view her in her inmost recesses and contemplate her with more delight in these original wilds than in the artificial labyrinths and feigned wildernesses of the palace. . . ." Similarly, Addison's architectonic apperception discerned formative principles at work in the universe; his habit of finding meaning in landscape and his taste for the endless, the remote, and the uninhabited are precursors to the aesthetic of the lonely infinite.

The Deistic poets, following the lead of Shaftesbury and Addison, preferred uncultivated portions of the globe, where evidence of the creator was least obscured by the hand of art.[24] The acme of primitive and secluded scenery, however, was attained in the 1760s by the international group

361

consequences. They rowed about for some time, making vain efforts to be heard, but all was silent about them. . . .
Georg Forster

of artists and authors drawing upon ghostly Ossianic subjects and their setting in a dim northern region. Somewhat later, Bernardin de Saint-Pierre imparted additional force to the notion that a spot is more true to itself when it is savage and bereft of human traces. In his *Voyage à l'Ile de France* there are several haunting evocations of the loneliness permeating a particular locality. The nocturne prompted by the sight of volcanic and barren Ascension Island serves as a telling case in point: "The moon rose and illuminated this solitude. Its light, which renders attractive sites more agreeable, made this one more terrible. . . ."[25]

Perhaps the earliest topography to gain the attention of the travel writers who were intent on more robust and Doric splendors, voided of any sign of domestication, was that of the High Alps. Concomitantly, the cult of beautiful and delectable valleys was abandoned to those of a gentler disposition. The Swiss professor and physician Scheuchzer and his poet-compatriot Haller sought out these formerly neglected areas in order "to see nature and not see men and their works." Compare the German landscape designer Hirschfeld's comments on the character of such naked asperities: In *Theorie der Gartenkunst* (1779), he declares that the rudeness (*Rauhigkeit*) and wildness peculiar to peaks, crevices, glaciers, and abysses is not only consonant with their idiosyncratic and sublime character but strengthened by the experience of solitude and stillness customarily associated with a rarefied atmosphere.[26]

Relying on firsthand knowledge of the Pyrenees (which were scorned by Guibert), Alexandre de Laborde counseled "a solitary course" at sunset, amid lengthening shadows, strange rocks, widening crevasses, and cool evening breezes. Climbing Chimborazo, Alexander von Humboldt was led to compare the majestic, isolated calm of this summit to those of Mont Blanc and Monte Rosa.[27]

Typically, from the seventeenth century to the start of the Victorian era, elevations and eminences were where society was not. The unpeopled crests of the Alps or the Cordillera—cold and glittering in their unstained whiteness—embodied remoteness. Even the bizarrely shaped Pyrenees, with their "barbaric architecture," epitomized seclusion. No height was more unsociable, however, than the upper reaches of the atmosphere, and no air was purer and less conducive to ordinary life. Pilâtre de Rozier, making his first ascent in a *montgolfière* on June 23, 1784, was impressed by the almost hallucinatory uniqueness of his position. Absconding into a fog bank, the balloon was suddenly engulfed by a thick mist. The aeronauts "wandered awhile, and [floated] for the first time over this more than savage theater." "Isolated and separated from all of nature," they "saw nothing beneath [their] feet except enormous masses of snow, which, reflecting the sunlight, infinitely irradiated the space [they] occupied." Lunardi, in his relation of the first aerial voyage made in England (on September 15, 1784), convincingly relates the "calm delight" and the "stillness, extent, and magnificence of the scene" at the moment when the horizon seemed to trace a perfect circle. London, usually a veritable beehive of activity, had all its industry suspended. "Thus tranquil, and thus situated," reports Lunardi, "how shall I describe to you a view such as the ancients supposed Jupiter to have of the earth, and to copy which there are no terms in any language? . . . [Here] everything wore a new appearance, and had a new effect. . . ." Thomas Baldwin's *Airopaidia* also gives voice to the euphoria or "peaceful serenity" that arises from absolute solitude and detachment.[28]

Utter tranquility, completely congruous with the spirit of the scenery stretching before one's eyes, could also be found in less exalted domains. The alpinists were accustomed to the feeling. Bourrit, in the *Nouvelle description des vallées de glaces* (1783), reflects on the celibate life led by shepherds ranging over this wilderness. Far above the sphere of earthly desires and passions, they enjoy "a peace, and stillness of soul resembling the air they breathe." Patrick Brydone, making his descent from the ethereal regions of Mount Etna, was equally aware that the mountaineer contracts something of its "invariable purity." Standing under a quiet sky and beholding unperturbed a storm gathering beneath his feet, the traveler occupies a privileged pinnacle uniquely suspending him in time and space.[29]

The experience of being set apart was often accompanied not by a sense of equilibrium but by one of retirement. Cornelius Le Bruyn, arriving at the threshold of Persepolis in 1704 was keenly sensible of his unqualified exposure in "such a solitary place." Monsieur de Ferriol, Louis XIV's ambassador to the Great Porte, records how, "solitary and alone," he pursued his drive "to see what outstanding things nature and art brought forth in [the] different lands" stretching along the Bosporus. Nearly a century later, Martin Sauer, exploring the Russian tundra, was struck by the eloquent "desolation" of the scenes surrounding him. During the same period, Mungo Park, proceeding through "the wilderness" of the Kingdom of Bambarra, was especially successful in conjuring up the burning barrens of Africa. Just after noon, when the heat of the sun was reflected with a violent intensity from the floor of the desert, the distant ridges of hills— seen through ascending vapors—began to wave and fluctuate like an unsettled sea. At that moment Park was parched with thirst and praying for the sight of a human habitation, but "nothing appeared all around but thick underwood, and hillocks of white sand."

Vivant-Denon furnishes the French counterpart to this potent image of wasteland. On the plain of Thebes he was inexorably attracted to the mutilated Colossi of Memnon (figure 108). Scarcely begun sketching these ruins, he "became conscious that [he] was alone with [his] stately characters and [with] the thoughts that their fate inspired." "Frightened of where I was," he continues, "I galloped to overtake my inquisitive companions. . . ."

Figure 243
George Back, *Preparing an Encampment on the Barren Grounds*, from John Ross's *Polar Sea*, 1823, pl. p. 412. Engraving by Edward Finden. Photo courtesy British Library.

Figure 244
H. W. Williams, *The Alps from Geneva*, from *Travels in Italy, Greece, and the Italian Islands*, 1820, I, pl. p. 36. Aquatint by J. Aberli (?). Photo courtesy Cabinet des Estampes, Bibliothèque Nationale.

Pagès, following the route from Bassora to Damascus, saw "immense plains" where the eye was arrested only by the horizon. An unrelentingly uniform surface, grayish in color, was matched by a profound silence, with "no four-legged beasts, no birds, not even insects to break it." The only experience comparable to this monotonous and dusty atmosphere was the "mournful silence of those whitened lands" at the poles.

The unrelieved solitude of scorching flats and "dreary" uniformities continued to be a pervasive motif during the first third of the nineteenth century. Three further examples will serve to demonstrate their perennial, if austere, attractiveness. Salt, in his *Voyage to Abyssinia* (1814), reminisces about Bruce's earlier (1770) lonely adventures in that realm and compares them to his own travels through "a sandy and barren district." Lichtenstein, traversing South Africa's broad treeless, grassless, and streamless hollows situated in plains even more denuded (if that is conceivable), was overcome by an oppressive melancholy. Experiencing an emotion antithetical to the balloonist's euphoria, the German explorer expressed "a quiet horror before this terrible solitude." The far-flung valleys occasionally glimpsed through gaps cutting their way through neighboring mountains looked like a petrified sea. Each bend disclosed a view opening onto a new twist in the endless labyrinth. No trace of human passage existed, although neither rocks nor shrubs barred the way. Even the Bushmen fled these canyons, and many, doubtless, were never trod by human feet. (See figure 101.) Burchell, taking a caravan across the identical red and naked soil, followed a course that "lay over a hard, even, bare, and open country, the surface of which was here and there relieved from its monotony, by a broad, and far-extended undulation." He continues:

The train of waggons, steadily following each other at equal distances drew a lengthened perspective line over the wide landscape, that presented the only object on which the eye could fix. While the van was advancing over the highest swell, the rear was still far out of sight in the hollow. Waggon behind waggon slowly rose to view. . . . Not a green herb enticed the eye; not a bird winged through the air; the creation here, was nought but earth and sky; the azure vault of heaven, expanded into the boundless aërial space, seemed lifted further from the globe.

Neither did Burchell and his men see a single human trace, only the footprints of a lion.[30]

Islands—particularly the "dreary" volcanic and nonparadisical sort frequently met with in the empty Pacific—were also apprehended as prime exemplars of isolation. (See figure 104.) Flinders's account of Kangaroo Island captures the forlorn flavor of such passages: "Certainly none more likely to be free from the disturbance of every kind could have been chosen, than these islets in a hidden lagoon of an uninhabited island, situated upon an unknown coast near the antipodes of Europe; nor can anything more consonant to the feelings, if pelicans have any, than quietly to resign their breath, whilst surrounded by their progeny, and in the same spot where they first drew it. . . ."[31]

SECTARIANS OF THE UNKNOWN

The secluded forest far exceeded the archipelago's occasional power. As Pierre Poivre disapprovingly notes, in its untilled depths one stumbles for miles across rank weeds and encumbering roots before catching even the faintest glimmer of rudimentary cultivation. Not only the virgin jungles of Africa, disdained by Poivre, but also Australia's lofty trees were thought to express the brute and primitive opacity of organic nature. D'Entrecasteaux terms them as ancient as the world because of their tightly plaited impenetrability. Flinders describes the same terrain: Wild nutmeg, fig, and two species of palm grow in abundance, but the heat is so suffocating and the mosquitos so rapacious that they create an environment that could prove delightful only "to a college of monks." In South America, Humboldt similarly (if less wryly) remarks on the impassable stretches of unrelieved and uninhabited greenery. Even in the best season the lush plants flanking the Pass of Quindiu cannot be skirted in less than ten to twelve days, and if any mishap should befall the helpless traveler he would find himself utterly isolated in a penumbrous and pathless wood overgrown by uncontrollable vegetation. The prospect of losing oneself under the cool arcades of the towering *ficus laurifolia* deep in the forests of Puerto Rico was not unpleasant, however, to André-Pierre Ledru, one of the naturalists on Nicolas Baudin's expedition. Indeed, he allies himself with the happily solitary botanists—"Tournefort in the Pyrenees, Jussieu in Peru, and Linnaeus in Lapland"—all "giving themselves up to the charming study of plants, forgetting to drink and to eat." "Here," Ledru goes on, "arrested by a thousand pictures which nature offers me at every step, I lost my way, and wandered completely preoccupied with the pleasure of gathering flowers. . . ." The aspect of such retreats may be diverse indeed. Belzoni, journeying to the Red Sea, came upon a "complete forest" of sunt trees exhibiting "the most beautiful and solitary scenes."[32]

Most celebrated, however, were the untouched wilds of North America. Jacques Milbert made a pilgrimage to the environs of Sandy Hill on the banks of the Hudson, "without a single soul to speak to." He responds to James Fenimore Cooper's vision—enunciated in *The Pioneers* (1823)— of being in the midst of a vast but alas rapidly disappearing solitude invaded by rampant and luxuriant overgrowth and in whose bosom repose the remains of the noble and fierce Indian. Much earlier, Chateaubriand, eluding the French Revolution, dreamed of going to the United States. The pretext for his voyage was the aim of discovering the fabled Northwest Passage, but his autobiographical *Mémoires d'outre-tombe* (1841) tell another tale: The future author of *Atala* (set in Louisiana) yearned to seek his fame "in solitude." He exalts not only North America's vacant forests (untouched by humanity except for the fleeting footfall of the "Red Skin") but also its marginless bodies of water. Nothing is more afflicting, he asserts, than the sight of Canadian lakes. The stark nakedness of their surface conjoined with an empty bank results in "solitudes that separate other solitudes." "Shores without inhabitants look out over seas without vessels; one floats down the deserted flood along deserted strands. . . ."

VOYAGE INTO SUBSTANCE

Equally moving is Cochrane's remembrance of Lake Guatavita on a lovely autumn day. Not a gust of wind rippled its liquid mirror; silently it reflected the thick groves straddling the beach. "Nought living moved, save a few waterfowl, that gently glided away from us as if wondering what creatures dared molest their solitary reign. . . ."[33]

A more "dismal" prospect than even the naked terminus of Tierra del Fuego existed at the poles, the acme of the lonely and the remote. (See figure 73.) The imagery used to portray the unfrequented voids of the far north and south is appropriately more austere than that used to characterize North America's unfurnished interior. Boisgelin de Kerdu occasionally spied Laplanders feeding their flocks, but more often than not these grueling marches through snow and glaciers and over deep and rapid rivers were conducted "without seeing a single human being during the whole of the route." What held true for the outer reaches of Norway was equally apt for craggy Iceland, called by Edy "that remote and secluded portion of the world."[34]

Wild terrain where man had rarely if ever set foot not only embodied the paradigm of solitude but was the setting for absolute or infrequently relieved silence. Here is Charles Darwin speaking:

Delight itself, however, is a weak term to express the feelings of a naturalist who, for the first time, has been wandering by himself in a Brazilian forest. Among the multitude of striking objects, the general luxuriance of the vegetation bears away the victory. The elegance of the grasses, the novelty of the parasitical plants, the beauty of the flowers, the glossy green of the foliage, all tend to this end. A most paradoxical mixture of sound and silence pervades the shady parts of the wood. The noise from the insects is so loud, that it may be heard even in a vessel anchored several hundred yards from the shore; yet within the recesses of the forest universal silence appears to reign. To a person fond of natural history, such a day as this, brings with it a deeper pleasure than he ever can hope again to experience. . . .

By contrast, the sense of immobility and frozen stasis implicit in absolute quiet is brilliantly diagnosed a half-century earlier by the younger Forster in the passage with which this section is prefaced. Completely vulnerable because totally exposed, two scientists (J. R. Forster and William Wales) sat in a tiny boat on an immense ocean encircled by ice. Nothing is more mournful than the naturalist's paratactic and sublime juxtaposition of bootless shouting with engulfing silence.

The aurora borealis unfurled noiselessly before Gmelin's and O'Reilly's wondering eyes. La Pérouse, exploring the coast of Alaska, came upon what he judged to be the most extraordinary and still place on the face of the earth. The depths of the Bay or Port des Français, surrounded by high snow-topped mountains, exhibited the visage of eternal sterility. "I have never," writes La Pérouse, "witnessed a breath of wind wrinkle the surface of this water. . . . The air is so tranquil and the silence so profound, that the ordinary voice of a man can be heard at half a league as can the sound of several seabirds. . . ." MacKenzie and Paul Gaimard were similarly impressed by "an awful profound silence" wrapping the grim, riven country of the "slumbering" ice-crowned Jokulls beyond Hecla. Both Pierre-Marie-François Pagès (in 1782) and Edme de La Poix de Fréminville (in 1819), slowly proceeding toward the North Pole, were stunned by the solitude and the profound silence permeating the vast domain of the Spitzbergen.[35]

Bourrit, in the Alps, pinpoints the source of a glacier's unequivocal fascination as the fact that nothing stirs in this boundless world in which all things harmonize with the "reigning and vast silence." Saussure also documents this alien and gigantic repose.[36]

The attribute of "solemn stillness" was believed to be congruent with the pictorialization of original creation as unseen and unspoiled. Thus, the untarnished image of the absolute, the premonition of infinite space, the sense of terrain as pure mirror reflecting the face of the earth at its genesis might be discovered anywhere. One moonlit night, William Alexander responded to the intangible presence of perfect peace while sailing undisturbed toward Peking. Chateaubriand, encamped in the dense thickets of the New World, awakened at midnight to find a reverberating calm weighing heavily on the forest: "One could say that silences succeeded silences. . . . Quiescence again invaded the desert. . . ."[37]

Silence receives its most antisocial interpretation in subterranean regions. Carl Lang records the tomblike atmosphere of the cavern at Castleton in whose unoccupied, flooded hall nothing is seen except steep escarpments erratically illuminated by flickering torchlight. Meditating on a lifetime of descents into the underworld, he praises those artless chambers consecrated to secrecy "where nature builds in quiet majesty." Hieroglyphs of its taciturn evolution surround the explorer in myriad incarnations: imperceptibly developing stalactites resembling rustling water, laconic mineral formations, and mutely growing crystals.[38]

Although the chill, alternatingly cramped and spacious confines of caves are scenically remote from the heat and horizontality of sandy wastes, both sites imply a fatal continuum. Lang makes clear how the numinous quality associated with grottos since time immemorial is due partly to the early awareness of their housing an indefinite and unimpeded lateral succession of perishing organisms. What is latent or covert in the still cavern becomes explicit and overt in the noiseless desert. Olivier, enduring violent summer winds in Egypt, cautions that one must immediately throw oneself on the ground to survive. The withering blast lasts 2–3 minutes at a time. During its brief passage, not only is the heat insupportable, but "the stillness of these deserts is uninterrupted except for plaintive cries, the sure announcement of danger menacing all living beings." Soon "an absolute stillness" ensues. As Mollien crossed the Desert of the Joloffs, his ear was also finely tuned to "the silence of death"; in these drought-stricken solitudes not an animal fixed its abode. Beechey, traveling over the "truly desolate and wretched" tracts of North Africa, listened to the lethal inarticulateness: "Marsh, sand, and barren rocks, alone met the eye: and not a single human being, or a trace of vegetation. . . . The stillness of the nights . . . was not even broken by the howlings of our old friends the jackalls and hyaenas. . . ."[39]

As the foregoing excerpt indicates, absolute quiet was often offset by noise. This antinomy emerges nowhere more clearly than in the narratives of the balloon ascents. The gala and earthy festivities that accompanied ascents—replete with fireworks and enthusiastic, clamorous crowds—contrast with the perfect calm and oblivion of space.

Faujas de Saint-Fond describes a highly unusual variant to this confusing and raucous scene: Pilâtre de Rozier's *montgolfière* was transported by night from the Place des Victoires to the Champ de Mars, illuminated by torches, flanked by a cortege, and escorted by a detachment of foot and horse guards. The silence and the late hour "tended to cast over this operation a singularity & a mystery truly designed to be imposing on those who had not been adverted." Faujas's awed description of the event indicates that a quiet gathering proved to be the exception. The balloonists' emphasis on detachment—both physical and psychic—gains added significance when pitted against this customary babble of ritualized solidarity. Baldwin, in the *Airopaidia*, remarks on the "soothing silence" that comes with being untethered: ". . . for a *while* detached, *far* detached from Earth, and *all* terrestrial Thoughts; wrapt in the *mild Azure* of the *ethereal* Regions; suspended in the Center of a vast and almost endless Concave; come as *mere* visitor, from *another* Planet; surrounded with the stupendous Works of *Nature*, yet *above* them. . . . a peaceful SERENITY OF MIND succeeded. . . ." High, but not high enough, this enviable and hushed euphoria was ruptured by the clatter of carriages moving along the turnpike below, "gratings of whose wheels on stones seemed uncommonly harsh although they could not be seen." Baldwin pointedly recalls the prior moment "when ALL AROUND was wrapt in the Sublimity of SILENCE which afforded a pleasureable Contrast; diffusing a DELICIOUS CALM"

A less pedestrian tumult might also be encountered in the reaches of the upper atmosphere. Blanchard, during his third aerial voyage, on July 18, 1784, was alerted by his companion to "the murmuring of a tempest." Typically, the pamphleteers and artists of the day portrayed the balloonists as soaring "to the seat of thunder." (See figures 154 and 156.) The aeronauts' epic adventures provoked a universal enthusiasm, which was focused on modern man set adrift in a cosmic din. Testu-Brissy's flamboyant equestrian flight of October 16, 1798, for which he educed a scientific reason, serves as a case in point. Fearing his balloon would explode, he made a hasty landing in a wheat field near Montmorency. He escaped

Figure 245
William Westall, *View on the North Side of Kangaroo Island*, from Matthew Flinders's *Voyage to Terra-Australis*, 1814, I, pl. p. 184. Engraving by W. Woolnoth. Photo courtesy British Library.

Figure 246
A. von Humboldt, *The Pass of Quindiu*, from *Vues des Cordillères*, 1814, pl. 5. Color aquatint by Duttenhofer. Photo courtesy British Library.

Figure 247
A. Mayer, *Glacier of Jöknll, Iceland*, from
Paul Gaimard's *Voyage en Islande et
Groenland*, 1838, II, pl. 80. Lithograph by
Sabatier and Bayot. Photo courtesy
Newberry Library.

Figure 248
Carl Lang, *Underground Boating in the
Cavern at Castleton*, from *Gallerie der
Unterirdischen Wunder*, 1806–1807, I, pl. p.
120. Color aquatint. Photo courtesy
Bibliothèque Nationale.

Figure 249
Anonymous, *View of Bastille Day
Celebration*, 1801. Color aquatint. Photo
courtesy Library of Congress, Tissandier
Collection.

Vue Brillante de l'Aniversaire du 14 Juillet 1801.

du 25 Messidor de l'An 9. Feu d'Artifice tiré a l'Etoille des Champs Elisées, sous le Consul Buonaparte premier de la Republique Française

A Paris chez J. Chereau Rue Jacques pres la Fontaine Severin N.º 257

Figure 250
H. G. Bertaux, *The Moment of Universal Exhilaration over the Triumph of Messrs. Charles and Robert at the Tuileries on October 1, 1783*. Etching. Photo courtesy Library of Congress, Landauer Collection.

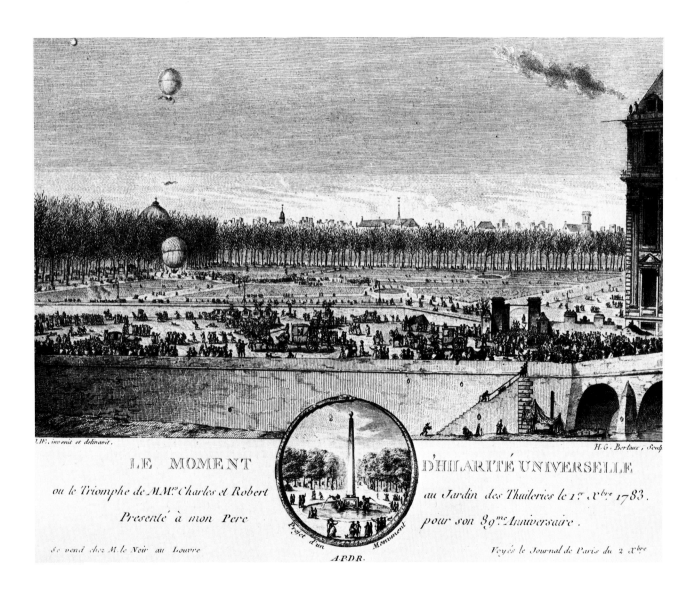

SECTARIANS OF THE UNKNOWN

the enraged peasants who wanted to drag him to a neighboring village in order to pay damages, only to rise into a storm cloud. He remained hidden within its unrelieved darkness for 3 hours, undaunted by rain, snow, lightning bolts, and resonating thunderclaps.[40]

A wide range of sounds, from deafening roars to scarcely audible whispers, reverberate through the pages of the factual travel accounts. The polarity between noise and stillness looms large in the portrayal of waterfalls. Describing the dense mangrove thickets of Mauritius, Bernardin de Saint-Pierre remarks how the encroaching sea snakes through entangled roots to form melancholy retreats and secluded streams, which silently twist and turn to plunge suddenly with a "muffled incoherent rumble" down the grassy slopes of a ravine. Sometimes, in addition, "the ear is wounded by the croak of the parrot, or by the shrill scream of the mischievous monkey."

Amid steep brown rocks and heaps of large stones dislodged from the mountains towering above Dusky Bay, New Zealand, Georg Forster heard the rending and splitting of a cascade. It was exceptionally loud because it repeatedly echoed from boulder to boulder, drowning out almost every other sound. Such thundering was especially noted in relations concerning the activity of Swiss cataracts. In their fugitive embodiment, as the result of an avalanche, they tumble by leaps and bounds from summit to crevice to plain, shattering to form a foaming sheet that precipitates into the adjoining valley. In their less ephemeral incarnation, as at the Staubbach, they brawl their way down established inclines. During the winter, however, this flow is peremptorily halted when the freeze sets in. Then, enormous icicles mold pendant shafts that frequently splinter with "a tremendous crash."[41]

But it was in North America that roiled water most consistently formed an effective foil to silent and tranquil pools. The Marquis de Chastellux was taken by the magnificent cataracts found along the Hudson River, wildly hurtling "with a ruckus" between boulders upheaved by ancient earthquakes. Once these obstacles are left behind, the stream peacefully and quietly glides into a deep valley. George Heriot insists upon the "solemn effect" produced by the "incessant sound" and rapid motion of the falls of the Saint Lawrence River. Approximately two miles in breadth, the torrent is accelerated both by the great declivity of its bed and the presence of three islands around which it must force passage. Masses of curling white spray tear, fracture, and dig cavities into the rocks below. Heriot uses analogous language to capture the ceaseless thunder of Niagara, "with the volumes of vapour darting upwards into the air, which the simultaneous report and smoke of a thousand cannon could scarcely equal."

Less terrifyingly sublime, perhaps, but magnificent nonetheless, was the waterfall at French Hoek on the Cape of Good Hope. Lord Valentia's

Voyages and Travels (1809) recounts how he and Henry Salt not only saw, but heard, it from afar. Through a cleft in the mountain a liquid column of considerable proportions dashed for 170 feet perpendicular and then "rolled over" large rocks overhung with brushwood. Even more massive was the confluence of the River Bogotà with that of the Magdalena. Charles Cochrane witnessed the initial commingling and subsequent divorce when the swollen stream issued untrammeled from the chasm at Toquendama. Darting white fumes, a fireworks of fanciful shapes, luxuriant vegetation, and the "deafening roar of the waters" heightened the loneliness of the situation.[42]

The boisterous clamor of the sea could be more vociferous than even the noisiness of the fall. Kaempfer, off the coast of Japan, braved the "remarkable and dangerous whirlpools" Faisaki and Narrotto, whose formidable aspect was considerably enhanced by a "rushing" noise like that made by spouting dragons. Le Gentil, coasting along the arid Ile de Bourbon in the Indian Ocean, observed the waves continuously sporting with large pebbles lining its margins. These were rhythmically lifted and dropped "with a kind of fury that produced a stunning noise." After quitting the Azores, Heriot gained an equally tempestuous shore. Lying 40 leagues from Newfoundland is the Great Bank, an enormous mountain beneath the surface of the Atlantic. Even in thick fogs sailors can detect the presence of these formidable shallows, because the din of the billows becomes more shrill as the ship approaches. Visitors to Fingal's Cave encountered a similar acoustical phenomenon: The surge of waves against basaltic pillars produced sonorous chords, transforming the grotto into a gigantic water organ—a colossal counterpart to the aeolian harp.[43]

The watery harmonies of the ocean contrasted with the jolting dissonances of glaciers. Gruner listened to their "perpetual creaking" in the valley of the Aar. Yet beneath this inhuman score existed the thread of a more subdued refrain: "the sad murmur" of water flowing under ice. Sherwill, climbing into the frozen wilderness of Mont Blanc, termed its unshapely melody of yawning rifts one of "uproarious desolation." As fugal counterpoint to this obstreperous and ungainly discord, he, too, cites the "strange sound" of the waters muttering and rustling within the flanks of the ice grottos of the Glacier des Bossons.

Concordances were impossible, however, in the harsh and unmelodious regions of the poles. Constantine Phipps describes the characteristic crunch of icebergs and the clatter occasioned by great chunks severing and then splashing into the sea. John Laing, in his *Voyage to the Spitzbergen* (1818), reproduces Captain Scoresby's memoir on Polar Ice, which permits the reader to experience the impact of "tremendous concussions" between battling floes: "A body of more than ten thousand millions of tons in weight, meeting with resistance, the consequences may possibly be conceived. The weaker field is crushed with an awful noise; sometimes the

Figure 251
G. S. Gruner, *Glacier with Subglacial Torrent*, from *Die Eisgebirge des Schweizerlandes*, 1760, pl. 2. Engraving by A. Zingg. Photo courtesy British Library.

Figure 252
M. Bravais, *Aurora Borealis to Northwest, Bossekop, Finnemark, December 30, 1838, 8:32 P.M.*, from Paul Gaimard, *Voyage en Scandinavie, Atlas*, 1839–1852, III, pl. 21. Lithograph by Lottin and Sabatier. Photo courtesy Library of Congress.

VOYAGE INTO SUBSTANCE

destruction is mutual. . . ." In Scoresby's own relation of the Arctic regions, he provides an explanation for the glistening and fantastic shapes exhibited by many bergs. Perforations, clefts, and hollows are the consequences of the sun's activity. The ice, thus rendered friable, "calves." Large pieces break off and plunge headlong into the sea with "a terrible crash which in some places produces an extraordinary echo in the neighbouring mountains." Wintering on the Saint Lawrence River, Isaac Weld reports a similar rasping at the moment when the ice begins to sunder, splitting from side to side "with a loud report." In terms of magnitude, Latin America's only equivalent is the earthquake. Captain Fitzroy of the *Beagle* was at Concepcion the morning of February 20, 1835. "Suddenly, an awful overpowering shock caused universal destruction—and in less than six seconds the city was in ruins. The stunning noise of falling houses; the horrible cracking of the earth, which opened and shut rapidly and repeatedly in numerous places; the desperate heart-rending outcries of the people; the stifling heat; the blinding, smothering clouds of dust; the utter helplessness and confusion, and the extreme horror and alarm can neither be described nor imagined. . . ."[44]

Resonance, resulting from the exertion of tremendous internal pressure, was also identified with "horrid subterranean noise." William Hamilton likens the periodic emissions of the hotspring called the Pisciarelli to the boiling and burbling of a gigantic cauldron. The warning hiss of the Great Geyser of Iceland (figure 168) was accompanied by escaping vapor forceful enough to pierce a beautifully crystallized crust of sulfur and clay. George MacKenzie minutely itemizes how this "dense column of steam, mixed with a little water," was "forcing its way impetuously through a crevice in the rock." "The violence with which it rushes out is so great," he notes, "that the noises thus occasioned, may often be heard at the distance of several miles. . . ." Typically, these intermittent eruptions took the form of incoherent stammers or gurgles, compounded by the "splashing and roar" of the jet pushing its way from the entrails of the earth into the open air.[45]

The explorer's sangfroid was most easily shattered, however, by beasts prowling in the wilderness. Climbing Table Mountain in the early hours of the morning, Bernardin de Saint-Pierre had his idyllic *clair de lune* violated by the howling of wolves; Williamson heard their cries as they were being smoked out of dens by hunters patrolling the edges of the Ganges. During a severe famine that struck Russia in the winter of 1788, Lesseps chronicled the plight of starving dogs become utterly uncontrollable, roaming the countryside, sinking teeth into anything and everything crossing their path, and even cannibalizing their weaker brethren. "To the horror of seeing them devour each other, succeeded the sad spectacle of those besieging the yurts where we dwelled. These poor beasts were so emaciated as to provoke compassion; they could barely move; their plaintive and persistent howls seemed to beg us to help them,

SECTARIANS OF THE UNKNOWN

& reproached us for the impossibility, because of where we were, of doing so. . . ."[46]

The prairies of North America, akin to the Eurasian continent, were also filled with clamorous creatures. Lewis and Clark saw vast herds of buffalo–ten thousand at a stretch—that "kept a dreadful bellowing during the night . . . so as to form an almost continued roar." These behemoths darkening the grasslands near the Medicine River, like the "snorting" hippo and the growling lion abiding in Africa's reedy plains or the whale "blowing among the numerous bergs," punctured the silence of the unknown.[47]

The travelers to the tropics seemed most attuned to the song of birds penetrating the dense vegetation and enlivening the wilderness. Yet Stedman, lying in his hammock in the jungles of Guiana, also listened to the flapping wings of the large, blood-sucking vampire bat, the incessant "touck, touck, touck" of the toad, the roaring of tigers, the shrieks of monkeys, and the hissing of snakes. Johnson, exploring Prince of Wales Island, was struck by the noise of water plummeting over rock fragments and the subdued rumble of a transient thunderstorm filtering through pine trees. In the eucalyptus stands of Australia's interior, Arago met with legions of blue-collared titmice, parakeets of all colors, and yellow-crested white cockatoos. He speaks for all his peers, hacking their way through "vast solitudes trodden only at long intervals by human feet" where "the cries of a bird, the whistling of a reed, the rustling of a piece of bark half torn off which the wind is gradually stripping, make a solemn impression on the mind, that involuntarily excites it to meditation and melancholy." For Arago neither silence nor sound produces the feeling of tranquility— as stillness might otherwise do when experienced, say, in a field located just outside a populous city. He astutely remarks that both quiescence and noise occasion painful emotions precisely because "there are no protectors in these profound and eternal forests."[48] With this reflection on ultimate exposure Arago illuminates and summarizes the necessary connection binding these two intangible, but perceptible, qualities. The tactile, that is, what is directly graspable, is not all that has a bearing on the characteristic aspect of a place. The invisible, in all its substantial epiphanies (the "prolonged vibration" of an echo, the constant "sweep" of the wind over an unbroken surface of water, the distant babble of a "rude chorus," the "tinkling of innumerable small bells," and even the "aromatic odors" of orange blossoms wafting over the surf) plays a decisive role in the apprehension of natural phenomena.[49]

The antithetical formula of void and plenum, and of inaudible and audible, touches upon the larger issue of all those sublimities that almost exceed our ability to copy them. By definition, enduring or fugitive solitude and silence—like height or depth—continually elude intellectual and physical pursuit. The eye laboring to penetrate wilderness is like the ear straining to hear stillness. The eye stretches to summits, sinks to abysses, and collapses underground just as the ear is receptive to high or low and obtrusive or muted pitch.

These spatial bearings and the aural range with which the scientific travelers adjusted themselves to the environment suggest the presence of another real world lying beyond the real world. Their experiences—neither dream nor mirage, because they were documented—confirmed the existence of a novel and marvelous realm alien to Europe's domesticated scenery.

The literary and pictorial tradition transmitted from antiquity of a bucolic and illusory setting, a fairyland in which nothing is quite what it seems, strips nature of its threatening power. It is a fictitious world made for the pensive and private man. Unapproachable and untouchable, the Virgilian landscape creates an asylum far from the actualities of life.[50] The acts of matter are of a different order.

The poetic device of the marvelous provides an exception to the rule of habitual experience. This *topos* may be identified with either form or content. The most significant aspect of the latter category for our purposes is not the divine, the human, or the miraculous but the natural marvelous founded on man's curiosity about the uncommon. It was the scientific bent of explorers that brought the extraordinary down to earth, that concretized and authenticated the foreign and the remote. The acuity of the scientific response was also reflected in the appropriation of the device of unpredictability. The element of surprise and instantaneity—a constant factor in exploration—is equally opposed to the expected and the tedious of everyday experience.[51]

Select examples will serve to indicate that travelers were at pains to show there was more to the phenomenal world than what met the unprobing eye and that this uncustomary aspect was also not illusory. Bourrit, gazing at the Mer de Glace of Montanvert, grappled with a "magical" scene unrolling at the border between France and Italy. The fractured mountains and wrathful frozen "sea" of ice revealed the face of nature as it must have appeared upon emerging from chaos. The *Journal des Voyages* (1825) extols in like manner the imposing face of Switzerland's hundred colossi, which metamorphose into "fantastic objects" and turn into "gigantic phantoms" when bathed by the rays of the setting sun. John Edy, describing the more tranquil physiognomy of Longsound Firth, focuses on the moment when profound silence prevails: "At these periods the objects reflected by the lake beneath have a magical effect; the extraordinary gleams of light, the great depth and purity of the water, the transient prismatic colouring, the mists or clouds, and other singular effects, tempt you to believe the whole to be a new creation. . . ." And Landmann, walking near Cintra in Portugal, surrendered to the serene, almond-and-pomegranate-scented air, which breathed of palpable enchantment.

Andrew Sparrman, herborizing on Table Mountain, underwent an analogous, if reverse, experience of agitated fugacity: "From the mist, or fog, which surround me . . . I perceived at times specks of clouds snatched off by the northwest wind, and driving along with violence through the air both above and below the spot I then stood upon, and directly followed by their shadows formed upon the same plains. In a word, this extensive and delightful spectacle was as enchanting as it was singular. . . ." Anders Skjöldebrand, in Finland, witnessed another evanescent landscape: the "enchanting prospect" of fogs collecting in the "soft brightness" of midnight and casting large shadows over mountains and rivers.[52]

The nocturnal or dimly lit scene seemed to be a particularly rich source of enchantment. Tuckey reports on a moonlit scene in which a vaporous play of smoky shapes deployed itself over slate and quartz cliffs lining the banks of the Congo.

The heavy obscurity of the cave was as filled with airy powers as the desert at nightfall. The gloomy vaults of the Durrenberg salt mines near Saltzburg were described in the *Journal des Voyages* (1819) as illuminated "by enchantment." One perceives neither entrance nor exit to this Stygian world. George Thompson, traveling in South Africa, explored a "remarkable cavern" first discovered in 1780. Its glistening stalactites reflected the glare of torches with "a very brilliant and enchanting effect." The beckoning "strangeness" of grottos, the "magical" otherness of blackened lava colonnades, was revealed only to those willing to enter the penumbra.[53]

The half-seen finds its counterpart in phenomena starkly disclosed in the bright, defining light of day. Malaspina comments on the hallucinatory power of Arctic light ruthlessly reflected from bergs or mists. Unlike caverns buried beneath the soil or tunneling into a hillside, grottos excavated into snow or floating ice (see figure 25) shine with the refulgence of a polished mirror. George Lyon delineated this "dazzling" scene in which the sun bore down powerlessly upon silvery icicles. Brooke employed a cognate image of reality to record flashing northern lights sighted in Lapland: pale sheets of flame combined visually with innumerable crystals created by hoarfrost to produce the effect of "an enchanted forest."[54]

Even a real object may appear fantastic; thus, these perceptual categories do not necessarily form mutually exclusive topics in the discourse of the nonfiction travel account. Rather, the marvelous, the enchanting, even the magical scene can represent not an invention or a vision but a mode of entry into what seems like another world—one that appears strange precisely because it is new and unassimilated. Within its ample confines, the scientific narrative demonstrates that there are many events occurring in nature that defy even the most feverish or effusive fancy. In short, more things are possible, comprehensible, and observable than are imaginable.[55]

The Navigation of Existence

What a noble study are the arts for those who cultivate them successfully! What a fine thing the sciences for those who know nothing of them! From how many troubles are the latter spared! From what toilsome labors are they exempt! They go not, like madmen, trusting to the stars and winds, to brave alternating frosts and storms. In their peaceful habitations, surrounded by constant friends, their lives flow smoothly on; and at the end of their career, when they fall asleep forever, their last thoughts are still endued with joy, their final recollection is an image of happiness! . . .
Jacques Arago

Jamais rien n'égalera ce moment d'hilarité qui s'empara de mon existence, lorsque je sentis que je fuyois la terre; ce n'étoit pas du plaisir, c'étoit du bonheur. . . .
Jacques Charles

The scientific desire to cut through appearances is closely allied to a methodology of quest. The entire enterprise of voyaging rested on the premise that each thing must be sought in its place, not within books or even within the compendious Picturesque garden.[56] The modern explorer was not to be confused with the stock type of the medieval wanderer, the exiled Jew Ahasuerus hounded and ekeing out a vagabond destiny beneath the stars. Nor did he fit the image of the mercenary seeker after fortune, leading an unstable, disorderly, and peripheral existence devoted to self-fulfillment and narcissistic individuality. The traveling naturalist or the scientific explorer was first and foremost a man in search of knowledge. He was distinct from other voyagers because he also worked "in the service of an organized vision of what might be found," seeking "to relate it to what is known." Unlike the wanderer, then, the explorer saw himself both as perceiving and as contributing to a sum of knowledge assessed beforehand. As Paracelsus already recognized in the sixteenth century,

He who wishes to explore nature must tread her books with his feet. Writing is learned from letters, nature however by traveling from land to land: one land, one page. This is the *Codex-Naturae*, thus must its leaves be turned.

Yet by the eighteenth century, Paracelsus's naive view that one observer could see and record it all was replaced by the realization that raw data had to be compiled from a variety of sources and published in order to be available for checking and confirmation by others.

Since Lucian's *True History*, the adventurer's fantastical exploits have been seen to stand outside the real meaning of life. Yet there are other aspects of his complex personality—as they emerge from literature—that illuminate the psychology of the traveler in search of unreduced visual detail. Engagement in the active life and willingness to enter experience bodily, to face constant risk, and to endure solitude and silence are capacities shared both by Casanova and Cook. In Hawkesworth's jaundiced appraisal of the unavailing search for the Great Southern Continent, the "persevering English navigator" Cook assumes epic stature. After fruitless traverses of the Pacific he dispelled error by declaring he found nothing but "barren rocks, scarcely affording shelter to penguins and seals; and dreary seas, and mountains of ice, occupying this immense space allotted to imaginary paradises."[57] Cook's intensity, devotion to truth, and unswerving sense of purpose simultaneously ally him with and distinguish him from the roving band immortalized in the Homeric epic.

Unlike the privateer Count Benyowsky, who reputedly possessed a disposition "singularly calculated for adventure" (brought up as he was in the school of mercenary, impromptu warfare), the leader of a serious expedition aspired to the qualifications of acquired genius. Claude-Adrien Helvétius's essay *De l'esprit* (1758) is particularly revealing on the point that, as with Bacon, genius is not the result of heredity but the effect of

SECTARIANS OF THE UNKNOWN

Figure 253
John Edy, *Scene in Longsound Firth,* from
Boydell's Scenery of Norway, 1820, II, pl. 39.
Color aquatint. Photo courtesy British
Library.

Figure 254
J. K. Tuckey, *Fisherman Inhabiting the Rocks of the Lovers Leap*, from *Voyage in Africa*, 1818, pl. p. 130. Engraving by W. Finden after sketch by Lt. Hawkey. Photo courtesy British Library.

Figure 255
B. Faujas de Saint-Fond, *Basaltic Pavement of the Bridge of Beaume*, from *Recherches sur les volcans éteints*, 1783, pl. 11. Engraving by Claude Fessard after drawing by J. F. Gautier-Dagoty. Photo courtesy British Library.

willed inquiry. This exponent of a radical form of materialism that differs in kind from that of his contemporaries Diderot and Saint-Lambert declares that the man of genius is produced solely by the peculiar circumstances in which he is placed. That is, the cultural climate must favor his development. Moreover, Helvétius notes that in his day circumstances are propitious for the nurturing of such an intellectual giant. He views with approval the fact that Europeans no longer interpret natural phenomena through imaginative means (the prerogative of the poet or the *littérateur*) but now employ study and application (the conceptual tools of the scientific genius). Only through experimentation does a great intellect uncover the secrets of nature, and, by extension, only through searching exploration does the voyager push back frontiers. One and the same methodology of fathoming the particulars of existence underlies both endeavors.[58]

Making genial discoveries, by definition, enlarges horizons; it impels one to become a citizen of the world, to inhabit both a spacious mental realm and a physical realm. According to William Sharpe, who was of the same mind as Helvétius, since the man of genius must acquire everything he is perpetually aware of his ignorance. By navigating through it, he interrogates the ambient. Hence, the quest is endless, extending beyond all boundaries. Limitations of a narrowly nationalistic or local attachment are effectively broken by the inventive and studious mind.

If all the world is his laboratory, then the self-made genius belongs to all mankind. He is the embodiment of the great and exemplary man, adulated in the latter part of the century, and not only his universality but also his fame places him beyond the borders of his homeland.[59] The discoverer, then, by aspiration, training, and temper, was considered singularly qualified to enter the lists as scientific genius, paladin, and cosmopolitan—indeed, as a modern Ulysses. The seafaring hero of the *Odyssey* was motivated to live his life as a series of energetic exploits at the margins of the world. Thus, he became the model for all who actively desired to plumb the unknown. As the archetypical adventurer, he could describe things for the first time as he encountered them. Similarly, the explorers of 1760–1800 were occasionally privileged to behold new portions of the globe.[60] It is not surprising, then, that avowals of originality are a refrain of voyage literature.

During his second voyage, Cook decided that the long months of the Antarctic winter should be spent not in lying at harbor—an idea repellant to his restless character—but in making two sweeps about the eastern and central island groups of the Pacific to make what new discoveries could be made. After narrowly escaping destruction outside the Barrier Reef in August 1770, he wrote

Such are the vicissitudes attending this kind of service and must always attend an unknown Navigation: was it not from the pleasure which naturly results to a Man from being the first discoverer, even was it nothing more than Sands and Shoals, this service would be insupportable especially in far distant parts, like this, short of Provision and almost every other necessary. . . .

The possibility of having such an unedited experience lured James Bruce into the deserts of Africa to undertake a journey that would yield "the first discovery" made in George III's reign. It drove Vincent Lunardi, who had "the ambition to be the first, not only to visit the English atmosphere, but to ascertain the practicability of rendering the balloon stationary," into the sky. It induced a host of artist-wanderers to pursue, on land, on sea, or in the air, the stable and dynamic aspects of nature. From alpine climbers like Wolf to sailing men like Hodges to high fliers like Charles, the chief motivation was to become the original visitor to an uncharted region. Valenciennes counseled the serious student of landscape to voyage—What could be more beneficial to the "inquisitive and philosophical artist" than to observe far-off lands at first hand?[61]

To be an initial witness implied at best that one was confronting a hitherto unseen region, at worst that the region had been unconsciously sighted or examined desultorily before. Chappe d'Auteroche declares California to be a land "so little known & because of that as worthy of curiosity!" Cook, who avers that his ambition had led him not only farther than any other man before him but as far as he thought it possible for man to go, carried the operations of his third and final voyage beyond his former discoveries and into "untrodden paths in the Northern hemisphere." Malaspina pushed his expedition to the far north to the very "limits of the ice fields." La Pérouse urges the reader of his *Voyage autour du monde* (1797) to scrutinize the wind charts; such close reading should prompt him to think not indifferently of those navigators "to the ends of the earth" who, "having struggled incessantly against fogs, bad weather and scurvy, scoured an unfamiliar coast."

Goethe delighted in his good fortune at having grown up during the latter part of the eighteenth century—specifically at having been a contemporary of the first balloonists. He explains why their discovery aroused an intense yearning in the thousands of spectators. The efforts of Pilâtre de Rozier and Charles excited universal admiration precisely because the moment was believed at hand when man would at last take possession of the unexplored atmosphere the way he had secured the sea.[62]

Variations on the theme of the attraction exerted by the strange are multiple. The American John Ledyard was animated by a "violent propensity" to explore the alien territory of Africa after having lived for several years among the American Indians. Alexander MacKenzie, in the preface to his *Voyages from Montreal* (1801), states that his journals will not gratify those who love to be falsely astonished or are enamored of romantic adventures. Nevertheless, he is cognizant of the scope and real merit of his achievement: "When it is considered that I explored those waters which had never before borne any other vessel than the canoe of the savage; and traversed those deserts where a European had never before presented himself to the eye of its swarthy natives . . . this work will, I flatter myself, be found to excite an interest, and conciliate regard. . . ." Under similar circumstances, Luigi Mayer declared the Ottoman Empire "a region so far from explored, that it has scarcely been visited by any European traveller." Seeking out "lonely" spots en route to Canada, George Heriot went "in search of new regions." Proceeding up the Congo, Tuckey too found himself "as in a new world." Within Brazil's primeval forest, Kotzebue also felt a gigantic and luxuriant "new creation" engulfing him; even the Andes, despite the numerous forays of Humboldt, offered to this scientific researcher and to his followers "a yet unexplored field," so fertile and unlimited were the generative powers of the South American soil. In sum: from Burckhardt's attempts to penetrate the "almost unknown districts" to the east of the Dead Sea to Lycett's maneuvers to reach the "unknown regions" of Australia's Outback discoverers were "electrified" by the thought that they might become harbingers of the new.[63]

Resembling the innovator or the solitary great man, the explorer—even when part of a collaborative venture—felt impelled "to do everything alone." The magnitude of his achievement, in his own eyes and in those of the world, seemed to hinge on its being an unexampled one. Martin Sauer iterated the special nature of his proposed undertaking, although he was but one member among many of a well-staffed geological and astronomical mission to northern Russia: "I would most willingly have stayed on the coast [of Alaska] alone to explore those unknown parts from tribe to tribe, until I had lost myself, or found my way to Europe through some of those cranny passages. I am aware, that I was thought a madman for it; but this madness, this enthusiastic confidence, would, I am certain, have assisted my success. . . ." Belzoni displays a lack of gregariousness similar to that coloring Sauer's account when he declares: "As I made my discoveries alone, I have been anxious to write my book by myself. . . ." Thus, from the beginning to the end of our period these studious and solitary explorers modeled themselves after the pattern of the self-formed scientific genius.[64]

Of greater consequence than the myth of singlehanded accomplishment, however, is the judgment that the committed explorer may never sink into repose. The traveler does not stay. Although it had not yet developed into the restless passion for increasingly extreme experiences associated with the Romantic wanderer, the voyager's search leading away from the quotidian and the banal was precursory of nineteenth-century escapism.

Again, the characterization of the self-made genius is apt. Bailly, echoing Bacon in his *Letters sur l'origine des sciences* (1777), stresses the danger posed to any form of progress by an indolent frame of mind that acknowledges only the dominion of the ancients. Upon the heels of such intellectual sloth, modern effort vanishes and is replaced by a languor that is detrimental to all creativity. Bailly's tone is appropriately hortatory. If the Western scholar had believed like the Chinese sage that everything must be stable and unchanging in the firmament, mirroring the structure of the Oriental family and state, then Europe would never have produced Descartes, Galileo, Cassini, or Newton. Correspondingly roused to the performance of exceptional, not sanctioned deeds, and avoiding life's tedium, the scientific traveler was prompt to assume his travail.[65]

Undeniably, travel for a purpose was hard work. In addition, it was fraught with discomfort and danger. More even than its Picturesque or Grand Tour antithesis, however, the voyage of discovery was difficult and filled with terrifying out-of-door encounters.

The perils of exploring the Pacific were apparent to the simplest eighteenth-century mariner. Absolutely cut off from their home ports for years at a time and navigating in largely uncharted waters strewn with newly formed atolls and submerged reefs, the small sailing vessels of the day were often impaled on rocks or left to the mercy of erratic winds and currents. Then there was the matter of crowded accommodations, strict discipline, hunger, and disease. In 1768, Bougainville, lying near the southern edge of New Guinea, was prevented from exploring the coast because his starving men were driven to eat the sealskins from off the yards and rigging. Kerguelen records that during his journey toward the North Pole his crew became frightened at the first sight of enormous mounds of ice "that frequently shattered around them with a horrible crash." Equally fearsome was the appearance of a single, unshivered sheet. Constantine Phipps describes the *Race Horse* and the *Carcass* trapped in floes: ". . . the ice closed fast, and was all around the ships; no opening to be seen anywhere. . . ." Georg Forster chronicles every conceivable danger awaiting the invader of the South Seas. Upon leaving Table Bay in November 1772 and beginning the long run to the Antarctic Circle, Cook's expedition also entered upon "an unexampled navigation." Suddenly, they ran into foul weather and high seas. The scientists, ignorant as to how to behave in this new situation, were the playthings of the storm. Decks were awash, floors of every cabin were inundated, and "the howl of the storm in the rigging, the roar of the waves, added to the violent agitation of the vessel, which precluded almost every occupation, were new and awful scenes, but at the same time severely felt, and highly disagreeable." In the thick fog enveloping Kerguelen's Land, the *Resolution* became separated from the *Adventure*. The former was thus obliged "to proceed alone on a dismal course to the southward," and the crewmen to expose themselves once more to "the dangers of that frozen climate" without "the hope of being saved by our fellow-voyagers in case of losing our own vessel." And when the company was not thus forsaken on "this vast and unexplored expanse," it had to contend with "naked and empty" islands, "dark and dismal lands," "heaps of rugged stones," and "filthy pits and ponds full of green, slimy aquatic plants, and stinking from its stagnation."[66]

Yet, as we know, there were Edenic exceptions. La Pérouse submitted to the "ravishing" sight of Maui, along whose verdant shores he coasted at a distance of one league. From such close quarters he could make out its amenities: "One must be a sailor and reduced, like us, in these scorching climates to a bottle of water a day, in order to conceive the sensations we felt. The trees that crowned the mountains; the vegetation, the banana trees observed surrounding the habitations, everything wrought an inexpressible charm upon our senses: but the ocean broke on the shore with great violence, and, new Tantaluses, we were reduced to desiring and devouring with our eyes that which it was impossible for us to attain. . . ."

George Vancouver feared not Hawaii's margins but its destructive volcano Maona Roa. Krusenstern and Lisiansky voiced more exacerbated premonitions of peril in the beautifully forested Sandwich Islands; nevertheless, the sight of cascades, winding rivulets, and coconut and breadfruit groves "assisted a great deal in removing" the "unpleasant sensations" they experienced upon reflecting that they were "amidst the dwellings of cannibals."

Then there was always the danger of shipwreck, if one had not already succumbed to hostile natives or wild beasts. William Westall, the draftsman accompanying Flinders's voyage, was nearly drowned at Madeira and lost all sketches made on the island. En route to Australia, the *Porpoise* ran aground on a reef. Moments later the *Cato* struck it, completely going to pieces (figure 164). Captain Palmer, in the *Bridgewater*, abandoned the helpless crew to shark-infested waters and steered for Batavia without having lifted a finger to give them assistance. He then bruited it about Calcutta that all had perished. What had been sacrificed to salt water, apart from Westall's sketches, were rare plants collected for the botanic gardens at Kew as well as dried specimens and Flinders's own small collection of minerals and shells.[67] Within this context, Lesseps's perceptive remarks on what might be termed the psychology of continuous suffering are appropriate. These trenchant ruminations—valid no matter what the mode of travel—were the product of daring overland explorations conducted on the Eurasian continent in the winter of 1788. Lesseps writes: "It seemed as if a wrathful nature conspired against us to multiply hindrances and prolong our woes. I appeal to anyone who has found himself in a similar situation; he will verify how cruel it is to find oneself shackled by ever-renewed obstacles. It is useless to distract oneself, to be patient; at length strength is exhausted and reason loses its grip. Nothing makes our torments more insupportable than the impossibility of foreseeing their end. . . ." Harsh winds, driving snow, "a horrible tempest," and famine were nothing, however, in comparison with Lesseps's hair-raising crossing of an ice ridge. Crawling on hands and knees high above a raging ocean and a sheer rock wall, he made his way across a ledge no more than two feet wide and one foot deep. His companions could neither see nor help him in his journey over gaping crevices and pounding surf, which took 45 minutes to accomplish. Not in the least discouraged that he had forgotten his dispatches on the other side, Lesseps bravely retraced his steps.

Lesseps's heroics share a kinship with the bold investigations of Vesuvius launched by William Hamilton at the time of the August 1779 eruptions. A solid ring of fire stretched from the crater and extended for a circumference of $2 1/2$ miles. It was the splendor and sublimity of this destructive scene, witnessed on the spot, that Hamilton tried to communicate in a letter to Sir Joseph Banks. As the emissions grew more furious, black and white smoke rose to a great height. Stones were ejected like bombs, tracing a parabola in the air. Meteors careened across the night sky. Falling stars shot in a horizontal direction, leaving behind a luminous wake.[68]

Faujas de Saint-Fond remarks that Blanchard's fifth aerial voyage, which lifted off from the Champ de Mars on March 2, 1784, required unsurpassed courage. Navigating those "solitudes of the air" at a height "no mortal had yet attained," and "alone, in the midst of silence, far from all human succor, & separated so to speak from the rest of nature," one might, if he did not take proper precaution, drift for a protracted period along a frightening and uncertain path. Under these adverse conditions the balloonist, become the mere sport of winds, would experience glacial cold or be choked by lack of oxygen, or be forced to spend the night in an exposed situation, surrounded by intangible perils. Sangfroid was a prerequisite for travelers. The *Mémoires* of Pilâtre de Rozier are replete with valorous adventures that caused public and scholars alike to bestow upon him the epithets "intrepid" and "indefatigable."

Analogous daring and stamina were required of those who moved across hotter terrain. Vivant-Denon recounts how, in the midst of arduous desert maneuvers, foot soldiers provided him with knees to serve as a table so that he might compose drawings and notes and bodies to afford shade from the sweltering heat. James Jackson, himself trapped on several occasions in the feverish "Shume" winds that cut swiftly across Morocco, relates how in 1805 an entire caravan proceeding from Timbuctu to Tafilelt could not find a drop of water. Two thousand people and 1,800 camels died of thirst "under the suffocating heat of the effulgent meridian sun." Vidal, in Paraguay, warned the visitor to expect intolerable summer heat and immoderate thirst.[69]

Continual rain likewise took its toll. Humboldt crossed the Pass of Quindiu in 1801, barefoot and exhausted, despite the persistent damp. Alexander Caldcleugh, also exploring in South America in the region of the Rio Colorado, amplified Humboldt's image of rugged roads torn up by mountain torrents. Caldcleugh was luckier than Humboldt; his guides prepared *ajotas* of sheepskin to wrap around the feet and *pilliones* to tie around the waist when they eventually reached the snow line. These precautions were taken so the body might keep dry in the event of the "extreme danger" of a fall down a precipice. During this climb, one of the mules slipped and rolled with a thousand turns to the bottom, but "miraculously got up and staggered about." Less fortunate were the porters when *puna* or diaphragmatic heaving set in. More insidious still was the exhaustion that attacked the *peones*; many lay down, gave themselves up for lost, and died before reaching the valley and safety.

Toil and suffering were also no strangers to those navigators charting the far north. Hudson's Bay and Davis Strait, according to Heriot, were beset by floating masses of ice that emitted an unspeakable cold and glinted whitely in the gloom of night, and overland journeys such as Franklin's afforded related, if different, perils of frozen water, naked cliffs, and treacherously compacted snow.[70]

Whereas certain characteristics, desires, and motives were shared by all classes of explorers, others were associated only with (or more readily apparent among) a specific type. The "new Icarus," flying into the rays of the sun, transcended his earthbound brethren not only by the certainty that he could accomplish with alacrity what the grounded observer and the mountaineer had to labor to attain but also by the fact that his Promethean performance was perceived as even more liberating than theirs. A host of "modern argonauts," like the ancient hero, stormed the sky and stole fire from its meteors. The balloonists, by their determined activity, redefined and recast the image of the Promethean inspired genius welcomed into the empyrean. This sedentary symbol of the enthusiastic poet, popular with critics from Shaftesbury on, was transformed into a concrete embodiment of life as lived, intertwined with the scientific goals of wresting from nature its dark secrets and from heaven its Franklinean electricity and its Apollonian light.

The titan, interpreted afresh as an apostle for progress, provided the late eighteenth century with a mythic figure that stood for enlightenment and science, not superstition. This humanitarian savior and secular messiah did not preach vassalage but urged the appropriation of nature through total saturation in physical abundance. What more striking sign of humanity's cosmic unfettering than the phenomenon of flight? This realization surfaces in a series of poems devoted to aerial navigation published in the *Almanach des Muses* for 1783. An anonymous rhymer assures his readers that "new Prometheuses" have bound the winds and subdued the seas. Then follows the crucial stanza:

It is in the century that we live,
That one has witnessed . . .
The eagle dispossessed of the air. . . .

      VOYAGE INTO SUBSTANCE

Similar language tinges the Abbé Hollier's "La navigation aérienne, ode," eulogizing the audacious Montgolfiers. By their momentous invention they pierced nature to arrive at its "darkest retreat," where "its secret is no longer concealed" and where

The element that
weighs upon the earth,
That rolls thunder in its flanks
And circulates in all its bodies,
Cedes its immense sway
And no longer opposes any barrier
To your impetuous assaults. . . .

Again, these "buoyant companions of clouds" are compared to Prometheus, who, like them, "create[s], invent[s], dispose[s]." By an extension of this thought, Verninac de Saint-Maur alludes to the "two new Icaruses" and Abbé Monti praises Robert as a "French Daedalus."[71]

To the extent that the Enlightenment explorer embodied in his person the conquest of the unknown, he forcibly grafted scientific invention onto poetic genius. In short, he "realized" what formerly could only be imagined. In this sense the balloonist-Prometheus incarnates unimpeded invention, the augmentation and corporealization of abstract knowledge through discoveries made in an arena hitherto reserved for the gods. In a manner more far-ranging and conspicuous than that of the sailor or the overland traveler, the aeronaut freed man from the crabbed narrowness and restrictions of a domesticated globe. By his exploits, he accustomed people to look up, to investigate the superior regions that J. M. W. Turner and John Ruskin would later make their own. He prepared the way for the nineteenth-century comic excursion as well as for serious open-ended exploration. The aeronaut exposed a truly naked nature and revealed the prospect of human liberty within it.[72]

The longing to break out and make contact with the world beyond the self is fundamentally connected with feelings of wanting to soar and feelings of not wanting to soar. To be rooted in place or to be lost in the great nowhere represents a bipolar tendency of the eighteenth century. As Addison puts it (*Spec.* 415), the mind hates anything that smacks of restraint, yet at the same time it fears what was just becoming an acknowledged reality in the critic's own time: the unfurnished depths of space. This tension between imprisonment and flight emerges clearly in the account given of the "experimental voyages" made in August and September 1804 by the physicists Gay-Lussac and Biot: "Confined to the surface of the globe we have no direct intimation of what passes in the lofty regions of the atmosphere. All the changes of the weather, which appear so capricious and perplexing, proceed no doubt, from the combination of a very few simple causes. Were the philosopher to penetrate beyond the seat of the clouds, to examine the circumstances of their formation, and mark the prevailing currents, he would probably remove in part, the veil that conceals those mighty operations. . . ."[73]

SECTARIANS OF THE UNKNOWN

Figure 256
A. Caldcleugh, *Crossing the Cordillera*, from *Travels in South America . . .* , 1825, II, frontispiece. Aquatint by Edward Finden after drawing by William Daniell. Photo courtesy British Library.

Figure 257
Anonymous, *Balloon over Mount Etna*, nineteenth century. Watercolor. Photo courtesy Library of Congress, Landauer Collection.

VOYAGE INTO SUBSTANCE

Figure 258
Naigeon, *Apollo Welcoming Charles as the New Prometheus,* eighteenth century. Aquatint by F. A. Tilly. Photo courtesy Library of Congress, Tissandier Collection.

Figure 259
Anonymous, *Caricature of Balloon Travel,* 1843. Engraving. Photo courtesy Library of Congress, Landauer Collection.

The freedom implicit in a panorama without qualification or obstruction and embodied in the balloon open-air festivities has antecedents in eighteenth-century urban planning, with its incorporation of wide squares within straitened cities, and in the dreams of demolition that haunted the architectural utopianists. As Mona Ozouf remarks, such an undelimited vacancy possessed the advantage of being without memory, that is, without any history or tradition. Hence its relevance for the aerial voyage in particular, and for all voyages into inhuman substance to a more general degree since it marks the entrance into a neutral world not characterized by social or cultural density. The radical absence of civilization renders the upper atmosphere strongly counter to anything Picturesque, that is, to anything layered over with conventions and mired in the patina granted by the ages.[74] The vision of untarnished freedom in the void was so intense that an anonymous bit of English doggerel issued in 1784 cautioned the "great monarch" to beware: "His subjects swear they wilt be free,/ And seek for freedom in the air. . . ."

On a more exalted plane, Goethe, in his letters from Switzerland—that legendary land of liberty—announced his desire to "plunge into boundless space." Plaintively, he inquired whether he was doomed perpetually to "crawl on high", to "stick" on the loftiest boulder the way he was "glued" to the meanest sod. This lament touches upon the balloonist's unique capability for defying centripetal force. The modern argonauts navigating across an untouched ocean, according to Gudin de La Brenellerie's poem "Sur le globe ascendant," at last served the Newtonian chain of gravity:

leave, soar, seek in the azure plains
. . . Glide with gentle motion over the austral ice.
Gambol amid the boreal flames,
These atmospheric fields formerly forbidden
Open through your exertions, and will be submissive to us
Enlarging the precinct prescribed for our elders,
. . . Attaining the utmost margins of our globe. . . .

"Perfectly unconnected with the earth, and unconcerned about it," in Thomas Baldwin's words, the aeronaut experienced a liberty impossible to realize in more mundane regions. Even the perilous life of the sailor (incarnated in Cook or La Pérouse), which bred an independence born of prolonged absence from land and of the ineluctable presence of a universe of water, could not rival the detachment that sprang from being baseless. Nor could the overland explorer like Humboldt, living in London while dreaming of the Tropics and striving after the terrestrially distant and the receding, escape into the foundationless.[75]

A major supposition underlying the discussion of the travelers' (especially the balloonists') desire to break out of confines into wide open spaces is that the entire enterprise of discovery depends on the existence of realms that allow some degree of individual freedom.

Since the seventeenth century, scientists had insisted on principles of unreserved thought and discussion. This frankness was requisite both to the undermining of the authority of antiquity and to the advancement of new findings against established ideas. Sir Francis Bacon's dictum that the same type of inquiry needed to compile a natural history would, in time, make man the master of nature melded well with the climatic theories of Mallet and Montesquieu.[76] According to these hypotheses, an organic relationship exists among an indwelling instinct for liberty, a simple life, and the native characteristics of a country. Thus we have the English myth of independence, the Swiss myth of the "barren, but sacred ramparts of liberty," the South Sea myth of an easeful paradise far from the complexities of European civilization, the Laplander myth of unobstructed wandering, and the African desert myth of "undisturbed tranquility and independence, and of freedom."[77]

Thus, as the explorer was lured to unoccupied areas where he might assert his topophilic desire for flight, he also contributed to the creation of the truism that certain regions—unlike his homeland—were exempt from the strictures of society. At the core of this duality, founded on the belief in an Arcadia of bounteous openness, lies the conviction that voyaging, in all its epiphanies, is capable of returning man to the pith of the physical world and to a primitive and unhedged purity of consciousness.

These restless seekers, whether clambering across mountain chains or absconding into the upper air, fled not only toward something (the unpenetrated plenum) but also away from something (claustrophobia). Recent criticism has shown that oppressive enclosure identified with the prison image is a tenacious soteriological symbol. It is elaborated most cogently in the Platonic and Neo-Platonic myth of the cave. In book VII of the *Republic*, fettered men see only spectral shadows flickering on a subterranean wall. This potent allegory objectifies spiritual blindness to deeper truths. Imprisoned in the world of the senses, according to Plato, man must undertake an arduous journey upward away from shifting appearances into the sphere of timeless reason and truth. This formula of an *anima* pent up in the body constituted a divisive fable that would nourish the entire literary tradition of the West, from the early Church Fathers down to Pascal, Voltaire, and Victor Hugo. It was the explorer in his role as navigator through phenomena that finally brought body and mind together.

In the realm of the fine arts, the immuring of the measureless, the embodiment of the elusively spiritual, occurs most memorably in Piranesi's *Carceri* etchings (1745, 1760). Not only do these penumbrous prisons perfectly anticipate Burke's definition of the Sublime born of terror, but by their colossal size and chthonic presence they suggest simultaneously inescapable infinity and dank organic decay. The Venetian architect's man-made chasms encompass not an abstract, sheltering and benevolent space but one that accentuates solitude, silence, and vulnerability as cor-

SECTARIANS OF THE UNKNOWN

poreally experienced. The untenanted void swells, multiplies, and dilates in a monstrous fashion, accompanied by physical distortions of time, which, like the chamber itself, either stretches or collapses. The invisible occupant of this artificial abyss cannot situate himself; he suffers from Pascal's predicament and has become a prisoner of space—now made tangible.[78]

Piranesi's powerful visualization of a cosmic dungeon finds an echo in the darker side of exploration. Unimpeded expansion could result not only in Jacques Charles's ebullient joy but also in total disorientation— a kind of Pascalian horror at, and shunning of, unknown and unknowable vistas. Paradoxically, too much space could be smothering. Endless traverses of the South American pampas, the Pacific Ocean, or the upper atmosphere—with their unvarying horizon or boundless prospect of air— were capable of eliciting the sensation of excessive freedom. Not only did this realization of perceptual ambivalence eventually lead exploration away from the external world into the private reaches of the mind, but, incongruously, this development came at the very moment when the idea of a closed space once again set in.

By 1800, the very fact of sustained and prolonged assaults on new terrain served to wall in fresh opportunities. What formerly was dispersed and unlimited now was codified and limited.[79] To the idea of free and progressive expansion succeeded the realization of enforced closure, due to laws inherent in the very nature of the activity. The appalling recognition dawned that the environment sets restrictions: What has been trodden once can never again be untrodden.[80]

This chapter has focused on ways in which the finite traveler coped with and ordered infinite perceptual information. His all-involving struggle to see and know belongs, as we have seen, to an overriding epistemological and ontological problem bedeviling eighteenth-century thought.[81] The traveler in search of fact illustrates the problematics of knowing and structuring the world in an exemplary fashion. By virtue of his profession, he asks persistently: What is real; how can relentless mental process and limitless physical flux become conjoined at any given moment?

VOYAGE INTO SUBSTANCE

6   *Hegemony of the External*

Faced with a proliferation of new scenery, travelers in search of substantiality pondered the problem of what was the correct, least distorting point of view from which to scrutinize the world. The foregoing chapter uncovered a shared repertoire of constructs patterning the spatial organization of the physical universe. Seeking to perceive the real forms of phenomena, natural historians conjoined the pursuit of empirical observation with a taxonomic principle of ordering. They attempted to ally information gleaned from analyses of repeatable experiences with personal studies of the natural world. This exploratory activity implies an awareness of the role played by perspective, i.e., the importance of taking into account not only shifting locations in space but also varieties of lived time—the very process of journeying. The traveler consciously observes himself in a situation and attempts to describe it accurately. Further, as he proceeds, both his eye and his judgment change with circumstances, and this whole visual and mental process changes at every instant. Thus, testing the flexibility of accurate perception against the changeableness of natural appearances is the tireless work of the serious observer.

It is the mind that, by induction, makes sense of the world. It is the intellect that binarily structures matter's continuum into discrete vertical and horizontal impulses through the act of visual excavation, just as it fragments time into segments to articulate the individual components of duration. However, the discoverer also tries to interpret phenomena according to their own internal time and space. In short, he is able to take his perspective from within objects—to show them from the inside, as it were. In making his perceptual processes coincide with the entropic structure of matter—revealed by Enlightenment philosophers—the voyager rejoined the divided world of matter and spirit. This procedure required that the traveler's gaze, his eyereach—more narrowly, his glance arrested at a precise moment in time—become congruent, if only fleetingly, with a specific moment of matter's existence, or an aspect of its history. Thus, personal, human perspective might harmonize with a span or an occasion in nature's behavior.

As two indispensable conditions for the integrated perception of the environment, space and time demand systematization if nature is not to appear chaotic. Although eighteenth-century voyagers were not yet functioning under the modern assumption that sight is culturally determined, they were sensible of the fact that there are differing styles of vision. Some individuals arrange the universe in great detail, some in broad outline, some in a mixture of both. There are styles of optical performance in which objects and events in the distance and in the future are given great attention, others in which immediate objects and events are deemed more important. In some visual modes, phenomena are perceived primarily in reference to the viewer rather than in terms of relationships among phenomena or in terms of themselves. Hence, the explorer selectively adjusts, fits, and connects himself to reality by consciously choosing to exclude the superaddition of the merely idiosyncratic while not avoiding particular assessment and judgment of how objects unbroken to civilization live in and move through a space and time determined and framed by them.

Prizing Immediacy

As you know, Mme. de Staël is bored if she has to pay attention to things, they seem to keep her from pursuing her thoughts. . . .
J. C. L. Sismonde de Sismondi

The traveler enjoys in anticipation the first sight of the constellation of the Cross, and the Magellanic clouds circling round the Southern Pole—the snow of Chimborazo, and the column of smoke ascending from the volcano of Quito—the first grove of tree ferns, and the Pacific Ocean; the days on which such desires are fulfilled form epochs in life. . . .
Alexander von Humboldt

The scientific traveler's inquisitive role within the physical world entails the use of a language of action that duplicates the bodily experience of immediacy. Thus, the flight of the explorer into the unknown, freed from the strictures of urban life, implies escape from conventional temporal restraints as well. Where everything is new, the use of the present tense becomes mandatory.

By frequently invoking the concept of reverie, eighteenth-century writers demonstrated their preoccupation with the fundamental distinction between rectilinear time and time immemorial. The first represents a succession of events that cannot be preserved intact, since its evolution is perpetually assailed and destroyed from without. The second embodies pure duration, an uncompounded plenum in which nothing is repeated; it continues as eternal and undifferentiated now. These temporal modes—taken absolutely—can be designated city time and natural time. The latter antedates all human records and therefore stands exempt from social and political vicissitudes. As Bonnet comments in his discussion of plants, their condition "seems to us less existence than simple abiding." Yet, as we have seen, their material and their "life" are both eternal and composed of expressive moments that point to deculturalization and regression toward the prelogical. Thus, natural phenomena embody the primitive and basic experience of being in the world.[1]

Mention of that elusive mental state to which Rousseau and Senancour (most prominently) gave themselves up appears warranted since it seems to imply an unmediated merging with the actual lived time of the landscape features themselves. But Rousseau's interlude on the Isle de Saint Pierre differs fundamentally from that of the traveler swiftly caught up in the intensity of the moment.

Reverie shuns clear thinking in favor of a welter of confused images. The daydreamer, lost among psychic impressions, does not look at phenomena; he remains undistracted by objects. To phrase it differently: He is not conscious of the spatial and temporal separateness of external things from his own consciousness but insinuates himself into a world to which he does not tangibly relate or penetrate. As Gaston Bachelard suggests, this act of immersion occurs most readily with fugacious things possessing the quality of enveloping softness. Fleeting mists, watery vapors, and melting fogs are conducive to a mood of seamless and inviolable dreaminess. Indeed, the venerable humor theory presupposed that a hidden sympathy was at work between the body and the mind, and that this relation was further affected by the influence of airs, waters, and places. The fragmentary writings of Heraclitus and Diogenes of Apollonia reveal the antiquity of the belief that moisture is unfavorable to thinking. Aqueous emanations inhibit intelligence; a dry soul is best for mental acuity.[2]

Standing in the shadow of this environmental theory is Dominique Bouhours's meditation on the sea (1671). Eugène and Ariste lapse into unfocused musing, hypnotized by the *je ne sais quoi* of the flux and reflux of the tide. Here, too, lies the source for Winckelmann's association of timelessness with imperceptibly moving water.[3]

To return to Rousseau's vision of fluid stasis, articulated in the *cinquième promenade*: The shimmering immediacy of the Lac de Bienne reverberates effortlessly through his consciousness. Rousseau informs the reader that his mind remained in this relaxed and floating state for several hours, "plunged in a thousand confused but delicious reveries without having any particularly determined or constant object [in view]." This uncritical self-absorption was induced by gazing at a clear sky and into a limpid lake, both of whom reflected back not themselves but Rousseau's tranquil fancies. When, from time to time, "a faint and feeble thought" reared its head, this slight impression was soon effaced in the continuous laving of the liquid that cradled him. Thus, his intellect remained suspended, forbidden from attaching itself to things.[4]

Rousseau's memorable boating excursion is the paradigm for those idle moments when, vacillating between waking and sleeping, perception and judgment are overcome gradually and without exertion, veiled by drifting ideas. Reverie thus represents not man's contact with nature but his removal from its dominion by means of intervening memory. As in the Picturesque garden, the imagination easily moves from one chimerical sensation to another. Flowing along, it does not encounter the external world but glides by it in a trice.[5]

HEGEMONY OF THE EXTERNAL

On the other hand, the apprehension of a striking detail in nature requires mental alertness, which is antithetical to reverie's protracted but objectless moment. Lingering in aesthetic appreciation over some aspect of the physical world is active contemplation. This demanding intellectual and spiritual exercise was recognized by Plato, Plotinus, Augustine, Bonaventure, Kant, and Schopenhauer. These disparate philosophers agreed that studying natural beauty fosters self-forgetfulness and the overcoming of that solipsistic self-consciousness that bedeviled Rousseau.[6]

To this venerable tradition of the cultivation of awe before the universe the eighteenth century added a further dimension. As remarked in chapter 1, scientific investigation also required a fundamental disinterestedness of inquiry, that is, a renunciation of easy self-expression. This exigency arose out of the desire to know, to match words with things, rather than the desire to praise God or to subjectify nature by projecting human perspectives. Quite literally, the cognizant beholder could locate his consciousness outside himself, in those objects that, for a period, absorbed him.[7]

Such wide-awake vision, by definition, denotes work and thus stands at the antipodes from reverie's passive ingestion. Once again, the theory of acquired genius proves helpful. In the words of the *Encyclopédie*, the man endowed with *génie* is "struck" by everything; he is perpetually forced to assimilate and adjust to incoming data. Further, his "taste for observation" implies temporality, since a delving glance "quickly" uncovers the interior of things. The language of swiftly probing perception is coupled by Bailly with a "restlessness of mind." This free-ranging intellect transports the extraordinary person not only beyond himself but "into regions of the world & into all the domains of nature." The Baconian ideal underlying this exhortation becomes evident when Bailly reiterates the powerful Victorine comparison of nature to a fortress continuously besieged since the beginning of time by those who wish to know.

The English also praised the nimbleness or agility of the great mind. Alexander Gerard contrasts this alacrity with "useless musings, or endless reveries" that hurry a man "over large fields, without any settled aim." True genius, says Gerard, "pursues a fixt direction." Indeed, this intellectual energy "can dart in an instant from heaven to earth." William Duff correspondingly declares that such intelligence "hurries the mind out of itself."[8]

Dynamic contemplation coupled with practical purpose was a hallmark of the Promethean hero of science. Centrifugal observations entail an analytical dedication to the external flow of things; hence, they are alien to the passivity implicit in reverie, and even to the quiet concentration on the self that is typical of religious meditation. This eighteenth-century entropic contemplation, which results in the observer's selective absorption in an external phenomenon, produces not only the temporary isolation of physical objects from out of the flux—the case of the natural masterpiece—but also a concomitant awareness of the actual second when the gaze became thus riveted.[9]

It now becomes apparent that the sublime immensity of the single, vital monument of earth not only isolated it in fact from the rest of the world but also contributed to a mental presence of ineluctable proximity. The time spent in registering the object involved both spatial and temporal coordinates. It is in identifying with precision this powerful moment of incursion that one source for the rising interest in the experience of instantaneity may be located. The voyager absorbed in the colossal monolith grasps its totality at first glance; that is, there is a coincidence or a congruity between the unity of an individual's initial perception and the unity of the object exhibited in its entirety at the instant in which it is perceived. This "pregnant moment"—here identified with the concrete impact that an actual object makes, not with a focusing device present in a literary or pictorial narrative—goes against the grain of a long temporal succession; it interrupts the uniform flow of sensations. The pinpointing and localizing of a spot in time as well as of a spot in space halts or suspends the discursive or associating motions of the mind and thereby creates a dense, enriched, tangible experience in which the segment of terrain communicates its meaning directly to a receptive consciousness.[10]

A second source for the valorization of the instant is the recognition on the part of the natural historian that transitory or conspicuously fluctuating phenomena, by definition, preclude any sense of wholeness or permanence. These effects disclose themselves as shifting aspects. Thus, Faujas de Saint-Fond, in his *Recherches sur les volcans éteints* (1783), can detect "the instant of disorder & of upheaval" imprinted within the fallen fragments of the basaltic Rocher de Mallias. (See figure 237.)

The occasion for noting mutations was even more propitious when a crater was still active. William Hamilton states that the observer must make haste to study the intermittent eruptions of Mount Vesuvius "at the moment" of their occurrence; the passage of "a few days only" can completely alter the "look" of the site, raising fumaroles and lava domes where there had been none. Houel adjusted to change by recording a shift in the tableau when his attentive contemplation of Stromboli was interrupted by the thunderous emission of stones into the atmosphere. (See figure 149.) Georg Forster, at Tanna in the New Hebrides, carefully clocked the visible fluctuations in the island's volcano during the course of a single day. Edy, in search of an islet that had abruptly formed in the vicinity of Iceland, commented on the universality of such fiery mountains bursting from "the mighty billows of the ocean" as well as from the plains.[11]

The eighteenth-century naturalists' anticipation of ever-impending destruction, couched in an idiom responsive to evanition, is everywhere apparent. At all points of the globe Forster spotted pinnacles that seemed to threaten downfall at "every moment." Deluc terms the Alpine avalanches that earsplittingly intrude upon the climber's silent ascent "detonations." Saussure reads yet another page written in Switzerland's natural history of mounting and ebbing destruction: The roiled sea of the Glacier of Montanvert, unlike the Grindelwald, was not frozen millenia ago at "the moment" when its surface was rutted and choppy, but "the instant" after, when the wind grew calm and the waves subsided into ruffled, well-worn crests. (See figures 197 and 198.) Scoresby notes that polar glaciers exhibit "the appearance of immense cataracts, suddenly arrested in their progress, and congealed on the spot, by the power of an intense frost." Even earthquakes, like the one that leveled Concepçion in the space of one and a half to two minutes, leave an indelible record of their "fatal convulsion" in the chaotic rubble created almost instantaneously.[12]

The tendency of geological activity to deposit its characterizing marks either rapidly or interminably was more than matched by constant shifts within meteorological phenomena. From Banks's journal kept on board the *Endeavour* we learn that "almost immediately on crossing the tropick the aire became sensibly much damper than usual, though not materially hotter." This sense of palpable "hereness" pervades Wallis's account of a meteor, encountered on the way to Patagonia, that "streaked with incredible (prodigious) rapidity across the sky in a horizontal line towards the southwest," taking "almost a minute in its trajectory." Le Gentil, in the Indian Ocean, pondered a strange luminous "smoke" that dawned "for the space of a minute." Although riveted to the waterless flats of the pampas, Vidal's exhausted and panting mules suddenly sniffed the air. At the moment, "not a cloud was to be seen," but in a few minutes "the most tremendous storm of thunder, lightning, and rain" came on. Major Thorn, with the British army in India, recorded the atmospheric peculiarities of the blank red desert stretching from the shores of the Indus to within a hundred miles of Delhi:

On our left appeared sand hills in endless succession, like the waves of the ocean, desolate and dreary to an immense extent, and scantily interspersed with the Bauboel, or *Mimosa Arabica*. While to the front and right of these immense wastes, the eye was deceived by those illusions, so frequent on the wild plains of Africa and Asia, known by the French term of "mirage," and in Persian, "Sirraub." These optical deceptions exhibited the representations of spacious lakes and rivers, with trees and other objects, in such a lively manner as almost to cheat the senses. . . . Often we were thus agitated between expectancy and disappointment, flattering our imaginations with a speedy indulgence; when just as the delightful vision appeared on the point of being realized, like the cup of Tantalus, the whole vanished, and left us nothing to rest upon but arid plains of glittering and burning sands. . . .

The balloonists, too, recorded such sudden cleavages in unfolding time. Pilâtre de Rozier exclaimed, concerning the swiftly unfurling scene viewed from an altitude of 11,732 feet, that "in a minute" he passed from winter to spring.[13] Undeniably, the aeronaut's scanning of nature was at once the most broad and the most narrow, and certainly the most fugitive, experience. Thomas Baldwin illustrates this curious antinomy in the notations he set down while sailing over Chester. The land below was alternately covered by an impenetrable white veil of clouds and exposed through rents gaping "for a few seconds." Earthly objects could now and again be discovered by "a Glance of the Eye" before "repeatedly escaping from Sight." (See figure 100.) Jacques Charles was equally susceptible to periodic glimpses of the prospect. Ascending at twilight on November 21, 1783, he had the pleasure of witnessing the sun set twice during the same 24-hour period. From his rapidly darkening vantage point he contemplated "for several instants the vacant air & the terrestrial vapors mounting from the heart of the valleys & rivers." The clouds "seemed to spring from the earth & heap themselves one on top of the other while preserving their wonted shape." In the midst of this "ineffable rapture & this contemplative ecstasy," the onset of an excruciating earache brought Charles back to himself. Monck Mason, recounting his flight in the balloon *Great Nassau*, remarks that it is "so entirely *sui generis*, so essentially distinct" a mode of transportation that the perceptions resulting from it are concordantly novel: "The moment the last hold upon the solid earth is cast off, all is perfect repose and stillness the most profound. . . . All [struggle, violent swaying connected with the launching] have ceased in an instant, and are succeeded by a degree of tranquility so intense, as for a moment to absorb all other considerations. . . . "[14]

A correlate of the theory that things actually change instantaneously is the observation that things change at every instant. Boisgelin de Kerdu, coasting along Malta's margins, remarked on the variety of rocks, mountains, gulfs, caverns, and grottos that border its shoreline and that manifested themselves "at every moment."[34] The phrase "*à chaque instant*" or its English equivalent is given added force when conjoined with a precise notation of time.[15]

This insistence on perceptual primacy is integral to the function of the travel relation whose overriding concern is to duplicate directly the temporal process of lived exploration. Consequently, in the interest of precision, natural phenomena were copied at an identifiable moment. "At three in the morning" Cornelius Le Bruyn began to climb Mount Taurus in Persia. Steep and pitted with rocks, the rugged precipices took on added "horror" in the night. On the evening preceding October 30, 1772, the elder Forster witnessed a flickering display of phosphorescence. The ocean had "the appearance of being all over on fire," and every wave that broke had "a luminous margin on top; wherever the sides of the ship came in contact with the sea."

The attempt to seize specific yet fleeting effects constrained the beholder to focus on their activity at a precise instant. Almost daily in these latitudes

Krusenstern observed a coldly illuminated sea, "composed of nothing but shining sparkles." At 8 o'clock on the night of October 8, however, he sighted a bright fireball interrupting the ubiquitous liquid glitter. As it streaked by, "the ship was quite lighted up . . . during the space of a half a minute." Although it quickly disappeared towards the northwest, the inflammable matter was "so strong that a broad clear line was visible in the same direction a whole hour afterwards." Lyon, in his *Private Journal* (1824), recorded the vanishing "by degrees and after the expiration of two hours" of a most perfect rainbow, whose contour was in no way affected by the blowing of a strong breeze and the presence of "mackerel and marestails." Garnerin, during his first nocturnal ascent from Tivoli on August 4, 1798, passed through dense clouds that concealed the twinkling lanterns below. However, he says, "about two, I perceived the stars, and saw several meteors dancing about the balloon. . . ."[16]

Expectation—as well as novelty, splendor, or danger—enhances and charges the moment. Having witnessed the eruption of the Great Geyser of Iceland, George MacKenzie longed for the repetition of an experience that he "could never tire of beholding." His appetite whetted by these wonders in potentia, he waited until 11:30 P.M. "At last," he reports, "the joyful sound struck my ear. . . . such a midnight scene as was now before us, can seldom be witnessed. . . . It raged furiously, and threw up a succession of magnificent jets, the highest of which was at least ninety feet. At this time I took the sketch from which the engraving [figure 168] is made. . . ." Eugène Robert, geologist on the French scientific expedition to Iceland and Greenland (1835–36), speaks of the "severe beauty" and the "imposing silence" experienced under the dome of that somber "volcanic aorta," the Cavern of Surtshellir. The snow accumulated in this abandoned place was lit through a hole punched in the vault. Robert writes: "At the moment when we were visiting this vast natural glacier, a ray of sunlight just penetrating obliquely by means of this opening, dimmed the torches with which we were all armed, and rendered the interior even more dark. . . ." J. R. Forster was similarly struck by the immense bergs floating in the high latitudes and vacancies of the Pacific. He notes in the *Observations Made during the Voyage* (1778) that on the morning of December 26, 1773, the crew counted 186 mountains of ice from the masthead. Rapid change—from nothing to something, in the preceding case—need not always be so dramatic, though. When in the same volume Forster discusses the color of the ocean, he notes that it varies in hue from place to place. Sometimes, he goes on to say, one comes across areas that are amazingly limpid and the bottom, at a depth of several fathoms, may be seen as plainly as if it were within a few yards' reach. At other instants, the same patch of ocean assumes a gray and turbid tinge, losing its clarity. The weather, of course, also contributes to a substance's mutability; a serene untroubled sky stains the waves with the finest berylline tint, but if a cloud should chance to pass, it "gives to a spot of the sea a hue quite different from the rest; and, if not well-

VOYAGE INTO SUBSTANCE

attended to, often alarms the navigator with the fear of soundings, or even shoals." "A judicious eye," Forster continues, "conducted by long experience, can alone distinguish properly in these cases...."[17]

The consciousness that things happen at a specific time did not mean merely that they happened at a specific moment. The very demands attendant upon certain types of exploration and the investigation of certain kinds of phenomena meant that the length of involvement could correspondingly be stretched out for greater or lesser periods. Maria Graham, climbing Cuesta de Prado in Chile, vertically itemizes—from the floor of the valley up—the variety of things encountered as they unfold: "We soon began to ascend the sharp and rugged mountain, and could not help stopping every now and then to admire the beautiful scene behind us, and to look down into the leafy gulfs at our feet.... At length, we reached the summit, and the Andes appeared in hoary majesty above a hundred ranges of inferior hills; but we had not yet come to the most beautiful spot...."

With a horizontally engaged vision, Volney, journeying toward Niagara Falls, discovered the cumulative cause of its voluminous waters: The plateau between Lake Erie and Ohio is higher than almost all the rest of the continent. On the north side of this tableland the ground suddenly gives way, dropping abruptly. This enormous plain covered with forests is the area through which the Saint Lawrence River threads at barely 3 miles per hour. Not until it is only 6 leagues below Lake Erie does the river swiftly gain momentum to plunge down the final slope.

Just as elevated or level terrain possesses its unfurling aspects, the monsoons that prevail on the western coast of India from June through August have a developmental chronology. Grindlay enumerates the visual stages, beginning with the first moments of the rain's lateral approach (indicated by sweeping masses of dimming clouds that collect "for many days previous") and ending with a climactic burst into transparency over the Ghauts or the Marhatta Mountains. (See figure 165.) The surface of the earth, which during the preceding four months has "presented a barren, burnt-up appearance," assumes, "in the space of three or four days," the "most brilliant verdure."

More ominous and considerably more dilatory in coming was the eruption of Vesuvius on August 4, 1779. William Hamilton chronicled the symptoms and portents that announced the nearing cataclysm. Throughout July, rumblings, explosions, accumulations of smoke above the crater, and emissions of red-hot scoriae intensified. By the end of the month these "increased to such a degree, as to exhibit in the night time the most beautiful fireworks, that can be imagined."

Finally, there are the accounts of returns to previously discovered regions. J. R. Forster's testimony to seasonal change will serve as a paradigm for that class of experience. When the *Resolution* first anchored at Tahiti, it was August and the hills were covered with shrivelled and dead herbage that imparted to the country "a barren and dreary look." But, writes Forster, "when we arrived eight months after, in April, the hills as far as their very summits were clad in the most agreeable verdure; the trees on the plains were bending under the weight of bread-fruit; in the valleys the largest apple trees were loaded with excellent fruit; all the shores were fringed by innumerable coconut trees. . . . "[18] (See figure 189.)

Whether experienced in a concentrated or a diluted form, the varieties of immediacy are based on a firsthand or close-up, not a secondary or remote, assault on the senses. With the crutch of memory avoided, on-the-spot perception is accomplished without loss of time (although it may take time to apprehend a continuously evolving reality). When the absorbed beholder deliberately enters into the activity or existence of a phenomenon, it seems to manifest itself nakedly without an intervening human screen. As a material presence, inescapably present now, the natural object is perceived—under conditions of absolute proximity and contiguity—as nothing but what it is.

An important sensation deriving from the apprehension of the immediate is that of the sudden. In this case, the brevity of the moment in which the apparition occurs is so condensed that the resulting encounter is heightened greatly. What is now under discussion is something that actually happens precipitously rather than something that is promptly perceived but does not occur at the instant of apprehension. The distinction is subtle but significant. The first lays stress on simultaneity; the phenomenal fact is both swiftly born and rapidly assimilated. The second emphasizes inconcurrency; the natural object, by an effort of the imagination, is violently wrested from its temporal sphere and made to obtrude into the beholder's. In short, there is a natural and an artificial way of making human and nonhuman perspectives coincide.

Burke, following on the heels of Shaftesbury, Addison, Pope, and Hutcheson, was most influential in propagating the idea that things that erupt without warning possess sublime character:

A sudden beginning or sudden cessation of sound of any considerable force has the same [Sublime] power. . . . Whatever either in sights or sounds makes the transition from one extreme to the other, easy, causes no terror, and consequently can be no cause of greatness. In everything sudden and unexpected, we are apt to start; that is, we have a perception of danger, and our nature rouses us to guard against it. It may be observed that a single sound, of some strength, though but of short duration, if repeated after intervals has a grand effect. . . . [19]

It was on this premise that William Chambers founded his Western interpretation of the Chinese garden as a theater filled with sudden transitions and striking formal oppositions. However, these paradoxical contrasts, in the British or the French Picturesque garden, were illusionistically contrived and produced a fabricated, not an authentic, presence.[20] The difference between the two perceptual attitudes—that is, between the unexpected stumbling upon the theatrical on the part of the spectator and the breaking into consciousness of a sought-after, just-discovered reality—was set forth cogently in Lord Kames's *Elements of Criticism* (1762). Kames takes up this issue within the framework of a protracted debate on the serial mechanism of Associationism. What is relevant about the theory is the claim that the mind's automatic propension to connect ideas among which it observes any similitude could be interrupted by the incursion of a fresh event. Novelty, the traveler's stock in trade, is defined as "the unexpected Appearance of Objects." A strange substance or unusual happening "produces instantaneously wonder," totally occupying the mind for a time and excluding all else. Kames, developing ideas proposed by Hume, specifically relates this nontransformative and nonreflective event to the activity of journeying: "Men tear themselves from their native country in search of things rare and new; and novelty converts into a pleasure the fatigues and even the perils of travelling. . . . " These "singular appearances" enflame curiosity "to know more of them." The argument is refined further. Surprise may be induced by a familiar object, if it is unawaited; a new object, however strange, will not astound the spectator who is prepared for the sight. Hence, the unforeseen is the source of surprise, but only true novelty yields wonder. Its temporal accompaniment is "momentary stupefaction," or a lapse out of human time. Basing his conclusions on this hierarchy of wonder, Kames decrees that its highest grade must involve an object that is unknown, that is, altogether new and seen by one person but once. Extending this hypothesis, Kames infers that, like surprise, wonder possesses "no invariable character," but "assumes that of the object which raises it."[21] In short, the traveler's gaze, at the very moment of alighting on a landscape feature, becomes allied with it both spatially and temporally. The profound recognition of alliance rather than of identity born in reverie is based not on mere tourist astonishment (that is, on things picturesquely appearing other than what or where they normally are) but on the knowledge of their being just what they seem.

As Kames's analysis indicates, the perception of anomaly is the peculiar prerogative of the traveler. However, discovery or scientific exploration extends beyond this, involving the long, "plain" process of observation and conceptual assimilation by many observers and also (by definition) placing value precisely on new phenomena, those for which one is unprepared. The change in perception was nothing short of revolutionary. The very existence of a taste for discovery was predicated on the proliferation of startling and informed revelations about the world. A structural parallel can be drawn between the scientific enterprise florescing in the years after 1760 and the procedure of exploration. Both developed a

HEGEMONY OF THE EXTERNAL

searching methodology for producing, not just eliciting, surprises—especially when they were working in tandem.[22]

The factual travel account fosters and documents an alertness to nature's unconventional, spur-of-the moment actions, which afford no time for preconception. A revealing example, deserving quotation in full, is found in Georg Forster's account of the passage from Dusky Bay to Queen Charlotte's Sound: At about 4:00 P.M., just opposite Cape Stephens,

> . . . on a sudden a whitish spot appeared on the sea in that quarter, and a column arose out of it, looking like a glass tube; another seemed to come down from the clouds to meet this, and they made a coalition, forming what is commonly called a water-spout. A little while after we took notice of three other columns. . . . The nature of water-spouts and their causes being hitherto very little known, we were extremely attentive to mark every little circumstance attendant on this appearance. Their base, where the water of the sea was violently agitated, and rose in a spiral form in vapours, was a broad spot, which looked bright and yellowish when illuminated by the sun. The column was of a cylindrical form. . . . These columns moved forward on the surface of the sea, and the clouds not following them with equal rapidity, they assumed a bent or incurvated shape, and frequently appeared crossing each other. . . .

The senior Forster corroborates his son's relation. The crew observed thick clouds gathering to the southwest, and to all appearances it rained on the southernmost margin of Cape Stephens. The "whitish spot on the surface" was recorded by Hodges in his painting of the episode.

On a less grandiose scale, Boisgelin de Kerdu studied the fountain produced as a side effect of a saltworks on the island of Malta. To the west of the mountain of Zebuccio, or Zebug, a long range of rocks sloped gently toward shore. Within 40 feet of sea level, they take on a perpendicular direction. A grotto under the boulders communicated with the ocean. Instead of evaporating, the trapped liquid was absorbed by the spongy stone; in winter, during rough and windy weather, storms drove waves into the cavern. The siphon thus produced forced its way through the natural well and "appeared like a beautiful wheatsheaf . . . rising perfectly entire to the height of sixty feet," and formed a "magnificent aigrette."[23]

Cook, on his third voyage, noted the brief adumbration of an immense floe in the otherwise chill void of the Pacific. The sharpness of the air, the gloominess of the weather, the brightness lying along the horizon "seemed to indicate some sudden change." "About an hour after, [came] the sight of a large field of ice . . . [which was] quite impenetrable, and extended from west by south, to east by north, as far as the eye could see. . . . " Webber captured an unanticipated incident that occurred on the following day; the ship ran into drift ice teeming with walrus.

Labillardière, about to sweep the South Seas in search of La Pérouse, seized in a lapidary juxtaposition the abrupt apparition of the aurora

Figure 260
William Hodges, *Waterspouts off Cape Stephens, New Zealand*. Oil, 53 1/2 × 76 inches. Photo courtesy National Maritime Museum.

Figure 261
John Webber, *Sea Horses*, B.M. Add. MS 23,921, 1778, fol. 112. Engraving by E. Scott. Photo courtesy British Library.

borealis: "The night was very dark, forthwith a luminous column of vast extent emerged from beneath the clouds and illuminated the surface of the water: the glittering sea still contained many shadowy intervals, when, all of a sudden, it seemed as if a sheet of fire unrolled [and moved] toward us. . . ."[24]

The advent and dispersion of fog was the maritime phenomenon most frequently described in a language embodying a sense of the unexpected. Wallis, the discoverer of Tahiti (or King George III Island), first sighted it in the early afternoon of June 18, 1767. He was forced to lie 5 leagues off shore because of the fog. When the pall finally lifted, the crew was startled to find itself surrounded by several hundred pirogues. La Pérouse, coasting along the perpetually mist-enshrouded margins of Alaska, was—like Cook before him—occasionally permitted to glimpse the austere contours of Mount Saint Elias when the vapors dissipated "tout d'un coup." (See figure 77.) Franklin, on his journey to the Polar Sea (1823), had the reverse experience. While the expedition was doubling Cape Barrow in the early morning hours, the shore party paddled briskly against a cold breeze until "the spreading of a thick fog" forced them to land. (See figure 139.) As Brooke's sleds glided across the empty reaches of Iceland, his guides discovered to their consternation that an obliterating haze was swiftly approaching. They urged the reindeer on, but to no avail: "All around us . . . quickly became obscured; the fog overtook us in our course; and in a few minutes the heavenly bodies were no longer visible: we were suddenly enveloped in a dense mist, and were unable to discern our closest neighbours. Our speed, notwithstanding was unrelaxed; and it was a complete helter-skelter race in the dark. . . . In this manner we scampered along the top of the Solivara and dreaded lest the mist should be succeeded by the snow-drift when our situation would have become much worse. . . . " (See figure 138.)

The encroachment of the vaporous need not be a terrifying experience, however. Grindlay took a view at the moment when daylight "bursts suddenly" upon the Ghauts—gigantic pinnacles "apparently floating in an ocean of white mist [figure 142] which, rising in successive rolling masses and dissipating under the increasing influence of the sun, gradually envelops the connecting range of mountains and the widespread plain below, studded with forests and cocoanut groves." Houel peered into the mouth of Etna. Mounting as high as possible in order to perfect his survey, he was "unable to tear his eyes away" from the abundant fumes filling the gaping crater, from whence a terrible noise resembling grating issued. When the wind scattered the smoke, he could glimpse a yawning void some 100 leagues in diameter.[25]

Other transient oddities of the atmosphere ranged from columnar electric corruscations "suddenly" standing above the pole (figure 158) to lowering thunderstorms "suddenly" descending in Taormina. In Greenland, boreal

VOYAGE INTO SUBSTANCE

light inundated the horizon, flashing brassy flames that soon died away; O'Reilly notes that "immediately after, from the westward there slowly extended upwards to the zenith four faintly marked radii, which diverged as they ascended. . . . One only remained, stretching in a magnificent arch over the zenith . . . and of a splendour exceedingly faint. . . . " (See figure 150.)

Weather conditions were the acme of unpredictability and instability, and were represented accordingly. When Lieutenant Tuckey crossed the Tropic of Cancer en route to the mouth of the River Zaire, not only did the ultramarine of the water unceremoniously change into a dark viridian, but Tuckey abruptly found himself in "that miserable region which has been so much spoken of as exposed to an everlasting calm." John Davy, exploring the interior of Ceylon, noted that its climatic transitions are actually "quite sudden," especially in the district of Doombera, where one side of the mountain is covered with vapors and drenched by rain and the other is parched with drought and scorched by an unclouded sun.

The fascination with the sudden appearance of a natural phenomenon is evident in the popular press. For example, *Le Magasin Pittoresque* cited admiringly Humboldt's description of artesian wells as "volcanos in miniature" that "suddenly" erupt as enormous columns of air.[26]

Sequence and Simultaneity

Our depths who fathoms, or our shallows finds
Quick whirls, and shifting eddies, of our minds?
Life's stream for Observation will not stay.
It hurries all too fast to mark their way.
In vain sedate reflections we would make,
When half our knowledge we must snatch, not take. . . .
Alexander Pope

The theme of "now" that shapes the voyager's commentary has, we recollect, a dual incarnation. The foregoing instances exemplified "moments" within the existence of phenomena. The following pages take up circumstances attendant upon another mode of perception; here, the spectator is temporarily stunned into aphasia. In this literal moment of transport, the intellect is whirled along, simultaneously lapsing out of discourse and out of contact with its analytical or perceptive self and with any object as connected to the continuum of the outer world.

The provocation of an immediate response as a criterion of aesthetic value was sustained in England from Addison to Coleridge.[27] In France, the *Encyclopédie* article devoted to *génie*—composed by either Diderot or Saint-Lambert—describes it as a natural gift, not an acquired talent. Hence, the person so endowed sees and is moved simultaneously. Unlike taste or erudition, which result from protracted effort and time, natural or original genius allows man to transplant himself instantaneously and with the heat of enthusiasm into any situation. It permits him to be beside himself, to hurry outside his train of consciousness. In contrast with the sudden apparition in which "excessive" presence or tangible character on the part of the object canceled the self-reflexive powers of the mind to awaken its critical forces, this instance has the imagination momentarily darting out and then falling back into itself before returning to the world. It is in this connection, too, that the eighteenth century conceived of the Sublime as a fusing antidote to boredom. That is, the sight of the uncommon in nature integrates strong mental and corporeal impressions in the evanescent effect of astonishment, thus typifying an alienation from those features that habit has turned stale or familiar.[28] Diderot's (and later Friedrich von Schlegel's) aesthetic of the interesting, as much as Addison's or Burke's celebration of the egregious, touches on the striking as a sensationalistic cure for visual ennui.

Diderot's *Salon* of 1767 contains several maxims making the point that one must ruin or individualize the totality of a building in order to convert it into an "object of interest." While praising Vernet's choice of "unheard of" things, discrete phenomena rarely viewed, and "singular and new images," Diderot admonished the artist to have recourse to nature's characteristic details as primary models. He contrasts the sudden pleasure instituted by such diversified and fragmented "original works" with the tedium inspired by comprehensive books that require one to think by following the argument serially. This comment prompts Diderot to a larger, audience-oriented reflection on the difficulty of arousing and maintaining interest while speaking or writing—both activities requiring the ingestion of a sequence.[29]

As these thinkers recognized, vast and unique objects seemed particularly likely to rupture the imprisoning chain of harmonious events by suddenly activating the mind wearied by successive sameness. The astounding and the colossal served to divide time by functioning as totally involving spurs to a violent, if brief, *stupore*. Johnson, in his *Oriental Voyager* (1807), finds the wild scenery of Ceylon's stark precipices and towering cliffs a delightful relief to the eye of the mariner "fatigued with the dull monotony of a long sea voyage." His eye fastens not on the entirety of nature but on "forms assuming bold—abrupt—grotesque. . . ."[30]

As with previously discussed motifs, however, temporal distinctions that break with a step-by-step sequence are not the sole prerogative of the seafarer but also inform the accounts of the mountain climber. The swift incursion of an intense, unalloyed present marks the discourses of Saussure, Ramond, Laborde, and Deluc. On the heights, these naturalists experienced a sudden physical (not just intellectual) revelation that fathomed in a flash the turbulent structural secrets of the world's great mountain chains. Deluc, in his *Lettre physiques et morales sur les montagnes* (1778), also snatches a complex moment of more superficial illumination. The rapid changes occasioned by shifting light in these rarified regions caused valleys to appear more deeply entrenched and hills and scarps to rise more steeply and to detach and distinguish themselves with greater clarity from their surroundings. In the end, they resembled the earth precipitously surfacing from primeval chaos, or, conversely, they seemed to have been visually excavated from out of the darkness.[31] Faujas de Saint-Fond, traveling among Scotland's tarns, was similarly transfixed by an isolated black boulder thrown up long ago by volcanic action. A closer parallel between ancient protracted occurrence and modern unitary experience was established by Cook in the rocky Marquesas. Here, a line of rugged hills rise steeply in ridges to be apprehended quickly from Resolution Bay as monolithic monuments readily graspable in a chunklike moment.

The thrust of such accounts of venerable and looming masses promptly perceived is that of vivid simultaneity, of the explorer's actual "now" made to merge with the extended "then" of their formation.[32] A representative selection of primal units joining thought and matter should highlight this theme of uncompounded perception. Approaching the great chain of Villequinskoi-khrebut in Russia, Lesseps registered "an enormous mass at least one hundred *toise* high and almost perpendicular, riddled with boulders and rocks on which snow—borne by the hurricane—cannot cling. . . . " James Dalloway was struck by the view of Brusa nestled "upon the roots of Olympus"—an especially remarkable scene because of a disruptive "sudden elevation" in the background. In the same year, 1797, Cassas traveled to Syria pursuing the course of its holy river. On the spur of the moment, his gaze chanced to alight upon and enormous and striking outcrop which, because of its height, he at first mistook for a cloud. An initial glance left Cassas ignorant as to what had created this unheaval—was it a trial sketch cast off by nature or the decaying remains of a ruin?[33] John Barrow admits that "the first appearance of so stupendous a mass of naked rock as the Table Mountain cannot fail to arrest, for a time, the attention of the most indifferent observer of nature from all inferior objects, and must particularly interest the mineralogist." Captain Robert Fitzroy reports that the crewmen of the *Beagle* assembled "and were watching the gradual appearance of snow-capped mountains which had previously been concealed, when, bursting upon our view, as if by magic, a lofty mountain [Mount Sarmiento] appeared towering among them; whose snowy mantle, strongly contrasted with the dark and threatening aspect of the sky, much enhanced the grandeur of the scene." William Burchell, describing the uniform mountains of the Karreeberge, remarks that, as his party reached the northern opening of the pass, a wide-extended prospect "burst at once" upon them.

While lying off the furrowed Korean coast, William Broughton spotted a crater 6 or 7 leagues in circumference broken into craggy points and riven by fissures that exposed variously colored earths, cinders, pumice, and sulfurous matter. Although this feature had been "suddenly thrown up" eons ago (as William Hamilton also recognized in the case of Vesuvius), the novelty lay in the paradoxical copulae; that is, the aspect of nature erupting with full force into the stream of present consciousness. Thus, the physical act of voyaging—penetrating matter over the course of time—is chronologically replicated in the visual process of being arrested by specific spots at certain moments. Those individual moments temporarily transform general sequence into simultaneity by offering all things immediately as if they are all at once present to the mind.

HEGEMONY OF THE EXTERNAL

In a congruous fashion, the imposing fragments of ancient Egypt dawned on Vivant-Denon. Passing over the granitic terrain environing the Cataracts, he discovered "all of a sudden" the moldering temple on the island of Philae. Unseizable shifts in scenery (that is, not forming a ready-made ensemble) also mark Vivant-Denon's speedy convergence on the plain of Thebes. Because Napoleon's army was perpetually on the march, Vivant-Denon lamented, scarcely had he copied a monument than he was "torn" from it: "There was a colossus that one could measure only by eye and by the sensation of surprise [it elicited]. . . . to the right hewn and sculpted mountains; to the left, temples which at more than one league still resembled boulders; palaces, other temples, from which I was torn. . . ."

Indeed, as Pope's "Epistle to Cobham" declares, "life's stream for observation will not stay." Edmond Temple, on his journey to La Paz, recorded the following about a sunrise that was "scarcely to be surpassed in the world":

As I rode thoughtlessly along, I perceived a brilliant streak resembling burnished gold, dazzling to look on, and wonderfully contrasted with the shades of night, which still lingered upon the world beneath; for to us the sun had not yet risen, though the somber profiles of the *Cordilleras* might be distinctly traced through the departing gloom. Imperceptibly, the golden effulgence blended with a field of white, glistening in vestal purity, and, expanding downwards, gradually assumed the form of a pyramid of silver of immeasurable base. . . . The sun then rose, or rather *rushed* upon the silent world, in a full blazing flood of morning splendour, and at the same moment the stupendous *Ylimani*, the giant of the Andes, in all the pomp of mountain majesty, burst upon my view. . . .

To cope with flux, the travelers identified with the single and the singular. William Orme, in Hindustan, speaks of the *choultry* (an open-air colonnade attached to a pagoda) that "abrupts" from the edge of the Rock of Tritchmopoly. Captain Charles Gold "came unexpectedly" upon a massive group of Hindu statuary, near the village of Manapar, that was revealed when Gold was only a few yards from the entrance to the area. James Forbes was taken with the blunt apparition of statues at Elephanta. William Hodges's earlier commentary on the subcontinent mentions "a few solitary wanderers" amid ruins of archaic masonry in a place "greatly gone to decay."[34]

Further, immense insulated masses perceived as disjointedly "rising abruptly," "rising at once," "rising immediately," or just "rising" were also characterized as quickly subsiding.[35] Both instances subverted the notion of time taken as a whole. Two anonymous letters published in the *Journal für die neuesten Land- und Seereisen* (1802) record that one stumbles upon Rügen's cliffs without prior warning: "Suddenly [*aufeinmal*] one steps out of the forest onto the ledge of an abyss; it is white, angular, with dreadfully fractured chalk spikes that plummet for three hundred

Figure 262
J.-B. de Laborde, *Singular Strata of
Calcareous Rocks,* from *Description de la
France,* 1781, II, pl. 7. Engraving by
C. Fessard after drawing by Ballin. Photo
courtesy Cabinet des Estampes,
Bibliothèque Nationale.

Figure 263
Carl Lang, *View of the Yellow Cavern of
Alcantara,* from *Gallerie der Unterirdischen
Wunder,* 1806–1807, I, pl. p. 152. Color
aquatint. Photo courtesy Bibliothèque
Nationale.

sedimentary layers of deposit until they reach the foaming sea. . . . This is the celebrated *Stubbenkammer*, in its way unique perhaps on the face of the known earth. . . ." Carl Lang also presses into service temporal and spatial division when he describes the limestone cave of Alcantara, near Lisbon. Its plunging depth is only occasionally broken with a floor rent by gaping holes. When Robert Ker Porter was lowered into Sweden's Dunamora iron mine, a disjunctive vista suddenly "struck" his sight; "mid-way suspended between the upper and nether world," he looked "towards the distant sky, or downwards into the regions of a lurid night." Caverns atomistically shatter the ground's continuity in every corner of the earth. Franz von Erdmann, in his *Beiträge zur Kentniss des Innern von Russland* (1822–1825), notes the welcome interruption of darkness provided by ice shining faintly from the bottom of the grotto near Tetjusch in Kasan. Raoul-Rochette, in his *Lettres sur la Suisse* (1823–1826), registers the discontinuous luminous effect of the calcine pavement of the Grotte du Dragon, on the outskirts of Stantz.

The balloon descent produced analogous prospects that quickly drew the attention downward, away from a rectilinear horizon. Baldwin remarks that, at an altitude of one mile, the sea (red in color) "suddenly" presented itself, and circular landscapes of distant countries filled the eye. The Roberts, during their October 15, 1784 flight, found themselves "suddenly involved in clouds of rain" when their descending path took them into a pocket of turbulence.[36]

Charles Cochrane, traveling in Colombia, spoke of exposed, wall-like strata. The valley, lying between these parapets, "must have been sunk by some sudden convulsion of nature, leaving the sides of these hills uncovered, whose bases were of more solid materials than itself."[37] In this instance, the voyager's descending perception mirrors the activity of a formerly unannounced geological plunge. Similarly, Johnson visually analyzes how conglomerate stones have fallen asunder over time to create the present hollows between the Lion's Head (on the Cape of Good Hope) and the sea. Hobhouse noted that when he veered left at the Stadium of Delphi he could search out a cleft splitting the mountain of Castri from summit to base. Gordale Scar in Yorkshire "burst upon" William Westall not only because the overhanging rocks seemed to be "torn" apart by some terrible concussion but also because they appeared to be in the momentary act of falling. Porter, viewing a basaltic valley in Armenia, was drawn along perpendicular beds demolished and tumbled together in a heap.[38]

Unforeseen depressions continuously forced travelers to look down. Hurrying toward the edge of a lake created by the spreading Gave, Dusaulx reached the Circus of Gavarnie. His gaze plummeted to the foundations of this amphitheater, following the trajectory of a bounding cascade. But it was the River Gave, not the waterfall, that was the "veritable agent"

Figure 264
Peter Schmidtmeyer, *Bridge of the Incas*,
from *Travels into Chile over the Andes*,
1824, pl. 11. Hand-colored lithograph by
A. Aglio. Photo courtesy British Library.

HEGEMONY OF THE EXTERNAL

of the magnificent forms dotting the valley: "The inexhaustible torrent is this primitive instrument and from the summits of Mardoré to Saint-Sauveur it rolls its turbulent waters into canals where the eye sometimes has great difficulty following it, and where the sun has never illuminated its depths. . . ."

Shortly after emerging from the Caucasus, Kotzebue encountered a granite barrier. In striking contrast with its precipitous rise was a narrow defile through which a relentless wind tunneled. The sudden view of the "gulph" of Etna after an arduous climb produced in Cockburn a sensation "really past description." He saw "most distinctly to the bottom of this wonderful and immense crater," which "contains several minor mountains, and their craters within it; some smoking like the most violent glass house, or steam-works." MacKenzie, in Iceland, compared the initial sight of a stream of lava at Havnefiord with the sunken "chasms and caverns" that now presented themselves on every side.[39]

The sight of a waterfall projecting from a perpendicular rock at Cascade Cove forced Cook to pursue visually its "great impetuosity." Mollien, clambering along trails in the mountains of Badet, discovered below what earlier had been concealed from view: the source of the Gambia and Rio Grande rivers. Standing on a similar eminence in Liverpool Plain, Oxley was "lost in astonishment" at the sight of Bathurst's Cataract cleaving the countryside in two and dividing it to its very roots. Lycett, also exploring Australia, encountered Beckett's Falls while pursuing the upper current of the River Apsley. He was astonished to see so many cascades, of which this one was perhaps the most important, and his eye was "arrested" by its 150-foot drop into an apparently bottomless abyss. In the less desolate Pyrenees, Heriot came upon the River of Eaux-Bonnes rolling through a ravine and abruptly hurtling down an incline to dissolve into foam.[40]

Life on board ship was especially conducive to the frequent riveting of attention to the ocean's floor. In June 1770, when Cook steered a dangerous course from Trinity Bay to the Endeavour River, the sea concealed dangerous shoals that seemed to project on the spur of the moment. To the unwary mariner, the deeps appeared to shallow "at once." Flinders, coasting off Australia's eastern shore, described its submerged coral reefs, which Westall illustrated as existing above the water's surface in order to give a better idea of their form. (See figure 164.) (In reality, however, the tide never leaves any considerable portion of the banks uncovered; hence the navigator is startled by their length as he peers some 150 fathoms beneath the waves.) Equally frightening to Anders Skjöldebrand was the spectacle of a frozen sea, an experience that must stand for this entire class of simultaneous perception. As his ship receded from Finland's coast, its glaciers were brusquely replaced by heaped mounds of floating ice. Their shattered heights were no match for their fractured depths, profundities that eluded even the most vigilant gaze.[41]

In sum: The voyager, by the work of exploration, reconciles in his body the experience of sequence with that of simultaneity. Long-standing phenomena, "rushing" or "bursting" in to overwhelm his consciousness, physically blend their moment with his. Such a spectator is, finally, as much in the thrall of a natural presence as the beholder who analyzes natural history precipitously in the making. Both types of dynamic perception involve incursions of an active matter into the psyche and run counter to the sluggish drifting of reverie. In the end, this bivalent construct of the sudden as fostering corporeal and mental unity represents a point of coincidence between matter and spirit.[42]

Topography Experienced in Context

... il faut pénétrer dans l'abîme des infiniment petits, ainsi que planer dans les désers incommensurab'ls du firmament: le monde d'une goutte d'eau, qu'on sçait peuplé de mille animaux de diverses espèces subit sans doute plus de révolutions que notre globe. ...
J. C. I. Delisle de Sales

Immediacy in time implies contiguity in space. Thus we find travelers assuring their readers that their notes and sketches were copied "on the spot." By this assertion, the eighteenth-century voyagers attempted to satisfy a further desideratum of simultaneity: that events portrayed should be "treated of" at the period when they occurred.[43]

Much has been written about the Romantics' obsession with specific places—for example, William Wordsworth's concentrated awareness of self buried at Grasmere. Nevertheless, a distinction must be drawn between such heartfelt attachments to a special place and the travelers' alertness to the characteristics of untrodden sites. The spiritual density and personalized texture associated with a familiar locale differs dramatically from the emotional vacancy of a new land. Virgin environments absorbed the attention of the modern explorer not by their well-loved and intimately known idiosyncrasies but by their very nakedness and absence of allusion.[44]

By definition, scenery once claimed or commemorated by feeling cannot again be experienced in an unmediated fashion. In contrast, the explorer—committed to the living of actuality, not to recollection; unwedded to the landscape; not endemic to his terrain—is an interloper in a raw world that functions without him. It is no wonder, then, that he sees every novel phenomenon as starting suddenly, even hieroglyphically, from the void. Moreover, the idea of an orderly plot in which man has sunk deep roots and to which he is somehow magically bonded, suggests a point of stasis. Like the ornamental garden, such private property is remote from the discoverer's dynamic response to the unenclosed wilderness.

The desire to provide firsthand geological evidence for the existence of uncultivated precincts inspired William Hamilton to descend into the mouth of Vesuvius just before its 1776 eruption; the text accompanying the plates asserts that the sketches were "taken on the spot." (See figure 148.) With similar intent, Valenciennes urged landscape painters to voyage in order to acquire the habit of sketching "at first sight." To capture accurately sky, sea, fog, and storms, he asserted, the artist must spend time not only coasting but on the high seas, out of the reach of land. Valenciennes's mind, stocked with the narratives of Forster and Bruce,

HEGEMONY OF THE EXTERNAL

also soared to the Asian and African plains, with their strange beasts. It was these unjaded sights that he wished the student of landscape painting to witness.[45] These are two telling examples of voyage literature's persistent theme that "nothing will be found there, but what I have seen with my own Eyes." In the same vein, Cornelius Le Bruyn declares that authors with whom he disputes "were not long enough upon the Spot, to be capable of making a just and accurate Description." Commodore Anson, according to the official historian of his circumnavigation, was rankled by those who deceived the public in the representation of views; Chaplain Richard Walter states that the only way to refute conjecture and fiction is "to go to the spot they described and to expose oneself to the risks which their false information always gives rise to."[46]

The acquisition of "thorough knowledge" unprejudicial to truth requires one to examine "on the spot," in the words of Aegidius Von Egmont's *Travels through Europe* (1759). The dual ambition to improve one's mind and to make discoveries is not without hazard; taking sketches directly "from nature" or crafting "a plain narrative of facts, written at the time when the occurrences happened" requires alacrity honed by an acute sense for the brevity and danger of the moment.

In the preface to his *Voyage en Egypte* (1802), Vivant-Denon is justifiably proud of the "immense" number of drawings he brought back to Europe—most of them executed while he was "on [his] knees, or standing, or even on horseback." Vivant-Denon was "never able to finish a single one according to [his] satisfaction," because for an entire year he "never once met with a table level enough to bear a ruler." He summed up consciousness of fugacity in this laconic statement: "I beheld a hundred things; a thousand escaped me. . . ." Burckhardt, similarly gifted with the tenacity needed to perform accurate observations, left a vivid account of how his memoirs of Nubia were composed: From notes hastily jotted on the spot, his journal was transcribed daily "in the corner of an open court, by the side of [the] camels, under the influence of the hot winds of the Desert, and under the sufferings of ophthalmia."[47]

Humboldt remarks that the sketches for the atlas to his voyage were not only marked by the greatest exactitude in the representation of objects but were created "at the spot" and "frequently under very afflicting circumstances." Arago adds an additional dimension to the voyager's constant and rapid collision with the random contingencies of new experience: Drawing with "unwearied zeal" in the open air (that is, utterly exposed) compounds the risk of being in an untried situation.[48] A great distance separates relations and delineations quickly fashioned "on the spot," "derived from living observation," and minutely studied "at the moment" from those fabricated later from memory. Recollection not only alters the arrangement of objects, "in order that they may be brought into view where they appear most interesting," but provides merely a "tolerably just" copy of appearances. Instead of the forcefully proximate, we are granted the filtered "seen after."[49]

Creating Finity

Rien de plus agréable que l'aspect de l'île . . .
L. A. de Bougainville

Balloon voyagers have likewise been particularly defective in their Descriptions of aërial Scenes and Prospects: those Scenes of majestic Grandeur which the unnumbered Volumes of encircling Clouds, in most fantastic Forms and various Hues beyond Conception glowing and transparent, portray to a Spectator placed as in a Center of the Blue Serene above them. . . .
Thomas Baldwin

Distinctive features of the late-eighteenth-century factual travel accounts are informed by an entropic, atheistic materialism. As noted in the discussion of natural effects, this philosophy stresses self-sufficient atomistic activity, ceaseless change, and constant struggle rather than the passive abiding of divinely controlled systems of the universe. To say this is also to raise the issue of a single, God-like perspective contravened by multiple natural aspects. By freeing himself of anthropomorphizing habits (that is, of the delusion of his uniqueness), the astute observer is able to enter and explore the history and present composition of the earth. In short: Liberated from the falsity of a panoptic perspective, man's individual eyereach and nature's characteristic aspects can at last intersect at an equally specific point in time and space.

Being "on the spot" and physically experiencing the manifold incursions of phenomena "suddenly" present meant that travelers gave shape and content to infinity.[50] They created finity by carving aspects and prospects out of a continuum. This representational act involved seizing monolithic formations witnessed instantaneously in isolation and recording complexly contrasted objects judged suddenly in relation.

A coda to the earlier discussion of the antinomies of vertical and horizontal suggests itself: Greatness, whether of height, depth, or lateral extension, is predicated on an individual's particular posture in space and shifting viewpoints in time.[51] In the operation of beholding a natural masterpiece or straining after a transitory effect there is a scale of diminishing degrees of optical acuity corresponding to the increasing distance (and temporal uninvolvement) from which the phenomenon is experienced.

Perspective, or *ars perspectiva*, derives from the Latin verb *perspicere*, meaning to see clearly, to examine, to see through, or to regard mentally. Before the fifteenth century the word was used to translate the Greek term for optics, the mathematical study of vision formulated by Euclid, preserved in Arabic texts, and revived for the Middle Ages in the writings of Roger Bacon, John Peckham, and Witelo.

The connection of vision and illumination was firmly established among the Romans. The Stoics were the first to utilize consistently the concept of light or *lumen* when outlining the various functions of the understanding. Thereafter it became a common thesis that sight shares knowing with the intellect; Descartes and Leibniz called reason *la lumière naturelle*. But it was Newton who fully incorporated the laws of optics into the laws of nature, thus initiating a widespread secularization of vision and, more important for our concerns, a fusion of style of vision with knowledge. It is not my purpose to provide the itinerary of the metaphor of perspective (so brilliantly analyzed by Guillén and others), but to pinpoint, whenever apt, a few moments of its fate in European culture.

It was the genius of Alberti and his successors to apply the Euclidean *prospectiva*—which in itself has nothing to do with art—to problems of artificial (that is, graphic) representation. By the seventeenth century, the English word *perspective* could mean the theory of linear perspective and could also be related to a telescope (a perspective glass), to a microscope or other refracting lens, to an expansive view in nature or a representation of such a view in a painting that made a conspicuous use of linear perspective, or to a perspective device. Out of this nexus of meanings spring certain issues of central interest to this study: distance (implied by the word *prospect*, meaning a real view), point of view, and truthfulness. All three are fundamentally related in that perspective—associated with optical or mirroring machinery—draws distant and confused truths (such as remote landscape elements) into a single image now made comprehensible from a single spot and near at hand.

Since the Renaissance, the hypothesis that space could be rationalized assumed the existence of a viewer at a definite distance, stationed in a specific and frozen position with respect to the world. A dual contradiction emerges from this theory, one realized by Leonardo. First, the ideal spectator, the fictitious single beholder posited in the Albertian scheme, assumes a unidirectional, fixed point of view, whereas in reality every scene generates multiple and even infinite aspects. Second, the more perfect the illusion of reality achieved in the perspective glass, the more perfect and facile the deception practiced on the viewer. Indeed, anamorphic games and chiromancy were based on visibly bending the rules of perspective in order to distort and conceal images, thus compelling the viewer to seek them out. On the other hand, refracting lenses could reveal the virtual terrain of the sun and the moon, with all their actual irregularities, and could mechanically extend sight downward to bodies invisible to the unaided eye. Yet, paradoxically, despite the testimony of the enhanced eye, the *trompe l'oeil* images that emerged from these instruments, and from others such as the camera obscura, possessed a dual nature: they appeared real only because they were so consummately fictitious. Because of doubts raised about the duplicitous games of optics during the early seventeenth century, the viewer could no longer confidently behold the world from the outside with the assured gaze of objective reason and from an elevated, Olympian, or totally embracing point of view.

On the other hand, the scientific perspicacity that this study has concentrated on—not that identified with wit, dexterously paradoxical in joining mentally the most varied and remote fancies, but that which enters the particularities of the world—scrutinized objects from alien perspectives: their own. Isolating and examining substances up close was tantamount to penetration and thus inaugurated a new visual habit of plainness or real transparency. The explorer-scientists carefully drew minute distinctions where a careless mind might have interjected broad associations. This scientific point of view developed during the seventeenth century, when

VOYAGE INTO SUBSTANCE

the availability of multiple psychic perspectives and personal identities rendered the very existence of outer things most problematic, most far off.

It was precisely in this area that the scientific gaze made its aesthetic contribution. The natural historian collapsed intervening space—both his and the external world's—in order to probe structure. Such judicious insight also subverted the generalized, surveying mode of perspective vision and focused attention on the partial aspect or charged fragment of the whole. The issue of perspective and distance from the audience can also be approached by the avenue of rhetoric. Wesley Trimpi distinguishes within Horace's commentary on Aristotle's *Rhetoric* two different types of oral composition: the political and the forensic. From this oratorical antithesis he demonstrates the establishment of a parallel—one that stretched well into the nineteenth century—between the skiagraphic work of art (distantly viewed, like the political speech meant to be heard or assimilated in the open) and the single display piece (scrutinized up close, like the forensic address employed for disputing a case in private chambers before a solitary judge). What Trimpi has to say about the stylistic or formal contrarieties between declamations made during public debates in the forum and pleas made to small gatherings in halls of recitation or *auditoria* may be gainfully extrapolated and applied to the perception of natural objects viewed *en plein-air* and the distant or close-up manner in which they were communicated.

Trimpi argues that Horace's distinction between a "written," private, refined style, requiring the concentrated attention of quiet, uninterrupted perusal, and a "spoken," public, less meticulous style was transplanted to Augustan literary convention. Yet in the eighteenth century the ostentatious style, suitable to close examination and interested in detail, began to shed its aura of art for its own sake, communicated in sheltered privacy. Simultaneously, the public or utilitarian style—formerly encountered at a distance and under the hot sun—narrowed its epic focus, as we have seen, to take in fragments, details, particulars.

Although mode of expression was the overriding issue in both instances, the selection of form had a concomitant bearing on the choice of subject. For example, Strabo in the *Geography* announces that he will omit the trivial and the inconspicuous and devote his attention instead to noble and great events. He uses a colossus as a visual analog for the longer narrative development of his extended work. Strabo's book is just such a giant in that it deals with facts about large things and wholes—viewed comprehensively and thus at a distance—and does not trouble itself with minutiae.[52] It was just this generalizing, far-off attitude of the ancients that the on-the-spot work of the explorers undermined.

It was in the pursuit of chorography, or specific topographies, not a hallowed abstract geography, that the artist-travelers set forth to experience

HEGEMONY OF THE EXTERNAL

the universe up close as a system of multiple and striking aspects demanding confrontation and collapse of interval. The masculine, trenchant, and plain style flexibly adapted itself to the adamantine qualities of the phenomena portrayed. Similarly, it forced the voyagers to learn through immersion the mutability of the material world by capturing in atmospheric sketches the specific transient effects or processes of a given moment. By the middle of the eighteenth century, Horace's polarities as well as the mechanism of unidirectional perspective were on the verge of foundering. During the course of an expedition, both the near and the far object were scrutinized, reciprocally "invaded," penetrated (at once or eventually), and copied as they were—not epideictically or with an overwhelming and hence screening display of technique.

These observations return us to a major theme of this book: the physiognomies of nature, or the assiduous attention paid to all its physical aspects. Scientific investigation as practiced by the travelers raised heedful observation to the status of art. By compelling the viewer to analyze (not just recognize) phenomenal reality, the activity of exploration suggested that there might be no significant distinction between scientific and aesthetic perception. Landscape studies especially emulated scientific goals: the willed seeing of an unravaged topography and the capacity for careful visual anatomization. Although the names of Alexander von Humboldt and John Ruskin have become synonymous with this "science of the aspect of things," their precursors were legion.[53]

The exercise of the experimental method—the only method that conforms to the business of duplicating constantly shifting reality viewed in a particular light and at a determinable moment—entails the careful notation of items as they are encountered, under as many conditions as possible. Only in this finite, inductive way, moving part by part, can one hope to arrive ultimately at a comprehensive picture, a total perspective. In the words of Georg Forster, "It was . . . requisite that [the scientific observer] should have penetration sufficient to combine different facts, and to form a general view from thence, which might in some measure guide him to new discoveries, and point out the proper objects of farther investigation. . . ."[54]

This methodology represents yet another revolution grounded in the fertile soil of the late eighteenth century. And, as Thomas Kuhn argues, during scientific revolutions experimentalists adopt new instruments to look in new places in order to see new and different things. All of this yields changes in outlook. Connected with the revolutionary transformation of vision brought about by travel narratives was the intensive use of optical instruments, both new and improved. What one sees depends not only on what one looks at and when, and on one's previous visual or conceptual experiences, but also on the tools with which one sees. The geognost in the alpine world, equipped with his camera obscura, or the balloonist, armed with his telescope, became an engrossed and augmented eye.

The camera obscura, as it was used notably by Jan Vermeer, resulted in a static projection that flatly mirrored the world in a preselected aspect. This frozen or "sustained" image likewise carried temporal overtones of isolated suspension usually associated with a "classical" landscape. That is, the time of the landscape painting was removed from its actual continuities in the real world. But the camera obscura could also be improved and made to seize transitory effects and agitated scenes; witness the paintings of the Guardi, Constable, Turner, and Delacroix.[55]

The popularity among travelers of the camera obscura (a device created to achieve verisimilitude) is an important gauge of their desire for exactitude. Since the beginning of its widespread use in the middle of the sixteenth century, it was professedly an empirical, not a supernatural, apparatus, intended to imitate the methods of the practical sciences in its replication of the matter of nature. The fundamental premise informing its employment was that knowledge gained through sensible experience was valuable and not illusory. Of course, this assumption ran counter to the belief mentioned earlier—inherited from Plato—that appearances, particularly visual ones, were undependable and meretricious. The notion that optical devices lead to truth, that the aspect of an object can reveal its inmost reality, belongs to an age convinced that the senses contribute to knowledge. Matter no longer—as in the Platonic and Neo-Platonic world view—veils the distant Idea dimly reflected within nature; it hieroglyphically contains everything, *is* that immanent, close-by concrete idea which only the scientist, not God, can decipher.

The camera obscura, then, was the perfect implement for naturalists seeking images of stark immediacy. In contrast with a mirror, which created a reversed and hence indirect reproduction of the world, with a camera obscura the artist could view the world directly and instantaneously without being disturbed by distortion or his own reflection.[56]

James Bruce offers a revealing example of the utilization of the camera obscura for the purpose of discovery. The introduction to the monumental *Narrative* chronicling Bruce's efforts to locate the source of the Nile records his lifelong devotion to drawing, mathematics, and astronomy. Like so many explorers of his generation, Bruce abandoned other undertakings when the 1768 transit of Venus was at hand. While serving as the British consul at Algiers, Bruce had a camera obscura constructed to his own specifications. With this compact, portable "delineator" a person of but moderate skill could do more work, of "the utmost truth," than the ablest draftsman. With the delineator, writes Bruce, "landscapes, and views of the country, which constitute the background of the picture, are real, and in the reality show, very strikingly indeed, in such a country as Africa,

HEGEMONY OF THE EXTERNAL

Figure 265
Thomas Wright, *A Perspective View of Visible Creation*, from *An Original Theory or New Hypothesis of the Universe*, 1750, pl. 17. Mezzotint. Photo courtesy Library of Congress.

abounding in picturesque scenes, how much nature is superior to the creation of the warmest genius or imagination," and "momentary masses of clouds, especially the heavier ones, of stormy skies, will be fixed by two or three unstudied strokes of a pencil."[57]

The telescope was fully comparable in seizing the peculiarities of a very different ambient. Like the camera obscura, it possessed the power of making the remote suddenly and unerringly proximate. The Countess in Fontenelle's *Une pluralité de mondes* (1686) protests that Newton's optical discoveries made the cosmos too large. The author retorts: "Dreadful, Madam, said I; I think it very pleasant, when the Heavens were a little blue Arch, stuck with Stars, methought the Universe was too strait and close, I was almost stifled for want of Air; but now it is enlarg'd in height and breadth, and a thousand & a thousand Vortex's taken in; I begin to breathe with more freedom, and think the Universe to be incomparably more magnificent than before. . . ." Toward the close of the eighteenth century a decisive shift occurred away from the chilling and timeless survey of "so vast a length, no eye can reach to the end of it," to an infinity made finite or brought up close. William Hamilton's *Supplement to the Campi Phlegraei* (1779) reflects this displacement. In the spirit of his alpinist brethren, Hamilton could, by using a good telescope, "distinguish as well, as if we had been actually seated on the summit of the Volcano." "In an instant," he notes, "a fountain of liquid transparent fire began to rise, and gradually increasing arrived at so amazing a height, as to strike everyone, who beheld it with the most awfull astonishment. . . ." (See figure 183.) Similarly, Deluc ponders how distance diminishes the visual force of large objects and how astonishment mounts as one approaches a colossal glacier. Obviously, the impact is more intense when the metamorphosis from small to large is instantaneous, when by looking through a glass the far suddenly stands near.

The dismay at ever-receding space voiced by Fontenelle's countess was fully dispelled only with the coming of the balloonist, equipped with barometer, hygrometer, and telescope. The account given by the *European Magazine* of Lunardi's voyage of September 15, 1784, should serve as a reminder of that entire class of experience. The reporter lists among the important aftermaths of this ascent that "the firmament fretted with golden fires will become an object of [the populace's] inquiry." Bernardin de Saint-Pierre was prepared to undertake a pilgrimage to England for the purpose of "seeing the sun in the telescope of Herschell, and [thanking] this illustrious man for having extended the sights and hopes of mankind into the firmament." Bernardin compares Herschel's invention to the solar microscope of Lieberkhun, which inflates a flea to the size of a sheep; both swiftly bring the diminutive and the distant powerfully adjacent. John Russell, with his detailed planispheres, brought the lunar disk "directly to earth."[58]

VOYAGE INTO SUBSTANCE

Figure 266
John Russell, *Moon in Plano*, from *The Lunar Planisphere*, 1809, pl. 1. Mezzotint. Photo courtesy British Library.

The precipitate collapse of the farthest far into the nearest near resulted in the dissolution of general nature into concrete sections or fragments. Fascination with the varieties of matter that demanded to be read myopically, with abbreviated spatial vectors as physical signs demarcating boundless extent, with immediacy as a token of temporal process, and with the intervention of magnifying optical instruments as devices for neutral vision all contributed to a nonanthropocentric perusal of particular aspects.

The classificatory approach of eighteenth-century science in general and geography in particular also tended to isolate individual occurrences within an environment. Careful analyses of land masses, such as Kerguelen's elevations of the Shetland Isles or Alexander's of the Heysan Islands, traced their discrete aspect. The determination of a place's "singular appearance" by "examining it narrowly" rapidly became a refrain. Dolomieu justifies the inspection of crude columns of prismatic basalt at the site of Vesuvius because it is more interesting to seize their appearance while they are still wedded to the spot. D'Entrecasteaux, speaking of the chain of reefs around New Caledonia, states that they characterize the "aspect of the coast." Flinders also seeks physiognomic identity when he painstakingly describes the "appearance" of Australia's hilly eastern shoreline. According to Forrest, the attentive observer must constantly be on the alert for a thousand "traits" visible in the country stretching along the banks of the Ganges and Jumna Rivers. This is the same visual alphabet of rocky features, bays, harbors, rivers, and headlands that Franklin identified while treading the coast from the mouth of the Coppermine River to the eastern tip of North America, the same rude mien that Brooke recovered in Scandinavia.[59] In short, the distinctive "face" or countenance of a province is reconstructed through the minute enumeration of salient forms and figures constituting an assemblage. When decoded, they provide a key to the terrain's dominant physiognomy, one that sums up its total history.

However, even singularities do not possess a unique aspect. (See figure 188.) Environmental perception involves alertness to multiplying perspectives. Ten leagues beyond Christmas Sound in Tierra del Fuego, Cook identified "Yorkminster," which alters its appearance "according to the different situations it is viewed from." The Marquis de Chastellux, congruously, notes how the aspects of Virginia's Natural Bridge unfold in time: On approaching the precipice laterally and from below, one first sees two rock masses that join to cover a ravine. Only later, from above, does one perceive that these twin pavements merge beneath the feet to form an arch. Then, at the base of the monument, yet another component— a small stream flowing under the distant vault—reveals itself. Kirkpatrick, in his *Account of Nepaul* (1811), remarks that Mount Jibjibia, towering above the other peaks of the Kuchar, is especially distinguishable from all points of view because of its curious aspect.

That shape is ever-changing as viewpoint is shifted struck Lycett in Van Diemen's Land, whose terminus is marked by asperities that present "a rugged and determined front to the icy regions of the South Pole." Australia abounds in gaps and fissures which, disdaining any semblance of uniformity, metamorphose with the slightest alteration in range.[60]

Prevailing aspect can also be contrasted with past aspect, not just by the method of physical encirclement but also by depth sounding. Houel's pictorial "map" of Mount Etna (figure 147) renders it simultaneously in three historic stages: its fiery genesis, the solid walls of its maturity, and the ongoing process of decay. The "new" visage is thus grafted onto the old—layered over, in a geological sense.

A less noble variation on the theme is the conferring of a modern face on the ancient land. Raoul-Rochette, touring the Jura, commented that industry bequeathed "a new physiognomy" to this region of venerable rock formations.

Not only constantly novel views of novel objects, but also the fresh incursion of vagrant ephemeral effects multiply aspect. As Charles Cochrane states concerning the appearance of Cape Blanco and La Guayra, when the sky is mottled the view is more remarkable than on serene days: "Accumulated clouds, strongly illuminated on their upper surface seem like floating islands of light on the surface of the ocean. Impending at various heights are columns of vapour between the eye of the traveller and the regions below. . . . Habitations and trees are, at intervals, visible through the spaces left by the clouds and vapours, which, urged by the wind, are perpetually changing forms and situation. Objects then seem deeper than when contemplated through a calmer and purer atmosphere. . . ."[61]

In sum: It would seem that two major suppositions underlie the travelers' interest in aspect. As Isaac Weld writes of Niagara Falls, "It is impossible for the eye to embrace the whole of it at once; it must gradually make itself acquainted in the first place with the component parts of the scene, each of which is in itself an object of wonder." Nature's immensity in general, and its individual colossi in particular, may be seized only as temporal and spatial fragments. Second, as tersely articulated by d'Entrecasteaux, "often the most pleasant objects glimpsed at a distance, cease to appear so when seen close up." To paraphrase, it is the ultimate delusion to imagine that what is snatched from afar reveals reality as it actually is.[62]

HEGEMONY OF THE EXTERNAL

These considerations, however, disclose only half the story. The terms *landscape* and *prospect* were often used interchangeably in the eighteenth century, but *prospect* typically connoted a more extensive view. A distinctive feature of both the popular prospect poem and the landscape garden was a lack of particularization; the gaze hurried over the brilliant profusion of the scene, occasionally pausing in its circular sweep to observe certain items in detail. This type of poetry or this way of experiencing the terrain tends to recognize rather than to scrutinize things on which the eye momentarily alights. The land belonging to the sphere of poem or garden, although without explicit margins, is not boundless in scope; it is punctuated by objects displaying a negligent order arranged according to a comprehensive and determinable pattern.[63]

As noted, the infinitely open because totally unknown prospect encountered by the voyager out in the world was breached through penetration, not by scanning from afar. During the second half of the century, then, not only artfully replenished but naturally stocked or even unimpeded vistas entered the aesthetic consciousness. The unfurling landscape was the perfect setting for the assertion of absolute freedom from civilizing restraints.

Witness the role played by natural "observatories," those imposing viewing stations planted in front of the major Swiss massifs. Travelers to the Bernese Oberland from Scheuchzer and Haller on sought belvederes from which to look up, down, or across at famous peaks. This does not imply, however, that they were content to see those mountains at a distance. The high, low, or level vantage point was merely one way among many for achieving visual access, for embracing vast spaces in a nonce.

Wolf and Raoul-Rochette spoke in favor of lofty locations from which the mountaineer could peer into crevasses and rents in the surfaces of glaciers.[64] Patrick Brydone enjoyed a corresponding view from on high. During his descent from Etna, all nature lay unfurled at his feet "united under one point of view." In the concurrent presence of "all seasons of the year, and all climates of the earth; with the whole variety of their productions," Brydone was roused by their unwonted compression. In such surroundings, he asks, "What mind can remain inactive?"

No matter whether the heights are situated in the Polar region or in the Burman Empire, judgment reacted with greatest freedom and vision functioned with swiftest acuity in those locations where the air was pure and free of gross vapors pressing upon the body. Landmann, leaning from the convent tower perched on the Rock of Lisboa, drank in a steep prospect and fragmented countryside. Humboldt, at once at the center and the circumference of the plateau of La Puebla, gazed from atop a natural colossus toward the east slope of the Cordillera. With the aid of a telescope his eye simultaneously and sharply registered dense forests and arid, pumice-strewn plains sparsely sprinkled with arborescent ferns and straggling mimosa. Johnson in Madeira and Hakewell in Jamaica similarly saw the distant brusquely approach, the ground rapidly rise, while peering at the prospect of Funchal and at the vale spreading out below Mount Diablo.[65]

The back-and-forth movement of the eye, darting downward from an elevated position and then precipitously across "a whole plain" or "an extensive country," tended to attribute importance to figures of large size soaring upward out of great flats. (See figures 16 and 19.) A significant variant of the expansive plain is the stretch of a submerged continent moving downward and laterally as far as the eye can see. While anchoring off the coast of Australia in January 1793, d'Entrecasteaux peered at "drowned lands spotted only when running traverse, . . . which vanished almost immediately."[66] In this moment of double vision, up and down or hither and yon meet in the spectator's awareness of an unequivocal present. Bernardin de Saint-Pierre, speaking from a different prospect-oriented perspective, suggests another location for achieving abrupt proximity between the externally remote and the indwelling senses. In *Harmonies de la nature* (ca. 1794) he discriminates between a mountain-climbing expedition and an ocean voyage. The bird's-eye view normal to lofty summits, one that unceremoniously confronts the observer with individualized formations starting upward, is contrasted with the "human view." Displaying his bias for the sea, Bernardin remarks that both the mariner and the hiker embosomed in a valley experience more fully, and at close quarters, the dynamic power of nature. It is especially on the coast, at the foot of that immense hollow containing the deep, that one beholds its effects unfolding at eye level: spectacular sunrises and sunsets, evanescent aerial meteors, tides, gaping mouths of rivers disgorging their flood, and mountain flanks ringed by waves and exposing their inmost mineral structure.

As one descends to the level of their manifestation, the most "pleasing prospects in the world" unravel with a kind of synchronous and isocephalic intensity. Jonathan Carver, spotting the entrance into Lake Superior from the Straits of Saint Marie, takes in the many "beautiful little islands that extend a considerable way before you." " . . . [On] the right," he continues, "an agreeable succession of small points of land that project a little way into the water, and contribute, with the islands, to render this bason [sic] . . . calm and secure from the ravages of those tempestuous winds by which the adjoining lake is frequently troubled. . . ." To be sure, watery stretches provided a multiplicity of "surrounding" prospects. George Dixon mocked the common wisdom that saw the Sandwich Islands as the Promised Land. Near Coal Harbour, he entered a dreary open area, which he beheld through uncomfortable conditions of cold and dank weather.[67]

HEGEMONY OF THE EXTERNAL

The view of mountains surging behind the pyramids and seen from the floor of Cairo's desert was called a magnificent prospect "composed of the most gigantic objects in nature" by Eyles Irwin. Landing on the shores of the Nile, Belzoni stared at "the distant view of Assouan," whose impact he thought increased because of the sterility of the lands through which he had just passed. Belzoni was conscious not only of the fringing curtain of granite mountains existing at a considerable remove from him, but also of an adjacent forest of palm trees and of the neighboring Island of Elephanta, which seemed to "interfere" with the impression made by the barren western bank.[68]

No matter how wide the prospect taken from the earth's great heights or from absolute sea level, it seemed somehow inadequate or restricted when compared with the glory of the age: the panorama experienced from a balloon. The aeronaut occupied the supreme vantage point, enabling him to survey the fullness of events while drifting within them. Unlike the navigator or the overland traveler (think of Brydone sailing in the middle of the Bay of Naples, Saussure at the heart of the Lac de Rousses, Vivant-Denon drifting in the Nile near Elephanta, or Forrest at the center of the Ganges), who is also bonded to his territory, the new Icarus occasionally realized his visual and sensory impressions completely.[69] (See figure 233.) He was not limited to aspects, to fragments set within the confines of an extensive whole, because his arena was nothing less than the actual totality of undivided space. This space, this marginless "spot" composed of "new airs" and "torrents of vapors," was tangibly present at every point in time during the course of the balloonist's progress through it. As Monck Mason aptly remarks, "all the ordinary qualifications of such scenes become, in fact, annihilated, and the eye for the first time beholds a picture of nature on the vastest scale, both as to size and magnificence, in the construction of which none of the complicated laws of linear perspective are at all involved. . . ."[70] Paradoxically, sharpness of contour, by which different features seen in prospect are qualified, is "strengthend with distance and remain[s] so as long as objects are distinguishable." Thus, not only does the most distant object appear with the greatest clarity, as if it were the most near, but it seems as if no interval actually exists. Thomas Baldwin contrasts journeys made by "conventional means" with balloon excursions. In the former, the time-consuming toil to attain a mountain panorama is endured not for the sake of "a complete Down Prospect, subject to a perpetual Variety," but merely for "an imperfect Side-View."[71] There comes a moment, Baldwin adds, when the telescope is useless. With increased elevation there is also an increasing accumulation of vapors. The ordinary telescope magnifies these clouds to the point that they are substituted in place of the object, under the form of opacity and cloudiness.[72] In short, the balloonist is eventually enveloped by a totally objectless panorama. The distant infinity hanging overhead, so feared by

Fontenelle's Countess, was replaced in the era of the aerial voyage by a more intimate conception of space, one that in no way belied its depth. This more proximate vision is plainly stated in a 1784 ode to the aerostatic globe: "Embrace the universe during the course of your brilliant flight,/ ... Far from feeble mortals, alone with nature. ..."

The anonymous French woman who accompanied Garnerin on an ascent made in 1798 adds the weight of actual experience to Paris's poem: "Nothing can be so fine, nothing so magnificent, as the spectacle of the universe, increasing in beauty and extent before the eyes of the aerial navigator. All was soon obscurity around us. We passed through dense vapors, and rose above the clouds. ..." Thus the "circular prospect" is either illuminated by the sun's rays, which permit objects to be distinguishable "at the Bottom of the Profound Abyss more than two miles in Diameter at one View," or "totally eclipsed as if by Haze or Vapour."[73] In either case, the balloonist is suddenly surrounded first by terrestrial things and then by outer space.

In short, it is in the aeronaut's extreme experience of panorama that the hegemony of the external receives its grandest apotheosis. No matter how rudely sublime or arresting the earthbound object, it cannot compete with the experience of being situated directly at the core of a living universe. Easefully drifting at the whim of winds, man and nature, consciousness and unconsciousness, are temporarily reconciled. Man's inner vitality and nature's dynamic powers are engaged in a profound exchange whose moment of barter perpetually takes place "now."

Yet this view or perspective taken from within matter, and other views from above (no matter how elevated the vantage), would prove to be the undoing of the scientific gaze. Certainly for the idealistic strain of nineteenth-century thought there was always the possibility of a loftier eternal viewpoint, one transcending the bounds of human sight to lodge in the divine.[74] According to this philosophy, the individual was doomed to a limited vision, one not sufficient to discover the structure of events, the connections among objects, the thing in itself. The realization that, no matter how high or low a perspective, it was always private, deeply subjective, and hence finite was countered by a realist tendency that looked levelly upon all phenomena, including man, and assessed them as equivalent aspects of an ongoing material continuum stretching horizontally and witnessed from the interior, from the narrow corner of a temperament.

With the nineteenth century, then, came an infinity of private perspectives and of material aspects corresponding to them. Thus, the eighteenth-century "moment," which struggled to get at a convention-free experience of the physical universe, passed into an endless series of temporal chunks and spatial units filtered and mediated by social and personal circumstance—in sum, by the exigent panorama of practical life.

Conclusion
The "Realization" of Nature

If these associations vary with the spirit of the poets, so much the more do they vary with the spirit of nations, which, having different customs, manners, and characters, could not associate all their ideas in the same way. So of two equally perfect languages, each has its beauties, each has expressions for which the other has no equivalent. . . . Whether [these] beauties belong exclusively to one language, or can pass from one language to another, they are equally natural, for nothing is more natural than associations of ideas that have become habitual. . . .
Abbé de Condillac

Je crois que ce fantôme [the Brocken Specter] est généralement une fidèle représentation de moi-même; mais aussi, de temps en temps, il est sujet à l'action du bon Phantasus, qui règne sur les songes. . . .
Charles Baudelaire

The most fundamental aim of the factual travel account as it was defined during the eighteenth and the early nineteenth century was the Baconian one of accurately impressing nature in the mind instead of the mind ignorantly propelling itself outward or fantastically receding inward. The stated objective of its creators was communication (through consummate description) of the things of this world. Because this genre of nature reportage intimately conjoined the verbal with the visual (and both with lived experience), and because it was an arm of natural history, its practitioners were continually in the position to test the inductive method put forward in the *Novum Organum*. More broadly, they reformulated the parameters of objectivity heralded by the propagators of the New Science, whose purpose had been to bring man out of the self-created cosmos deduced by the ancients and the Scholastics—founded on half-truths and imaginative lies—into a pristine, more knowing, original state. Whatever else getting back to the primitive meant for the enlighteners, it also denoted getting back to the real. The investigative tool of the scientific gaze, trained to penetrate, aided the explorer as it helped the mineralogist not only to fathom the present landscape but also to decode the archaic state of the earth with eyes that could discern the substance of things nearly as distinctly as had Adam's.

Nourished by the competitive and proliferating sciences, the habit of discovery—vital to all fields of empirical endeavor that wanted to lay claim to being progressive and meaningful—entailed the invention of new models and methods to understand and assimilate new things. Concomitantly, the enterprise of giving to findings about the natural world a substantial form demanded and elicited a "transparent" discourse for universal communicability and comprehension. The stylistic reform that had arisen in the seventeenth century from the debate between a "plain" and a "metaphysical" style, given point by the Royal Society and still a manifest concern to eighteenth-century linguistic remodelers, seemed tailor-made for the construction of mental and perceptual implements for getting those two very different systems, mind and nature, together without distortion.

The dictum that on a deep level the function of natural philosophy was the impartial imaging of nature readily allied itself with a verbal and visual style of recording. The pairing of these representational concerns—which the ambitions of science raised to an aesthetic level—occurred in Bacon's *Advancement of Learning* (1605) and in Hobbes's *Leviathan* (1651), where it was asserted (inverting the message of Quintilian's *Institutes*) that words were but the images of matter. This asseveration was matched by the growing desire of the Royal Society—and, by extension, all other scientific academies—to make words and pictures (that is, any artificial constructs) match things in order to make concrete a true model of the physical world.

This program for establishing inner and outer correspondences was complicated by the fact that the very notion of matter (that is, the actual stuff forming natural phenomena) and the apperceptive faculty itself were undergoing profound changes as a result of the scientific discoveries of the eighteenth century. One strategy for bringing about the marriage of the human intellect and the external world was to narrow the gulf between epistemology (that is, how one construes the mind's way of knowing nature) and the definition of what actually constitutes that nature. The discoveries about matter's lifelike, dynamic, organic properties, on the rise from the middle of the eighteenth century onward, temporarily served to stop the breach. If natural objects were condemned to be seen solely as compounded of primary qualities (Descartes)—that is, of a bare, lifeless, extended substratum—then they could be judged mentally impenetrable. This rationalistic interpretation dooming matter to being unknowably inert and opaque was challenged by a number of interlocking and materialistic developments. Even the natural masterpiece, the lithic or corpuscular monument in its most radical form, had its intractability softened, "ruined," during the course of the eighteenth century. It became perceptually permeable through the revolutionary discovery—a Copernican epiphany attributable to natural philosophers in conjunction with explorers—that it possessed a sometimes quiescent, sometimes violent, corporeous history of its own. In the second half of the eighteenth century, the monument that endured the earth's travails was increasingly undermined by its "accidents" or the volatilization of the "substratum" into fugitive effects, defined here as the nonauthorial "acts" of matter. The dissemination of Newtonianism, and the recrudescence of ancient hylozoism and its commingling with French biological vitalism and Leibnizian dynamism, provided an alternative vision of a world in dissolution, a realm of physical substance shot through with transmaterial forces and hence more readily graspable by an increasingly complex psychology and a more perspicuous eye.

The headlong pursuit after and duplication of natural monuments and ephemera were predicated on the belief in the possibility of knowing the world. Generically speaking, the Picturesque aesthetic—representative of the second strategy—embodies by contrast a tactic of evasion, the manifest loss of confidence in man's ability to know what lies outside himself and to understand it. Its theories are firmly embedded in subjectivist classifications of knowledge and are the logical issue of a path leading inexorably from the Cartesians, through Locke, to reach a dead end in Hume. At the hinge of these programs for skepticism aggregate "ideas," "concepts," and "names," all tending to mediate between the mind and the world of things. Thus, serial reflections, musings, reveries, and associations were more real for the seeker after the Picturesque because they were more accessible, more akin to and proximate to the sequential mechanism of his brain. Nor do they point beyond themselves, either to a transcendental sphere or to a spot lying outside the intellect, as had been the case in older philosophies.

Paradoxically, the retraction of the gaze from objects to rest on percepts and concepts dwelling only within the mind coexisted with the historical moment when objects asserted themselves, achieving the status of documents—uncontaminated, because uncontrolled, sources of evidence independent of man. It was precisely the discoverer's appropriation of Baconian methodology for a "Natural and Experimental History" (that is, the firsthand, sensuous acquaintance with phenomena; a bodily lowering into matter conducive to a visceral form of knowledge) that suggested a third strategy for grappling with the nonhuman world. By dint of the explorer's physical collusion with matter, he succeeded in striking a dual blow against the doctrines concerning the relativity of knowledge and the theories that man possessed the means to think only in abstractions and to perceive only habitually. Natural history acquired for physical phenomena the equivalent if not superior status formerly allocated to human events. The voyager penetrated nature as a repository and archive, elevating the wild, brute, or "naive" specimen to the position of rival or primitive twin to mankind's entire cultivated and artificial achievement.

After this momentous recognition of ontological separateness and distinctness, nature, as Kant observed in *Critique of Pure Reason* (1784), must be allowed free play to do its mobile work unhampered, behind man's back (so to speak), and man must be left to pursue his own transformational art according to his culture, his language, and the *a priori* rules of space and time that govern his understanding. The long-standing assumption that man and the phenomenal world naturally belong together (the argument revolved around how)—to which the empirically based travel account contributed its share by the systematic investigation of nature down to its most subtle particles—broke apart. In the nineteenth century, nature and art increasingly came to express alien languages; their fusion had to be created. This polarization represents in essence the tension

CONCLUSION: THE REALIZATION OF NATURE

between an autonomous environmentalist and an "art for art's sake" aesthetic.

Today, against the backdrop of the new hermeneutics, we may smile at the explorers' presumed attempt at suppression of the idiosyncratic in viewing, and we may even think it heroic. Yet it cannot be denied that this desire constituted a major component in the history of perception of the eighteenth and nineteenth centuries. Indeed, can one understand modern hyperbolic relativism without it? The quest for a purity of experience—whether achieved in the mind or out in the world—reposes at the core of most eighteenth-century thought. When philosophy and human history taught that all experience is mediated by ideas and conventions—in short, by self-reflexive interpretations—only the natural sciences and their implementors, the discoverers, could point refreshingly to the fact that nature was palpably, hence immediately, available to them in their privileged role as conscious observers, probers, delvers. By dint of being on location, riveted to the aspect of the present but not unmoored from the perspective of the terrain's past, and in a state of emphatic attentiveness, the explorer moved along with the changing shapes of natural particulars. Thus, he could embody and transmit their fragmentary appearance.

Against a larger backdrop, such pictured narratives (making use of repeatable pictorial and verbal statements, to quote William Ivins) stand as a testament to the Western European preoccupation with verisimilitude. The travel account, functioning as a conveyor of visual information newly apprehended, had an advantage over other forms of literary illustrated books based on copies of copies, translations of translations, and schemas of seeing and delineating. In some measure it was spared this fate by its very purpose: the sharp-sighted voyager's actual firsthand and physical acquaintance with phenomena whose personality, not his own virtuosity, he felt scientifically bound to report through copying and description. The discoverer realized—and here lies his importance—that it was necessary for accuracy's sake to verify any qualitative visual information by going to where the thing was and looking at it.

Yet the logical outcome of this long-felt desire to reproduce autonomous images free of subjective entanglements only first and inarguably displayed itself for the reading and viewing public not in etchings, aquatints, engravings, or lithographs, nor even in a "transparent" text, but in William Henry Fox Talbot's "photogenic drawings." *The Pencil of Nature* (1844–1846) reproduced natural images, among them landscapes, that to Talbot's contemporaries seemed bereft of any translator. According to Talbot's introductory remarks, "They are impressed by Nature's hand; and what they want as yet of delicacy and finish of execution arises chiefly from our want of sufficient knowledge of her laws. . . ." More so than in the calotype or in Niépce's "heliography," it was in the documentary photograph of the 1860s (the work of the Western Geological Survey photographers T. H. O'Sullivan and John Hillers springs to mind) that selectivity appeared laid to rest and it was assumed that nature could finally portray itself liberated from the trammels of art.

What follows by way of conclusion is an attempt to establish some specific points of contact between the kinds of nature imagery that emerged from the travel accounts (or, more broadly, the aesthetic ramifications inherent in the entire enterprise of voluntary perception and active deciphering) and some fundamental tenets regarding nature that are evident in the artistic and literary movements of the late eighteenth century and the first half of the nineteenth. These come to grips in revealing ways with key assumptions at work in, and questions ineluctably posed by, voyages in search of fact. To wit: One must know, through careful seeing, a vast deal about natural things in the performance both of art and science; further, landscape can function as the decultured antithesis to the conventionality of the human world; finally, there is a need for "plainness" or willed depersonalization to restructure the universe aright. Unavoidably and as the result of a cumulative process reaching deep into the seventeenth century, the illustrated factual narratives, by virtue of their popularity (with a public interested in pictorial information no matter the method of reproduction) and the sheer scale of their output, focused attention on what would become the nub of the representational issue of the nineteenth century: Where and what is reality?

The Nominal Mode

. . . il ne restoit plus que la tâche de visiter avec soin et dans la plus grand détail, les côtes de ces mêmes terres dont les navigateurs n'avoient pas encore pû faire la reconnoissance. . . .
Antoine Raymond Joseph de Bruny, Chevalier d'Entrecasteaux

Do not all charms fly
At the mere touch of cold philosophy
. . . Philosophy will clip an Angel's wings
Conquer all mysteries by rule and line,
Empty the haunted air, and gnomed mine—
Unweave a rainbow. . . .
John Keats

The popularity of the nonfiction travel account—documented by modern scholars such as Atkinson, Parks, Adams, and Batten—hinged in part on the genetic desire of the explorers and the public to return to an almost mythical apprehension of the earth as it might have been or as it unfolded before human consciousness appeared in it. The brunt of my argument has been to demonstrate the development of penetrative strategies to convey facts about an alien, unadorned, fluctuating universe. The voyagers succeeded in some measure in recovering the naked individuality of the land in its historical uniqueness and concreteness. The visible result of their exertions was to dissolve the formerly intractable physiognomy of nature into a complex field of eroding discrete and epic fragments and into tangible forces now thought expressive of nature's entropic power, not of God's. Accumulating specific instances of monumental and ephemeral phenomena contributed to the formulation of pictorial constructs coincident with the paradigms of duration and process simultaneously being created by science.[1]

Ironically, one of the explorers' abiding cultural legacies was a detached interest (that is, one freed of the possessive pronoun) turned primarily upon uncultivated individualities—upon the formulation of descriptions of a congeries of undomesticated particulars, each recognized as living independent of man in the long life of the planet. To state it differently: The scientific explorer sanctioned a noninterfering posture subversive of

CONCLUSION: THE REALIZATION OF NATURE

human autonomy by the very fact that he chose to employ a "neutral" or nominal style for recording and getting into natural processes. This unmanipulative or antipsychological aesthetic was strengthened by the Enlightenment's dyspeptic view of the petty actions of men in comparison with the grandiose, heroic, and liberated performances of nature.[2]

Increasingly under attack by epistemological skepticism, however, was the notion that the writer or artist ever could—even if he was properly wary of the Idols—produce an authentic duplication, a verifiable equivalent to the complexities of external reality, not merely his idiosyncratic or otherwise conditioned imitation of it. The factual travel account, perhaps better than any other genre, exposes this quandary. As long as the object was unstudied and hence in some sense new (that is, heretofore not discovered or incorporated into a general design), it defied and challenged by its sudden difference any idea preexisting in the mind of the beholder. However (as d'Entrecasteaux laments in the passage quoted at the beginning of this section), when all great land masses have been sighted and trod, when the era of primary discoveries comes to a halt, the belief in the possibility of reproduction or congruity is seriously undermined.[3] In point of fact, one must again relearn the world.

In short, the problem with novel content qua content, as with external things qua things, is that after marvelous items have once been found they become only a springboard for commonplace, secondary associations. By the same token, in order for the matter reckoned appropriate to a literature and an art of fact to be conveyed stylistically as through a window unstained by subjectivity, both its aesthetic and its informational value must be contingent on the experiential freshness of that matter. Persuaded of the importance of the natural object on a variety of fronts, the eighteenth-century travelers engaged in the intense activity of discovering new landscapes, paying heed to the multifarious appearances of the earth in the fashion of their great contemporaries who were chronicling the manners of men: the antiquarian historians Ludovico Antonio Muratori, Curne de Sainte-Palaye, Edward Gibbon, and Bernard de Montfauçon.

Although the scientific travel account as codified during the Enlightenment remained vital in the age of the industrial revolution, during the opening decades of the nineteenth century its synthetic merits were increasingly disunited and two other types of narrations achieved ascendancy: the purely entertaining travel book and the instructive guide (the ancestor of the Baedeker volumes). This division occurred simultaneously in scientific tracts; pleasure was no longer inextricably tied to instruction. Utilitarian navigations by sea or air and pragmatic overland explorations, which had managed to both inform and delight during the preceding period, were overshadowed by the sentimental, self-projecting, or autobiographical journey, tour, or circuit. Descendants and continuators of the aboriginal seekers after the Picturesque, the new tourists felt the landscape without precisely seeing it.[4]

Eugène Fromentin's lyrical *Un été dans le Sahara* (1856) and *Une année dans le Sahel* (1858) succinctly illuminate the gulf between the earlier generation of explorer-scientists, with their "passion for discoveries," their quest after facsimile and document, and the later generation of poetic travelers. The motivating desire is no longer the Baconian one to "communicate to all" the wondrous details of nature (as Cassas and Sonnini put it), but rather "a certain manner of seeing, of feeling and of expressing what is personal to me and has not ceased to be mine." Fromentin, in advance of Baudelaire's, "Invitation to a Voyage" brilliantly analyzes the self-reflexive significance illustrated travels might hold in the second half of the nineteenth century. Places once fraught with novelty have long since changed and lost their mystery, thereby disenfranchising those who would describe rather than recount, who would minutely study and reproduce external nature. While giving tongue-in-cheek praise to the descriptive school of literalistic genre painters who felt the need "to imitate everything" (Gérôme and the *Orientalistes*), Fromentin cautions that the language that speaks to the eyes is not the same one that addresses the soul.

Fromentin's choice of the epistolary mode flouts the trend toward informative notation as it simultaneously subverts the superficial meanderings of the eighteenth-century Picturesque. His letters and accompanying sketches were not jotted daily or on the spot because, thus composed, they would have lost the quality of being "refracted images" or the "distillation of things." Noted down after a lapse of months or even years, without recourse to anything but personal memories and in a genre favorable to "condensed recollections," this style of narration confirms that we possess of nature only what our sensibilities, not our senses, furnish. Fromentin was therefore constrained to seek truth outside external resemblance. In his account the conviction of perfect sincerity is coupled with the unqualified preeminence of the imagination. Time has selected the souvenirs; "a grain of art has slipped in." Gone too is the value placed on the unaltering scientific gaze and the standardized scientific method that insisted all observations be reported in full and naturalistic detail, that was predicated on repeatable verbal and pictorial statements capable of moving across linguistic frontiers, and that provided (in the words of Joseph Banks) "one common measure which speaks universally to all mankind." Instead, the new internal eye is "faceted," and its prisms are brought to bear not on objects but on sensations experienced in depth and in evolution during the course of a long voyage. The new method does not focus but, in musical fashion, transposes so that "frequently emotion supplants the image":

What good is it to multiply remembrance, to accumulate facts, to run after unedited curiosities, to weigh oneself down with nomenclatures, itineraries and lists? The external world is like a dictionary; it is a book filled with repetitions and synonyms: many equivalent words for the same idea. Ideas are simple, forms are multiple; it is for us to choose and summarize. As for famous spots, I compare them to rare, rare locutions, a useless luxury of which human language can deprive itself without losing anything. . . . All is in all. Why is the quintessence of the Algerian countryside contained in the small space framed by my window, and can I not hope to see the Arab people filing under my gaze along the great highway or in the meadows that border my garden? Here, as usual, I trace a circle around my house, I extend it as far as needed so that the entire world is more or less contained within its circumference. . . .

Thus Fromentin raises anew the issue of point of view. Both as artist and as writer he selects his vantage. Now, however, the procedure has become entirely productive, even spiritual, a mental process of indicating things by ellipses to make the spectator imagine that which he no longer needs to see. It is a method, as Fromentin's British contemporary Edward Lear remarked, of imbibing the general forms of a place and then disengaging from it personal impressions.[5]

Paradoxically, as Fromentin intimates, the example and the explicit purpose of the nonfiction travel account predicated on the voluntary subservience of art to nature may be held in some degree responsible both for driving the artist or writer away from the optical riches of external nature into a created world of the "artificial ideal"—toward the Scylla of Baudelaire's solipsistic, dreaming hashish eater, incapable of the externally directed civic action of the wine drinker—and conversely for forbidding him to wander up and down in the bodiless void, near the Charybdis of his sightless fancy.[6]

If new earth formations and dramatic effects began to vanish or turn humdrum, the preeminence of the scientific explorer, too, was challenged by an itinerant band of wanderers, as Fromentin suggests. The transformation of travel with a purpose into the ideal of life as a game parallel to the activity of endless voyaging, that is, the continual psychic movement toward an ever-receding existential goal, is already discernible during the 1790s.

Chateaubriand's untrammeled roamings, however, still imply that passage entails the actual traversing of physical space. The Romantic quest ultimately leads, not unidirectionally out into the blank plains, dense forests, or nebulous skies of a beckoning or unknown land, but back into the tangled self.[7] Yet it was the importance of scientific exploration—seen as another form of the experimental method—that it foreshadowed and even legitimized the Romantic mania for contextual and stylistic innovation. The discoverers' unimpeded freedom to penetrate outer barriers could be metamorphosed by a sleight of hand into the justification for autonomous fabrications, a kind of imaginative trespassing beyond established norms or borders. Formal originality and phantasmagorical subject matter represent a transplanting of the natural to the sphere of the artful, a transmutation of robust external phenomena precipitated out of aesthetic matter as tangible chimeras to stock a created universe.[8]

All levels of society were engrossed by the spectacle of cosmic energies harnessed in Franklin's lightning rod, Volta's battery, and Mesmer's baton. Below the sphere of stellar effluvia lay the fugitive gases revealed by Lavoisier and Priestley and the exquisite crystal structures exposed by Romé de l'Isle.[9] Further, the Baconian injunction to observe, amplified by the Enlightenment, was predicated on visible action, on the propension to "establish and extend the power and dominion of the human race itself over the universe." However, it was the unabated activity of scientific expeditions, sponsored by European academies from the 1760s on, that turned the Lord Chancellor's utopia into concrete reality.[10]

The illustrated travel account was the scientific backbone of the formulation of "plain" approaches to nature, the studious ocular investigations that extended well into the nineteenth century. Unlike the wholly Picturesque tour or diary of the alienated and exiled wanderer, who preferred graceful or highly wrought apologias for a retiring sensibility's being in the world, the nonfiction relation is frankly structured. A "plain-speaking" methodology, in contrast with the inventive overlayering "styles" of the fine arts, flexibly corresponds to the characteristics of the object falling under its perusal.[11]

Art as scientific language, as limpid and democratic medium for the transcription of ipseity, does not self-expressively alter the pure presence of the properties it remands. In the latter half of the eighteenth century, the work of art—whether poetry or painting—approached the status of tangible embodiment exhibiting a reciprocal resonance between mind and thing, not just the condition of idealized imitation of a distant divine or a normative aesthetic model. Impelled by students of natural history, artists were induced to seize the world out there, to grasp *natura naturata*.[12] A logical outgrowth of the Baconian conviction that the external world is the real world and that our senses, when trained, can provide a replica of it—especially as words move closer to things—was the circumstance that art could for a brief moment be regarded as the crown of science. No longer a handmaiden, it was an equal partner in the great undertaking of visual discovery. By this felicitous alliance, art was liberated from its derisory consortment with empty fancying and was elevated to the task of picturing reality.[13]

Although Wordsworth predicted at the beginning of the nineteenth century that the imaginations of the artist and the scientist would meld, his prophecy did not materialize along Baconian lines. The longed-for fusion between these common seekers of connections between "particular parts" and

CONCLUSION: THE REALIZATION OF NATURE

"general nature" never came about in the form of transparent mirroring, largely because the language of science during the course of its development became increasingly opaque to the uninitiated (that is, increasingly quantified and mathematical, and hence qualitatively nonmimetic). Sadly, the disciplines that had been visibly accessible to a broad spectrum of eighteenth-century readers precisely because of their sensuous empiricism were judged around 1800 to be paradigms of desiccated abstract knowledge. As Chateaubriand unequivocally asserts in his *Génie du christianisme* (1802), science—unlike religion—dries up the heart and removes the enchantment from nature.[14]

At bottom, the "classical" or "plain" methodology of the scientist, his apparent commitment to cool observation and measured transcription, is at one with a basic structural tenet of Neoclassical painting: that the visible is amenable to radical, even puristic, articulation through the procedure of partition. *Trompe l'oeil* object and external thing refer to one another by means of a style that excludes all incertitude. Further, the insertion of such painted replicas of reality forces the spectator to explore close up the surface of the canvas. In the nominal mode, each portion of an aggregate is made visibly distinct; its anatomy is coterminously dissected and lucidly displayed.[15] The traditional connection between such an analytical style and certain literary genres devoted to the transmission of sequences of events (such as the history, the memoir, the scientific *compte-rendus*, and the factual travel account) is patent. Indeed, the Neoclassical style may be termed the natural history of art.

Verulam's insistence on clarity and distinctness in language gave rise to systems devoted to relocating the universal in the concrete. Important linguistic developments occurred during the seventeenth and eighteenth centuries precisely because of the utilitarian requirement for an invisible or unobtrusive idiom. The discovery of a plenitude composed of heterogeneous parts dictated the use of parataxis for recording. Thus armed, writers and artists rose to meet the flood of incoming data. In the case of Classicism *redivivus* in the late 1770s and the 1780s, the pull of accurately noting down facts—whether in contemporary, ancient, or natural history— was a device for embodying abstractions, making them present and alive. Though the tragedies of Corneille and Racine prefigure a type of later stilled action characterized by an atmosphere of separation comparable to the isolating procedures of modern scientific experimentation, they still operate discursively. Passions are juxtaposed and analyzed as if in a vacuum, with no disturbing, extraneous factors allowed to mar their pure and simple exposition within a rationally constructed space. To be sure, Racine's elevated tragedies consist of a few clearly interrelated events unobtrusively manipulated to reveal what moves men's hearts.[16] But by the late eighteenth century it is not the autonomous human actor woven into a narrative who alone dominates the compressed foreground. Natural philosophers and explorers ensured that the heroic relics of nature increasingly and singly occupied a shallow stage that brought occurrences up close. This shift—both in human and natural affairs—was based on an acute sense of irreducible and individual presence. A far greater number of phenomenal things existed (because they were intellectually and perceptually assimilated) than before—things that had been replicated in utterable and paintable images.

This hypothesis helps in some measure to situate the wide gamut of naturalistic elements—precipitated out, not organically melded—discoverable in Jacques-Louis David's major history paintings of the 1780s. David's plain style is identical to the nominalist mentality of the crystallographer laboring during the waning years of the *ancien régime*. Not only does he paratactically and antithetically isolate—as under a bell jar—the discontinuous figures which we must work to add up into a unitary aggregate, but by means of the inclusion of myopically rendered arresting cracks, fissures, and lithic surroundings he anchors them in a tangible moment of the historical continuum materially captured in paint. To enhance a sense of immediacy with respect to the beholder, to be convincing as to the verisimilitude and "objectivity" of the pictorial statement in his major history paintings of the 1780s, David deliberately avoids stylistic variations, conspicuous or blatant formal touches, in order to convey through stone-by-stone reconstruction a pristine specimen of ancient life. His is an instrumental, optical language—building by accretion—that aims at transparency, the concealing of manner, to transmit matter. (The changed atmosphere of the new public Salon—as opposed to the traditional aristocratic *cabinet* of the connoisseur, collector, amateur, or *curieux*—in which David's works were displayed also served to turn his paintings into physical objects viewed in a neutral "deflated" space, much like the rock sample "democratically" studied in the laboratory.)

From another vantage, that of social history, scholars have suggested that one deeply ingrained reason that helped make the academic system the natural pattern of organization for high culture, particularly in France, was that Classicism had been the predominant cultural mode or expressive tool of society since the late seventeenth century. The formulation of a *goût* or an *esprit classique* was, in part, one of the academies' first significant by-products, and it was maintained as the prevailing style of French life during the Enlightenment, when the Académie des Sciences enjoyed its greatest success. Both in France and in England (remember Bishop Sprat's support for a new form of probative statement expressed in a plain style) it was articulated as a set of rules defining artistic, ethical, linguistic, and philosophical norms; in short, it established a common methodology for analyzing a broad range of topics. Classicism fostered not only an orderly arrangement of data fluidly chained together to forge a unity out of an aggregate, but also a style unadorned by personal exhibitionism. In art as in life, masculine sobriety, balance, and restraint were thought necessary for the new ventures in cooperative data collecting, and, more generally, for the universal and cumulative cognitive advance of mankind.[17] In Neoclassicism, however, the links were broken and the fragments of the composition abruptly confronted each other aphoristically and simultaneously, thus asserting their material autonomy and activity congruent with the probative methodology of the Enlightenment mineralogist or chemist.[18]

All this is by way of saying that the scientifically shaped eighteenth-century mentality, whether evinced in social institutions, in "high" art, in natural-history illustrations, or in certain literary genres, represents a commitment to cloaking ideas with bodies communicated in a mode that suppresses the exhibition of self to reveal the system of the other. In addition to parataxis or partition, the nominal or operative style of representation employs the trope of metonymy, that rhetorical device by which contiguous entities can be reduced to the status of exact functions of one another. More pertinent, the name of a part or aspect of a thing is made to stand for the whole. The preoccupation with such charged and juxtapositive contractions distinguished the grammarians' search for a universal hieroglyphic, the natural historians' search for the characteristic essences of organic species bodied forth in their fragmentary particularities, and the artists' (especially the landscapists') search for the deep design of the entire earth pictured in its shattered physiognomies. Hence, as a style free of the showy and obscuring displays of psychological idiosyncracies, Neoclassicism closely approximates the experimental method, namely that exacting vision and toil needed in the unearthing of things. The exploratory technique permits the bold assertion of their individual existence as discrete units.

The nominal mode, of which Neoclassicism is but a late variant, can be identified, then, as a major stylistic tool of the expedition artist-writer bent on being "plain." Depicting natural monuments with fidelity, drawing out nature's divided truths, was concomitant with the suppression of any hint of the toll that making them took on the observer. The penetration of geological formations and of other natural effects dictated that the depths of the perceiver remain inscrutable in the work. Further, nominalism as a mode of entry into the world focused on actual morphological structures deemed concretely "prototypical," as opposed to merely general. The earth's masterpieces, then, entered the pictorial vocabulary by means of a precariously balanced tension between a transparent expression and the disruptive declaration of subjectivity on the part of the self-eloquent specimen.

Not only did the scientist and the explorer render the strange familar by bringing it literally close up in the text, on the picture plane, and into the European consciousness, but together they bequeathed to the nineteenth century the realization that nature should be interpreted historically—

indeed, that this was the only way by which it might be properly understood for itself and in relation to humanity. The interest in merely Picturesque landscapes ebbed almost at the moment of the advent of Davidian ideas. Artists began to paint not just historiated landscapes in the time-honored vein of Claude and Poussin but epic scenes of imposing geological and meteorological phenomena. Imbued by this new attitude, Valenciennes declared that the painter was "the historian of nature" and that no phenomenon—whether witnessed in the Alps, in the Pyrenees, in Asia, or in Africa—was alien to his brush. Each region unfurls "a new physiognomy" and possesses a discoverable "territorial aspect": the searing climate of Egypt, the burnt desert of Syria with its corrosive simoon, the parched plains and watery mirages of Africa described by Bruce and Volney, the glittering crystallizations of Antiparos, and the abrupt rock formations upheaved by earthquakes in Calabria.[19]

The explorers' assiduous chronicling of the gigantic and persistent "war of nature," which was recognized by Erasmus Darwin and which cropped up again in the evolutionary views of his grandson Charles, resulted in the aesthetic outstriding of the ruins of art by those of the earth. Natural history, more even than ancient history, was seen to occupy itself with sublime forces made concrete, with the abstract, remote, or primitive idea of the earth made tangibly present in images evidencing change.[20] In sum: The nominal representation of the varieties of the elemental demonstrated, through minute recreation, specific events and historic facts as important as concrete episodes in the life of Belisarius, Brutus, or the Horatii.

Layers of Earth, Strata of Mind

Was bildet denn Landschaftmalerei, als die grosse, irdische, uns umgebende Natur? Und was ist erhabener, als die Erfassung des geheimnissvollen Lebens dieser Natur?
C. G. Carus

Aux mines de sel de Saltzbourg, on jette, dans les profondeurs abandonnées de la mine, un rameau d'arbre effeuillé par l'hiver; deux ou trois mois après, on le retire couvert de cristallisations brillantes: les plus petites branches, celles qui ne sont pas plus grosses que la patte d'une mésange, sont garnies d'une infinité de diamants, mobiles et

It might appear that a study of the scientifically inspired discovery and gathering of phenomena stands at the antipodes of the Romantic creative enterprise. By the late eighteenth century, in that Ossianic and "Gothick" period of sensibility, there already was a clear sense of literature and art as dealing with energetic states of mind and not mirroring outer objects. With the following generation, the empiricist concern with optical procedures for correct knowledge and the confident delight in visibility was further complicated by an overriding interest in the internal process of conversion. Now, not the object of the material world but the complexities of the productive imagination were difficult to see. As inheritors of the eighteenth-century struggle to fuse the experience of sequence into simultaneity, the Romantics deemed perception to be an essentially personal and inventive effort, a constructive seeing from a particular and transforming point of view. Instead of reduplicating the natural world, the mind dissolved it in order to reformulate it.

Moreover, the notion of mimesis acquired in Romantic theory a heavily derogatory sense understood to mean either thoughtless quotation of preexisting works or unaltered copies taken from the "dictionary" "out there."

CONCLUSION: THE REALIZATION OF NATURE

éblouissants; on ne peut plus
reconnaître le rameau primitif. . . .
Stendhal

The word *art*, which traditionally meant mechanical skill, had already risen in value during the eighteenth century, when the emphasis on reproductive technical dexterity was undercut by the developing estimation for an "original" genius. A potential danger in laying stress on the overwhelming strength of the imagination can be seen in one nineteenth-century tendency to isolate art and to specialize the imaginative "aesthetic" faculty to this one kind of activity, thus weakening the bond forged earlier between the subjective, fancying fine arts and the objective, perceptual sciences. As Condorcet clairvoyantly lamented, much is given up when knowledge becomes relative entirely to man, to his sensations and ideas, and to the world around him only insofar as it can be inferred from these sensations and ideas.

Commercial publishing, on the rise since the late eighteenth century, with its limitless possibilities for mechanical reproduction and the widespread dissemination of information to a mass audience (all part of the initial travel-book boom), stood at the poles of the Romantic conception of a judicious audience of "the cultivated few." Historically, the notion of culture as the total body of the arts, pitted against the standards of capitalist commodities and the marketplace, occurred precisely at the moment when the artist emerged as "a special kind of person," distinctly at odds with an existing world (one that just is). It follows that, within this exclusive milieu, a naturalistic and conspicuously unrearranged denotative art was not in favor. Furthermore, the close connection assumed for didactic purposes to exist in the scientific travel account between image and word, between percepts addressed to the senses and concepts directed to the mind, was anathema to artists and writers interested in the autonomy of their respective arts.

The point of juncture for these disparate activities lay not in illustration but in the process of restructuring experiences. Coleridge and Blake, among other British thinkers fed by the German philosophy of Boehme, Kant, Schelling, and Baader, treasured the reconstitutive powers of the imagination, not the naked inlet of the senses. In an 1815 letter to Wordsworth, Coleridge castigates the "philosophy of mechanism," which strikes death, "cheats itself by mistaking clear images for distinct conceptions," and "idly demands conceptions where intuitions alone are possible or adequate to the majesty of the Truth." And in an 1801 letter to Poole, Coleridge asserts that "deep thinking is attainable only by a man of deep feeling," and that "all Truth is a species of revelation." Percy Shelley's aesthetic doctrines, articulated in the *Defence of Poetry*, come to rest too on the model of the shaping imagination as that capacious faculty crafting tangible expressions of invisible truth. Art is the energetic projection of an individual mind into the world; thus, it behooves one to "imagine intensely." These men, then, fought against the soul's domination by what they took to be an automatic procession of dead (that is, unregenerated) outer things: the pernicious bequest of Newtonian transmaterialism, Lockean empiricism, and, we might add, unimpeded traveling. The volitional, outward-directed clarity of the scientific gaze was countered by a dimming of merely physical sight to concentrate deliberately on the organic faculties of the mind, on Chateaubriand's "chiaroscuro truth" lodged within.[21] Already with the 1800 edition of the *Lyrical Ballads*, Wordsworth was committed to the view of self-projection, to the importance of recollection in tranquility. The "inward eye" of the Lake Poet, the visionary acuity of Blake, the "secondary imagination" of Coleridge, and the superior intellect of Chateaubriand that knows when to shut its eyes all variously represent a reaction to the cult of popular science and the tendency to equate optical discovery and the correct recording of visual experience—the first step in the creative process—with the end result of art.[22]

In France, the seeds of dissent had been sown by one of the most ardent exponents of the sciences. Diderot, by forging a compelling image of the autonomous genius, held that the true creator could not be molded by circumstances or observations. Simultaneously, Rousseau raised severe doubts concerning the desirability of scientific and artistic progress. Together they laid the foundations for the attacks against reason grounded in nature that emerged during the revolutionary period. Yet Diderot, as a biological vitalist and a student of Spinoza and Leibniz, was aware how psychology and physiology pass into each other. Nature is intimately related to the creating individual because they are both in process. This intersection of self with world at the particulate level was not to be the case with Chateaubriand. He journeyed to the Holy Land as pilgrim and knight with Bible, Gospels, and Crusades in hand, as Lamartine picturesquely commented. It was the "poetic," subjective testimony of the *Itinéraire* rather than of the more factual *Mémoires d'outre-tombe*—composed by a man in exile from European civilization and thus forced into confronting "the other"—that would take root in the following generation.

Alphonse de Lamartine's *Voyage en Orient* (1832–33), a rich welter of "landscapes and reflections, " is a salient example. Consciously following Chateaubriand's precedent, Lamartine brought back "profound impressions" in his heart and "lofty and terrible lessons" in his mind. What is important is not the clear-eyed recording of phenomena stripped of human history but a study of comparative conventions and cultures—"that intimate education of thought by thought, by places, events, by juxtapositions of epochs with epochs, mores with mores, beliefs with beliefs, none of this is lost for the voyager, poet or philosopher; these constitute the rudiments of his future poetry and philosophy. . . ." On the banks of the Jordan, Lamartine was incapable of resisting the impression of sadness and horror which the surrounding volcanic terrain and corrugated mountains of Judea inspired. Whether he was at Jericho or toiling toward the temples of Baalbek, it was the grave, the sad—nature lulled or startled by human passage—that arouses in Lamartine a "melancholy withdrawal." Evident in his narrative are both a sense of self-discovery and one of

CONCLUSION: THE REALIZATION OF NATURE

private discovery, not a sense of a first discovery made once and for all valid for public consumption. To that end, Lamartine frankly admits that he is not attempting to describe the thousands of astonishing and wonderful objects that strike his eye at Baalbek: "I am neither sculptor nor architect; I do not know the name given to stones in such and such a place, in such and such a form. I speak inadequately an unknown tongue;—but that universal language which the beautiful addresses even to the most ignorant eye, that the mysterious and the antique speaks to the soul and to the philosophic spirit, I understand it; and I never understood it as strongly as in this chaos of marbles, shapes, enigmas which litter this marvelous court. . . ." In the same poetic quest, Théophile Gautier undertook frequent journeys, first to Spain, then to Algeria (sent by Louis-Philippe), and subsequently to Turkey, Russia, and Egypt. His distinctively individual picturesque voyage to Algeria (1845) and his *Souvenirs* of the Nile deeply marked Maxime du Camp's sensual reminiscences stemming from a trip to Egypt, in 1849, accompanied by Flaubert. Common to all their musings is an inchoate feeling of melancholy, not an ocular joy in reaching out of the self in exploration. Eugène Delacroix experienced a nameless sadness while gazing upon the "immense and uninhabited" plain at Reddat in Algeria, whose stillness was punctured only by the intermittent cries of frogs and other animals; Maxime du Camp underwent it in the country of the pharoahs, that "dying land whose life is sapped little by little."[23]

In opposition to those English and French writers who operated on the assumption that the imagination was an untutored faculty, qualified not only to appropriate nature's powers but to rival them, stands the thought of the younger Goethe. On sketching trips made to the Harz mountains during his Weimar years (1775–1786), Goethe was apparently content to record the superiority of natural productions over those of art.

In Germany, Goethe's youthful copyist stance with respect to natural phenomena was systematically eroded by the dissemination of Friedrich Schelling's *Naturphilosophie* and of Kantian and (especially) Fichtean philosophy. According to the results of the search for the unconditional or last ground of reality of our knowledge, nature is but the product of the ego; it exists merely as a willed limit set by the thinking self. For the Schelling of the *Naturphilosophie* it is the mind that builds up a comprehensive picture of reality. The gulf stretching between the radically perceptual and the constructivist view can be gauged by comparing Goethe's need to "cling to one or a few objects, or see them from all sides and to become one with them" with Heinrich Heine's patently subjective memory of a *Harzreise* taken in 1824. In an occasionally ironic account redolent of Wertherian references, mountains, fir forests, and "bizarrely shaped" clouds are constrained to bend to a musical analogy, to blend harmoniously yet silently with the blue sky and green earth. For Heine, nature creates in the manner of a great poet (not the reverse) and knows how to produce the most sublime effects with a minimal number of elements. Goethean morphological particularity is replaced by "sun, trees, flowers, water, and love." The inclusion of pathos highlights the dependence of physical phenomena on human intervention, the slighting of visual for psychological fact. Without love in the heart of the beholder, Heine declares, "the sun is only so and so many miles in diameter, and trees are useful for heating, and flowers will be classified according to their pistils, and water is wet."[24]

From such literary evidence we may infer that the rise of an internalized landscape is, in part, an unbalanced reaction against the hegemony of the external. The discrepancy between an overwhelming and complex environment and the increasingly problematic will or capability of mirroring it must surely have contributed to the desire of remaking reality mark by mark. The struggle to reproduce an infinite and mutable nature, one that could not be dominated in its panoramic totality or captured aspect by aspect through the mimicking force of one's pen, points to a search for structural congruities between mind and matter. On one hand, the interiorization of images of vastness in the Romantic consciousness heralds a focal shift away from the immensity of outer space to an exploration of inner deeps. On the other hand, the emphasis on the creative imagination offers an architectonic analogy between the tiered mental faculties (building upward from sensible perceptions) and the physical world (actively subsuming, while retaining, its lower forms).[25] Both processes are replicated in the material formation of a work of art stroke by stroke, layer by layer, pigment by pigment.

Although Wordsworth, Lamartine, and Heine may sometimes have felt constrained to shut out strange beauties in order to heed the murmur of the invisible soul, Blake and Coleridge demanded relentless accuracy in creative works. As Mary Shelley warns, "invention, it must be humbly admitted . . . can give form to dark, shapeless substances, but cannot bring into being the substance itself." The greatest Romantic poetic and artistic productions are distinguished by the concreteness of their detail, by the self-sufficient coherence, the discoverable logic, and the integrity of their invented world—by, precisely, their paradoxical truthfulness. William Hazlitt's *Essays on Reynolds' Discourses* (1814–15) are especially revealing on this score. Hazlitt castigates the erstwhile president of the Royal Academy for urging the student artist to give himself up to the non-sensuous, the abstract, the "empty void of his imagination": "Stripping nature of substance and accident, he is to exhibit a decompounded, disembodied, vague ideal nature in her stead, seen through the misty veil of metaphysics, and covered with the same fog and haze of confusion. . . ."[26]

It is in this specific context of prizing the phenomenal that the factual travel account was to exert its most decisive and positive aesthetic influence. The uncompromising Romantic valuation of the exquisite uniqueness of a myriad of natural forms lovingly reinvented, its incorporation of the substantial with the symbolical, its embracing of radical individuality both

CONCLUSION: THE REALIZATION OF NATURE

in the concrete expression of the work of art and the living of a life, return us to the quest for particulars that was the fundamental motivation informing exploration. Even the pantheistic insinuation of self into terrestrial manifestations through sympathy (as practiced by Runge), or the division of nature into materially expressed polarities of solid and impalpable, dark and light (as achieved by Constable and Turner), or the collapse of antitheses such as the sublime and the grotesque, the gigantic and the diminutive (as embarked upon by Victor Hugo)—all these strivings toward completeness are based on the desire to create tangible signs for natural processes as they are encountered. They embody diverse attempts to discover an aesthetic capable of signifying artificially the totality of the natural universe fabricated without neutralizing its constituent components.[27]

For its first interpreters, the term *romantic* did not denote that which was wildest in the terrain but rather that which was most particular. Both the French word *romanesque* and the English word *romantic* were employed to designate idiosyncratic places, sites, aspects of the land. These, unlike the *pittoresque* or Picturesque, did not speak to the eyes alone but also poetically engaged the soul.[28]

A small but telling selection of images will serve to suggest the afterlife of the lone and striking natural masterpiece in the landscape painting of the early nineteenth century. A good point of departure is Caspar David Friedrich's preoccupation, recorded in a series of sepia drawings dating from ca. 1801–02, with the rude and solitary icons of Rügen. At the turn of the century this island was a great drawing card, as travel literature shows. The moving encounter with the enigmatic Stubbenkammer and Arkona stimulated an abiding interest in specific landmarks such as isolated oak trees, gaping chasms, and ambiguous prehistoric cairns, the standard items of Friedrich's repertory.

Friedrich's monological involvement with natural wonders centrally positioned on the canvas and exerting an immediate impact on the beholder seems conditioned by the illustrated voyage. Consequently, his attentiveness to individual rock morphologies should not be interpreted in the exclusively religious sense that has become customary among contemporary German scholars, whereby every particularity is wrenched to conform with a parable of spiritual loss and redemption.[29] Friedrich's contemporary G. H. Schubert, in *Ansichten von der Nachtseite der Naturwissenschaft* (1808), points toward a surer path of decipherment. In a vision of Genesis that is reminiscent of Maillet's cosmic musings, Schubert conjures up an image of the earth as a gigantic alembic. When the waters of the prehistoric ocean began their retreat, the will to form or to actualization (*Bildungstrieb*) of our planet was first articulated in highly individualized mountain peaks; these were the waves of that primitive and chaotic sea become rigid. Today's unyielding masses once belonged to an animating flood and still testify to realities formerly obtaining on our ancient globe. The chalk cliffs of Rügen are no exception. Although by comparison with porphyry outcrops they are of a fairly recent date, these calcinations appear like "lofty tombstones of a sunken colossal world, with megalithic graves [presiding] over it." Aptly, Schubert cites Friedrich as having best captured the character of such archaic and artless fragments.[30]

The close connections between art and science, between attentive scrutiny and travel, and between natural history and a "speaking" terrain are reflected in Carl Gustav Carus's remarks on the marvels of Rügen, which he first visited in 1819. In the *Neun Briefe über Landschaftmalerei* (1831), Carus, like Schubert before him and Friedrich (whom he met in 1817) even earlier, employs the visual method of comparative geomorphology in order to record the singularity of the site. Whereas basaltic mountains exhibit only lines that strive steeply toward the heights, "here everything moves toward the broad and the flat." Whereas Schubert descried the lingering legacy of the cliffs' initial formation, Carus perceives the long-term effects of change and erosion. Rain causes deep furrows to splinter the surface of the glistening white chalk fields, exposing innumerable flintstones—a circumstance minutely attended to in Friedrich's painting of two years later. This ensemble of traits taken together produces the unusual "physiognomy" of the region, augmented by the presence of huge granite blocks driven ashore by powerful currents flowing from Sweden.[31]

Carus's influential letters on landscape painting (composed between 1815 and 1824) called for a deep inquiry into the process of nature, showing that passion for research into its mutable language that distinguished his countryman and contemporary Alexander von Humboldt. Emulating the great explorer with his summons for "paintings of the life of the earth," he followed in the footsteps of the late-eighteenth-century artist-scientist who studied plants like a botanist, optical effects like an "electrician," and, above all, rocks like a geologist. His pragmatic interest in basalt outcrops took tangible shape in the "geognostic" landscapes he painted in the wake of a trip to the Riesengebirge. It was on those heights that Carus, like Goethe in the Harz Mountains, became convinced of the importance of capturing the material life of nature in landscape paintings. His conviction that an informed approach to the significant behavior of phenomena was necessary for profound insight—bolstered by his readings in Humboldt's *Physiognomik der Gewächse (1800)*—found its way into the *Überlegungen in dem Aufsatz, Andeutungen zu einer Physiognomik der Gebirge* (begun ca. 1820), which would eventually constitute part of the *Neun Briefe*.[32]

Many motifs initially introduced in eighteenth-century voyage literature are alive in the pages of Carus's manifesto. First and foremost is the theme of the life states of the earth as it is, not as a projection or personification. Carus employs the vitalist language of hylozoism when he defines the landscape artist's task as that of seizing "the secret life" of nature. Mountainous terrain "speaks distinctly," declaring the "history" of the land as bodied forth in expressive dispositions and specific configurations: "Firm ground, with all its various manifestations, such as boulder and mountain and valley and plain, still and moving waters, airs and clouds, with their myriad effects, these are, as nearly as possible, the forms in which the life of the earth announces itself, a life of such immeasurability that men hardly dare recognize or count it as existence. . . ." Carus emphasizes that the cultivation of such a perceptive, scientific gaze does not come easily. The eye must be rigorously "trained" to observe phenomena not as "arbitrary, indistinct, lawless, and, therefore, senseless" apparitions of the "diversity of substance." Landscape painters in the past, wallowing in scientific ignorance and conventionalized routine, had succumbed, for example, to depicting the highly individualized contours of ridges in such a way that "barely any trace remained of their peculiarly characteristic figures." Preserving the likeness and dignity of nature meant not just the limning of its grandiose aspects, such as alpine regions, storms at sea, penumbrous forests, active volcanos, and springing waterfalls. Pressing his point, Carus encourages the artist not to neglect the quiet and simple vitality of the earth enunciated in a gentler, less obtrusive organic speech.[33]

Carus, as a probing investigator of natural history, like Johann Christian Dahl, Karl Blechen, Ludwig Richter, and Johann Heinrich Ramberg, is bent upon making a region's osteology the basis for descriptive sincerity in landscape art. Yet even Friedrich's patently symbolic or allegorical work evinces the notation of the idiosyncratic morphologies of boulders, mountains, and singular rock fragments, based on the close study of natural forms and forces. Friedrich was open to the lure of primitive material substances, although he painted ascetically by purging the oil medium of any physicality. This formal fascination was based on a fact proved incontrovertibly within the pages of the nonfiction travel accounts: that endurance is inscribed hieroglyphically in matter's very grain. Civilized man, as the epitome of the impotent and the impermanent, is obliged by Friedrich to confront schematically, and not interact with, unpeopled strata that constantly defy his powers of penetration. There is no meeting point or possibility for dialogue established between the enclosed self and the charged fragment located out "there." For Friedrich the numbing and self-sufficient drama of landscape is one to which the human being is only marginally juxtaposed.[34]

That the earth speaks with a powerful voice, even through layers of silt, was especially evident in the case of the prehistoric mound of compacted soil or rock. The theme of primitive cairns, popular with the Dresden circle of Romantics, was an important aftermath not just of the "discovery" of Rügen but of the entire eighteenth-century "ruinist" tradition of mouldering memorials. Retaining a sense of the artless and the numinous, they functioned in the paintings of Friedrich and Carus as potent relics, lonely stubs embodying a particular moment of natural evolution. In them the hand of the artificer was seen to defer again to the ground's gifts.[35]

The survival down to the modern period of dolmens, menhirs, kistvaens, and barrows stemming from an era in advance of the first great civilizations demonstrated that in nature the sculptural was often wed to the tectonic. Indeed, their forms originated in the same myth: stones springing oracularly out of the soil. Thus, Herder's aesthetic endorsement of crude markers, voiced in the *Älteste Urkunde des Menschengeschlechts* (1774), is based on their being not symbols but incarnations of things themselves, the earliest wholly material monuments. As such, they appear not only in German paintings of the early nineteenth century but in sculptural and architectural projects as well.[36] By the very fact of the medium that architecture is forced to employ, as Arthur Schopenhauer was to comment derisively, it cannot escape the inert qualities of brute stuff from which it is fashioned. Anachronistically defining the primary properties of physical substance as unreactive weight, density, rigidity, and hardness—bereft of the *Form-trieb*—Schopenhauer states that it is perforce incapable of embodying the spiritual. According to his scheme, architecture, like the fragments of the earth from which it is constructed, concretely pictures the raw condition of a brute and unregenerated world.[37]

The notion that an unretouched terrain and a "natural" or naturalized architecture were mutually enhancing, creating a total physical environment, was another legacy left by the travel narratives. These relations fostered admiration for monolithic and colossal blocks, which were valued for their historical testimony and their personalized physiognomy—attributes dependent upon their being discovered still rooted to the site.

Paradoxically, a vivid awareness of the colossal mound of indistinguishable earth lurks behind the gigantic and classicizing sculptural projects submitted for the competitions held at the Institut National from the time of the French Revolution until 1830. Antoine-Chrysostôme Quatremère de Quincy, as a student of ancient Egypt, gave the theory its formal enunciation in the *Encyclopédie méthodique*. He points to the evocative ambiguity of tumuli offering an exact simulacrum of natural buttes, hills, and a host of other elevations scattered almost universally throughout the lands of antiquity.[38] François Rude testifies to the vitality of this conception in the second version of his *Napoleon awakening to Immortality* (1845, Louvre), in which Bonaparte, draped in the cloak he wore at Marengo, is shown starting from the abrupt basaltic cliffs of Saint Helena.[39]

It is the conjunction of unhewn monument with sublime scenery that most clearly exhibits the debt to voyage literature. Napoleon was thought a particularly appropriate figure to station amid the giants of nature. The *Magasin Pittoresque* (1841) offers the following detailed report, contributed by the Swiss artist Rodolfe Töppfer, concerning the celebrated Napoleon of Mont-Blanc. Some 10 years earlier, a traveler from Lyon had noticed the striking resemblance of the peaks (viewed collectively from the rear slope of Mont Salève at sunset) to the invincible conqueror: ". . . the closed eye, the nose, the requisite pallor of the face, and I know not what solemn and grandiose repose completed the illusion. Certainly, there is something which grips the imagination in this accident of one colossus impersonating another. . . ." The same journal also communicates the vogue for erecting a "simple stone," a "massif," to the memory of the incomparable leader, an honorable "pendant" to the austere slab on Saint Helena attesting to the transitoriness of human glory.[39] Long after his death, nothing seemed more apposite to Napoleon's historic stature as indomitable hero than the lonely singularities of an enduring, "suffering" nature. Aptly, these were the same rugged wonders Napoleon himself had admired in 1791, while still a young lieutenant. Quartered at Valence, he climbed one of the highest peaks of the Drôme; later, sequestered in the forest of Mortefontaine, he strolled among its rocks.[40]

David d'Angers's lifelong pursuit of the physiognomies of his renowned contemporaries best illuminates this continuing aesthetic conjunction of powerful, history-shaping individuals with historic heaps of primitive rock. His *Carnets* afford abundant evidence for the seductiveness to the sculptor of the changing shapes of experience embodied in stone. In 1844, while wandering across the peaks near Barèges, David d'Angers came upon an immense granite boulder. Deeply stirred at its sight, he immediately connected it—as had Quatremère and Eméric David—with archaic memorials: "Thus must have been that of Moses on Mount Nebo. I thought that this monument would suit one of the immortal *montagnards* of the Convention, and the idea came to me to trace the name of Robespierre which I surmounted with a liberty cap, [placing] a star at its summit. Several days later, I saw that a slavish hand had erased this exalted name. . . ." Some 12 years prior to that event, the sculptor had already counseled a bereaved Vendéean to replace the conventional and imitative sarcophagus he had planned to erect to the memory of his father with the eloquent and unmediated reality of a boulder ("*un gros rocher*"). It was logical that, in searching for an objective correlative to match the energy, worth, and substantiality of his illustrious peers, David d'Angers should be driven to appropriate highly individualized mountain fastnesses. These are "beautiful and poetic" only when they furnish large prominent points composed of "jutting or vast rectilinear contours, like gigantic pedestals, so that the human imagination can place on them the statues of heroes or of beings whose perpetuation is dear to it." Their heads "lose themselves in the sky, their country," and the clouds are "at their feet." Again, in the Pyrenees, rendered famous by the accounts of Ramond, David d'Angers spotted a colossal boulder, a veritable socle, awaiting the statue of a great man. In the vicinity of the Cirque at Gavarnie, the strange and chaotic crests suggested the shape of a recumbent effigy, thus enabling the sculptor to dispense with art altogether. The optical match was so perfect that he thought he "beheld the tomb of a great man." As might be expected, only masculine mountains of primary rock engaged his attention, since these quickly dispossess themselves through the evolutionary process of anything that hints at a "soft physiognomy"; "they grow bold, they appear to menace heaven with their needles; they are riddled with torrents, crevasses; yet in this they resemble the dynamic man whose tears inspire respect. . . ."[41]

The French Utopian architects equally pressed into service the language of an animated matter promulgated by the factual travel accounts. The theme of colossal buildings subsiding into earth shares an affinity with sculptural monoliths (natural and artificial) merged with the environment. Claude-Nicolas Ledoux, in the *Cemetery* destined for Chaux (1773–1789), Etienne-Louis Boullée, in the *Temple of Reason* and the *Cenotaph for Newton* (1784), and Jean-Jacques Lequeu, in his mysterious subterranean cities, all displayed a distinct partiality to enormous artifacts resistlessly gliding downward.[42] In their most advanced productions, not only did these "visionaries" favor pure, luminous stereometric bodies—sanctioned by the sciences of astronomy and crystallography—but they were likewise intrigued by the endless fertility and protean metabolism of physical substance before manipulation or fabrication. Most conspicuously, in the *Temple of Reason*, Boullée exploits the visual tension between an underground basement formed of rude boulders and the scintillant perfection of a soaring sphere above. Resembling a radiant crystal towering over its rayless and shapeless matrix (figure 216), this temple pits pellucid formal definition and natural expressiveness against obscure prehistoric chaos. The testament of natural history, of Romé de l'Isle and Dolomieu, also stands behind the ingenious motif of petrified, crystal-laden water spouting from the unadorned planar wall of Ledoux's *Workshop destined for the Fabrication of Salts at Chaux*. The image is inspired—as Stendhal's powerful metaphor of the "crystallization of love" would be—by accounts of descents into mines.[43] Nonetheless, it is Lequeu who most often employs the grotesque and irregular aspects of the earth captured in dim, cavernlike structures. Copious notations accompanying his unrealized projects indicate a persistent interest in the immense diversity of nature's chthonic language. His penchant for congelations, for the rebarbarized decorative "skin" of a building, is related to the larger aesthetic issue illuminated by the travel account, namely the rivalry between the artificial and the natural. This leads him to petrify the flowing furnishings of grottos, gulfs, and labyrinths, the mobile and sometimes even fragile entities constituting the organic and inorganic world. Spurning Quatremère de Quincy's Platonic judgment concerning the "poverty of nature," Lequeu pushed his ocular researches to embrace the smallest minutiae of epidermic detail.[44]

The vogue for subterranean chambers can also be seen in the taste for images of caves; both architecture and painting reflect the antimonies of

CONCLUSION: THE REALIZATION OF NATURE

the highly finished and artificial pitted against the spontaneous and un-refined trials of nature. By association (that is, by a baptism in soil), the artifact achieves a deconventionalization, attaining an unaffected and truthful character that derives from having been cradled in the lap of natural history.[45]

The fusion of the monumental, the artless, and the vital subsisted in England at least since the time of William Stukeley's publication *Stonehenge* (1740), and certainly since Joseph Banks's 1772 discovery of prismatic columns of basalt at Staffa. The primitive prototype continued to play a role in the archaizing conceptions of John Soane and up to and including John Martin's underworld paintings, with their tunnels snaking through abandoned mines.[46]

The sanction given by the factual travel accounts to a genre in which rock, mountain, or cavern is self-justificatory may best be identified in a select group of works by Turner and Constable. During his first visit to Switzerland, in 1802, Turner produced a series of watercolors and oils devoted to capturing the glacial scenery. The *St. Gothard and Mont Blanc Sketchbook* (British Museum), in particular, records his intense dialogue with the summits ringing Chamonix. These are shown as cleft fragments, rents in the ice, or as solitary monoliths witnessed up close. Following Saussure's lead, Turner trained a penetrating and frequently vertical gaze on the imposing aspects and presences of the Alpine world, rendering them with immediacy and acuity. Each item of this frozen region is isolated so that the resulting image becomes an abiding specimen, a heroic survivor or aspect of a specific catastrophe endured by the terrain.[47] In certain late paintings, Turner's archrival Constable also focuses on the natural object as self-contained historical phenomenon, not on a humanized rural milieu. *Hadleigh Castle* (Paul Mellon Center for British Art, Yale University) depicts two hollow towers going down to earth. Borrowing the mode of vision established in the travel account, Constable invests the taller remnant—tellingly stationed in the foreground of the picture plane—with a sudden and powerfully nonhuman presence in relation to the absorbed beholder. The dominating position assigned this witness to the world's past is not owed to the Picturesque rubric of ruinist painting as practiced by Paul Sandby, Thomas Hearne, Michel Angelo Rooker, and Thomas Girtin, which is predicated on establishing a fixed, optimal distance between monument and viewer. On the contrary, the naturalized masterpiece is made dynamically both to rise from and sink into the slope directly before one's eyes, thus unavoidably taking on the stature of a strongly silhouetted butte or hillock seen up close. Viewed as an abandoned monolith "with presence," then, it establishes a direct lineage between one of the greatest nineteenth-century masters of landscape painting and the eighteenth-century seekers after vital truths lodged within a charged particular.[48] The isolation of single embryonic elements continues in Constable's watercolors of two mysterious colossi: *Stonehenge* and *Old Sarum* (Victoria and Albert

Museum). By emphasizing the stones' rudimentary quality and their separateness from any current human affairs, Constable shows himself aware of their profoundly ambiguous character, somewhere between art and nature, between trackless city and pathless site. The appearance of being stranded in a vast, featureless plain, "a desolation," unmistakably incorporates the visual vocabulary of an endless, deserted "sea of ruins." (See figure 208.) Thus, at the close of his career, Constable deliberately concentrated on a "barren," "deserted," "earthy" object, and found it to be irreducible and densely here, unavoidably mired in the living matrix of the world. The local and regional flavor of his earlier art, the "home landscape" surrounding the River Stour, had deepened to a recognition of nature's history.[49]

The nineteenth-century students of nature, then, fell heir to a rich bequest left by the voyagers: the profound apprehension that the Material Sublime must have a local habitation and a specific name.

A further consequence of the illustrated travel account emerges in the increasing pictorial sensitivity to fugitive effects. Expedition scientists amply demonstrated that no contradiction existed between their discipline and high art. Optical experiments conducted the world over to investigate the source of auroras, Brocken Specters, parhelia, mirages, and countless other atmospheric and terrestrial phenomena indicated nature's potential for aesthetic expression. Paradoxically, while artists were differentiating themselves from "mechanical" scientists, the practical works of these natural historians were informed by a high consciousness of beauty and a reaching out to explore the dynamic principles of nature. Their revelation of phenomenal behavior resulted in two modes of representation: as a spectacular visual rhetoric or as a delicate meteorological nuance.

An essential ingredient of surprise and astonishment—evident in the French melodrama of René-Charles Guilbert de Pixérécourt, manifest in the "Byronic" paintings of the young Delacroix, reflected in periodicals and reviews, and crowned by the interest in things exotic during the first third of the nineteenth century—is a rational extension of the eighteenth-century belief that the universe is conspicuously pervaded by stunning forces. Travel reports promoted a view of the explorer in a state of exaltation, living in a heightened reality where hyperbole is a "natural" form of experience; anything less would not only appear inauthentic but banal.[50]

Nonetheless, the transition from Diderot's aesthetics of the interesting and from Mercier's appreciation of "férocité" in nature to a bombastic sublimity in which astounding natural evanescences were fully acted out in art, completely re-presented before our eyes, was accomplished only in the nineteenth century. One can trace in certain British paintings, in particular, the deliberate avoidance of finesse or shading, the forcing of tone, the constant reaching toward the grandiloquent, and vying with the real thought indispensable for the blow-by-blow replication of phantasmagoria.

Turner's youthful cataclysmic history pieces, including *Smiting of the First-Born in Egypt*, *Tenth Plague*, *Destruction of Sodom*, and *Deluge* (Tate Gallery), already exhibit what was to become a lifelong fascination with cosmic spasms expressed hyperbolically to produce wonderment. The detailed portrayal of earthquakes, avalanches, waterspouts, volcanic eruptions, and other temporary convulsions of the earth emanating from the steady fount of travel literature fed Turner's master theme of relentless and omnipresent disaster.[51]

The hallucinatory landscape of feverish effect and mirror surface, however, reached its acme with the theatrical world created by John Martin and the British and American School of Apocalyptics. Martin claimed accuracy for his images of boundless subterranean caverns—verging on the caricaturization of nature's "character"—illuminated by a fiery glare the color of molten lava. His overstated illustrations to Milton's *Paradise Lost* (1824) are filled with exaggerated settings intended to compete with and surpass the explorers' views of quarries, mines, and shafts fitfully lit by torches. Moreover, Martin's obsessive concern for geological change as it related to the popular subject of the Flood was fed by narratives devoted to images of prehistoric mountains and swamps. His interest in the deluge was shared by Soane, Turner, Benjamin West, John Linnell, William Westall, and Francis Danby. Danby's firsthand observation of strong effects amid the high and rocky wastes of Norway, coupled with evidence couched in travelogs, produced the extravagant *Opening of the Sixth Seal* (Tate Gallery).[52]

The elimination of an overdrawn or strained rhetoric and of the last vestiges of solid form (still implicit in the overwhelming material motif chosen by the catastrophists) occurred, in Constable's words, when the artist attended to "the natural history of the skies." When the obduracy of the isolated thing is volatilized, vision embraces the interconnected complexity of light, space, and time expressed physically. The travel account was responsible equally for drawing attention to the sudden fugitive luminous or meteorological occurrence. In short, it was as successful in evoking the particularity of this insubstantial sphere as it had been in presenting a more robust universe.

The preoccupation with the faint, the drifting, the least tangible parts of nature has long been acknowledged to exist in the "fusive" poetry of Shelley, Coleridge, and Keats. Uncoalesced fragrances and floating phantasms form the poetic counterpart to the several theories of mind as subtle matter and matter as etherealized flux current in the eighteenth century. One is reminded of Newton's "electric spirit" and elastic principle and of Lavoisier's gas. It is typical of the dualistic attitude of these authors to blur the phenomenal world with transcendence by suggesting its organic processes.

The staples of the Romantic landscape thus exist within the framework of an eroding or dynamic antithesis; the partitions separating a resisting object are abolished by a permeating ether. As the nineteenth century wore on, both writer and artist placed more emphasis on the fleeting instead of the timeless, further rupturing Cartesian dualism.[53]

Any complex description of terrain that wishes to approximate reality must also include representations of barely perceptible phenomena. Even in the desert, as Vivant-Denon and Burckhardt noted, the crystalline clarity of dawn metamorphoses rapidly into the shimmering heat of a dust-laden atmosphere. At sea, as the Forsters and Hodges showed, gales, waves, clouds, and hazes are among the countless fleeting ways in which nature punctuates each passing moment. The dynamism of constant, conspicuous variation is matched by the graphic animism hidden in the generative particles of matter.[54]

One result of this double perception was that the early-nineteenth-century painter of the weighty and somber singularity could also be the master of the landscape of mist. On numerous occasions throughout his career, Friedrich was drawn to the vaporous. His paintings of fog wreathing an anchor, silently stealing into a valley, obscuring the Riesengebirge, or condensing into northern lights fastidiously record its caliginous powers. It cloaks massifs like a blanket, drips from trees, or hangs disembodied overhead. Its impalpable and achromatic presence enhances the uninhabitedness of Friedrich's world, an enclosed and enclosing domain which man is privileged to observe from without but which—unlike the Enlightenment scientific traveler—he can no longer enter. An especially telling juxtaposition occurs in *Wanderer above a Sea of Fog* (1818, Hamburg Kunsthalle), in which the incorporeal mist is made to mingle with the dense and assertive corporeality of compacted boulders. The formless is coeval with the formed in nature. Only man is alien; his sharply defined black silhouette assumes the geometrical shape appropriate to an artifact.[55]

In France, "delicate use of gray" belongs to its artistic patrimony, to the taste for mists and luminous effects. By the late eighteenth century, however, the *Ossian* forgeries of MacPherson, the fashion for Gothic penumbra, the emanations dear to science and pseudo-science, and above all the balloon ascents had deepened those irradiated Rococo mists.[56]

Just as Friedrich or Runge responded to both the intransigent and the melting features of physical substance, Boullée was inspired by the crystalline clarity and the stability of inorganic forms and by the cloudy shadows playing over them. His theories and projects, formulated in the treatise *Architecture, Essai dur l'art*, reflect the longing to integrate colossal stone monuments with the changeableness and the primitive vitality of natural forces. Typically, Boullée employs an antithetical formula whereby pyramids, truncated towers, and spheres sink into a dry landscape of sand while their summits are surrounded by an incongruously wet atmosphere, more diffuse than Constable's or Turner's clouds.[57] In the *Essai*, Boullée pointedly invokes the *aérostat* because it provides the architect with the requisite image of immensity made tangible and with the real picture of nebular space. The invention of the balloon stands behind his drawing for Newton's cenotaph (ca. 1784) both in terms of its *charliére* shape and in the milky exhalations staining the circumscribed infinity of the *Night* version. Moreover, scientific travel accounts most probably are the source for Boullée's placement of the empty sarcophagus in the interior of the planetarium, like the Pole Star, at the center of "a great plain" or on "a vast sea."[58]

Ledoux's *L'architecture considérée sous le rapport de l'art, des moeurs et de la législation* (1804) contains corresponding divigations on natural effects recorded by voyagers. His landscape descriptions move swiftly from arid deserts, to sunlight mirrored on the ocean's waves, to phosphorescent furrows, to the explosion of thunder, to the vagaries of blazing corruscations deployed against an immense firmament. His experience of fumes, in particular, was garnered not only from balloon excursions but also from the descents into mines—all part of the research he conducted on European saltworks in preparation for the designs of the "ideal" city of Chaux. Ledoux's initial transports concerning quarries quickly became dampened when he learned of their actual state: walls dirtied by "vapors," vaults lost in "clouds" that were "exhaled" by clayey soil, and "thick smoke [that] made figures disappear, by blending them with nocturnal chimeras."[59]

Anne-Louis Girodet-Trioson most closely approximated the condition of being pleasantly involved in dim exhalations. Influenced by the transparencies of de Loutherbourg, the *fantasmagories* of the Belgian balloonist Robertson, and the experience of being "in the midst of the air's waves" recounted by French aeronauts, he succeeded in creating a tenebrous view of the atmosphere seen from above, with its chiaroscuro effects.[60] A marked affinity for the scientific observation of all manner of aqueous meteors is cogently featured in two master paintings of Girodet's youth: *Apotheosis of the French Warriors* (1802, Malmaison) and *Endymion* (1791, Louvre). In these works, fugitive fogs, vapors, dews, and nightly precipitations have their temporality heightened by the sudden incursion of streaking stellar apparitions, gauzy ghosts, phosphorescent lights, and momentary gusts of wind—all observed at close hand and for the first time by the aeronaut. This important source of Girodet's aerial conceptions is also revealed in a series of "portraits-visions" composed much later, which present famous men borne aloft "on clouds." Girodet deliberately borrows

Figure 267
E. L. Boullée, *Cenotaph for Newton: Exterior View*, from *Essai sur l'art*, 1784, Ha, 57, no. 7. Watercolor. Photo courtesy Cabinet des Estampes, Bibliothèque Nationale.

Figure 268
E. L. Boullée, *Cenotaph for Newton: Interior, "Night" Effect*, from *Essai sur l'art*, 1784, Ha, 57, no. 8. Watercolor. Photo courtesy Cabinet des Estampes, Bibliothèque Nationale.

popular imagery found in late-eighteenth-century engravings showing the profiles of illustrious balloonists "swimming" in the atmosphere. Pilâtre de Rozier, Charles, Lalande, Sadler, Garnerin, and Luder were thus honored, surrounded by the very mists and vapors over which they had triumphed.[61] (See figures 161 and 232.)

The peculiarly French artistic heritage that scientifically transforms Rococo sunny haze into a belt of encircling gases extends well past the middle of the eighteenth century. It was not Claude Monet and the Impressionists who discovered the fugitive and the instantaneous. Although Monet undeniably, during the 1870s, rendered nature's effects in a seemingly summary technique congruent with the fleeting motif he selected (a practice not instituted by the illustrated travel acccount), he was the culminator and not the instigator of a tradition that viewed water as variable matter, existing as mobile transparent sheets that eventually condense into droplets of foam or mist.

Broadly speaking, the persistent Gallic interest in unstable aqueous meteors must be distinguished from the more robust English passion for clouds.[62] Although Constable shares in the period's burgeoning concern for meteorology, his devotion to natural science—displayed in the Hampstead *Lectures on Landscape* (1833)—takes a form quite at variance with that of the French artists under review. Constable seems to dismiss Deluc's or Cotte's theory that clouds are the result of constant evaporation, that is, perpetual exhalations streaming from the surface of the earth. Rather, he appears to favor the hypothesis, put forward by Thomas Forster in *Researches about Atmospheric Phenomena* (1813) and by Luke Howard in *Climate of London* (1818–1820), that they are produced by electrical fluctuations within the aerial ocean. The Constablean cloud, as a vehicle to convey the chiaroscuro of nature, is less rarified ascending vapor than churning, evanescent, but indestructible *substance*, compactly present overhead. It lacks the ghostly or gaseous visionariness of the French incarnation.[63]

The late landscapes of Turner, on the other hand, suggest a comparison, precisely in the representation of the vague as physical energy, between the two countries. Whereas Constable portrays nature in the concrete act of becoming (trees are severed, and cirro-stratus clouds scud off the canvas, unimpeded by the frame), Turner spatially insulates his scenery through light. Exploiting the travel account's discovery of the optical power of singular effects, he apotheosizes scintillating luminosity, converting it into a major genre.

Hazlitt's perceptive recognition that Turner's landscapes are full of gossamer colors, or the "picture of nothing and very like," links the British master to a major eighteenth-century scientific polarity, an antithetical formula that underlay the illustrations of nature that were to emerge from the nonfiction travel account: the materialization of spirit and the im-materialization of substantiality. A poem composed by Turner and attached to a painting of London exhibited in 1809 best illuminates this shared persuasion with the French, an affiliation that harks back to joint roots in voyage literature:

Where burthen'd Thames reflects the crowded sail,
Commercial care and busy toil prevail,
Whose murky veil, aspiring to the skies,
Obscures thy beauty, and thy form denies,
Save where thy spires pierce the doubtful air,
As gleams of hope amidst a world of care. . . .

Fume, fog, electric and phosphorescent phenomena, and "tinted steam" belong to the preceding era's view of the atmosphere as a stream of living atoms lost in the vapory distances of an ever-expanding universe.[64] Like Shelley's watery, misty, and ethereal impressions grounded in precise scientific and atmospheric studies, Turner's *Polyphemus* (National Gallery of Art, London) and his paintings from the 1840s of Venetian lagoons and harbors are primarily the record of an aerial and fluid conflict harmoniously resolved through pigment application. This strife "stain[s] the dead, blank, cold air with a warm shade/ Of unentangled intermixture, made/ By love, of light and motion: one intense/ Diffusion, one serene Omnipresence. . . ."[65]

It is as just such a painter of inchoate process or of the nebulous, not of clouds per se, that Ruskin valued Turner over Constable. In *Modern Painters*, Ruskin asserts that contemporary artists are concerned not only with their sensible appearance and objective configuration but also with the effects of obscuring mists and the ephemeral appearance of things glimpsed through the screen of the atmosphere. Indeed, it is the task of the modern landscapist to capture those things that are not only difficult to comprehend but are, in the traditional sense, unpaintable: wind, lightning, refractions, transparencies, cloud shadows: "With these striking differences in color, [the rain cloud] presents no fewer nor less important in form, chiefly from losing almost all definiteness of character and outline. It is sometimes nothing more than a thin mist, whose outline cannot be traced. . . . In fact, it rather partakes of the nature, and assumes the appearance, of real water in the state of spray, than of elastic vapor. . . . They are not solid bodies borne about with the wind, but they carry the wind with them. . . ." Yet there is a deeper opposition at work in Ruskin's unflattering comparison of the two masters, one that again devolves on the contraries of art and nature. Constable's fundamental thesis (declared in his second lecture on landscape) that the painting of natural phenomena might legitimately be regarded as experimental science, that is, involved with "a constant process of learning through close observation of the phenomena in nature," becomes by the time of the last lecture overtly seditious to art precisely on the question of the role of tradition and convention. How could Ruskin, as advocate of the eminently artful Turner (so visibly devoted in his youth to Claude), respond favorably to the revolutionary idea attacking mimesis

Figure 269
A. L. Girodet, *Apotheosis of the French Warriors*, 1802. Oil, 75.8 × 72.4 inches. Photo courtesy Musée de Malmaison, Malmaison-Rueil.

VOYAGE INTO SUBSTANCE

Figure 270
A. L. Girodet, *Sleep of Endymion*, 1793. Oil,
77.6 × 102.4 inches. Photo courtesy
Documentation Photographieque de la
Réunion des Musées Nationaux.

first encountered within the pages of the factual travel account? Constable bluntly states:

> It appears to me that pictures have been over-valued; held up by a blind admiration as ideal things, and almost as standards by which nature is to be judged rather than the reverse; and this false estimate has been sanctioned by the extravagant epithets that have been applied to painters as "the divine," "the inspired," and so forth. Yet, in reality, what are the most sublime productions of the pencil but selections of some of the forms of nature, and copies of a few of her evanescent effects; and this is the result, not of inspiration, but of long and patient study under the direction of much good sense.[66]

The impalpabilities of the English painter of flowing nebulosities were exceeded only by the ineffabilities captured by the American Luminists. The silence and stillness that had once reigned over North American lakes—first extolled by eighteenth-century travelers—took on transcendent overtones in the writings of Thoreau and Emerson. The Quietism pervading the hushed paintings of Fitz Hugh Lane, Martin Heade, and William Kensett protracts the initial experience of explorers lost in the solitudes of the New World.[67]

Travel as Metaphor for Art and Life

The cause of the evil lies, I believe, deepseated in the system of ancient landscape art; it consists, in a word, in the painter's taking upon him to modify God's work at his pleasure, casting the shadow of himself on all he sees, constituting himself arbiter where it is honor to be a disciple, and exhibiting his ingenuity by the attainment of combinations whose highest praise is that they are impossible. . . . The sense of artificialness, the absence of all appearance of reality, the clumsiness of combination by which the meddling of man is made evident, and the feebleness of his hand branded on the inorganization of his monstrous creature, is advanced as a proof of inventive power, as an evidence of abstracted conception; — nay, the violation of specific form, the utter abondonment of all organic and

The long-standing struggle between the acts of nature and those of man were to be resolved in the modern period by the progressive building up, in words or in paint, of a concrete picture of what was in the world. Thus, in literature and in art, there was strong reaction against the exclusive claims of the external object. However, this is only half the story. The early nineteenth century also reveled in the likenesses painstakingly created by Madame Tussaud. Such flawless replicas are as endemic to the period as the puppets or automata celebrated in Heinrich von Kleist's *Über das Marionettentheatre* (1810), a parable on the loss of natural innocence and the discovery of highly self-conscious powers of reflection.[68]

The interest in duplicating the human body in wax or in manufacturing a seamless identity was, like the contemporaneous mania for panoramas, dioramas, or daguerrotypes, predicated on the desire for totally accurate representation. The illusion of actual presence—nature so successfully artifactualized that there was no suspicion of gap—entranced the spectator precisely because it stepped beyond all limits, especially the traditional mimetic limitations of art. Verism as the fabrication of pure facsimile, as "absolute" copy without apparent recourse to invention or to personal mark, was coextensive with the estimation of the creative imagination.[69]

It has been argued that nineteenth-century European culture displayed everywhere the compulsion toward a realistic understanding of the world. However, this designation meant something other than the all-embracing comprehension of nature sought by the voyager who was conditioned by the ideas of the Enlightenment *philosophes*. With the increasing value placed on subjectivity, and with the separation of disciplines formerly considered mutually interdependent wholes, this mode of perception gave

*individual character of object
(numberless examples of which from
the old masters are given in the
following pages), is constantly held
up by the unthinking critic as the
foundation of the grand or historical
style, and the first step to the
attainment of a pure ideal. Now,
there is but one grand style, in the
treatment of all subjects whatsoever,
and that style is based on the
perfect knowledge, and consists in
the simple, unencumbered
rendering, of the specific characters
of the given object, be it man, beast,
or flower. . . .*
John Ruskin

*. . . Je reconnais à tout être sa
fonction naturelle; je lui donne une
signification juste dans mes
tableaux; je fais même penser les
pierres. . . .*
Gustave Courbet

way to differing personal viewpoints of the world as a sum of aspects or fragments seen from the corner of a temperament. The Positivists and the Social Darwinians identified their "realism" with the analysis of natural laws carried out by scientists. In this frame of reference, realism in the natural sciences could still be identified with the "scientific method" that had been developing since Bacon's time for the analysis of natural processes.

For the researcher into the mysteries of natural history, to be a realist meant both to see things plainly, as they really are, and to draw appropriate judgments from this correct apprehension. For the artist or the writer, to be a Realist meant not simply to reproduce landscape in all its manifestations (usually the most ordinary), but also to capture truth in surface appearances (that is, in the complex actuality of the modern social milieu). The aesthetic exigency of truth signified that the beautiful and the ugly were factors of equal importance in the work of art, no matter what "one must be of one's time."[70]

Champfleury, who was among the most astute critics of the Realist school and an apologist for a popular, naive art freed of the impulse to "make pretty pictures" best illuminates this attitude. In the study "Courbet en 1860" and in the Saint-Simonian vision of "Pictures for the Future" from the *Histoire de l'imagerie populaire*, he declares that the landscape appropriate to the nineteenth century is one of industrialization. Certainly this assertion stands at the antipodes of Rousseau's shocked discovery of a stocking factory amid the Alps. The motif of traveling and a hatred for the conventionality of the Picturesque loom large in Champfleury's attempt to entice the painter of *Burial at Ornans* and *Young Girls of the Village Giving Alms* to create vast murals for railroad stations. These frescos were to alleviate the boredom of waiting by depicting the actual movements of urban passengers in tireless transit—"The machine [the train] and the role which it plays in the landscape, is that not sufficient to make a beautiful painting?"

To Champfleury's mind, Gustave Courbet as a "powerful" landscapist is the appropriate artist for this type of modern image-making liberated from traditional symbolism. His characteristic painterly mode is *"forte,"* and thus congruent with the iron physiognomy of the grubbing regions through which courses the "mastodon of iron running along rails, cleaving trees, rocks, leaving behind villages on one side, passing over a village on an audacious bridge, snorting, hissing, sweating; and [then] the arrival of the big crowd, bustling and noisy, stupefied, crying, embracing, who come and go."

The shift underway at midcentury from the discovery of physical space to that of social space, apparent in the Impressionists' paintings of Baron Haussmann's Parisian boulevards as if they were landscapes and in Champfleury's call for the representation of a toiling nature penetrated by an engine carrying displaced city masses, was couched parodically in the language of voyage literature: "taking possession of a new world." Further, the apprehension of nature's wide-flung particularity was transformed into susceptibility to a profound but narrow localism: Courbet's paintings are inextricably intertwined with his native region of the Franche-Comté and its mores. For Champfleury, all natural phenomena, earlier encountered on the spot or in the wild in travel accounts, are now chained to human use: "Is the search for products extracted from the earth not interesting to paint on the walls of a train station? Beautiful paintings: those of the labor of men in mines!"

On a deeper level, one that underlies his major writings devoted to the history of caricature and other forms of popular illustration, Champfleury again brings us face to face with the issue of a conventionless art. The new (or rather, old) barbarism of ancient *grilli*, of *images d'épinal* dating from the Middle Ages, and of crude faience ware produced during the French Revolution fascinates the critic of modern life precisely because their very stylistic and thematic rudeness and naiveté permit contemporary man to "penetrate profoundly into the rudimentary embryos" of human nature. Popular imagery reveals that "the stammering of children is the same in all countries; in spite of its arrested development it offers, nevertheless, the charm of innocence, and what constitutes the charm of modern image-makers [Honoré Daumier and the circle of lithographers around Charles Philipon] is that they have remained children, that is to say, they escape the progress of the city arts."

In a notable inversion, physical topography had been replaced with human geography or demography. What the eighteenth-century traveler in search of fact sought in a mineral and vegetable primitivism and attained through a science of nature, the nineteenth-century archaeologist of popular sentiment discovered in folk art and a science of man.

Yet Champfleury was of two minds on the question of what constitutes a real nature. In "Brumes et rosées: Chintreuil," he praises a landscape painter who escaped the city to work on the margins of its encroaching suburbs. Confronting this visualization of a Bérangeresque countryside, Champfleury evokes an Edenic experience that had become increasingly elusive in the face of spreading urbanization: "Walking alone, confronting nature, in the open air, under the sun. . . ." Chintreuil's landscapes reveal the artist to be "a friend of solitude . . . where broom and hawthorn grow freely." Champfleury continues: "No one is seated beside the serene pond over which scud glancingly lazy clouds. No one [is] at the foot of the tall poplars gently inclining their heads beneath the wind's caresses. . . ." What are we to make of this idyllic appreciation of a Corot-like landscape depicting rural matters that were no more? It is nature painting—not freed of culture, convention, and the entire freight of corrupt human history as the Enlightenment envisaged it, but offering respite from *actualités*, from nature modernized. This form of landscape, too, according to Champfleury, represents a "nature stripped of all artifice." It was the type of painting practiced by the Barbizon School, and on occasion it could entail traveling. From 1857 to his death in 1878, Charles-François Daubigny rambled along the waterways of France in his houseboat, accompanied by a constantly changing and motley crew of family and friends. Integrating himself totally in a localized world of streams and rivers, the artist memorialized the watery topography of his *pays*. Voyage after voyage, year after year, he sketched along the same stretches of the Seine and the Oise. Typically, when lured by a friend to make an impromptu trip to Spain in 1869, he left that country after less than two weeks to return to the familiar and the local. For Daubigny, travel was no longer for the purpose of discovering yet another exotic motif (Fromentin's insight) but for deepening the individual experience of one's native land over the course of a lifetime.[71]

Although the Realists of 1848–1857 (Courbet, Jean-François Millet, the Barbizon "bohemians," Champfleury) and the Naturalists of 1850–1895 (Adalbert Stifter, the Victorian Genre Painters, Emile Zola, Gerhard Hauptmann) shared a common ideational germ in wanting to re-present the truth of their time as experienced, their methods differed. Zola's critical writings, spanning 30 years, illuminate the subtle distinctions between nineteenth-century Realism and Naturalism, distinctions which depend on Hippolyte Taine's milieu theory and on Claude Bernard's epochal statement of the experimental method. Already in the early "Deux définitions du roman" (1866), Zola enunciates the master themes of his future apologia for literary Naturalism. Composed for the thirty-third session of the Congrès scientifique de France, held at Aix, the essay tackles the metamorphoses undergone by that venerable genre. Central to Zola's argument is the theory that the Greeks, constantly preoccupied with their gods, created "no exact painting of real life." Among the Romans, Petronius was one of the few to eschew pure fictions. The *Satyricon* wins Zola's approval because the voyages of its hero are used as simple pretexts for placing before the reader's eyes scenes actually observed by the author. Only in modern times, however, does the novel cease being merely a pleasing lie, a potpourri of marvelous adventures taking place in a fantasy world bearing no resemblance to our own. The modern novel, defined by Zola as a product of observation and analysis, is singularly suited to chronicle the life of urban man irrevocably "living here now, in a corner." The time-honored *conte*, under the pressure of dominating scientific trends and methodology, became in the writings of Honoré de Balzac a treatise on moral anatomy. In a revolutionary passage concluding the essay, Zola predicts the breakup of worn-out rhetorical classifications and artificial separations of literary genres and hypothesizes a new, comprehensive formulation of human thought modified by society and milieu. Young writers, he exhorts, "need only look around then state what they have seen."

Although the projected *Essai de rhétorique historique* was not to be, Zola fleshed out his youthful divigations in *Le roman expérimental* (1880). In a minute analysis of Claude Bernard's *Introduction à l'étude de la médecine expérimentale*, he makes the great positivist physiologist's methodology his own. At the outset, he, like Bernard, distinguishes between the procedures of observation and experimentation. The naturalist novelist (and painter, as is evident from the art criticism) does not merely observe or "photograph" in the manner of the Enlightenment natural historian; rather, he intervenes. Using Baron Hulot from *La cousine Bette* as an example, he praises Balzac's technique of placing him in a situation (analogous to the scientist's "instigating observation") over which the narrator retains control. What might be called the antinomy between nature observed on the spot and reality manipulated is thus firmly established at the outset. The subtle implications of Bernard's distinction are expounded at great length. The observer patiently studies phenomena which he does not alter, whereas the experimenter—although also without preconception—varies for a specific purpose what nature presents. Consequently, for the scientific experimenter as for the creator of an experimental art, natural phenomena are artificially arranged so as to appear different from how they look in nature. Yet, Bernard-Zola cautions, the moment the result of the experiment manifests itself the experimenter as interpreter must vanish, must transform himself instantaneously back into pure observer. The experiment Zola sees the modern novelist engaging in is performed on man; clearly this is not simply a matter of copying or of "photographing" but rather one of that very modification, interpretation, or "experimentation" that is made by a specific temperament. The personal nature of such alteration constitutes genius, for "to see is to invent."

Zola's discussion deals not with the itemization of natural phenomena but with the actualities of human physiology. He alludes to a familiar polemic. The new "science of phenomena of life," according to Bernard-Zola, is founded on the science devoted to the study of brute phenomena. In both instances, whether in the natural sciences or in the anatomy of contemporary mores, one must reattach phenomena through the process of experimentation to their conditions of existence or their immediate causes. Reviving the vitalist materialist-mechanist antithesis central to much of eighteenth-century philosophy, Bernard proposes a positivist resolution. He suggests that on a physico-chemical or molecular level an intimate conjoining of these two disparate milieus (physiological and psychological with inorganic, internal with external) is possible. Physiologist and critic thus confront directly the eighteenth-century struggle to merge a fluid epistemology with entropic theories of matter. Indeed, the language employed is that of the French materialists, of La Mettrie's *L'Homme machine*, even of Hartley's mechanical "vibrations": "the same determinism ought to rule the stone of the highway as the brain of man." With this premise heeded, a common ground can be located between the intricate inner and interorganic milieu of man and the outer and extraorganic milieu of purely physical nature. Clearly, as was the case for Champfleury, mineralogical complexity is far less great than that of living beings. The task of the experimental novel, then, is not to study that inorganic or organic nature of the phenomenal world, but the natural (not the abstractly idealized or metaphysical) man, just as the Enlightenment attempted to study a "natural" or naked nature. Zola uses the idiom forged during the post-Baconian age of discovery: All labor in the nineteenth century funnels into the great scientific work that is "the conquest of nature." By this, of course, was meant the conquest of the human unknown teeming around him, the physiological penetration of the actors in their social setting as they wandered through a *Comédie humaine*.

In this connection, Zola takes up the question of style. Naturalism is a method of plain observation and judicious experimentation, one characterized by an absence of personal fantasy, by the presence of scientific criteria operating in the place of individual authority. Subject matter and style are inseparable. He declares unequivocally that ostentatious rhetoric and scientific method are distinct. It is at this juncture that Zola and Bernard part ways. Apparently, Bernard was deluded, on the basis of idiosyncratic stylistic considerations, into thinking that the fine arts do not lend themselves to the transparency of the experimental method, whereas Zola (setting aside the question of the kind of specimen under scrutiny) states emphatically that their domain is at one with that of the physiologist.

Identical suppositions concerning the elaboration of a concrete model of reality function in Zola's *Salons* and art criticism. For the critic, the naturalist artist (Eduard Manet, Camille Pissarro) is a painter of man, not a maker of tableaux (that is, a conspicuous user of style). Although it is not explicitly stated, the idea unmistakably corresponds to Bernard's definition of the experimental scientist interpreting, transforming, and filtering reality through his temperament. To wit: "Le moment artistique" records Zola's irritation at the imprecision of Realism and its conceptual limitations. Zola insists that there are two components essential to the work of art, just as in the milieu: the real ingredient (phenomenal nature) and the individual ingredient (man). In an inversion that is by now typical, nature, however, is "fixed, always identical," it "remains the same for all the world"; on the contrary, "man is variable to infinity: so many works and so many different minds; if the temperament did not exist, all paintings necessarily would be simple photographs." Thus, from the vantage of Bernard's determinist physico-chemical perspective (true for the macrocosm and microcosm of internal and external), Zola defines the work of art as the product of the momentary collocation of changeable, living, variable humanity with a fixed atomic nature. What is significant for Zola, therefore, it is not a Realism of contemporary topic or neutral style (i.e., "photography"), not the Dutch "sauces" of François Bonvin or the tedious minutiae of Jean-Louis-Ernst Meissonnier and Jean-Léon Gérôme, but a modern methodology, a creative reaction in the face of the infinite complexities of the human temperament—in short, the genius of Manet or Degas.

The implication for Naturalist (Impressionist) landscape painting, as well as for the *"actualistes"* who interpret their era, is that the great artist provides the receptive observer (not the ignorant public, for which Zola has only disdain) with a new and personal translation. Man assigns nature its character, character is not inherent in nature's aspects. Stated otherwise: The meaningless panorama of organic flux is given concrete aspects, point.

Though Zola's Positivism underscores observation as both the locus for departure and the point of conclusion in his program for contemporary art, phenomenal nature is to be totally reconstituted by an intimate alliance forged between a fluctuating consciousness and externalities. Landscapists can avoid being imitative only by retaining their individuality, by commingling their unique humanity with the matter of this world. For Zola and the artist-writer of a naturalist persuasion, there is no landscape freed of culture; it is as much a mirage as is the absolute Beautiful. If truth for the Realist consists in the recording of *actualités*, for the Zolaesque Naturalist it lies in a "plain" method, in a scientific language reminiscent of that proposed by Condillac, stipulating the perceiver's exploration of the world as lived in and his discoveries about all types and classes of humanity.[72]

The merger between the discourse of the laboratory and that of the studio is also evident in Adalbert Stifter's serenely radical and totally un-French Biedermeier "Naturalism." This Austrian master of the painted and written sketch praised the wondrous "thingness" of the inorganic and organic world in an 1855 collection of short stories evocatively entitled *Bunte Steine* (Colorful Stones). Stifter's aim in these novellas (in truth, travel pieces from the Tyrol) is to tell of the great and the small, the extraordinary and the familiar: "of the agitation of the air, the rippling of water, the growing of plants, the swelling of the ocean, the green of the earth, the shimmer of the sky, the glitter of the stars. . . ." The power that causes milk to boil over in a housewife's humble pot is one and the same with that forcing lava to rupture the firm contours of a mountain. The latter seems more striking and draws the attention of an untutored and careless spectator, but the scientific investigator's searching look is capable of extending "to the whole and the universal," in which all particulars, even the most ordinary, are eventually subsumed. Stifter urges a marriage between these two visions. If the human gaze—so sensitive to light— could also be sharpened to perceive electricity and its magnetic streams, "what a grand world, what a plenum of boundless appearances would open for us." Although we do not possess a corporeal eye efficient enough for such refined apprehension, we do enjoy "the intellectual eye of science," and it informs us that invisible energies course through the universe, flowing around, enveloping, and perpetually altering all things. Lightning is only a tiny token or bare wisp of an effect indicative of this formidable spirit in nature. It is at this point that Stifter blends his aesthetic philosophy with the scientific outlook of the nineteenth century:

Since science accumulates only kernel upon kernel, only makes observation after observation, only stitches together the general out of particulars, and since ultimately the mass of phenomena and the field of the given are so endlessly vast, God perforce made the joy and happiness of research commensurately inexhaustible; we, too, in our [artistic] studies can hope to represent only the particular, never the general, since that would be Creation: thus the history of the great in nature is constructed from the continual metamorphoses of opinions concerning that grandeur....

Though the optimistic lyricism of Stifter's *Bergkristall* (mountain crystal) or even the darker note of his *Turmalin* differs absolutely from Zola's deterministic physiological method, Stifter attempts the same wedding of external nature with the inner life of man. Both a human temperament stamped by judiciousness, simplicity, and laboriousness and a vehemently agitated, moody character, disquieting, envious, ambitious, destructive, and even suicidal, find their inhuman counterparts in a petrified and animate nature: in ice grottos, blocks of black granite, storms, lava-spewing mountains, and earthquakes. According to Stifter, the correspondence between these two realms operates on the deepest level. In opposition to raw, uncivilized individuality and egoism there exist benevolent social forces that collectively touch humanity and are not threatened by solitary barbaric energies. Stifter is speaking of a newly moralized nature, nature revealed as intensely *bieder* through the lawlike discoveries of science, just as mankind predictably progresses simultaneously toward a condition of ethical probity and rectitude. As was the case with Zola, modern art and modern narrative do not function for Stifter at the level of the epic or the tragic; rather, their content is shaped by "the ordinary, the quotidian," because human affairs resemble "the million root hairs" of the tree of life. Moral law functions like natural law; it plays itself out in the infinite business contracted by men with men. In a futuristic vision, Stifter foresees the evolution of man and art in nature as the movement away from the one-sided, sensual, fantastical individuality of single vision to a polyphony of points of view trained on attaining a common good. His work bears the mark of this belief. The utterly ordinary pebbles, grasses, stones, and odd bits of glass gathered on mountain excursions during his youth are varnished to let their "beautiful blue, green, and red lineaments shine through." The act of collecting (here practiced not upon precious gems but on the meanest minerals) that motivates the amassing of particulars is subsequently modified by the transparent glaze of art. From rambles originally undertaken unthinkingly and without purpose, Stifter crafted an edifying, ethical natural history, a thoroughly nineteenth-century *Bildungsreise* for the youth of tomorrow.[73]

But it is Ruskin who is most crucial to any definition of Naturalism at the middle of the nineteenth century. His complex and shifting opinions

CONCLUSION: THE REALIZATION OF NATURE

reflect, refocus, and recast many major themes encountered in the factual travel account. Like Stifter, he can on occasion record the complete otherness of an alien nature, the sheer horror of a landscape untouched by human life. In Stifter's *Bergkristall*, a tale of two children lost on Christmas eve in a monstrous glacial world where they exist merely as tiny wandering specks, the familiar Tyrolean valleys and meadows are transformed into a hostile Arctic waste furrowed by crevasses, avalanches, and ice grottos. Ruskin, gazing upon the limestone summits of the inaccessible range of the Rochers des Fys above the Col d'Anterne, evokes (in highly wrought language unconnected with the nominalistic and plain-speaking idiom of the Biedermeier) a similar experience. A "ghastly range of pinnacles" is utterly shorn, "to the utmost desolate, knowing no shaking of leaves in the wind, nor of grass beside the stream—no motion but their own mortal shivering, the deathful crumbling of atom from atom in their corrupting stones; knowing no sound of living voice or living tread. . . ."

Not limited to Stifter's regionalism and taste for the homespun, Ruskin could foresee a greater terror when he was reminded, while climbing through a pine forest, how even scenes that seem independent of any interest other than that elicited by themselves are, in fact, dependent on the warmth of recollection. As he cast about to discover with greater precision the sources of the terrain's impressiveness, he resorted to the ruse of imagining it for a moment as if it were "a scene in some aboriginal forest of the New Continent." This apparently innocuous mental transposition threw over the wooded ravine of the Jura "a sudden blankness" and "chill": "The flowers in an instant lost their light, the river its music; the hills became oppressively desolate; a heaviness in the boughs of the darkened forest showed how much of their former power had been dependent upon a life which was not theirs, how much of the glory of the imperishable, or continually renewed, creation is reflected from things more precious in their memory than it, in its renewing. . . ."

Ruskin was perpetually torn between praising the structuring powers of the imagination (which he employed to such splendid rhetorical effect in his prose style) and calling for humility in the plain observation of natural phenomena; in short, he vacillated between Switzerland's "cultured" Alps and the explorer's inhuman vacancy. This polarity also assumed another guise. Whereas Mount Cervin and the Zmutt glacier at times rendered him uncomfortable, because their blocks of reddish gneiss and slatey crystalline rocks presented a changeless and soundless scene "so removed, not merely from the presence of men, but even from their thoughts," the watery (though defaced) historiated landscape of Venice aroused instead the "great charities of the imagination." It is the bonding of associative trains of ideas with a unique moral sensibility that Ruskin always finds impossible at the antipodes and occasionally elusive atop European summits. In his densely physical description of Venice's uncivilized incarnation as prehistoric, lifeless, impassable, and unvoyageable swamp, the compulsion to read God's purpose in nature—and therefore an instance of the critic's psychological distance from eighteenth-century secularism—is amply evident: "How little could we have known, any more than what now seems to us most distressful, dark, and objectless, the glorious aim which was then in the mind of Him in whose hand lay all corners of the earth! How little imagined that in the laws which were stretching forth the gloomy margins of those fruitless banks, and feeding the bitter grass among their shallows, there was indeed a preparation, and *the only preparation possible,* for the founding of a city which was to be set like a golden clasp on the girdle of the earth. . . ."

Despite a literary preference for urban or natural scenes in which one can discover some personal, historical, or pious reflection, Ruskin champions equally pictorial phenomena "for which there are no words in language, and no ideas in the mind"—things that "can only be conceived while they are visible." Constant vigilance in observation led to Ruskin's perception of a cosmic dualism between enduring moments and fugitive effects. *Modern Painters* is rife with examples of the "two eternities," of "the Vacancy and the Rock" pitted against transitory manifestations, the colored "gradations" of clouds, sunsets, and storms. These opposites, through their reconciliation, would transcend the beauty of material things by adding their force to individual consciousness. Many examples are spun out in Ruskin's writings, from the cold, slow, unaware metamorphosis of crystals expounded to schoolgirls in *The Ethics of the Dust* to the contrasts of fragility and strength, softness and vigor, uprightness and wandering, cleaving and binding of *Praeterita's* rekindled memories.

Treading Saussure's and Humboldt's intellectual trail, Ruskin cleaves nature into its northern and southern and its male and female aspects. He juxtaposes the glittering gems, supple sculpture, jaspar pillars, and sunlit, cloudless skies of Italy with the "uncouth animation" of rocks torn from the Moorland—"creations of ungainly shape and rigid limb but full of wolfish life." Further, in a manner reminiscent of Forster's musings on a larger perspective, he meditates on the proper distance at which to observe natural objects:

If you desire to perceive the great harmonies of the form of a rocky mountain, you must not ascend upon its sides. All is there disorder, accident, or seems so. . . . Retire from it, and, as your eye commands it more and more, as you see the ruined mountain world with a wider glance, behold! dim sympathies begin to busy themselves in the disjointed mass; line binds itself into stealthy fellowship with line; group by group, the helpless fragments gather themselves into orderly companies; new captains of hosts and masses of battalions become visible, one by one, and far away answers of foot to foot, and bone to bone, until the powerless chaos is seen risen up with girded loins, and not one piece of all the unregarded heap could now be spared from the mystic whole. . . .[74]

Perhaps the most significant legacy of the factual travel account evident in Ruskinian thought, however, is the dictum of truth to the material.[75] In the *Poetry of Architecture*, Ruskin engages in a comparative analysis of Swiss and Westmoreland cottages with an eye to their connection with and their effect on the scenery. His severe criticism of the former hinges in part on their "rawness," their fatal neatness, and their lack of gradation— in short, their refusal to conceal art and to blend into or be cowed by the surrounding motionless colossal scenery. Such a dwelling is content neither to unite with the mountain spectacle nor to sink unobtrusively into a quiet corner of the land. Because of this repudiation of the ambient, the Swiss cottage paradoxically annihilates the sense of solitude, one of the principal charms of all heights. The color and the building material of the ideal cottage must, therefore, fit in well with the environment so that only by the closest inspection can the fact of its being a habitation be ascertained. The Westmoreland cottage, built of slate and greywacke, responds admirably to such a demand. This leads Ruskin to reflect that "the material which Nature furnishes, in any given country, and the form which she suggests will always render the building the most beautiful, because the most appropriate." The color of such a primitive hut is the same as the surrounding soil, exquisitely mottled by the *Lichen geographicus*, mingling "as on a native rock": "the mass, consequently at a distance, tells only as a large stone would, the simplicity of its form contributing still farther to render it unconspicuous. . . ." Ruskin marvels at the microscopic as well as the macroscopic truth. Each stone lodged in the cottage's wall activates its surface because it is a miniature study revealing the infinite delicacy and complexity of structure present in all minerals, from the pebble to the mountain. Armed with a history of nature in which no material is inert, Ruskin strikes yet another blow against the merely Picturesque. The abominable Swiss cottages of Britain, embellished with green shutters and circumscribed by a garden of flintstone, bear no resemblance to the chalets of the Alps; Ruskin urges instead the creation of a vernacular "humble" building style without pretension or ostentatious "taste," exhibiting no "kind of ornament, but what nature chooses to bestow." Such a dwelling, says Ruskin, "wears all its decorations wildly, covering its nakedness, not with what the peasant may plant, but with what the winds may bring."

Ruskin's momentous realization—explicitly stated in the section on chimneys in *The Poetry of Architecture* and in the lecture "Iron in Nature" in *The Two Paths*—is that a nonimitative or convention-free art "must not be built of civilised materials"; it must be intimately connected with the characteristic substance, the very regional stuff of the country in which it is to be raised. In contrast with the "elevated" mountain villa of the gentleman—formulated according to the whimsical, idiosyncratic dictates of taste (not chorographic particularity or the specific physical properties of the local soil) and generalizing, eclectic principles—the "low" rustic genre of the vernacular—originally fit only for the untutored boor but now made apt for the lover of raw nature—embodies a humility before matter's constituent particles. This perspicuous observation is congruent with Champfleury's advocacy of a new and invigorating primitivism to revitalize nineteenth-century painting. Thus, barbarism and naiveté of topic and style were to emerge from an unstylish or tasteless popular art first formulated by a preindustrial folk.

What makes Ruskin's view distinctive is that he grounds such building types in nature, not in art (no matter how crude). He admonishes architects that a redeeming sensitivity for material, for its inmost character and qualities, should be melded with artistic energy just as the body must be bonded to the soul for life: ". . . Nature is always carrying on very strange work with this limestone and flint of hers: laying down beds of them at the bottom of the sea; building islands out of the sea; filling chinks and veins in mountains with curious treasures; petrifying mosses, and trees, and shells; in fact, carrying on all sorts of business, subterranean or submarine, which it would be highly desirable for us, who profit and live by it, to notice as it goes on. . . ."

Fully in tune with these materialistic convictions was Ruskin's disdain for the horde of wanton tourists who were desecrating his eighteenth-century vision of the Swiss Alps as a sublime domain of rock and ice. To rectify this sacrilege, he urged in *Modern Painters* that more and more topographically accurate pictures—not cavalier "combinations"—be made of alpine subjects. Indeed, Ruskin's conception of historical landscape painting embraced the purpose of "giving persons who cannot travel trustworthy knowledge." Ruskin undertook the encouragement and even patronage of John William Inchbold and John Brett to further detached scientific observation and the making of consciously detailed geographical and geological statements.[76]

Yet, despite these firm ties to the aesthetic of a preceding generation, Ruskin's thought emancipates itself from that of his acknowledged precursors. Gone is that intense secular delight in nature experienced in a more adventurous era by observers no longer obligated to extract religious feelings from mountains and glens. Gone, too, not just from Ruskin but from the Victorian Age as a whole, is the innocent prelapsarian belief that geological strata embody and articulate primarily the history of their own formation and evolution.

Despite his manifest interest in the close observation and the fastidious reproduction of a multiplicity of geological formations, Ruskin did not reject human society for the dangerous austerity of an unmediated, solitary relationship with the varieties of inorganic life. He transformed nature not (as Wordsworth had) into self-serving visible signs of subjective states, but in order to incorporate it into the fabric of moral life. Thus, the industrial world that saw pampas grass brought to the front lawns of staid villas and a howling wilderness procured for the suburbs could countenance only the marriage of the exotic with the domestic, the natural redeemed by the ethical.

CONCLUSION: THE REALIZATION OF NATURE

Ruskin's chronic vacillation between functioning as seer and as thinker, his precipitous alternation between observing something and telling it "in a plain way" and analyzing and describing an emotion, brings us to the ultimate Naturalistic enterprise: the lucid art of the satirist. Even on Olympian heights and during inspired flights of fancy, Ruskin realized that the imagination is a wearable faculty; periodically it must be "laid down on the grass, among simple things, and left quiet for a while." The recollection that on occasion the mass of the Aiguille de Varens, the jagged range of the mountains of the Réposoir, and all the needles of Mont Blanc aroused no joy led to Ruskin's most astute observation about the psychic attrition wrought by travel: When inventive powers faint away, commerce with "a little thing,—a tuft of moss, or a single crag at the top of the Varens, or a wreath or two of foam at the bottom of the Nant d'Arpenaz" will revive it.[77]

Ruskin's insight that Mont Blanc and its superb pine forests cannot be found everywhere and that the human mind must be happy, in antlike fashion, "with the bits of stick and grains of crystal that fall in its way to be handled, in daily duty," lies at the heart of Rodolphe Töpffer's gentle caricatures of the literature of exploration in his *Voyages en zigzag*. These represent a creative reaction in the face of the shifting appearances of the "real" world. Ironically, it is in nineteenth-century satire that the depth of knowledge about externalities, the emphasis on the phenomenally concrete, and the stress on visibility endemic to the factual travel account achieve their gravest incarnation. Creating a heroic-comic amalgam of the directed scientific gaze, the wayward lateral movement of the Picturesque tour, and the erudite intention of the *Bildungsreise*, Töpffer gave birth to a novel genre of illustrated voyage. Neither straight-as-an-arrow travel for a purpose, nor aimless meandering nor voyage into self, his account presents the natural history "pedestrian" excursion pursued "in zigzag."

As Sainte-Beuve noted in 1853, Töpffer, a Genevan landscape painter, draftsman, physiognomist, and intrepid hiker, had marched in the wake of the physicist-voyager Saussure. However, the rustic style of Töpffer's alpine narratives and the accompanying sketches reveal a taste not only for the *fruste* (Töpffer's favorite expression) or for the "rude" traits of nature's masterpieces but also for the rough, "unpolished," countrified aspects of human character. Töpffer's verbal and visual descriptions give the splendors of mountain scenery full-page representation (engraved on wood by Alexandre Calame or François and Jean-Louis Disday, but these are always balanced, and even undermined or challenged, by humorous, quotidian, lively vignettes and anecdotes devoted to the foibles of a perambulating schoolmaster and his irrepressible charges. The animation of the landscape arises from the comic adventures of this noisy troop, not from the sublime physiognomy of the Cervin or from the "brute existence and mute grandeur of these [mountainous] creations without life."

Nowhere is the mixing of high and low topic and style, of the risible, all-too-human actuality and a serious, knowing love of pure nature, more in evidence that in Töpffer's meditations on what it means to sketch on the spot and to stroll. Contrary to what the strict, unidirectional voyager in search of fact might maintain, the *flâneur* engages in an activity diametrically opposite to doing nothing. Initiating his vacation hikes in 1823, while an assistant master at a boarding school, Töpffer came to realize—in the manner of "nobler" explorers—that traveling on foot without the paraphernalia of the Grand Tourist's servants, luggage, and uncomfortable and confining conveyances meant blissful independence. One might "freely go to the right, to the left, down, up, wherever one could walk or climb," rest in a comfortable hostel and, above all, regale one's appetite.

Töpffer's love of freedom, his compulsion to decamp, to escape from the narrow confines of scholarly life in order to "evade the tyranny of memory" over nature's realities, his passion for carrying out these alpine excursions year after year, no matter what the hardship, fatigue, or privation—all are from the legacy of the taste for discovery. Töpffer even provides his own witty riposte to the academic "instructions, reports, and notices on questions to resolve during scientific voyages." Almost the exact contemporary of François Arago, he captures the flavor of that famous explorer-scientist's directives to officers bound for the Far North and Algeria while subtly subverting them.

Töpffer's inimitable "theory of excursions" entails three conditions upon which depend the success of an outing of some 20 days. First, the dozen or more voyagers must be youthful, filled with an insouciant gaiety, an elastic vigor, while still retaining an unspoiled love for what is truly pleasurable. A critical number of participants is necessary, Töpffer insists, not only to provide him with the joy of observing his pupils' emancipation in the open air but also to introduce a diversity of relationships, viewpoints, and conversations that foster a sense of community. Second, the leader must be blessed with an indefatigable, courageous, and supportive fellow-traveler. Nothing is more desirable or essential than to have for the companion of one's voyage one's life companion, another adult to help govern and console the unruly bunch and with whom to share intimate thoughts and feelings stirred by the spectacle of grand and new things. Third, the excursion on foot offers a playful occasion for exploring freely, "without the control of fixed and methodical guidance." Indeed, Töpffer approaches Arago's assertion that "most great discoveries happen spontaneously, without anyone having foreseen them, or suspected them."

Töpffer's natural-history voyage, like life itself, is conducted in zigzag fashion. Escaping from the Linnaean schema of dry systematic gathering, Töpffer cheerfully watches his ebullient charges impulsively lured "to the right, to the left, there where the insect chirps, there where scent betrays a flower, there where remnants of a rock hint at some discovery." Töpffer continues: "One goes from ravine to plain, from glade to underbrush, from amusement to treasure, and excessively long days would seem to the apprentice naturalist a too brief promenade, if, happily, he did not still have to count and classify his riches, to locate for them a safe place beneath the leather of his knapsack, or, even better, in some box bought en route, then consolidated, then enlarged, then divided into compartments, object of constant improvements, of pleasure and strict surveillance. . . ."

The charm and wisdom of Töpffer's unorthodox pedagogy conducted as sport results in an explosion of "scientific ardor:" everyone is digging for plants, turning up stones, helping one another, developing into a "researcher," a "happy or able discoverer." The Genevan schoolmaster, in language conditioned by the venerable Baconian summons to a collective investigation of the natural world, applies the "high" art of the scientific reformer to his lowly band. His "caravan of voyagers" metamorphoses through the joy of being on the spot into "merry colonials" whose purpose is to conquer the physical world. And the leader of this "gay science" collects not plants and insects but views, landscapes, mores—everywhere he is drawing, sketching, critically and comically inspecting the trivia and grandeur of the world.[78]

The feasibility of a science without pedantry (inconceivable to Ruskin), and of travel or life, as a serious game, was the dream of Nadar, a French photographer, balloonist, and lifelong apostle of heavier-than-air flight who composed a "heroic-comic" history of that mode of exploration outlining his instrumental role in its evolution. In his *Mémoires du Géant*, written after the balloon disaster near Hanover on October 19, 1863, Nadar records the trials and tribulations of experimental aviation in a colloquial style reminiscent of Töpffer's. He laments that aerial locomotion has not advanced one iota since the days of the Montgolfiers, Pilâtre de Rozier, Charles, Conté, and Dupuis-Delcourt. In fact, by the middle of the nineteenth century this "sublime and execrable discovery" had become the almost exclusive property of acrobats and circus performers, manipulators of flying nymphs and fish. Nadar satirized these "balloon-operators" and, with the invention of the colossal *Géant*, "threw a huge stone into the pond of aerial fish, though not yet having done with all that ichthyology." Nadar deserves, along with Töpffer, to be seen as a true successor to the Enlightenment travelers. He bankrupted himself time and time again in his devotion to flight, and he proselytized before the *Académie des Sciences*, in the pages of his journal, the *Aéronaute*, and through the *Société d'encouragement du plus lourd que l'air*. His zeal as balloonist-photographer is worthy of the inventors of 1783.

By means of caricature, Nadar, like Töpffer, pithily summarizes the history of modern scientific exploration, not only placing it within his own contemporary milieu but trenchantly reshaping it to create a new genre. With great verve he records the comedy and tragedy of getting aloft, improbably yet veristically stringing together financial dealings, unruly crowds, unreliable pilots, sublimely phosphorescent nocturnal scenery, and air disasters. Nothing is too trivial for Nadar's pen; everything is fully actualized in line with his aesthetic belief that a photograph should not be retouched. For our purposes, his most pungent and telling parody is that provoked by a stalwart member of the *Géant's* crew: the hilariously monomaniacal cook and Lucullian quartermaster of the first flight, Eugène Delessert. Nadar unleashes his full satiric arsenal on this "model" traveler who circumnavigated the globe "ten or twelve times" but only visited California five times and Australia six:

He speaks all known languages and perhaps even Javanese. He hunted the prairie buffalo with the Delawares and the O Jib Be Was, the white bear in Norway, the blue fox in Greenland, and he lit his cigar with the last incandescent lava to emerge from the extinguished volcanos of the Himalaya; Vice-President for the Committee of Vigilantes in San Francisco; he had hung or hung himself ten or twelve rascals, whose rope, I think, he held himself, and, mixing the useful with the pleasurable, he founded the first French hospital in California. He has manufactured munitions, ridden horseback, loaded boats, drafted commercial agreements and paints watercolors. He has seen everything, knows everything. . . .

Nadar encountered considerable difficulty in convincing his expedition's provisioner, who was accustomed to lengthy and probing explorations among savages, that the crew of fourteen would not be spending six months floating between heaven and earth. Every morning as Nadar arrived at the maneuvering ground, Delessert greeted him with a steady procession of victuals to be squeezed into the passenger basket. On parade were "hampers of dishes, Bordeaux glasses, champagne glasses, liqueur glasses, tinned vegetables, smoked meats, alcohol burners. . . ." "The moment has finally come," Nadar goes on, "to declare, in the face of God and before man, that it is to Delessert that we owed the legs of mutton, lobsters, chickens, and radishes triumphantly festooning our outer casing at the time of the first ascension. . . . I have basked too long in the public approbation of this exhibition not to regard it as a duty to restitute to Delessert today the glory which belongs to him alone. . . ." This humorous anecdote epigrammatically sums up the entire history of travel for a purpose (use and beauty, to be sure) in the person of Delessert. Moreover, this passage contains yet another nugget of the serious: a glancing reference to Nadar's central theme that Delessert "played" at ballooning with the naive, fresh intensity of a child mustering his soldiers. Just as Nadar's ideal of science without pedantry is embodied by the diverting Jacques Babinet—a member of the august Académie des Sciences, yet a popularizer capable of great wit, pursuing his zigzag researches by "halting according to whim at spots which please him, gathering to the left and to the right of his path, in his seeming distraction, pebbles or flowers"—so, too, Nadar's proposed solution to the vexing problem to steering is discovered in a toy.

Nadar's passionate advocacy of the "sacred helix" (a kind of helicopter) came about through the "testing" of playthings. From pinwheels (*stropheors*) he had purchased while roaming France, Belgium, and Germany, Nadar sought to fashion the science of aviation, to make of balloon exploration a serious game. This solemn sport even had its own rules (the published *Règlement de bord de l'aérostat Le Géant*) and an immediate popularizer (the American journalist Robert Mitchell).[79]

In sum: The factual travel account made significant contributions to nineteenth-century aesthetics on a variety of fronts. Better than any other genre, it demonstrated that art involves the direct encounter of nature with the self in the constantly adjusting act of living. Perhaps its most striking legacy, then, was in the area of methodology. The traveler in search of fact inaugurated the habit of constructing a never-ending series of hypotheses concerning physical reality on the basis of constant exposure to and scrutiny of its mutable data. At a fundamental perceptual level, therefore, the scientific discoverer promulgated an exploratory way of looking at the world. Penetrating phenomena opened a new perspective on the actual shape of existence, now viewed as an open-ended and intersecting sequence of experiences momentarily "realized" in concrete fragments of reality and shifting aspects.

As an extension of this thought, it was the voyaging artist who first turned his studio into a laboratory devoted to the minute examination of palpable externalities out "in the field."[80] He not only positioned himself in front of the world; he entered the world. Similarly, the mid-nineteenth-century painters' and writers' commitment to exposing the unadorned substantiality of appearances as it resides in tangible surfaces, embodied in the conspicuous and parallel materiality of the aesthetic medium manipulated, was the result of the travelers' discovery of nature's autonomous marks. In short, it was the traveler's wariness of the unguided and "self-projecting" heart, his reliance on empirical observation rather than preconception, that first permitted a nonanthropocentric universe to declare itself in full force.

Even the habit of collecting contributed to the democratization or leveling of visible objects,[81] both natural and artificial, and to the undercutting of farfetched sublimities by the ordinary and the comic. Extending investigative sight into all reaches of nature's archive, into its behavior as embodied in imprints and traces, the explorer established an optic that was antithetical both to the Olympian perspective of distant, uninvolved contemplation and to the narrowly subjective convention of personification. It was the voyager, then, who paved the way for the works of nature to be validated aesthetically and to assume their place beside artifacts as equal but distinct partners in the real world.

VOYAGE INTO SUBSTANCE

Notes

Introduction

1. For discussions of the Picturesque and *pittoresco* in relation to travel literature see Jean Adhémar, "Les lithographies de paysage en France à l'époque romantique," *Archives de l'art français* 19 (1938), 268; *Le voyage pittoresque* (London: Arts Council Gallery, 1967); Ingrid G. Daemmrich, "The Ruins Motif as Artistic Device in French Literature," *Journal of Aesthetics and Art Criticism* 30 (summer 1972), 454–455; R. K. Raval, "The Picturesque in Knight, Turner, and Hipple," *British Journal of Aesthetics* 18 (summer 1978), 249–250.

2. J. Hardy, *A Picturesque and Descriptive Tour in the Mountains of the High Pyrenees: Comprising Twenty-Four Views of the Most Interesting Scenes, from Original Drawings taken on the Spot; With Some Account of the Bathing Establishments in that Department of France* (London: R. Ackermann, 1825), p. 1. For a recent discussion of the Picturesque and the Pyrenees see Marguerite Gaston, *Images romantiques des Pyrénées, Les Pyrénées dans la peinture et dans l'estampe à l'époque romantique* (Pau: Amis du Musée Pyrénéen, 1975), pp. 62–70.

3. William Gilpin, *Remarks on Forest Scenery, and Other Woodland Views relative chiefly to Picturesque Beauty. Illustrated by the Scenes of New Forest in Hampshire*, third edition (London: T. Cadell and W. Davies, 1808), 9. For an analysis of Gilpin's contributions to the aesthetic of the Picturesque see Luke Hermann, *British Landscape Painting of the Eighteenth Century* (Oxford University Press, 1974), pp. 111–112; Russell Noyes, *Wordsworth and the Art of Landscape* (Bloomington: Indiana University Press, 1968), p. 24. Shaftesbury provides an important antecedent for the idea of a rustic style as one composed of a mixture of dissonances; see Anthony, Earl of Shaftesbury, *The Moralists, A Philosophi-*cal Rhapsody (Indianapolis: Bobbs-Merrill, 1964; first published in 1709), part iii, section ii, pp. 130–132.

4. Uvedale Price, *On the Picturesque*, 1810 edition (Edinburgh: Caldwell, Lloyd, and Co., 1842), pp. 77–82. For an excellent analysis of the opposing varieties of the Picturesque espoused by Knight and Price see Martin Price, "The Picturesque Moment," In *From Sensibility to Romanticism. Essays presented to Frederick A. Pottle*, ed. Frederick W. Hilles and Harold Bloom (Oxford University Press, 1965), pp. 259–260; Raval, "The Picturesque," p. 253.

5. Dora Wiebenson, *The Picturesque Garden in France* (Princeton University Press, 1978), pp. 7–9.

6. The idea that the Englishman's attitude toward nature was to use it as an escape from the spiritual aridity of the age has been discussed by diverse authors. Chief among them are H. F. Clark ["Eighteenth-Century Elysiums. The Role of 'Association' in the Landscape Movement," *Journal of the Warburg and Courtauld Institutes* 6 (1943), 189], Christopher Hussey [*English Gardens and Landscapes, 1700–1750* (New York: Funk and Wagnalls, 1967), p. 101], John Dixon Hunt ["Gardening, and Poetry, and Pope," *Art Quarterly* 37 (spring 1974), 4], and Peter Willis [see *The Genius of the Place: The English Landscape Garden, 1620–1820*, ed. John Dixon Hunt and Peter Willis (London: Paul Elek, 1975), pp. 15–16]. Despite divergencies in interpretation, all these authors agree that, as in a painted landscape by Claude or Poussin, the aim of the Picturesque gardener is to raise nature to the human mind.

7. R. P. Knight, *The Landscape, a Didactic Poem* (London: W. Bulmer and Co., 1794),

ii, 156–161. That in the Picturesque mode the landscape garden is no longer organized into *a priori* shapes is discussed by John Dixon Hunt [*The Figure in the Landscape: Poetry, Painting, and Gardening during the Eighteenth Century* (Johns Hopkins University Press, 1976), p. 120] and by John Gage ["Turner and the Picturesque, I and II," *Burlington* 107 (January and February 1965), 17].

8. H. Newton Barker, "Sir Joseph Banks and the Royal Society," in *Employ'd as a Discoverer*, ed. J. V. S. Megaw (Sydney: A. H. and A. W. Reed, 1971), p. 84. On the difference between scenic travel and travel for a purpose see John Barrell, *The Idea of Landscape and the Sense of Place, 1730–1840: An Approach to the Poetry of John Clare* (Cambridge University Press, 1972), p. 92.

9. For a discussion of the Wittgensteinian idea that the forms of experience indicate there is more than one way of seeing an object, and of this idea's relation to eighteenth-century theories of perception, see H. W. Piper, *The Active Universe: Pantheism and the Concept of Imagination in the English Romantic Poets* (Athlone Press of University of London, 1962), pp. 209–215.

10. For a survey of Associationist doctrines see Martin Kallich, "The Association of Ideas and Critical Theory: Hobbes, Locke, and Addison," *ELH* 12 (December 1945), 291–314 passim.

11. The vogue for topiary, like that for the Picturesque garden, was based on a distate for more unembellished nature. See Miles Hadfield, *Topiary and Ornamental Hedges: Their History and Cultivation* (London: Black, 1971), pp. 47–48. It will be my argument throughout that the European doctrines of Associationism and the Picturesque are intrinsically inimical to the new environments discovered by eighteenth-century explorers—environments bereft of relics, myths, and legends connected with the history of the West. Jay Appleton [*The Experience of Landscape* (New York: Wiley, 1975), p. 41] suggests that it is precisely because of its initial lack of associations that the raw American landscape had to be argued into aesthetic respectability.

12. Gerald Finley ["The Encapsulated Landscape: An Aspect of Gilpin's Picturesque," in *City and Society in the Eighteenth Century*, ed. Paul Fritz and David Williams (Toronto: Hakkert, 1973), 197–202] analyzes the Picturesque "methodology" as it is seen through the eyes of William Combe's satirical *Tour of Dr. Syntax in Search of the Picturesque* (1812). Although Gilpin perceptually isolates that part of the landscape with Picturesque potential, the process of "encapsulation" requires a reorganization and a synthesis of the basic ingredients found in nature.

Hence the traveler must have a pictorial scheme in back of his mind with which to reconstruct the entirety of the scene.

13. On the increasing particularity in characterization as a literary phenomenon see W. Houghton Taylor, " 'Particular Character,' An Early Phase of a Literary Evolution," *PMLA* 60 (March 1945), 161–171 passim. For Reynolds (who rejected the characteristic for landscape painting) and for Gilpin (who subordinated, not freed, the objects in his Picturesque composition), landscape elements could not exist independent of human imagination (see Barrell, *Idea of Landscape*, pp. 51–54).

14. Hunt and Willis, *Genius of the Place*, pp. 3, 31–35.

15. On the notion that the garden could be not merely a land of illusion but a "museum" of matter see Hunt, *The Figure in the Landscape*, p. 32, and, especially, *Jardins en France, 1760–1820. Pays d'illusion. Terre d'expériences* (Paris: Caisse Nationale des Monuments Historiques et des Sites, 1977), pp. 18–19. In the early nineteenth century, the garden might even provide the geography and history of an entire region; see Alfred Hoffmann, *Der Landschaftsgarten* (Hamburg: Broschek, 1963), p. 271.

16. Pierre-Henri Valenciennes, *Eléments de perspective pratique à l'usage des artistes, suivis de réflexions et conseils à un élève sur la peinture et particulièrement sur le genre du paysage* (1800) (Geneva: Minkoff Reprint, 1973), p. 351. Even earlier, Blondel had voiced similar reservations about the potpourri of the English garden; see J. F. Blondel, *Cours d'architecture civile* (Paris: Chez la Veuve Desaint, 1773), IV, p. 6. On the incorporation of wilder scenery into the French garden see Wiebenson, *Picturesque Garden in France*, pp. 105–106; on the English desertion of the garden for travel see Hunt and Willis, *Genius of the Place*, p. 33.

17. François Le Vaillant, *Voyage de . . . dans l'intérieur de l'Afrique, par le Cap de Bonne-Espérance, dans les années 1780, 81, 82, 83, 84, & 85* (Paris: LeRoy, 1790), I, pp. 166–167. The experience was not unusual. In 1738 Thomas Herring, the bishop of Bangor, made a diocesan journey through Wales and found the magnificence of nature such that he feared the sight of Stowe afterward would make him smile; see Elizabeth W. Manwaring, *Italian Landscape in Eighteenth-Century England* (Oxford University Press, 1925), pp. 170–171.

18. Désiré Raoul-Rochette, *Lettres sur la Suisse* (Paris: G. Engelmann, 1824), I, part II, pp. 10–11.

19. On the Picturesque garden as *décor* see E. de Ganay, "Les rochers et les eaux dans les jardins à l'anglaise," *Revue de l'art Ancien et Modern* 66 (July 1934), 66–69; Wie-

benson,, *Picturesque Garden in France*, pp. 104–105. For the inherently dramatic struggle obtaining in the English Picturesque garden, whereby the energies of art wrestle with the resistant materials of nature, see Price, "The Picturesque Moment," p. 277. The association of garden with theater goes back to the Italian Renaissance; see Hunt and Willis, *Genius of the Place*, p. 36.

20. For a general survey of this tradition see E. H. Gombrich, *The Heritage of Apelles, Studies in the Art of the Renaissance* (Cornell University Press, 1976), pp. 13, 32–33; Kenneth Clark, *Landscape into Art*, second edition (London: Murray, 1976), p. 17.

21. Robert A. Koch, *Joachim Patinir* (Princeton University Press, 1968), p. 19. Koch's assertion that Patinir's "constructions" defy optical reality because he gives as much detail to distant and rocky masses as to those nearby should be contrasted with the careful analyses of Henrich Gerhard Franz [*Niederländische Landschaftsmalerei im Zeitalter des Manierismus* (Graz: Akademische, 1969), I, p. 42].

22. William Smiley Eddelmann III, Landscape on the Seventeenth- and Eighteenth-Century Italian Stage, Ph.D. diss., Stanford University, 1972, pp. 52–72. On the development and evolution of the "satyric" landscape see E. H. Gombrich, *Norm and Form, Studies in the Art of the Renaissance* (London: Phaidon, 1966), pp. 119–121; John Reese Rothgeb, The Scenographic Expression of Nature (1545–1845): The Development of Style, Ph.D. diss., Case Western Reserve University, 1971, pp. 102–120, 152–160 passim; S. Lang, "The Genesis of the English Landscape Garden," in *The Picturesque Garden and its Influence outside the British Isles*, ed. Nikolaus Pevsner (Washington, D.C.: Dumbarton Oaks, 1974), p. 18.

23. For a discussion of Juvarra's innovations see M. Viale Ferrero, *Filippo Juvarra, scenegrafo e architetto teatrale* (Turin: Pozzo, 1970). On the dialogue between theater and reality during the eighteenth century see Herbert Dieckmann, "Die Wandlung des Nachahmungsbegriffes in der Französischen Ästhetik des 18. Jahrhunderts," in *Nachahmung und Illusion*, ed. H. R. Jauss (Munich: Wilhelm Fink, 1965), pp. 47–49; Osvald Siren, *China and the Gardens of Europe of the Eighteenth Century* (New York: Ronald, 1950), pp. 104–105; E. H. Gombrich, *Meditations on a Hobby Horse* (London: Phaidon, 1968), chapter "Imagery and Art in the Romantic Period."

24. On Burke's and Chambers's invocation of the Chinese garden because of the relation of its "terrible" scenes to the Sublime see Dora Wiebenson, " 'L'architecture terrible' and the 'jardin anglo-chinois,' " *Journal of the Society of Architectural Historians*, 27 (May 1968), 138.

25. On the rise of exoticism in seventeenth-century France see Geoffroy Atkinson, *Les relations de voyages du XVIIᵉ siècle et l'évolution des idées* (Paris: Librairie Ancienne Edouard Champion, 1924), pp. 171–174; Martin Eidelberg, "A Chinoiserie by Jacques Vigouroux Duplessis," *Journal of the Walters Art Gallery* 35 (1977), 72.

26. John Nieuhof, *An Embassy from the East-India Company of the United Provinces to the Grand Tartar Cham, Emperor of China*, tr. John Ogilby (London: John Macock, 1669), pp. 50–55, 64–65. For a modern analysis of the famous T'ai hu stones, regarded as unexcelled masterpieces of nature since the Sung period, see Osvald Siren, *Gardens of China* (New York: Ronald, 1949), pp. 21–28. On the role of the Jesuits in transmitting to the West the Chinese veneration for mountains see D. F. Lunsingh Scheurleer, *Chinese Export Porcelain Chine de Commande* (Salem, N.H.: Faber and Faber, 1974), p. 81.

27. For a survey of the rise of the belief in the intimate relation between man and nature (one of the unique characteristics of Chinese thought) and its relation to landscape painting see Michael Sullivan, "Pictorial Art and the Attitude toward Nature in Ancient China," *Art Bulletin* 36 (March 1954), 1–2. On the infiltration into the eighteenth century of the Taoist idea that the breath of nature's own pulsating life must be captured in painting see Siren, *Gardens of China*, pp. 17–19; Numa Broc, *La géographie des philosophes. Géographes et voyageurs français au XVIIIᵉ siècle* (Paris: Ophrys, 1975), p. 407.

28. On the Japanese use of nature as the matter of art see Gérard Barrière, "L'emotion que peut donner un arpent de terre quand on sait ce que signifie un jardin au Japon," *Connaissance des arts* 270 (August 1974), 62–63; Toshio Takeuchi, "Die Schönheit des Unbelebten," in *Proceedings of the Sixth International Congress of Aesthetics*, ed. Rudolf Zeitler (University of Uppsala Press, 1972), pp. 670–671.

29. Jean Ehrard, *L'idée de la nature en France dans la première moitié du XVIIIᵉ siècle* (Paris: S.E.U.P.E.N., 1963), II, p. 742.

30. The classic discussion remains Arthur O. Lovejoy and George Boas, *Primitivism and Related Ideas in Antiquity* (Johns Hopkins University Press, 1935). A more recent survey is R. G. Collingwood, *The Idea of Nature* (Oxford University Press, 1960).

31. Philostratus, *The Life of Apollonius of Tyana*, tr. F. C. Conybeare (London: William Heinemann, 1926), I, p. 309. On the persistence of the idea of the universe as a great animal see Marjorie Hope Nicolson, *The Breaking of the Circle: Studies in the Ef-*

fect of the "New Science" upon Seventeenth-Century Poetry (Columbia University Press, 1960), p. 2.

32. Jan Bialostocki, "The Renaissance Concept of Nature and Antiquity," in Acts of the Twentieth International Congress of the History of Art (Princeton University Press, 1963), pp. 19–20, 23–24. Also see Hiram Haydn's excellent discussion of the Renaissance conception of the nature of nature, "Il Controrinascimento e la natura della natura," in Problemi del Manierismo, ed. Amadeo Quondam (Naples: Guida, 1975), pp. 186, 190–195, 205–206. Haydn groups Renaissance thinkers into five categories based on their views of nature: the Christian Humanists Martin Luther and John Calvin, the Christian Occultists Cornelius Agrippa and Paracelsus, the ultra-Naturalists (including Michel de Montaigne), the Romantics Pico della Mirandola and Giordano Bruno, and the Materialists Niccolò Machiavelli and Francesco Guicciardini. Montaigne's primitivistic naturalism—more secular than Pico's symbolic pantheism—is of interest. For him, nature is a mighty Venus Genetrix, an indifferent mother who gives rise to the infinite diversity and mutability of the world. Montaigne's naturalistic bent, which was expressed in a profound interest in the customs and costumes of the inhabitants of the New World (as reported by Jean de Léry and André Thévet), opposes the "typical nudity" of the Brazilians (i.e., Nature) with the characteristic overdressing (i.e. Art) of the Europeans. In the eighteenth century this attitude was to be expanded to include an unvarnished, uncosmeticized landscape, i.e. a naked nature freed of culture. See chapter 4 of the present volume.

33. Also see Götz Pochat's discussion in Der Exotismus des Mittelalters und der Renaissance (Stockholm: Almquist and Wiksell, 1970), p. 46.

34. Lester G. Crocker, Diderot's Chaotic Order, Approach to Synthesis (Princeton University Press, 1974), p. 71.

35. On the concept of energeia, recognized by Plutarch and Horace and vital to Renaissance, Baroque, and eighteenth-century aesthetics, see Mary E. Hazard, "The Anatomy of 'Liveliness' as a Concept in Renaissance Esthetics" (to appear in the Journal of Aesthetics and Art Criticism); Bernard Teyssèdre, Roger de Piles et les débats sur le coloris au siècle de Louis XIV (Paris: Bibliothèque des Arts, 1957), p. 68, n. 3; Eric Rothstein, " 'Ideal Presence' and the 'Non-Finito' in Eighteenth-Century Aesthetics," Eighteenth-Century Studies 9 (spring 1976), 320–322; Rose Frances Egan, "The Genesis of the Theory of 'Art for Art's Sake' in Germany and England," Smith College Studies in Modern Language 2 (July 1921), 60.

36. The Works of the Right Honourable Joseph Addison, coll. Mr. Ticknell (London: Vernor and Hood, 1804), II, 367, Spec. 414. A perceptive discussion of the pleasures of the imagination provided by Addison's "accidental landskips" can be found in Ernest Lee Tuveson's The Imagination as a Means of Grace, Locke and the Aesthetics of Romanticism (University of California Press, 1960), pp. 115–117, and in Hans-Joachim Possin's Natur und Landschaft bei Addison, ed. Gerhard Müller-Schwefe and Friedrich Schubel (Tübingen: Niemeyer, 1965), pp. 157–158.

37. That nature could be aesthetically vindicated because of the regularity of its "architecture" has been discussed by Arthur O. Lovejoy ["The Chinese Origin of a Romanticism," Journal of English and Germanic Philology 32 (January 1933), 11] and by Gary Iseninger ["The Work of Art as Artifact," British Journal of Aesthetics 19 (spring 1979), 148–151].

38. Henri Focillon, The Life of Forms in Art, tr. Charles Beecher Hogan and George Kubler, second English edition (New York: Wittenborn, Schultz, 1948), p. 33. On the Western tradition see H. W. Janson, "The 'Image made by Chance' in Renaissance Thought," in De Artibus Opuscula, Essays in Honor of Erwin Panofsky, ed. Millard Meiss (Zurich: Buehler, 1960), pp. 254–255. The history of the Renaissance and post-Renaissance Kunst- und Wunderkammer is central to this development, since such "rooms" or "cabinets" artfully juxtaposed shells, corals, and marine plants with the most contrived art in the manner of the Elder Pliny, who treated the history of art as an appendix to the study of metals and gems, naturalia mingled with artificilia, science with art, the true with the false. Not until the seventeenth century did the natural-history cabinet separate itself out of such a mixture and this was largely due to the impetus of science. See Julius von Schlosser, Die Kunst- und Wunderkammern der Spätrenaissance. Ein Beitrag zur Geschichte des Sammelwesens, ed. Jean-Louis Sponsel (Leipzig: Klinkhardt and Biermann, 1908), pp. 73–76, 101.

39. There is a profound difference between the "chance-image theory" followed by Leonardo and Michelangelo (discussed by Janson) and the perception of real beauty lodged in the relief of the terrain. It is in this spirit that Erasmus Warren in his Geologia of 1690 praises "that roughness, brokenness, and multiform confusion in the surface of the Earth . . . which will appear to be as the . . . Carvings, and Ornamental Sculptures; that make up the Lineaments and Features of Nature, not to say her Braveries" [cited in Marjorie Hope Nicolson's Mountain Gloom and Mountain Glory. The Development of the Aesthetics of the Infinite (Cornell University Press, 1959), p. 267]. William Hamilton's Campi Phlegraei, Observations on the Volcanos of the Two Sicilies (Naples, 1776), II, pl. V, testi-

fies to the growing scientific curiosity for actual "distinctive marks" of nature that prod the desire to replicate rather than *phantasia*.

40. In 1772 Joseph Banks journeyed to Iceland, stopping at Staffa on the way. His account of Staffa, with detailed descriptions, illustrations by John Frederick Miller, and measurements of basaltic formations, was published in Thomas Pennant's *A Tour in Scotland and Voyage to the Hebrides* (Chester: John Monk, 1774), 262–263. William Daniell, in his important *Illustrations of the Island of Staffa, in a Series of Views* (London: Longman, Hurst, Rees, Orme, and Brown, 1818), p. 5, revoices Banks's initial enthusiasm, declaring that "this piece of nature's workmanship far surpasses everything that invention, luxury, and taste ever produced among the Greeks." Charles Bonnet, in a similar vein, speaks of microscopic salt crystals as "Obélisques" superior to those fashioned by art [*Contemplation de la nature*, second edition (Amsterdam: Marc-Michel Rey, 1769), I, pp. 236–238].

41. Jean-Baptiste-Joseph Le Gentil, *Voyage dans les mers de l'Inde fait par ordre du roi à l'occasion du passage de Vénus, sur le disque du soleil, le 6 juin 1761 & le 3 du même mois 1769* (Paris: Imprimerie Royale, 1779), II, p. 641.

42. George Vancouver, *A Voyage of Discovery to the North Pacific Ocean, and Round the World; in which the Coast of North-West America has been carefully Examined and Accurately Surveyed, Undertaken by His Majesty's Command, principally with a View to Discover the Existence of Any Navigable Communication between the North Pacific and North Atlantic Oceans; and Performed in the Years 1790, 1791, 1792, 1793, 1794, and 1795* (London: G. and G. and J. Robinson and J. Edwards, 1798), III, pp. 334–335.

43. Carl Lang, *Gallerie der unterirdischen Schöpfungswunder und des menschlichen Kunstfleises unter der Erde* (Leipzig: Karl Tauchniss, 1806–1807), I, p. 101.

44. Shaftesbury, *The Moralists*, part iii, ii, p. 125. The continuing account in the eighteenth century of customary associations led increasingly to the notion that the standard of "nature" in art is a function of habits formed by association in the mind. As we have seen, this notion did not go unopposed. Shaftesbury, with his combination of Platonic Idealism and psychological intuitionism, was determined to reassert not only the formal criterion of nature in the face of the relativism, which went hand in hand with Associationism, but also its "real" status outside the mind of the beholder. Thus he provides a vital critical alternative to those thinkers committed to the conventionality of seeing. See Lawrence Manley, *Convention, 1500–1750* (Harvard University Press, 1980), pp. 340–341.

45. Denis Diderot, *Le rêve de D'Alembert* (1782), ed. Paul Vernière (Paris: Marcel Didier, 1951), p. 4. For analogous ideas see Jean-Baptiste-René Robinet, *Considérations philosophiques de la gradation naturelle des formes de l'être, ou les essais de la nature qui apprend à faire l'homme* (Paris: Charles Saillant, 1768), pp. 14–15. The new theories furthered by Newton's famous General Scholium to the 1713 edition of the *Principia* had much to do with encouraging the attribution of supernatural characteristics to the physical world; see Ernest Tuveson, "Space, Deity, and the 'Natural Sublime,'" *Modern Language Quarterly* 12 (March 1951), 32.

46. Wolfgang Herrmann, *Laugier and Eighteenth-Century French Theory* (London: Zwemmer, 1962), pp. 197–198, 215.

47. Roseline Bacou, *Piranesi, Etchings and Drawings* (Boston: New York Graphic Society, 1975), pp. 19, 154. See also John Wilton-Ely, *The Mind and Art of Giovanni Battista Piranesi* (London: Thames and Hudson, 1978), p. 119. Here the cyclopean town walls of Cori from the *Antichità di Cora* (1764) clearly appear to be more the work of nature than of man. Many more examples of this type could be educed.

48. Jean Houel, *Voyage pittoresque des isles de Sicile, de Malte et de Lipari, où l'on traite des antiquités qui s'y trouvent encore; des principaux phénomènes que la nature y offre; du costume des habitans & de quelques usages* (Paris: De l'Imprimerie de Monsieur, 1782), IV, p. 32.

49. Ibid., I, p. 28, pl. 20.

50. *Oeuvres complètes de Jacques-Henri Bernardin de Saint-Pierre* (1784), ed. Louis Aimé-Martin (Paris: Méquigonon-Marvis, 1818), V, pp. 93–95 and the entire section entitled "Ruines de la nature." Gilpin, in his *Observations on the Mountains and Lakes of Cumberland* (1808 edition), likewise comments that we consider ruins more the work of nature than of art; see Noyes, *Wordsworth and the Art of Landscape*, p. 25.

51. W. D. Robson-Scott, *The Literary Background of the Gothic Revival in Germany* (Oxford: Clarendon, 1965), pp. 101–103.

52. Ibid., pp. 96–97. For a discussion of Herder's influence on the young Goethe's idea of art as another manifestation of nature see Egan, "The Genesis of the Theory of 'Art for Art's Sake,'" p. 48.

53. Samuel Simon Witte, *Ueber die Bildung und der Ursprung des keilformigen Inschriften zu Persepolis, Ein philosophisch-geschichtler Versuch* (Rostock and Leipzig: Karl Christop Stiller, 1799), pp. 1–2. In the preface, Witte alludes to his earlier hypothesis in which he attempts to interpret cuneiform as the result of natural causes. By the time of this study, however, he has

altered his view and no longer claims that the cuneiform inscriptions are necessarily connected with the origin of the ruins of Persepolis. As testimony to the tenacity of Witte's early ideas I cite two notable travelers who took him to task: Alexander von Humboldt, *Zerstreute Bemerkungen über den Basalt der ältern und neuern Schriftsteller* (1800), pp. 23–33 passim; Luigi Mayer, *Views in Egypt from the Original Drawings in the Possession of Sir Robert Ainslie, Taken during his Embassy to Constantinople by . . . ; Engraved by and under the Direction of Thomas Milton; with Historical Observations, and Incidental Illustrations for the Manners and Customs of the Natives of This Country* (London: R. Bowyer, 1801), p. 17. Mayer points out that Witte was not alone in his beliefs: James Bryant (the mythographer) imagined that the three largest pyramids were not artificial structures of stone and mortar, but solid rock cut into a pyramidal shape, and James Bruce (the explorer) supported this opinion when he suggested that the lower course of the pyramids was an actual stratum of rock.

54. Marjorie Hope Nicolson, *Science and Imagination* (Hamden, Conn.: Archon, 1976), pp. 206–209. For the change in axis of interest in natural history between the seventeenth and the eighteenth centuries as revealed through microscopy see François Delaporte, "Des organismes problématiques," *Dixhuitième Siècle* 9 (1977), 58.

55. Johann Beckmann, *Beyträge zur Geschichte der Erfindungen* (Leipzig: Paul Gotthelf Kummer, 1799), IV, p. 225; V, pp. 144–146.

56. Antoine Sabatier, *Dictionnaire des origines, découvertes, inventions, et établissemens* (Paris: Moutard, 1776), III, p. 240.

57. *Voyage de d'Entrecasteaux, envoyé à la recherche de La Pérouse. Publié par order de sa majesté l'Empereur et roi, sous le ministère de S. E. le vice-amiral Decrés, Comte de l'Empire*, ed. M. de Rossel (Paris: Imprimerie Impériale, 1801), I, p. 55. The eighteenth-century developments traced here seem to be singularly prescient of 1960s "earth works" sculpture. On the environment defining what is sculptural see Jack Burnham, *Great Western Salt Works, System Esthetics. Essays on the Meaning of Post-Formalist Art* (New York: Braziller, 1974), p. 20.

58. Jean-Baptiste-René Robinet, *De la nature* (Amsterdam: E. van Harrevelt, 1763–1766), IV, 111–112. Part of the problem must be seen within the context of art's inability to divest itself of customary habit, so that both in the making and in the perceiving of the artifact vision became mechanical. Paradoxically, the whole rhetorical tradition of the artlessness of art—the creation of the illusion that things could not be otherwise, such that the effect of the finished product is "natural"— was seen by midcentury to rest on a mechanical convention. That is to say, art's "second nature" was seen as purely rhetorical in character, sanctioned by custom rather than by an empirical experience of actual particulars; art had become a technical curiosity. See Manley, *Convention*, pp. 176–177, 343.

59. Jörg Garms, "Machine, Composition und Histoire in der Französischen Kritik um 1750," *Zeitschrift für Asthetik und allgemeine Kuntswissenschaft* 16, no. 1 (1971), 28–33.

60. This idea culminated in the eighteenth-century fascination with the automaton, that "machine which moves by itself, & which possesses within itself the principle of its own movement. . . ." (Sabatier, *Dictionnaire des origines*, I, pp. 154–156). It is interesting to juxtapose this ultimate machine with Edmund Burke's appraisal of the utterly "natural" Stonehenge: " . . . the rudeness of the work increases the cause of grandeur, as it excludes the idea of art and contrivance; for dexterity produces another sort of effect, which is different enough from this" [*A Philosophical Inquiry into the Origin of Our Ideas of the Sublime and the Beautiful* (1757) (New York: Harper and Brothers, 1844), part ii, section xiii, p. 98.

61. Barthélemy Faujas de Saint-Fond, *Essai de géologie ou mémoires pour servir à l'histoire naturelle du globe* (Paris: Gabriel Dufour, 1803–1809), II, pp. 197–199.

62. Robert Ker Porter, *Travelling Sketches in Russia and Sweden during the Years 1805, 1806, 1807, 1808* (London: John Stockdale, 1813), I, pp. 31–34. For a modern discussion of the French sculptor's project of a rearing horse on the edge of a rocky elevation—inspired by Bernini's dramatic effects at the Piazza Navona in the *Fountain of the Four Rivers*—see George Levitine, *The Sculpture of Falconet* (Greenwich, Conn.: New York Graphic Society, 1971), pp. 55–59.

63. Porter, *Travelling Sketches in Russia*, I, pp. 34–35.

64. Ronald Paulson has identified the polysemous forms of the Augustans—the puns, zeugmas, and juxtapositions of Butler, Dryden, Swift, and Pope ["Hogarth and the English Garden: Visual and Verbal Structures," in *Encounters: Essays on Literature and the Visual Arts*, ed. John Dixon Hunt (London: Studio Vista, 1971), pp. 84–90; *Emblem and Expression: Meaning in English Art of the Eighteenth Century* (London: Thames and Hudson, 1975), p. 43].

65. On the Mannerist love of ambiguity in architectural grottos see Lucile M. Golson, "Serlio, Primaticcio and the Architectural Grotto," *Gazette des Beaux-Arts* 70 (February 1971), 95–96; Erik Forssman, *Säule und*

Ornament. Studien zum Problem des Manierismus in den Nordischen Säulenbüchern und Vorlageblättern des 16. und 17. Jahrhunderts (Stockholm: Almquist and Wiksell, 1956), pp. 140–144; Ernst Guldau, "Das Monster-Portal am Palazzo Zuccari in Rom," *Zeitschrift für Kunstgeschichte* 32, no. 3–4 (1969), 249–250.

66. Ernst Kris, "Der Stil 'rustique,' die Verwendung des Naturabgusses bei Wenzel Jamnitzer und Bernard Palissy," *Jahrbuch der Kunsthistorischen Sammlungen in Wien*, N.F., I (1926), 179–196 passim.

67. Bernard Palissy, *Oeuvres complètes*, ed. Paul-Antoine Cap (Paris: J.-J. Dubochet et Cie, 1844), p. xii. Also see Henri Delange, *Monographie de l'oeuvre de Bernard Palissy, suivie d'un choix de ses continuateurs ou imitateurs* (Paris: Quai Voltaire, 1862), pp. 28–29; Serje Grandjean, *Bernard Palissy et son école* (Paris: Au Pont des Arts, 1952), pp. 23–36 passim.

68. Peter Ward-Jackson, "Some Mainstreams and Tributaries in European Ornament, 1500–1750: Part III," *Victoria and Albert Museum Bulletin* 3 (October 1967), 123–124.

69. For the best modern evaluation of Palissy's "science" see H. R. Thompson, "The Geographical and Geological Observations of Bernard Palissy the Potter," *Annals of Science* 10 (June 1954), 149–165. On the larger issue of the formation of the "stilo non-finito" see Elisabeth Herget, *Die Sala Terrena im Deutschen Barock* (Frankfurt-am-Main: Vita, 1954), pp. 69–73; Bertha Harris Wiles, *The Fountains of Florentine Sculptors and their Followers from Donatello to Bernini* (Harvard University Press, 1933), pp. 80–85.

70. On the Mannerist love for metamorphic forms, for *grilli* and chimeras, see Thomas DaCosta Kaufmann, "Arcimboldo's Imperial Allegory," *Zeitschrift für Kunstgeschichte* 39, no. 4 (1974), 281–286.

71. Georges Marlier, "Pourquoi ces rochers à visages humains?" *Connaissances des Arts* 124 (June 1962), 90–91. Also see Pochat, *Exotismus*, p. 177.

72. Ludwig von Baldass, "Die Niederländische Landschaftsmalerie von Patinir bis Brueghel," *Jahrbuch der Kunsthistorischen Sammlungen des allerhöchsten Kaiserhauses, Wien* 34 (winter 1918), 113.

73. Eva-Maria Schenck, *Das Bilderrätsel* (Cologne: Kleikamp, 1968), p. 108.

74. Stuart Cary Welch, *Wonders of the Age. Masterpieces of Early Safavid Painting, 1501–1576* (Cambridge, Mass.: Fogg Art Museum, Harvard University, 1979), pls. 24, 27, 37, 51. These miniatures, among many others, illustrate strange gatherings of rock spirits, earth spirits, and ghouls lurking in the terrain.

75. *Anamorfosen, Spel met Perspectief* (catalog), Rijksmuseum, Amsterdam, 1975–76.

76. Heinrich Gerhard Franz, "Meister der Spätmanieristischen Landschaftsmalerei in den Niederlanden," *Jahrbuch des Kunsthistorischen Institutes der Universität Graz* 3–4 (1968–69), 21, 44–48.

77. Olaf Koester, "Joos de Momper, the Younger, Prolegomena to the Study of His Paintings," *Artes* 2 (1966), 14–17.

78. Herget, *Sala Terrena*, p. 65.

79. Roger de Piles, *Cours de peinture par principes* (1708) (Paris: Barrois l'aîné, Firmin-Didot, 1791), pp. 158–160 (see the section entitled "Du paysage").

80. Dean Tolle Mace, "Ut pictura poesis, Dryden, Poussin, and the Parallel of Poetry and Painting in the Seventeenth Century," in *Encounters*, pp. 73–77.

81. Cited in Manwaring, *Italian Landscape*, pp. 49–50. For Joshua Reynolds's discussion of the "original" or "characteristical" style and Rosa's embodiment of its "irregular, wild, and incorrect" qualities see *Discourses on Art*, ed. Robert R. Wark (Yale University Press, 1975), pp. 84–85.

82. Joseph Lycett, *Views in Australia or New South Wales, & Van Diemen's Land, Delineated, in Fifty Views with Descriptive Letter Press, Dedicated by Permission, to the Right Hon. Earl Bathurst, etc. by . . . Artist to Major-General Macquarie, Late Governor of These Colonies* (London: J. Souter, 1824), pl. 17. The view on the Wingeecarrabee River is worthy of Rosa's "transcendant genius," whose "representations of some of the rudest scenes of nature" approach "so near to the sublimity of Nature itself."

83. Bernhard Fehr, "The Antagonism of Forms in the Eighteenth Century," in *Von Englands geistigen Beständen* (Frauenfeld: Huber, 1944), p. 86.

84. Albert Ilg, *Die Fischer von Erlach* (Vienna: Carl Konegen, 1895), I, 532–534.

85. Ibid., 527.

86. Johann Bernhard Fischer von Erlach, *Entwurff einer historischen Architektur* (Vienna, 1721), pl. 18. For a modern evaluation of the influence of Deinocrates's project on the Baroque period see Werner Körte, "Deinocrates und die Barocke Phantasie," *Die Antike* 13 (1937), 290–293.

87. Axel Janeck, "Naturalismus und Realismus. Untersuchungen zur Darstellung der Natur bei Pieter van Laer und Claude Lorraine," *Storia dell'Arte* 28 (1976), 287. This excellent article poses the question whether the far-reaching topographic exactitude in seventeeth-century art might not be related to the then-emerging modern sciences.

88. Modern scholarship has not explained the reason or illuminated the source for the specimenlike formations in Mantegna's paintings. See Paul Kristeller, *Andrea Mantegna* (Berlin and Leipzig: Cosmos, 1902), pp. 174, 239–240; Andrew Martindale, *The Complete Paintings of Mantegna* (New York: Abrams, 1972), pp. 89, 113, 117.

89. As with Mantegna, the literature on such key works as Leonardo's *Madonna of the Rocks* offers no comprehensive explanation of the setting. See A. Richard Turner, *The Vision of Landscape in Renaissance Italy* (Princeton University Press, 1966), pp. 19–27. More recently, Martin Kemp discussed the Marian imagery—especially dear to the Immaculatists—of "dove-cleft of rocks" and "cavities of walls," metaphors taken from the *Song of Songs*. See Kemp's *Leonardo da Vinci, The Marvellous Works of Nature and Man* (Harvard University Press, 1981), p. 96. On the empirical foundation for Leonardo's and Dürer's botanical studies see Brian Morley, "The Plant Illustrations of Leonardo da Vinci," *Burlington* 121 (September 1979), 553–560. Leonardo's drawings were rediscovered shortly after the accession of George III in 1760. See Arthur S. Marks, "An Anatomical Drawing by Alexander Cozens," *Journal of the Warburg and Courtauld Institutes* 30 (1967), 437–438.

90. Koch, *Patinir*, p. 19.

91. Arthur K. Wheelock, Jr., *Perspective, Optics, and Delft Artists around 1650* (New York: Garland, 1977), p. 49. Even earlier, science, technology, and magic were closely connected at the court of Rudolf II. See Maria Poprzecka, "Le paysage industriel vers 1600," *Bulletin du Musée National de Varsovie* 14 (1973), 46.

92. Clarence J. Glacken, *Traces on the Rhodian Shore; Nature and Culture in Western Thought from Ancient Times to the End of the Eighteenth Century* (University of California Press, 1967), p. 25. Glacken writes from the perspective of a cultural geographer. For the best art-historical analysis of the rise and development of ancient landscape painting see Peter Heinrich von Blanckenhagen and Christine Alexander, *The Paintings from Boscotrescase* (Heidelberg: Kerle, 1962), pp. 26–30, 55–57; Peter Heinrich von Blanckenhagen, "The Odyssey Frieze," *Mitteilungen des Deutschen Archaeologischen Instituts Roemische Abteilung* 70 (1963), 112–115.

93. Since the literature on topography is significantly large, I will mention only a few salient, recent examples: Luigi Salerno, "La pittura di paesaggio," *Storia dell'Arte* 24–25 (1975), 111–124; Germain Bazin, "Paesaggio redivivo," *L'Oeil* 258–259 (January–February 1977), 2–9; Rosario Assunto, *Speccio vivente del mondo (Artisti stranieri in Roma)* (Rome: De Luca, 1978), pp. 25 ff.

94. Philip Conisbee, "French Landscapes in London," *Burlington* 120 (January 1978), 43–44.

95. Giovanni Paolo Lomazzo, *Idea del Tempio della Pittura*, ed. Robert Klein (Florence: Nella Sede dell'Institute Palazzo Strozzi, 1974), I, p. 298; see chapter xxxii, "Paesi e loro forme diverse" and "Paesi e loro forme applicate ai Dei."

96. Hunt, *Figure in the Landscape*, p. 39. It is interesting to compare this eighteenth-century habit of mind with that espoused by Ruskin when he drew an analogy between the passion for minuteness of the landscape painter and that of Louis Agassiz. See W. F. Axton, "Victorian Landscape Painting: A Change in Outlook," in *Nature and the Victorian Imagination*, ed. Ulrich Knoepflmacher and G. B. Tennyson (University of California Press, 1977), p. 291.

97. Iola A. Williams, *Early English Watercolours and Some Cognate Drawings by Artists Born not later than 1785* (London: The Connoisseur, 1952), pp. 5–8, 43.

98. Janeck, "Naturalismus und Realismus," pp. 285–287.

99. Dorothea Nyberg, *Meissonnier, an Eighteenth-Century Phenomenon. Oeuvre de Juste-Aurèle Meissonier* (New York: Blom, 1969), p. 38.

100. On the history and tradition of the *locus amoenus* in pastoral art and literature see Rensselaer W. Lee, *Names on Trees. Ariosto into Art* (Princeton University Press, 1977), pp. 29–30.

101. Oliver T. Banks, *Watteau and the North: Studies in the Dutch and Flemish Baroque Influences on French Rococo Painting* (New York: Garland, 1977), pp. 69–70. Also see Nyberg, *Meissonnier*, p. 37; Ward-Jackson, "Mainstreams and Tributaries," part III, pp. 124–129.

102. Georg Weise, "Vitalismo, animismo e panpsichismo e la decorazione nel Cinquecento e nel Seicento," *Critica d'Arte* 6 (November–December 1959), part I, 386–388.

103. Hermann Bauer, *Rocaille, zur Herkunft und zum Wesen eines Ornament-Motivs* (Berlin: de Gruyter, 1962), pp. 56–58. For a broader discussion of the aesthetic of ruins see Paul Zucker, *Fascination of Decay. Ruins: Relic-Symbol-Ornament* (Ridgewood, N.J.: Gregg, 1968), p. 3.

104. Marianne Roland Michel, "Le cabinet de Bonnier de La Mosson, et la participation de La Joue à son décor," *Bulletin de la Société de l'histoire de l'art français* 1975 (1976), 220. Schlosser, in his *Kunst- und Wunderkammern* (pp. 98–100), notes the connection between the Mannerist collector's love of the unusual, refined, and complex *scherzo* and the ornamental forms

of the Rococo. Indeed, one might even suggest a parallel between the Rudofinian love of a "courtly" technology, embodied in automata, and the "galant" science of Algarotti's Newtonianism "pour les dames." Further, the important idea of moving out from the confines of the natural-history cabinet into the wide world itself was cogently expressed in Albertus Seba's *Locupletissimi Rerum naturaliam Thesauri accurata Descriptio et Iconibus artificiosissimis expressin, per universam Physices historiam* (Amsterdam: Janssonio-Waesbergios, & J. Wetstonium, & Gul. Smith, 1734–1765), I, p. 2. Indeed, Seba notes that one of the advantages of the moderns over the ancients, and particularly the moderns of the eighteenth century, is that they rely on their own eyes, not solely on the eyes of others. According to Seba, however, no single person can exhaust the vast treasure of nature or order the immense divisibility of matter. Hence the importance of the discoveries made by members of scientific academies and the new itineraries formulated by physicists and mathematicians who voyage at these academies' expense and record what they behold.

105. Between 1660 and 1800, collections of voyages were very popular. By the middle of the eighteenth century the great voyages of study, which undertook and largely achieved a vast description of the sensible universe, were underway. See Percy G. Adams, *Travelers and Travel Liars, 1600–1800* (University of California Press, 1962), p. 88; Albert Béguin, *L'âme romantique et le rêve. Essai sur le romantisme allemand et la poésie française* (Paris: Editions des Cahiers du Sud, 1937), I, p. 113; Michel Duchet, "L'histoire des voyages: Originalité et influence," in *L'Abbé Prevost* (Aix-en-Provence: Ophrys, 1965), p. 154; Paul van Tieghem, *Le sentiment de la nature dans le préromantisme européen* (Paris: Nizet, 1960), pp. 97–98.

106. André Chenier, *L'invention, poème*, ed. Paul Dimoff (Paris: Nizet, 1966), pp. 116–118.

107. P. L. Moreau de Maupertuis, "Lettre sur le progrès des sciences," in *Oeuvres* (Hildesheim: Olms, 1965), pp. 378–388.

108. Ibid., p. 391.

109. Ibid., 423–430.

110. Denis Diderot, *Pensées sur l'interprétation de la nature* (Paris, 1755), p. 14.

111. "Découverte," in *Encyclopédie, ou dictionnaire raisonné des sciences, des arts et métiers*, 1754, IV, p. 705.

112. Charles de Brosses, *Histoire des navigations aux terres australes. Contenant de ce que l'on sçait des moeurs & des productions des contrées découvertes jusqu'à ce jour; &*

où il est traité de l'utilité d'y faire de plus amples découvertes, & des moyens d'y former un établissement (Paris: Durand, 1756), I, pp. 11–12.

113. Edward Young, *Conjectures on Original Composition* (1759) (Leeds: Scholar, 1966), p. 48.

114. William Duff, *An Essay on Original Genius; and Its Various Modes of Exertion in Philosophy and the Fine Arts, particularly in Poetry*, second edition (London: Edward and Charles Dilly, 1767), p. 86.

115. John Hawkesworth, *An Account of the Voyages Undertaken by the Order of His Recent Majesty for Making Discoveries in the Southern Hemisphere, and Successively Performed by Commodore Byron, Captain Wallis, Captain Carteret, and Captain Cook, in the Dolphin, the Swallow, and the Endeavour; Drawn Up from the Journals Which Were Kept by the Several Commanders and from the Papers of Joseph Banks, Esq.* (London: W. Strahan & T. Cadell, 1773), I, p. iii.

116. Cited in Mona Ozouf, *La fête révolutionnaire, 1789–1799* (Paris: Gallimard, 1976), p. 16.

117. Andrew Sparrman, *A Voyage to the Cape of Good Hope, towards the Antartic Polar Cicle, and round the World; But chiefly into the Country of the Hottentots and Caffres from the Year 1772 to 1776*, tr. from the Swedish (London: G. G. J. and J. Robinson, 1777), p. iii. For a perceptive modern assessment of this period, in which everything seemed novel and was greeted with enthusiasm, see Broc, *La géographie des philosophes*, p. 9.

118. Cornelius Le Bruyn, *Travels into Muscovy, Persia, and Part of the East-Indies, Containing an Accurate Description of Whatever is Most Remarkable in Those Countries, and Embellished with Three Hundred and Twenty Copper Plates, Representing the Finest Prospects, and Most Considerable Cities in Those Parts; The Different Habits of the People; the Singular and Extraordinary Birds, Fishes and Plants which are There to be Found: As Likewise the Antiquities of Those Countries . . . The Whole Being Delineated on the Spot, from the Respective Objects*, tr. from the French (London: A. Bettesworth and C. Hitch, S. Birt, C. Davis, J. Clarke, S. Harding, D. Browne, A. Millar, J. Shuckburgh, and T. Osborne, 1737), I, p. 2. The plates in this edition retain the French captions.

119. *A Voyage to the Pacific Ocean, Undertaken by the Command of His Majesty, for Making Discoveries in the Northern Hemisphere. To Determine the Position and Extent of the West Side of North America; Its Distance from Asia; and the Practicability of a Northern Passage to Europe, Performed under the Direction of Captains Cook, Clerke, and Gore in H. M. Ships the Resolution and*

Discovery, In the Years 1776, 1777, 1779, and 1780 (London: W. and A. Strahan, 1784), I, p. xxvi.

120. Vancouver, *Voyage of Discovery*, I, p. i.

121. Richard Colt Hoare, *The History of Modern Wiltshire* (London: John Nichols and Son, 1825), II, p. 57.

122. A. J. von Krusenstern, *Voyage round the World in the Years 1803, 1804, 1805, & 1806 by Order of His Imperial Majesty Alexander the First, on Board the Ships* Nadeshda and Neva, tr. Richard Belgrave Hoppner (London: John Murray, 1813), p. vi.

123. John Franklin, *Narrative of a Journey to the Shores of the Polar Sea; in the Years 1819, 20, 21, and 22. With an Appendix on Various Subjects relating to Science and Natural History. Illustrated by Numerous Plates and Maps* (London: John Murray, 1823), p. 237.

124. "Machine aérostatique," *Journal de Monsieur, Frère du Roi*, April 1783, pp. 64–69.

125. De Brosses, *Histoire des navigations*, I, p. 5. On the Baconian contribution to eighteenth-century thought see Edgar Zilsel, "The Genesis of the Concept of Scientific Progress," in *Roots of Scientific Thought: A Cultural Perspective*, ed. Philip P. Wiener and Aaron Noland (New York: Basic, 1957), p. 259.

126. L'Abbé des Granges Gagnière, "Lettre sur le globe aérostatique du 21 décembre 1783," *Journal Encyclopédique*, January 1784, p. 293.

127. G.-H. Le Roy, "Le globe Montgolfier, ode," *Journal Encyclopédique*, January 1784, p. 293.

128. Pierre Bertholon, *Des avantages que la physique, et les arts qui en dépendent, peuvent rétirer des globe aérostatiques* (Montpellier: Jean Martel aîné, 1784), p. 62.

129. Antoine de Parcieux, *Dissertation sur les globes aérostatiques* (Paris: de Parcieux, 1783), p. 13.

130. Bertholon, *Avantages*, pp. 17–21, 25–27, 37–40.

131. Tiberius Cavallo, *The History and Practice of Aerostation* (London: C. Dilly, 1785), p. 322.

132. Eric Nørgaard, *The Book of Balloons*, translated and revised by Eric Hildesheim (New York: Crown, 1971), p. 38.

133. Gaston Tissandier, *Simples notions sur les ballons et la navigation aérienne* (Paris: Librairie Illustrée, 1876), pp. 53–60.

134. Bertholon, *Avantages*, p. 24. For the most comprehensive and most recent survey of these popular ascents see *Leichter als Luft. Zur Geschichte der Ballonfahrt* (Münster: Landschafts-Verband Westfalen-Lippe, 1978).

135. Cited in N. Horwood's "James Cook and His Predecessors in Australian Discovery," in *Employ'd as a Discoverer*, p. 21.

136. M. L. A. Milet-Mureau, ed., *Voyage de La Pérouse autour du monde* (Paris: Imprimerie de la République, An V), I, p. lxxi; Samuel Hearne, *A Journey from Prince of Wales's Fort, in Hudson's Bay to the Northern Ocean, Undertaken by Order of the Hudson's Bay Company. For the Discovery of Copper Mines, a North West Passage, etc. in the Years 1769, 1770, 1771, 1772* (Dublin: P. Byrne, 1796), p. xxvii.

137. James Bruce, *Travels to Discover the Source of the Nile, in the Years 1768, 1769, 1770, 1771, 1772, 1773* (Edinburgh: G. G. J. and J. Robinson, 1790), I, "Dedication to the King."

138. Broc, *Géographie des philosophes*, pp. 284–286.

139. Cook, *Voyage to the Pacific*, I, p. iii.

140. J. S. Bailly, "Eloge du Capitaine Cook," in *Discours et mémoires, par l'auteur de l'Histoire de l'astronomie* (Paris: de Bure, 1790), I, p. 348.

141. On the ancient tradition of geographical description see Batten, *Pleasurable Instruction*, pp. 41–44; George P. Parks, "The Turn to the Romantic in the Literature of the Eighteenth Century," *Modern Language Quarterly* 25 (March 1964), 23.

142. Adams, *Travels and Travel Liars*, pp. 223–236. Adams identifies three kinds of travel books on the basis of their contents: true travel accounts accurately reporting genuine experiences (such as William Dampier's *New Voyage round the World*), imaginary or "extraordinary" voyages (like Swift's *Gulliver's Travels*), and the "travel lie" (such as William Symson's *New Voyage to the East Indies*, i.e. a work of fiction about a pretended voyage with facts stolen from other writers). For a discussion of the many imaginary voyages published at the close of the eighteenth century, see also Gilbert Chinard, *L'Amérique et le rêve exotique dans la littérature française au XVIIᵉ et au XVIIIᵉ siècle* (Paris: Droz, 1934), pp. 408–409.

143. Auguste LeFlamanc, *Les utopies prérévolutionaires et la philosophie du dixhuitième siècle* (Paris J. Vrin, 1934), pp. 145–147.

144. Van Tieghem, *Le sentiment de la nature*, p. 178.

145. Dora Wiebenson, *Sources of Greek Revival Architecture* (Pennsylvania State University Press, 1969), pp. 13–25, 39.

146. Richard Pococke, *A Description of the East and Some Other Countries. Observations in Palestine or the Holy Land, Syria, Mesopotamia, Cyprus and Candia* (London: Pococke, 1745), II, part I, p. iv.

147. Adam Neale, *Travels through some Parts of Germany, Poland, Moldavia and Turkey* (London: Longman, Hurst, Rees, Orme and Brown, 1818), p. 195.

148. La Pérouse, *Voyage*, I, p. ii. See also *Crozet's Voyage to Tasmania, New Zealand, the Ladrone Islands, and the Philippines in the Years 1771–1772*, tr. H. Ling-Roth (London: Truslove and Shirley, 1791), pp. 68–69.

149. George Levitine, *The Dawn of Bohemianism. The Barbu Rebellion and Primitivism in Neoclassical France* (Pennsylvania State University Press, 1977), pp. 14–20. Levitine makes the interesting point that in the late eighteenth century traces of the old confusion between the fine arts and the mechanical arts still lingered. Like the actor, the professional artist remained stigmatized for a long time. Levitine argues that, because of the prevailing stereotypes associated with manual work, unwarranted heroics were unthinkable for an artist, in contrast with a writer or a poet. The painter could expose himself voluntarily to danger only for the purpose of study, thus following the example of great explorers like La Pérouse and Dolomieu.

Chapter 1

1. M. H. Abrams, *Natural Supernaturalism. Tradition and Revolution in Romantic Literature* (New York: Norton, 1971), p. 341. Blake's spurning of a vision that saw reality as a multitude of isolated individuals was certainly not unique to the period. Reynolds declared in the eighth *Discourse* (p. 151) that "Simplicity, when so very inartificial as to seem to evade the difficulties of art, is a very suspicious vertue," and Kames, in his discussion of the two kinds of beauty of physical objects, declares that the first kind, intrinsic to a single object viewed apart without any relation to another, is "an object of sense merely" and "no more is required but singly an act of vision" [Henry Home, Lord Kames, *Elements of Criticism* (1762) (New York: S. Campbell & Son, E. Duyckinck, G. Long, Collins & Co., Collins & Hannay, and W. B. Gilley, 1823), I, p. 166].

2. Sparrman, *Voyage to the Cape of Good Hope*, I, pp. v–vi. For an excellent discussion of Coleridge's un-Blakean attempt to reconcile visionary insight with scientific reasoning see Thomas McFarland, "The Origins and Significance of Coleridge's Theory of the Secondary Imagination," in *New Perspectives on Coleridge and Wordsworth*, ed. Geoffrey H. Hartman (Columbia University Press, 1972), pp. 214–216; and Bernard Smith, "Coleridge's "Ancient Mariner" and Cook's Second Voyage," in *The Antipodean Manifesto; Essays in Art and History* (Oxford University Press, 1976), pp. 176–177.

3. For the development of the scientific method in the late eighteenth century and its attempt to focus on the concrete individual see, in particular, Michel Foucault, *The Birth of the Clinic: An Archaeology of Medical Perception*, tr. A. M. Sheridan Smith (New York: Pantheon, 1973), pp. xiii–xv; Northrop Frye, "The Imaginative and the Imaginary," in *Fables of Identity, Studies in Poetic Mythology* (New York: Harcourt, Brace & World, 1963), pp. 151–153; Hans Sachsse, "Naturwissenschaft, Technik und Wirklichkeit," in *Zum Wirklichkeitsbegriff*, ed. Günter Bandmann (Mainz: Steiner, 1974), pp. 12–14; Trevor H. Levere, "The Rich Economy of Nature: Chemistry in the Nineteenth Century," in *Nature and the Victorian Imagination*, pp. 192–193.

4. Alexander Gerard, *An Essay on Genius* (London and Edinburgh: W. Strahan, T. Cadell, and W. Creech, 1774), pp. 367–368.

5. On the tranquility of the scientific observation of nature with its focus on the operations of things placed in an eternal foreground, see: Erich Auerbach, *Mimesis: The Representation of Reality in Western Literature*, tr. Willard R. Trask (Princeton University Press, 1953), pp. 3–15 passim; Harcourt Brown, "Tensions and Anxieties: Science and the Literary Culture of France," in *Science and the Creative Spirit. Essays on the Humanistic Aspect of Science*, ed. Harcourt Brown (University of Toronto Press, 1958), pp. 107–108; Van Tieghem, *Le sentiment de la nature*, p. 252. For the connection of Goethe with this tradition see W. D. Robson-Scott, *The Younger Goethe and the Visual Arts* (Cambridge University Press, 1981), pp. 85–89. Robson-Scott sees this attitude as the particular hallmark of his Weimar (and thus pre-Italian) period.

6. F. E. L. Priestley, " 'Those Scattered Rays Convergent': Science and Imagination in English Literature," in *Science and the Creative Spirit*, pp. 62–64; H. Newton Barber, "Sir Joseph Banks and the Royal Society," in *Employ'd as a Discoverer*, pp. 66–70. For a survey of the role played by scientific academies and their directives in the mounting of expeditions see Percy G. Adams, "The Achievements of James Cook and His Associates in Perspective," in *Exploration in Alaska: Captain Cook Commemorative Lectures, June–November 1978* (Anchorage, Alaska: Cook Inlet Historical Society, 1980), pp. 19–23. Also see in this connection Urs Bitterli, *Die "Wilden" und die "Zivilisierten." Grundzüge einer Geistes- und Kulturgeschichte der Europäische-Über-*

seeischen Begegnung (Munich: Beck, 1976), pp. 28–35. On the Restoration history of the Royal Society and its affinities with Puritanism see Charles Webster, The Great Instauration. Science, Medicine, and Reform, 1626–1660 (London: Duckworth, 1975), pp. 88–89.

7. See Thomas Sprat, The History of the Royal Society of London, for the Improving of Natural Knowledge (London: F. Martyn, 1667), pp. 61–62, 111–114; Charles Perrault, Paralèlle des anciens et des modernes, en ce qui regarde les arts et les sciences. Dialogues. Avec le poëme du Louis Le Grand, et une epistre en vers sur le génie (Paris: Jean Baptiste Coingard, 1688), preface. This "plain style" should be contrasted with the wiry, knotty style of the Metaphysical poets; see George Williamson, "Strong Lines," English Studies 18 (August 1936), 153; R. F. Jones, "The Background of the Attack on Science in the Age of Pope," in Pope and His Contemporaries. Essays Presented to George Sherburn, ed. James L. Clifford and Louis A. Landa (Oxford: Clarendon, 1949), pp. 99–104. An interesting attempt to vindicate the ancients from the ubiquitous criticism that they knew nothing of science is to be found in A. L. Millin, Minéralogie homérique, ou essai sur les minéraux, dont il est fait mention dans les poèmes d'Homère (1790), second edition (Paris: C. Wasermann, 1816), pp. xi–xiii.

8. Lynn Thorndike, "Newness and Novelty in Seventeenth-Century Science and Medicine," in Roots of Scientific Thought, pp. 444–450. For discussion of the fact that the sense of being a professional in the sciences was growing at the same time that the publication of scientific works had become a profitable branch of the book trade with international connections, see Harcourt Brown, Science and the Human Comedy: Natural Philosophy in French Literature from Rabelais to Maupertuis (University of Toronto Press, 1976), pp. 84–92, 130–131. Also see François-Marie-Arouet de Voltaire, Letters Concerning the English Nation (London: C. Davis and A. Lyon, 1733), pp. 242–243.

9. Edgar Zilsel, "The Genesis of the Concept of Scientific Progress," in Roots of Scientific Discovery, pp. 253–274 passim. For a criticism of Zilsel's thesis that the idea of progress appears in prescientific writings alone see A. C. Keller, "Zilsel, the Artisans, and the Idea of Progress," in Roots of Scientific Discovery, pp. 283–285. Despite this dispute, it cannot be doubted that Bacon in England and Descartes in France defined the ideal of scientific progress. On this point see Paolo Rossi, Francis Bacon: From Magic to Science, tr. Sacha Rabinovitch (London: Routledge & Kegan Paul, 1968), p. 25; Pierre Garari, "Le cartésianisme et le classicisme anglais," Revue de Littérature Comparée 31 (July–September 1957), 375–380.

10. That the Baconian tradition established not only a separation but an antithesis between art and science is fully discussed in Priestley's " 'These Scattered Rays Convergent,' " in Science and the Creative Spirit, pp. 56–61. By the middle of the eighteenth century this popularly held view that the mind is capable of only one activity at a time (the scientist reasons without feeling and without flights of imagination while the poet imagines but cannot think) was being undermined. Thus, Duff (Essay on Original Genius, pp. 115–120) and Young (Conjectures on Original Composition, pp. 69–71) praise the sublime imaginations of Bacon and Newton. Conversely, Hume, Gerard, and Chambers argue that in the perception of beauty identified with the fine arts one must employ much right reasoning in order to feel the proper sentiment; see Eileen Harris, "Burke and Chambers on the Sublime and Beautiful," in Essays in the History of Architecture Presented to Rudolf Wittkower (London: Phaidon, 1967), p. 211.

11. Jones, "Background of the Attack on Science," in Pope and His Contemporaries, p. 104. [The end result of this Baconian attitude may be seen in the contemporary art movement interested in earthworks. Representation is diminished and real things take its place; illusion withdraws in favor of concrete actuality composed of the basic substances of the earth. See Virginia Gunter, Earth, Air, Fire, Water: Elements of Art (Boston: Museum of Fine Arts, 1971), I, p. 7.]

12. Cecil Albert Moore, Backgrounds of English Literature, 1700–1760 (New York: Octagon, 1969), pp. 76–77.

13. Garai, "Cartésianisme et classicisme," pp. 384–387. For a recent survey of the empirical tradition see Dorion Cairns, "An Approach to Phenomenology," in Philosophical Essays in Memory of Edmund Husserl, ed. Marvin Farber (New York: Greenwood, 1968), pp. 4–12.

14. Martin Kallich, "The Association of Ideas and Critical Theory: Hobbes, Locke, and Addison," ELH 12 (December 1945), 306–308. Also see on this point Wallace Jackson, Immediacy: The Development of a Critical Concept from Addison to Coleridge (Amsterdam: Rodopi, 1973), p. 103. The crucial passages are to be found in John Locke's "Essay Concerning Human Understanding," in Works (London: Thomas Tegg; W. Sharpe and Son; G. Offer; G. and J. Robinson; J. Evans and Co., 1823), I–II, 4.3.6, 4.10. 10–17, pp. 120–126, 330–332, 359–367, and in his Second Reply to Stillingfleet, IV, pp. 460–469, and in Nicolas Malebranche's De la recherche de la vérité. Ou l'on traite de la nature de l'esprit de l'homme, & de l'usage qu'il en doit faire pour éviter l'erreur dans les sciences (Paris: André Pralard, 1678), 3.2.1, section 1, pp. 188–190. On the empiricist

struggle, see the comments of Manley, *Convention*, pp. 241–242, 282–285. On the different "worlds" perceived in France and England see Voltaire, *Letters*, p. 11. I would like to express my deep gratitude to Professor John Yolton and the members of his seminar Space and Time, Matter and Motion, held at the Folger Institute in the fall of 1981, for helping to clarify these difficult concepts.

15. Collingwood, *Idea of Nature*, pp. 70 ff., 113–115. (Note in particular the discussions of Plato's mature conception of forms and the philosophy of Berkeley.) Also see Wheelock, *Perspective, Optics*, p. 113.

16. Guy Sircello, *Mind and Art* (Princeton University Press, 1972), pp. 3–6.

17. Kallich, "Association of Ideas," pp. 302–309. For the suggestion that Associationist doctrine might somehow be connected with the growing ascendancy of the physical sciences in its concern with the sensory origins and manifestations of knowledge as opposed to Johnson's and Burke's preoccupation with the "general" in art see Walter J. Ong, "Psyche and the Geometers: Associationist Critical Theory," in *Rhetoric, Romance, and Technology* (Cornell University Press, 1971), pp. 213–223. In the end, however, Ong concludes that Associationism is not markedly more empirical than Aristotle, Quintilian, or Fénélon. For a discussion of the role of memory in classical aesthetics, ensuring that the mind will not be disturbed by the intrusion of physical objects, see Steffi Röttgen, "Mengs, Alessandro Albani und Winckelmann—Idee und Gestalt des Parnass in der Villa Albani," *Storia dell'Arte* 30–31 (1977), 154–155.

18. Herrmann, *Laugier*, pp. 35–36.

19. L. Rosenfield, "Condillac's Influence on French Scientific Thought," in *The Triumph of Culture: Eighteenth-Century Perspectives*, ed. Paul Fritz and David Williams (Toronto: Hakkert, 1972), pp. 158–162. Also see Frederick Charles Green, *Minuet: A Critical Survey of French and English Literary Ideas in the Eighteenth Century* (St. Clair Shores, Mich.: Scholarly Press, 1971), pp. 267–268.

20. Isabel F. Knight, *The Geometric Spirit. The Abbé de Condillac and the French Enlightenment* (Yale University Press, 1968), p. 16.

21. Etienne Bonnot, Abbé de Condillac, "Essai sur l'origine des connaissances humaines" (1746) and "Traité des sensations" (1754), in *Oeuvres philosophiques*, ed. Georges LeRoy (Paris: Presses Universitaires de France, 1947), I, pp. 61–73, 254–256. Also see Jacques Derrida, *L'archéologie du frivole* (Paris: Galilée, 1973), pp. 11–26 passim; Rosenfield, "Condillac," pp. 163–164.

22. Jacques Derrida, *De la grammatologie*, Collection "Critique" (Paris: Minuit, 1967), pp. 194–200. Also see Leland Thielemann, "Diderot and Hobbes," in *Diderot Studies* 2 (1952), 221–231 passim.

23. Newton Barber, "The Botany of the South Pacific," in *Captain Cook, Navigator and Scientist*, ed. G. M. Badger (Canberra: Australian National University Press, 1970), p. 88. That the act of discovery entails a shift in perception was noted by Thomas S. Kuhn in *The Structure of Scientific Revolutions* (University of Chicago Press, 1962), p. 121.

24. Barrell, *Idea of Landscape*, pp. 22–23. Barrell makes the point that such eighteenth-century terms as *view, prospect*, and *scene* depend upon a habit of perception that passes over objects as the eye journeys toward the horizon. My point is that the explorer subverted this form of vision in which the eye was not seriously engaged or halted by the object.

25. J. B. Pujoulx, *Paris à la fin du XVIIIᵉ siècle, ou esquisse historique et morale des monuments et des ruines de cette capitale; de l'état des sciences, des arts et de l'industrie à cette époque, ainsi que des moeurs et des ridicules de se habitans* (Paris: Brigite Mathé, 1801), p. 376.

26. H. W. Beechey, *Proceedings of the Expedition to Explore the Northern Coast of Africa, from Tripoly Eastward; in MDCCCXXI and MDCCCXXII. Comprehending the Greater Syrtis and Cyrenaica; and of the Ancient Cities Composing the Pentapolis* (London: John Murray, 1828), p. v.

27. R. P. du Fesc, "Dissertation sur la lumière septentrionale, avec l'explication de ses divers phénomènes," *Journal de Trévoux* (July 1732), 1205 ff.

28. P. Cotte, *Mémoires sur la météorologie pour servir de suite & de supplément au Traité de météorologie publié en 1774* (Paris: Imprimerie Royale, 1788), I, p. ix.

29. *The Endeavour Journal of Joseph Banks, 1768–1771*, ed. J. C. Beaglehole (Sydney: Trustees of the Public Library of New South Wales in Association with Angus and Robertson, 1962), I, pp. 19, 29. Also see Brown, *Science and the Human Comedy*, pp. 141–144.

30. Heinrich Bosse, "The Marvellous in Romantic Semiotics," *Studies in Romanticism* 14 (summer 1975), 225.

31. Duff, *Original Genius*, p. 97. Also see Gerard, *Essay on Genius*, pp. 415–434. Gerard notes that a genius for the arts is, nonetheless, not incompatible with a genius for science. To prove his point he cites Pamphilus, Metrodorus, Leonardo da Vinci, Agostino Carracci, Parmigianino, and Edmond Halley. He attributes these

dual talents to the flexibility of imagination natural to genius; however, he is forced to admit that such geniuses excel only in one department and are inferior in the other area. For a discussion of Gerard and his influence, see: Howard Mumford Jones, *Revolution and Romanticism* (Belknap Press of Harvard University Press, 1974), p. 271.

32. Rémy-Gilbert Saisselin, *Taste in Eighteenth-Century France. Critical Reflections on the Origin of Aesthetics* (Syracuse University Press, 1965), pp. 67–71.

33. George P. Landow, *The Aesthetic and Critical Theories of John Ruskin* (Princeton University Press, 1971), pp. 32–33, 378–384. According to Ruskin there are three classes of perception: that of the man who perceives rightly because he does not feel, and to whom the primrose is merely a primrose because he does not love it; that of the man who perceives wrongly because he feels, and to whom the primrose is anything but a primrose, the sun, a star, and so on; and that of the man who perceives rightly in spite of his feelings, to whom the primrose is forever nothing less than itself.

34. Hélène Metzger, "La littérature scientifique française au XVIIIᵉ siècle," *Archeion* 16 (1934), 14–15.

35. William Thorn, *Memoir of the Conquest of Java; With the Subsequent Operations of the British Forces in the Oriental Archipelago, to Which is Subjoined a Statistical and Historical Sketch of Java; Being the Result of Observations Made in a Tour through the Country; With an Account of Its Dependencies* (London: T. Egerton, 1815), p. vii.

36. Horace-Bénédict de Saussure, *Voyage dans les Alpes, précédes d'un essai sur l'histoire naturelle des environs de Génève* (Neufchâtel: Louis Fauché-Borel, 1779–1796), I, p. i. For a discussion of Saussure as the instigator of a new scientific Romanticism see Helmut Rehder, *Die Philosophie der unendlichen Landschaft, Ein Beitrag zur Geschichte der Romantischen Weltanschauung* (Halle/Saale: Max Neumeyer, 1932), pp. 31–35. For the Johnsonian conception of "passionate intelligence" and its relation to exploration see Hans-Joachim Possin, *Reisen und Literatur: Das Thema des Reisens in der Englischen Literatur des 18. Jahrhunderts* (Tübingen: Max Niemeyer, 1972), pp. 80–82; Schwartz, "Johnson in an Age of Science," in *Johnson and Science*. Also see Samuel Johnson, *The Rambler*, ed. W. J. Bate and A. B. Strauss (Yale University Press, 1969), 2, p. 187.

37. Jacques-Henri Bernardin de Saint-Pierre, *Voyage à l'Isle de France, à l'Isle de Bourbon, au Cap de Bonne-Espérance* (Amsterdam and Paris: Merlin, 1773), I, p. 94. For Bernardin's role in rectifying the conceptual insufficiency of eighteenth-century French landscape vocabulary see Louis Roule, *Bernardin de Saint-Pierre et Harmonie de la nature* (Paris: Flammarion, 1930), p. 192; Broc, *Géographie des philosophes*, p. 477; Daniel Mornet, *Le sentiment de la nature en France de J. J. Rousseau à Bernardin de Saint-Pierre* (Paris: Hachette, 1907), pp. 435–436.

38. *Voyage de Humboldt et Bonpland. Relation historique* (Paris: Gide, 1814–1834), I, p. 4. On Humboldt's quarrel with Burke see Douglas Botting, *Humboldt and the Cosmos* (New York: Harper & Row, 1973), p. 260. For the aesthetic tradition of disinterestedness, stretching from Addison to Ruskin, see Martin Price, *To the Palace of Wisdom: Studies in Order and Energy from Dryden to Blake* (Garden City, N.Y.: Doubleday, 1964), p. 361; Robert Hewison, *John Ruskin: The Argument of the Eye* (Princeton University Press, 1976), p. 20; Kermal, "Natural Beauty," p. 149.

39. Georg Forster, *A Voyage round the World in His Britannic Majesty's Sloop, Resolution, Commanded by Captain James Cook, during the Years 1772, 3, 4, and 5* (London: B. White, J. Robson, P. Elmsly, and G. Robinson, 1777), I, p. xi.

40. Mungo Park, *Travels in the Interior Districts of Africa: Performed under the Direction and Patronage of the Africa Association in the Years 1795, 1796, and 1797*, fifth edition (London: W. Bulmer, 1807), p. 2.

41. Harold Fisch, "The Scientist as Priest: A Note on Robert Boyle's Natural Theology," *Isis* 44 (September 1953), 259; Jacques Proust, *L'encyclopédie* (Paris: Colin, 1965), pp. 131–133. That the eighteenth century saw nonfiction travel literature as a science connected with events, and the explorer as a "researcher," "sucking" intelligence from different geographical regions, is a point made by Batten (*Pleasurable Instruction*, pp. 7, 49).

42. Sparrman, *Voyage to the Cape of Good Hope*, I, p. 81; Alfred Orian, *La vie et l'oeuvre de Philibert Commerson des Humbers* (Mauritius Printing Co., 1973), p. 16.

43. Barthélemy Faujas de Saint-Fond, *Recherches sur les volcans éteints du Vivarais et du Vélay; avec un discours sur les volcans brûlans* (Grenoble and Paris: Chez Joseph Cuchet, Nyon aîné, Née et Masquelier, 1778), p. 364.

44. Le Vaillant, *Voyage dans l'Afrique*, p. ix.

45. Ibid., p. x. Le Vaillant's zeal becomes even more comprehensible when it is placed in the context of the *Encyclopédie* and the high praise meted out by the *philosophes* for inventions and discoveries of all kinds. See "Invention," *Encyclopédie*, 1765, XIII, p. 849; "Découverte," *Encyclopédie*, 1754, IV, p. 706.

46. Paulson, *Emblem and Expression,* p. 51.

47. Carol T. Christ, *The Finer Optic: The Aesthetic of Particularity in Victorian Poetry* (Yale University Press, 1975), p. 13.

48. Robert Aubin, *Topographical Poetry in XVIII-Century England* (New York: Modern Language Association of America, 1936), p. 57.

49. Reynolds, *Discourses,* pp. 59–60.

50. Williams, *English Watercolors,* p. 38.

51. Pococke, *Description of the East,* I, p. v.

52. George Heriot, *A Picturesque Tour Made in the Years 1817 and 1820 through the Pyrenean Mountains, Auvergne, the Departments of the High and Low Alps, and in Part of Spain* (London: R. Ackermann, 1824), p. i.

53. Michel Faré, "De quelques termes désignant la peinture d'object," in *Etudes d'art français offertes à Charles Sterling,* ed. Albert Châtelet and Nicole Renaud (Paris: Presses Universitaires de France, 1975), pp. 271–274.

54. Ong, *Psyche and the Geometers,* pp. 223–224; Dieckmann, "Wandlung des Nachahmungsbegriffes," in *Nachahmung und Illusion,* pp. 29–30.

55. Aristotle, *Poetics,* IX. 1451 b 5–10. See also Scott Elledge, "The Background and Development in English Criticism of the Theories of Generality and Particularity," *PMLA* 62 (March 1947), 167–169.

56. Wesley Trimpi, "The Meaning of Horace's *Ut pictura poesis,*" *Journal of the Warburg and Courtauld Institutes* 36 (1973), 22 ff. Trimpi provides an excellent discussion of the ancient literary and rhetorical tradition celebrating an exactitude of art that demands close examination.

57. Walter Jackson Bate, "The Sympathetic Imagination in Eighteenth-Century English Criticism," *ELH* 12 (June 1945), 158–159. Also see Barrell, *Idea of Landscape,* pp. 2–3; Aubin, *Topographical Poetry,* pp. 46–47. On the French tradition of descriptive poetry, which owes to an impetus coming from England and, to a lesser extent, from Germany, see Guitton, *Jacques Delille,* pp. 65–70, 263–265. For the idea that regions, like people, have personalities, and that the geographical term *landscape* designates the state of being or the reality of a region, see Douglas Crary, "A Geographer Looks at the Landscape," *Landscape* 9 (autumn 1959), 23.

58. Johann Wolfgang Goethe, *Dichtung und Wahrheit,* in *Goethes Werke in sechs Bänden,* ed. Erich Schmidt (Leipzig: Insel, 1940), V, 115.

59. Valenciennes, *Eléments de perspective,* pp. 279–280. Valenciennes cites the search for veracity in these matters by Giovanni Maria della Torre, William Hamilton, and Déodat de Dolomieu.

60. Paul Fussell, Jr., "Patrick Brydone, the Eighteenth-Century Traveller as Representative Man," in *Literature as a Mode of Travel: Five Essays and a Postscript* (New York Public Library, 1963), p. 55. Lockean psychology is not wholly committed to the external world. Critics have noted Locke's implicit critique of Newtonian science: that the components of experience called particulars in the external world are the only reality, yet they are unknowable and have nothing knowable to connect or support them but the mind's own functions. See Donald P. Ault, *Visionary Physics: Blake's Response to Newton* (University of Chicago Press, 1974), p. 66. Despite this skepticism, it is undeniable that mariners, overland travelers, miners, and balloonists acted as if it were possible to pierce to the root and record of every phenomenon; see Gaston Bachelard, *La terre et les rêveries de la volonté* (Paris: José Corti, 1948), pp. 260–261.

61. Richard Walter, *Voyage autour du monde fait dans les années 1740, 1, 2, 3, 4,* tr. from the English (Amsterdam and Leipzig: Arkste'e & Merkus, 1751), pp. xiii–xiv. Walter, the chaplain aboard the *Centurion,* from whose journals and other papers much of Anson's account was drawn, is at pains to undermine the common view of the sailor as someone as rough as the element upon which he sails. He reminds the reader that the king had established a drawingmaster at Portsmouth for those destined to fill different positions in the Royal Navy. Furthermore, he asserts that the day of the illiterate or uncultivated seaman is past; that even the most ordinary navigation requires the knowledge of several branches of science.

62. Michel Adanson, *Histoire naturelle du Sénégale. Coquillages avec le relation abrégée d'un voyage fait en ce pays, pendant les années 1749, 50, 51, 52 & 53* (Paris: Claude-Jean-Baptiste Bauche, 1757), p. 1.

63. Banks, *Endeavour Journal,* p. 263.

64. Joseph Acerbi, *Travels through Sweden, Finland, and Lapland, to the North Cape, in the Years 1798 and 1799* (London: Joseph Mawman), I, p. viii.

65. Jacques-Gérard Milbert, *Voyage pittoresque à l'Ile de France, au Cap de Bonne-Espérance et à l'Ile de Teneriffe* (Paris: A. Nepveu, 1812), I, p. viii.

66. J. E. V. Arago, *Narrative of a Voyage round the World in the Uranie and Physicienne Corvettes, Commanded by Captain Freycinet, during the Years 1817, 1818, 1819, and 1820; on a Scientific Expedition Undertaken by Order of the French Government, In a Series of Letters to a Friend by ....*

Draughtsman to the Expedition, tr. from the French (London: Truettel and Wurtz, 1823), p. ii.

67. Henry James, "The Real Thing," in *Selected Short Stories*, ed. Quentin Anderson, revised edition (New York: Holt, Rinehart and Winston, 1961), pp. 124, 131.

68. Wilbur Samuel Howell, "De Quincey on Science, Rhetoric, and Poetry," in *Poetics, Rhetoric, and Logic: Studies in the Basic Disciplines of Criticism* (Cornell University Press, 1975), pp. 192–200. For the now much-debated study of the two ancient characters of style (the *genus grande* or *nobile*, devoted to the general and communal ideas of oratorical style, and the *genus humile* or *submissum*, originating in philosophy and devoted to expressing individual variances of experience) see Morris William Croll, " 'Attic' Prose in the Seventeenth Century," in *Style, Rhetoric, and Rhythm; Essays*, ed. J. Max Patrick (Princeton University Press, 1966), pp. 59–61. Croll's interpretation of the classical "plain" style has been severely challenged by Robert Adolph in *The Rise of the Modern Prose Style* (MIT Press, 1968), pp. 272–285. Adolph notes that there are two contradictory features in it. During the pre-Restoration period, the plain style followed the usage of Cicero and Quintilian, in which words imitated mental things. During the post-Restoration period, and specifically in Bacon's and the Royal Society's probative style, words were to be reduced to external things. Further, Adolph claims that Bacon used many styles, depending on his aims and audience; his use of a very un-Senecan style, stripped of connotations to remove the "contract of error" between deliverer and receiver, in the *Advancement* was bound up with a utilitarian purpose. For the larger distinction between a "rhetorical" and a "serious" view of life and art stretching back to antiquity see Richard A. Lanham, *The Motives of Eloquence: Literary Rhetoric in The Renaissance* (Yale University Press, 1976).

69. Howell, *De Quincey on Science*, pp. 210–211.

70. See, in particular, Wesley Trimpi, *Ben Jonson's Poems, A Study of the Plain Style* (Stanford University Press, 1962), pp. viii–ix and 4–32 passim. Trimpi discusses the antirhetorical reaction against florid stylistic models (wrongly associated with Cicero) and the espousal of a classical plain style. The distinction between the Asiatic and Attic styles hinges on a dichotomy of denotation (content) and connotation (expression). *Denotation* usually refers to the simple referent of a word, *connotation* to its context and the qualifications that context imposes. Connotation came to be extended to include not only associations legitimately offered by the context, but any associations that the individual talent of the reader was able to provide.

Much as in late-eighteenth-century Associationism, such associations usually were described as *feelings*. Therefore, the term *connotation* came to mean emotions enjoyed by the reader whether they were relevant to the context or not. In the plain style, the denotative and the connotative most nearly approached each other in the exclusion of irrelevant associations from the context. Further, the linguistic characteristics of the plain style were modesty in metaphor, sparing use of archaisms, and lack of adornment in other figures of speech. In short, it was not to be "colored."

71. Elledge, "Generality and Particularity," pp. 157–159. On the Baconian requirements for scientific discourse see Rossi, *Bacon*, pp. 197–201.

72. Paul Bénichou, *Le sacre de l'écrivain, 1750–1830* (Paris: José Corti, 1973), pp. 48–50. On the late-eighteenth-century conviction that there are active powers of the mind that stand outside the law of Associationism and that function in science and poetry see McFarland, "Origin and Significance of Coleridge's Theory of the Secondary Imagination," p. 235.

73. Schenck, *Das Bilderrätsel*, p. 166.

74. Dean Tolle Mace, "Ut Pictura Poesis," in *Encounters*, pp. 63–65. For the concepts of energeia and enargeia I am grateful to Mary E. Hazard, who permitted me to consult the typescript of her article "The Anatomy of 'Liveliness' as a Concept in Renaissance Esthetics." On this point see Eric Rothstein, " 'Ideal Presence' and the 'Non Finito' in Eighteenth-Century Aesthetics," *Eighteenth-Century Studies* 9 (spring 1976), 318–319.

75. Auerbach, *Mimesis*, pp. 110, 116, 120–121, 166–167. For a discussion of the rise of the concept of replication in poetry and drama during the second half of the eighteenth century and the concomitant move away from involuntary illusion see Marian Hobson, *The Object of Art: The Theory of Illusion in Eighteenth-Century France* (Cambridge University Press, 1982), p. 209.

76. Forster, *Voyage round the World*, I, pp. vi, xiv. Also see Louis-Antoine de Bougainville, *Voyage autour du monde par la frégate du roi la Boudeuse et la Flûte l'Etoile, en 1766, 1767, 1768, & 1769*, second revised edition (Paris: Saillant & Nyon, 1772), I, pp. xi, xxxix; James Morier, *A Journey through Persia, Armenia, and Asia Minor, to Constantinople, in the Years 1808 and 1809; in which is Included Some Account of the Proceedings of H. M.'s Mission, under Sir Harford Jones, Bart. K. C. to the Court of the King of Persia* (London: Longman, Hurst, Rees, Orme, and Brown, 1812), p. vii; George Landmann, *Historical, Military, and Picturesque Observations on*

Portugal, Illustrated by Seventy-Five Coloured Plates, Including Authentic Plans of the Sieges and Battles Fought in the Peninsula during the Late War (London: T. Cadell and W. Davies, 1818), I, preface, p. vi; and *Voyage de Humboldt et Bonpland*, II, pp. iii–iv.

77. Jacob Opper, *Science and the Arts. A Study in Relationships from 1600–1900* (Rutherford, N.J.: Fairleigh Dickinson University Press, 1973), pp. 67–68. For a contemporary discussion of metaphoric displacement see Donald A. Schon, *Invention and the Evolution of Ideas* (London: Tavistock, 1963), pp. 35, 51–53, 68–72.

78. Derrida, *De la grammatologie*, pp. 412–413.

79. Denis Diderot, *Salons*, ed. Jean Séznec and Jean Adhémar (Oxford: Clarendon, 1963), III, 153.

80. Duff, *Original Genius*, pp. 34–36, 39.

81. De Brosses, *Histoire des navigations*, I, p. ix; La Pérouse, *Voyage autour du monde*, I, p. v. The Admiralty did not feel that Cook was capable of editing his own journal for publication. Thus, they hired Dr. John Hawkesworth, a literary figure of the time and friend to Dr. Johnson, to amend the navigator's style as he saw fit. Hawkesworth also had access to Banks's papers from the first voyage. He turned a plain, unvarnished tale into a proto-Grecian fairy tale. In addition, he had Alexander Buchan's and Sidney Parkinson's drawings "edited" for European sensibilities. See Judith Nash, "Homage to James Cook," *Connoisseur* (February 1979), 79.

82. Matthew Flinders, *A Voyage to Terra Australis; Undertaken for the Purpose of Completing the Discovery of that Vast Country, and Prosecuted in the Years 1801, 1802, and 1803, in His Majesty's Ship the* Investigator, *and Subsequently in the Armed Vessel* Porpoise *and* Cumberland *Schooner. With an Account of the Shipwreck of the* Porpoise, *Arrival of the* Cumberland *at Mauritius, and Imprisonment of the Commander during Six Years and a Half in that Island* (London: W. Bulmer, 1811), I, p. lx.

83. Otto von Kotzebue, *A Voyage of Discovery into the South Sea and the Beering's Straits, for the Purpose of Exploring a North-East Passage, Undertaken in the Years 1815–1818* (London: Longman, Hurst, Rees, Orme, and Brown, 1821), I, p. vi.

84. The most intelligent attempts at separating and defining the terms *naturalism* and *realism* in the visual arts have emanated from German critics. See in particular J. A. Schmoll, gen. Eisenwerth, "Naturalismus und Realismus: Versuch zur Formulierung verbindlicher Begriffe," *Städel-Jahrbuch*, N.F., V (1975), 252–253; Winfried Nerdinger, "Zur Entstehung des Realismus-Begriffes in Frankreich und zu seiner Anwendung im Bereich der ungegendständlichen Kunst," *Städel-Jahrbuch*, N.F., V (1975), 230–231. For an extended discussion, see the conclusion of the present volume. On the important contribution of seventeenth-century technical literature (including the celebrated *Mutus Liber* published in La Rochelle in 1677 by Jacob Sulatus and the earlier engravings from the workshop of Theodore de Bry and Matthaeus Merian) to the formulation of naturalism, see Lee Stavenhagen, "Narrative Illustration and the Mute Books of Alchemy," *Explorations in Renaissance Culture* 5 (1979), 58–65. Sulatus's volume, in particular, was free of needless chatter and could be "read" as such by all nations regardless of language. The engravings of laboratory procedures were intended to convey discursive empirical information without resorting to words. De Bry and his followers, however, were interested in narrative techniques and serial illustration. Nonetheless, their interest in the temporal and real world—associated with their Protestant background—relates to the phenomenon of naturalism in its European context.

85. Vivant-Denon, *Voyage en Egypte*, I, pp. 1–2.

86. G. A. Olivier, *Voyage dans l'Empire Othoman, l'Egypte et la Perse, fait par L'ordre du gouvernement, pendant les six premières années de la République* (Paris: H. Agasse, 1801), I, p. xi.

87. A. F. Skjöldebrand, *Description des cataractes et du canal de Tröllhatta en Suède; avec un précis historique* (Stockholm: Charles Delen, 1804), p. 11.

88. Günther Bandmann, "Das Kunstwerk und die Wirklichkeit," in *Zum Wirklichkeitsbegriff*, pp. 28–38; Herbert Spiegelberg, "The 'Reality-Phenomenon' and Reality," in *Husserl*, pp. 86–87. On nineteenth-century literary Realism see George Levine, *The Realistic Imagination: English Fiction from Frankenstein to Lady Chatterly* (University of Chicago Press, 1981), pp. 67–70, and Hans Robert Jauss, *Literaturgeschichte als Provokation* (Frankfurt-am-Main: Suhrkamp, 1970), pp. 107–143.

89. It is interesting to contrast Reynolds with Hazlitt on this score. In the fourth Discourse, Reynolds takes up the question of invention and concludes that it is the power of representing a mental image on canvas: " . . . as in the conception of this ideal picture, the mind does not enter into the minute peculiarities of the dress, furniture, or scene of action; so when the Painter comes to represent it, he contrives those little necessary concomitant circumstances in such a manner that they shall strike the spectator no more than they did himself in his first conception of the story." (Reynolds, *Discourses*, p. 59) Haz-

litt, in discussing a portrait of an English lady by Anthony Van Dyke, takes up the issue of the importance of individual expression: " . . . the imitation of external and visible form is only correct or nearly perfect, when the information of the eye and the direction of the hand are aided and confirmed by the previous knowledge and actual feeling of character in the object represented. . . . "[*The Complete Works of William Hazlitt*, ed. P. P. Howe (London: J. M. Dent, 1931), XII, p. 289]

90. On the larger question of description versus narration in art see Svetlana Alpers, "Describe or Narrate? A Problem in Realistic Representation," *New Literary History* 8 (autumn 1976), 15–27 passim.

91. Ralph Cohen, "Literary Criticism and Artistic Interpretation: Eighteenth-Century English Illustrations of 'The Seasons,' " in *Reason and the Imagination: Studies in the History of Ideas, 1600–1800*, ed. J. A. Mazzeo (Columbia University Press, 1962), pp. 280–281. On the connection between word and print see Aubin, *Topographical Poetry*, pp. 48–51.

92. Ibid., pp. 290, 305–306. Also see C. V. Deane, *Aspects of Eighteenth-Century Nature Poetry* (Oxford: Blackwell, 1935), pp. 63–64; James Malek, "Charles Lamotte's 'An Essay upon Poetry and Painting' and Eighteenth-Century British Aesthetics," *Journal of Aesthetics and Art Criticism* 29 (summer 1971), 472.

93. Batten, *Pleasurable Instruction*, pp. 82–84.

94. Banks, *Endeavour Journal*, pp. 110–111.

95. Alexandre Cioranescu, "La découverte de l'Amerique et l'art de la description," *Revue des Sciences Humaines* 104 (April–June 1962), 163–168. Cioranescu describes the perceptual and linguistic revolution that occurred in the wake of Columbus's voyages. Much of what he says is relevant to the second half of the eighteenth century: The art of observation prompted writers to learn how to individualize objects. This innovation was a response to the desire for precision in order better to comprehend a new reality. The same desire to imitate nature and to grasp it in all its multifariousness was aided by the proliferation of optical devices and graphic techniques in the eighteenth century, which stressed absolute fidelity in transcription with far less emphasis on the use of hoary exemplars. See Joan Friedman, "Every Lady Her Own Drawing Master," *Apollo* 105 (April 1977), 265–266.

96. Forster, *Voyage round the World*, I, p. iv.

97. Denis Diderot, *Pensées sur l'interprétation de la nature* (Paris, 1754), p. 105. Also see Pujoulx, *Paris*, pp. 227–228. For the long tradition in France (established since the last third of the seventeenth century) that encouraged the participation of a wide segment of the educated public in physical, chemical, and anatomical experiments, see Hans Kortum, *Charles Perrault und Nicolas Boileau, Der Antike-Streit im Zeitalter der klassischen Französischen Literatur* (Berlin: Rütten & Loening, 1966), pp. 28–29. Levitine (*Dawn of Bohemianism*, pp. 33–34) decries the popularity of science at the beginning of the nineteenth century in France.

98. Paul Dimoff, *La vie et l'oeuvre d'André Chenier jusqu'à la révolution française, 1762–1790* (Paris: Droz, 1936), II, pp. 38–39. Also see Jones, *Revolution and Romanticism*, pp. 373–374.

99. Metzger, "La littérature scientifique," pp. 11–14. On the popularity of science in the second half of the eighteenth century, see especially Robert Darnton, *Mesmerism and the End of the Enlightenment in France* (Harvard University Press, 1968), pp. 2–45.

100. Philip Wiener, "Leibniz's Project of a Public Exhibition of Scientific Inventions," in *Roots of Scientific Thought*, pp. 460–461. Also see Adrienne L. Kaeppler, "Ethnography and the Voyage of Captain Cook," in *Artificial Curiosities," An Exposition of Native Manufactures Collected on the Three Pacific Voyages of Captain James Cook* (Honolulu: Bishop Museum Press, 1978), pp. 37–48 passim.

101. Barthélemy Faujas de Saint-Fond, *Description des expériences de la machine aérostatique de MM. de Montgolfier et de celles auxquelles cette découverte a donneé lieu* (Paris: Cuchet, 1783), I, p. 10.

102. Edouard Guitton, "Un thème 'philosophique': 'l'invention' des poètes de Louis Racine à Népomucène Lemercier," *Studies on Voltaire and the Eighteenth Century* 88 (1972), 693.

103. Daniel Mornet, *Le romantisme en France au XVIIIᵉ siècle* (Geneva: Slatkine Reprints, 1970), p. 27. Also see Le Flamanc, *Les utopies prérévolutionnaire*, pp. 92–93; Rehder, *Unendlichen Landschaft*, p. 15. Also note the important Renaissance precedent that contrasted the "ordinary nudity" of the recently discovered Brazilian Indians (i.e., nature) with the overdressing of the Europeans (i.e., art). Jodelle's verse appended to the frontispiece of André Thévet's *Singularités de la France Antarctique* (1557) makes this rhetorical opposition plain: "Ces barbares marchent tous nus,/ Et nous, nous marchens inconnus,/ Fardés, masqués . . . " (cited in Haydn, "La Natura naturata," p. 206). I will try to show in chapter 4 how this "nudity" becomes transferred from primitive man to his ambient, a landscape freed of the trappings of Western culture.

104. *L'invention humaine: technique, morale, science: Leurs rapports au cours de l'évolution*. Dix-septième semaine de synthèse (Paris: Albin Michel, n.d.), p. 71. Also see Joseph Warren Beach, *The Concept of Nature in Nineteenth-Century English Poetry* (New York: Macmillan, 1936), p. 4. Beach makes the point that the Romantic pantheist poets stressed elements in the concept of nature that derived from science. By the middle of the nineteenth century, when science had advanced beyond its earlier descriptive and classificatory phase, its mythic potential continued as it revealed a world picture made up of ruthlessly struggling forces. See Hewison, *Ruskin*, p. 20.

105. Michel Foucault, *Les mots et les choses, une archéologie des sciences humaines* (Paris: Gallimard, 1966), pp. 141–142.

106. Ibid., pp. 142–145. Also see Glacken, *Traces*, pp. 508–509.

107. Jan Huizinga, "Naturbild und Geschichtsbild im achtzehn Jahrhundert," in *Parerga* (Basel: Burg, 1945), pp. 166–172. On the great interest in history and its varieties in the eighteenth century see Bertha Bessmertny, "Les principaux ouvrages sur l'histoire des sciences parus en France pendant le XVIIIᵉ siècle," *Archeion* 16 (1934), 325–328; Karl Kroeber, "Romantic Historicism: the Temporal Sublime," in *Images of Romanticism: Verbal and Visual Affinities*, ed. Karl Kroeber and William Walling (Yale University Press, 1978), pp. 149–150. In his otherwise stimulating discussion, Kroeber errs when he states that Neoclassicism had no historical equivalent for the physical, topographical, and material sublimity in which it delighted; its art and history remained distinct. As I will show in chapter 4, the natural-history text (and, by extension, the nonfiction voyage) filled this role.

108. T. D. Kendrick, *The Lisbon Earthquake* (London: Methuen, 1956), pp. 133–140. That travelers were keenly aware of such metamorphoses is recorded by Mayer (*Egypt*, p. 3): "From a concatenation of moral and physical causes, which we shall not attempt to trace, the face of Egypt has been changed like the features of its inhabitants. . . ."

109. Rehder, *Unendlichen Landschaft*, p. 30.

110. Philibert Commerson, "Lettre de . . . à M. de Lalande," in *Supplément au voyage de M. de Bougainville; ou journal d'un voyage autour du monde, fait par MM. Banks & Solander, Anglois, en 1768, 1769, 1770, 1771*, tr. M. de Fréville (Paris: Saillant & Nyon, 1772), p. 256. This work, published anonymously, is attributed to Cook or Hawkesworth.

111. Georg Weise, "Vitalismo, animalismo e panpsichismo e la decorazione nel Cinq-uecente e nel Seicento," *Critica d'Arte* 7 (March–April 1960), part II, 89–90. On the continuation of vitalist tendencies during the eighteenth century see J. L. Carr, "Pygmalion and the *Philosophes*. The Animated Statue in Eighteenth-Century France," *Journal of the Warburg and Courtauld Institutes* 23 (1960), 250–252.

112. Patrick Coleman, "The Idea of Character in the *Encyclopédie*," *Eighteenth-Century Studies* 13 (fall 1979), 28–29.

113. Carl Linnaeus, *Reflections on the Study of Nature*, tr. from the Latin (London: George Nicol, 1785), p. 20.

114. Georges-Louis LeClerc, Comte de Buffon, "Histoire naturelle," in *Oeuvres complètes avec les supplémens* (Paris: P. Dumenil, 1835), I, p. 43.

115. Francis X. J. Coleman, *The Aesthetic Thought of the French Enlightenment* (University of Pittsburgh Press, 1971), pp. 131–133. Also see Bénichou, *Le sacre de l'écrivain*, p. 131; Brown, *Science and Creative Spirit*, p. 93.

116. Gustav Solar and Jost Hösli [*Hans Conrad Escher von der Linth, Ansichten und Panoramen der Schweiz. Die Ansichten 1780–1822* (Zurich: Atlantis, 1974), pp. 79–81] point out that Escher saw Picturesque drawings of Switzerland and its wonders as mere embellishment when compared with his own unconventionalized geological and topographical documentation. Indeed, they conclude (as do I) that scientific studies of the terrain can be more emotionally charged and possess greater aesthetic sensitivity than Picturesque *vedute* precisely because they take on the geognostic character of the land.

117. Sparrman, *Voyage to the Cape of Good Hope*, I, pp. iii–v.

Chapter 2

1. Walter Burkert, *Lore and Science in Ancient Pythagoreanism*, tr. Edwin L. Minar, Jr. (Harvard University Press, 1972), pp. 28–38; Nicolson, *Breaking of the Circle*, pp. 1–2.

2. Ralph Cudworth, *The True Intellectual System of the Universe* (London: Richard Royston, 1678), pp. 105–108; *Mr. Bayle's Historical and Critical Dictionary, The Second Edition to Which is Prefixed, the Life of the Author*, by Mr. Des Maizeaux, Fellow of the Royal Society (London: J. J. and P. Knapton, D. Midwinter, J. Brotherton, 1735–1738), II, pp. 657–661.

3. Weise, "Vitalismo," part I, pp. 385–386.

4. Jean-Claude-Izouard de l'Isle de Sales, *De la philosophie de la nature, ou traité de morale pour l'espèce humaine, tiré de la philosophie et fondé sur la nature*, third edition (London, 1777), II, pp. 411–412.

5. Antoine Fabre d'Olivet, *The Golden Verses of Pythagoras. Explained and Translated into French and Preceded by a Discourse upon the Essence and Form of Poetry among the Principal Peoples of the Earth*, tr. Nayan Louise Redfield (New York: G. P. Putnam's Sons, 1917; first published in 1813), pp. 275 ff. A typical account of metempsychosis and its attendant belief in universal animism is the report of John Henry Grose, *A Voyage to the East-Indies with Observations on Various Parts There* (London: S. Hooper and A. Morley, 1757), p. 297.

6. M. Raymond, "Saint-Martin et l'Illuminisme contre l'Illuminisme," in *Sensibilità e Razionalità nel Settecento*, ed. Vittore Branca (Venice: Sansoni, 1967), I, p. 47. Also see Locke, *Essay*, in *Works*, II, 4.10.14–17, 4.3.6, pp. 331–336, 359. On the *Principate* of Newton and the controversy that the theory of gravitation aroused—particularly among the Cartesians—see A. Rupert Hall, *The Scientific Revolution, 1500–1800. The Formation of the Modern Scientific Attitude*, second edition (Boston: Beacon, 1962), pp. 258–265; Alexandre Koyré, *Newtonian Studies* (University of Chicago Press, Phoenix Books, 1965), pp. 15–17. On the conviction that Newton's theory of matter and its actions, which pervades both the *Principia* and the *Opticks*, is to be found in most of the scientific writing of the eighteenth century, see Schofield, *Mechanism and Materialism*, p. 4.

7. Marx W. Wartofsky, "Diderot and the Development of Materialistic Monism," *Diderot Studies* II (1952), 286–287.

8. Diderot, *Le rêve de D'Alembert*, p. 70.

9. G. W. Leibniz, *On the Reform of Metaphysics and on the Notion of Substance* (1694), in *Philosophical Works*, ed. George Martin Duncan (second edition) (New Haven: Tuttle, Morehouse & Taylor, 1908), pp. 75–76. For an exposition of Leibniz's belief in the "beautiful pre-established Order" and his opposition to Newton's supposed mechanism see *A Collection of Papers, Which Passed between the Late Learned Mr. Leibniz and Dr. Clarke, in the Years 1715 and 1716. Relating to the Principles of Natural Philosophy and Religion. With an Appendix* (London: James Knapton, 1717), pp. 7–11.

10. Diderot, *Le rêve de D'Alembert*, p. 70.

11. Bonnet, *Contemplation de la nature*, I, p. 221. Also see Aram Vartanian, "Trembley's Polyp, La Mettrie and Eighteenth-Century French Materialism," in *Roots of Scientific Thought*, pp. 497–513 passim.

12. Nicolson, *Science and Imagination*, p. 211.

13. Bonnet, *Contemplation de la nature*, I, 31.

14. Louis-Sebastien Mercier, *Mon bonnet de nuit* (Neufchâtel, 1784–85, I, pp. 21–22.

15. For mention of eighteenth-century views of the "feminine" and "masculine" characteristics of matter see Ault, *Visionary Physics*, p. 119; P. M. Heiman and J. E. McGuire, "Newtonian Forces and Lockean Powers: Concepts of Matter in Eighteenth-Century Thought," in *Historical Studies in the Physical Sciences*, III, ed. Russell McCormmach (University of Pennsylvania Press, 1971), pp. 236–237.

16. A.-F. Frézier, *Relation du voyage de la mer du sud aux côtes du Chily et du Pérou fait pendant les années 1712, 1713, & 1714* (Paris: Jean-Géoffrey Nyon, Etienne Ganeau, Jacque Quillau, 1716), p. 146: "Dans la suite des temps on est venu de reföuillir les mêmes mines, & l'on a trouvé dans le bois, dans les crânes, & dans les os, des filets d'argent qui les pénétroient comme la veine même. . . ."

17. Robinet (*De la nature*, I, p. 223) cites a bell tower in Derby, England, that became visible from a certain distance; this was not the case a hundred years earlier. He attributes the alteration to the lowering of a mountain that had intervened between the viewer's line of sight and the church and the concomitant rising of the mound on which the church stood. Further, he points out that Santerini did not exist before the time of Seneca and that it continues to "grow" beneath the feet of its present inhabitants.

18. Claude-Henri Watelet, *L'art de peindre. Poème avec des réflexions sur les différentes parties de la peinture* (Paris, 1760), pp. 123–124: "L'expression s'étend des objets les plus simples, aux objets les plus composés; des corps les moins susceptibles d'action, à ceux qui sont les plus animés; enfin de la matière à l'esprit. . . ."

19. T. Takeuchi, "Die Schönheit des Unbelebten," in *Proceedings of the VIth International Congress of Aesthetics*, ed. Rudolf Zeitler (Uppsala, 1972), p. 669.

20. Teyssèdre, *Roger de Piles*, p. 66.

21. See in particular Piper, *Active Universe*, p. 4. For the scientific roots of eighteenth-century vitalism see Elizabeth L. Haigh, "The Vital Principle of Paul-Joseph Barthez: The Clash between Monism and Dualism," *Medical History* (Great Britain) 21 (January 1977), 1–14; "The Roots of the Vitalism of Xavier Bichat," *Bulletin of the History of Medicine* 79 (spring 1975), 72–86. Paul-Joseph Barthez was the most influential vitalist at the University of Montpellier. In 1778 he published his theories in *Nouveaux éléments de la science de l'homme*, attributing functions of the living body to the action of the vital principle. Barthez thought evidence indicated that the vital principle existed separately from

the human body and that it might emanate from a universal principle created by God to animate the world. Haigh's discussion of Bichat not only locates him within the Montpellier tradition but also analyzes his stance in relation to the physiologists Hermann Boerhaave, Georg-Ernst Stahl, Albrecht von Haller, and Barthez. Although her articles do not develop the aesthetic ramifications of this principle, she notes that La Mettrie and Diderot were influenced by it. One wonders how much the important French notion of *sensibilité* owes to the concept of irritability and the prescient idea that a latent force of sensibility exists in all the material of the universe.

22. William Borlase, *Antiquities Historical and Monumental of the County of Cornwall* (London: W. Bowyer and J. Nichols, 1769), pp. 211–222; A. C. Quatremère de Quincy, *Encyclopédie méthodique* (Paris: Henri Agasse, 1788–1825), III, p. 541. For a controversial modern discussion of this phenomenon see Vincent Scully, *The Earth, the Temple, and the Gods: Greek Sacred Architecture* (Yale University Press, 1962), pp. 19 ff.

23. Nieuhof, *Embassy*, p. 269. When the wealthy Chinese intend to create a tomb "they diligently examine the shape and nature of the Hill for its situation, and are very solicitous to discover a happy piece of Earth: and such they esteem, so which has the resemblance of the Head, Tayl, or Heart of a Dragon; which once found, they imagine that according to wish, all things shall go well with their Posterity. . . ."

24. Siren, *Gardens of China*, pp. 17 ff. For a more recent discussion see Patrick Conner, "China and the Landscape Garden: Reports, Engravings and Misconceptions," *Art History* 2 (December 1979), 429–440.

25. Barbara Maria Stafford, "Toward Romantic Landscape Perception: Illustrated Travel Accounts and the Rise of 'Singularity' as an Aesthetic Category," *Art Quarterly*, N.S., 1 (autumn 1977), 89–124.

26. Tuveson, "Space, Deity, and the 'Natural Sublime,' " p. 32.

27. Vartanian, *Diderot and Descartes*, pp. 47–49, 129, 135–137. Vartanian's discussion of the influence of Cartesian physics on the *philosophes* (especially Diderot and his circle) stresses that it reduced natural science exclusively to a consideration of the components of matter. Thus, nature was seen as the proper object of science and as unrelated in any fundamental sense to problems of a theological kind. On the changing views of matter see Günther Bandmann, "Der Wandel der Materialbewertung in der Kunsttheorie des 19. Jahrhunderts," in *Beiträge zur Theorie der Künste im 19. Jahrhunderts*, ed. Helmut

Koopmann and J. Adolf Schmoll, gen. Eisenwerth (Frankfurt am Main: Vittorio Klostermann, 1971), I, pp. 1301–1302. Clearly, one result of the aesthetic vindication of matter is the possibility of a masterpiece freed of culture and craft. For the history of its opposite, the quasi-divine work of man, see Walter Cahn, *Masterpiece: Chapters on the History of an Idea* (Princeton University Press, 1979), pp. 29, 47, 89, 91 ff. For the related construct of *mirabilia*, embodied at first in the seven architectural wonders of the ancient Greek and Near Eastern world and later in Roman antiquities, see Maria Luisa Madonna, " 'Septem Mundi Miracula' come Templi della Virtu. Pirro Ligorio e l'Interpretazione cinquecentesca della meraviglio del Mondo," *Psicon* (1976), 25–33. For eighteenth-century views concerning the "immaterialism" of the contour see Barbara Maria Stafford, "Beauty of the Invisible: Winckelmann and the Aesthetics of Imperceptibility," *Zeitschrift für Kunstgeschichte* 43, no. 1 (1980), 65–78.

28. Bonnet, *Contemplation de la nature*, I, pp. 33–36. Also see Wilson L. Scott, "The Significance of 'Hard Bodies' in the History of Scientific Thought," *Isis* 50 (June 1959), 199–200. Although Scott is discussing atomic theory, in which until 1850 atoms were often considered hard and elastic, his statements corroborating a view of matter as solid, massy, hard, and impenetrable are relevant to this chapter.

29. Marcia Pointon, "Geology and Landscape Painting in Nineteenth Century England," *British Society for the History of Science* 1 (1979), 93. Although this essay ignores the eighteenth-century tradition, it is useful to remember at this juncture that Ruskin, in reviewing John Brett's *Val d'Aosta*, drew attention to the theory of historical landscape. By this term was meant the pictorial representation of an environment in which the physical history of the landscape is manifest.

30. Georges-Louis Le Rouge, *Jardins anglochinois* (Paris, 1775–1788), VII, pl. 22: "Dessinées d'après nature dans le Forest de Fontainebleau en 1734 par . . . alors Ingenir Géographe de S.A.S. M. le Comte de Clermont. Idées pour la construction des Rochers dans les jardins anglais." This search for rocks "with character" is discussed in E. de Ganay, "Les rochers et les eaux dans le jardins à l'anglaise," *Revue de l'art ancien et moderne* 66 (July 1934), 66, and C. C. L. Hirschfeld, *Theorie der Gartenkunst* (Leipzig: M. G. Weidmanns Erben und Reich, 1779–1785), I, p. 192.

31. De Piles, *Cours de peinture*, pp. 173–174. On an early apologist for rocks and crags, naked and broken cliffs, see Francis Edward Litz, "Richard Bentley on Beauty, Irregularity, and Mountains," *ELH* 12 (December 1945), 327–332.

32. Hubert Burda, *Die Ruine in den Bildern Hubert Roberts* (Munich: Wilhelm Fink, 1969), p. 56.

33. P. G. Anson, "Rocks and Gardens," *Landscape* 11 (winter 1961–62), 3. Two helpful books dealing with the largely unstudied area of the pictorial connections between the East and the West during the eighteenth century are Cécile and Michel Beurdeley, *Castiglione, peintre jésuite à la cour de Chine* (Paris: Bibliothèque des Arts, 1971), and Lunsingh Scheurleer, *Chine de Commande*.

34. Bashō, *"The Narrow Road to the Far North" and Selected Haiku*, tr. Dorothy Britten (Tokyo: Kodansha, 1974), pp. 33–34, 37.

35. Le Bruyn, *Travels*, I, p. 176. Also see Frederick Lewis Norden, *Travels in Egypt and Nubia*, tr. Peter Templeman (London: Lockyer; Davis and Charles Reymers, 1756–57), pl. 74, fig. b. For a discussion of such "singular rocks" and their descriptions in the accounts of Le Bruyn, Norden, and Keyt see L. L. Viel de Saint-Maux, *Lettres sur l'architecture des anciens* (Brussels, 1779–1784), pp. 24–25.

36. William Marsden, *Views of Sumatra* (London, 1799), pl. 7.

37. John Barrow, *A Voyage to Cochin China in the Years 1792 and 1793* (London: T. Cadell and W. Davies, 1806), plate facing p. 5. This book documents a trip to Vietnam and Java, with additional accounts of journeys to Africa, the Canary Islands, Rio de Janeiro, Madiera, and Tristan de Cunha.

38. John Barrow, *An Account of Travels into the Interior of Southern Africa, in the Years 1797 and 1798; Including Cursory Observations on the Geology and Geography of the Southern Part of that Continent; The Natural History of Such Objects as Occurred in the Animal, Vegetable, and Mineral Kingdoms; and Sketches of the Physical and Moral Characters of the Various Tribes of Inhabitants Surrounding the Settlement of the Cape of Good Hope* (London: T. Cadell, Jr., and W. Davies, 1801), I, p. 60. Barrow was secretary to the Earl of Macartney and Auditor-General of Public Accounts at the Cape.

39. George Hutchins Bellasis, *Views of Saint Helena* (London: John Tyler, 1815), pl. 5. These six views, aquatinted by Robert Havell, were dedicated to the Duke of Wellington, through whose efforts "the Island of Saint Helena is at this time an object of interest to the whole world." Also see Clarke Abel, *Narrative of a Journey in the Interior of China, and of a Voyage to and from that Country in the Years 1816 and 1817* (London: Longman, Hurst, Rees, Orme, and Brown, 1818), p. 193.

40. Thomas and William Daniell, *Oriental Scenery; One Hundred and Fifty Views* (London: T. and W. Daniell, 1816), part V, pls. 9, 10. Thomas (1749–1840) and William (1769–1837) Daniell published their monumental work in six parts between 1795 and 1808. It has recently been interpreted in light of India's history and the maturation of British power in the region. Such a vast topographical work represents a means of grasping an unknown territory and provides a document of possession. See Kenneth Bendiner, "Thomas and William Daniell's 'Oriental Scenery': Some Major Themes," *Arts* 55 (December 1980), 98–103.

41. Thomas Sutton, *The Daniells, Artists and Travellers* (London: The Bodley Head, 1954), p. 19. Also see Anson, *Voyage*, p. 278.

42. Neale, *Travels*, pp. 71–72.

43. J. K. Tuckey, *Narrative of an Expedition to Explore the River Zaire, usually Called the Congo, in South Africa, in 1816, under the Direction of . . . to which is Added the Journal of Professor Smith; Some General Observations on the Country and Its Inhabitants; and an Appendix: Containing the Natural History of that Part of the Kingdom of the Congo through which the Zaire Flows* (London: John Murray, 1818), p. 95. The fourteen engravings were made after Lt. John Hawkey's sketches.

44. George Waddington, *Journal of a Visit to Some Parts of Ethiopia* (London: John Murray, 1822), p. 125; John William Edy, *Boydell's Picturesque Scenery of Norway with the Principal Towns from the Naze, by the Route of Christiana, to the Magnificent Pass of the Swinesund; from Original Drawings Made on the Spot, and Engraved by . . . With Remarks and Observations Made in a Tour through the Country, and Revised and Corrected by William Tooke, F.R.S., Member of the Imperial Academy of Sciences, and of the Economical Society at Saint Petersburg* (London: Hurst, Robinson, and Co.; Late Boydell and Co., 1820), pl. 63 and letterpress; Robert Melville Grindlay, *Scenery, Costumes, and Architecture, Chiefly on the Western Side of India* (London: R. Ackermann, 1826–1830), I, pl. 15.

45. Albert V. Carozzi, "Rudolph Erich Raspe and the Basalt Controversy," *Studies in Romanticism* 8 (summer 1969), 239, 245.

46. John Whitehurst, *An Inquiry into the Original State and Formation of the Earth*, second edition (London: W. Bent, 1786; first published in 1778), pp. 251, 256–257. On the Neptunist-Vulcanist controversy and its specific connection to eighteenth-century illustrations of the Giant's Causeway see Martyn Anglesea and John Preston, " 'A Philosophical Landscape': Susanna Drury and the Giant's Causeway," *Art History* 3 (September 1980), 252–273.

47. Jean-Benjamin de Laborde, *Description générale et particulière de la France* (Paris, 1781–1796), II, pl. 3 and letterpress.

48. Houel, *Voyage*, II, pl. 112, pp. 71–74.

49. *Voyage de Humboldt et Bonpland*, atlas, pl. XXII, pp. 123–124. For the same point see Jacques-Gérard Milbert, *Itinéraire pittoresque du fleuve Hudson et des parties latérales de l'Amerique du Nord, d'après les dessins originaux pris sur les lieux* (Paris: Henri Gaugain et Cie, 1828), p. 51.

50. Cook, *Voyage*, I, pp. 314–315. Much later, the Russian artist Louis Choris produced beautiful sketches of corals when he accompanied Captain Otto von Kotzebue's expedition that left Saint Petersburg in July 1815 in the brig *Rurik*. See Louis Choris, *Vues et paysages des regions équinoxiales, recueillis dans un voyage autour du monde . . . avec un introduction et un texte explicatif* (Paris: Paul Renouard, 1827), pl. 10. This brilliant color lithograph depicting red corals and madrepores is based on a wonderful watercolor sketch of coral reefs in the Choris Sketchbook, now in the Fuller Collection of the Bishop Museum in Honolulu.

51. La Pluche, *Spectacle de la nature*, III, p. 241.

52. H. Diane Russell, *Jacques Callot: Prints & Related Drawings* (Washington, D.C.: National Gallery of Art, 1975), figs. 229, 240, 241,; p. 283.

53. Sydney Parkinson, *A Journal of a Voyage to the South Seas in His Majesty's Ship, the* Endeavour, *Faithfully Transcribed from the papers of the Late . . . Draughtsman to Joseph Banks, Esq. on His Late Expedition, with Dr. Solander, round the World. Embellished with Views and Designs, Delineated by the Author, and Engraved by Capital Artists* (London: Stanfield Parkinson, 1773), pls. 20, 24; pp. 99, 117. Also see Bernard Smith, *European Vision and the South Pacific, 1768–1850. A Study in the History of Art and Ideas* (Oxford: Clarendon, 1960), pp. 17–18. Smith interprets this passage as illustrating the conflicting ideals of art and science.

54. John Henry Grose, *A Voyage to the East-Indies, with Observations on Various Parts there* (London: S. Hooper and A. Morley, 1757), p. 89; Cook, *Voyage*, I, pl. 4, p. 66; Charles Cordiner, *Remarkable Ruins and Romantic Prospects of North Britain. With Ancient Monuments and Singular Subjects of Natural History* (London, 1791), viz. *Rock of Dunby*; William Alexander: 870 Drawings Made during Lord Macartney's Embassy to the Emperor of China, 1792–1794, India Office Library, III, fol. 21 v, no. 68.

55. Louis-François Cassas, *Voyage pittoresque de la Syrie, de la Phénicie, de La Palestine, et de la Basse Egypte* (Paris: Imprimerie de la Republique, An VI), II, pl. 67, p. 8; W. F. W. Owen, *Narrative of Voyages to Explore the Shores of Africa, Arabia, and Madagascar* (London: Richard Bentley, 1833), I, pp. 280–281. The Memorandum issued from the Admiralty, reproduced in the preface, indicates the Royal Navy's desire to have the coast of Africa between Sierra Leone and the River Gambia completely surveyed and explored. Despite this fact, Owen's tone is markedly different from those of earlier scientific voyagers to the River Zaire (e.g., Tuckey in 1816); his language displays the hallmarks of the Picturesque. Also see Arthur de Capell Brooke, *Travels through Sweden, Norway, and Finmark to the North Cape in the Summer of 1820* (London: Rodwell and Martin, 1823), pls. 7, 8; pp. 208–210.

56. Yves-Joseph, Baron de Kerguelen-Trémarec, *Relation d'un voyage dans la mer du Nord aux côtes d'Islande, du Greenland, de Férro, de Schettland, des Orcades & de Norwège; fait en 1767 & 1768* (Paris: Prault, 1771), pl. 10, p. 158; also see pl. V, fig. 18, and pl. IX, fig. 19. The fascination for such hollowed out rocks continued in the nineteenth century, both in the popular press and in the landscapes of Claude Monet. For the former see "Les Feroe," *Le Magasin Pittoresque* 35 (1840), 297.

57. De Laborde, *Description*, II, pl. 14. N.B.: After volume IV the title becomes *Voyage pittoresque de la France, avec la description de toutes ses provinces.*

58. Alexander von Humboldt, *Researches concerning the Institutions and Monuments of the Ancient Inhabitants of America*, tr. Helen Maria Williams (London: Longman, Hurst, Rees, Orme & Brown, J. Murray, & H. Colburn, 1814), I, pls. 4, 53. Also see Jean-Benjamin de Laborde, *Tableaux topographiques, pittoresques, physiques, historiques, moraux, politiques, littéraires de la Suisse et de l'Italie, ornée de 1200 estampes . . . d'après les dessins de MM. Robert, Perignon, Fragonard, Paris, Poyet, Raymond, Le Barbier, Berthelemy, Menageot, Le May, Houel. etc.* (Paris: Née & Masquelier, 1777), I, part II, pl. 163. On the European interest in Swiss bridges (natural and artificial) see Pierre du Prey, "Eighteenth-Century English Sources for a History of Swiss Wooden Bridges," *Zeitschrift für Schweizerische Archäologie und Kunstgeschichte* 36, no. 1 (1979), 51–63. Among the earliest illustrations of these are the copper engravings by F. Melchior Füssli found in Johann Jacob Scheuchzer, *Beschreibung der Natur-Geschichten des Schweizerlandes* (Zurich: Scheuchzer, 1706–1708), III, pls. facing p. 27; p. 42.

59. National Maritime Museum, Greenwich, "Anson's Voyage. Lieut. Brett's Original Drawings, Dec. 1740–July 1743. Engraved for the Narrative, 1748." See, further, Richard Walter, *A Voyage round*

the World in the Years 1740, I, II, III, IV (London: John and Paul Knapton, 1744), I, p. 260.

60. Alexander, Drawings, III, fol. 79, no. 252; George Staunton, An Authentic Account of an Embassy from the King of Great Britain to the Emperor of China (London: W. Bulmer and Co., 1797), I, pp. 94–98.

61. Louis-François Cassas, Voyage pittoresque et historique de l'Istrie et Dalmatie, ed. Joseph Lavallée (Pierre Didot-l'aîné, 1802), p. 156.

62. De Laborde, Description de la France, II, pl. 5; Park, Travels, p. 53.

63. William Daniell, Interesting Selections from Animated Nature with Illustrative Scenery (London: T. Cadell, 1807–1812), pl. 29; Tuckey, River Zaire, pp. 131–132.

64. Robert Smith, Views of Prince of Wales Island (London, 1821), plate entitled View of Mt. Erskine and Pulo Ticoose Bay, Prince of Wales Island. In 1813 Robert Smith was surveying on the Mirzapur southern frontier. In 1814 he became the superintending engineer on Prince of Wales Island (Penang), to which he returned in 1818. Here he made the sketches used by William Daniell for his large and extremely handsome engravings. Also see John Davy, An Account of the Interior of Ceylon, and of Its Inhabitants (London: Longman, Hurst, Rees, Orme, and Brown, 1821), pp. 6 ff.; James Pattison Cockburn, Views to Illustrate the Route of the Simplon Pass (London: Rodwell and Martin, 1822); Robert Ker Porter, Travels in Georgia, Persia, Armenia, Ancient Babylonia (London: Longman, Hurst, Rees, Orme, and Brown, 1822), pl. 59, pp. 146, 150–151; Charles Forrest, A Picturesque Tour along the Rivers Ganges and Jumna, in India: Consisting of Twenty-Four Highly Finished and Coloured Views, a Map, and Vignettes, from Original Drawings made on the Spot; With Illustrations, Historical and Descriptive (London: R. Ackermann, 1824), pl. 7, pp. 140–141.

65. Acerbi, Travels, I, pp. 182–184.

66. Two surveys dealing with the exploration of Switzerland are John Grand-Carteret, La montagne à travers les ages: Rôle joué par elle; façon dont elle a été vue (Grenoble: H. Falque et F. Perrin, 1903), and Numa Broc, Les montagnes vues par les géographes et les naturalistes de langue française au XVIIIe siècle, Mémoires de la section de géographie, IV (Paris: Bibliothèque Nationale, 1969). The earliest visual record of Alpinism, replete with mountains and chamois hunting, is Das Jagdbuch Kaiser Maximilians I (Brussels). In 1510, Dürer's pupil Hans Leonard Schaüfelen received the commission to illustrate the allegorical poem Theuerdank (1517), which places the emperor in an Alpine world. Leonard Beck and Hans Burgkmair were also involved in the project. See Conrad Gesner, On the Admiration of Mountains . . . (1543); A Description of the Riven Mountain, Commonly Called Mount Pilatus (1555), tr. from the Latin by H. B. D. Soulé and ed. W. Dock and J. Monroe Thorington (San Francisco: Grabhorn, 1937), pp. 44–45.

67. Parks, "Turn to the Romantic," p. 27.

68. Koester, "Joos de Momper," pp. 11–13. Also see Palissy, Oeuvres complètes, p. 31.

69. Diderot, Salons, II, p. 167. This panegyric follows hard on the heels of Diderot's apostrophe to the painter Philippe-Jacques de Loutherbourg. Also see Friedrich Kammerer, Zur Geschichte des Landschaftsgefühls im Frühen achtzehnten Jahrhundert (Berlin: S. Calvary, 1909), p. 79. Kammerer makes the point that the taste for mountains as colossal masses was eminently suited to the Baroque style of the seventeenth century, with its fascination for monstrous dimensions. For the Baroque precedent, see further Katherine Brownell Collier, Cosmogonies of Our Forefathers. Some Theories of the Seventeenth and Eighteenth Centuries (New York: Octagon, 1968), pp. 59–61.

70. Glacken, Traces, pp. 408–427 passim; Litz, "Richard Bentley," pp. 327–331; Vartanian, Diderot and Descartes, pp. 67–68.

71. W. R. Schweizer, "The Swiss Print," Connoisseur 130 (November 1952), 85–86; Les joies de la nature au XVIIIe siècle, Exhibition Bibliothèque Nationale (Paris, 1971), pp. 8–12; Jean Furstenberg, La gravure originale dans l'illustration du livre française au dix-huitième siècle (Hamburg: Dr. Ernst Hauswedell & Co., 1975), p. 295. For Caspar Wolf's contribution, in particular, see Yvonne Boerlin-Brodbeck, Caspar Wolf (1735–1783), Landschaft im Vorfeld der Romantik, exhibition, Kunstmuseum (Basel, 1980), and Willi Raeber, Caspar Wolf, 1735–1783, Sein Leben und Sein Werk, (Munich: Sauerländer, 1979). For early Alpine documentation see Gustav Solar, Hackaert. Die Schweizer Ansichten, 1653–1656. Zeichnungen eines Niederländischen Malers als frühe Bilddokumente der Alpenlandschaft (Dietikon-Zurich: Josef Stoeker, 1981). The young Jan Hackaert was one of twelve Dutch artists working on commission for the Amsterdam lawyer Laurens van der Hem, whose holdings were incorporated into the famous atlases compiled by the seventeenth-century Amsterdam cartographer Joan Blaeu. The bulk of the Swiss views were drawn in 1655 during a journey of four months from Zurich to the Grisons, undertaken with the Zurich draftsman Conrad Mayer and their pupil Hans Rudolf Werdmuller. The most fascinating result of Solar's study is to show how this young student of Jan Both became involved in the nationalist interests of the Dutch in the source of the Rhine, and, above all, in the commercial

and economic interests of Dutch merchant circles behind Van der Hem's commission for the exploration of the most strategic spots in the Grison's crucial north-south passage of the Alps.

72. Broc, *Les montagnes*, pp. 67–68; Mornet, *Le sentiment de la nature*, pp. 261–274 passim; Van Tieghem, *Préromantisme*, p. 169.

73. Solar, Hösli, *Escher von der Linth*, p. 67. For a discussion of the varieties of eighteenth-century Swiss engravings destined primarily for an English clientele see T. S. R. Boase, *Les peintres anglais et la vallée d'Aoste*, tr. A. P. D'Entrèves (Novara: Département du Tourisme, des Antiquités et Beaux-Arts Région Autonome Vallée d'Aoste, 1959), pp. 5–6.

74. Mercier, *Mon bonnet de nuit*, II, pp. 123–125. On the continuation of Mercier's "scientific" imagery in the Romantic writings of Hugo see Helen Temple Patterson, "Poetic Genesis: Sebastien Mercier into Victor Hugo," *Studies on Voltaire and the Eighteenth Century* 11 (1960), 68–70.

75. Broc, *Les montagnes*, p. 62.

76. Louis-François Elizabeth, Baron Ramond de Carbonnières, *Observations faites dans les Pyrénées, pour servir de suite à des observations sur les Alpes, insérées dans un traduction des Lettres de W. Coxe, sur la Suisse* (Paris: Belin, 1789), pp. 35–36. Also see Gaston, *Images romantiques des Pyrénées*, p. 12; Boase, *Vallée d'Aoste*, pp. 20–25.

77. Ramond de Carbonnière, *Observations*, pp. 71–73, 195–197. For an excellent discussion of Ramond and his contribution to the rise of "Pyreneeism" see Cuthbert Girdlestone, *Poésie, politique, Pyrénées. Louis-François Ramond (1755–1827). Sa vie, son oeuvre littéraire et politique* (Paris: Minard, 1968), pp. 146 ff. Ramond's "spirit of observation" was aided and abetted by J. Dusaulx's *Voyage à Barège et dans les Hautes Pyrénées, fait en 1788* (Paris: Didot jeune, 1796) and François Pasumot's *Voyages physiques dans les Pyrénées en 1788 et 1789. Histoire naturelle d'une partie de ces montagnes; particulièrement des environs de Barège, Bagnères, Cantères et Gavarnie. Avec des cartes géographiques* (Paris: Le Clare, 1797).

78. Gaston, *Images romantiques de Pyrénées*, pp. 75–80. On Constant Bourgeois, the inventor of the French panorama and one of the first artists to render the Pyrenees "scientifically" in the 1790s, see Marcel Durliat, "Alexandre du Mège, ou les mythes archéologiques à Toulouse dans le premier tiers du XIXe siècle," *Revue de l'Art* 23 (1974), 32–33.

79. Pierre Bouguer, *La figure de la terre, determinée par les observations des Messieurs . . . & de La Condamine, de l'Académie Royale des Sciences, envoyés par ordre du Roy au Pérou, pour observer aux environs de l'équateur. Avec une relation abrégée de ce voyage, qui contient la description du pays dans lequel les opérations ont été faites* (Paris: Charles-Antoine Jombert, 1749), pl. p. cx; pp. xxix–xxx.

80. William Inglis Morse, ed., *Letters of Alejandro Malaspina (1790–1791)*, tr. Christopher M. Dawson (Boston: McIver-Johnson, 1944), pp. 27, 32. For the official account of the expedition see Alejandro Malaspina, *Viaje al Rio de La Plata en el Siglo XVIII*, ed. Hector R. Ratto (Buenos Aires: "La Facultad," 1939). For a reproduction of the *View* attributed to Ravenet see Jose Torre Revello, *Los Artistas Pintores de la Expedicion Malaspina* (Buenos Aires: Jacobo Pevser, 1944), pl. XXXIX.

81. Halina Nelken, *Humboldtiana at Harvard* (Cambridge, Mass.: Harvard University Press, 1976), pp. 8–9, 17.

82. *Voyage de Humboldt et Bonpland*, I, p. vi.

83. Ibid., pls. X, XVI; pp. 42, 102–104.

84. Alexander Caldcleugh, *Travels in South America, during the Years 1819, 20, 21, Containing an Account of the Present State of Brazil, Buenos Ayres, and Chile* (London: John Murray, 1825), I, pl. p. 319: *View of the Great Chain of the Andes*; Charles Stuart Cochrane, *Journal of a Residence and Travels in Colombia, during the Years 1823 and 1824* (London: Henry Colburn, 1825), I, pp. 177–179; and Conrad Martens, "*Beagle* Watercolours from *The Beagle Expedition and Survey to Southern Australia, 1837–1843*," National Maritime Museum, Greenwich, no. 13: *Cordillera of the Andes Seen from the East from Mystery Plain*. For a recent biography of Charles Darwin and a concise summary of his expedition see John Chancellor, *Charles Darwin* (New York: Taplinger, 1976). The most basic document of that expedition compiled from the original manuscripts is Nora Barlow, ed., *Charles Darwin's Diary of the Voyage of the H.M.S. Beagle* (Cambridge University Press, 1933). Also see the standard account by Robert Fitzroy, *Narrative of the Surveying Voyages of His Majesty's Ships* Adventure *and* Beagle, *between the Years 1826 and 1836, Describing Their Examination of the Southern Shores of South America, and the* Beagle's *Circumnavigation of the Globe* (London: Henry Colburn, 1839), II, pp. 338, 349–350. Volume III of the Fitzroy account contains Charles Darwin's *Journal and Remarks, 1832–1836*. For the most complete account of Conrad Martens, the English artist of German stock whom Fitzroy engaged as draftsman at Monte Video in 1832, see Lionel Lindsay, *Conrad Martens: The Man and His Art*, ed. Douglas Dundas, second revised edition (Sydney: Angus and Robertson, 1968).

85. Jerome Lobo, *A Voyage to Abyssinia*, tr. M. Le Grand (London: A. Bettesworth, 1735), p. 204.

86. Patterson, *Poetic Genesis*, p. 70.

87. Bruce, *Travels*, III, pp. 64, 125.

88. George Annesley, Viscount Valentia, *Voyages and Travels to India, Ceylon, the Red Sea, Abyssinia, and Egypt* (London: William Miller, 1809), III, pl. 5.

89. Charles Gold, *Oriental Drawings: Sketched between the Years 1791 and 1793* (London: Bunney, 1806), pl. 34 and glossary.

90. Grindlay, *Western India*, I, pls. 8, 9 and commentary.

91. William Hodges, *Select Views in India, Drawn on the Spot in the Years 1780, 1781, and 1783, and Executed in Aqua Tinta* (London: J. Edwards, 1786), pls. 8, 9, 16, 22. For Hodges's itinerary in India see William Foster, "William Hodges, R.A., in India," *Bengal Past & Present* 30 (July–September 1925), 1–8.

92. Alexander Allan, *Views in the Mysore Country* (London: A. Allan, 1794), pl. 4. My illustration reproduces the pen-and-ink drawing for that plate (WD 107), now in the India Office Library. For information on Allan, who took part in the third and fourth Mysore wars, and on these artists in India, see Mildred Archer, *British Drawings in the India Office Library* (London: Her Majesty's Stationery Office, 1969), I, pp. 93 ff.

93. Robert Home, *Select Views in Mysore, the Country of Tipoo Sultan; from Drawings Taken on the Spot by . . . ; With Historical Descriptions* (London: Bowyer, 1794), p. 9; Daniell, *Oriental Scenery*, II, part III, pl. 13; Robert Elliott, *Views in the East: Comprising India, Canton, and the Shores of the Red Sea; With Historical and Descriptive Illustrations* (London: H. Fisher, 1833), II, plate and text: *Hill Fortress of Dowlutabad*.

94. William Orme, *Twenty-Four Views in Hindostan from the Original Pictures Painted by Mr. Daniell & Col. Ward now in the Possession of Richard Chase, Esq.* (London: Edward Orme, 1805), pl. 10 and p. 4. In 1664 François Bernier, physician to the Grand Mogul, had journeyed to Kashmir and reported his findings to the Académie des Sciences; see his *Voyages de . . . , docteur en medécine de la Faculté de Montpellier, contenant la description des états du Grand Mogul, de l'Hindoustan, du Royaume de Kachemire, etc.* (Amsterdam: Paul Marret, 1699), II, p. 270. Unfortunately, although the book is illustrated with copper engravings, the plate on p. 268 supplies only a map showing the Caucasus and the mountains of Tibet. On Bernier's place in the large picture of

French scientific exploration see P. Huard and M. Wong, "Les enquêtes scientifiques françaises et l'exploration du monde exotique aux XVIIe et XVIIIe siècles," *Bulletin de l'Ecole Française d'Extrême-Orient* 52, no. 1 (1964), 143–144.

95. William Kirkpatrick, *An Account of the Kingdom of Nepaul; Being the Substance of Observations Made during a Mission to That Country in the Year 1793* (London: William Miller, 1811), pp. v–xiv; pls. pp. 153, 158.

96. J. B. Fraser, *Views in the Himala Mountains* (London: Rodwell & Martin, 1820). Also see Albert W. Bettex, *L'invention du monde*, tr. Armel Guerne (Paris: Delpire, 1960), p. 96. Although the fascination with "the snowy ridge of old Imaus, or the modern Himalaya Mountains" continued to grow, no descriptions or illustrations in the first half of the nineteenth century exceeded those of Fraser. See for comparison William Thorn, *Memoir of the War in India, Conducted by General Lord Lake, Commander-in-Chief and Major-General Sir Arthur Wellesley, Duke of Wellington; from Its Commencement in 1803, to Its Termination in 1806, On the Banks of the Hyphasis. With Historical Sketches, Topographical Descriptions, and Statistical Observations* (London: T. Egerton, Military Library, 1818), p. 488; Robert Elliot, *Views in the East; Comprising India, Canton, and the Shores of the Red Sea. With Historical and Descriptive Illustrations* (London: H. Fisher, 1833), I, plates *Grass Rope Bridge at Teree, in the Province of Gurwall* (D. Cox, dr., W. Taylor, engr.) and *Jerdair* (D. Cox, dr., W. Higham, engr.); Carl, Freiherr von Hügel, *Kaschmir und das Reich der Siek* (Stuttgart: Hallberger'sche Verlagshandlung, 1840–1842). The last volume reduces the grandeur of the immense rocky masses to the confines of the vignette.

97. James Manson, "Twelve Drawings of Almorah," ca. 1826, accompanying the *Report of the Mineral Survey of the Himalaya Mountains Lying between the Rivers Sutlej and Kalee*, India Office Library, MSS Eur. E. 96, fols. 6, 12. Also see Archer, *British Drawings*, II, pp. 558–559.

98. Francis Hamilton (formerly Buchanan), *An Account of the Kingdom of Nepal, and of the Territories Annexed to This Dominion by the House of Gorkha* (Edinburgh: Archibald Constable, 1819), pp. 89–90; pls. 1, 2.

99. Pococke, *Description of the East*, II, part I, p. 95.

100. Bruce, *Travels*, III, pp. 582–583.

101. James Grey Jackson, *An Account of the Empire of Marocco, and the Districts of Suse and Tafilelt; Compiled from Miscellaneous Observations Made during a Long Residence in, and Various Journies through, These Countries. To which is Added an Account of Shipwrecks on the Western Coast of Africa,*

and an *Interesting Account of Timbuctoo, the Great Emporium of Central Africa*, second revised edition (London: J. Bulmer, 1811), pp. 10–11.

102. George Heriot, *Travels through the Canadas, Containing a Description of the Picturesque Scenery on Some of the Rivers and Lakes; With an Account of the Productions, Commerce, and Inhabitants of Those Provinces; to which is Subjoined a Comparative View of the Manners and Customs of Several of the Indian Nations of North and South America* (London: Richard Phillips, 1807), pp. 2–3.

103. Abel, *China*, pl. 2 and pp. 184–185.

104. Heinrich Lichtenstein, *Reisen im Sudlichen Africa in den Jahren 1803, 1804, 1805, und 1806* (Berlin: C. Salfold, 1811), I, pl. i, p. 102.

105. John Oxley, *Journals of Two Expeditions into the Interior of New South Wales, Undertaken by Order of the British Government in the Years 1817–1818* (London: John Murray, 1820), pl. p. 235 and p. 236.

106. Davy, *Ceylon*, pl. 13 and p. 4.

107. Pococke, *Description of the East*, II, part I, pl. 5 and pp. 20, 65; Broc, *La géographie des philosophes*, p. 280.

108. Jacques-Gérard Milbert, *Voyage pittoresque à l'Ile de France, au Cap de Bonne-Espérance et à l'Ile de Teneriffe* (Paris: A. Nepveu, 1812), I, p. 53. After studying landscape painting with Valenciennes, Milbert states, he immediately began voyaging. Despite the title of his work, he was part of an expedition of discovery ("un veritable voyage", as he puts it). He became ill during Péron's expedition to the southern lands, a voyage of discovery ordered by Napoleon when he was still First Consul, and had to be put ashore on Mauritius. This work is the result of that enforced two-year sojourn.

109. "William Alexander's Journal of a Voyage to Pekin in China on Board the *Hindostan* which Accompanied Lord Macartney on His Embassy to the Emperor," British Library, Add. Mss. 35174, fol. 3.

110. Le Gentil, *Voyage*, II, pp. 644–646.

111. Bernardin de Saint-Pierre, *L'Isle de France*, II, pp. 28–29; Forster, *Voyage round the World*, I, pp. 63–64; Thomas and William Daniell, *A Picturesque Voyage to India by Way of China* (London: Longman, Hurst, Rees, and Orme, 1810), pl. 7. Also see Abbé de La Caille, *Journal historique du voyage fait du Cap de Bonne-Espérance* (Paris: Guillyn, 1763), pp. 148–149, 155–156.

112. Jacques-Julien, Houton de Labillardière, *Atlas pour servir à la relation du voyage à la recherche de La Pérouse par . . . en 1791, 1792, et pendant la 1ᵉʳᵉ et 2ᵉᵐᵉ année de la République* (Paris: H. Jansen, An VIII), I, p. 430; Vancouver, *Voyage of Discovery*, I, pl. 3, p. 268; Cassas, *L'Istrie et Dalmatie*, pl. 33 and pp. 119–120; Alexandre-Louis-Joseph de Laborde, *Voyage pittoresque et historique de l'Espagne* (Paris: Pierre Didot l'aîné, 1806–1818), I, part I, p. 75; James Cordiner, *A Description of Ceylon, Containing an Account of the Country, Inhabitants and Natural Productions* (London: Longman, Hurst, Rees, and Orme, 1807), I, p. 200; Valentia, *Voyages and Travels*, I, pl. p. 266; *Voyage de Humboldt et Bonpland*, I, *Supplément*, pl. 64 and p. 296; Edmond Temple, *Travels in Various Parts of Peru, Including a Year's Residence in Potosi* (London: Henry Colburn and Richard Bentley, 1830), I, pp. 283–285; H. A. West, *Six Views of Gibraltar in Two Parts with Six Views Each* (London: R. Ackermann, 1828), part II, pl. 11.

113. James Pattison Cockburn, *Swiss Scenery* (London: Rodwell and Martin, 1820), pp. 165–166; J. J. Wetzel, *Voyage pittoresque au Lac des Waldstettes ou des IV Cantons* (Zurich: Orell, Fussli et Compagnie, 1820), II.

114. On the discovery of Wales by Richard Wilson, George Barrett, Paul Sandby, and Thomas Pennant see Peter Hughes, "Paul Sandby and Sir Watkin Williams-Wynn," *Burlington* 114 (July 1972), 460–463; Robert Rosenblum, "The Dawn of British Romantic Painting, 1760–1780," in *The Varied Pattern: Studies in the Eighteenth Century*, ed. Peter Hughes (Toronto: Hakkert, 1971), pp. 191–192; Daniel Stempel, "Revelation on Mount Snowdon: Wordsworth, Coleridge, and the Fichtean Imagination," *Journal of Aesthetics and Art Criticism* 29 (spring 1971), 381.

115. Eugenio Battisti, *L'Antirinascimento* (Milan: Feltrinelli, 1962), pp. 182–184. Also see Wolfgang Kemp, "Die Höhle der Ewigkeit," *Zeitschrift für Kunstgeschichte* 32, no. 2 (1969), 135–148. For an exhaustive early-eighteenth-century discussion of "the vegetative ferment"—bolstered by recent travel accounts—see the writings of F. M. P. Colonna (Crosset de La Haumerie): *Les principes de la nature ou de la génération des choses* (Paris: André Cailleau, 1731), pp. 271–276; *Les secrets les plus cachés de la philosophie des anciens, découvertes et expliqués, à la suite d'une histoire des plus curieuses* (Paris: d'Houry, 1722), pp. 59 ff.; *Histoire naturelle de l'univers, dans laquelle on rapporte des raisons physiques, sur les effets les plus curieux, & les plus extraordinaires de la nature* (Paris: André Cailleau, 1734), I, pp. viii–ix.

116. Delange, *Palissy*, p. 19; Herget, *Sala Terrena*, pp. 134–135. See especially Salomon de Caus, *Les raisons des forces mouvantes* (Paris: Hierosme Droüart, 1624).

117. Benjamin Boyce, "Mr. Pope in Bath Improves the Design of His Grotto," in *Restoration and Eighteenth-Century Literature*, ed. Carroll Camden (University of Chicago Press, 1963), pp. 144–151; Robert A. Aubin, "Grottoes, Geology, and the Gothic Revival," *Studies in Philology* 31 (July 1934), 408–410, 412; Alexandre-Louis-Joseph, Comte de Laborde, *Description des nouveaux jardins de la France et de ses anciens châteaux* (Paris: Desmarquette, 1808–1815), pl. 67.

118. Johannes Langner, "Architecture pastorale sous Louis XVI," *Art de France* 3 (1963), 182–183.

119. Joseph Pitton de Tournefort, *Relation d'un voyage du Levant, fait par ordre du roy. Contenant l'histoire ancienne & moderne de plusieurs isles de l'Archipel, de Constantinople, des côtes de la Mer Noire, de l'Armenie, de la Géorgie, des frontiers de Perse & de l'Asie Mineure . . . enrichie de descriptions & de figures d'un grand nombre de plantes rares, de divers animaux; et de plusieurs observations touchant l'histoire naturelle* (Paris: Imprimerie Royale, 1717), I, pls. 187, 190, and pp. 190–192; M. G. F. A. Choiseul-Gouffier, *Voyage pittoresque de la Grèce* (Chez Tilliard, Graveur, De Bure Père et Fils, Tilliard Frères, 1782–1809), I, pls. 36, 37, 38, and pp. 71–76. On the continuing French fascination with grottos see the work of Claude-Louis Châtelet, an illustrator for the Abbé de Saint-Non, discussed in Philippe Huisman's *French Watercolors of the Eighteenth Century*, tr. Diana Imber (New York: Viking, 1969), p. 127.

120. Lang, *Unterirdischen Wunder*, I, pl. p. 100 and pp. 105–106.

121. Partha Mitter, European Attitudes to Indian Art from the Mid-Thirteenth to the End of the Nineenth-Century, Ph.D. diss., University of London, 1970, pp. 181–184; Martin Hardie and Muriel Clayton, "Thomas Daniell, R.A. (1749–1840), William Daniell, R.A. (1769–1837)," *Walker's Quarterly* 35–36 (1932), 74; James Wales, *Hindoo Excavations in the Mountain of Ellora near Aurungabad in the Decan, in Twenty-Four Views. Engraved by and under the Direction of Thomas Daniell* (London, 1803), pls. IX, XX. For reproductions of all Daniell aquatints, arranged according to their journey in India, see Mildred Archer, *Early Views of India* (London: Thames and Hudson, 1980).

122. William Hodges, *Travels in India during the Years 1780, 1781, 1782, and 1783*, second revised edition (London: J. Edwards, 1794; first published in 1793), p. 71. For a discussion of the late-eighteenth-century taste for the chthonic—to which the fascination with all forms of caverns belongs—see Frederic V. Bogel, "The Rhetoric of Substantiality: Johnson and the Later Eighteenth Century," *Eighteenth-Century Studies* 12 (summer 1979), 457–480.

123. James Forbes, *Oriental Memoirs, Selected and Abridged from a Series of Familiar Letters Written during Seventeen Years Residence in India: Including Observations on Parts of Africa and South America* (London: T. Bensley, 1813), I, pp. 423–425.

124. Thomas Anburey, *Hindoostan Scenery Consisting of Twelve Select Views in India, Drawn on the Spot by . . . of the Corps of Engineers, Bengal, during the Campaign of the Most Noble Marquis Cornwallis Shewing the Difficulty of a March thro' the Gundecotta Pass* (London, 1799), pl. 7; Thomas Postans, 212 Drawings and Twelve Lithographs Depicting Costumes, Occupations, Scenery, and Buildings in Sind, Cutch, and Bombay, 1830–1845, India Office Library, W.D. 485, fol. 74 b. For a biography of Postans see Archer, *British Artists*, I, pp. 278 ff.

125. Joseph Aignan Sigaud-Lafond, *Dictionnaire des merveilles de la nature* (Paris: Rue et Hotel Serpente, 1781), pp. 97–98; Louis Boisgelin de Kerdu, *Ancient and Modern Malta: Containing a Description of the Ports and Cities of the Islands of Malta and Goza, together with the Monuments of Antiquity still remaining, The Different Governments to which They Have Been Subjected, Their Trade and Finances, and History of the Knights of St. John of Jerusalem and a Particular Account of the Events which Preceded and Attended Its Capture by the French and Conquest by the English* (London: G. & J. Robinson, 1804), I, pl. 16 and p. 46; Botting, *Humboldt*, pp. 84–85.

126. Jan Knops, *Misighit Sela, Nusa Kambangan, Java (Indonesia)*, ca. 1815, The Raffles Drawings, India Office Library, W.D. 2991, fol. 23. Also see Mildred Archer and John Bastin, *The Raffles Drawings in the India Office Library, London* (Oxford University Press, 1975), p. 54. The collection is made up of 38 pencil, wash, and watercolor drawings, most of them made in Singapore, Penang, Bencoolen, and Java between 1804 and 1841. They are commonly referred to as the Raffles Drawings since they are said to have been the property of Sir Shamford Raffles (1781–1826), Lieutenant Governor of Java (1811–1816) and Bencoolen (1818–1824) and founder of Singapore. Their history is complicated and involved. Suffice it to say that these drawings constitute the main body of work by Captain G. P. Baker for use as illustrations to Raffles's *The History of Java* (London, 1817). Knops's drawing is inscribed in Captain Baker's hand.

127. William Westall, *Views of the Caves near Ingleton, Gordale Scar, and Malham Cave in Yorkshire* (London: John Murray, 1818), pp. 4–5; Hodges, *Travels in India*, pp. 73–74; William Mariner, *Voyage aux Iles des Amis, situées dans l'Océan Pacifique fait dans les années 1805 à 1810, avec l'histoire des habitans depuis leur découverte par le Capitaine Cook*, second edition (Paris: J. Smith, 1819), I, p. 277.

128. Botting, *Humboldt*, p. 22. On its founder and first director see W. Mühlfriedel and M. Guntau, "A. G. Werner's Wirken fur die Wissenschaft und sein Verhältnis zu den geistigen Strömungen des 18. Jahrhunderts," in *Abraham Gottlob Werner Gedenkschrift* (Leipzig: UEB, 1967), pp. 9–46.

129. Le Bruyn, *Travels*, II, pls. 250, 251, and pp. 189–191.

130. Heinrich Winkelmann, *Der Bergbau in der Kunst* (Essen: Glückauf, 1958), pp. 84–88; Poprzecka, "Le paysage industriel," p. 42.

131. *French Painting 1774–1830: The Age of Revolution*, exibition at Grand Palais, Paris, Detroit Institute of Arts, and Metropolitan Museum of Art (1975), pl. p. 94, cat. no. 101, pp. 493–494; Rüdiger Joppien, *Philippe-Jacques de Loutherbourg, R.A., 1740–1812*, exhibition at Iveagh Bequest (Kenwood: Greater London Council, 1973); Winkelmann, *Bergbau*, pp. 332, 373; Michael McCarthy, "Sir Roger Newdigate: Some Piranesian Drawings," *Burlington* 120 (October 1978), fig. 39 and pp. 671–672.

132. Daniell, *Animated Nature*, I, pl. 18; Pierre Boisgelin de Kerdu, *Travels through Denmark and Sweden, to which is Prefixed a Journal of a Voyage down the Elbe to Hamburgh; Including a Compendious Historical Account of the Hanseatic League . . . With Views from Drawings Taken on the Spot by Dr. Charles Parry* (London: Wilkie and George Robinson, 1810), II, pp. 199–204, 222–235; Porter, *Russia and Sweden*, II, pp. 193–194; Edy, *Norway*, I, pp. x–xiii; Beechey, *Northern Coast of Africa*, pp. 317–318. On the significance of the theme of mining in German Romantic literature see Josef Durler, *Die Bedeutung des Bergbaus bei Goethe und in der Deutschen Romantik* (Frauenfeld and Leipzig: Huber, 1936), p. 196, and Pierre-Maxime Schuhl, "La machine, l'homme, la nature, et l'art au XVIIIᵉ siècle, in *Rappresentazione artistica e Rappresentazione scientifica nel "Secolo dei Lumi,"* ed. Vittore Branca (Venice: Sansoni, 1970), pp. 117–118.

133. T. M. Perry and Donald H. Simpson, *Drawings by William Westall, Landscape Artist on Board H.M.S.* Investigator *during the Circumnavigation of Australia by Captain Matthew Flinders R.N. in 1801–1803* (London: Royal Commonwealth Society, 1962), pp. 14–21, 25–26; Jane Roundell, "William Hodges' Paintings of the South Pacific," *Connoisseur* 200 (February 1979), 86. For a French example of these handsome and accurate coastal profiles see Jules Dumont D'Urville, *Voyage de la corvette l'Astrolabe exécuté pendant les années 1826-1827-1828-1829 sous le commandement de . . . capitaine de vaisseau* (Paris: J. Tastu, 1830–1834), atlas, pls. 43, 44.

134. Blanckenhagen, "The Odyssey Frieze," p. 129.

135. J. C. Beaglehole, *The Journals of Captain James Cook*, vol. IV: *The Life of Captain James Cook* (London: Black, 1974), p. 228.

136. Adanson, *Senégalé*, pp. 57–58, 67–68; Constantine John Phipps, *A Voyage towards the North Pole Undertaken by His Majesty's Command, 1773* (London: W. Bowyer and J. Nichols, 1774), p. 44. On the Phipps-Banks connection see A. M. Lysaght, *Joseph Banks in Newfoundland and Labrador, 1766. His Diary, Manuscripts, and Collections* (London: Faber and Faber, 1971), pp. 59–62.

137. On the ill-fated Kerguelen-Trémarec see Crozet, *Voyage to Tasmania*, p. 7, n. 1, and Forster, *Voyage round the World*, I, pp. 110–112. La Pérouse's disappearance is treated in René Pomeau's "La Pérouse philosophe," in *Approches des Lumières, Mélanges offerts à Jean Fabre* (Paris: Klincksiek, 1974), pp. 357–358. On the gloom of Japan's volcanic shores see La Pérouse, *Voyage*, III, p. 29; William Robert Broughton, *A Voyage of Discovery to the North Pacific Ocean . . . Performed in His Majesty's Sloop* Providence *and Her Tender in the Years 1795, 1796, 1797, 1798* (London: T. Cadell and W. Davies, 1804), pl. p. 141 and pp. 140–141.

138. Daniell, *Voyage to India by Way of China*, pl. 43; Alexander, "Drawings Made during Lord Macartney's Embassy," fol. 40, no. 128. On Alexander's (1767–1816) training see Herrmann, *British Landscape Painting*, p. 131.

139. Vancouver, *Voyage of Discovery*, III, pl. 2, p. 150; pl. 3, p. 204; Krusenstern, *Voyage round the World*, I, p. 129; Franklin, *Journey to the Polar Sea*, pl. p. 366 and pp. 364–366.

140. Morier, *Journey through Persia*, pl. p. 5 and pp. 3–5; Lycett, *Australia*, pl. 14; François Péron, *Mémoires du Capitaine . . . sur ses voyages* (Paris: Brissot-Thivars, 1824), I, p. 233; Beechey, *Northern Coast of Africa*, pl. p. 112 and p. 140; J. B. Debret, *Voyage pittoresque et historique au Brésil depuis 1816 jusqu'à 1831. Séjour d'un artist français au Brésil* (Paris: Firmin-Didot, 1834–1839), II, pls. 1–2, and I, p. 4. For a modern study of this student of David and the popularity of his work in Europe see Alfonso Arinos de Melo Franco, *J. B. Debret: Estudios ineditos*, tr. John Knox (Rio de Janeiro: Fontana, 1974).

141. Bougainville, *Voyage autour du monde*, II, pp. 24–25. For a discussion of Bougainville and the impact of his voyage see L. Davis Hammond, ed., *News from New Cythera. A Report of Bougainville's Voyage, 1766–1769* (University of Minnesota Press, 1970), pp. 3–4, 53–55.

142. Parkinson, *Journal of a Voyage*, p. 13.

143. Johann Reinhold Forster, *Obervations made during a Voyage round the World, on*

Physical Geography, Natural History, and Ethic Philosophy, Especially on 1) the Earth and Its Strata 2) Water and the Ocean 3) the Atmosphere 4) the Changes of the Globe 5) Organic Bodies, and 6) the Human Species (London: G. Robinson, 1778), pp. 15–16, 105–107.

144. Forster, *Voyage round the World*, I, p. 556; Pennant, *Scotland and the Hebrides*, pl. 29 and p. 264; James Wales, *Twelve Views of the Island of Bombay and Its Vicinity Taken in the Years 1791 and 1792* (London: R. Goodwin, 1804), pl. 12; Flinders, *Voyage to Terra Australis*, II, pl. p. 172 and pp. 168–172; Henry Salt, *A Voyage to Abyssinia and Travels into the Interior of That Country. Executed under the Orders of the British Government in the Years 1809 and 1810; In Which Are Included an Account of the Portuguese Settlements on the East Coast of Africa, Visited in the Course of the Voyage* (London: F. C. and J. Rivington, 1814), pl. a, p. 169; Edy, *Norway*, I, p. xxxviii; Brooke, *Travels*, p. 373 and vignette p. 376; Davy, *Ceylon*, p. 2; Kotzebue, *Voyage of Discovery*, III, p. 229.

145. Arago, *Voyage round the World*, I, p. xxiv.

146. Saussure, *Voyage dans les Alpes*, I, pp. ii–vi.

147. Le Bruyn, *Travels*, II, pp. 12, 24, 30 and pl. 148. On the accuracy of Le Bruyn's account see Johannes Dobai, *Die Kunstliteratur des Klassizismus und der Romantik in England* (Berne: Benteli, 1974), I, p. 880.

148. W. G. Browne, *Travels in Africa, Egypt, and Syria, from the Year 1792 to 1798* (London: T. Cadell, Jr., and W. Davies, 1799), p. 134; Mayer, *Views in Egypt*, p. 2, pl. p. 22, and pp. 22–23. On the theme of ruins rooted to the site see Robert Ginsberg, "The Aesthetics of Ruins," *Bucknell Review* 18 (winter 1970), 100–102.

149. "Les ruines de Petra," *Magasin Pittoresque* 46 (1836), p. 367 and fig. p. 368.

150. William Hamper, *Observations on Certain Ancient Pillars of Memorial Called Hoar-Stones* (Birmingham: William Hodgetts, 1820), p. 4; Borlase, *Antiquities of Cornwall*, pp. 175–182; Thomas Pennant, *The Journey to Snowdon* (London: Henry Hughes, 1781), pp. 261–262; Pierre-François Hugues, called d'Hancarville, *Recherches sur l'origine, l'esprit et les progrès des arts* (London: B. Appleyard, 1785), I, p. viii; Richard Payne Knight, *The Symbolical Language of Ancient Art and Mythology, an Inquiry* (New York: J. W. Bouton, 1876), pp. 147–149; Jacob Grimm, *Teutonic Mythology*, tr. James S. Stallybrass (London: George Bell and Sons, 1882), II, pp. 529–532.

151. Borlase, *Antiquities of Cornwall*, pl. 20, fig. 7, and pp. 240–256; Laborde, *Espagne*, I, pl. 41 and pp. 25–26. For an additional discussion of "Rock-basons" see William Borlase, *Observations on the Ancient and Present State of the Islands of Scilly and Their Importance to the Trade of Great Britain* (Oxford: W. Jackson, 1756), p. 22.

152. Barthélemy Faujas de Saint-Fond, *Voyage en Angleterre, en Ecosse et aux Iles Hébrides* (Paris: H. J. Janson, 1797), I, pp. 354–355; Hoare, *Wiltshire*, II, pp. 49–50; William Stukeley, *Stonehenge, A Temple Restored to the British Druids* (London: W. Innys and R. Manby, 1740), p. 8; M. Cambry, *Monumens celtiques, ou recherches sur le culte des pierres* (Paris: Chez Mad. Johanneau, 1805), pls. 1, 3, 5; Godfrey Higgins, *The Celtic Druids* (London: R. Hunter, 1829), pls. 42, 44. For a modern discussion of the Enlightenment vogue for these rude stones see Stuart Piggott, *William Stukeley, an Eighteenth-Century Antiquarian* (Oxford: Clarendon, 1950).

153. Cordiner, *Ceylon*, II, 122, 139; Porter, *Russia and Sweden*, II, p. 181; M. Taylor, Baron de Roujoux and Charles Nodier, *Histoire pittoresque de l'Angleterre et de ses possessions dans les Indes* (Paris: Administration de l'Histoire Pittoresque d'Angleterre, 1835), I, pp. 17–18. As late as Taylor's work, dolmens were still regarded as ambiguous monuments.

154. Rosario Assunto, *Il Paesaggio e l'Estetica*, Geminae Ortae, XIV, ed. Raffaello Franchini (Naples: Giannini, 1973), I, pp. 317–319. Although several art historians have discussed the interest of such artists as Thomas Girtin, J. S. Cotman, and Thomas Rowlandson in the "mysterious and astonishing relicks of Druidism," they have not connected these "Sublime"—and, by implication, violently produced—formations to the aesthetic vindication of the plain. See in particular Herrman, *British Landscape Painting*, pp. 123–124; Adele M. Holcomb, "*Devil's Den*: An Early Drawing by John Sell Cottman," *Master Drawings* 2, no. 4 (1973), 393–396; Eugenie de Keyser, *The Romantic West, 1789–1850* (Geneva: Skira, 1965), pl. 122.

155. Chappe d'Auteroche, *Voyage en Sibérie*, I, p. 86; Neale, *Travels*, I, pp. 154, 249–250; *Histoire des kosaques, epreuve* (Paris, 1813), pp. 200–201; Staunton, *Embassy to China*, II, pp. 82–83; Cook, *Voyage*, III, pl. 70 and pp. 201–202.

156. Jonathan Carver, *Travels through the Interior Parts of North America in the Years 1766, 1767, 1768* (London: Carver, 1778), pp. 173–174; Constantin-François Chasseboeuf, Comte de Volnay, *Tableau du climat et du sol des Etats-Unis d'Amerique* (Paris: Chez Courcier, Chez Dentu, An XII), I, p. 30; Paul Allen, ed., *History of the Expedition under the Command of Captains Lewis and Clark, to the Sources and down the River Columbia to the Pacific Ocean. Performed during the years 1804-5-6. By order*

of the Government of the United States (Philadelphia and New York: Bradford and Inskeep, 1814), I, pp. 51, 121, 199.

157. *Voyage de Humboldt et Bonpland*, I, p. 20; Vancouver, *Voyage of Discovery*, III, pl. 5 and pp. 412–414; E. E. Vidal, *Picturesque Illustrations of Buenos Ayres and Monte Video Consisting of Twenty-Four Views: Accompanied with Descriptions of the Scenery, and of the Costumes, Manners, etc. of the Inhabitants of Those Cities and Their Environs* (London: R. Ackermann, 1820), pls. pp. 53, 67, 85, 91 and pp. 94–95; Fitzroy, *Narrative of a* Beagle *Voyage*, II, pp. 93–94, 338; Darwin, *Narrative of Voyages of the* Beagle, III, pp. 87–88.

158. Vincent Lunardi, *An Account of the First Aerial Voyage in England. In a Series of Letters to his Guardian, Chevalier Gherardo Compagni* (London: Lunardi, 1784), p. 36; Hatton Christopher Turnor, *Astra Castra. Experiments and Adventures in the Atmosphere* (London: Chapman and Hall, 1965), p. 357 (reproduces Monck Mason's 1837 *History of Aerostation* in an appendix); Thomas Baldwin, *Airopaidia: Containing the Narrative of a Balloon Excursion from Chester, the Eighth of September, 1785. Taken from Minutes Made during the Voyage* (Chester: J. Fletcher, 1786), pls. pp. 58, 154 and pp. 81–83.

159. Cook, *Voyage*, II, pls. 35, 50 and pp. 111, 204; *Proceedings of the Association for Promoting the Discovery of the Interior Parts of Africa* (London: W. Bulmer, 1810), I, p. 25.

160. J. C. Hobhouse, *A Journey through Albania, and Other Provinces of Turkey in Europe and Asia, to Constantinople, during the Years 1809 and 1810* (London: James Cawthorn, 1813), pl. p. 433 and pp. 428–430; R. H. Colebrook, *Twelve Views of Places in the Kingdom of Mysore, the Country of Tippoo Sultan, from Drawings Taken on the Spot* (London: Edward Orme, 1805), pl. 3; Hamilton, *Nepal*, p. 62; Browne, *Travels*, p. 175; Lichtenstein, *Reisen*, I, pp. 607–608, 685; *Voyage de Humboldt et Bonpland*, I, pl. 26 and p. 204; Temple, *Peru*, II, pp. 60–62; Smith, *Antipodean Manifesto*, p. 160; Oxley, *Journals*, pp. 26–27; G. Belzoni, *Narrative of the Operations and Recent Discoveries within the Pyramids, Temples, Tombs, and Excavations in Egypt and Nubia; and of a Journey to the Coast of the Red Sea, in Search of the Ancient Berenice; and Another to the Oasis of Jupiter Ammon* (London: John Murray, 1820), pp. 79, 86–90.

161. George Steuart MacKenzie, *Travels in the Island of Iceland, during the Summer of the Year 1810* (Edinburgh: Thomas Allan and Company, 1811), p. 109; Porter, *Russia and Sweden*, II, p. 185.

162. Forster, *Voyage round the World*, I, pp. 93–94, 97–98; Bailly, *Discours et mémoires*, I, p. 333; Franklin, *Polar Sea*, p. 277. On

Cook's heroic endurance on the second voyage, the one on which he laid the foundations for future Antarctic oceanography, see J. C. Beaglehold, "Cook the Man," in *Captain Cook Navigator and Scientist*, p. 19. Later explorers such as Ross and Parry knew more about ice navigation, and their expeditions were commemorated in panoramas of the day. See Richard D. Altick, *The Shows of London* (Belknap Press of Harvard University Press, 1978), pp. 128 ff. Eric Adams, *Francis Danby: Varieties of Poetic Landscape* (Yale University Press, 1973), p. 74.

163. Flinders, *Voyage to Terra-Australis*, II, pp. 115–116; Kotzebue, *Voyage of Discovery*, II, p. 366. See also Dorothy Hill, "The Great Barrier Reef," in *Captain Cook Navigator and Scientist*, pp. 70–71; Daniell, *Animated Nature*, I, pl. 47.

164. Appleton, *Experience of Landscape*, p. 241. On the sublimity implicit in "vastness of extent" see Burke, *Sublime and Beautiful*, part II, secs. vii–viii, pp. 61–62.

165. Forster, *Voyage round the World*, II, p. 407; Cordiner, *Ceylon*, I, pp. 285–286; Davy, *Ceylon*, p. 68; *Voyage de Humboldt et Bonpland*, I, p. 4; Cook, *Voyage*, I, pl. 49 and p. 288; La Pérouse, *Voyage*, II, p. 81.

166. Wiebenson, *Picturesque Garden in France*, p. 29; Addison, *Works*, II, p. 358. The desert, because of its association with antiquity and the Holy Land, looms large—at least in terms of verbal description—in early travel accounts. See, for example, Bernhard von Breydenbach, *Le Saint voiage et pélérinage de la cité saincte de Hierusalem*, tr. Jean de Hersin (Lyons, 1489); *Les saintes pérégrinations de Bernard de Breydenbrach* (1483), tr. F. Larrivaz (Cairo: Imprimerie Nationale, 1904), p. 40. En route to Cairo, the Dean of the Cathedral of Mainz expressed his distaste for "the horror of the immense solitude and the aridity of deserts" and contrasted them with Cairo's refreshing gardens and fertile soil. Also see D'O. Dapper, *Description de l'Afrique, contenant les noms, la situation & les confins de toutes ses parties, leurs rivières, leurs villes & leurs habitations, leurs plantes & leurs animaux; les moeurs, les coutumes, la langue, les richesses, la religion & le gouvernement de ses peuples*, tr. from the Flemish (Amsterdam: Wolfgang, Waesberge, Boom & Van Someren, 1686), pl. 58 and pp. 203–204. The etching showing a caravan marching from Cairo to Mecca expends most of its attention on the wondefully caparisoned camels and Turks moving not through a desert but across a mountainous landscape. The description of the Sahara (there is no plate) refers to it by its Arabic name as the "Path of Storms," a land that is "sandy," "meager," and "uncultivated."

167. Le Rouge, *Jardins anglo-chinois*, VIII, pp. 5–6. On the connection of "natural

wildness" with the vogue for Chinese Gardens see Arthur O. Lovejoy, "The Chinese Origin of a Romanticism," *Journal of English and Germanic Philology* 32 (January 1933), 13–20. Also see Laborde, *France*, V, pl. 25 and p. 32.

168. Strabo, *The Geography* 2. 5, 33; 17. 1, 52; 1. 2, 25. For an interesting discussion of wilderness as chaos "where order and shaping are not" see John R. Stilgoe, *Common Landscape of America, 1580 to 1845* (Yale University Press, 1982), pp. 7–12.

169. Le Bruyn, *Travels*, I, pp. 161–164; Bernard Maillet, *Telliamed, ou entretiens d'un philosophe indien avec un missionnaire françois sur la diminution de la mer, la formation de la terre, l'origine de l'homme* (Amsterdam: Chez l'Honoré & fils, 1748), I, pp. 133–135.

170. Eyles Irwin, *A Series of Adventures in the Course of a Voyage up the Red-Sea on the Coasts of Arabia and Egypt; And of a Route through the Desarts of Thebais, hitherto unknown to the European Traveller, in the Year 1777* (London: J. Dodsley, 1780), p. 310; Bruce, *Travels*, IV, pp. 552–553; I, "Dedication to the King"; Park, *Africa*, pl. p. 338 and pp. 493, 506.

171. Vivant-Denon, *Voyage en Egypte*, I, p. 141, 150–152; Mayer, *Egypt*, pp. 9–10. On Vivant-Denon's role in the Napoleonic campaign and his influence on the taste for ruins prevalent in France during the Directoire and Empire periods see René Jullian, "Le Thème des ruines dans la peinture de l'époque néo-classique en France," *Bulletin de la Société de l'histoire de l'art français* 1976 (1978), 271. It is instructive to compare the contemporaneous, inferior, and considerably less extensive survey made when the British army occupied Egypt; see Thomas Walsh, *Journal of the Late Campaign in Egypt: Including Descriptions of that Country, and of Gibraltar, Minorca, Malta, Marmorice, and Macri; With an Appendix Containing Official Papers and Documents* (London: T. Caddell, Jr., and W. Davies, 1803), pls. 48, 49 and pp. vi–viii. Captain Walsh, of His Majesty's 93rd Regiment of Foot and Aide-de-Camp to Maj. Gen. Sir Eyre Coote, provides a "simple narrative" of the events that occurred from October 24, 1800 (the day on which sailing orders arrived at Gibraltar) to the final conquest of Egypt by the British. His drawings, in contradistinction to those made by Vivant-Denon, were taken "in perfect security, and with all necessary deliberation; they are, at least, not the hasty sketches of a solitary traveller, who holds the pencil with a trembling hand. . . ." Yet, like those of the Frenchman, they, too, are not "the productions of reminiscence, executed in the retirement of the closet, from a few strokes made by stealth. . . ." For anything comparable to the desert views stemming from the Egyptian Campaign, the British had to await

William Burchell's *Travels in the Interior of Southern Africa* (London: Longman, Hurst, Rees, Orme, and Brown, 1822) (I, pl. 4 and pp. 282–284; II, pp. 27–28). Also see Helen M. McKay, *The South African Drawings of William J. Burchell* (Johannesburg: Witwatersrand University Press, 1952), II, introduction, and, most notably, David Roberts, *The Holy Land, Syria, Idhumia, Egypt and Arabia. With Historical Descriptions by the Rev. George Croly, L.L.D. Lithographed by Louis Haghe* (London: F. G. Moon, 1842), II, pls. 46, 50. Roberts's handsome publications differ in two major respects from the turn-of-the-century French work: The religious overtone is unmistakable, and the lithographic technique—despite the beauty of the plates—imparts a generalized aura to the desert's features.

172. Luigi Mayer, *Views in Palestine, from the Original Drawings by . . . . with an Historical and Descriptive Account of the Country, and Its Remarkable Places* (London: T. Bensley for R. Bowyer, 1804), pp. 1–4; Olivier, *L'Empire Othoman*, III, pp. 168–171; *Proceedings of the Africa Association*, I, pp. 121–122, 173.

173. Jackson, *Marocco*, pp. 107–108; M. Saugnier, *Relations de plusieurs voyages à la côte d'Afrique, à Maroc, au Sénégal, à Gorée, à Galam, etc., avec des détails intéressans pour ceux qui se destinent à la traite des nègres, de l'or, de l'ivoire, etc., tirées des journaux de . . . qui a été long-temps esclave des maures et de l'empereur de Maroc* (Paris: Gueffier Jeune, 1791), pp. 103–105; *Proceedings of the Africa Association*, I, 112, 120–121; Browne, *Travels*, pp. 184–185; John Leyden, *A Historical & Philosophical Sketch of the Discoveries and Settlements of the Europeans in Northern & Western Africa at the Close of the Eighteenth Century* (Edinburgh: J. Moir, 1799), pp. 33–34.

174. James Grey Jackson, *An Account of Timbuctoo and Housa, Territories in the Interior of Africa by El Hage Abd Salam Shabeeny, with Notes, Critical and Explanatory. To which Is Added Letters descriptive of Travels through West and South Barbary, and across the Mountains of Atlas* (London: Longman, Hurst, Rees, Orme, and Brown, 1820), pp. 2–6; G. F. Lyon, *A Narrative of Travels in Northern Africa, in the Years 1818, 19, and 20; Accompanied by Geographical Notices of Soudan, and of the Course of the Niger* (London: John Murray, 1821), pl. p. 325 and pp. 323–327.

175. John Leyden, *Historical Account of Discoveries and Travels in Africa, by the late. . . , Enlarged, and Completed to the Present Time, with Illustrations of Its Geography and Natural History, as well as of the Moral and Social Condition of Its Inhabitants by Hugh Murray, Esq. F.R.S.E.* (Edinburgh: George Ramsay, 1817), I, pp. 417–420; John Lewis Burckhardt, *Travels in Nubia; by the Late . . . . Published by the Association*

for *Promoting the Discovery of the Interior Parts of Africa*, ed. Col. Leake (London: John Murray, 1819), pp. v–vi, xlvii–xlix; Belzoni, *Narrative*, pl. 25 and pp. 146–147.

176. Beechey, *Northern Coast of Africa*, pl. p. 112 and pp. 106–107; Lycett, *Australia*, p. 2; Robert Mignan, *Travels in Chaldea, Including a Journey from Bussorah to Bagdad, Hillah, and Babylon, Performed on Foot in 1827* (London: Henry Colburn and Richard Bentley, 1829), p. 5.

177. Pococke, *Description of the East*, I, pl. 30 and pp. 97–99; Fifty Drawings of the Landscapes and Antiquities of Southern India, 1784–1818, India Office Library, MacKenzie Collection, W.D. 625–674, portfolio 3. On Colin MacKenzie (1754–1821) of the Madras engineers, later Surveyor-General of India, who amassed a large number of manuscripts, copies of inscriptions, and drawings during his years of service, see Archer, *British Artists*, II, pp. 472 ff. Many of MacKenzie's drawings and those of his assistants were made in 1784 and in 1787–88 during his surveys.

178. Hodges, *Select Views in India*, pl. 27; Daniell, *Oriental Scenery*, II, part IV, pl. 15.

179. Annesley, *Voyages and Travels*, I, pl. 1 and p. 18; *Voyage de Humboldt et Bonpland*, I, pl. 4 and p. 9; Lichtenstein, *Reisen*, II, pl. p. 338 and p. 341.

180. Allen F. Gardiner, *Narrative of a Journey to the Zoolu Country in South Africa, Undertaken in 1835* (London: William Crofts, 1836), pl. p. 334; Belzoni, *Narrative*, pl. 1 and p. 124; Lyon, *Northern Africa*, p. 23.

181. Stuart Piggott, *The Druids* (New York: Praeger, 1975), pp. 48, 80.

182. "Religion des gaulois," *Magasin Pittoresque* 41 (1836), 331–333. On the refuge symbolism of forests see Appleton, *Experience of Nature*, p. 104. On the developing tradition of forest landscape representation ca. 1600 see Terez Gerszi, "Brueghels Nachwirkung auf die Niederlandischen Landschaftmäler um 1600," *Oud Holland* 90, no. 4 (1976), 229.

183. Le Flamanc, *Les utopies prérévolutionnaires*, p. 79; André Monglond, *Le préromantisme français* (Grenoble: B. Arthaud, 1930), II, pp. 427–428; Philip C. Ritterbush, *Overtures to Biology, The Speculations of Eighteenth-Century Naturalists* (Yale University Press, 1964), pp. 143–151.

184. Isaac Weld, *Travels through the States of North America, and the Provinces of Upper and Lower Canada, during the Years 1795, 1796, and 1797* (London: John Stockdale, 1799), pp. 2, 23; Alexander MacKenzie, *Voyages from Montreal, on the River St. Lawrence, through the Continent of North America to the Frozen and Pacific Oceans in the Years 1789 and 1793. With a Preliminary Account of the Rise, Progress, and Present Stage of the Fur Trade of That Country* (London: T. Cadell, Jr., and W. Davies, 1801), p. vi; Volney, *Tableau*, I, pp. 7–8; Milbert, *Hudson*, I, pp. xxi–xxiv. For the view that forests were noxious see Glacken's discussion of the French Forest Ordinance of 1669 in *Traces*, pp. 485–489. On the aesthetic impact of deforestation see Nicolai Cikovsky, Jr., " 'The Ravages of the Axe': The Meaning of the Tree Stump in Nineteenth-Century American Art," *Art Bulletin* 61 (December 1979), 611–617. Deforestation was not limited to North America. Captain Thomas Williamson, in his *Oriental Fieldsports; Being a Complete, Detailed, and Accurate Description of the Wild Sports of the East and Exhibiting, in a Novel and Interesting Manner, the Natural History* (London: Edward Orme, 1807) (see letterpress for pl. 23), laments the disappearance of "those close woods" and "large grass jungles" near the banks of the Baugratty River that had teemed "with tigers, buffaloes, etc." Williamson adds: ". . . The improvements which have taken place in the Cossimbazar Island, in general owing to the many speculators in indigo, have annihilated many of the grass covers, they being converted into arable lands, and as the population increased, the underwoods, with perhaps many of the trees, were cut for fuel . . . [and] dealt forth destruction in such an unprecedented style as, in the course of a few years, absolutely cleared the country within twelve or fifteen miles of . . . [the] station at Daudpore. . . ." C. S. Sonnini, in his *Voyage en Grèce et en Turquie, fait par ordre de Louis XVI, et avec l'autorisation de la cour ottomane* (Paris: F. Buisson, An IX) (I, pp. 96–97) speaks of the deforestation of the once beautifully wooded island of Cyprus and voices the fear that it might well occur in France.

185. Forster, *Voyage round the World*, I, p. 207; Cook, *Voyage*, I, pp. 95, 198–200; Hawkesworth, *Carteret, Relation des voyages . . . Carteret*, I, p. 277; Crozet, *Tasmania*, pp. 85–89; Lesseps, *Journal*, I, pp. 187–188; Franklin, *Polar Sea*, p. 97.

186. Louis O'Hier de Grandpré, *Voyage à la côte occidentale d'Afrique, fait dans les années 1786 et 1787 . . . Suivi d'un voyage fait au Cap de Bonne-Espérance, contenant la description militaire de cette colonie* (Paris: Dentu, 1801), I, p. 10, II, pl. p. 49; John Lewis Burckhardt, *Travels in Syria and the Holy Lands by the Late . . . Published by the Association for Promoting the Discovery of the Interior Parts of Africa* (London: John Murray, 1822), p. 488.

187. Miguel Rojas-Mix, "Die Bedeutung Alexander von Humboldts für die künstlerische Darstellung Latein Amerikas," in *Alexander von Humboldt—Werk und Werkgeltung*, ed. Hanno Beck (Munich: Piper, 1969), pp. 112–114. For a reprint of the account of the voyage see João Mauricio

Rugendas, *Viagem Pitoresca a travês do Brasil*, ed. Rubens Borba de Morals (Saõ Paolo: Martins, 1940). Also see *Voyage de Humboldt et Bonpland*, I, pl. 41; Kotzebue, *Voyage of Discovery*, III, pp. 6–9; Caldcleugh, *South America*, I, pp. 13–14. It was natural after the publication of Humboldt's work, however, that the tropical rain forest entered landscape painting. See Albert Berg, *Physiognomy of Tropical Vegetation in South America; A Series of Views Illustrating the Primeval Forests on the River Magdalena and in the Andes of New Granada with a Fragment of a Letter from Baron Humboldt to the Author and a Preface by Frederick Klotzsch* (London: Paul and Dominic Colnaghi and Co., 1854). Theodor de Bry's earlier monumental series on the New World provides only a slight sense of its primeval forests; see de Bry, *Dritte Buch Americae, darinn Brasilia durch Johann Staden von Homberg aus eigener Erfahrung in Teutsch beschrieben. Item Historia der Schifffahrt Joannis Lerii in Brasilien Welche Er selbst publiciert hat* (Frankfurt-am-Main, 1593), pl. p. 54. A century later, in Captain Thomas Bowery's journal "Asia: Wherein is Contained ye Scituation, Comerse, etc. of Many Provinces, Isles, etc., in India, Per., Arabia, and ye South Seas—Experienced by Me T.B. in ye Aforementioned India. Viz. from Anno MDCLXIX to MDCLXXIX" (ms. EUR D782, India Office Library), fol. 95, two wild beasts (perhaps a lion and a wild boar) are still shown in the most rudimentary of "woods" in Bengal. By the close of the eighteenth century, although George Staunton described the Brazilian forest, his artist William Alexander did not copy it. See *Embassy to China*, I, pp. 177–178.

188. Engelbertus Kaempfer, *The History of Japan, Giving an Account of the Ancient and Present State and Government of that Empire; of Its Temples, Palaces, Castles and Other Buildings; of Its Metals, Minerals, Trees, Plants, Animals, Birds, and Fishes . . . Together with a Description of the Kingdom of Siam*, tr. J. G. Scheuchzer (London: Scheuchzer, 1727), I, pp. 14, 26; Lt. J. Moore and Capt. Marryat, *Views of Rangoon and Combined Operations in the Burman Empire* (London, 1825–26), pls. 4, 16; J. Grierson, *Twelve Selective Views of the Seat of War, Including Views Taken at Rangoon, Cachar and Andaman Islands from Sketches Taken on the Spot by . . .* (Calcutta: Asiatic Lithographic Press, 1825), pl. *View on a Lake near Rangoon*; J. Kershaw, *Description of a Series of Views in the Burman Empire, Drawn on the Spot by . . . and Engraved by William Daniell, R.A.* (London: Smith, Elder, and Co., [1831?], pl. 1; Captain Trant, *Two Years in [J]ava. From May 1824 to May 1826. By an Officer on the Staff of the Quarter-Master General's Department* (London: John Murray, 1827), pp. 278–279, 439–440; Hodges, *Select Views in India*, pl. 91; Williamson, *Oriental Fieldsports*, pl. 22 and p. 87; J. G. Stedman, *Voyage à Surinam et dans l'intérieur de La

Guiane, contenant la relation des cinq années de courses et d'observation faites dans cette contrée intéressante et peu connue; avec des détails sur les Indiens de la Guiane et les nègres*, tr. P. F. Henry (Paris: F. Buisson, An VII), atlas, pls. 13, 25, 32.

189. James Johnson, *The Oriental Voyager; or, Descriptive Sketches and Cursory Remarks, on a Voyage to India and China in His Majesty's Ship Caroline, Performed in the Years 1803–4–5–6* (London: James Asperne, 1807), p. 348.

190. Daniel Beeckman, *A Voyage to and from the Island of Borneo, in the East-Indies. With a Description of the Said Island: Giving an Account of the Inhabitants, Their Manners, Customs, Religion, Product, Chief Ports, and Trade* (London: T. Warner and J. Batley, 1718), pl. p. 37 and pp. 35–37. Also see the useful compilation by John Bastin and Pauline Rohatgi, *Prints of Southeast Asia in the India Office Library* (London: Her Majesty's Stationery Office, 1979).

191. Lysaght, *Banks in Newfoundland*, p. 144; Neale, *Travels*, p. 153; Georg Forster, "Ein Blick in das Ganze der Natur. Einleitung zu Anfangsgründe der Tiergeschichte," in *Schriften zu Nature, Kunst, Politik*, ed. Karl Otto Conrady (Reinbeck bei Hamburg: Rowohlt, 1971), p. 60; *Voyage round the World*, II, pp. 117, 424; Weld, *Travels*, pp. 102–103; Milbert, *Hudson*, I, pp. 93–94.

192. Pococke, *Description of the East*, I, p. 142; La Pluche, *Spectacle de la nature*, III, pl. p. 243 and pp. 241–243; Le Gentil, *Voyage*, II, p. 657. An early precedent for such underwater scenes may be found in the drawings by Jacques LeMoyne and John White engraved by Theodor de Bry and published in the *Voyages en Virginie et en Floride* (Paris: Duchartre et Van Buggenhoudt, 1585), pls. 17, 27.

193. De Piles, *Cours de peinture*, pp. 184–191; Bashō, *Narrow Road to the Far North*, introduction and pp. 35, 40, 44; Macartney, *Embassy to China*, I, pp. 428–431.

194. Le Bruyn, *Travels*, II, pl. p. 233 and pp. 132–133; Hodges, *Travels in India*, pl. p. 26; Gold, *Oriental Drawings*, pl. 39; Sir Charles D'Oyly, *Scrap-Book*, India Office Library, fol. 72; Maria Graham, *Journal of a Residence in India* (Edinburgh: George Ramsay and Company, 1812), pl. p. 7; *Journal of a Residence in Chile, during the Year 1822, and a Voyage from Chile to Brazil* (London: Longman, Hurst, Rees, Orme, Brown, and Green, 1824), pl. 2, p. 85; pl. 4, p. 135; Grierson, *Seat of War*, letterpress for plate *Port Cornwallis, Andaman Islands*.

195. Pococke, *Description of the East*, II, part I, pp. 104–105; Louis Moland, ed., *Oeuvres poètiques de André Chenier* (Paris: Garnier Frères, 1884), II, p. 72; *Lewis and Clark Expedition*, II, p. 155.

196. Weld, *Travels*, p. 39; Heriot, *The Canadas*, pp. iii, 35; Carver, *North America*, pp. 167–168; Frédéric Gaetan, Marquis de La Rochefoucauld-Liancourt, *Voyage dans les Etats-Unis d'Amerique fait en 1795, 1796, et 1797* (Paris: Du Pont, Buisson, Charles Pougens, An VII), I, pp. 358–359; Houel, *Voyage*, I, pl. 63 and p. 116.

197. Landmann, *Portugal*, II, pl. p. 124; Wetzel, *Lacs de Suisse*, II, p. 7; Brooke, *Travels*, pp. 352–353.

198. Tuckey, *Expedition to Zaire*, p. 116; Elliott, *Views in the East*, I; Vidal, *Buenos Ayres*, p. vi; Cochrane, *Journal*, II, pp. 177–178; Le Bruyn, *Travels*, I, p. 63.

199. Browne, *Travels*, pp. 65, 121; Vivant-Denon, *Voyage en Egypte*, I, p. 4; Burckhardt, *Travels in Nubia*, pp. 16, 42, 350–351; *Proceedings of the Africa Association*, I, p. 123.

200. Cook, *Voyage*, I, p. viii; Crozet, *Voyage*, p. 71; *Lewis and Clark Expedition*, II, p. 110; Pococke, *Description of the East*, II, part I, pp. 34–35. On the popularity of marine subject matter in the late eighteenth century see Broc, *La géographie des philosophes*, pp. 280–281.

Chapter 3

1. Stephen Toulmin and June Goodfield, *The Architecture of Matter* (New York: Harper & Row, 1962), pp. 202–208; Heiman and McGuire, "Newtonian Forces and Lockean Powers," pp. 242–260 passim. On the rise of interest among artists and writers in a wide gamut of substances which affect the senses, see Jacques Guillerme, "Le malsain et l'économie de la nature," *Dixhuitième Siècle* 9 (1977), 61–62.

2. Scott, "Significance of 'Hard Bodies,'" p. 203; Colm Kiernan, *Science and the Enlightenment in Eighteenth-Century France, Studies on Voltaire and the Eighteenth Century* 59 (1968), 167; Jérôme Richard, *Histoire naturelle de l'air et des météores* (Paris: Saillant & Nyon, 1770), I, pp. 37, 61, 128. For the most illuminating discussion of this aspect of Newton's thought and its afterlife see Alexandre Koyré, *From the Closed World to the Infinite Universe* (Johns Hopkins University Press, 1957), pp. 159–178, 252, passim; *Newtonian Studies*, appendixes A–D, pp. 115–169 passim. Also see Isaac Newton, *The Mathematical Principles of Natural Philosophy*, tr. Andrew Motte, third edition (London: B. Motte, 1729), I, pp. 8–17. This edition is especially valuable because it contains Roger Cotes's preface, with its important reformulation of Newton's principles and its vehement denial (against the attacks of the Cartesians and Leibniz) that gravity is an "occult" property. For Voltaire's rephrasing see *Letters*, pp. 136–138, 147–148.

3. Henry Guerlac, "An Augustan Monument: The Optics of Isaac Newton," in *The Varied Pattern*, pp. 155–161; John Wild, "Husserl's Critique of Psychologism: Its Historic Roots and Contemporary Relevance," in *Philosophical Essays*, pp. 28–29.

4. David B. Wilson, "Concepts of Physical Nature: John Herschel to Karl Pearson," in *Nature and the Victorian Imagination*, pp. 202–203.

5. Shaftesbury, *Moralists*, p. 102, part iv; John Stewart, *The Revelation of Nature with the Prophecy of Reason* (New York: Stewart [1813]), p. 7.

6. Albert Bettex, *The Discovery of Nature* (New York: Simon and Schuster, 1965), p. 73; Le Flamanc, *Les utopies prérévolutionnaire*, pp. 135–138; H. A. M. Snelders, "Romanticism and Naturphilosophie and the Inorganic Natural Sciences, 1797–1840," *Studies in Romanticism* 9 (summer 1970), 200–202. Also see Koyré, *Closed World*, pp. 221–222, 258. Leibniz also seems to wish to reduce material nature to a pure, self-sustaining, and self-perpetuating mechanism, such that the intervention in nature of nonmechanical and therefore nonmaterial agencies becomes a miracle; see *Clarke-Leibniz Correspondence*, p. 27. At the same time, Leibniz's contribution to the Great Chain of Being thesis made him important to the French vitalists.

7. Balloon ascents, made with increasing frequency from 1783 on, were matched by other inventions that rendered the impalpable palpable. For example, the steam engine represented an analogous harnessing of a puzzling vapor, the demystification of an incomprehensible pneuma. See *Decouvertes et inventions depuis les temps les plus anciens jusqu'à nos jours*, third revised edition (Paris, 1846), pp. 7, 107–113.

8. Kiernan, *Enlightenment and Science*, pp. 165–166; Le Flamanc, *Les utopies prérévolutionnaire*, p. 60; Guitton, *Jacques Delille*, pp. 118–119; Guillerme, "Le Malsain," p. 68.

9. Louis S. Greenbaum, "The Humanitarianism of Antoine-Laurent Lavoisier," *Studies on Voltaire and the Eighteenth Century* 88 (1972), 653–656; Pierre Bertholon, "De la salubrité de l'air des villes, & en particulier des moyens de la procurer," *Journal Encyclopédique* (May 1787), 408–410; "Lettre à M.C. par P.C.J.," *Journal de Trévoux* (December 1722), 2087–2089. For a discussion of late-eighteenth-century science, considerations of urban hygiene, and their bearing on architectural and urban planning, see Richard A. Etlin, *The Architecture of Death: The Transformation of the Cemetery in Eighteenth-Century Paris* (Cambridge, Mass.: MIT Press, 1983).

10. Glacken, *Traces*, pp. 489–490; "Lettre à M.C.," pp. 2075–2086; Guillerme, "Le malsain," p. 63; Bernardin de Saint-Pierre,

Harmonies de la nature, in *Oeuvres complètes,* VII–VIII, pp. 47–49.

11. Glacken, *Traces,* pp. 430, 460.

12. La Pluche, *Spectacle de la nature,* III, pp. 248–254, 290; *Table analytique et raisonnée du Dictionnaire des sciences, arts et métiers* (Paris and Amsterdam: Chez Panckoucke, Marc-Michel Rey, 1780), I, pp. 39–40.

13. Béguin, *L'âme romantique,* I, p. 118; Kiernan, *Enlightenment and Science,* pp. 170–171; Ritterbush, *Overtures to Biology,* pp. 5–7.

14. A. F. G. Gode-von-Aesch, *Natural Science in German Romanticism* (New York: AMS, 1941), pp. 201–203; Gaston Bachelard, *The Poetics of Reverie,* tr. Daniell Russell (New York: Orion, 1969), p. 180; John Arthos, *The Language of Natural Description in Eighteenth-Century Poetry* (New York: Octagon, 1966), pp. 342–343; Alfred Biese, *Das Naturgefühl im Wandel der Zeiten* (Leipzig: Quelle & Meyer, 1926), p. 137.

15. Fabre d'Olivet, *Pythagoras,* pp. 226–229; J.-L. Vieillard-Baron, "Hemsterhuis, platonicien, 1721–1790," *Dixhuitième Siècle* 17 (1975), 142; Bettex, *Discovery of Nature,* pp. 17–18.

16. Béguin, *L'âme romantique,* I, p. 100; Robert Klein and Henri Zerner, "Italian Art 1500–1600," *Sources and Documents in the History of Art,* ed. H. W. Janson (Englewood Cliffs, N.J.: Prentice-Hall, 1966), p. 185; Kiernan, *Enlightenment and Science,* pp. 167–168.

17. G. W. von Leibniz, *On the Reform of Metaphysics and on the Notion of Substance,* in *Philosophical Works,* pp. 75–76; *Considerations on the Principles of Life, and on Plastic Natures,* p. 251; Johann Gottfried von Herder, *Vom Erkennen und Empfinden der menschlichen Seele; Bemerkungen und Träume,* in *Gesammelte Werke* (Potsdam: Rütten & Loening, 1939), I, pp. 119, 128. For a history of these proponents of modern dynamism and vitalistic activity see Max Jammer, *Concepts of Force: A Study in the Foundations of Dynamics* (Harvard University Press, 1957), pp. 158–166; M. H. Abrams, *The Mirror and the Lamp* (Oxford University Press, 1953), p. 202. For Hartley's emphasis—in contradistinction to Hume's focus in the *Enquiry Concerning the Human Understanding* (1748)—on the physiological cause of association, and his doctrine of "vibrations," see David Hartley, *Various Conjectures on the Perception, Motion, and Generation of Ideas* (1746), tr. Robert E. A. Palmer (Los Angeles: Augustan Reprint Society, 1959), p. vii.

18. Wallace E. Anderson, "Immaterialism in Jonathan Edwards' Early Philosophical Notes," *Journal of the History of Ideas* 25 (April–June, 1964), 181–200 passim; Herbert Piper, "The Pantheistic Sources of Coleridge's Early Poetry," *Journal of the History of Ideas* 20 (January 1959), 48–50. Among the best discussions of the nature and kind of Berkeley's Immaterialism and its visual implications are I. C. Tipton, *Berkeley, the Philosophy of Immaterialism* (London: Methuen, 1974); Gary Thrane, "Berkeley's 'Proper Object of Vision'," *Journal of the History of Ideas* 38 (April–June 1977), 243–260; John W. Yolton, "As in a Looking Glass: Perceptual Acquaintance in Eighteenth-Century Britain," *Journal of the History of Ideas* 40 (April–June, 1979), 207–234.

19. "Vapeurs, vaporeux," *Encyclopédie,* XVI, p. 836; "Evaporation,"VI, p. 124; "Crépuscule," IV, p. 455; Valenciennes, *Eléments de perspective,* pp. 260–263. For a discussion of the newer concern to illustrate different times of day and a variety of atmospheric effects by a realistic method, see P. Walton, "The Educated Eye: Neo-Classical Drawing Masters & Their Methods," in *The Triumph of Culture: Eighteenth-Century Perspectives* (Toronto: Hakkert, 1972), pp. 113–115.

20. Richard, *Histoire naturelle de l'air,* V, p. 311; Jan Hendrik van Swinden, *Mémoires sur les observations météorologiques* (Amsterdam: Marc-Michel Rey, 1780), p. 72; Alexandre-Guy Pingré, "Précis du mémoire sur l'isle qui a paru en 1783, au sud-ouest de l'Islande, lu par . . . dans la séance publique de l'académie royale des sciences de Paris, tenue le 12 novembre dernier," *Journal Encyclopédique* (January 1784), 116–118.

21. Rudolf Tombo, *Ossian in Germany* (New York: AMS, 1966), pp. 95–101; Gaston Bachelard, *L'air et les songes. Essais sur l'imagination du mouvement* (Paris: José Corti, 1943), pp. 227–229; Bachelard, *L'eau et les rêves, Essai sur l'imagination de la matière* (Paris: José Corti, 1942), p. 29. These eighteenth-century theories sound very much in tune with Baudelairean and Ruskinian aesthetics as interpreted recently by Lee McKay Johnson, *The Metaphor of Painting. Essays on Baudelaire, Ruskin, Proust, and Pater* (Ann Arbor, Mich.: UMI Research Press, 1980), pp. 11–146 passim.

22. Marjorie Hope Nicolson, *Newton Demands the Muse. Newton's "Opticks" and the Eighteenth-Century Poets* (London: Archon, 1963), p. 32; Louis Hourticq, "L'exposition du paysage français de Poussin à Corot, 1ere partie," *Revue de l'art ancien et moderne,* 48 (June 1925), 5–6; James Dallaway, *Constantinople Ancient and Modern, with Excursions to the Shores and Islands of the Archipelago and to the Troad* (London: T. Bensley for T. Cadell, Jr., and W. Davies, 1797), p. 180.

23. Gombrich, *Heritage of Apelles,* p. 17.

24. Blanckenhagen, "Odyssey Frieze," p. 119; *Paintings from Boscotrecase,* pp.

36–37; Rothgeb, "Scenographic Expression of Nature," p. 32.

25. Beurdeley, *Castiglione*, pp. 81–87.

26. Damisch, *Théorie du nuage*, p. 192; Guitton, *Jacques Delille*, p. 533; Biese, *Naturgefühl*, p. 145.

27. "Effet," *Encyclopédie*, V, p. 406. For the nexus of meanings inherent in the eighteenth-century concept of *effet* see Albert Boime, *The Academy and French Painting in the Nineteenth Century* (London: Phaidon, 1971), p. 167.

28. Anne-Marie Chouillet-Roche, "Le clavecin-oculaire du Père Castel," *Dix-Huitième Siècle* 8 (1976), 158; Alexandre Ananoff, "Effets d'aquarelle et de gouache," *Connaissance des Arts* 197 (July–August 1968), 101; Charles-Yves Cousin d'Avallon, *Lingetiana, ou recueil* (Paris: Vater Jouannet, 1801), pp. 63–64.

29. Richard Bruce Carpenter, The Dutch Sources of the Art of J.-H. Fragonard, Ph.D. diss., Harvard University, 1955, pp. 11, 166–169; Pierre Rosenberg and Isabelle Compin, "Quatre nouveaux Fragonard au Louvre," *Revue du Louvre* 2, no. 4–5 (1974), 274–275; Arlette Serullaz, "Dessins inédits Nathalie Volle de Fragonard, David, et Drouais," *Revue du Louvre* 2 no. 4-5 (1974), 77–78; Carol Greene Duncan, The Persistence and Re-Emergence of the Rococo in French Painting, Ph.D. diss., Columbia University, 1969, pp. 180–189; Robert Raines, "Watteaus and 'Watteaus' in England before 1760," *Gazette des Beaux-Arts* 93 (February 1977), 60–61. For a discussion of the suppression of a rational, specific space in Rococo painting, see Norman Bryson, *Word and Image: French Painting of the Ancien Régime* (Cambridge University Press, 1981), pp. 95–96.

30. Jean Cailleux, "Les artistes français du dix-huitième siècle et Rembrandt," in *Etudes d'Art offertes à Charles Sterling* (Paris: Presses Universitaires de France, 1975), p. 290; Bernard Hercenberg, *Nicolas Vleughles, peintre et directeur de l'Académie de France à Rome* (Paris: Léonce Laget, 1975), pls. 24, 28; Martin Kemp, "A Date for Chardin's 'Lady Taking Tea,'" *Burlington* 120 (January 1978), 22. On Diderot's materialistic language, called into existence by the need to analyze Chardin's sensuous facture, see Else Marie Bukdahl, *Diderot critique d'art*, tr. from the Danish by Jean-Paul Faucher (Copenhagen: Rosenkilde et Bagger, 1980), I, pp. 339–344.

31. Ann Percy, *Giovanni Benedetto Castiglione (1616–1670)* (Philadelphia: Museum of Art, 1971), pp. 17–20; Jonathan Scott, *Piranesi* (New York: St. Martin's, 1975), pp. 50–52; Roseline Bacou, *Piranesi, Etchings and Drawings* (Boston: New York Graphic Society, 1975), pls. 6, 10; *Piranèse et les français, 1740–1790* (Rome: Elefante, 1976),

catalog nos. 6, 144 and pp. 41–42, 273. On the greatness of the dim see Burke, *Sublime and Beautiful*, pp. 114–119; Marcia Allentuck, "Sir Uvedale Price and the Picturesque Garden: The Evidence of the Coleorton Papers," in *Picturesque Garden*, p. 60. Beyond the artistic evidence, it is important to bear in mind that there was a technological source for the representations of smoke and steam: the plates in the *Encyclopédie* devoted to manufacture, especially to the dyeing of cloth at the Gobelins or to the making of glass. See *Recueil de planches sur les sciences, les arts liberaux, et les arts méchaniques* (Paris: Briassen, 1772), X, pls. 1, 10–14.

32. Bernardin de Saint-Pierre, *Harmonies de la nature*, in *Oeuvres complètes*, IX–X, p. 430; Goethe, *Dichtung und Wahrheit*, in *Werke*, IV, p. 109; Deane, *Nature Poetry*, pp. 97–98; Hunt, *Figure in the Landscape*, pp. 107–108. For a discussion of the new aesthetic of the fugitive see Fernand Maury, *Étude sur la vie et les oeuvres de Bernardin de Saint-Pierre* (Geneva: Slatkine Reprints, 1971), pp. 422, 426.

33. Hugh Blair, *A Critical Dissertation on the Poems of Ossian the Son of Fingal*, second edition (London: T. Becket and P. A. De Hondt, 1765), p. 29; Mornet, *Romantisme en France*, pp. 117–118; Paul van Tieghem, *L'Année Littéraire (1754–1790) comme intermediaire en France des littératures étrangères* (Geneva: Slatkine Reprints, 1966), no. 39, p. 63. On the influence of the Ossian mania on art see Henry Okum, "Ossian in Painting," *Journal of the Warburg and Courtauld Institutes* 30 (1967), 328, 333, 336; *Ossian und die Kunst um 1800* (Munich: Prestel, 1974), catalog nos. 6, 8, 9 and pp. 61–63, 66.

34. Roger Mercier, "La Théorie des climats des 'Reflexions critiques' à 'L'esprit des lois,'" *Revue d'Histoire Littéraire de la France* 53 (1953), part I, 23; Marcel Raymond, "Entre la philosophie et le romantisme: Senancour," in *Sensibilità e Razionalità*, p. 39.

35. Gode-von-Aesch, *Natural Science in German Romanticism*, pp. 163–164; Ernest Hauterive, *Le merveilleux au XVIIIᵉ siècle* (Geneva: Slatkine Reprints, 1973), pp. 213–216; Béguin, *L'âme romantique*, I, pp. 7–10; [Jérôme] Richard, "La théorie des songes," *Journal de Trévoux* (June 1766), 2484–2485. On dream imagery see *Ossian und die Kunst*, pp. 43, 47–49; *Johan Tobias Sergel 1740–1814* (Munich: Prestel, 1975), pls. 80, 82, 83.

36. Moore, *Backgrounds of English Literature*, pp. 190, 195; Glacken, *Traces*, p. 457. For a recent discussion of "the English Malady" see Vieda Skultans, *English Madness, Ideas on Insanity 1580–1890* (London: Routledge & Kegan Paul, 1979), chapter 3. Among the more interesting, and early, eighteenth-century discussions of dreams

and their connection to hypochondria (i.e., their dependency on the tone and texture of the humoral "spirits") is to be found in Bernard Mandeville's *Treatise of the Hypochondriae and Hysterick Diseases. In Three Dialogues*, second revised edition (London: J. Tonson, 1730), pp. 231–236. Among the most important ancient sources for the variety of images and phantasms possible is Cicero, *De Divinatione*, i.3. The issue for the eighteenth century, as Mandeville and Bayle (*Dictionary*, II, p. 660) make plain, is whether a dreamer has thoughts that are not material; that is, whether his soul is perfectly disengaged from all commerce with the body. Is the alienation of mind from matter possible, or is the soul material as well?

37. A. S. P. Woodhouse, "The Poetry of Collins Reconsidered," in *Sensibility to Romanticism*, pp. 104–105; Duff, *Original Genius*, pp. 138–141, 177; Thielemann, "Diderot and Hobbes," p. 257; Jean Seznec, *L'ombre de Tiresias*, in *Essais sur Diderot et l'antiquité* (Oxford: Clarendon, 1957), pp. 54–56.

38. Seznec, *L'ombre de Tiresias*, pp. 53–54; James Henry Rubin, "Endymion's Dream as a Myth of Romantic Inspiration," *Art Quarterly*, N.S., 2 (spring 1978), n. 90, p. 83; Giuliano Briganti, *I pittori dell'immaginazio. Arte e rivoluzione psicologica* (Milan: Electa, 1977), p. 167; Geoffrey Hartman, *Romantic Poetry and the Genius Loci*, in *Beyond Formalism. Literary Essays 1958–1970* (Yale University Press, 1970), pp. 325–330. The best modern study of the history of incarnating abstractions is to be found in the essays of Robert Klein. See especially "L'imagination comme vêtement de l'âme chez Marsile Ficin et Giordano Bruno," in *La forme et l'intelligible. Ecrits sur la renaissance et l'art moderne*, ed. André Chastel (Paris: Gallimard, 1970).

39. Nicolas Lenglet-Dufresnoy, *Recueil de dissertations anciennes et nouvelles sur les apparitions, les visions & les songes* (Avignon and Paris: Jean-Noël Leloup, 1751), pp. 246–249. In the course of his exposition, Lenglet-Dufresnoy often takes to task the work of his famous Benedictine precursor. See Augustin Calmet, *Traité sur les apparitions des esprits, et sur les vampires ou les révénans de Hongrie, de Moravie, etc.* (1754), revised and augmented edition (Senonnes: Joseph Pariset, 1754), I, pp. 381, 403–406. Though Dom Calmet often has recourse to religious principles in order to explain specters, he devotes chapter 48 of his treatise to "the secrets of physics & of chemistry taken for supernatural things." Here he delights in describing "an infinity of marvelous effects" produced by phosphorus, "the flow of corpuscles," and the "insensible transpiration of bodies." He suggests that the ashes of the dead arrange themselves into the shape with which the author of nature imprinted them, and that human blood, still warm and still filled with spirits or volatile sulfuric acid, gives rise to the "ideas" or phantoms of people interred in cemeteries. Both authors are endebted to Artemidorus's *Interpretation of Dreams*, Robert J. White (Park Ridge, N.J.: Noyes, 1975).

40. M. Roux, "Historie naturelle, chymique & médicinale des corps des trois règnes de la nature, ou abrégé des oeuvres chymiques de M. Gaspard Neumann," *Journal de Monsieur* (February 1781), 349–350; J. L. D'Alembert, C. Bossut, and J.-J. Lalande, *Dictionnaire encyclopédique des mathématiques* (Paris: Panckoucke, 1789), I, p. 24; "Gaz," *Encyclopédie*, VII, p. 520; Guerlac, "Optics of Newton," pp. 141, 147, 150; Robert E. Schofield, *The Lunar Society of Birmingham, A Social History of Provincial Science and Industry in Eighteenth-Century England* (Oxford: Clarendon, 1963), pp. 181–182; Jean-Louis Carra, *Nouveaux principes de physique, ornés de planches* (Paris: Esprit, 1781), III, pp. 236–237; Toulmin and Goodfield, *Architecture of Matter*, p. 214.

41. Pliny, *Natural History* 35.10. Also see Franciscus Junius, *The Painting of the Ancients, in Three Bookes: Declaring by Historical Observations and Examples, the Beginning, Progresse, and Consummation of that Most Noble Art* (London: Richard Hodgkinsonne, 1638), pp. 5, 17–19, 223. Also see Pliny, *Natural History*, 35.10; Quintilian, *Orat. Inst.*, 12.10. On the realization of unrealizable things see also Athanesius Kircher's discussion of catoptric magic (i.e., the "capturing" of things by mirrors) in *Ars magna lucis et umbrae* (1646). Kircher's catoptric theater—both game and instrument of instruction in the mechanics of sight—was mounted on a cabinet lined with 60 mirrors. With the front shutter lowered it would reflect simultaneously the sky and the lid, thus mirroring comets, flying bodies, and other meteorological phenomena in addition to objects standing below, which now seemed reversed and suspended in the air. For a discussion of how nature fared in this *galerie des glaces* see Jurgis Baltrušaitis, "Un musée des miroirs," *Macula* 2 (1977), 2–16.

42. Lomazzo, *Idea*, I, p. 126; Erwin Panofsky, " 'Nebulae in Pariete,' Notes on Erasmus' Eulogy on Dürer," *Journal of the Warburg and Courtauld Institutes* 14 (1951), 35–40; Damisch, *Théorie du nuage*, pp. 50, 180–183; Janson, " 'Image Made by Chance,' " p. 264; Andrea Busiri Vici, *Trittico paesistico romano del '700. Paolo Anesi—Paolo Monaldi—Alessio de Marchis* (Rome: Bozzi, 1976), pp. 163–165; Martin Hardie, *Water-Colour Painting in Britain* (New York: Barnes & Noble, 1967), III, p. 134.

43. Clovis Whitfield, "Nicolas Poussin's 'l'Orage' and 'Temps calme,' " *Burlington* 119 (January 1977), 10; Oskar Bätschmann,

"Poussins Narziss und Echo im Louvre: Die Konstruktion von Thematik und Darstellung aus den Quellen," *Zeitschrift für Kunstgeschichte* 42 (June 1979), 38. For an extended discussion of the ubiquity of these unpaintable beauties see Louise Vinge, *The Narcissus Theme in Western European Literature up to the Early Nineteenth Century*, tr. Robert Dewsnapt and Lisbeth Grönlund (Lund: Gleerups, 1967).

44. De Piles, *Cours de peinture*, pp. 164–167, 198–200; Jean Bernard Le Blanc, *Lettre sur l'exposition des ouvrages de peinture, sculpture, de l'année 1747. Et en général sur l'utilité de ces sortes d'expositions* (Paris, 1747).

45. Rothgeb, "Scenographic Expression of Nature," pp. 306–313, 327–330; Rüdiger Joppien, "Philippe Jacques de Loutherbourg's Pantomime 'Omai, or a Trip round the World' and the Artists of Captain Cook's Voyages," *British Museum Yearbook* III, 85–86, 94–95; M. and W. G. Archer, *Indian Painting for the British 1770–1880* (Oxford University Press, 1955), p. 24.

46. Valenciennes, *Eléments de perspective*, pp. 244–250, 264–266; "Exhalaison," *Encyclopédie*, VI, p. 253.

47. Louis Cotte, *Traité de météorologie* (Paris: Imprimerie Royale, 1774), p. xvii; *Mémoires sur la météorologie*, I, pp. iii–vii; J. A. Deluc, *Recherches sur les modifications de l'atmosphère*, revised edition (Paris: Chez la Veuve Duchesne, 1784), III, pp. 238–239; N. Rouland, *Tableau historique des propriétés et des phénomènes de l'air* (Paris: Gueffier, 1784), pp. 450–451. The best discussion of the early students of the atmospheric sciences in France is to be found in Broc's *Géographie des philosophes*, pp. 435–440.

48. Thomas Forster, *Researches about Atmospheric Phaenomena* (London: Thomas Underwood, 1813), pp. 12–13; James Capper, *Meteorological and Miscellaneous Tracts Applicable to Navigation, Gardening and Farming, with Calendars of Flora for Greece, France, England, and Sweden* (Cardiff: J. D. Bird, ca. 1800), pp. 149–150. For a modern discussion of the mechanics of cloudiness see H. H. Lamb, *Climate: Present, Past and Future* (London: Methuen, 1972), I, pp. 46–47, 56–57, 361. For an explanation of English weather and its relation to the representation of the countryside, see David Lowenthal and Hugh C. Prince, "The English Landscape," *Geographical Review* 54 (July 1964), 315–316.

49. Aristotle, *Meteorologica*, 3; "Estimation de la temperature de différens dégrés de latitude par Richard Kirwan, écuyer de la société royale de Londres," *Journal Encyclopédique* (May 1790), 196–199. Although the Aristotelian classification of meteors was cited often in seventeenth-century illustrated treatises, it was not generally depicted until the eighteenth century. See,

for example, Gaspar Schott, *Physica curiosa, sive Mirabilia naturae et artis* (Herbipol: Johannis Andreae Endteri & Wolf, 1667), book XI: *De Mirabilibus meteororum*, pp. 1181 ff. A major exception is Descartes's 1637 treatise *Les météores*, which is stunningly illustrated with engravings of vesicular *"tourbillons"* indicating vapor formation in the atmosphere.

50. Richard, *Historie naturelle de l'air*, V, pp. 21, 45–46; Arthur de Capell Brooke, *Winter Sketches in Lapland, or Illustrations of a Journey from Alten on the Shores of the Polar Sea in 69° 55" North Latitude through Norwegian, Russian, and Swedish Lapland to Tornea at the Extremity of the Gulf of Bothnia Intended to Exhibit a Complete View of the Mode of Travelling with Rein-Deer, the Most Striking Incidents that Occurred during the Journey, and the General Character of the Winter Scenery of Lapland* (London: J. Rodwell, 1827), pl. 22 and p. 532; Phipps, *North Pole*, p. 71; Smith, *Antipodean Manifesto*, p. 186.

51. Pierre Bertholon, *De l'électericité des météores* (Paris: Croullebois, 1787), II, pp. 122–128; "Remarques adressés aux auteurs de ce journal sur la cause des chaleur excessives des brouillards, etc., de l'été dernier, & sur celle du rigoureux hiver qu'on a essuyé cette année," *Journal Encyclopédique* (May 1784), 303–306. [In pre-revolutionary France the Illuminati were struck by the harmony thought to exist between meteorological phenomena and political events. See Le Flamanc, *Les utopies prérévolutionnaire*, p. 78. Joseph Priestley, the British Deist, chemist, and rival of Lavoisier, was an important precursor of Bertholon in the "electrical" field. See his *History and Present State of Electricity, with Original Experiments* (1768), second revised edition (London: J. Dodsley, J. Johnson and J. Payne, and T. Cadell, 1769), pp. ix–xi. Priestley exudes enthusiasm for this branch of natural history so rich in discoveries made "in so short a space of time, and all so recent." The "philosophical instruments" it employs—unlike the globe or orrery—reflect not human ingenuity but exhibit the very operations of nature. "By the help of these machines," Priestley writes, "we are able to put an endless variety of things into an endless variety of situations, while nature herself is the agent that shows the result. . . ."]

52. Lesseps, *Journal historique*, I, p. 146; Brooke, *Winter in Lapland*, pls. 9, 11 and pp. 451–455; William Scoresby, *An Account of the Arctic Regions, with a History and Description of the Northern Whale-Fishery* (Edinburgh: Archibald Constable and Co., 1820), I, p. 163; John Franklin, *Narrative of a Second Journey to the Shores of the Polar Sea, in the Years 1825, 1826, and 1827. Including an Account of the Progress of a Detachment to the Eastward, by John Richardson, M.D., F.R.S., F.L.S.* (London: John Murray, 1828), pl. p. 155 and pp. 154–155.

NOTES

53. La Pérouse, *Voyages autour du monde*, II, pp. 10, 248; G. Mollien, *Travels in the Interior of Africa, to the Sources of the Senegal and Gambia; Performed by Command of the French Government, in the Year 1818*, ed. T. E. Bowdich (London: Henry Colburn & Co., 1820), p. 270; Graham, *Chile*, pp. 154–156, 351–353; *Journal of a Voyage to Brazil, and Residence There, during Part of the Years 1821, 1822, 1823* (London: Longman, Hurst, Rees, Orme, Brown, and Green, 1824), pls. 6, 8 and pp. 170, 220; Cochrane, *Colombia*, I, p. 14.

54. Kaempfer, *History of Japan*, I, p. 105; Daniell, *Oriental Scenery*, II, part IV, pl. 22; Grindlay, *Western India*, I, pl. 18; Wales, *Hindoo Excavations*, pl. 24; Henry Salt, *These Twenty-Four Views Taken in Saint Helena, the Cape, India, Ceylon, Abyssinia, and Egypt* (London: William Miller, 1809), pls. 21, 22.

55. Bruno Weber, "Die Figur des Zeichners in der Landschaft," *Zeitschrift für Schweizerische Archäologie und Kunstgeschichte* 34, no. 1 (1977), 48–49; Richard, *Histoire naturelle de l'air* 7, 223–234; Rodolphe Hentzi, *Vues remarquables des montagnes de la Suisse* (Berne: Wagner, 1776), pl. 5 and p. 14; Raoul-Rochette, *Lettres sur la Suisse*, I, part I, pp. 39–40. Also see Etienne-Pivert de Senancour's *Oberman* (1804), letter 84, in which the author meditates before the cascade of the Pissevache and interprets its rustling waters as the symbol of dematerialization and ultimate dispersal (cited by Raymond, "Senancour," in *Sensibilità e Razionalità*, I, p. 30). Among the earliest views of Swiss falls are those in Scheuchzer's *Natur-Geschichte des Schweizerlandes*, II, p. 44, and Gottlieb Siegmund Gruner's *Eisgebirge des Schweizerlandes: beschrieben von . . . Fürsprech vor den Zweyhunderten des Freystaates Bern* (Bern: Abraham Wagner, Sohn, 1760), I, plate facing p. 104.

56. Bruce, *Travels*, III, p. 425; Cochrane, *Colombia*, II, pp. 178–179.

57. Grose, *East Indies*, p. 17; Le Gentil, *Les mers de l'Inde*, II, pl. 1, and p. xiv.

58. Chappe d'Auteroche, *Voyage en Siberie*, III, pl. 15 and pp. 342–343; Giovanni Maria della Torre, "Incendio del Vesuvio accadute li 19 d'octobre del 1767," *Journal des Sçavans* 36 (1769), 46–55; Cook, *Voyage*, II, pl. 59 and pp. 61–62; Patrick Brydone, *A Tour through Sicily and Malta, in a Series of Letters to William Beckford, Esq. of Somerly in Suffolk* (London: W. Strahan and T. Cadell, 1773), I, pp. 195–196. Also see the plates illustrating a wide variety of volcanic activity in Jean Blaeu's *Nouveau théâtre d'Italie, ou description exacte de ses villes, palais, églises, etc. Et les cartes géographiques de toutes ses provinces* (Amsterdam: Pierre Mortier, 1704), III, pls. 9, 13.

59. Dürler, *Bedeutung des Bergbaus*, pp. 187–191; Boisgelin de Kerdu, *Travels in Denmark and Sweden*, II, pl. p. 221 and pp. 220–221; William Borlase, *The Natural History of Cornwall* (Oxford: W. Jackson, 1758), p. 12. For a volume that traces mining imagery through the ages see Marcel N. Barbier, *Les mines et les arts à travers les âges* (Paris: Société de l'Industrie Minérale, 1956). The arch-exponent of the Picturesque, William Gilpin, in his *Observations on the Highlands of Scotland* (1789) and in his *Observations on the Mountains and Lakes of Cumberland and Westmoreland*, finds no picturesque beauty in the interior regions of the earth, only in the entrances to caverns. It was in German Romantic literature, with Novalis (Count Friedrich von Hardenberg), Schubert, and especially E. T. A. Hoffmann, that the depths of the mine took on special significance. See, in particular, "The Mines of Falun," in *The Best Tales of Hoffmann* (1819), ed. E. F. Bleiler (New York: Dover, 1967), pp. 285 ff.

60. Damisch, *Théorie du nuage*, pp. 54–55, 258; Appleton, *Experience of Landscape*, p. 113; Bachelard, *L'air et les songes*, pp. 218–219.

61. "Nuée," *Encyclopédie*, XI, p. 278; Richard, *Histoire naturelle de l'air*, V, pp. 308–309; J. Frederic Daniell, *Meteorological Essays and Observations* (London: Thomas and George Underwood, 1823), p. 110. Although the eighteenth century was content with using the very vague term *air*, progress was made during that period in the study and measurement of atmospheric phenomena; see Broc, *Les montagnes*, pp. 173–174.

62. Macartney, *Embassy to China*, I, p. 103; Forster, *Voyage round the World*, I, p. 65; Barrow, *Southern Africa*, I, pp. 38–40; Johnson, *Oriental Voyager*, pp. 17, 49–50.

63. Bernard O'Reilly, *Greenland, the Adjacent Seas, and the North-West Passage to the Pacific Ocean, Illustrated in a Voyage to Davis's Strait during the Summer of 1817, With Charts and Numerous Plates from Drawings by the Author Taken on the Spot* (London: Baldwin, Cradock, and Joy, 1818), pls. p. 196 and pp. ii–iv, 37–38.

64. Faujas de Saint-Fond, *La machine aérostatique*, I, pp. 1–2; II, frontispiece and p. 19; "Notices diverses concernant la machine aérostatique," *Journal Encyclopédique* (January 1784), 306–307; M. Laudier, "Expériences & observations concernant la machine aérostatique, adressés aux auteurs de ce journal," *Journal Encyclopédique* (April 1784), 299–300; "Discours de M. Montgolfier (l'aîné) sur l'aérostat, prononcé dans un des séances de l'académie des sciences, belles-lettres & arts de la ville de Lyon, en novembre 1783," *Journal Encyclopédique* (April 1784), 10–14; "Letter to Charles," Library of Congress, Tissandier Collection. That the balloon *fêtes* shared the exuberant spirits of other large public manifestations taking place during the an-

cien régime is confirmed by Alain-Charles Gruber, *Les grandes fêtes et leurs décors à l'époque de Louis XVI* (Paris: Droz, 1972), p. 22.

65. François Bruel, *Histoire aéronautique par les monuments peints, sculptés, dessinés et gravés des origines à 1830* (Paris: André Marty Imprimerie de Frazier-Soye, 1909), pl. 92 and pp. 18, 59; Baldwin, *Airopaidia*, pp. 57–58, 110, 128–141.

66. "Rapport fait par MM. Duhamel du Monceau & Tillet, présenté à l'Académie par le Père Cotte, prêtre de l'Oratoire, & correspondent de cette Académie," *Observations sur la physique, sur l'histoire naturelle et sur les arts* 2 (April 1772), 11; Richard, *Histoire naturelle de l'air*, VII, p. 329. On the belief that "majestic truth dwelt in sublime light" see Nicolson, *Newton Demands the Muse*, p. 121. On the increasing frequency of aqueous and meteorological imagery in poetry see Guitton, *Jacques Delille*, p. 101.

67. Kerguelen-Trémarec, *Relation*, p. 9; Richard, *Histoire naturelle de l'air*, VII, pp. 357–360: Bouguer, *Figure de la terre*, p. xii; Thorn, *Java*, p. 286; O'Reilly, *Greenland*, pl. p. 46 and p. 161. On the ancient and medieval interest in such light "mirroring" prodigies see Jurgis Baltrušaitis, *Essai sur une légende scientifique. Le Miroir. Révélations, science-fiction et fallacies* (Paris: Elmayan, Le Seuil, 1978), pp. 49–65. The latter also provides a number of mid-nineteenth-century illustrations.

68. Richard, *Histoire naturelle de l'air*, VII, pp. 224–225; "Le spectre du Brocken," *Magasin Pittoresque* 43 (1833), pl. p. 341; Smith, *Antipodean Manifesto*, pp. 177–179. See also Lawrence Rooke, "Directions for Seamen Bound for Long Voyages," *Philosophical Transactions of the Royal Society* 1 (1666), 50–51. The latter are a set of instructions on what seamen should take note of on their travels—including luminous phenomena—and how they should keep records. A brief preface clearly states the aims of the Royal Society. For a French example see the instructions given by Antoine-Laurent de Jussieu to the naturalists aboard Boudin's expedition: André-Pierre Ledru, *Voyage aux Iles de Ténériffe, la Trinité, Saint-Thomas, Sainte-Croix et Porte-Ricco, exécuté par ordre du gouvernement français, depuis le 30 septembre 1796 jusqu'au 7 juin 1798 sous la direction du Capitaine Baudin, pour faire des recherches et des collections relatives à l'histoire naturelle* (Paris: Arthus Bertrand, 1810), I, p. xvii. The Brocken Specter and its kin were neatly classified by Sir David Brewster, *Letters on Natural Magic, Addressed to Sir Walter Scott, Bart.* (London: John Murray, 1834), pp. 127–148. The topography of the moon, with its mountains, craters, and "spots," was illustrated with increasing frequency and accuracy from the mid-

dle of the seventeenth century on. See in particular Gaspar Schott, *Iter Extaticum coeleste, quo Mundi opificium, id est, Coelestis Expansi, siderung . . .* (Herbipoli: Scumptibus Joh. Abdr. & Wolffg. Jun. Endterorum, 1660), pl. 3, p. 64; Tobias Mayer, *Bericht von den Mondskugeln, welche bey der kosmographischen Gesellschaft in Nürnberg, aus neuen Beobachtungen verfertigt werden durch . . .* (Nuremberg: Homännischen Officin, 1750), pls. 1, 2. The most handsome of these lunar portraits, however, is that of John Russell, *The Lunar Planispheres, Engraved by the Late . . . , Esq., R.A. from His Original Drawings. With a Description* (London: William Bulmer and Company, 1809), pls. 1, 2. This folio edition had been preceded in 1797) by Russell's *Lunar Globe*.

69. Bernardin de Saint-Pierre, *Harmonies de la nature*, in *Oeuvres complètes*, IX–X, p. 320; Barrow, *Southern Africa*, I, pp. 40–41.

70. Forster, *Observations made during a Voyage*, pp. 120–121; Chauncey C. Loomis, "The Arctic Sublime," in *Nature and the Victorian Imagination*, pp. 100–102. Joseph Priestley's *History and Present State of Discoveries Relating to Vision, Light and Colours* (London: J. Johnson, 1772) provides a compendium of the state of knowledge in the latter part of the eighteenth century; J. R. Forster owned a copy of this and probably took it with him on Cook's second voyage.

71. Ritterbush, *Overtures to Biology*, pp. 25–26; R. P. du Fesc, "Dissertation sur la lumière septentrionale, avec l'explication de ses divers phénomènes," *Journal de Trévoux* (July–September 1732), 1216–1217, 1575–1576; Fredrich Daniel Behn, *Das Nordlicht* (Lübeck: Christian Gottfried Donatus, 1770), pp. 27–29. Priestley concludes, with Beccaria, that the more unusual appearances in the earth and the heavens, from the aurora borealis and falling stars to waterspouts, whirlwinds, hurricanes, and earthquakes, are caused by electricity. See *History of Electricity*, pp. 341–361 passim. Thus, in order to make discoveries in this new experimental science he urges sapient observers to make "an expedition into [its] undiscovered reaches." See Joseph Priestley, *Experiments and Observations on Different Kinds of Air, and Other Branches of Natural Philosophy* (Birmingham: Thomas Pearson, 1790), I, p. xxv.

72. Roger-Joseph Boscovich, "Dissertatio de Lumine," *Journal de Trévoux* (July 1750), 1654–1656; Bertholon, *Électricité des météores*, II, p. 39; Carra, *Nouveaux principes physiques*, III, p. 174. On Carra see Thomas Crow, "The *Oath of the Horatii* in 1785, Painting and Pre-Revolutionary Radicalism in France," *Art History* 1 (December 1978), 440.

73. Jean-Jacques Dortous de Mairan, *Traité physique et historique de l'aurore boréale* (Paris: Imprimerie Royale, 1733), pp. 65–66, 245–251. For modern discussions of this phenomenon see John A. Eddy, "The Maunder Minimum," *Science* 192 (June 18, 1976), 1189–1202; Emmanuel Le Roy Ladurie, *Histoire du climat depuis l'an mil* (Paris: Flammarion, 1967), p. 222. For an eminently readable and informative account of the aurora borealis, written by a scientist for the layman, see Robert H. Eather, *Majestic Lights. The Aurora in Science, History, and the Arts* (Washington, D.C.: American Geophysical Union, 1980), pp. 2–3. The modern explanation of the phenomenon is that it is the result of solar-wind particles streaming out from the sun in all directions. When they encounter the earth's magnetic field, the trajectories of electrically charged particles are affected. The shape of the earth's magnetic field acts to guide particles to two oval regions around the poles, and this is where auroras occur every night of the year. As those particles collide with the oxygen and nitrogen of the earth's upper atmosphere, they impart some of their energy to the gas which is then radiated in the form of colored light.

74. Forster, *Voyage round the World*, I, pp. 115–116; Kerguelen-Trémarec, *Relation*, p. 165; Franklin, *Journey to Polar Sea*, p. xii; Brooke, *Winter in Lapland*, pl. 18 and pp. 125–126; Turnor, *Astra Castra*, pp. 123–124. For the most stunning folio illustrations (lithographs after M. Bevalet) of the aurora borealis, see Paul Gaimard's *Voyages de la commission scientifique du Nord en Scandanavie, en Laponie, au Spitzberg et aux Feröe pendant les années 1838, 1839, et 1840 sur la corvette* La Recherche, *commandé par M. Fabvre, Lieutenant de vaisseau. Publiés par ordre du roi sous la direction de . . . , président de la commission scientifique du Nord* (Paris: Arthus-Bertrand, 1842–1852), in which 12 plates (unnumbered) in the Atlas de Physique are devoted to the appearance of the aurora over Bossekop in Finland.

75. Cotte, *Traité de météorologie*, p. 90; Thomas Wright, *An Original Theory or New Hypothesis of the Universe* (London: Wright, 1750), pp. 24, 59–61; Bettex, *Discovery of Nature*, pp. 118–119; La Pluche, *Spectacle de la nature*, III, p. 483; D'Alembert, *Dictionnaire encyclopédique*, II, pp. 443–445; Skjöldebrand, *North Cape*, pp. 8–9, 19.

76. Sigaud-Lafond, *Dictionnaire des merveilles*, p. 65; Bertholon, *Électricité des météores*, I, pp. 1–3; Valenciennes, *Eléments de perspective*, p. 257. On the new sensibility of post-Newtonian man and his taste for a colossal and infinite nature, see Tuveson, "Space, Deity, 'Natural Sublime,' " p. 21.

77. Rooke, "Directions for Seamen," p. 52; Cotte, *Traité de météorologie*, pp. 79–82; Ritterbush, *Overtures to Biology*, pp. 21–23.

78. Belzoni, *Narrative*, p. 33; Kaempfer, *History of Japan*, I, 45.

79. Pujoulx, *Paris*, p. 33; C. L. Berthollet, *Essai de statique chimique* (Paris: Imprimerie de Demonville et Soeurs, 1803), I, pp. 257–258; François Péron, *Voyage de découvertes aux terres australes, exécuté par ordre de sa majesté l'empereur et Roi, sur les corvettes* Le Géographe, Le Naturaliste, *et la goelette* Le Casuarima, *pendant les années 1800, 1801, 1802, 1803, 1804* (Paris: Imprimerie Impériale, 1807), I, pp. 40–41; Forster, *Observations Made during a Voyage*, pp. 65–66; Beaglehole, *Endeavour Journal of Banks*, p. 179. Also see Marie Louise Hemphill, "Le carnet de croquis du séjour en Angleterre en 1815 de Charles-Alexandre Lesueur (1778–1846)," *Bulletin de la Société de l'histoire de l'art français* 1975 (1976), 239. For an exhaustive modern study of the phenomenon see Harvey E. Newton, *The History of Luminescence from the Earliest Times until the Present* (Philadelphia: American Philosophical Society, 1957).

80. Bernardin de Saint-Pierre, *Voyage à l'Ile de France*, I, p. 37; *Harmonies de la nature*, in *Oeuvres complètes*, VII–VIII, pp. 114–117. Similarly, Erasmus Darwin, in both sections of *The Botanic Garden* ("The Economy of Vegetation" and "The Loves of the Plants"), refers to phosphorescent effects.

81. *Noctiluca*, or fire of the sea, was first given prominence by Robert Boyle in a series of published experiments. See *The Aerial Noctiluca or Some New Phenomena and a Process of a Facetious Self-Shining Substance* (London: T. Snowdon, 1680); *New Experiments and Observations Made upon the Icy Noctiluca* (London, 1681–82). The issue that was hotly debated, from Boyle and—even earlier—Descartes (*Les météores*, 1637) to the close of the eighteenth century was the source (putrescence, friction, or dinoflagellates) of this cold light. Also see Macartney, *Embassy to China*, I, p. 295; Brooke, *Winter in Lapland*, pp. 53–54.

82. Broc, *La géographie des philosophes*, p. 438; Jean D'Alembert, "Réflexions sur la cause générale des vents," in *Histoire de l'Académie des sciences* (1750), pp. 41–47; Rouland, *Phénomènes de l'air*, pp. 528–533; Gaspard Monge, Jean-Dominique Cassini, Pierre Bertholon, *Dictionnaire de physique* (Paris: Hotel de Thou, 1793), I, p. 227.

83. Forster, *Voyage round the World*, I, p. 253; Kaempfer, *History of Japan*, I, pp. 50–53; Louis de Grandpré, *Voyages dans l'Inde et au Bengale, fait dans les années 1789 et 1790 . . . Suivi d'un voyage fait*

dans la Mer Rouge, contenant la description de Moka, et du commerce des Arabes de l'Yemen; des détails sur leur caractère et leurs moeurs (Paris: Dentu, 1801), II, p. 125; Perry and Simpson, Drawings by William Westall, p. 28; Daniell, Oriental Scenery, V, pl. 8; Grindlay, Western India, II, pl. 21.

84. Brydone, Sicily and Malta, II, pp. 63, 139; Jackson, Marocco, pp. 283–284; Belzoni, Narrative, p. 195. Also see Thorn, Memoir of the War in India, pp. 345–346; Fitzroy, Narrative of a Beagle Voyage, II, p. 93.

85. "Trombe," Encyclopédie, XVI, p. 689; Recueil de planches, IV, pl. 2, figs, 3–4; Bertholon, Eléctricité des météores, II, pp. 216, 221–223; William Dampier, A Collection of Voyages (London: James and John Knapton, 1729), I, p. 451; Forster, Voyage round the World, I, p. 193; F. W. Beechey, Narrative of a Voyage to the Pacific and Beering's Strait, to Co-Operate with the Polar Expeditions: Performed in His Majesty's Ship Blossom, under the Command of . . . in the Years 1825, 26, 27, 28 (London: Henry Colburn and Richard Bentley, 1831), pl. p. 149 and p. 5; Le Gentil, Voyage, II, pls. 1, 9 and p. xv; M. La Place, Voyage autour du monde par les mers de l'Inde et de la Chine de la corvette de sa majesté La Favorite, exécuté pendant les années 1830, 1831, 1832 (Paris: Arthus Bertrand, 1835), pls. 3, 4: Johnson, Oriental Voyager, p. 136; Peter Schmidtmeyer, Travels into Chile, over the Andes, in the Years 1820 and 1821, with Some Sketches of the Productions and Agriculture; Mines and Metallurgy; Inhabitants, History, and Other Features of America; particularly of Chile and Aranco (London: S. McDowall, 1824), pl. p. 8. On the waterspout as a marine phenomenon that elicited considerable attention in the late eighteenth century—particularly from Coleridge—see Smith, Antipodean Manifesto, pp. 181–182.

86. Forster, Observations Made during a Voyage, pp. 43–44; Martin Sauer, An Account of a Geographical and Astronomical Expedition to the Northern Parts of Russia, for Ascertaining the Degrees of Latitude and Longitude of the Mouth of the River Kovima; of the Whole Coast of the Tshutski, to East Cape and of the Islands in the Eastern Ocean, Stretching to the American Coast, by Command of Catherine II, by Commodore Joseph Billings in the Years 1785, etc. (London: T. Cadell, Jr., and W. Davies, 1802), pl. p. 303; MacKenzie, Iceland, pls. pp. 224–225 and p. 224; "Voyage de M. Monge en Islande," Journal des Voyages de Découvertes et Navigations Modernes, ou Archives Géographiques du XIXᵉ Siècle 6 (1820), 15–17; "Voyage en Islande et au Mont Hécla en 1827," pl. p. 128 and pp. 124 ff; An Historical and Descriptive Account of Iceland, Greenland, and the Faroe Islands; with Illustrations of Their Natural History, second edition (Edinburgh and

London: Liver & Boyd; Simpkin, Marshall, & Co., 1841), pl. 3 and p. 56.

87. Dominique Bouhours, La mer, in Les entretiens d'Ariste et d'Eugène (Amsterdam: Jacques Le Jeune, 1671), pp. 24–29; De Piles, Cours de peinture, pp. 177–179; Valenciennes, Eléments de perspective, p. 215; Bettex, Discovery of Nature, pp. 139–142. On the role played by watery metaphors in eighteenth-century art and theory see Stafford, "Beauty of the Invisible," pp. 65 ff.

88. Grandpré, Voyage dans l'Inde et au Bengale, II, pp. 184, 265–267; Valenciennes, Eléments de perspective, p. 216; Cordiner, Remarkable Ruins, plates "Findlater Castle" and "Coast of Moray"; Forrest, Ganges and Jumna, pl. 7 and p. 141.

89. Le Flamanc, Les utopies prérévolutionnaire, p. 64; Jack Lindsay, J. M. W. Turner, His Life and Work, a Critical Biography (Greenwich, Conn.: New York Graphic Society, 1966), pp. 50–51; Chappe d'Auteroche, Voyage en Siberie, II, p. 713; Smith, European Vision, pp. 41, 52; Geoffrey Callender, " 'Cape Town' by William Hodges, R.A.," Burlington 79 (September 1941), 93–94; Bernardin de Saint-Pierre, Voyage à l'Isle de France, I, pp. 60–61; Basil Hall, Account of a Voyage of Discovery to the West Coast of Corea, and the Great Loo-Choo Island; with an Appendix Containing Charts, and Various Hydrographical and Scientific Notices (London: John Murray, 1818), frontispiece and pp. 58–59; Krusenstern, Voyage round the World, I, pp. 228–229.

90. Broc, Les montagnes, pp. 147–154; Biese, Naturgefühl, p. 144; David Irwin, "Jacob More, Neo-Classical Landscape Painter," Burlington 114 (November 1972), 778; "Charles Steuart, Landscape Painter," Apollo 104 (October 1977), 302; Liselotte Fromer-Im-Obersteg, Die Entwicklung der Schweizerischen Landschaftsmalerei im 18. und frühen 19. Jahrhundert (Basel: Birkhauser, 1945), pp. 73–77; F. C. Lonchamp, Un siècle d'art suisse (1730–1830). L'estampe et le livre à gravures. Guide de l'amateur (Lausanne: Librarie des Bibliophiles, 1920), p. 66; J.-L. Aberli (1723–1786), son temps, sa vie et son oeuvre (Paris and Lausanne: Librairie des Bibliophiles, 1927), p. 39; "J.-L. Aberli Engravings," Cabinet des Estampes, Bibliothèque Nationale, Paris, yb.³ 2069, pl. 15; Cockburn, Simplon Pass.

91. Skjöldebrand, Cataractes de Trollhätta, pl. 3 and pp. 8–9. For the first accounts the English public received of "romantic" Norway see Adams, Francis Danby, p. 55. Boisgelin de Kerdu, Denmark and Sweden, II, pl. 3 and pp. 24–25.

92. Cassas, L'Istrie et Dalmatie, pl. 30 and pp. 105–106, 157. Also see Colin McMordie, "Louis-François Cassas: The Formation of a Neo-Classical Landscapist," Apollo 3 (March 1976), 228–230.

93. Bougainville, *Voyage autour du monde*, II, pp. 213–214; Cook, *Voyage*, I, pp. 73, 77; Forster, *Voyage round the World*, I, pp. 136, 143.

94. Carver, *North-America*, pl. p. 70 and p. 69; François-Auguste Chateaubriand, *Mémoires d'outre-tombe*, ed. Maurice Le Vaillant, second revised edition (Paris: Flammarion, 1964), I, pp. 302–306; Heriot, *Canadas*, pls. pp. 161, 171 and pp. 159–161; Milbert, *Hudson*, I, pp. 198–201.

95. Annesley, *Voyages and Travels*, I, pl. 2 and p. 39; pl. p. 444 and p. 443; Pococke, *Description of the East*, I, p. 122; Mayer, *Views in Egypt*, p. 8; Vivant-Denon, *Voyage en Egypte*, I, p. 160.

96. Hamilton, *Campi Phlegraei*, II, pl. 38; Laborde, *Tableaux de la Suisse*, I, pp. 86–88; *France*, I, pl. 15; J. B. L. Romé de l'Isle, *Cristallographie, ou description des formes propres à tous les corps du règne minéral, dans l'état de combinaison saline, pierreuse, ou métallique* (Paris: De l'Imprimerie de Monsieur, 1783), I, pp. 51–52; Lang, *Unterirdischen Wunder*, I, pl. p. 24 and pp. 24, 28. Subterranean falls, mimicking their above-ground counterparts, were known since antiquity. See Kenneth Woodbridge's discussion of just such a cascade at the Villa Maecenas, Tivoli, in *Landscape and Antiquity, Aspects of English Culture at Stourhead 1718-1838* (Oxford: Clarendon, 1970), pp. 96–97.

97. D'Avallon, *Linguetiana*, pp. 73–74; Athanasius Kircher, *Mundus Subterraneus* (Amsterdam: Joannis Janssonÿ et Elizaei Weyerstraet, 1665), I, pls. pp. 16, 180, 186; Valenciennes, *Eléments de perspective*, pp. 224–225. On the importance of the last of the Renaissance polymaths see Joscelyn-Godwin, *Athanasius Kircher, A Renaissance Man and the Quest for Lost Knowledge* (London: Thames and Hudson, 1979), pp. 84 ff; Nicolson, *Mountain Gloom and Mountain Glory*, p. 168. On the mid-eighteenth-century discovery of Sicily's convulsive beauty see Rose Macaulay, *Pleasure of Ruins* (New York: Walker, 1966), pp. 222–226.

98. E. H. Gombrich, "Renaissance Artistic Theory and the Development of Landscape Painting," *Gazette des Beaux-Arts* 41 (May–June 1953), 353; Busiri Vici, *Trittico paesistico*, pp. 179–182; Pascal de La Vaissière, "Passagistes et paysages voyageurs, Philibert-Bénoit Delarue et l'Encyclopédie," *Nouvelles de l'Estampe* 29 (September–October 1976), 17. See also Alexandra R. Murphy, *Visions of Vesuvius* (Boston: Museum of Fine Arts, 1978).

99. Hamilton, *Campi Phlegraei*, II, pls. 34, 35; Brydone, *Sicily and Malta*, I, pp. 24, 30; Fussell, "Patrick Brydone," in *Five Essays*, pp. 58–61; Houel, *Voyage*, I, pl. 69 and pp. 130–131. On Houel's new technique of mixing watercolor and gouache to render light effects more easily, and his success at the Salon, see J.-F. Méjanès, "A Spontaneous Feeling for Nature: French Eighteenth-Century Landscape Drawings," *Apollo* 103 (November 1976), 403; Diderot, *Salons*, IV, p. 264.

100. Faujas de Saint-Fond, *Volcans éteints*, pls. 7, 10, 19 and pp. 285, 297–298, 365–366. On Julien-Victor Veyrenc, the gifted amateur who turned Faujas's field sketches into drawings for plates, see Denys Sutton, "Enchantment and Intellectualism," *Apollo* 97 (January 1973), 8. On the larger issue of the basalt controversy and its role in the scientific vulcanological literature of the 1780s, see Grand-Carteret, *La montagne*, I, pp. 487–489.

101. *Voyage de Humboldt et Bonpland*, I, pl. 10 and pp. 44–46; Landmann, *Portugal*, II, pl. p. 168 and p. 167; Arago, *Voyage round the World*, I, pl. 5, p. 206, pp. 205–206. The painting *Crater in the Pacific* (Art Gallery and Museum, Brighton), usually ascribed to William Hodges, has been reattributed to John Knox. Doubt has been cast on this work because Cook's party never visited the interior of a crater during the second voyage. See Isabel Combs Stuebe, *The Life and Works of William Hodges* (New York: Garland, 1979), p. 357.

102. Carozzi, "Basalt Controversy," pp., 236–238; Forster, *Voyage round the World*, I, pp. 371, 267–268; Sparrman, *Cape of Good Hope*, I, p. 96; La Pérouse, *Voyage*, II, pp. 97–100; Louis Choris, *Voyage pittoresque autour du monde, avec des portraits de sauvages d'Amerique, d'Asie, d'Afrique, et des Iles du Grand Océan; des paysages, des vues marines* (Paris: Firmin-Didot, 1820), pl. 5; Péron, *Mémoires*, p. 285; Bernardin de Saint-Pierre, *Voyages à l'Isle de France*, I, p. 28; Le Gentil, *Voyage*, II, pp. 635–636. On the late-eighteenth-century notion that the myriad islands of the Pacific were the visible fragments of Plato's lost Atlantis, see Barbara Maria Stafford, *Symbol and Myth: Humbert de Superville's Essay on Absolute Signs in Art* (Cranbury, N.J.: Associated University Presses, 1979), pp. 123–127.

103. Beaglehole, *Endeavour Journal of Banks*, pp. 83–84; MacKenzie, *Iceland*, pl. 3 and p. 108; Paul Gaimard *Voyage en Islande et Groënland* (Paris: Arthus Bertrand, 1838–1842), I, pl. 32; Edy, *Norway*, I, pp. xli–xliv; P. Gaimard, *Voyage en Islande et au Groënland publié par ordre du roi sous la direction de M . . . Atlas historique. Lithographié d'après les dessins de M.A. Meyer* (Paris: Arthus Bertrand, 1838–1842), II, pl. 132. Also see the geological description by Eugène Robert accompanying *Voyage en Islande et au Groënland, exécuté pendant les années 1835 et 1836 sur la corvette La Recherche . . . dans le but de découvrir les traces de La Lilloise . . . Publié . . . sous la direction de M.P.G.* (Paris: Arthus Bertrand, 1838–1852), II, pp. 293–294.

104. Broc, *Les montagnes*, p. 173; *La géographie des philosophes*, p. 198; Kendrick, *Lisbon Earthquake*, pp. 25, 156; Sebastien Mercier, *Tableau de Paris* (1782), II, p. 312; Cochrane, *Colombia*, I, pp. 37–41; Déodat de Dolomieu, *Mémoire sur les îles Ponces et catalogue raisonné des produits de l'Etna; pour servir à l'histoire des volcans* (Paris: Cuchet, 1788), n. 1, p. 291; Laborde, *France*, I, pl. 6; Grandpré, *L'Inde et Bengale*, II, p. 268.

105. Marc-Théodore Bourrit, *Nouvelle description des vallées de glace et des hautes montagnes qui forment la chaîne des Alpes Pennines & Rhétiennes* (Geneva: Paul Barde, 1783), I, pp. 219–220; Anson, *Voyage*, pp. 62–63; A. J. Pernety, *Journal historique d'un voyage fait aux îles Malouînes en 1763 & 1764* (Berlin: Etienne de Bourdeaux), II, p. 526; Hodges, *Travels in India*, p. 72; Laborde, *Nouveaux jardins*, pl. 20 and p. 76.

106. Gottfried Siegmund Gruner, *Histoire naturelle des glacières de Suisse*, tr. M. de Keralio (Paris: Panckoucke, 1770), pls. 2, 12, 16, 17; Broc, *Les montagnes*, pp. 197–204; Van Tieghem, *Sentiment de la nature*, pp. 185–186; Walter Schmid, *Romantic Switzerland, Mirrored in the Literature and Graphic Art of the Eighteenth and Nineteenth Centuries* (Bern: Hallwag, 1965); Caspar Wolf, *Vues remarquables des montagnes de la Suisse avec leur description, Iere partie* (Bern: Wagner, 1778), preface. For a modern discussion of Alpine glacier retreat see LeRoy Ladurie, *Histoire du climat*.

107. Bourrit, *Nouvelle description*, III, p. 37; Markham Sherwill, *Mont Blanc. Fourteen Narratives Written by Those Travellers who Have Successfully Attained the Summit of This Mountain, between the Years 1786 and 1838 . . . Accompanied by a Series of Views, Portraits, and Original Letters Collected by . . .* (1840), I, pl. p. 336 and pp. 334–340; Wolf, *Vues remarquables*, p. 10; Laborde, *Tableaux de la Suisse*, I, p. xxv. On the Swiss print's increasing focus on such scenery during the nineteenth century see Alfred Schreiber-Favre, *La lithographie artistique en Suisse au XIX^c siècle. Alexandre Calame: le paysage* (Neuchâtel: A la Baconnière, 1966).

108. Cockburn, *Swiss Scenery*, p. 65; John Ross, *Voyage of Discovery Made under the Orders of the Admiralty in His Majesty's Ships Isabella and Alexander for the Purpose of Exploring Baffin's Bay and Inquiring into the Probability of a North-West Passage*, second edition (London: John Murray, 1819), pl. p. 161; Gaimard, *Islande et Groënland*, II, pl. 80.

109. LeRoy Ladurie, *Histoire du climat*, pp. 116–122, 140–141; Weber, "Zeichner in der Landschaft," p. 56; Bashō, *Narrow Road to the Far North*, p. 42; *Voyages de M. le Marquis de Chastellux dans l'Amerique Septentrionale dans les années 1780, 1781 &*

1782 (Paris: Prault, 1786), I, pp. 301–302; Friederika Brun, "Reise von Genf auf dem See durch die Westliche Schweiz," *Journal für die neuesten Land- und Seereisen und das Interessanteste aus der Völker- und Länderkunde* 1 (1808), 313.

110. Mercier, *Mon bonnet de nuit*, IV, p. 37; Cockburn, *Swiss Scenery*, p. 70; Raoul-Rochette, *Lettres sur la Suisse*, I, part I, pl. 21 and p. 72; Hilaire Sazerac, *Un mois en Suisse, ou souvenirs d'un voyageur* (Paris: Sazerac & Duval, 1825), pl. 29; Gruner, *Glacières de la Suisse*, p. 55; Wolf, *Vues remarquables*, p. 11; Johann George Sulzer, *Tagebuch einer von Berlin nach den mittäglichen Ländern von Europa in den Jahren 1775 und 1776 gethanen Reise und Rückreise* (Leipzig: Weidmanns Erben und Reich, 1780), pp. 374–375.

111. Loomis, "Arctic Sublime," pp. 96–98; Cook, *Voyage*, I, pl. 30 and p. 37; Roundell, "Hodges' Paintings of the South Pacific," p. 86; Forster, *Voyage round the World*, I, p. 96; *Observations Made during a Voyage*, p. 70; Phipps, *North Pole*, pl. 7 and p. 70; Edward Chappell, *Narrative of a Voyage to Hudson's Bay in His Majesty's Ship* Rosamond, *Containing Some Account of the North-Eastern Coast of America and of the Tribes Inhabiting That Remote Region* (London: J. Mauwman, 1817), pls.: *View of the* Rosamond *Passing to Windward of an Iceberg, Cape Saddleback*, and *The* Rosamond *Grappled among Close Ice*; John Laing, *A Voyage to Spitzenbergen, Containing an Account of That Country*, second revised edition (Edinburg: Adam Black, 1818), p. 48.

112. Ross, *Voyage of Discovery*, pp. lxv, 5–6, and pls. 47, 48; William Parry, *Journal of a Voyage for the Discovery of a North-West Passage from the Atlantic to The Pacific, Performed in the Years 1819–20* (London: John Murray, 1821), pl. 17; Scoresby, *Arctic Regions*, II, pl. 14; I, pp. 205, 252, 502; George Back, *Buchan's Voyage towards the North Pole* (London, 1818), pls.: *H.M. Brig* Trent *in the Ice off Spitsbergen, June, 1818, H.M.S.* Dorothea *Nipped in the Ice off Spitsbergen, June 10, 1820; Expedition to the McKenzie River 1824–27* (London: G. Murray, 1828), pl. 20.

113. Ross, *Voyage of Discovery*, pl. p. 139 and pp. 138–139; P. S. Pallas, *Nouveau voyage dans les gouvernemens méridionaux de l'Empire de Russie dans les années 1793 et 1794*, tr. from the German (Paris: Amand Koenig, 1801), I, p. 41 and vignette p. 60. For Pallas's Russian emulators in exploration note Tachoff's *Travels to the Icy Sea* (1770–1773) and Chvoinoff's *Journey to the Icy Sea* (1775), cited in Sauer, *Geographical and Astronomical Expedition*, pp. 163 ff.

114. Adanson, *Sénégale*, pp. 24, 48; Jackson, *Marocco*, pp. 46–47; Lyon, *North Africa*, pl. p. 70 and p. 211; Bruce, *Travels*,

IV, pp. 557, 553–556, 582; Moritz von Kotzebue, *Narrative of a Journey into Persia in the Suite of the Imperial Russian Embassy in the year 1817* (London: Longman, Hurst, Rees, Orme, Brown, 1819), pp. 217, 261; Vidal, *Buenos Ayres*, pl. p. 91 and p. 92.

115. Belzoni, *Narrative*, p. 196; Brydone, *Sicily and Malta*, I, pp. 86–89; Houel, *Voyage*, II, p. 21; P. Domenico Giardina, *Discorso sopra la Fata Morgana di Messina, comparsa nell'anno 1644 al di XIV d'agosto . . . della Compagnia di Gesu, con alcune note dell'eruditissimo Sig. Andrea Gallo, Messinese*, in *Opuscoli di Autori Siciliani*, I (Catania: Giachimo Pulejo, 1753), pp. 125–129; Bernardin de Saint-Pierre, *Harmonies de la nature*, in *Oeuvres Complètes*, IX–X, pp. 55, 65–66; *Voyages à l'Île de France*, I, p. 51. Valenciennes warns his students to be wary of such optical illusions and to avoid representing them in paintings since "this effect is disagreeable and false when in nature [and] it will become more ridiculous in Painting"; the illusion will appear to be the fault of the artist, and since not the slightest falsity (*fausseté*) is permissible in a picture, and even less in perspective (which has science as its principle), it is best to avoid these errors. See *Eléments de perspective*, pp. 212–213. One of the best early compendia of ancient and modern ideas concerning watery optical illusions was gathered by Pierre Perrault, the black sheep of that famous seventeenth-century French family of scholars. See *On the Origin of Springs*, tr. Aurèle La Rocque (New York: Hafner, 1967), pp. 58–59.

116. Cook, *Voyage*, I, p. xx; Hawkesworth, *Relation . . . Byron*, I, p. 12; Le Gentil, *Voyage*, II, pl. 8 and p. 725; Turnor, *Astra Castra*, p. 383. One of the earliest accurate scientific studies of the varieties of mirage—based on precise documentation offered by Humboldt, Arago, and Le Gentil—is that of Jean-Baptiste Biot, *Recherches sur les réfractions extraordinaires qui ont lieu près de l'horizon* (Paris: Bachelier, 1810).

117. Henry G. Van Leeuwen, *The Problem of Certainty in English Thought, 1630–1690*, second edition (The Hague: Martinus Nijhoff, 1970), pp. 2–9, 106–120. For a different perspective, namely the battle between the ancients and the moderns, see Richard Foster Jones, *Ancients and Moderns: A Study of the Rise of the Scientific Movement in Seventeenth-Century England*, second revised edition (St. Louis: Washington University, 1961), pp. 41–61. For the important contribution made by seventeenth-century French particulate philosophies and Gassendian atomism to the British explanation of the myriad new facts educed in the chemical and biological sciences, see Robert G. Frank, Jr., *Harvey and the Oxford Physiologists: A Study of Scientific Ideas* (University of California Press, 1980), pp. 90–97. On the Newtonian revolution as seen by some of Newton's French successors (Bailly, Maupertuis, Clairaut, D'Alembert), see I. Bernard Cohen, *The Newtonian Revolution* (Cambridge University Press, 1980), pp. 120–127; Hahn, *Anatomy*, p. 94.

1. Lee, *Names on Trees*, pp. 3–9; Plotinus, *Ennead*, II, 3.7; Maillet, *Telliamed*, I, pp. 125–126; Whitehurst, *Original State and Formation of Earth*, pp. 257–258. For the analogy of geology with linguistics—in the sense of the geologist's deciphering the past history of nature contained in its "monuments"—see Martin J. S. Rudwick, "Transposed Concepts from the Human Sciences in the Early Work of Charles Lyell," *British Society for the History of Science* 1 (1979), 69–72. On how this "new kind of antiquary," reconstructing the prediluvial scene with vivid immediacy, was responsible for creating a new visual language, see Rudwick, "The Emergence of a Visual Language for Geological Science," *History of Science* 14 (1976), 149–195 passim. In reality, the idea is quite old. Seba (*Locupletissimi*, IV, 123) describes fossil shells discovered in the mountains near Avignon as "antiquities or monuments of Nature." See also Niebuhr, *Description de l'Arabie*, p. 348.

2. "Sur les races d'animaux perdues," *Magasin Pittoresque* 26 (1834), pl. p. 204 and pp. 204–205. In identifying the eighteenth-century fascination with the natural hieroglyph, this chapter will take to task the view that the "matter" of this world was seen primarily as a spiritual analogue, that is, as a commentary on the mind of God. See Earl R. Wasserman, "Nature Moralized: The Divine Analogy in the Eighteenth Century," *ELH* 20 (March 1953), 39–41, 55–61, 65, 76. My thesis is that by the middle of the century the Baconian notion that the "show of things belong to the domain of science" had been accepted by an advanced sector of artists and the public as not needing an idealized or transformational translation.

3. Rehder, *Unendlichen Landschaft*, pp. 37–38; Whitehurst, *Original State and Formation of Earth*, pp. 119–120; Maillet, *Telliamed*, II, pp. 99, 108. The middle of the eighteenth century saw the publication of a number of books on cosmology. Maillet, who was French consul-general in Egypt, produced a work that, in its stress on the idea that the history of the earth was not just a study of its past but also one of its present, should be compared to Maupertuis's *Essai de cosmologie* (Leiden, 1751) and Nicolas Boulanger's *Anecdotes de la nature* (ca. 1750). See Collier, *Cosmogonies of Our Forefathers*, pp. 219–227; Ehrard, *Idée de la nature*, I, p. 204.

4. Buffon, *Les époques de la nature*, in *Oeuvres complètes*, II, pp. 73 ff.; Daniel Mornet, *Les sciences de la nature en France au XVIIIᵉ siècle, un chapitre de l'histoire des*

Chapter 4

VOYAGE INTO SUBSTANCE

idées (Paris: Armand Colin, 1911), pp. 117–126; Jacques Roger, "Le Feu et l'histoire: James Hutton et la naissance de la géologie," in *Approches des Lumières*, pp. 417–423; John Playfair, *Illustrations of the Huttonian Theory of the Earth* (London: Cadell and Davies; Edinburgh: William Creech, 1802), pp. 97, 483 ff.; Monglond, *Préromantisme*, I, pp. 135–137; Mircea Eliade, *Cosmos and History, The Myth of the Eternal Return* (New York: Harper & Row, 1959), pp. 87, 145.

5. Paracelsus [Theophrastus, Philip of Hohenstein], *A New Light of Alchymie: Taken out of the Fountaine of Nature, and Manuall Experience. To Which Is Added a Treatise of Sulphur: . . . Also Nine Books of the Nature of Things*, tr. Gerardus Dorn (London: Richard Cotes, 1650), pp. 101–130. For the best modern discussion of the aesthetic influence of the Paracelsian theory of signs see Michael Baxandall, *The Limewood Sculptors of Renaissance Germany* (Yale University Press, 1980), pp. 32–40, 161. Even chiromantic games were popular by the early eighteenth century. See F. M. P. Colonna [Crosset de la Haumerie], *Le nouveau miroir de la fortune, ou abrégé de la géomance. Pour la récréation des personnes curieuses de cette science* (Paris: André Cailleau, 1726).

6. For a survey of the interpretation of fossils from Pliny to the close of the eighteenth century see Emile Guyénot, *Les sciences de la vie aux XVIIᵉ et XVIIIᵉ siècles. L'idée d'évolution* (Paris: Albin Michel, 1941), pp. 341–343. The inscription endemic to the mineral or fossil, and, by extension, to the natural monument, is to be distinguished from the epigram carved by the hand of man on tree, rock, or statue. A special form, the elegiac nature inscription, is related to eighteenth-century gardens. See Geoffrey H. Hartman, *Wordsworth, Inscriptions, and Romantic Nature Poetry*, in *Beyond Formalism*, pp. 207–210.

7. Bachelard, *La terre et les rêveries de la volonté*, pp. 17–21; Bauer, *Rocaille*, pp. 25–26. Blake offers the most unflattering images of petrification and crystallization, through which "the jewels of light" become hardened or, as in *Jerusalem*, "every Minute Particular [is] hardened into grains of sand" (cited in Ault, *Visionary Physics*, p. 147). On Newton's influential if confusing desire to have it both ways—to have small, hard particles that simultaneously possess "certain Powers, Virtues, or Forces"—see Query 31 in *Opticks, or a Treatise of the Reflections, Refractions, Inflections & Colours of Light* (New York: Dover, 1951), pp. 375–376; and *Principles of Natural Philosophy*, II, p. 393 (A certain most subtle Spirit, which pervades and lies hid in all gross bodies . . .). Two modern commentators who trace the influence of these ideas on eighteenth-century thought are Ernan McMullin [*Newton on Matter and Activity* (University of Notre Dame Press, 1978), pp. 54–55] and Arnold Thackray [*Atoms and Powers: An Essay on Newtonian Matter-Theory and the Development of Chemistry* (Harvard University Press, 1970), pp. 134 ff.]. Thomas McFarland, on the other hand, in his otherwise stimulating *Romanticism and the Forms of Ruin: Wordsworth, Coleridge, and Modalities of Fragmentation* (Princeton University Press, 1981), pp. 5–55 passim, does not connect the ruin aesthetic with current debates on the nature of matter.

8. Battisti, *Antirinascimento*, n. 73, p. 437; Paul Zucker, "Ruins—An Aesthetic Hybrid," *Journal of Aesthetics and Art Criticism* 20 (winter 1961), 128–129; André Chastel, "Le fragmentaire, l'hybride, et l'inachevé," in *Das Unvollendete als künstlerische Form: Ein Symposion*, ed. J. A. Schmoll, gen. Eisenwerth (Bern and Munich: Francke, 1959), pp. 87–88. The conception of the "ruins of nature" seems to have arisen in the later seventeenth century with the "Diluvialists," among them Thomas Burnet. See Aubin, "Grottoes, Geology," p. 414. Their continuing fascination and their prod to aesthetic speculation is seen in J. B. Jackson's *The Necessity for Ruins, and Other Topics* (University of Massachusetts Press, 1980).

9. Macaulay, *Pleasure of Ruins*, pp. 128–129; Burda, *Die Ruine*, pp. 35–36.

10. On the notion of the decay of nature and its role in the polemic between the ancients and the moderns see Richard Foster Jones, *Ancients and Moderns: A Study of the Rise of the Scientific Movement in Seventeenth-Century England*, second edition (St. Louis: Washington University, 1961), pp. 22–40. On the need for a reassessment of the whole ancient-versus-modern controversy and its continuation into the eighteenth century see Joseph M. Levine, "Ancients and Moderns Reconsidered," *Eighteenth-Century Studies* 15 (fall 1981), 72–89. See further Glacken, *Traces*, pp. 124, 69–72; Diderot, *Salons*, III, pp. 228–229. For a discussion of Diderot's biological dynamics hinging on a concept of universal process embodied in the two opposing forces of energy and change, see Lester G. Crocker, *Diderot's Chaotic Order, Approach to Synthesis* (Princeton University Press, 1974), pp. 9, 29–30. Also note the presence of vitalism in Mercier's *Mon bonnet de nuit* (I, p. 47) and Desmond King-Hele's *Erasmus Darwin* (New York: Scribner, 1963) (pp. 71–72).

11. *Pythagoron. The Religious, Moral, and Ethical Teachings of Pythagoras*, reconstructed and edited by Hobart Huson (1947), pp. 3, 15, 17, 19, 21. On the popularity and availability of literature about Pythagoras during the eighteenth century see Carlos Sommervogel, *Table méthodique des Mémoires des Trévoux* (Geneva: Slatkine Reprints, 1969), p. 133. Also see Le Bruyn, *Travels*, II, pp. 13–14, 19–20. For

the theme of sculpture partially submerged in the site see Ernst Guldan, "Das Monster-Portal am Palazzo Zuccari in Rom," *Zeitschrift für Kunstgeschichte* 32, no. 3–4 (1969), 243–245; Körte, "Deinocrates," pp. 304–306.

12. Daemmrich, "Ruins Motif," Part II, p. 35; Ginsberg, "Aesthetic of Ruins," p. 90; Roland Mortier, " 'Sensibility,' 'Neoclassicism,' or 'Preromanticism,' " in *Eighteenth-Century Studies Presented to Arthur M. Wilson*, ed. Peter Gay (University Press of New England, 1972), p. 158; Carra, *Physique*, I, pp. 87–88; Van Tieghem, *Sentiment de la nature*, p. 195; Glacken, *Traces*, p. 119.

13. For a discussion of how, both in England and France, earlier material concepts were reified in the second half of the eighteenth century into "imponderables," and even Newton's theory of dynamic corpuscularity was reinterpreted to lessen its material and heighten its immaterial content, see Schofield, *Mechanism and Materialism*, pp. 162–169; Robert Darnton, *Mesmerism and the End of the Enlightenment in France* (Harvard University Press, 1968), pp. 2–45. For the most broad-based study devoted to one kind of "energy," see J. L. Heilbron, *Electricity in the 17th and 18th Centuries: A Study of Early Modern Physics* (University of California Press, 1979), pp. 436–448.

14. Snelders, "Romanticism and Naturphilosophie," p. 194; Dürler, *Bedeutung des Bergbaus*, pp. 91–93; Wolf von Engelhardt, "Schönheit im Reiche der Mineralien," *Jahrbuch für Ästhetik und Allgemeine Kunstwissenschaft* 4 (1958–59), 56–57. On the growing interest in mineralogy, not just in Germany but in France, marked by the introduction of a course on the topic by Buffon in 1745 at the Jardin du Roi and by the increasing number of major collections, see Kiernan, *Enlightenment and Science*, pp. 152–153.

15. Junius, *Painting of the Ancients*, pp. 94–96. Also see Seneca *De. Benef.* 4.7 and *Quaest. nat.* 2. 45; Pliny, *Nat. hist.* 1.7, 1. For several key post-antique treatises discussing the issue of natural markings see Giambattista della Porta, *Phytognomonica* (Naples: Apud Horatium Saluianum, 1588); Schott, *Physica curiosa*; Robert Boyle, *An Essay about the Origine & Virtues of Gems. Wherein Are Propos'd and Historically Illustrated Some Conjectures about the Consistence of the Matter of Precious Stones, and the Subjects wherein Their Chiefest Virtues Reside* (London: William Godbid, 1672); Philippo Bonanni, *Musaeum Kircherianum sive Musaeum A. P. Athanasio Kirchero in Collegio Romano Societatis Jesu jam pridem incoeptum nuper restitutum, auctum, descriptum, & Iconibus illustratum* (Rome: Typis Georgii Plachi Caelaturam Profitentis, & Characterum, 1709).

16. Louis Bourget, *Traité des pétrifications avec figures* (Paris: Briasson, 1742), pp. 54–55; Johann Jacob Scheuchzer, *Natur-Geschichte des Schweizerlandes, samt seinen Reisen über die Schweizerische Gebürge*, ed. Johann Georg Sulzer (Zurich: David Gessner, 1746), I, pp. 8–10; II, p. 127. A key figure in developing this surprisingly modern view appears to have been a prolific Roman physician and chemist, the Sieur de Colonna. See his *Histoire naturelle de l'univers*, II, pp. 300–319 passim. For his seminal influence see the tribute paid him by Antoine-Joseph Dézallier d'Argenville, *L'Histoire naturelle éclaircie dans une de ses parties principales, l'Oryctologie, qui traite des terres, des pierres, des métaux, des minéraux, et autres choses* (Paris: De Bure l'aîné, 1755), p. 29. Also see, for its discussion of fossil shells, his *La Conchyliologie, ou histoire naturelles des coquilles de mer, d'eau douce, terrestres et fossiles; avec un traité de la zoomorphose, ou représentation des animaux qui les habitent: Ouvrage dans lequel on trouve une nouvelle méthode de les diviser* (Paris: De Bure l'aîné, 1780), I, pp. 88–89. D'Argenville was the first Frenchman to offer a general history of the fossils of France. Also note Johann Friedrich Henckel, *Flora Saturnis; Die Verwandschaft des Pflanzen mit dem Mineral-Reich* (Leipzig: Johann Christian Martini, 1722), pp. 550–553.

17. Nicolson, *Mountain Gloom*, p. 148; *Breaking of the Circle*, pp. 143–145; Weise, "Vitalismo," part I, pp. 394–396; Jurgis Baltrušaitis, *Le moyen âge fantastique, antiquités et exotismes dans l'art gothique* (Paris: Armand Colin, 1955), p. 216; Heinrich Gerhard Franz, "Niederländische Landschaftsmaler im Künstlerkreis Rudolf II," *Uměni* 18 (1970), 224; Jacques Guillerme, "LeQueu et l'invention du mauvais goût," *Gazette des Beaux-Arts* 66 (September 1968), 161. The later eighteenth century replaced Palissy's hypothetical lapidary sap with the Newtonian "law" of elective affinity. See René-Just Haüy, *Traité de minéralogie* (Paris: Louis, 1801), I, p. 1.

18. Kircher, *Mundus subterraneus*, II, pls. 23, 24, 30–36. These ideas continued into the eighteenth century; see Sherwill, *Mont Blanc*, I, p. 83; *Voyages de Mr [Jean] Du Mont, en France, en Italie, en Allegmagne, à Malthe, et en Turquie. Contenant les recherches & observations curieuses qu'il a faites en tous ces païs: Tant sur les moeurs, les coütumes des peuples, leurs différens gouvernemens & leurs religions; Que sur l'histoire ancienne & moderne, la philosophie & les monumens antiques* (The Hague: Etienne Foulque & François L'Honoré, 1699), I, p. 27; Colonna, *Les secrets*, pp. 86–87, pls. pp. 112, 114; M. E. Bertrand, *Recueil de divers traités sur l'histoire naturelle de la terre et des fossiles* (Avignon: Louis Chambeau, 1766), pp. 152–153. It is significant that Agricola's *De Ortu et Causis subterraneorum* became the object of renewed attention

during the second half of the eighteenth century; see, for example, *Georg Agricola's aus Glauchau mineralogische Schriften, übersetzt und mit erläuternden Anmerkungen und Excursionen von Ernst Lehmann* (Freiburg: Craz und Gerlach, 1806–1812), I, pp. 201–209.

19. Bourguet, *Pétrifications*, pp. 56, 61; Perrault, *Origin of Springs*, pp. 35–37; Johann Georg Freüdenberg, *Dissert. physicomedica de Filtre Lapide* (Giessen: Typis Henningi Mülleri, 1702), pp. 13–15; Colonna, *Principes de la nature*, pp. 271–274. On the longevity of the idea that stones generate see Marjorie Nicolson and G. S. Rousseau, *"This Long Disease, My Life": Alexander Pope and the Sciences* (Princeton University Press, 1968), pp. 256–258.

20. Frézier, *Relation*, pp. 146–147; Robinet, *De la nature*, I, p. 203; Johannis Philippi Breynii, *Epistola de melonibus petrefactis Montis Carmel vulge creditis* (Leipzig: Literis Immanuelis Titii, 1722), pp. 9–11; Pitton de Tournefort, *Voyage du Levant*, I, pl. p. 190 and pp. 187–192; Robinet, *De la nature*, IV, p. 203; Laborde, *Espagne*, I, pp. 10–13; Lang, *Unterirdischen Wunder*, I, pl. p. 76 and pp. 43, 49, 76–77.

21. De l'Isle de Sales, *Philosophie de la nature*, II, pp. 411–413; Diderot, *Rêve de D'Alembert*, p. 59; Mercier, *Mon bonnet de nuit*, I, pp. 21–22; Robinet, *Considérations philosophiques*, pp. 6–7, 16–18, 59 and pl. 4, p. 54; *De la nature*, IV, pp. 21–26. On the importance of Robinet see Gode-von-Aesch, *Natural Science*, p. 141; A. J. L. Busst, "The Image of the Androgyne in the Nineteenth Century," in *Romantic Mythologies*, ed. Ian Fletcher (New York: Barnes & Noble, 1967), p. 2. The Pythagorean foundations of this theory can be found in book XV of Ovid's *Metamorphoses*. Here, the Samian philosopher expounds his doctrine of metempsychosis and decries the eating of animals: "All things are changing; nothing dies. The spirit wanders, comes now here, now there, and occupies whatever frame it pleases. From beasts it passes into human bodies, and from our bodies into beasts, but never perishes. . . . " [Ovid, *Metamorphoses*, tr. Frank Justus Miller (Harvard University Press, 1944), II, pp. 377, 391]. However, unlike eighteenth-century theorists, Pythagoras does not envisage the possibility of stones possessing a life of their own. "Slimy mud" contains seeds that produce "green frogs," i.e., animals higher than its inorganic self. See, for example, Bernardin de Saint-Pierre, *Voyage à l'Isle de France*, I, pp. 120–122 and pl. 3, p. 122.

22. *The Select Works of Antony van Leeuwenhoek, Containing His Microscopical Discoveries in Many of the Works of Nature*, tr. Samuel Hoole (London: Henry Fry, 1798), I, p. v; Jan Swammerdam, *Histoire générale des insectes. Ou l'on expose clairement la manière lente & pres'qu'insensible de l'accroissement de leurs membres, & ou l'on découvre evidemment l'erreur ou l'on tombe d'ordinaire au sujet de leur prétendue transformation* (Utrecht: Guillaume de Walcheren, 1682), p. 28. For the aesthetic ramifications of microscopic discoveries see the hand-colored copper plates illustrating Jacob Christian Schäffer's *Die Blumenpolypen der süssen Wasser beschrieben und mit den Blumenpolypen der salzigen Wasser verglichen* (Regensburg: Emanuel Adam Weiss, 1755), pls. I–III. Also see Vartanian, "Trembley's Polyp," in *Roots of Scientific Thought*, pp. 497–501; Bonnet, *Contemplation de la nature*, I, p. 221; Diderot, *Rêve de D'Alembert*, pp. 69–70. On the popularity of these ideas in English circles, see Peter S. Dance, *Shell Collecting, A History* (University of California Press, 1966), pp. 58–59. The Salons reflected this naturalist curiosity of the period in the *trompe-l'oeil* still-life paintings of Anne Vallayer-Coster and Antoine Berjon. See *French Painting, 1774–1830*, pp. 309–310, 615–617, 638–640.

23. La Pluche, *Spectacle de la nature*, III, p. 386; Eugène-Mélchior Patrin, *Histoire naturelle des minéraux* (Paris: Crapelet, An IX), III, pl. p. 280 and pp. 281–282.

24. Collier, *Cosmologies of Our Forefathers*, pp. 443–447; Ehrard, *Idée de la nature*, I, p. 201; "Le cabinet de Courtagnon, poëme," dédié à Madame la Douairière de Courtagnon, avec un discours préliminaire sur l'histoire naturelle *Dea Fossilea* de Champagne (Challons: Seneuze, 1763), pp. 15–16.

25. Linnaeus, *Reflections on the Study of Nature*, pp. 5–14.

26. Romé de l'Isle, *Cristallographie*, I, pp. xv–xvi; n. 20, p. 19; 106–109.

27. Jean-Claude de La Métherie, *Analyse des travaux sur les sciences naturelles pendant les années 1795, 1796 & 1797* (Paris: A. J. Dugour, 1798), pp. 77–78; Patrin, *Histoire naturelle*, II, pp. 203–205; Bachelard, *La terre et les rêveries de la volonté*, p. 282.

28. Romé de l'Isle, *Cristallographie*, I, n. 4, p. 24; A. G. Werner, *On the External Characters of Minerals*, tr. Albert V. Carozzi (University of Illinois Press, 1962), chapter 1. For a provocative discussion and critique of Werner's characterology see Déodat Guy Sylvain Tancrède de Gratet de Dolomieu, *Sur la philosophie minéralogique et sur l'espèce minéralogique par le citoyen . . . , membre de l'Institut National et un de professeurs-administrateurs du Jardin des Plantes* (Paris: Bossange, An 9), pp. 16–17, 37–41, 60. While praising Werner for introducing an analytical procedure into research concerning a mineral's properties, Dolomieu objects to his relating everything to external characters. The

Frenchman claims that the newly developing science of chemistry has come to the rescue of mineralogy, helping the researcher in his quest to discover the individual form of each species. Thus, Dolomieu is interested not in surface manifestations but in the fundamental chemical composition, "the characterizing causes" lurking in the interior of all crystals. The larger implication of this theory—namely, that the form or shape of any figured thing is due to the mutual attraction of its parts (affecting the smallest atoms as well as the largest bodies)—is discussed in Joseph Priestley's *Disquisitions Relating to Matter and Spirit. To which Is Added the History of the Philosophical Doctrine Concerning the Origin of the Soul, and the Nature of Matter; With Its Influence on Christianity; Especially with Respect to the Doctrine of the Pre-Existence of Christ* (London: J. Johnson, 1777), p. 5. In the German Romantic theory of the following generation, art—not matter—becomes that which is configured; see Karl Phillip Moritz, *Schriften zur Ästhetik und Poetik*, ed. Hans Joachim Schrimpf (Tübingen: Niemeyer, 1962), pp. 93–99.

29. Janson, " 'Image Made by Chance,' " p. 255; Pliny, *Natural History*, 36.5; 37.1; Faujas de Saint-Fond, *Essai de géologie*, II, pp. 178–182; Patrin, *Histoire naturelle*, I, pl. p. 101 and pp. 100–102; Jean-Fabien Gautier-D'Agoty, *Histoire naturelle ou exposition générale de toutes ses parties. Gravées et imprimées en couleurs naturelles; avec des notes historiques; Première partie: Règne minéral* (Paris: D'Agoty, 1781), pls. 11, 12, 16, 17, 27, 29, 30, 47, 65. The notes for the plates were provided by Romé de l'Isle. On the large and confusing Dagoty or D'Agoty family see E. Bénézit, *Dictionnaire des peintres, sculpteurs, dessinateurs, et graveurs* (1776), IV, 646–647. For a discussion of other French natural-history illustrators (e.g. Jean-Jacques de Boissieu and Delarue) working around 1767 on the *Minéralogie* section of the *Encyclopédie*, see Pascal de La Vaissière, "Un regain d'activité graphique de Philibert-Benôit Delarue. Une recherche d'Absolu," *Gazette des Beaux-Arts* 90 (October 1977), 120–121; "Paysagesistes et paysages voyageurs," p. 17. The British were also active as natural-history illustrators; see, in particular, Borlase, *Natural History of Cornwall*, pls. 15, 16, figs. 28, 29, 35, and pp. 121–122, 137. The leading German figure was the Nuremberg naturalist George Wolfgang Knorr; see his *Recueil de monumens des catastrophes que le globe de la terre a essuiées, contenant des pétrifications dessinées, gravées, et enluminées, d'après les originaux commencé par . . . , et continué par ses hérétiers avec l'histoire naturelle de ces corps* (Nuremberg, 1768–1775), especially I, pp. 44, 55.

30. Samuel Simon Witte, *Über den Ursprung der Pyramiden in Egypten und der Ruinen von Persepolis, ein neuer Versuch*

(Leigzig: J. G. Müllerischen Buchhandlung, 1789), pp. 21–27. That Witte's ideas enjoyed considerable currency is proved by Alexander von Humboldt's lengthy refutation of them in *Zerstreute Bemerkungen über den Basalt*, p. 38. Also see Hamilton, *Campi Phlegraei*, II, pl. 46.

31. For a brilliant analysis of Cozens's aesthetic see Jean-Claude Lebensztejn, "En blanc et noir," *Macula* 1 (1977), 4–13. On a literary parallel, an interest in the physical facts of language (punctuation, blanks, typography), see Roger B. Moss, "Sterne's Punctuation," *Eighteenth-Century Studies* 15 (winter 1981–82), 179–200. The text of *A New Method of Assisting the Invention in Drawing Original Composition of Landscape* is reproduced in A. P. Oppé's *Alexander and Robert Cozens* (London: Black, 1952): "A true blot is an assemblage of dark shapes made with ink upon a piece of paper, and likewise of light ones produced by the paper being left alone. All the shapes are rude and unmeaning, as they are formed with the swiftest hand. But at the same time there appears a general disposition of the masses, producing one comprehensive form, which may be conceived and purposely intended before the blot is begun. . . . " (p. 2)

32. *Narrative of A. Gordon Pym*, in *The Complete Tales and Poems of Edgar Allan Poe (1809–1849)* (New York: Vintage, 1975), p. 873. John Irwin, in his *American Hieroglyphics, The Symbol of the Egyptian Hieroglyphics in the American Renaissance* (Yale University Press, 1980), does not seem to be aware of the eighteenth-century tradition that matter writes its own history. (See Irwin, pp. 167–177.)

33. Gary Shapiro, "Intention and Interpretation in Art: A Semiotic Analysis," *Journal of Aesthetics and Art Criticism* 33 (fall 1974), 33–34, 38–39; J. H. Lambert, *Anlage zur Architectonic, oder Theorie des Einfachen und des Ersten in der philosophischen und mathematischen Erkenntniss* (Riga: Johann Friedrich Hartknoch), II, pp. 276–277; Wilhelm Mrazek, "Metaphorische Denkform und Ikonologische Stilform. Zur Grammatik und Syntax bildlicher Formelelemente der Barockkunst," *Alte und Moderne Kunst* 9 (March–April 1964), 15, 21–23; and Joseph H. Summers, "The Poem as Hieroglyph," in *Seventeenth-Century English Poetry: Modern Essays in Criticism*, ed. William R. Keast (Oxford University Press, 1962), pp. 215–216.

34. Coleman, "Idea of Character," pp. 23, 26, 30, 36, 40. On the distinction between seventeenth- and eighteenth-century language schemes see Murray Cohen, *Sensible Words: Linguistic Practice in England, 1640–1785* (Johns Hopkins University Press, 1977), pp. 60–69; 80 ff.; James Knowlson, *Universal Language Schemes in England and France, 1600–1800* (University of Toronto Press, 1975), pp. 139 ff. By the

late eighteenth century the image of "writing" had expanded until all physical shapes became dimly meaningful forms of script, and each of these forms (physiognomics, botany, mineralogy, or geology) had its own science of decipherment.

35. Marianne Thalmann, *Zeichensprache der Romantik* (Heidelberg: L. Stiehm, 1967), pp. 27–30; Ludwig Volkmann, "Die Hieroglyphen der Deutschen Romantiker," *Münchner Jahrbuch der Bildenden Kunst*, N.F., 3 (1926), 174–178.

36. Jones, *Ancients and Moderns*, pp. 49, 57; Leeuwen, *Problem of Certainty*, pp. 49–56; Williamson, *Senecan Amble*, pp. 154–158; Francis Bacon, *Advancement of Learning, Novum Organum, New Atlantis* (Chicago: Encyclopaedia Britannica, 1952), pp. 12, 16.

37. William Warburton, *The Divine Legation of Moses Demonstrated (1741)* (New York: Garland, 1978), II, pp. 65–167 passim. On the traditional allegorical and emblematic role played by Egyptian hieroglyphics—especially in Renaissance art and Humanism since the fourteenth century—see Karl Giehlow, "Die Hieroglyphenkunde des Humanismus in der Allegorie der Renaissance besonders der Ehrenpforte Kaisers Maximilian I; mit einem Nachwort von Arpad Weixlgärtner," *Jahrbuch der Kunsthistorischen Sammlungen des Allerhöchsten Kaiserhauses Wien*, 32, no. 1 (1915), 1–232. Also see Clifton Cherpack, "Warburton and Some Aspects of the Search for the Primitive in Eighteenth-Century France," *Philological Quarterly* 36 (April 1957), 221–231 passim; Derrida, *De la grammatologie*, pp. 398–402, 408. On the interest of European *savants* in pictograms, at least since the early seventeenth century, and their reproduction in travel literature, see Rüdiger Joppien, "Etude de quelques portraits ethnologiques dans l'oeuvre d'André Thevet," *Gazette des Beaux-Arts* 89 (April 1978), 132. Also see Etienne Bonnot de Condillac, *Oeuvres philosophiques*, ed. Georges Le Roy, in *Corpus Général des philosophes français* (Paris: Presses Universitaires de France, 1974), I, 61–64.

38. Antoine Court de Gebelin, *Monde primitif, analysé et comparé avec le monde moderne, considéré dans son génie allégorique et dans les allégories auxquelles conduisit ce génie* (Paris: Court de Gebelin, 1773–1782), I, pp. 11–13; III, pls. 4, 5. On the significance of Court's views of the primitive world and his idea that the subjects of mythology were personifications of natural objects, see Le Flamanc, *Les utopies prérévolutionaire*, pp. 101–103, 115–116, 157–159, n. 1, p. 83; Guitton, *Jacques Delille*, pp. 415–416; Piper, *Active Universe*, p. 139; Rehder, *Unendlichen Landschaft*, p. 44. Athanasius Kircher is Court's most notable intellectual precursor. See *Oedipus Aegyptiacus* (Rome: Vitalis Mascardi,

1652–1654), II, p. 106; *Turris Babel sive Archontologia* (Amsterdam: Janssonie-Waesbergiana, 1679), p. 177; *China Monumentis*, p. 227.

39. Arthur H. Scouten, Review of *Vico and Herder: Two Studies in the History of Ideas* by Isaiah Berlin, *Comparative Literature Studies* 15 (1978), 336–340; Patrick Hutton, "The New Science of Giambattista Vico: Historicism in Its Relation to Poetics," *Journal of Aesthetics and Art Criticism* 30 (spring 1972), 361–363. On the idea that mythology is a work of art produced by nature see Wolfgang Kayser, *The Grotesque in Art and Literature*, tr. Ulrich Weisstein (New York: McGraw-Hill, 1963), p. 50.

40. Paulson, *Emblem and Expression*, pp. 91–92; Terence Doherty, *The Anatomical Works of George Stubbs* (Boston: Godine, 1974); C. Neue, "Dog beneath the Skin: Stubbs' Dog Portraits," *Country Life* 157 (February 6, 1975), 314–315; Valenciennes, *Eléments de perspective*, p. 223; *Les carnets de David d'Angers*, ed. André Bruel (Paris: Plon, 1958), II, pp. 274–275, 335.

41. Rehder, *Unendlichen Landschaft*, p. 179; Annedore Müller-Hofstede, *Der Landschaftsmaler Pascha Johann Friedrich Weitsch (1723–1803)* (Braunschweig: Waisenhausbuchdrückerei und Verlag, 1973), pp. 133–136.

42. Piggott, *Druids*, pp. 156–158, 168–170; Borlase, *Antiquities of Cornwall*, pp. 172, 160.

43. Paul Shepherd, Jr., "The Cross Valley Syndrome," *Landscape* 10 (spring 1961), 4–5; "Formes singulières des rochers," *Magasin Pittoresque* 46 (1840), 363–366. For the application of the concept of physiognomics to land masses see Patterson, *Poetic Genius*, pp. 50–51; Gode-von-Aesch, *Natural Science*, p. 239; Rehder, *Unendlichen Landschaft*, pp. 38–39, 107; Broc, *Les montagnes*, p. 56; Dürler, *Bedeutung des Bergbaus*, p. 84; Alfred G. Roth, *Die Gestirne in der Landschaftsmalerei des Abendlandes* ed. Hans R. Hahnloser (Bern-Bümpliz: Benteli, 1945), p. 83.

44. Bourrit, *Mont-Blanc*, p. 142; Laborde, *Tableaux de la Suisse*, I, p. lv; Raoul-Rochette, *Lettres sur la Suisse*, I, part 2, p. 28; II, part 4, p. 40; Wetzel, *Lac de Suisse*, I, p. 30; Macartney, *Embassy to China*, II, p. 205; Bernardin de Saint-Pierre, *Etudes de la nature*, in *Oeuvres*, V, p. 96.

45. Forster, *Voyage round the World*, I, p. 453; Faujas de Saint-Fond, *Essai de géologie*, II, pp. 2–3; Samuel Georg Gmelins, *Reise durch Russland zur Untersuchung der drey Natur-Reiche. Reise von St. Petersburg biss nach Ischerkask, der Hauptstadt der Donsichen Kosacken in den Jahren 1768 und 1769* (St. Petersburg: Kayserliche Akademie der Wissenschaft, 1770–1774), II, p. 12; "Petrifications de Chiramyn en Perse,"

NOTES

Journal des Voyages de Découvertes, I
(1819), 197; Cook, *Voyage*, II, p. 485; Forster, *Observations*, p. 19.

46. Edy, *Norway*, I, pl. 23; Kotzebue, *Voyage of Discovery*, II, p. 404.

47. Burke, *Sublime and Beautiful*, part II,
section v, p. 72; Gotthilf Heinrich Schubert, *Ansichten von der Nachtseite der Naturwissenschaft* (Darmstadt: Wissenschaftliche
Buchgesellschaft, 1967), pp. 191–192;
Romé de l'Isle, *Cristallographie*, I, p. ix.
The mineralogist and the geologist, in
probing the "osteology" of rocks, bor-
rowed vocabulary and method from their
fellow scientists in the disciplines of anatomy and biology; see Toby Gelfand, "The
Paris Manner of Dissection: Student Anatomical Dissection in Early Eighteenth-
Century Paris," *Bulletin of the History of
Medicine* 46 (1972), 99–130 passim; William Le Fanu, "Natural History Drawings
Collected by John Hunter F.R.S.
(1728–1793) at the Royal College of Sur-
geons of England," *Journal of the Society
for the Bibliography of Natural History*
(Great Britain) 8, no. 4 (1978), 319–333.

48. Shepherd, "Cross Valley Syndrome,"
p. 708; Yi-Fu Tuan, *Topophilia, A Study of
Environmental Perception, Attitudes, and
Values* (Englewood Cliffs, N.J.: Prentice-
Hall, 1974), pp. 27–29; *Carnets de David
d'Angers*, II, p. 15; I, p. 24.

49. Jürgen Paul, "Die Kunstanschauung
John Ruskins," in *Theorie der Künste*, I,
p. 292; Levere, "Rich Economy of Nature,"
and Bruce Johnson, " 'The Perfection of
the Species' and Hardy's Tess," in *Nature
and Victorian Imagination*, pp. 191,
259–261. Ruskin's persuasion was not the
only one, however. The nineteenth-
century view of the scientist as amoral pe-
netrater (replete with sexual overtones) of
the mysteries of nature is embodied in the
account of Victor Frankenstein's study of
chemistry at Ingolstadt. See Mary Wollstonecraft Shelley, *Frankenstein or the Modern Promotheus* (New York: Harrison Smith
and Robert Haas, 1934; first published in
1817), pp. 41–42.

50. Foucault, *Birth of the Clinic*, pp. 88–90,
135–137, 162–169.

51. Herder, *Erkennen und Empfinden*, in
Werke, I, p. 145; Chenier, *Oeuvres poétiques*, II, pp. 67–68.

52. Gerard, *Genius*, pp. 322–323; Duff,
Original Genius, p. 35.

53. Bate, "Sympathetic Imagination," pp.
144, 147–149. On the French tradition of
absorption, from Diderot to Courbet, see
Michael Fried, *Absorption and Theatricality:
Painting and Beholder in the Age of Diderot*
(University of California Press, 1980),
chapter 1, "The Primacy of Absorption."
Although Fried discusses paintings rather

than natural objects and is exclusively concerned with developments in France beginning at mid-century, the phenomenon of
rapt attention (which he identifies in the
paintings of Chardin, Greuze, Vien, and
Carlo van Loo) can be transposed to the
oubli de soi that characterizes an international "style" of scientific observation of
nature. Nevertheless, Fried's analysis,
which extends to considerations of reverie
and dreams, seems to have more in common with the ideas put forth in John Baillie's 1747 discussion of the sublime. In this
treatise Samuel Monk locates the crucial
transitional moment when speculation
withdrew from the search for sublimity in
the object and began to be centered in the
emotions of the subject. My use of the
term *absorption* is, by contrast, centrifu-
gally oriented. See Thomas Weiskel, *The
Romantic Sublime: Studies in the Structure
and Psychology of Transcendence* (Johns
Hopkins University Press, 1976), p. 14.

54. Bate, "Sympathetic Imagination," pp.
161–162; Biese, *Naturgefühl*, p. 143; Stafford, "Beauty of the Invisible," n. 106, p.
73.

55. Daniell, *Oriental Scenery*, II, part IV, pl.
X; Maurice Shellim, *The Daniells in India
and the Waterfall at Papanasam* (Calcutta:
The Statesman Ltd., 1970), pp. 9–10; Si-
ren, *China and Gardens of Europe*, p. iv;
Beurdeley, *Castiglione*, p. 138.

56. Forster, *Ein Blick*, pp. 49–53; Takeuchi,
"Schönheit des Unbelebten," p. 669; Carr,
"Pygmalion and *Philosophes*," p. 255; Gaston Bachelard, *La terre et les rêveries du répos* (Paris: José Corti, 1948), pp. 77–11.

57. Bachelard, *La terre et rêveries de la volonté*, pp. 32–33; James Hakewell, *A Picturesque Tour of the Island of Jamaica, from
Drawings Made in the Years 1820 and 1821
by . . . Author of "The Picturesque Tour of Italy"* (London: Hurst and Robinson, 1825),
p. 3; Glacken, *Traces*, p. 391. I have altered Ruskin's terms *Imagination Associative* and *Imagination Penetrative* to fit the
late-eighteenth-century aesthetic of discovery. See Piper, *Active Universe*, pp.
215–220.

58. P. L. M. de Maupertuis, *Lettre sur le
progrès des sciences* (1752), pp. 53–54; Mercier, *Mon bonnet de nuit*, I, p. 22. On the
topic of subterranean geography, also see
Jean-Claude-Izouard Delisle de Sales, *Histoire philosophique du monde primitif (1780)*,
fourth revised edition (Paris: Didot l'Aîné,
1793), I, pp. 39–46. This popular study
contains 30 plates taken from Faujas de
Saint-Fond, Saint-Non, Pennant, Palissy,
Court de Gebelin, and Knorr.

59. Jean-Jacques Rousseau, *Les rêveries du
promeneur solitaire* (Paris: Bibliothèque Indépendante d'Édition, 1905), pp. 255–256;
Christophe Traugott Delius, *Anleitung zu
der Bergbaukunst nach Ihrer Theorie und*

Ausübung, nebst einer Abhandlung von den Grundsätzen der Bergkammerwissenschaft (Vienna: Joh. Thomas Edlen v. Tratternern, 1773), pp. 1–2. Unlike Werner, Delius espoused a matrix theory of minerals, that is, one according to which the earth contains the fundamental matter of all minerals within the cores of mountains. See Dürler, Bedeutung des Bergbaus, pp. 19–24. This literature should be distinguished from more technology-oriented treatises whose illustrations focus on mining equipment and distilling and metal-refining processes. See, for example, Lazarum Ercker, Aula subterranea Domina dominantium subdita subditorum. Das ist: Untererdische Ofhaltung ohne Welche weder die Herren regiren/noch die Unterthanen gehorchen können. Oder gründliche Beschreibung derjenigen Sachen/ so in der Tiefe der Erde wachsen/ als aller Ertzen der königlichen und gemeinen Metallen/ auch fürnehmster Mineralien/ durch Welche/ nächst Gott/ alle Künste/ Übungen und Stände der Welt gehandhabet und erhalten werden/ . . . (Frankfurt: Johann David Sunners and Johannes Haass, 1684), frontispiece.

60. Eugenio Battisti, "Natura Artificiosa to Natura Artificialis," in The Italian Garden, ed. David Coffin (Washington, D.C.: Dumbarton Oaks, 1972), pp. 30–32; Claudia Lazzaro-Bruno, The Villa Lante at Bagnaia, Ph.D. diss., Princeton University, 1974, pp. 195–196; Kris, "Stil 'rustique,'" pp. 200–201.

61. Leyden, Discoveries and Travels in Africa, II, p. 372; Pitton de Tournefort, Voyage du Levant, I, "Éloge."

62. Bonnet, Contemplation de la nature, I, p. 232; Saussure, Voyage dans les Alps, I, pp. ii–iv.

63. La Pérouse, Voyage autour du monde, II, p. 109; D'Entrecasteaux, Voyage, I, p. x. Also see Sauer, Geological and Astronomical Expedition to North Russia, p. 230.

64. Bailly, Discours et mémoires, I, pp. 322–323; Broc, La géographie des philosophes, pp. 298–299, 304–305, 311. For a "Romantic" "seeker after images" like Chateaubriand, the desire to penetrate took on a more personal quality: the wish to insinuate himself into the presence of a place. See Paul Viallaneix, "Chateaubriand voyageur," in Approaches des Lumières, pp. 564–565; Clarence J. Glacken, "On Chateaubriand's Journey from Paris to Jerusalem, 1806–07," in The Terraqueos Globe: The History of Geography and Cartography (Los Angeles: William Andrews Clark Memorial Library, 1969), p. 50.

65. Broc, Les montagnes, pp. 19–20, 65; La géographie des philosophes, pp. 314–315.

66. W. B. Carnochan, Confinement and Flight: An Essay on English Literature of the Eighteenth Century (University of California Press, 1977), p. 103. The desire to immerse oneself in the atmosphere should be related to the ancient conception of the feminine nature of the air (Plato, Empedocles, Cicero). In post-classical times, the air was deemed feminine less for the attractive reason of its virginity than for its unpredictability, sudden changes of mood, and liability to storms. Thus, the mixed nature of the atmosphere suggested the duality of virgin and whore. See Clive Hart, "Flight in the Renaissance," Explorations in Renaissance Culture 5 (1979), 20–32.

67. Bertholon, Avantages des globes aérostatiques, pp. 36–37; de Villers, Le Camus, and Le Fevre, Dissertation sur le fluide. Principe de l'ascension des aérostats de MM. Montgolfier (Paris, 1784), p. 19.

68. Rouland, Propriétés de l'air, p. 311; Monge, Cassini, and Bertholon, Dictionnaire de physique, I, p. 223.

69. Faujas de Saint-Fond, La machine aérostatique, I, p. 199. As late as Monck Mason's 1837 History of Aerostation (cited in Turnor, Astra Castra, p. 368) there was still discussion about the peculiarities of a medium into which the balloonist was about to "intrude." For a modern analysis of the euphoria associated with such an "aerial vision," see Roland Barthes, The Eiffel Tower and Other Mythologies, tr. Richard Howard (New York: Hill and Wang, 1979).

70. "Particulars of the Parachute, with a Circumstantial Account of Mr. Garnerin's Ascent in the Balloon, and His Descent in the Parachute, on Tuesday, September 21, 1802," European Magazine 44 (1802), 515. Also see aquatint by Simon Petit, Expérience du parachute (October 22, 1797). That this immersion in air fostered the infant science of meteorology from 1783 onward is attested to by Tissandier, Simples notions, pp. 66–67.

71. Kotzebue, Voyage of Discovery, III, p. 261; Martha Noel, "Le thème de l'eau chez Senancour," Revue des Sciences Humaines 107 (July–September 1962), 361–363; MacKenzie, Iceland, pl. p. 119. Also see "Les geysers, sources d'eau bouillante en Islande," Magasin Pittoresque 28 (1833), 224.

72. Jean-Claude-Richard, Abbé de Saint-Non, Voyages pittoresque ou description des royaumes de Naples et de Sicile (Paris, 1781–1786), I, p. 181. For the rare subject in art of Empedocles leaping into the active volcano, see Michael Kitson, Salvator Rosa (London: Arts Council of Great Britain, 1973), catalog 44, pl. 35 and p. 36.

73. Hamilton, Supplement to Campi Phlegraei, pp. 3–4; Campi Phlegraei, II, pls. 9, 10; Houel, Voyage, I, II, pl. 123 and p. 105. For the persistence of this tradition note the description by Eugène Robert, geolo-

gist on France's monumental expedition to Iceland and Greenland, of the ancient currents of lava that had flowed from the magnificent Klofa-Jökull. In striding across Iceland he wades "through plains of animated scoriae." See Gaimard, *Voyage en Islande; Histoire du voyage*, II, p. 237.

74. Forster, *Voyage round the World*, I, pp. 191–192; Lesseps, *Journal historique*, I, pp. 72–73.

75. Revello, *Expedicion Malaspina*, pls. 44, 45 and p. 89; Morse, *Malaspina Letters*, pp. 22–25; *The Malaspina Expedition: "In the Pursuit of Knowledge . . ."* (Santa Fe: Museum of New Mexico Press, 1977), pp. 4–10; Otto von Kotzebue, *Entdeckungs-Reise in die Süd-See, und nach der Berings-Strasse* (Weimar: Gebr. Hoffmann, 1821), I, pp. 145, 147; Franklin, *Second Journey to Polar Sea*, pl. p. 171 and pp. 169–170. Also see Gaimard, *Islande et Greenland*, II, pl. 137: "La Corvette *La Recherche* au milieu des glaces."

76. George Adams, *Lectures on Natural and Experimental Philosophy, Considered in Its Present State of Improvement* (London: R. Hindmarsh, 1794), V, pp. 462–465.

77. Bernardin de Saint-Pierre, *Harmonies de la nature*, in *Oeuvres*, IX–X, pp. 74–75; Macaulay, *Pleasure of Ruins*, pp. 229–230; Forbes, *Oriental Memoirs*, p. 311.

78. Pococke, *Description of the East*, II, part I, p. 36; Jean Chappe d'Auteroche, *Voyage en Californie pour l'observation du passage de Vénus sur le disque du soleil, le 3 juin 1769; contenant les observations de ce phénomène, & la description historique de la route de l'auteur à travers le Mexique*, ed. Jean-Dominique Cassini (Paris: Charles-Antoine Jombert, 1772), pp. 13–14; Sparrman, *Cape of Good Hope*, I, pp. 4, 6; Milbert, *Ile de France*, I, pp. 111–112. For a good contemporary survey of the varieties of phosphorescence see Joseph Placidus Heinrich, *Die Phosphorescenz der Körper oder die Dunkeln bemerkbaren Lichtphänomene der anorganischen Natur* (Nuremberg: Johann Leonhard Schrag'schen Buchhandlung, 1811).

79. Carver, *North-America*, pp. 48, 132–133; Milbert, *Hudson*, I, p. 127; Houel, *Voyage*, III, pp. 67–68.

80. Salt, *Abyssinia*, pl. p. 357 and pp. 354–356.

81. Jackson, *Marocco*, p. ix; *Timbuctoo*, p. ix; *Proceedings of the Association for Promoting the Discovery of the Interior Parts of Africa* (London: C. Macrae, 1790), pp. 3, 6–8.

82. Saugnier, *Relations*, p. ii; Grandpré, *Afrique*, I, p. iii; Leyden, *Discoveries and Travels*, I, pp. 397–398; Philip Beaver, *African Memoranda: Relative to an Attempt to* establish a British Settlement on the Island of Bulama on the Western Coast of Africa, in the Year 1792. With a Brief Notice of the Neighbouring Tribes, Soil, Productions, etc., and Some Observations on the Facility of Colonizing That Part of Africa, with a View to Cultivation; and the Introduction of Letters and Religion to Its Inhabitants; but more particularly as the Means of Gradually Abolishing African Slavery *(London: C. and R. Baldwin, 1805), p. iii; Mollien, *Interior of Africa*, pp. v, 1; T. Edward Bowditch, *Mission from Cape Coast Castle to Ashantee, with a Statistical Account of That Kingdom, and Geographical Notices of Other Parts of the Interior of Africa* (London: John Murray, 1819), p. 5.

83. Leyden, *Discoveries and Travels*, II, pp. 365–370, 312–321; Beechey, *Northern Coast of Africa*, p. v; Thomas Legh, *Narrative of a Journey in Egypt and the Country beyond the Cataracts* (London: John Murray, 1816), pp. vi–vii; Burckhardt, *Nubia*, p. xlix.

84. *The Narrative of the Honourable John Byron (Commodore in a Late Expedition round the World) Containing an Account of the Great Distresses Suffered by Himself and His Companions on the Coast of Patagonia, from the Year 1740, till Their Arrival in England, in 1746, with a Description of St. Jago de Chile* (London: S. Baker and G. Legh and T. Davies, 1768), p. iii; *Supplément au voyage de Bougainville*, p. 258.

85. Forster, *Voyage round the World*, I, p. 197; Oxley, *Journals of Two Expeditions*, pp. vii–ix; Lycett, *Australia*, p. 4.

86. Forster, *Voyage round the World*, I, pp. 567, 269; Cook, *Voyage*, I, pp. xi, lx.

87. MacKenzie, *Montreal*, p. iv; Milbert, *Hudson*, I, p. viii; Samuel Davis, *Views in Bootan: From the Drawings of . . . by William Daniell* (London, 1813), letterpress; "Antiquités trouvés dans l'île de Java," *Journal des Voyages de Découvertes* 3 (1819), 373; Arago, *Voyage round the World*, I, p. 280; James Johnson, *N° 1 of a Series of Views in the West Indies: Engraved from Drawings Taken recently in the Islands: With Letter Press Explanations Made from Actual Observations* (London: Underwood, 1827), plate "View in the Tortola from Ruthy Hills," letterpress.

88. Cook, *Voyage*, I, p. lx.

89. Arthos, *Language of Natural Description*, p. 64; Peter Hughes, "Language, History & Vision: An Approach to Eighteenth-Century Literature," in *Varied Pattern*, pp. 83, 91.

90. Forster, *Ein Blick*, p. 54; Cassas, *Istrie et Dalmatie*, pl. 30 and p. 107; Lewis and Clark, *History of Expedition*, I, pp. 263, 310; Vidal, *Buenos Ayres*, p. 100.

Chapter 5

91. Brydone, *Sicily and Malta*, I, p. 174; Houel, *Voyage*, I, pl. 62 and p. 115. On the eternal metamorphosis of matter see Houel's description of a voyage to the summit of Mt. Etna (II, p. 100).

92. Faujas de Saint-Fond, *Volcans éteints*, pls. 2, 11 and pp. 271, 300; *Essai de géologie*, III, pl. 25 and pp. 412–415; Borlase, *Natural History of Cornwall*, pl. 13 and pp. 125–127.

93. J. F. Henckel, *Unterricht von der Mineralogie oder Wissenschaft von Wassern, Erdsäfften, Sältzen, Erden, Steinen und Ertzen* (Dresden: Joh. Nicol Gerlachen, 1747), pp. 32–33; Bourguet, *Pétrifications*, p. 32; Romé de l'Isle, *Cristallographie*, I, pp. 6–7; Daniell, *Staffa*, pp. 7–9; *Animated Nature*, I, pl. 24.

94. Edy, *Norway*, I, pl. 1 and letterpress; "Action destructive de l'océan," *Magasin Pittoresque* 16 (1836), pl. p. 44; "Changemens de forme des continens," ibid. 15 (1835), 115; Barrow, *South Africa*, I, pp. 34–35.

95. Kendrick, *Lisbon Earthquake*, pp. 112, 118–124; Le Flamanc, *Les utopies prérévolutionnaire*, p. 66; Henry F. Majewski, "Mercier and the Preromantic Myth of the End of the World," *Studies in Romanticism* 7 (autumn 1967), 1–2. For an early appreciation of "the incessant changes of this earth's surface," see Shaftesbury, *The Moralists*, part III, section i, pp. 122–123. For a modern assessment of how the descriptive sciences of the later eighteenth century—especially geology—were continually revolutionizing their basic conceptions on the basis of scrutiny of actual earth events, see Charles Coulston Gillispie, *Genesis and Geology. The Impact of Scientific Discoveries upon Religious Beliefs in the Decades before Darwin. A Study in the Relations of Scientific Thought, Natural Theology, and Social Opinion in Great Britain, 1790–1850* (New York: Harper, 1959), pp. 41–72, 98–120 passim; *The Edge of Objectivity: An Essay in the History of Scientific Ideas* (Princeton University Press, 1960), pp. 260–302 passim. On the long-standing association of vehemence and impetuosity with the word *violence*, see Williams, *Keywords*, pp. 278–279.

96. This premise should be related to the late-eighteenth-century idea that in the history of language is history itself. See Cohen, *Sensible Words*, pp. 122–127; Arthur O. Lovejoy, *A Documentary History of Primitivism and Related Ideas* (Baltimore: Johns Hopkins University Press, 1935), I, pp. 103–117; " 'Nature' as Aesthetic Norm," *Modern Language Notes* 42 (1927), 444–450.

97. Eisenstein, *Printing Press*, I, pp. 272–284. Also see Uwe Japp, "Aufgeklärtes Europa und natürliche Südsee. Georg Forster's *Reise um die Welt*," in *Reise und Utopie. Zur Literatur der Spätaufklärung*, ed. Hans Joachim Piechotta (Frankfurt-am-Main: Suhrkamp, 1976), pp. 14–30. Japp takes up the issue of the polarization between reason and nature during the Enlightenment, the perception of civilization as "denaturing," and the attendant difficulties this brought for the observation and description of alien settings.

1. See Mandeville, *Treatise of Hypochondriac*, p. 232; Forster, *Voyage round the World*, I, p. iv. The chief modern student of art and perception is Sir Ernst Gombrich. See, in particular, his *Art and Illusion: A Study in the Psychology of Pictorial Representation* (New York: Pantheon, 1961), chapter 4, and *The Sense of Order: A Study in the Psychology of Decorative Art* (Ithaca, N.Y.: Cornell University Press, 1979), introduction. In both these chapters Gombrich discusses—from a Neo-Positivist and anti-Hegelian vantage—the nature of "realistic" representations. The latter book recapitulates the arguments of the former and brings them up to date. He reasserts his fundamental premise that man tends to probe the real world and make representations with a hypothesis of regularity in mind. This hypothesis is not abandoned unless refuted; thus, making comes before matching—that is, seeking precedes seeing. Consequently, a schema is constructed before one matches it against reality. For a subtle analysis of what is a genuinely "historical" conception of "reality" and a comparison of Gombrich's and Auerbach's divergent views, see Hayden White, *Metahistory: The Historical Imagination in Nineteenth-Century Europe* (Johns Hopkins University Press, 1973), pp. 3 ff.

2. Gombrich, *Sense of Order*, p. 105. Also see I-Fu Tuan, *Topophila: Study of Environmental Perception, Attitudes, and Values* (Englewood Cliffs, N.J.: Prentice-Hall, 1974), pp. 59 ff., for a discussion of "Culture, Experience, and Environmental Attitudes."

3. Jean Babelon, "Découverte de monde et littérature," *Comparative Literature* 2 (spring 1950), 166; Moore, *Backgrounds of English Literature*, p. 71. Also see the sociological study by Hugh Allen West, *From Tahiti to Terror: George Forster, the Literature of Travel, and Social Thought in the Late 18th Century*, Ph.D. diss., Stanford University, 1980, pp. 84–105. West discusses how private ambition and scientific aspirations were inextricably tangled in Forster's intellectual and political career. From the larger perspective of the historian of science of the Enlightenment, see Charles Coulston Gillispie, *Science and Polity in France at the End of the Old Regime* (Princeton University Press, 1980), pp. 77–78. Gillispie discusses the dual imperative that motivates scientific discoverers (but which might be extended to embrace discoverers of all classes), namely, the absorption in the study of nature for

NOTES

its own sake and for the good of humanity and the premium the entire scientific enterprise places on originality.

4. Forster, *Voyage round the World*, I, pp. viii–ix, 125, 244–245, 117, 104–105, 250.

5. Arago, *Voyage round the World*, I, p. 211; Porter, *Russia and Sweden*, II, p. 31; Landmann, *Portugal*, II, pl. p. 62 and p. 63; Belzoni, *Narrative*, p. 109.

6. Concerning a "psychological scenery," see Hunt, *Figure in the Landscape*, pp. 175–180; Broc, *Géographie des philosophes*, p. 219; Lambert, *Anlage zur Architectonic*, I, p. 372.

7. Moore, *Backgrounds in English Literature*, pp. 219–220, 226–229; Rouland, *Phénomènes de l'air*, p. 86.

8. Forster, *Voyage round the World*, I, p. xii–xiii.

9. Auerbach, *Mimesis*, pp. 307–310, 321–322.

10. Appleton, *Experience of Landscape*, p. 127; Giulio Carlo Argan, "Lo Spazio 'oggetivo' nella pittura Inglese dell Settecento: La teorica del Pittoresco," in *Sensibilità e Razionalità*, pp. 305–306; Ozouf, *La fête révolutionnaire*, p. 150; Atkinson, *Relations de voyages*, p. 3. Some modern anthropoligists and linguists have argued that a binary organization of experience (the structuring of language and the ordering of space on the analogy of up-down, front-back, night-day, left-right) is an intrinsic part of human perception. See Roman Jakobson and Morris Halle, *Fundamentals of Language* (The Hague: Mouton, 1956), pp. 44–49; Claude Lévi-Strauss, *The Raw and the Cooked* (New York: Harper and Row, 1969).

11. Weiskel, *Romantic Sublime*, pp. 4–5, 19–21; Karl Viëtor, "De Sublimitate," *Harvard Studies and Notes in Philology and Literature* 19 (1937), 268–274. On the long rhetorical tradition behind such counterpositions see David Summers, "Contrapposto: Style and Meaning in Renaissance Art," *Art Bulletin* 59 (September 1977), 360.

12. Guitton, *Jacques Delille*, p. 111; Pitton de Tournefort, *Voyage du Levant*, I, pl. p. 190 and pp. 189–191; Boisgelin de Kerdu, *Denmark and Sweden*, II, pp. 203–205. The royal imprimatur was placed on such ventures by Peter the Great, who descended into German mines, and by Gustave III, who explored Sweden's mines and was commemorated in the act in a series of aquatints by Elias Martin (1739–1818). See *La gravure en Suède*, exhibition at Bibliothèque Nationale (Paris, 1980); Per Bjurström, "La gravure en Suède," *Nouvelles de l'Estampe* 51 (May–June 1980), 10–11. Concerning the late-eighteenth-century quest after the prototype, or fundamental form of all organisms, hidden beneath the confusing miscellany of surface traits, see Bettex, *Discovery of Nature*, p. 168; Dürler, *Bedeutung des Bergbaus*, pp. 108, 122–123. That caves, chasms, ravines—any orifice that allows someone to enter physically into the fabric of the earth—are potent refuge symbols is a point made by Appleton, *Experience of Landscape*, p. 103.

13. Lycett, *Australia*, pl. 23 and letterpress; Turnor, *Astra Castra*, p. 356.

14. Bachelard, *La terre et les rêveries de la volonté*, pp. 357–359; Belzoni, *Narrative*, pp. 156–157; De Piles, *Cours de peinture*, p. 163.

15. Bougainville, *Voyage autour du monde*, II, pp. 69–70; Hammond, *News from New Cythera*, p. 44. Also see J.-E. Martin-Allanic, Bougainville navigateur et les découvertes de son temps, Ph.D. diss., University of Paris, 1964.

16. J. F. Pilâtre de Rozier, *Premier expérience de la montgolfière construite par l'ordre du roi*, second edition (Paris: De l'Imprimerie de Monsieur, 1784), pp. 13–14.

17. W. H. Auden, *The Enchafèd Flood, or, the Romantic Iconography of the Sea* (New York: Random House, 1950), pp. 16–20; Vivant-Denon, *Voyage en Egypte*, I, pl. 73 and pp. 169–170, 188; Beechey, *Northern Coast of Africa*, pl. p. 113 and p. 39; Oxley, *New South Wales*, pl. p. 235 and p. 234; Lycett, *Australia*, p. 1. Moreover, that in the late eighteenth century the atmosphere came to be designated as "this vast expanse of air" is attested to by Richard, *L'air et des météores*, VII, p. 12.

18. Bachelard, *La terre et les rêveries de la volonté*, pp. 379–380; Appleton, *Experience of Landscape*, pp. 89–91; Michel Foucault, *Folie et deraison. Histoire de la folie à l'âge classique* (Paris: Plon, 1961), p. 172; Faujas de Saint-Fond, *La machine aérostatique*, I, pp. 19–20; Antoine de Parcieux, *Dissertation sur les globes aérostatiques* (Paris: de Parcieux, 1783), pp. 18, 28.

19. Abrams, *Natural Supernaturalism*, pp. 171, 290–291; Arthos, *Language of Natural Description*, p. 54. My thesis differs from that recently put forward by Peter Schwenger in "The Masculine Mode," *Critical Inquiry* 5 (summer 1979), 622–625. Here and in a projected book on "phallic critiques," Schwenger examines the relation between masculinity and literary style, that is, the infusion of a particular sense of the body into the attitudes and encounters of a life. His premise is that the underlying fact of one's sexuality must affect perceptions not only of oneself but of the world. Thus, the writer's style conforms to his body's own qualities; it is a male style marked by deliberate distancing from self-

VOYAGE INTO SUBSTANCE

awareness and by the characteristics of spareness, reserve, omission, and noncommital surface. Sandra M. Gilbert and Susan Gubar, in their *Madwoman in the Attic: The Woman Writer and the Nineteenth-Century Literary Imagination* (Yale University Press, 1978), similarly argue for the existence of a distinctly female imagination. My argument follows the opposite tack and demonstrates the masculine solidity and confidence thought to reside not in the male ego but in the pure phenomenal object. However, Schwenger's undeniable assertion that one of the most powerful archetypes of manhood is the belief that a real man acts rather than contemplates is applicable to the true explorer.

20. Arnold van Gennep, *The Rites of Passage*, tr. Monika B. Vizedom and Gabrielle L. Caffee (University of Chicago Press, 1960), pp. 15–17; Virginia Bush, *Colossal Sculpture of the Cinquencento* (New York: Garland, 1976), pp. 37, 51; Borlase, *Antiquities of Cornwall*, pl. 17, fig. 1, and p. 188; Pennant, *Journey to Snowdon*, pl. 9 and pp. 174–175; Bellasis, *Saint Helena*, pl. 5, and letterpress.

21. Acerbi, *Travels*, I, p. x. For the comparison between the virile and majestic Alps and the "smiling and more fertile" Pyrenees made by the inspector of the Compagnie détachées des Invalides, see *Voyages de Guibert, dans diverses parties de la France et en Suisse. Faits en 1775, 1778, 1784 et 1785. Ouvrage posthume, publié par sa veuve* (Paris: D'Hautel, 1806), pp. 329–331. On the contrary, his compatriot Dusaulx, in his *Voyage à Barège* (II, p. 79), finds the mountains of the Gèdres district "more male, more pronounced" than those of other valleys carved out by the River Gave.

22. Mercier, "La théorie des climats," pp. 31–32.

23. In the doctrines of the semilegendary Lao-tzu (an official during the Chou dynasty who grew weary of court life), *Tao*, the indefinable, is likened to water, the source of life. Further, Lao-tzu articulated a basically sexual concept of the living landscape in which the stream-filled valley was female and the mountain male. It is hard to say, however, how present in the minds of Western artists and writers was this dual vision of yin and yang. See Michael Sullivan, "Pictorial Art and the Attitude toward Nature in Ancient China," *Art Bulletin* 36 (March 1954), 4–5. Also see Adam Müller, *Von der Idee der Schönheit. In Vorlesungen gehalten zu Dresden im Winter 1807/1808* (Berlin: Julius Eduard Hitzig, 1809), pp. 154–155; Bachelard, *L'eau et les rêves*, pp. 49–52, 175–180. Bachelard discusses the literary convention—especially popular among Romantics like Novalis—of referring to water as a form of "feminine" matter in its immaculate quiescent (and

aquiescent) incarnation and as "masculine" in its roiled waves. On the equally "soft" realm of atmospheric fogs and exhalations see Cotte, *Traité de météorologie*, pp. 47–48. See Hart, "Flight in the Renaissance," pp. 22–29, for the associations of flight with the attainment of bliss.

24. Shaftesbury, *Moralists*, part III, section i, p. 122. Further, see the passage where Shaftesbury declares that "space astonishes; silence itself seems pregnant, whilst an unknown force works on the mind, and dubious objects move the wakeful sense" (cited in Moore, *Backgrounds of English Literature*, pp. 73, 89–95; Possin, *Nature und Landschaft bei Addison*, p. 132).

25. *Ossian und die Kunst um 1800*, p. 57; Roy Harvey Pearce, "The Eighteenth-Century Scottish Primitivists: Some Reconsiderations," *ELH* 12 (September 1945), 216–219; Bernardin de Saint-Pierre, *L'Ile de France*, in *Oeuvres*, I, pp. 66–67. On Bernardin de Saint-Pierre as a "scientific" eulogist of the savage landscape empty of human traces, see Monglond, *Le préromantisme*, I, p. 139; Mornet, *Les sciences de la nature*, pp. 155–157. For Bernardin, primitive nature and society were superior to their civilized incarnations. This view is in contrast with that espoused by the Scots Dugald Stewart, Adam Ferguson, and James Dunbar, who found nothing good in primitive society and opposed the extravagances of Hugh Blair and James Macpherson.

26. Grand-Carteret, *La montagne à travers les âges*, I, pp. 362, 371; Hirschfeld, *Theorie der Gartenkunst*, I, pp. 194–195.

27. Laborde, *Espagne*, I, p. 18; *Voyage de Humboldt et Bonpland*, I, pl. 25 and p. 200.

28. George Levine, "High and Low: Ruskin and the Novelists," in *Nature and the Victorian Imagination*, pp. 137–138; Pilâtre de Rozier, *Premier expérience*, pp. 11–12; Lunardi, *First Aerial Voyage in England*, pp. 32–33; Turner, *Astra Castra*, p. 92.

29. Bourrit, *Nouvelle description*, I, p. 59; Brydone, *Sicily and Malta*, I, pp. 201–212.

30. LeBruyn, *Travels*, II, p. 7; Sauer, *Expedition to Russia*, pl. p. 44 and p. 47; Park, *Interior of Africa*, pp. 264–266; Vivant-Denon, *Voyage en Egypte*, I, pl. p. 44 and p. 145; Salt, *Abyssinia*, pl. p. 352 and p. 352; Mollien, *Interior of Africa*, p. 209; Lichtenstein, *Reisen*, II, pl. p. 338 and pp. 339–340; *Wahreste und neueste Abbildung des Türckischen Hofes/Welche nach denen Gemählden der königliche Französische Ambassadeur, Monsr, de Ferriol, Zeit seiner Gesandtschafft in Constantinopel im Jahr 1707 und 1708. Durch einen geschickten Mahler [J.-B. Vanmour] nach den Leben hat verfertigen lassen in fünff und sechzig Kupffer-Blatten gebracht werden. Nebst einer aus dem Französischens ins Teutsche übersetzen Be-*

schreibung (Nuremberg: Adam Jonathan Felssecker, 1719), p. 1. On Vanmour's contribution—primarily costume studies with landscapes, engraved by C. Weigel—see R. van Luttervelt, De "Turkse" Schilderijen van J. B. Vanmour en zijn Schoel. De Verzameling van Cornelis Calkoen, Ambassadeur bij de Hoge Porte, 1725–1743 (Istanbul: Nederlands Historisch-Archaeologisch Instituut in het Nabije Oesten, 1958), pp. 2, 46; A. Boppe, Les peintres du Bosphore au dix-huitième siècle (Paris: Hachette, 1911), pp. 1–55 passim. On the silence of the desert, also see Pierre-Marie-François, Vicomte de Pagès, Voyages autour du monde, et vers les deux Pôles, par terre et par mer, pendant les années 1767, 1768, 1769, 1770, 1771, 1773, 1774 & 1776 (Paris: Moutard, 1782), I, pp. 304, 315–316; Burchell, Southern Africa, I, pp. 282–286, 288.

31. William Bligh, A narrative of the Mutiny on Board His Britannic Majesty's Ship Bounty; and the Subsequent Voyage of Part of the Crew from Tofoa, One of the Friendly Islands, to Timor, a Dutch Settlement in the East-Indies (Philadelphia: William Spotswood, 1790), p. 11; James Wathen, Journal of a Voyage in 1811 and 1812, to Madras and China, Returning by the Cape of Good Hope and Saint Helena (London: J. Nichols, Son, and Bentley), p. 233; Flinders, Terra Australis, I, pl. p. 184 and p. 183.

32. Pierre Poivre, Voyage d'un philosophe, ou observations sur les moeurs & les arts des peuples de l'Afrique, de l'Asie, et de l'Amerique (Yverdon, 1768), pp. 7–8; D'Entrecasteaux, Voyage, I, p. 54; Flinders, Terra Australis, II, p. 236; Voyage de Humboldt et Bonpland, I, pl. 5 and pp. 14–15; Ledru, Voyages aux Iles de Ténériffe, II, p. 67; Belzoni, Narrative, p. 308.

33. Milbert, Hudson, I, p. 104; Kynaston McShine, The Natural Paradise: Painting in America 1800–1950 (New York: Museum of Modern Art, 1976), p. 102; Chateaubriand, Mémoires d'outretombe, I, pp. 240–241, 320–321. Chateaubriand muses that the Canadian lakes in his day are no longer what they were in the days of Jacques Cartier's first voyage to Canada (1534–35), Samuel Champlain's Relation des voyages (1640), Louis-Armand de Lom d'Arce, Baron de La Hontan's Nouveaux Voyages (1703), Joseph-François Lafitau's Moeurs des sauvages americains (1724), or Pierre-François-Xavier de Charlevoix's Histoire et description générale de la Nouvelle France (1744). On the importance of Chateaubriand in the propagation of American scenery see Hugh Honour, The European Vision of America (Kent State University Press, 1975), pp. 286 ff. For Thomas Jefferson's contributions to the admiration for American scenery see William Howard Adams, ed., The Eye of Thomas Jefferson (Washington, D.C.: National Gallery of Art, 1976), pp. 314 ff. Also see Cochrane, Colombia, II, p. 200.

34. Parkinson, Journal, p. 10; Boisgelin de Kerdu, Denmark and Sweden, II, pl. p. 260 and pp. 263–264; Edy, Norway, I, p. xxxvii.

35. See Darwin, Narrative of Voyages of Beagle, III, p. 11. See Viëtor, "De Sublimitate," p. 276, for the classic association of Sublimity with stillness by Baumgarten in his Aesthetica (1750–1758) (before Winckelmann). Also see Forster, Voyage round the World, I, p. 99; Gmelin, Reise durch Sibirien, IV, p. 163. The discussion as to whether auroral sounds existed was particularly lively during the eighteenth century. The absence of any clear physical mechanism for producing them yielded doubt. Nonetheless, a faint rustling, hissing, swishing, or cracking was often described. Samuel Hearne, in his Journal from Prince of Wales Fort in Hudson's Bay to the North Ocean (1759), compares the rustling and crackling noises of the aurora to the waving of a large flag in a fresh gale of wind. See Eather, Majestic Lights, pp. 154–155. Also see La Pérouse, Voyage autour du monde, II, p. 158; MacKenzie, Iceland, p. 243; Gaimard, Voyage en Islande, Géologie et minéralogie, I, p. v; Pagès, Voyage autour du monde, II, p. 135; Chevalier de La Poix de Fréminville, Voyage to the North Pole in the Frigate the Syrene (London: Sir Richard Phillips and Co., 1819), p. 84.

36. Bourrit, Nouvelle description, I, pp. 61–62; Saussure, Voyages dans les Alpes, II, p. 562.

37. Mieczystawa Sekrecka, "L'expérience de la solitude dans Obermann de Senancour," in Approches des Lumières, pp. 449–450; Levine, "High and Low," pp. 140–142; Alexander, Voyage to Pekin, p. 32; Chateaubriand, Mémoires d'outre-tombe, I, pp. 325, 327–328. My examples, drawn from wildernesses all over the world and recorded as early as the first Alpine explorations of the mid-eighteenth century, should help to dispel the uniqueness claimed for the American Luminist tradition of painting, at least on this score. On the Luminists' fascination with the "poetry of things themselves" and their stillness captured in "luminist light," see Barbara Novak, American Painting of the Nineteenth-Century: Realism, Idealism, and the American Experience, second edition (New York: Harper & Row Icon Editions, 1979), pp. 92 ff. In a recent essay, "On Defining Luminism" (American Light, pp. 24, 27–28), Novak has softened her view of the "unique" qualities possessed by works executed by John Frederick Kensett, Fitz Hugh Lane, Martin J. Heade, and William Stanley Haseltine. In addition, Novak expands her earlier implications of silence and states that a key "correlative of luminism" is silence. For the theological implications of stillness in American Landscape painting, see Novak's Nature and Culture: American Landscape Painting 1825–1875 (Oxford University Press, 1980), pp. 47–50.

VOYAGE INTO SUBSTANCE

38. Lang, *Unterirdischen-Wunder*, I, pl. p. 120, pp. 121, 25–26, pl. p. 34, p. 34. Also see Sulzer, *Natur-Geschichte des Schweizerlandes*, I, p. 7.

39. On the numinous properties of caves and the ancient role of grotto as sanctuary see Naomi Miller, *Heavenly Caves: Reflections on the Garden Grotto* (New York: Braziller, 1982), pp. 13–29. Also see, on the infinity of the desert, Lang, *Unterirdischen-Wunder*, I, pp. 22–23; Olivier, *L'Empire Othoman*, III, p. 241; Mollien, *Interior of Africa*, p. 97; Beechey, *Northern Coast of Africa*, pp. 210–211.

40. Ozouf, *La fête révolutionnaire*, pp. 49–54, 67–69; Guitton, *Jacques Delille*, p. 419; Faujas de Saint-Fond, *La machine aérostatique*, I, p. 17; Baldwin, *Airopaidia*, pp. 84–85, 108–109; "An Exact Narration of M. Blanchard's Observations during His Third Aerial Voyage, on the 18th of July 1784," *Universal Magazine* (September 1784), p. 357; Bruel, *Histoire aéronautique*, numbers 39, 173.

41. Bernardin de Saint-Pierre, *L'Ile de France*, in *Oeuvres*, I, pp. 100–103; Forster, *Voyage round the World*, I, p. 148; Hentzi, *Vues remarquables*, p. 7, plates 6, 10, p. 15. Also see H. W. Williams, *Travels in Italy, Greece, and the Ionian Islands* (Edinburgh: Archibald Constable, 1820), I, p. 37.

42. *Voyages de Chastellux*, I, p. 96; Heriot, *The Canadas*, pl. p. 120 and pp. 119–120, 163; Valentia, *Voyages and travels*, I, pl. p. 39 and pp. 39–40; Cochrane, *Colombia*, II, pp. 178–180.

43. Kaempfer, *History of Japan*, I, pp. 102–103; Le Gentil, *Les mers de l'Inde*, II, p. 652; Heriot, *The Canadas*, p. 17; "Grotte basaltique de l'Ile de Staffa, en Ecosse," *Magasin Pittoresque* 5 (1833), pl. p. 37 and pp. 36–37.

44. Gruner, *Histoire naturelle*, p. 43; Sherwill, *Mont Blanc*, III, p. 163; I, p. 341; Phipps, *North Pole*, pl. p. 70 and p. 70; Laing, *Spitzbergen*, pp. 149–151; Scoresby, *Arctic Regions*, I, p. 254; Weld, *North America*, p. 228. Also see Fitzroy, *Narrative of Beagle Voyages*, II, p. 403.

45. Hamilton, *Campi Phlegraei*, II, pl. 21, and letterpress; MacKenzie, *Iceland*, pl. p. 119, pp. 118, 196, pl. 4, p. 116; "Voyage de M. Monge en Islande," *Journal des Voyages de Découvertes* 6 (1820), 18.

46. Bernardin de Saint-Pierre, *L'Ile de France*, II, in *Oeuvres*, I, pp. 29–30; Williamson, *Oriental Field Sports*, pl. 34, p. 123; Lesseps, *Journal historique*, 1, pp. 150–152, 254–256.

47. Lewis and Clark, *History of the Expedition*, II, pp. 339–340, 395; Tuckey, *River Zaire*, p. 96; Mollien, *Interior of Africa*, p. 93; O'Reilly, *Greenland*, p. 177.

48. Johnson, *Oriental Voyager*, p. 120; Stedman, *Surinam*, I, pp. 330–332, 339; Arago, *Voyage round the World*, II, pl. 24 and pp. 204–205.

49. Sparrman, *Cape of Good Hope*, II, p. 271; William Henry Smyth, *Memoir Descriptive of the Resources, Inhabitants, and Hydrography of Sicily and Its Islands, Interspersed with Antiquarian and Other Notices* (London: John Murray, 1824), pl. 13 and pp. 167–168; Kotzebue, *Voyage of Discovery*, II, p. 361; III, p. 76; Salt, *Abyssinia*, pl. p. 399 and pp. 398–399; Kershaw, *Burman Empire*, pl. 2 and p. 2. For a defense of the aesthetic relevance of the imperceptible see Joseph Margolis, "Aesthetic Appreciation and the Imperceptible," *British Journal of Aesthetics* 16 (autumn 1976), 306–308.

50. Viëtor, "De Sublimitate," p. 264; Blanckenhagen, *Paintings from Boscotrecase*, pp. 35, 50–53, 58–61. For a discussion of the characteristics of the "Virgilian" landscape see Clark, *Landscape into Art*, p. 128.

51. Bosse, "The Marvellous," pp. 213–216. For seventeenth-century usage see Bouhours, *Entretiens d'Ariste et d'Eugène*, pp. 273–274. The most sophisticated and comprehensive analysis of the marvelous and related literary genres is Tzvetan Todorov's *The Fantastic: A Structural Approach to a Literary Genre*, tr. Richard Howard (Press of Case Western Reserve University, 1973), pp. 41–57.

52. Bourrit, *Nouvelle description*, III, p. 68; "La Suisse," *Journal des Voyages de Découvertes* 26 (1825), 351–352; Edy, *Norway*, II, letterpress for pl. 39; Landmann, *Portugal*, II, pl. p. 166 and p. 166; Sparrman, *Voyage to Cape of Good Hope*, I, p. 36; Skjöldebrand, *Journey to North Cape*, pp. 50–51.

53. Tuckey, *Expedition to Zaire*, p. 173; "Description des salines de Durrenberg, près de Hallein dans le pays de Saltzbourg," *Journal des Voyages de Découvertes* 2 (1819), 379; George Thompson, *Travels and Adventures in Southern Africa by ... Eight Years a Resident at the Cape. Comprising a View of the Present State of the Cape Colony. With Observations on the Progress and Prospects of British Emigrants*, second edition (London: Henry Colburn, 1827), I, pls. pp. 276, 280 and pp. 275–277; "Le basalte," *Magasin Pittoresque* 9 (1839), 67–69; "Grotte des Demoiselles ou des Fées," *Magasin Pittoresque* 9 (1839), 373; "Les montagnes trachytiques," *Magasin Pittoresque* 11 (1840), 87–88.

54. Malaspina, *Letters*, p. 47; Lyon, *Journal*, p. 274; Brooke, *Lapland*, pl. p. 518 and pp. 517–518.

55. Duff, *Original Genius*, pp. 86–97 passim; Bosse, "The Marvellous," pp. 218–220; Hunt, *Figure in the Landscape*, pp. 183–184.

56. For a summary and review of the idea that by the help of an artificial landscape the beholder's thoughts are taken to distant climes, see Siren, *China and the Gardens of Europe*, pp. 88, 153–155; Harris, "Burke and Chambers," pp. 208–213; Jurgis Baltrušaitis, "Lands of Illusion: China and the Eighteenth-Century Garden," *Landscape* 11 (winter 1961–62), 10–11; Hirschfeld, *Theorie der Gartenkunst*, I, p. 193. On the importance to the Romantics of the idea that every object must be seen in its natural habitat, see Eveline Schlumberger, "La foi artistique de Chateaubriand," *Connaissance des Arts* 197 (July–August 1968), 130–131. Also see James H. Bunn, "The Aesthetics of British Mercantilism," *New Literary History* 11 (winter 1980), 303–321. Bunn suggests that, between 1688 and 1763, so prodigious yet so patternless seemed the importation of luxuries from exotic lands that they appeared to lead a life of their own. The trader's taste for collecting odds and ends, which he identifies as part of a general economics of gathering without any consideration of a unifying principle and which necessarily ignores the native ground from which these artifacts had been removed, finds an aesthetic equivalent in Picturesque gardens. These are open-air equivalents of private curio collections. Torn from their cultural or natural contexts, these assemblages of curios deny the individual's usefulness. This is an attitude counter to that espoused by the explorer, for whom the value of the individual specimen grows in proportion to an examination of its context. An extension of this "mercantile aesthetic" might be seen in the fate of the "original" work of art after it has undergone a range of "reproductions," from lithography to photography. As Walter Benjamin has pointed out, techniques of reproduction can bring the image of the original into situations in which the original would never be found. In short, reproduction removes the object from its ground and its tradition, or rather, liquidates its traditional value and "aura," See Benjamin, *Das Kunstwerk im Zeitalter und seiner technischer Reproduzierbarkeit. Drei Studien zur Kunstsoziologie* (Frankfurt-am-Main: Suhrkamp, 1963), pp. 15–16.

57. Carnochan, *Confinement and Flight*, pp. 21–28; Duchet, "L'histoire des voyages," pp. 153–154; Alan D. McKillop, "Local Attachment and Cosmopolitanism in the Eighteenth-Century Pattern," in *Sensibility to Romanticism*, p. 201; Paul Zweig, *The Adventurer* (London: Dent, 1974), pp. 4–9; Auerbach, *Mimesis*, pp. 135, 267–270; Cook, *Voyage*, I, p. lvii. Also see George Sarton, *Six Wings: Men of Science in the Renaissance* (Bloomington: Indiana University Press, 1957), p. 137; Eisenstein, *Printing Press as an Agent of Change*, II, pp. 472–478.

58. Mauritius Augustus Benyowsky, *The Memoirs and Travels of . . . , Magnate of the Kingdoms of Hungary and Poland, One of the Chiefs of the Confederation of Poland, etc., etc.* (London: G. G. J. and J. Robinson, 1789), I, p. i; C. A. Helvétius, *De l'Esprit, or Essays on the Mind and Its Several Faculties* (1758) (New York: Bert Franklin, 1970), pp. 96–97, 359–365, 372; Gerard, *Essay on Genius*, pp. 8–9; William Sharpe, *A Dissertation upon Genius* (1755) (New York: Scholars' Facsimiles & Reprints, Delmar, 1973), p. 56. Sharpe differs from Gerard and Duff in emphasizing education. Like the French encyclopedist Claude-Adrien Helvétius, Sharpe is less interested in "original genius" than in the power for acquiring knowledge. He argues for the innate equality of all minds and the consequent necessity of education as a guide to genius. He would agree with Helvétius that the man of genius takes advantage of everything and is perpetually sensible of his ignorance, finding instruction everywhere.

59. McKillop, "Local Attachment and Cosmopolitanism," pp. 196–197. Also see Charles Dédéyan, *Le cosmopolitisme européen sous la révolution et l'empire* (Paris: Société d'Edition d'Enseignement Superieur, 1976), II, pp. 588–591. On the concept that great men transcend national boundaries see Leopold Ettlinger, "Denkmal und Romantik, Bemerkungen zu Leo von Klenze's Walhalla," in *Festschrift für Herbert von Einem zum 16. Februar 1965*, ed. Gert von der Osten (Berlin: Mann, 1965), pp. 65–66.

60. Zweig, *Adenturer*, pp. 15–16; Batten, *Pleasurable Instruction*, p. 96; Atkinson, *Relations de voyages*, pp. 16–17; Girdlestone, *Ramond*, p. 94.

61. Beaglehole, "Cook the Man," in *Captain Cook Navigator and Scientist*, pp. 20–21; Bruce, *Travels*, I, "Dedication to the King"; Lunardi, *Account of the First Aerial Voyage in England*, p. 11; Weber, "Die Figur des Zeichners in der Landschaft," p. 54; Valenciennes, *Eléments de perspective*, pp. xxvii–xxviii, 519–521.

62. Chappe d'Auteroche, *Voyage en Californie*, p. 5; Beaglehole, "Cook the Man," in *Captain Cook Navigator and Scientist*, p. 21; Cook, *Voyage*, I, p. iv; Malaspina, *Letters*, p. 38; La Pérouse, *Voyage autour du Monde*, II, p. 134; Rudolf Braunburg, *Leichter als Luft. Aus der Geschichte der Ballonluftfahrt* (Hamburg: Marion von Schröder, 1963), p. 17; Tissandier, *Simples notions sur les ballons*, pp. 30–31.

63. Leyden, *Historical and Philosophical Sketch of Discoveries*, p. 6; MacKenzie, *Voyages from Montreal*, pp. vii–viii; Luigi Mayer, *Views in the Ottoman Empire, Chiefly in Caramania, a Part of Asia Minor hitherto Unexplored; with Some Curious Selections from the Islands of Rhodes, and Cyprus, and the Celebrated Cities of Corinth, Carthage, and Tripoli: from the Original*

Drawings in the Possession of Sir. R. Ainslie, Taken during his Embassy to Constantinople by . . . With Historical Observations and Incidental Illustrations of the Manners and Customs of the Natives of the Country (London: R. Bowyer, 1803), pp. 1, 17–21; Heriot, *The Canadas*, p. 2; Tuckey, *Expedition to Zaire*, pp. 285–286; Kotzebue, *Voyage of Discovery*, III, p. 5; Cochrane, *Colombia*, I, p. 3; Burckhardt, *Travels in Syria and the Holy Land*, p. 311; Lycett, *Australia*, p. 1; Milbert, *Hudson*, I, pp. xii–xiii.

64. Johann Georg Gmelin, *Reise durch Sibirien, von dem Jahr 1733 bis 1743* (Göttingen: Verlegts Abram Bandenhoecks Seel., Wittwe, 1751–1752), I, preface; Sauer, *Expedition*, p. 196; Belzoni, *Narrative*, p. vi; Gerard, *Essay on Genius*, p. 319.

65. Jean-Baptiste Tavernier, *Recueil de plusieurs relations et traitez singuliers et curieux de . . . Escuyer, Baron d'Aubonne, qui n'ont point esté mis dans ses six premiers voyages*, second edition (Paris: Chez la Veuve Clouzier, Pierre Aubouyn, Pierre Emery, 1685), p. iii; Jean-Sylvain Bailly, *Lettres sur l'origine des sciences et sur celle des peuples de l'Asie adressés à M. de Voltaire* (London: Elmsley; Paris: De Bure l'aîné, 1777), pp. 21–25. On the notion of travel and discovery as an antidote to ennui see Young, *Conjectures on Original Composition*, pp. 12–13; Ozouf, *La fête révolutionnaire*, p. 205; Parks, "Turn to the Romantic," p. 23; Levine, "High and Low," in *Nature and the Victorian Imagination*, p. 146.

66. Atkinson, *Les relations de voyages*, p. 186; Pomeau, "La Pérouse philosophe," in *Approches de Lumières*, pp. 359–360; Cook, *Voyage*, I, pp. vi, xiv, xviii; Kerguelen, *Voyage*, p. 67; Phipps, *North Pole*, pl. p. 60 and p. 61; Forster, *Voyage round the World*, I, pp. 87–88, 114–115, 569–570; Forster, *Observations*, p. 107.

67. La Pérouse, *Voyage autour du monde*, II, p. iii; Vancouver, *Voyage of Discovery*, III, pl. I and p. 14; Krusenstern, *Voyage round the World*, I, p. 125; Flinders, *Voyage to Terra Australis*, II, pl. p. 312 and pp. 300–311. Also see Perry and Simpson, *Drawings by William Westall*, pp. 12–13.

68. Lesseps, *Journal historique*, I, pp. 264–265, 173–178; Hamilton, *Supplement to Campi Phlegraei*, pp. 13–15. Also see Landmann, *Portugal*, II, pl. p. 202 and p. 202.

69. Faujas de Saint-Fond, *La machine aérostatique*, II, pp. 161–164; *La vie et les mémoires de Pilâtre de Rozier, écrits par lui-même, publiés par Tournon de la Chapelle* (Paris, 1786), pp. 54–55; Vivant-Denon, *Voyage en Egypte*, I, p. 141; Jackson, *Marocco*, pp. 284–285. Accidents of this sort accord with the great quantities of human and other bones found in various parts of the desert. However, Burckhardt and Belzoni also mention fierce tribesmen. See Burckhardt, *Travels in Nubia*, pp. 348–349; Belzoni, *Narrative*, p. 155; Vidal, *Buenos Ayres*, pl. p. 91 and p. 193.

70. *Voyage de Humboldt et Bonpland*, I, pl. 5 and pp. 15–16; Caldcleugh, *South America*, II, frontispiece and pp. 105–109; Heriot, *Canadas*, p. 32; Franklin, *Polar Sea*, pl. p. 412 and p. 412; *Second Journey to Polar Sea*, p. x.

71. Gaston Tissandier, *Voyages dans les airs* (Paris: Hachette, 1898), pl. 8 and pp. 20–28; Raymond Trousson, *Le thème de Promethée dans la littérature européene* (Geneva: Droz, 1964), pp. 225–227, 381–384; "A l'année 1783," *Almanach des Muses* (Paris: Lalain l'aîné, 1785), pp. 3–4; Abbé Hollier, "La navigation aérienne, ode," pp. 91–92; Raimond Verninac de Saint Maur, "Le siècle de Louis XVI," p. 102; Abbé Monti, "La navigation aérienne," p. 53.

72. Addison, *Spec.* 415. Also see Guitton, "Un thème 'philosophique,'" pp. 678–680; *Jacques Delille*, p. 361. On the Renaissance roots of the modern hero-traveler, who counts the world as his home, in contradistinction to the cosmic traveler—as I am defining the aeronaut—see Thomas Goldstein, "The Role of the Italian Merchant Class in Renaissance and Discoveries," *Terrae Incognitae* 8 (1976), 23.

73. Jackson, *Immediacy*, p. 17; Damisch, *Théorie du nuage*, p. 258; Carnochan, *Confinement and Flight*, pp. 7–12, 157–160; Turnor, *Astra Castra*, p. 121.

74. Ozouf, *La fête révolutionnaire*, pp. 151–156, 120.

75. "Carruthers Scrapbook," National Air and Space Museum, Washington, D.C.; Goethe, *Briefe aus der Schweiz* (1779), in *Werke*, VI, pp. 93, 119; Braunburg, *Leichter als Luft*, pp. 15–17; M. Gudin de La Brenellerie, "Sur le globe ascendant," *Almanach des Muses* (1784), pp. 25–27; Baldwin, *Airopaidia*, p. 128; Helen Rosenau, "The Sphere as an Element in the Montgolfier Monuments," *Art Bulletin* 50 (March 1968), 65; Chateaubriand, *Mémoires d'outre-tombe*, I, pp. 254–255; Kurt R. Biermann and Fritz G. Lange, "Alexander von Humboldts Weg zum Naturwissenschaftler und Forschungsreisenden," in *Alexander von Humboldt Festschrift, aus Anlass seine 200. Geburtstages* (Berlin: Akademie-Verlag, 1969), pp. 97, 101.

76. For a discussion of the supposition that it requires civilizations with some degree of individual freedom to bring about inventions, see Crosby Field, Invention through the Ages, address to Patents and Research Seminar of National Association of Manufacturers, Cleveland, June 21, 1948, pp. 3–18; Boime, *Academy and French Painting*, pp. 175–176; Jones, "Background on the Attack on Science," in

Chapter 6

Pope and His Contemporaries, p. 97; A. C. Quatremère de Quincy, *Architecture*, in *Encyclopédie Méthodique* (Paris: Henri Agasse, An IX), II, pp. 570–571; T. J. Beck, *Northern Antiquities, French Learning and Literature (1755–1855): A Study in Preromantic Ideas* (Columbia University Press, 1934), pp. 60–61, 121, 126.

77. Brydone, *Sicily and Malta*, II, p. 26; Forster, *Voyage round the World*, I, p. 303; Bougainville, *Voyage autour du monde*, II, p. 45; Acerbi, *Travels*, II, pl. p. 107 and p. 106; Beechey, *Northern Coast of Africa*, p. 40.

78. Victor Brombert, "Pascal's Happy Dungeon," in *The Classical Line: Essays in Honor of Henri Peyre*, Yale French Studies 38 (1967), pp. 231–242; Lorenz Eitner, "Cages, Prisons, and Captives in Eighteenth-Century Art," in *Images of Romanticism*, pp. 26–27; George Poulet, *Trois essais de mythologie romantique* (Paris: José Corti, 1966), pp. 143–146; Brown, "Tensions and Anxieties," in *Science and the Creative Spirit*, pp. 99–100; Gaston Bachelard, *The Poetics of Space*, tr. Maria Jolas (New York: Orion, 1964), p. 221; Carole Fabricant, *Swift's Landscapes* (Johns Hopkins University Press, 1982), pp. 43–54. On the importance of Piranesi's post-1760 etchings in the construction of the spatially dense romantic landscape see Norbert Miller, *Archäologie des Traums* (Munich: Hanser, 1978), pp. 325–353; Bruno Reudenbach, *G. B. Piranesi Architektur als Bild. Der Wandel in der Architekturauffassung des achtzehn Jahrhunderts* (Munich: Prestel, 1979), pp. 41–53.

79. Glacken, *Traces*, pp. 623–635. This view should be contrasted with that of Bayle at the beginning of the eighteenth century. Bayle lauded nature's energies and an endlessly dynamic universe. See Crocker, *Diderot's Chaotic Order*, pp. 4–6.

80. Le Flamanc, *Les utopies prérévolutionnaires*, pp. 143–144; H. F. Clark, "Eighteenth-Century Elysiums. The Role of 'Association' in the Landscape Movement," *Journal of the Warburg and Courtauld Institutes* 6 (1943), 174; Schubert, *Ansichten*, p. 179.

81. It is Hume, however, who carries Locke's skepticism regarding the possibility of ever knowing the external world to its logical conclusion, declaring that it is absurd to imagine that the senses can ever distinguish between ourselves and the external world. See David Hume, *A Treatise of Human Nature*, ed. L. A. Selby-Bigge (Oxford: Clarendon, 1949), p. 190. His view should be contrasted with that of his compatriot, composed some thirty years later. See Joseph Priestley, *The History and Present State of Discoveries Relating to Vision, Light, and Colours* (London: J. Johnson, 1772), pp. 30, 390–394. Writing from the vantage point of a chemist, Priestley declares that no bounds can be set to the advances of knowledge and that "every new discovery is but an opening to several more," and this progress is expected to accelerate. Later in the treatise, espousing the ideas of the Croatian astronomer and mathematician Roger Joseph Boscovich (so important in France), he declares that matter is not impenetrable but material, like the brain, and thus knowable by it.

1. Assunto, *Il paessagio e l'estetica*, I, pp. 64–67; Bonnet, *Contemplation de la nature*, II, pp. 104–105. For a parallel with the modern movement of earthworks see Germano Celant, ed., *Art Povera, Conceptual, Actual or Impossible Art?* (London: Studio Vista, 1969), p. 230. This art that recognizes the value of the elements represents "a moment that tends towards deculturization, regression, primitiveness and regression toward the pre-logical and pre-iconographic stage, toward elementary and spontaneous politics and a tendency toward the basic elements in nature (land, sea, snow, minerals, heat, animals) and in life (body, memory, thought), and in behaviour (family, spontaneous action, class struggle, violence, environment)." For the modern theory of vision as based on neurological reflexes and also as a process intricately involved with the whole body system in both present functioning and past experience, see Arnold Gesell, Frances L. Ilg, and Glenna E. Bullis, *Vision, Its Development in Infant and Child* (New York: Paul B. Hoeber, 1949), p. vi; Vasco Ronchi, *Optics: The Science of Vision* (New York University Press, 1957), pp. 67–123 passim; Ward C. Halstead, *Brain and Intelligence: A Quantitative Study of the Frontal Lobes* (University of Chicago Press, 1947), p. 61.

2. Béguin, *L'âme romantique*, II, pp. 329–332; Noel, "Le thème de l'eau chez Senancour," pp. 357–358, 364; Bachelard, *Poetics of Reverie*, pp. 29–34, 185. For a survey of ancient humoral theory see Glacken, *Traces*, pp. 81–82.

3. Bouhours, *Les entretiens*, pp. 2–4, 10; Hermann Bauer, "Architektur als Kunst. Von der Grösse der idealistischen Architektur-Ästhetick und ihrem Verfall," in *Probleme der Kunstwissenschaft* (Berlin: de Gruyter, 1963), I, n. 9, p. 136.

4. Rousseau, *Les rêveries*, pp. 177–182, 251–255. Also see Derrida, *La grammatologie*, pp. 200–206; Jean Starobinski, "Rousseau's Happy Days," *New Literary History* 11 (autumn 1979), 153, 157–159; James S. Hans, "Gaston Bachelard and the Phenomenology of the Reading Consciousness," *Journal of Aesthetics and Art Criticism* 35 (spring 1977), 322; Vinge, *Narcissus Theme*, p. 308.

5. Jacques G. Benay, "L'honnète homme devant la nature, ou la philosophie du

Chevalier de Méré," *PMLA* 79 (March 1964), 26; Ralph Cohen, "Association of Ideas and Poetic Unity," *Philological Quarterly* 36 (October 1957), 470–474; Derek Clifford, *A History of Garden Design* (New York: Praeger, 1963), p. 145; Hunt and Willis, *Genius of the Place*, p. 38; Paulson, *Emblem and Expression*, p. 57.

6. Mary Carmen Rose, "Nature as Aesthetic Object: An Essay in Meta-Aesthetics," *British Journal of Aesthetics* 16 (winter 1976), 6–7; Maren-Sofie Røstvig, *The Happy Man: Studies in the Metamorphoses of a Classical Idea*, second edition (New York: Humanities Press, 1971), II, pp. 93–94. On the important role played by Kant's *Critique of Judgment* in formulating reflection rather than emotion as the distinctive mark of aesthetic pleasure, see Rose Frances Egan, "The Genesis of the Theory of 'Art for Art's Sake' in Germany and in England," *Smith College Studies in Modern Language* 2 (July 1921), 34–37. By way of reminder, see Sprat, *History of Royal Society*, p. 72, on the "Race of Inquisitive Minds."

7. Foucault, *Birth of the Clinic*, pp. 121–122. See Friedrich Schlegel's *Kölner Vorlesungen* (1804–1805) (cited in Bosse, "The Marvellous in Romantic Semiotics," pp. 227, 234) for the expression of the Romantic fear that man's being would lose itself into the object if it were not for the image of that object which will take its place. The image thus functions as a kind of counter-object (*Gegen-Ding*) produced by the ego so as to preserve its freedom (i.e., distance) and so still hold fast to the object. Since the sensual impact is so overwhelming, the image alone will be too weak to resist. Countering this fear is Wordsworth's belief that the poet finds his lost identity with nature in that moment when he is penetrated by a sense of nature's "huge and mighty forms" [cited in Northrop Frye, *A Study of English Romanticism* (New York: Random House, 1968), p. 19].

8. *Encyclopédie*, VII, pp. 583–584; Bailly, *Lettres*, pp. 21, 25–30; Gerard, *Essay on Genius*, pp. 31, 58; Duff, *Original Genius*, p. 171.

9. Trousson, *Le thème de Prométhée*, p. 210; Jack J. Spector, *Delacroix: The Death of Sardanapalus* (London: Allen Lane, 1974), pp. 104–105; Bate, "Sympathetic Imagination," p. 156. It is interesting to compare Ruskin's distinctions (*Modern Painters*, III) of inactive reverie, useful thought, and higher contemplation (cited in Frederick Kirchoff, "A Science against Sciences: Ruskin's Floral Mythology," in Knoepflmacher and Tennyson, *Nature and Victorian Imagination*, p. 146).

10. Deane, *Aspects of Nature Poetry*, pp. 93–95; Bush, *Colossal Sculpture*, p. 154; Michael Fried, "The Beholder in Courbet: His Early Self-Portraits and Their Place in his Art," *Glyph* 4 (1978), n. 35, p. 128. I am grateful to Francis H. Dowley for letting me consult his book-length manuscript "The Moment in Seventeenth and Eighteenth-Century Art Criticism," which focusses on the moment as "a pivot in the unification of a work of sculpture or painting." Also see Du Bos's statement (cited in Dieckmann, "Wandlung Nachahmungsbegriffes," in Jauss, *Nachahmung and Illusion*, pp. 43–44) that the impression an imitation makes is not as strong as that made by the actual object. The superficial impression made by an imitation is quickly erased; thus, the greater energy of nature corresponds to a stronger, more enduring, and overwhelming impression. For the continuing perception of the sudden looming quality of the natural masterpiece see Léon de Laborde, *Voyage de l'Arabie Pétrée par . . . et Linant* (Paris: Giard, 1830), preface.

11. Faujas de Saint-Fond, *Volcans éteints*, pl. 4 and pp. 278–279; Hamilton, *Supplement to Campi Phlegraei*, pl. 2, and letterpress; *Campi Phlegraei*, II, pls. 13, 14, and letterpress; Houel, *Voyage*, I, pl. 72 and pp. 133–134; Forster, *Voyage round the World*, II, p. 282; Edy, *Norway*, I, p. xlv.

12. Forster, *Voyage round the World*, I, pp. 268–269; J. A. Deluc, *Lettres physiques et morales sur les montagnes et sur l'histoire de la terre et de l'homme* (The Hague: Detune, 1778), p. 152; Saussure, *Voyages dans les Alpes*, II, p. 7; Scoresby, *Arctice Regions*, II, pl. 5 and p. 159; Fitzroy, *Narrative of Beagle Voyages*, II, plate facing p. 404 and p. 403.

13. Banks, *Endeavour Journal*, pp. 177–178; Hawkesworth, *Relation des Voyages*, II, p. 9; Le Gentil, *Voyage*, II, pl. 8 and pp. 660–661; Vidal, *Buenos Ayres*, pl. p. 91 and pp. 96–97; Thorn, *War in India*, p. 485; Pilâtre de Rozier, *Premier expérience*, p. 13.

14. Baldwin, *Airopaidia*, pp. 71–73; "Notices diverses concernant la machine aérostatique," pp. 313–315; Turnor, *Astra Castra*, p. 356. Also see Tissandier, *Les ballons*, pp. 82–83.

15. Boisgelin de Kerdu, *Malta*, I, p. 74; Milbert, *Hudson*, I, p. 191. Valenciennes (*Eléments de perspective*, p. 219) alerts the apprentice landscape painter that clouds change every moment and that the artist must be especially attentive in studying them.

16. Le Bruyn, *Travels*, I, p. 171; Forster, *Observations*, p. 64; Krusenstern, *Voyage round the World*, I, p. 40; Lyon, *Private Journal*, p. 204; "Garnerin's Nocturnal Ascension," Carruthers Scrapbook, National Air and Space Museum, Washington, D.C.

17. MacKenzie, *Iceland*, pl. p. 224 and pp. 222–224; Gaimard, *Voyage en Islande; His-*

torie du voyage, II, atlas, pls. 130–132, and pp. 293–294; Forster, *Observations*, pp. 69–70, 55–56.

18. Graham, *Chile*, pls. 3, 4 and pp. 196–197; Volney, *Tableau des Etats-Unis*, I, pl. 3, p. 112, and pp. 107–110; Grindlay, *Western India*, I, pl. 2 and pp. 3–4; Hamilton, *Supplement to Campi Phlegraei*, pl. 3 and pp. 5–6; Forster, *Observations*, pp. 104–105.

19. Burke, *Sublime and Beautiful*, part II, section xviii, p. 58. On Herder's, Goethe's, and Coleridge's predilection for the phenomenal, the immediately experienced fact associated with a biologically oriented cosmology, see Opper, *Science and the Arts*, pp. 40–43. On Mme. de Staël's boredom if she had to pay attention to things, see R. G. Saisselin, "Tivoli Revisted or the Triumph of Culture," in Fritz and Williams, *Triumph of Culture*, p. 15.

20. Jacques Guillerme, "Lequeu, entre l'irregulier et l'éclectique," *Dix-Huitième Siècle* 6 (1974), 176; Dora Wiebenson, " 'L'architecture terrible' and the 'Jardin anglo-chinois,' " *Journal of the Society of Architectural Historians* 27 (May 1968), 137; *Picturesque Garden in France*, p. 35.

21. Kames, *Elements of Criticism*, I, pp. 211–219. For a discussion of Kames's distinction between "ideal presence" and "real presence" (the former being the Associationists' imaginative unity and the latter the factual existence of things, and, further, of "reflective presence," or events called up by reflection) see Cohen, "Association of Ideas," p. 470. Hume is an important precursor of Kames in the analysis of the "passion" of surprise. Although agreeable in itself, surprise puts the spirits in agitation, augmenting both agreeable and painful affections. 'Hence everything, that is new, is most affecting, and gives us either more pleasure or more pain, than what, strictly speaking, naturally belongs to it. . . .' When it often returns, novelty wears off, passions subside and "we survey the objects with greater tranquility." See Hume, *Treatise on Human Understanding*, p. 423. Also see Hayden White's discussion of the "astonishing" and "remarkable" (but not "surprising") facts invoked by Charles Darwin in his natural history-writings, especially in the *Origin of the Species*: "The Fictions of Factual Representation," in *The Literature of Fact: Selected Papers from the English Instutute*, ed. Angus Fletcher (New York: Columbia University Press, 1976), p. 39.

22. Kuhn, *Structure of Scientific Revolutions*, pp. 52–57, 91; Gaston Bouthoul, *L'invention* (Paris: Marcel Giard, 1930), pp. 4–6. On voyaging as part of the general eighteenth-century enthusiasm for science, and on the popularity of voyage literature as resting upon its promise to resolve scientific debates, see Roger Hahn, *The Anatomy of a Scientific Institution* (University of California Press, 1971), p. 90.

23. Forster, *Voyage round the World*, I, pp. 190–191; Forster, *Observations*, pp. 109–112; Boisgelin de Kerdu, *Malta*, I, pl. 7, p. 69, and pp. 68–70.

24. Cook, *Voyage to Pacific*, II, pl. 51 and p. 455; Labillardière, *Voyage*, I, p. 43.

25. Hawkesworth, *Relation des Voyages*, II, p. 92; La Pérouse, *Voyage autour du monde*, II, pp. 136–137; Franklin, *Journey to Polar Sea*, pl. p. 366 and p. 367; Brooke, *Lapland*, pp. 443–444, and *Atlas*, pls. 7, 11; Grindlay, *Western India*, I, pl. 18, and letterpress; Houel, *Voyage*, I, pl. 66 and p. 120.

26. O'Reilly, *Greenland*, pl. p. 46 and p. 32; George Cockburn, *A Voyage to Cadiz and Gibraltar up the Mediterranean to Sicily and Malta, in 1810, & 11, Including a Description of Sicily and the Lipari Islands, and an Excursion in Portugal* (London: J. Harding, 1815), pl. p. 252 and p. 252; Tuckey, *Expedition to River Zaire*, pp. 235, 253; Davy, *Ceylon*, p. 53. Also see "Puits de feu, Souvenirs de Chine," *Magasin Pittoresque* 4 (1833), 30–31.

27. De Piles, *Cours de peinture*, p. 109; Weiskel, *Romantic Sublime*, pp. 29–30, 18–24; Jackson, *Immediacy*, pp. 5–6, 23.

28. *Encyclopédie*, VII, p. 582. On the origin of the concept of personal identity or of the self-in-consciousness in the second (1694) edition of Locke's *Essay*, see Christopher Fox, "Locke and the Scriblerians: the Discussion of Identity in Early Eighteenth-Century England," *Eighteenth-Century Studies* 16 (fall 1982), 1–25. Fox notes that Locke's dismissal of the substantial self and his new criterion of identity opened the possibility for an alienation of consciousness; i.e., that the "same Man" can, quite literally, be *"not himself"* or *"beside* himself."

29. Diderot, *Salons*, III, p. 156; *Recherches philosophiques sur l'origine et la nature du Beau*, in *Oeuvres complètes*, ed. J. Assezat (Paris: Garnier, 1876), X, p. 42. For the category of the "interesting," see Burda, *Die Ruinen*, n. 390, p. 87. For Friedrich Schlegel's notion that the categories of the "characteristic" and the "interesting" are the hallmark of modern poetry, see his *Die Griechen und Römer*, in *Kritische Friedrich-Schlegel Ausgabe*, ed. Ernst Behler (Neustrelitz: Michaelis, 1797), I, 213–223.

30. For a discussion of the High Renaissance use of the word *stupore* and such attendant terms as *meraviglia* and *terribilità* to describe the effect of the work of art, see David Summers, *Michelangelo and the Language of Art* (Princeton University Press, 1980), pp. 171–173. According to Vincenzo Borghini, advisor to Vasari, when an artist does more than is expected

of him he causes marvel by the defeat of matter. *Stupore* is a state resulting from the perception of a thing that exceeds the limits of our senses, such as the metaphorical brilliance of artifice that dazzles the eye by a display of virtuosity on a very small and on a very large scale. Whereas Summers traces the rhetorical tradition (dating from Longinus's *De sublimitate*) esteeming the artificial construction that could be made grand and splendid through the sheer force of art, scientific explorers are speaking not of metaphorical size but of the actual magnitude of real objects. Also see Carl Lamb, *Die Villa d'Este in Tivoli, ein Beitrag zur Geschichte der Gartenkunst* (Munich: Prestel, 1966), p. 94; Elledge, "Generality and Particularity," p. 166; Johnson, *Oriental Voyager*, p. 65.

31. Broc, *Les montagnes*, p. 42; Deluc, *Lettres physiques*, p. 127.

32. Faujas de Saint-Fond, *Voyage en Angleterre*, II, p. 117; Cook, *Voyage*, I, pl. 33 and p. 306.

33. Lesseps, *Journal*, II, pp. 140–143; Dallaway, *Constantinople*, p. 179; Cassas, *Voyage en Syrie*, II, pl. 62 and p. 11.

34. Barrow, *Travels*, I, p. 33; II, frontispiece; Fitzroy, *Narrative of* Beagle *Voyage*, I, plate facing p. 26 and pp. 26–27; II, plate facing p. 360; Burchell, *South Africa*, I, pp. 297–298; Broughton, *Voyage of Discovery*, p. 288; Hamilton, *Campi Phlegraei*, II, pl. 11 and letterpress; Vivant-Denon, *Voyage en Égypte*, I, pl. 69 and pp. 160–161, 3; Temple, *Peru*, II, vignette p. 55 and pp. 54–55; Orme, *Hindostan*, p. 3; Gold, *Oriental Drawings*, pl. 45 and letterpress; Forbes, *Oriental Memoirs*, p. 434; Hodges, *Select Views in India*, pl. 32 and letterpress.

35. Flinders, *Terra Australis*, II, p. 111; "N. Perrin voyage inédit: Notice sur l'Ile-Barbe, près de Lyon," *Journal des Voyages de Découvertes* 7 (1820), 211; Henry Ellis, *Journal of the Proceedings of the Late Embassy to China; . . . Interspersed with Observations upon the Face of the Country, the Polity, Moral Character, and Manners of the Chinese Nation* (London: John Murray, 1817), p. 332; Lichtenstein, *Reisen im Südlichen Africa*, II, pl. p. 338 and p. 336; John M'Leod, *Narrative of a Voyage in His Majesty's Late Ship* Alceste, *to the Yellow Sea, along the Coast of Corea, and through Its Numerous Hitherto Undiscovered Islands, to the Island of Lewchew, with an Account of Her Shipwreck in the Straits of Gaspar* (London: John Murray, 1817), p. 27.

36. "Zwei Briefe über die Insel Rügen," *Journal für die neuesten Land- und Seereisen* 1 (1802), 9; Lang, *Unterirdischen-Wunder*, II, plate facing p. 152, p. 155; Porter, *Russia and Sweden*, II, pp. 178–180; "Description d'une grotte près de Tetjusch, Kasan" [from Franz von Erdmann's *Beytrage*], *Jour-*

nal des Voyages de Découvertes 27 (1825), 336–338; Raoul-Rochette, *Lettres sur la Suisse*, II, part III, pl. 7, and vignette p. 21; Baldwin, *Airopaidia*, pp. 89–91; "Mr. Smeathams Account of the Balloon Ascent at Paris," *Morning Chronicle*, October 15, 1784, in Carruthers Scrapbook, National Air and Space Museum, Washington, D.C.

37. Cochrane, *Colombia*, I, pp. 178–179.

38. Johnson, *Oriental Voyager*, pp. 45–47; Hobhouse, *Albania*, pl. p. 246 and p. 246; Westall, *Caves in Yorkshire*, p. 8; Porter, *Travels in Georgia*, II, pl. 85 and pp. 624–625.

39. Dusaulx, *Voyage à Barège*, II, p. 58; Kotzebue, *Journey into Persia*, p. 75; Cockburn, *Voyage to Cadiz*, I, pl. p. 137 and p. 137; MacKenzie, *Iceland*, pl. p. 101 and pp. 100–101. Also see Gaimard, *Voyage en Islande*; *Histoire du Voyage*, II, pp. 149–150 and atlas, pls. 77–79.

40. Forster, *Voyage round the World*, I, pp. 146–147; Mollien, *Interior of Africa*, pl. p. 233 and pp. 233–234; Oxley, *New South Wales*, pl. p. 300 and p. 299; Lycett, *Australia*, pl. 24 and letterpress; Heriot, *Pyrenean Mountains*, pl. p. 46 and pp. 45–46.

41. John Hawkesworth, *An Account of a Voyage round the World with a Full Account of the Voyage of the* Endeavour *in the Year 1770 along the East Coast of Australia by Lt. James Cook, Commander of His Majesty's Bark* Endeavour. *Compiled by D. Warrington Evans, Illustrated with a Variety of Cuts and Charts Related to the Country Discovered* (1773) (Brisbane: Smith & Paterson, 1969), pl. p. 545 and pp. 544–545. The journals of Cook and Banks were handed over to Dr. John Hawkesworth, who was commissioned to draw up an account of the voyage. In 1774, German and French editions were published. This facsimile was taken from the first edition, held in the library of the Royal Historical Society of Queensland, Newstead House, Brisbane. I have also been citing in earlier references Hawkesworth's three-volume (French) edition of the Admiralty's official collection, which includes in addition to Cook's the voyages of Byron, Wallis, and Carteret. For examples of an acute vision in depth also see Flinders, *Terra Australis*, II, pl. p. 312 and pp. 311–312; Skjöldebrand, *North Cape*, p. 5.

42. Rehder, *Unendlichen Landschaft*, pp. 205–206; Piper, *Active Universe*, pp. 3–5. This late-eighteenth-century animism should be contrasted with that of Victorians such as Tennyson and William Holman Hunt, who, while they zealously pursued accurate observation of nature, decreasingly felt its sympathetic power. Their acute sensitivity to natural detail thus often became curiously detached from any real interest in nature itself. See Christ, *Finer Optic*, pp. 17–20.

43. Batten, *Pleasurable Instruction*, p. 70. Whereas Batten seems to suggest that such an emphasis on presence and the present is a pose, I have argued throughout that discovery requires being on the spot. Those explorers committed to the Baconian ideal that knowledge of nature and discovery of truth was meant to be a public affair felt impelled to give a firsthand account of their experiences. For the new standing given to knowledge in the Enlightenment see Hahn, *Anatomy of a Scientific Institution*, pp. 36–37.

44. Geoffrey H. Hartman, *Wordsworth's Poetry: 1787–1814* (Yale University Press, 1964), pp. 85–86, 166–173; *Beyond Formalism*, pp. 207–208; Lowenthal, "English Landscape," p. 310; George H. Ford, "Felicitous Space: The Cottage Controversy," in Knoepflmacher and Tennyson, *Nature and Victorian Imagination*, p. 48. On the seventeenth-century identification of wilderness with the unadorned, the naked, the decrepit, the decultured, the monstrous—i.e., with that which lies outside the order of nature—see Bernadette Bucher, *Icon and Conquest: A Structural Analysis of de Bry's Great Voyages*, tr. Basia Miller Gulati (University of Chicago Press, 1981), pp. 107–113. For a discussion of the rise of subjectivity and point of view—that is, of a world seen and constituted from the standpoint of the individual, or, to put it another way, the growth of "intellectual eyesight" or "insight"—see Summers, *Michelangelo and Language of Art*, p. 133; Claudio Guillén, "On the Concept and Metaphor of Perspective," in *Literature as System: Essays toward the Theory of Literary History* (Princeton University Press, 1971), p. 309. The notable precursor to these studies is Murray Wright Bundy's *Theory of Imagination in Classical and Mediaeval Thought* (Folcroft, Pa.: Folcroft Library Editions, 1976), pp. 51–59. Here, Bundy analyzes the concept of "phantasy" in Plato and outlines the power of vision as that of insight or intuition.

45. Weber, "Figur in der Landschaft," pp. 44–48; Valenciennes, *Eléments de perspective*, pp. 490–493, 508.

46. Le Bruyn, *Travels*, preface; Bouguer, *Figure de la terre*, pp. lvii, xliv; Anson, *Voyage*, p. vii.

47. J. Aegidius van Egmont, *Travels through Part of Europe, Asia Minor, the Islands of the Archipelago; Syria, Palestine, Egypt, Mount Sinai, etc., Giving a Particular Account of the Most Remarkable Places, Structures, Ruins, Inscriptions, etc. in These Countries*, tr. from the Dutch (London: L. Davis and C. Reymers, 1759), I, pp. vi, viii; Forster, *Voyage round the World*, I, p. 427; George Dixon, *A Voyage round the World, Performed in 1785, 1786, 1787, and 1788 in the King George and Queen Charlotte* (London: G. Goulding, 1789), p. xxiii; Vivant-Denon, *Voyage en Egypte*, I, pp. 2–3; Burckhardt, *Travels in Nubia*, p. xci.

48. *Voyage de Humboldt et Bonpland*, I, p. v; Arago, *Voyage round the World*, I, p. xxvi.

49. Landmann, *Portugal*, I, preface; Boisgelin de Kerdu, *Denmark and Sweden*, I, p. x; Heriot, *Canadas*, pp. iv–v; Milbert, *Ile de France*, II, p. 64; Hobhouse, *Albania*, p. 242; Schmidtmeyer, *Chile*, p. 222. For Fuseli's judgment that "the last branch of uninteresting subjects [is] that kind of landscape which is entirely occupied with the tame delineation of a given spot," see Perry and Simpson, *Drawings by William Westall*, p. 21.

50. Cohen, *Sensible Words*, pp. 60, 76, and the entirety of chapter 3 ("Theories of Language and the Grammar of Sentences, 1740–1785," pp. 78–136).

51. Longinus, *On the Sublime*, tr. A. O. Prickard (Oxford: Clarendon, 1906), p. xix; Weiskel, *Romantic Sublime*, pp. 25–26; Possin, *Nature und Landschaft bei Addison*, pp. 106–108.

52. My review of perspective theory has been freely drawn from the following works: Guillén, "Metaphor of Perspective," in *Literature as System*, pp. 284–321 passim; Ernest B. Gilman, *The Curious Perspective: Literary and Pictorial Wit in the Seventeenth Century* (Yale University Press, 1978), pp. 17–47, 76–77, 228–229; James Turner, "Landscape and the 'Art Prospective' in England, 1584–1660," *Journal of the Warburg and Courtauld Institutes* 42 (1979), 290–293; Joel Snyder, "Picturing Vision," in *The Language of Images*, ed. W. J. T. Mitchell (University of Chicago Press, 1980), pp. 219–246. For the rhetorical dimension, see Trimpi, "Ut pictura poesis," pp. 1–34; Summers, *Michelangelo and the Language of Art*, pp. 17–18; Wendy Steiner, *The Colors of Rhetoric: Problems in the Relation between Modern Literaure and Painting* (University of Chicago Press, 1982), pp. 62, 87–90.

53. Rojas-Mix, "Alexander von Humboldt's Künstlerische Darstellung," in Beck, *Alexander von Humboldt*, pp. 106–111; Halina Nelken, *Humboldtiana at Harvard* (Harvard University Press, 1976), pp. 21–22; *Alexander von Humboldt. His Portraits and Their Artists: A Documentary Iconography* (Berlin: Dietrich Reimer, 1980), pp. 68–73; *Voyage de Humboldt et Bonpland*, I, pp. 122–124 and atlas, pl. 22; Kirchoff, "Science against Sciences," in Knoepflmacher and Tennyson, *Nature and Victorian Imagination*, pp. 250–251; Hewison, *Ruskin*, pp. 29–31; Brown, *Science and Creative Spirit*, p. 111. For Blake's criticism of this one-sided view of the world (which he thought perceived only its front side) and his distaste for "empirical perception" (which gives a sense of definiteness, concreteness, vividness, but not completeness), see Ault, *Visionary Physics*, p. 175. Ruskin's essence/aspect distinction did not hold for pre-Victorian observers. For Dolomieu, Goethe, or

Humboldt the "central being" of a natural phenomenon can be discerned by the scientific observer from a deeper investigation of its surface characteristics. See chapter 4 of this volume.

54. Auerbach, *Mimesis*, p. 292; Forster, *Voyage round the World*, I, p. xii.

55. Kuhn, *Structure of Scientific Revolutions*, pp. 110–111; Weber, "Figur in der Landschaft," pp. 60, 88; Schmoll, "Naturalismus und Realismus," p. 257; Finley, "Encapsulated Landscape," in Fritz, *City and Society*, pp. 204–205. Also see William K. Carr and Amiel W. Francke, "Culture and the Development of Vision," *Journal of the American Optometric Association* 47 (January 1976).

56. Wheelock, *Perspective*, pp. 115, 143–162 passim.

57. Bruce, *Travels*, I, pp. i–x.

58. Bernard Bouvier de Fontenelle, *A Plurality of Worlds* (1686), tr. John Glanville (London: Nonesuch, 1929), p. 115; Perrault, *Paralèlle*, p. 3; Hamilton, *Supplement to Campi Phlegraei*, pp. 9–10; Deluc, *Lettres physiques*, p. 146; Tuckey, *Expedition to River Zaire*, p. 257; "A View and Description of Mr. Lunardi's Aerial Voyage, from the Artillery-Ground, London, to a Field near Ware, in Hertfordshire, on Wednesday the 15th of September," *European Magazine* (September 1784), in Carruthers Scrapbook, National Air and Space Museum, Washington, D.C.; Bernardin de Saint-Pierre, *Harmonies*, IX–X, in *Oeuvres*, VII–VIII, pp. 321–322; Russell, *Lunar Planisphere*, pls. 1 and 2 and pp. 1–3. On the ambiguity caused by certain features of the moon see "Habitans lunaires," *Journal des Voyages de Découvertes* 24 (1824), 120.

59. Bernardin de Saint-Pierre, *Voyage à l'Ile de France*, in *Oeuvres*, I, pp. 89–92; Pernety, *Iles Malouïnes*, II, p. 526; Kerguelen-Trémarec, *Voyage*, pls. 10, 11 and pp. 156–157; Dixon, *Voyage round World*, pl. p. 206 and p. 205; Gratet de Dolomieu, *Mémoire sur Iles Ponces*, p. 455; D'Entrecasteaux, *Voyage*, I, p. 106; Flinders, *Terra Australis*, II, pl. p. 38 and p. 36; Forrest, *Ganges and Jumna*, p. 1; Franklin, *Journey to Polar Sea*, p. xii; Brooke, *Sweden, Norway*, pp. 137–138.

60. Cook, *Voyage*, II, pl. 32 and p. 185; Chastellux, *L'Amerique Septentrionale*, II, pls. 1, 2 and pp. 69–71; Kirkpatrick, *Nepaul*, p. 124; Lycett, *Australia*, p. 10. For the suggestion that there is a typical "movement of thought" in the reaction to and description of experiences of nature such as these (especially Chastellux's description of the natural bridge), see Garry Wills, *Inventing America: Jefferson's Declaration of Independence* (New York: Doubleday, 1978), chapter 19. I am grateful to J. Carson Webster for drawing my attention to this reference. For a sensitive discussion of "environmental perception" as an intensification of attitude toward nature see Glacken, "Chateaubriand's Journey to Jerusalem," pp. 50–51.

61. Houel, *Voyage*, II, pl. 102 and p. 58; Raoul-Rochette, *Lettres sur la Suisse*, I, part II, p. 29; Milbert, *L'Ile de France*, I, p. 216; Cochrane, *Colombia*, I, pp. 11–12.

62. Weld, *North America*, pp. 314–320; D'Entrecasteaux, *Voyage*, I, p. 117.

63. Deane, *Aspects of Nature Poetry*, pp. 103, 106; Røstvig, *Happy Man*, II, pp. 37, 41–42.

64. Broc, *Les montagnes*, p. 31; Hentzi, *Vues remarquables*, pl. 1 and p. 11. On the difficulty of establishing a point of view, especially in the mountains, see Grand-Carteret, *La montagne*, I, p. 490.

65. Brydone, *Sicily and Malta*, I, pp. 200–201; Kershaw, *Burman Empire*, p. 5; Franklin, *Second Journey to Polar Sea*, pl. p. 4 and p. 4; Landmann, *Portugal*, II, pl. p. 168 and p. 167; *Voyage de Humboldt et Bonpland*, I, p. 233, and atlas, pl. 34; Johnson, *Oriental Voyager*, pp. 8–9; Hakewell, *Jamaica*, pl. 14 and letterpress.

66. Forster, *Voyage round the World*, I, p. 349; Johnson, *West Indies*, plate: *English Harbour, Antigua from Great George Fort*, and letterpress; D'Entrecasteaux, *Voyage*, I, pp. 218–219.

67. Bernardin de Saint-Pierre, *Harmonies*, IX–X, in *Oeuvres*, VII-VIII, pp. 192–193; Carver, *North-America*, p. 143; Cook, *Voyage*, I, p. xxvii; Dixon, *Voyage round the World*, p. 61.

68. Irwin, *Voyage up Red Sea*, p. 329; Belzoni, *Egypt and Nubia*, p. 59. Also see Fréminville, *Voyage to North Pole*, p. 88.

69. *Leichter als Luft*, p. 115; Brydone, *Sicily and Malta*, I, pp. 18–19; Saussure, *Voyages dans les Alpes*, I, p. 307; Forrest, *Ganges and Jumna*, p. 136.

70. *Rapport fait à l'Académie des sciences sur la machine aérostatique, inventée par MM. de Montgolfier* (Paris: Moutard, 1784), pp. 11, 23–26; George Adams, *An Essay on Electricity*, second revised edition (London: Logographic Press, 1785), p. 250; Buhan Armand-Gouffé, *Des fougerais, Gilles aéronaute, ou l'Amerique n'est pas loin* (Paris: Logerot, 1799), p. 34; Turnor, *Astra Castra*, pp. 363–364.

71. Baldwin, *Airopaidia*, n. 5, pp. 141–142. Something of this experience of total encirclement was approximated in mountain panoramas; see Solar and Hösli, *Panoramen der Schweiz*, pp. 65, 82; Faujas de Saint-Fond, *Essai de géologie*, I, pp. 2–3; Williams, *Travels*, I, p. 36.

72. Baldwin, *Airopaidia*, p. 171.

73. E. Salchi, *L'origine de l'univers, ou la philosophie des voyages autour du monde* (Bern: Emmanuel Haller, 1799), pp. 3–4; M. Paris, "Le globe aérostatique, ode," (1784), p. 64; "Account of a French Lady in a Balloon with Mr Garnerin [1798]," Carruthers Scrapbook, National Air and Space Museum, Washington, D.C.; Baldwin, *Airopaidia*, plate facing p. 58 and pp. 75, 81. This new experience of space had a parallel in stage design. The extreme spatial depth and more distant infinities of seventeenth-century settings were replaced by more intimate and proximate spatial conceptions in the eighteenth century. See Eddelman, "Landscape on Stage," p. 238.

74. On Romanticism's (especially German Romanticism's) view from a height, both in art and in literature, see Marshall Brown, *The Shape of German Romanticism* (Ithaca, N.Y.: Cornell University Press, 1979), pp. 42–47. On the "failure" of the Enlightenment system—once it had drawn the distinction between mythical thinking and scientific thinking—to see how these might be bound up with one another as phases in the history of single culture, society, or individual consciousness, see White, *The Irrational and Historical Knowledge*, in *Tropics of Discourse*, p. 143.

Conclusion

1. For a discussion of culturally determined habits of analysis, i.e., the shared disposition to address visual experience in or out of a picture in special ways, see Michael Baxandall, *Painting and Experience in Fifteenth-Century Italy: A Primer in the Social History of Pictorial Style* (Oxford: Clarendon, 1972) pp. 89, 101.

2. White, *Metahistory*, pp. 50, 69–79; *Tropics of Discourse*, pp. 231–236; "Fictions of Factual Representation," in Fletcher, *Literature of Fact*, pp. 33–36. On the importance of science and natural history as subject matter in English poetry (especially descriptive poetry) during the years 1760–1800, and their usefulness in helping the writer penetrate farther into the secrets of nature, see William Powell Jones, *The Rhetoric of Science: A Study of Scientific Ideas and Imagery in Eighteenth-Century English Poetry* (University of California Press, 1966), pp. 182–185.

3. White, *Tropics of Discourse*, pp. 239–251 passim; Richard Woodfield, "Thomas Hobbes and the Formation of Aesthetics in England," *British Journal of Aesthetics* 20 (spring 1980) 146–152; Carolyn Korsmeyer, "The Two Beauties: A Perspective on Hutcheson's Aesthetics," *Journal of Aesthetics and Art and Art Criticism* 38 (winter 1979), 146–150; Batton, *Pleasurable Instruction*, p. 92; D'Entrecasteaux, *Voyage*, I, pp. ix–x. Hobbes was an important early challenger of the notion that the artist could produce an accurate representation of nature rather than only his perception of it. The "inner sense" psychologists (in-

cluding Francis Hutcheson), while holding that a disinterested enjoyment of an object's perceptual qualities was possible, declared nonetheless that beauty did not belong to an object but was an idea in the mind of the perceiver. On the idea that after the Fall man abandoned immediacy in the communication of the concrete and fell into the abyss of the mediateness of all communication, see Walter Benjamin, *Reflections, Essays, Aphorisms, Autobiographical Writings*, ed. Peter Demetz and tr. Edmund Jephcott (New York: Harcourt Brace Jovanovich, 1978), p. 328.

4. White, "Fictions of Factual Representation," in Fletcher, *Literature of Fact*, pp. 37–38. On this point, White's discussion of Darwin's *Origin of the Species* is especially illuminating. The naturalist, desiring to remain within the ambit of plain fact, insisted that there is a real order in nature, not one that is the result of some spiritual or teleological power. The order he sought in the data must be manifest in the facts themselves. Like Kant, Darwin insisted that the source of all error is semblance; thus, he was against analogy, the merely metaphorical characterizations of facts. As a scientist and explorer he wanted to make the case for real affinities; everything must be entertained as what it manifestly seems to be. Also see White, *Metahistory*, p. 51; Batten, *Pleasurable Instruction*, pp. 6, 30–38, 72–81, 107; Viallaneix, "Chateaubriand voyageur," p. 563; Grand-Carteret, *La montagne*, II, p. 40; Gerald Finley, "The Genesis of Turner's 'Landscape Sublime,'" *Zeitschrift für Kunstgeschichte* 42, no. 2–3 (1979), 153, 163. On the travel book as part of the expanding nineteenth-century publishing enterprise, whereby the public's contact with book and periodical illustrations vastly outnumbered their encounter with original drawings, see Clive Ashwin, "Graphic Imagery, 1837–1901: A Victorian Revolution," *Art History* 1 (September 1978), 360.

5. Eugène Fromentin, *Sahara & Sahel*, third edition (Paris: Plon, 1879), I, pp. vii–xi; II, pp. 195, 339–343; Cassas, *Voyage de la Syrie*, I, p. 2; Sonnini, *Voyage dans l'Egypte*, I, p. 4; Edward Lear, *Journals of a Landscape Painter in Southern Calabria* (London: Richard Bentley, 1852), pp. 111–112. For Lear's method in action also see *Views in Rome and Its Environs. Drawn from Nature and on Stone* (London: T. M'Lean, 1841), pl. 5; John Carne, *Syria, The Holy Land, Asia Minor, etc. Illustrated. In a Series of Views Drawn from Nature [by] W. H. Bartlett, William Purser, etc. With Descriptions of the Plates by . . . Author of "Letters from the East"* (London: Fisher, 1836), I, pl. p. 46; *Memoir and Letters of the Late Thomas Seddon, Artist. By His Brother (1854–1856)* (London: James Nisbet, 1858), pp. 52–53. Also note the shared attitude toward nature and travel of Fromentin and Delacroix; see Eugène Delacroix, *Journal*,

1822–1852, ed. André Joubin (Paris: Plon, 1950), I, pp. 124–127, 137, 147, 152. It is entirely dissimilar from the journalistic treatment of exotic inhabitants as practiced by Gérôme and the *Orientalistes*; see Philippe Jullian, *Les orientalistes. La vision de l'Orient par les peintres européens au XIXe siècle* (Freiburg: Office du Libre, 1977), pp. 58–61; Gerald M. Ackermann, *Jean-Léon Gérôme (1824–1904)* (Dayton, Ohio: Dayton Art Institute, 1972), pp. 11–12, 16–26. Edward Said [*Orientalism* (New York: Pantheon, 1978), p. 42] would have it that such "imperial" representations involve the appropriation of one culture by another.

6. Charles-Pierre Baudelaire, *Paradis artificiels* (1851), in *Oeuvre complètes*, ed. Y.-G. Le Dantec and Claude Pichois (Paris: Gallimard, 1961), pp. 342–343, 348–350. Doubtless the negative reaction of the Romantics to the nonfiction travel account was in part due to their perception of it as mere scientific illustration. For the history and importance of the latter from the Renaissance onward and its concern with communicable descriptive techniques, precise and full reporting of observations, and new possibilities of duplicating detailed naturalistic images, see Eisenstein, *Printing Press as Agent of Change*, II, pp. 468–470. Analogously, for Hegel's conception of the varieties of historical writing, divided into prosaic statement of fact and poetic recreation, see White, *Metahistory*, pp. 86–88.

7. Smith, *European Vision and South Pacific*, p. 251; Viallaneix, "Chateaubriand voyageur," pp. 569–573; Carnochan, *Confinement and Flight*, p. 104.

8. On the enthusiasm for and the opposition to innovation, see A. C. Quatremère de Quincy, *Considérations sur les arts du dessin en France* (Paris: Desenne, 1794), pp. 44–45; Etienne-Louis Boullée, *Architecture. Essai sur l'art*, ed. J.-M. Pérouse de Montclos (Paris: Hermann, 1968), pp. 43–44; Boime, *Academy and French Painting*, p. 178; Emil Kaufmann, *Architecture in the Age of Reason* (Cambridge, Mass.: Archon, 1966), pp. 146, 161–166. On the Romantic poetic as the poetic of the technological age, growing out of the same ground although they appear diametrically opposed, and each, in its own way growing out of noetic abundance, see Ong, *Rhetoric, Romance, and Technology*, p. 279.

9. For the rapidly mounting literature concerning the seductiveness of science for the eighteenth-century mind, see especially Darnton, *Mesmerism*, pp. 2–45; Gillespie, *Edge of Objectivity*, pp. 151–201 passim; Heilbron, *Electricity*, pp. 344–372. Also see Hahn, *Anatomy*, pp. 257–261, 274–275; Ann Lorenz Van Zanten, "The Palace and the Temple: Two Utopian Architectural Visions of the 1830s," *Art History* 2 (June 1979), 179–187.

10. Eisenstein, *Printing Press as Agent of Change*, II, pp. 465–469; Robert McRae, "The Unity of the Sciences: Bacon, Descartes, Leibniz," in Wiener and Noland, *Roots of Scientific Thought*, pp. 390–397. For the continuing importance of Bacon's ideas to the making of art, see Elizabeth Sewell, *The Orphic Voice: Poetry and Natural History* (Yale University Press, 1960), pp. 57–62.

11. Foucault, *Birth of the Clinic*, pp. 113–120; Raymond Williams, *Keywords: A Vocabulary of Culture and Society* (Oxford University Press, 1976), pp. 233–234. The word *science* came into English in the fourteenth century from French as a term for knowledge. Thereafter, it became more generally used, often interchangeably with "art," to describe a particular body of knowledge or skill (*scientia*). But from the middle of the seventeenth century certain changes are evident; a distinction between science and art is made on the basis of difficulty (i.e., a skill requiring theoretical knowledge versus a skill requiring only practice). By the early eighteenth century, at a theoretical level, *science* denoted a kind of knowledge, argument, or method rather than a kind of subject.

12. Guitton, *Jacques Delille*, p. 558; Frye, *English Romanticism*, pp. 10–12; Albert Boime, "Marmontel's *Bélisaire* and the Pre-Revolutionary Progressivism of David," *Art History* 3 (March 1980), 81. For the seventeenth-century background of the idea that a study of the arts and sciences as intellectual disciplines in themselves might be useful to the practicing painter, see Charles Dempsey, *Annibale Carracci and the Beginnings of Baroque Style* (Glückstadt: J. J. Augustin, 1977), p. 47.

13. Walter R. Davis, "The Imagery of Bacon's Late Work," in *Seventeenth-Century Prose: Modern Essays in Criticism*, ed. Stanley E. Fish (Oxford University Press, 1971), pp. 239–250; Badt, *Constable's Clouds*, p. 27; White, *Metahistory*, pp. 51–54.

14. Knoepfelmacher and Tennyson, *Nature and Victorian Imagination*, pp. xviii–xix; Frye, *English Romanticism*, p. 88; Bénichou, *Le sacre de l'écrivain*, pp. 130–133; François-August Chateaubriand, *Génie du christianisme, ou beautés de la religion chrétienne. Edition abrégée à l'usage de la jeunesse* (Paris: d'Herhan, 1807), II, pp. 163 ff.

15. Foucault, *Les mots et les choses*, pp. 146–147; Anthony D. Smith, "The 'Historical Revival' in Late Eighteenth-Century England and France," *Art History* 2 (June 1979), 162.

16. Fletcher, *Literature of Fact*, pp. viii-xii, xxii-xxiii; Auerbach, *Mimesis*, pp. 374–390 passim. Also see the following essays pub-

lished in Fish's *Seventeenth-Century Prose*:
R. F. Jones, "Science and Language in
England of The Mid-Seventeenth-Cen-
tury," pp. 94–111; Perry Miller, "The Plain
Style," pp. 147–186; A. C. Howell, "*Res et
Verba*: Words and Things," pp. 187–199.

17. Remy G. Saisselin, "Néoclassicisme,
discours et temps," *Gazette des Beaux-arts*
94 (July–August 1979), 21–23; "Tivoli Re-
visited," in Fritz, *Triumph of Culture*, pp.
20–22; Hahn, *Anatomy*, pp. 48–49; Baker,
Condorcet, pp. 120–122. For the observation that the private collector dreams that
he is not only in a distant or past world
but also, at the same time, in a better one
where things are freed of the drudgery of
being useful, see Benjamin, *Reflections*,
p. 155.

18. Fredrick Accum, *Elements of Crystallography, After the Method of Haüy; With or
Without a Series of Geometrical Models*
(London: Longman, Hurst, Rees, Orme,
and Brown, 1813), pp. 5–9. The difference
between an organic (biological) model and
an inorganic (crystallographic) model operates, I believe, in late-eighteenth-century
aesthetic discussions. If the Romantic work
of art denotes a composition akin to the
complex mechanism of vegetable and animal substances, then the Neoclassical
sense of structure is analogous to the arrangement of solids which combine and
multiply geometrically. The distinction
may be summed up as one between a
principle of organization and a system of
aggregation.

19. Adhémar, "Lithographies de paysage,"
p. 204; Valenciennes, *Eléments de perspective*, pp. 453, 476, 528, 538–543, 567, 573,
615. See Harold Osbourne's interesting attempt to relate the scientist's quest for rational understanding and search for order
to the artistic enterprise in "Concepts of
Order in the Natural Sciences and in the
Visual Fine Arts," *Leonardo* 14 (autumn
1981), 290–294.

20. Peter Gay, *Art and Act. On Causes in
History—Manet, Gropius, Mondrian* (New
York: Harper & Row, 1976), pp. 3–7; King-
Hele, *Erasmus Darwin*, p. 87; Nicolson,
Mountain Gloom, p. 379; David Watkin,
*Thomas Hope (1769–1831) and the Neo-Clas-
sical Idea* (London: Murray, 1968), p. 113.
For the contrary notion that the landscape
is not alive, see the essay by Delécluze
published in the *Journal des Débats*, June
22, 1861, and cited in Pierre Miquel's *Le
paysage français au XIXᵉ siècle, 1824–1874.
L'école de la nature* (Maurs-La-Jolie: Marti-
nelle), I, pp. 56, 73. For Ruskin's belief,
cited in *Modern Painters*, that specific and
historic facts (lichen, rock striations) are
more important than general or transitory
ones (light, atmosphere), see Allen Staley,
The Pre-Raphaelite Landscape (Oxford:
Clarendon, 1973), p. 51.

21. Guillén, *Literature as System*, pp. 287,
330–332, 310–311; Summers, *Michelangelo
and Language of Art*, pp. 166–167, 181;
Raymond Williams, *Culture and Society,
1780–1950* (London: Chatto & Windus,
1973), pp. xv–xvii, 32–38, 43–44, 67–70;
Keywords, pp. 28, 34–35; Baker, *Condorcet*,
p. 189; Eisenstein, *Printing Press as Agent
of Change*, II, pp. 559–563; R. G. Saisselin,
"Neo-Classicism: Images of Public Virtue
and Realities of Private Luxury," *Art History* 4 (March 1981), 34; Dorothy Walsh,
"Some Functions of Pictorial Representation," *British Journal of Aesthetics* 21 (winter 1981), 33–34; Michael Kitson, "Painting
from Nature," *Burlington* 123 (February
1981), 112; Gilman, *Curious Perspective*,
pp. 70–71; Marc H. Bernstein, "The Ecological Approach to Visual Perception,"
Journal of Aesthetics and Art Criticism 39
(winter 1980), 204. For an important antecedent to the Romantic "voyage in the
mind" see Hobbes's discussion in the *Leviathan* and the *de Homine* of the "vast
spaces" the animal spirits cover as they
speedily range in thought from phantasm
to phantasm. Hobbes's unguided mental
discourse (that is, wit bereft of judgment)
follows a careening path parallel to that of
mental operations. See Elizabeth J. Cook,
"Thomas Hobbes and the Far-Fetched,"
*Journal of the Warburg and Courtauld Insti-
tutes* 44 (1981), 231–232.

22. On Coleridge's central role in demanding a mind not passive but active and constituent, as in Kant, and an imagination
not decorative but creative in the highest
sense, see Basil Willey, *Samuel Taylor Coleridge* (New York: Norton, 1972), pp.
88–89. For a complex formulation of a
"Romantic" theory of the creative imagination, see James Engell, *The Creative
Imagination: Enlightenment to Romanticism*
(Harvard University Press, 1981), pp.
338–353. See also Frye, *Fables of Identity*,
pp. 135–137; McFarland, "Coleridge's Theory of Secondary Imagination," in Hartman, *New Perspectives*, pp. 195–200;
Werner Hofmann, "Les écrivains-dessinateurs, I: Introduction," *Revue de l'Art* 44
(1979), n. 9, p. 18; Levitine, *Dawn of Bohemianism*, p. 132. Also see the introductory
essay by George Levitine to the exhibition
catalogue by Melinda Curtis, *Search for Innocence: Primitive and Primitivistic Art of
the Nineteenth Century* (College Park: University of Maryland Art Gallery, 1975).

23. Alphonse de Lamartine, *Souvenirs,
impressions, pensées et paysages pendant un
voyage en Orient 1832–1833, ou notes d'un
voyageur*, in *Oeuvres complètes* (Paris: de
Lamartine, 1862), I, pp. 5–6; II, pp. 5–9,
154, 160, 169–170; Théophile Gautier,
Voyage pittoresque en Algérie (1845), ed.
Madeleine Cottin (Geneva: Droz, 1973), p.
64; Delacroix, *Journal*, I, p. 147; Maxime
du Camp, *Le Nil. Egypte et Nubie*, fourth
edition (Paris: Hachette, 1877), p. 9. The

etcher Prosper Méryon, who circumnavigated the globe between 1842 and 1846, speaks of the 200 passengers on board the *Rhin* as each experiencing individually the "strong poetry" born "of the contact of our senses, our imagination, with the grandeur of nature." See Philippe Néagu, "Méryon: le voyage en Océanie. Lettres de Méryon à l'Administration des Beaux-Arts concernant la publication de son *Voyage en Océanie*," *Nouvelles de l'Estampe* 58–59 (July–October, 1981), 16.

24. Robson-Scott, *Goethe and Visual Arts*, p. 85. For a discussion of how, after Descartes, the appearance-reality distinction began to slip out of focus and was replaced by the inner-outer distinction, which was left for Kant to resolve, see Richard Rorty, *Philosophy and the Mirror of Nature* (Princeton, N.J.: Princeton University Press, 1979), pp. 160–164. Rorty notes that, by the time of Kant, it looked as if there were two alternative foundations for knowledge: One had to choose between the interiorized version of the Platonic Forms, Cartesian clear and distinct ideas, on the one hand, and Humean "impressions" resulting from external nature, on the other. Kant, in rejecting both these putative objects as incomplete unless combined in "synthesis," was the first to think of the foundations of knowledge as the rules, not the objects, which the mind had set up for itself. Kant's system, which permits us to decide what nature was allowed to be like, was developed to the point of radical subjectivity, especially by Johann Gottlieb Fichte and Friedrich Schelling. See Schelling, *The Unconditional in Human Knowledge. Four Early Essays (1794–1797)*, tr. Fritz Marti (Bucknell University Press, 1980), pp. 71–72. On the Romantics' journey into the interior, see the many essays by Erich Heller, especially those collected in *The Artist's Journey into the Interior, and Other Essays* (New York: Random House, 1965) and *The Disinherited Mind; Essays in Modern German Literature and Thought* (Cambridge: Bowes & Bowes, 1952), and the more recent writings of Marshall Brown, *The Shape of German Romanticism* (Cornell University Press, 1979), pp. 142–160. For the opposition between Goethe's clear, "Greek" vision and Heinrich Heine's irony, see Heine's *Die Harzreise*, in *Werke* (Munich: Beck, 1973), I, pp. 288–289.

25. Foucault, *Les mots et les choses*, p. 150; Béguin, *L'âme romantique*, II, p. 328; Jörg Traeger, *Philip Otto Runge und sein Werk, Monographie und kritischer Katalog* (Munich: Prestel, 1975), p. 38; Gaston, *Pyrénées*, p. 47; Peter Brooks, "Godlike Science / Unhallowed Arts: Language and Monstrosity in *Frankenstein*," *New Literary History* 9 (spring 1978), 591–592; Bachelard, *Poetics of Space*, p. 205.

26. Guitton, " 'L'invention,' " p. 697, *William Hazlitt's Essays on Reynolds' Discourses, Written for the Champion*, in Wark, *Discourses*, pp. 331–332; Martin Meisel, " 'Half Sick of Shadows': The Aesthetic Dialogue in Pre-Raphaelite Painting," in Knoepflmacher and Tennyson, *Nature and Victorian Imagination*, n. 3, p. 311; Mary Poovey, "Mary Shelley and the Feminization of Romanticism," *PMLA* 95 (May 1980), 345.

27. Hugh Honour, *Romanticism* (New York: Harper & Row, 1979), p. 17; Traeger, *Runge*, pp. 39, 45; J.-L. Vieillard-Baron, "Hemsterhuis, platonicien, 1721–1790," *Dix-Huitième Siècle* 7 (1975), 144–145; Leslie Parris, Ian Fleming-Williams, and Conal Shields, *Constable: Paintings, Watercolours & Drawings* (London: Tate Gallery, 1976), entries for catalog nos. 263, 311, 331 and pp. 156, 174, 188; Andrew Wilton, *Turner and the Sublime* (London: British Museum, 1980), pp. 25 ff.; Pierre Georgel, "Le romantisme des années 1860 et la correspondance Victor Hugo–Philippe Burty," *Revue de l'Art* 20 (1973), 33; Patterson, *Poetic Genius*, p. 70.

28. Mongland, *Le préromantisme français*, I, pp. 12, 114–115; Mornet, *Romantisme en France*, pp. 35–38. Also see Williams, *Culture and Society*, pp. 45–47, for an explanation of Keats's romantic designation of "negative capability": " . . . when a man is capable of being in uncertainties, mysteries, doubts, without any irritable reaching after fact and reason."

29. Werner Sumowski, *Caspar David Friedrich-Studien* (Wiesbaden: Steiner, 1970), pp. 7, 116; Helmut Börsch-Supan, *Caspar David Friedrich* (Munich: Prestel, 1973), pp. 16–20, 29, 46–48, 138, 154; "L'arbre aux corbeaux de Caspar David Friedrich," *Revue du Louvre* 4 (1976), 285–289. Among recent critics, only Werner Hofmann and William Vaughan deny to Friedrich's paintings the religious significance that Börsch-Supan, in particular, would see everywhere. See Werner Hofmann, *Caspar David Friedrich und die Deutsche Nachwelt* (Frankfurt-am-Main: Suhrkamp, 1977). Nonetheless, his Marxist slant and purely socio-political interpretation strike me as equally inadequate. Also see William Vaughan, *German Romantic Painting* (Yale University Press, 1980), p. 74.

30. Schubert, *Nachtseite der Naturwissenschaft*, pp. 184–188, 192–196.

31. Carl Gustav Carus, *Neun Briefe über die Landschaftsmalerei* (Leipzig: Gerhard Fleischer, 1831), pp. 182–184; Marianne Prause, *Carl Gustav Carus: Leben und Werk* (Berlin: Deutscher Verlag für Kunstwissenschaft, 1968), pp. 15–16, 26; Sumowski, *Friedrich-Studien*, pp. 19–20.

32. Nelken, *Humboldtiana at Harvard*, pp. 21–26; Prause, *Carus*, pp. 44, 104; Carus, *Neun Briefe*, pp. 173–179.

33. Carus, *Neun Briefe*, pp. 27, 50, 108–109, 118–119, 135, 139–141.

34. Badt, *Constable's Clouds*, pp. 22–23; Prause, *Carus*, pp. 42–43, 53; Marie Bang, "Two Alpine Landscapes by C. D. Friedrich," *Burlington* 107 (November 1966), 571–572; Helmut Börsch-Supan, "Caspar David Friedrich et Carl Friedrich Schinkel," *Revue de l'Art* 45 (1979), 9, 11, 18; Eva Börsch-Supan, "Architektur und Landschaft," in *Karl Friedrich Schinkel. Werke und Wirkungen* (Berlin: Martin-Gropius-Bau, 1981), p. 55; Müller-Hofstede, *Weitsch*, pp. 146–147, 164–180; Börsch-Supan, *Friedrich*, pp. 98, 108, pls. 15, 20; Bachelard, *La terre et rêveries de la volonté*, pp. 201–203. For a documented, if late, instance of the influence of travel literature on Friedrich (Parry's 1819–20 expedition in search of the Northwest Passage), see Wolfgang Stechow, "Caspar David Friedrich und der 'Griper,'" in *Festschrift für Herbert von Einem*, ed. Gert von der Osten and Georg Kauffman (Berlin: Mann, 1965), pp. 241–245.

35. *Ossian und die Kunst um 1800*, pp. 90–93; Prause, *Carus*, p. 28; Otto Schmitt, "Ein Skizzenbuch C. D. Friedrichs im Wallraf-Richartz Museum," *Wallraf-Richartz Jahrbuch* 11 (1930), 292; Andreas Aubert, *Caspar David Friedrich: Gott, Freiheit, Vaterland* (Berlin: Bruno Cassirer, 1915), pls. 7, 8.

36. Wilhelm Weber, "Luther-Denkmäler—Frühe Projekte und Verwirklichungen," in *Denkmäler im 19. Jahrhunderts, Deutung und Kritik*, ed. Hans Ernst Mittig and Volker Plagemann (Munich: Prestel, 1972), pp. 183, 187; Nikolaus Pevsner, "The Egyptian Revival," in *Studies in Art, Architecture and Design* (New York: Walker, 1968), I, p. 233; Robson-Scott, *Literary Background of Gothic Revival*, p. 63; Maurice Rheims, *La sculpture au XIXᵉ siècle* (Paris: Arts et Métiers Graphiques, 1972), p. 45; Fred Licht, *Sculpture, Nineteenth and Twentieth Centuries* (Greenwich, Conn.: New York Graphic Society, 1967), pp. 308, 318; "Vue de Corse: Le lion de Bastia," *Magasin Pittoresque* 39 (1833), 232.

37. Bauer, "Architektur als Kunst. Von der Grösse der Idealistischen Architektur-Asthetik und ihrem Verfall," in *Kunstgeschichte*, pp. 147–152; Béguin, *L'âme romantique*, I, p. 102; Burda, *Die Ruine*, p. 21.

38. James Fergusson, *Rude Stone Monuments in All Countries; Their Age and Uses* (London: John Murray, 1872), pp. 43–44, 57–58; Friedrich Piel, *Das Ornament-Groteske in der Italienishen Renaissance; zu Ihrer Kategorialen Struktur und Entstehung* (Berlin: De Gruyter, 1962), pp. 8, 44–45; Bush, *Colossal Sculpture*, pp. 13, 18–36;

René Schneider, *L'esthétique classique chez Quatremère de Quincy* (Paris: Hachette, 1910), p. 70; Quatremère de Quincy, *Encyclopédie méthodique*, III, p. 542; J. F. Sobry, *La poétique des arts ou cours de peinture et de littérature comparée* (Paris: Delaunay, 1810), p. 302; Jean Humbert, "Les obélisques de Paris—projets et réalisations," *Revue de l'Art* 23 (1974), 16–17. Also see the section "In Praise of Hands" in Henri Focillon's *The Life of Forms in Art* (New York: Wittenborn, Schultz, 1948), p. 71, where he states: " . . . for long ages it [the hand] piled unhewn boulders one upon the other to commemorate the dead and to honour the gods. Using vegetable juices to brighten the monotony of such objects, the hand deferred once again to the Earth's gifts. . . ."

39. Alexis Bertrand, *François Rude* (Paris: Librairie de l'Art, 1888), pp. 69–71; Licht, *Sculpture*, p. 313; "Le Napoleon du Mont-Blanc," and "Un monument en l'honneur de Napoleon," *Magasin Pittoresque* 48 (1841), 8, 311; Grand-Carteret, *La montagne*, I, pp. 28–29. For the longevity of this idea of literally merging man with mountain and its international scope, see Emil Nolde's 1894 illustrations of Alpine monoliths transformed into gigantic supernatural creatures. [Cited in Robert Rosenblum's *Modern Painting and the Northern Romantic Tradition: From Friedrich to Rothko* (New York: Harper & Row, 1975), p. 135.] Diane Lesko, in "Cézanne's 'Bather' and a Found Self-Portrait," *Artforum* (December 1976), pp. 53–54, n. 9, p. 57, argues that such anthropomorphic imagery is hidden in the post-Impressionist landscapes of Cézanne and Gauguin. During the 1960s, Robert Smithson and Hans Hacke created enormous land masses that merged with the environment. (See Celant, *Art Povera*, pp. 139, 179.) On the revival of such anamorphic figures at the turn of the nineteenth century and their importance to Romanticism see Baltrušaitis, *Anamorphoses*, pp. 74–76, the introduction and chapter 2 of the present volume.

40. "Napoleon et l'écologie," editorial, *Gazette des Beaux-Arts*, 90 (November 1977), 1–2. Perhaps the political lesson—the painful need for tearing order out of chaotic matter—was learned here.

41. *Les carnets de David d'Angers*, I, pp. 50, 165; II, pp. 4–35, 187, 190, 213. The Pyrenees and their gigantic incarnations play a striking role in Francisco de Goya's imagery, both early and late in his career. See F. D. Klingender, *Goya in the Democratic Tradition* (New York: Schocken, 1968), pp. 207–208; José Gudiol, *Goya, 1746–1828, Biography, Analytical Study and Catalogue of his Paintings*, tr. Kenneth Lyons (Barcelona: Poligrafa, 1971), I, pls. 863–866, 325; II, pls. 965, catalog no. 610.

42. Werner Oechslin, "Pyramide et sphère. Notes sur l'architecture révolutionnaire du

XVIIIe siècle et ses sources italiennes," *Gazette des Beaux-Arts* 77 (April 1971), 204; Oscar Reutersvärd, "De 'sjunkande' Cenotafierna hos Moreau, Fontaine, Boullée och Gay," *Konsthistorisk Tidskrift* 28 (1959), 125–126; Majewski, "Mercier," n. 13, p. 21; Viel de Saint-Maux, *Lettres*, p. 7. For a discussion of eighteenth-century materialist aesthetics—as expressed in the architectural writings of Carlo Lodoli and Marc-Antoine Laugier—see Joseph Rykwert, *The First Moderns: The Architects of the Eighteenth Century* (MIT Press, 1980), pp. 288 ff.

43. Kaufmann, *Architecture in Age of Reason*, p. 151; J.-M. Pérouse de Montclos, *Etienne-Louis Boullée (1728–1799), de l'architecture classique à l'architecture révolutionnaire* (Paris: Arts et Métiers Graphiques, 1969), pp. 200–202; Boullée, *Architecture*, pp. 25, 33; Klaus Lankheit, *Der Tempel der Vernunft. Unveröffentliche Zeichnungen von Etienne-Louis Boullée* (Basel: Birkhäuser, 1968), pp. 20–22; Barbara Maria Stafford, "Science as Fine Art: Another look at Boullée's *Cenotaph for Newton*," *Studies in Eighteenth-Century Culture* 11 (1981); Allan Braham, *The Architecture of the French Enlightenment* (London: Thames and Hudson, 1980), pp. 181–182; Michel Gallet, *Claude-Nicolas Ledoux, 1736–1806* (Paris: Picard, 1980), pp. 12–14, 104–125. For a study of the role of crystals in German Expressionist architecture and design (but one that does not seem to recognize the eighteenth-century prototype), see Rosemary Haag Bletter, "The Interpretation of the Glass Dream—Expressionist Architecture and the History of the Crystal Metaphor," *Journal of the Society of Architectural Historians* 40 (March 1981), 20–43. Among the most significant Romantic uses of the metaphor of crystallization—seen as a process of accretion or layering—which, Bletter does not mention is Stendhal's view of love as a process of endless crystallization, an intuition inspired by his descent into a salt mine at Salzburg. See Stendhal [Henri Beyle], "De l'amour," in *Oeuvres complètes*, ed. Daniel Muller and Pierre Jourda (Paris: Librairie Ancienne Honoré Champion, 1926), I, pp. 33–34.

44. Jacques Guillerme, "Lequeu, entre l'irregulier et l'éclectique," pp. 167–173; "Lequeu et l'invention du mauvais goût," p. 161; Jean-Jacques Marty, "Les cas de Jean-Jacques Lequeu," *Macula* 5–6 (1979), 140–141, 149.

45. The sensation of boundlessness sought by the revolutionary architects and their quest for *caractère* modeled after nature's powerful effects were presaged in Le Camus de Mézières's *Le génie de l'architecture ou l'analogie de cet art avec nos sensations* (Paris, 1780) and cited in Erik Forssman's *Dorisch, Jonisch, Korinthisch. Studien über den Gebrauch der Säulenordnungen in der Architektur des 16.-18. Jahrhunderts* (Stockholm: Almquist & Wiksell, 1961), pp.

121–124. On the encouragement of invention in the creation of new orders from the middle of the seventeenth century on, see J. M. Pérouse de Montclose, "Le sixième order d'architecture, ou la pratique des ordres suivants les nations," *Journal of the Society of Architectural Historians* 36 (December 1977), 226–227, 232, 240. On the Romantic taste for "darksome rocks" and "secret caves" see G. Wilson Knight, *The Starlit Dome: Studies in the Poetry of Vision* (London: Oxford University Press, 1941), pp. 183–186; Rosenblum, *Northern Romantic Tradition*, pp. 102, 112; Inge Eichler, "Die Cervarafeste der Deutschen Künstler in Rom," *Zeitschrift des Deutschen Vereins für Kunstwissenschaft* 31, no. 1 (1977), 82.

46. Lister, *British Romantic Painting* (London: Bell, 1973), pp. 43–44, 107; Geoffrey Grigson, "Fingal's Cave," *Architectural Review* 104 (August 1948), 51–54; Hardie, *Water-Colour Painting in Britain* II, pls. 12, 18, 20, 76, 77; Adele M. Holcomb, *John Sell Cotman* (London: British Museum, 1978), pls. 23, 33, 160, 161; John Summerson, "Le tombeau de Sir John Soane," *Revue de l'Art* 30 (1975), 52; William Feaver, *The Art of John Martin* (Oxford: Clarendon, 1975), pp. 88–89, 98, 149.

47. Wilton, *Turner and the Sublime*, catalog nos. 19–31 and pp. 116–122; John Russell and Andrew Wilton, *Turner in der Schweiz* (Dübendorf: De Clive, 1976), pp. 9–11.

48. See Louis Hawes, "Constable's *Hadleigh Castle* and British Romantic Ruin Painting," *Art Bulletin* 65 (September 1983), 455–470.

49. John Constable, *Discourses*, ed. R. B. Beckett (Suffolk Records Society 1970), XIV, pp. 24–25, 82. Also see Adele M. Holcomb, "The Bridge in the Middle Distance: Symbolic Elements in Romantic Landscape," *Art Quarterly* 37 (spring 1974), 43–46; Louis Hawes, *Constable's Stonehenge* (London: Her Majesty's Stationery Office, 1975), pp. 3–5, 12; John Dixon Hunt, "Wondrous Deep and Dark: Turner and the Sublime," *Georgia Review* 30 (spring 1976), 152. On the similarity between this kind of perception and that used in viewing a colossal monument, see Marvin Trachtenberg, "The Statue of Liberty: Transparent Banality or Avant-Garde Conundrum," *Art in America* 62 (May–June, 1974), 36–37.

50. C. J. Wright, "The 'Spectre' of Science. The Study of Optical Phenomena and the Romantic Imagination," *Journal of the Warburg and Courtauld Institutes* 43 (1980), 193–199; D. H. Carnahan, "The Romantic Debate in the French Daily Press of 1809," *PMLA* 53 (June 1938), 475, 483, 488; Peter Brooks, "The Aesthetics of Astonishment," *Georgia Review* 30 (fall 1976), 615, 617, 627–639; Mercier, *Mon bonnet de nuit*, II, pp. 145–146.

51. Jack Lindsay, *Turner*, pp. 77, 89–90, 156, 179, 186, 193. Also see Wilton, *Turner and the Sublime*, pp. 72–76, for an attempted classification of Turner's varieties of the Sublime, including the horrific and the terrific. It would be fruitful to examine such catastrophic paintings against the background of the larger category of the "spatial" landscape of melancholy—humid, heavy, cold, and quasi-diluvial—as described in Foucault's *Folie et déraison*, p. 121.

52. Feaver, *John Martin*, p. 72; Richard Green, "John Martin Rediscovered," *Connoisseur* 181 (December 1972), 250–252; Curtis Dahl, "Bulwer-Lytton and the School of Catastrophe," *Philological Quarterly* 32 (October 1953), 428–434; "The American School of Catastrophe," *American Quarterly* 11 (fall 1959), 380–388; Adams, *Danby*, pp. 56–58; Hardie, *British Water-Colour Painting*, II, pp. 27–28, 46–47.

53. Wilson, *Starlit Dome*, pp. 181–182, 188, 220; W. K. Wimsatt, Jr., "The Structure of Romantic Nature Imagery," in *The Verbal Icon: Studies in the Meaning of Poetry* (Lexington: University of Kentucky Press, 1954), pp. 111–116; Jackson, *Immediacy*, pp. 57, 62, 69; Marcia Pointon, "Pictorial Narrative in the Art of William Mulready," *Burlington* 122 (April 1980), 230; Steven Z. Levine, *Monet and His Critics* (New York: Garland, 1976), pp. 223 ff.

54. Crary, "Geographer Looks at Landscape," p. 23. For recent interest in the aesthetic possibilities of fog dripping on exposed surfaces, the "growth" of natural crystals, and the patterns formed by bubbling water, see *Earth, Air, Fire, Water: Elements of Art*, I, pp. 74, 78, 87–90, 107.

55. Werner Hofmann, *Caspar David Friedrich, 1774–1840* (Hamburg: Kunsthalle, 1974), p. 18; *Friedrich und die Nachwelt*, pp. 20–21; Börsch-Supan, *Friedrich*, pp. 53, 90, 110, 118–122; Helmut Börsch-Supan and Karl-Wilhelm Jähnig, *Caspar David Friedrich: Gemälde, Druckgraphik und bildmässige Zeichnungen* (Munich: Prestel, 1973), pp. 295–300, 342, 349, 364, 380.

56. Hourticq, "Poussin à Corot," II, pp. 112–114; *Ossian und die Kunst um 1800*, pp. 56, 63–64; *Carnets de David d'Angers*, I, p. 274; Schlumberger, "La foi artistique de Chateaubriand," pp. 133–134; Raymond, "Senancour," in Branca, *Sensibilità e Razionalità*, p. 41. Also see Smith, "The 'Historical Revival,' " p. 167, for the increase by one-third of landscapes exhibited in the Salons from the mid-1760s. Smith comments, however, that the English taste for the theater, the Picturesque, and the atmosphere found little counterpart in France. My point, on the contrary, has been that the balloon voyages were instrumental in the recognition of atmospheric effects by the French.

57. Traeger, *Runge*, p. 57; Helen Rosenau, *The Ideal City, Its Architectual Evolution* (New York: Harper & Row, 1972), pp. 93–94; *Piranèse et les français*, p. 61; Rosenblum, *Northern Romantic Tradition*, p. 31.

58. Adolf Max Vogt, *Boullées Newton-Denkmal. Sakralbau und Kugelidee* (Basel: Birkhäuser, 1969), pp. 362, 372–375; Pérouse de Montclose, *Boullée*, pp. 194, 198; Braham, *Architecture of French Enlightenment*, pp. 115–116.

59. Yvan Christ, *Projets et divations de Claude-Nicolas Ledoux, architecte du roi* (Paris: Minotaure, 1961), pp. 42, 60, 73, 118, 122; Braham, *Architecture of French Enlightenment*, pp. 180–181. For a discussion of the more general trend (evident by the 1770s) of creating urban monuments to recall not the glory of ancient Rome but that of nature and sentiment, see Wiebenson, *Picturesque Garden in France*, pp. 118–119.

60. Sarah Burns, "Girodet-Trioson's *Ossian*: The Role of Theatrical Illusionism in a Pictorial Evocation of Otherworldly Beings," *Gazette des Beaux-Arts* 95 (January 1980), 17–19; J. J. L. Whiteley, "Light and Shade in French Neo-Classicism," *Burlington* 117 (December 1975), 771–772. On the role of Girodet's relation to English art and its importance in the introduction of early Romantic themes and styles to France, see James Henry Rubin, "Gros and Girodet," *Burlington* 121 (November 1979), 719–721.

61. George Levitine, "Quelques aspects peu connus de Girodet," *Gazette des Beaux-Arts* 65 (April 1965), 237, 240–241; Barbara Maria Stafford, "Les météores de Girodet," *Revue de l'Art* 46 (1979), 51 ff.; "Endymion's Moonbath: Art and Science in Girodet's Early Masterpiece," *Leonardo* 15, no. 3 (1982), 193–198. Also see Sir David Salomon's Balloon Collection, Cabinet des Estampes, Bibliothèque Nationale, Ib. 18, III, fols. 6, 37.

62. Nørgaard, *Book of Balloons*, pp. 51–52; Hendrik de Leeuw, *From Flying Horse to Man in the Moon* (New York: St. Martin's, 1963), p. 15; Levine, *Monet and His Critics*, pp. 20, 23, 33–34; Michel Butor, "Monet, or the World Turned Upside Down," *Art News Annual* 34 (1968), 21–32; Bernard Dorival, "Ukiyo-e and European Painting," in *Dialogue in Art: Japan and the West* (Tokyo: Kodansha, 1976), pp. 47–48, 59; Alberto Wirth, "Kandinsky and the Science of Art," *British Journal of Aesthetics* 19 (autumn 1979), 362–364.

63. Constable, *Discourses*, pp. 68–69. Also see John Thornes, "Constable's Clouds," *Burlington* 121 (November 1979), 698–704. Thornes disagrees with Louis Hawes ["Constable's Sky Sketches," *Journal of the Warburg and Courtauld Institutes* 32 (1964), 344–365] that Luke Howard's classification

could have stimulated Constable's studies of 1821–22. Also see Cotte, *Traité de météorologie*, pp. 49, 50, 63; Daniel, *Meteorological Essays*, pp. 2–3. Note the parallel with Shelley, who in *Mont Blanc* conceives of the cloud as an eternal though changing substance, scintillating, evanescent, dissolving yet indestructible. See Knight, *Starlit Dome*, pp. 198–199. A parallel can also be drawn with the Wordsworthian attempts at creating an unghostly kind of visionariness, cited in Hartman, *Beyond Formalism*, p. 331.

64. Finley, "Encapsulated Landscape," in Fritz, *City and Society*, p. 211; Adams, *Danby*, pp. 139–140; R. K. Raval, "The Picturesque: Knight, Turner, and Hipple," *British Journal of Aesthetics* 18 (summer 1978), 255; John Gage, "Turner and the Picturesque—II," *Burlington* 107 (February 1965), 80; J. R. Watson, "Turner and the Romantic Poets," in Hunt, *Encounters*, pp. 111, 115, 122.

65. John Gage, *Colour in Turner, Poetry and Truth* (London: Studio Vista, 1969), pp. 128–132; Ritterbush, *Overtures to Biology*, pp. 203–205; Damisch, *Théorie du nuage*, pp. 259–261, Ruskin, *Modern Painters*, part II, section III, chapter 4, p. 255. Also note the persistence of the Winckelmannian tradition of "blurred equivocal beauty," and its influence in France on Théophile Gautier and the 1830s *l'art pour l'art* aesthetic of the Parnassian poets. See Raymond Giraud, "Winckelmann's Part in Gautier's Conception of Classical Beauty," in *The Classical Line: Essays in Honor of Henri Peyre* (Yale French Studies, 1967), pp. 179–181.

66. Ruskin, *Modern Painters*, part II, section III, chapter 4, p. 242; Constable, *Discourses*, p. 68.

67. *The Natural Paradise*, pp. 74, 79–80; Barbara Novak, "On Defining Luminism," in John Wilmerding, *American Light: The Luminist Movement, 1850–1875. Paintings, Drawings, Photographs* (Washington, D.C.: National Gallery of Art, 1980), pp. 27–28; Novak, *American Painting of the Nineteenth Century*, pp. 92–98. Also see Henry David Thoreau, *Walden or, Life in the Woods* (New York: Libra, 1960); see especially "The Ponds," pp. 155–178.

68. Heather Martienssen, "Madame Tussaud and the Limits of Likeness," *British Journal of Aesthetics* 20 (spring 1980), 128–133; Heinrich von Kleist, *Über das Marionettentheater* (Zurich: Flamberg, 1971), pp. 18, 25; Erich Heller, "The Dismantling of a Marionette Theatre; or, Psychology and the Misinterpretation of Literature," *Critical Inquiry* 9 (spring 1978), 420.

69. On the Western European preoccupation with verisimilitude and how this relates to the history of the original print

and the taking of a photograph, see William M. Ivins, Jr., *Prints and Visual Communication* (Cambridge, Mass.: Harvard University Press, 1953), pp. 3–24, 50–69; M. Daguerre, *Diorama, Regent's Park. Two Views: Ruins of Holyrood Chapel, A Moonlight Scene . . . and the Cathedral of Chartres* (London: C. Schulze, 1825), p. 8; *Historique et description des procédés du daguerréotype et du diorama*, revised edition (Paris: Alphonse Giroux et Cie, 1839), pp. 1–2, 19–32, 73 ff.; William Henry Fox Talbot, *The Pencil of Nature* (1844–1846) (New York: Da Capo, 1969). That the early expedition photograph was thought to realize scientifically the notion of art as a transcript of what actually happened or what really was seen is a point made by Weston J. Naef and James N. Wood in their *Era of Exploration: The Rise of Landscape Photography in the American West, 1860–1885* (Boston: New York Graphic Society, 1975), p. 133. Also see Joel Snyder and Doug Munson, *The Documentary Photograph as a Work of Art: American Photographs, 1860–1876* (David and Alfred Smart Gallery, University of Chicago, 1976), pp. 11–13. For contemporary skepticism concerning the nineteenth century's naive faith in photographic realism see Bob Rogers, "Realism and the Photographic Image," *Gazette des Beaux-Arts* 98 (September 1981), 89–94.

70. Among the most recent, if unsatisfactory, attempts to survey the nineteenth-century "movements" of Realism and Naturalism is Gabriel P. Weisberg, *The Realist Tradition: French Painting and Drawing, 1830–1900* (Indiana University Press, 1980). Only Petra T. D. Chu's essay "Into the Modern Era: The Evolution of Realist and Naturalist Drawing" tries to come to grips with the stylistic divergences between the two. Naturalism is given exceedingly short shrift in the catalog (pp. 188–189), where it is treated as a phenomenon endemic to the 1870s—one often confused with Impressionism. For an analysis of Victorian Realism in literature, and to some extent in art, and its historical antecedents, see Christ, *Finer Optic*, pp. 3–5. For a reminder of the long tradition of studying nature analytically see Kenneth Clark and Carlo Pedretti, *Leonardo da Vinci Nature Studies from the Royal Library at Windsor Castle* (New York: Johnson Reprint, 1980), pp. 9–11, 29–46. To date, Schmoll's "Naturalismus und Realismus" remains the best discussion of the current confusion existing between these two terms. Also see F. W. J. Hemmings, "The Origins of the Terms *naturalisme, naturaliste*," *French Studies* 8 (April 1954), 111–114; H. U. Forest, "Théodore Jouffroy et le problème de l'imitation dans les arts," *PMLA* 56 (February 1941), 1095–1101.

71. Champfleury [Jules Fleury], *Le réalisme*, ed. Geneviève and Jean Lacambre (Paris: Hermann, 1973), pp. 180–192, 88–90; *His-*

toire de l'imagerie populaire, new and revised edition (Paris: Dentu, 1886), pp. xii, 159–174; Histoire des faiences patriotiques sous la révolution (Paris: Dentu, 1867), pp. v–vii, x; Histoire de la caricature antique, third revised edition (Paris: Dentu, 1879), p. xv. Also see Madeleine Fidell-Beaufort and Janine Bailly-Herzberg, Daubigny (Paris: Geoffroy-Dechaume, 1975), pp. 48–49; Robert Hellebranth, Charles-François Daubigny, 1817–1878 (Morges: Matute, 1976), pp. xvii–xx; T. J. Clark, The Absolute Bourgeois: Artists and Politics in France, 1848–1851 (London: Thames and Hudson, 1973), pp. 78, 102–103; Petra T. D. Chu, French Realism and the Dutch Masters: The Influence of Dutch Seventeenth-Century Painting on the Development of French Painting between 1830 and 1870 (Utrecht: Haentjens, Dekker and Gumbert, 1974), p. 18.

72. Emile Zola, Oeuvres complètes, ed. Henri Mitterand (Paris: Cercle du Livre Précieux, 1968), X, pp. 277–282, 1175–1201; XI, pp. 286–287, 339; XI, pp. 796–797, 808–853, 860–879.

73. Adalbert Stifter, "Bunte Steine," in Gesammelte Werke (Wiesbaden: Im Insel-Verlag, 1959), III, pp. 7–17, 19, 133–240. Also see Herbert von Einem, Deutsche Malerei des Klassizismus und der Romantik, 1760 bis 1840 (Munich: Beck, 1978), pp. 164–168; Fritz Novotny, Adalbert Stifter als Maler, second revised edition (Vienna: Schroll, 1941), pp. 40–68. For the Germanic tradition, stretching from Goethe to Stifter, that valued the close observation and accurate description of natural phenomena, see Herbert von Einem, "Das Auge, der edelste Sinn," in Goethe-Studien (Munich: Wilhelm Fink, 1972), pp. 14–15; Günter Weydt, Naturschilderung bei Annette von Droste Hülshoff und Adalbert Stifter (Berlin: Emil Ebering, 1930), pp. 62–65, 71–82; Christine Oertel Sjögren, The Marble Statue as Idea: Collected Essays on Adalbert Stifter's Der Nachsommer (University of North Carolina Press, 1972), pp. 2–7, 52–61.

74. John Ruskin, Selections from the Writings (New York: Wiley, 1890), pp. 5–15, 20–29, 33–35, 56–58, 71, 94–99, 441–458; Modern Painters, part IV, chapter 1, sections 1–5, pp. 266–269; The Ethics of the Dust: Ten Lectures to Little Housewives on the Elements of Crystallisation, second edition (New York: Wiley, 1886), pp. 57–58, 219; Praeterita. Outlines of Scenes and Thoughts Perhaps Worthy of Memory in My Past Life (London: Rupert Hart-Davis, 1949), pp. 93–102, 150–156.

75. David J. DeLaura, "The Context of Browning's Painter Poems: Aesthetics, Polemics, Historics," PMLA 95 (May 1980), 370–379; Bandmann, "Wandel der Materialbewertung," in Koopmann, Theorie der Kunst, I, pp. 133–139, 141, 151; G. L. Hersey, High Victorian Gothic; A Study in Asso-

ciationism, ed. Phoebe Stanton (Johns Hopkins University Press, 1972), pp. 28–32; Nicholas Penny, "Ruskin's Ideas on Growth in Architecture and Ornament," British Journal of Aesthetics 13 (summer 1973), 277–279; Ellen E. Frank, "The Domestication of Nature: Fine Houses in the Lake District," in Knoepflmacher and Tennyson, Nature and Victorian Imagination, pp. 68–69. In addition to Bandmann's sensitive analysis of the origin and development of the positive estimation of matter—a tradition to which the authors under discussion belong—see Friedrich Piel, "Anamorphose und Architektur," in Festschrift Wolfgang Braunfels, ed. Friedrich Piel and Jörg Traeger (Tübingen: Wasmuth, 1977), pp. 292–293. Piel addresses the opposite issue, namely, how the illusionistic vault painting of the Baroque period—which he relates to an extension of the Mannerist anamorphic "stretching of perspective"—produces the effect of denying the physical substance of the painted architecture, transforming space into an "imaginary realm." In the process of dematerialization a unity is brought about among the various arts, thus creating the theoretical foundation for the Gesamtkunstwerk. The materialist tradition, as I have tried to demonstrate, focuses on the contrary on the individual properties and substantiality of the object.

76. John Ruskin, The Poetry of Architecture: or, The Architecture of the Nations of Europe Considered in Its Association with Natural Scenery and National Character (Sunnyside, Orpington: George Allen, 1893), pp. 41–43, 48–49; The Two Paths: Being Lectures on Art, and Its Application to Decoration and Manufacture, Delivered in 1858–9 (New York: Wiley, 1876), pp. 117, 132, 134, 140, 146, 153–160; Modern Painters, part II, chapter 2, section 5. Also see David Robertson, "Mid-Victorians amongst the Alps," J. Hillis Miller, "Nature and the Linguistic Moment," and Walter L. Creese," "Imagination in the Suburb," in Knoepflmacher and Tennyson, Nature and Victorian Imagination, pp. 113, 443, 54–55; Staley, Pre-Raphaelite Landscape, pp. 117–132. Most recently, Elizabeth K. Helsinger has developed Ruskin's use of an "excursive vision" in both his verbal descriptions and his experience of a landscape painting. See her Ruskin and the Art of the Beholder (Harvard University Press, 1982), especially pp. 63–84. I disagree, however, with her view that this form of visual discovery is allied with a Picturesque aesthetic. On the merger of high and low taste, see Daniel Cottom, "Taste and the Cultivated Imagination," Journal of Aesthetics and Art Criticism 134 (summer 1981), 376–380. Cottom suggests that in the eighteenth century there occurred a general convergence between the very refined and the very ignorant, between the man whose taste was so fine as to reject almost everything and the man who would reject those same things in the

same language because he had so little taste. Clearly Ruskin, too, does not pit his aristocratic aesthetic values against the ordinary but incorporates it. He refines art to the point of artlessness, i.e., to the point where the Westmoreland cottage appears so natural that it aids in discovering the art of nature.

77. Ruskin, *Selections*, pp. 396–397.

78. Rodolphe Töpffer, *Nouveaux voyages en zigzag à la Grande Chartreuse, autour du Mont Blanc, dans les vallées d'Herenz, de Zermatt, au Grimsel, à Gênes et à La Corniche, précédés d'une notice par Sainte-Beuve. Illustrés d'après les dessins orginaux de . . .* (Paris: Victor Lecou, 1854), pp. iii–xiii, 57–67; *Premières voyages en zigzag, ou excursion d'un pensionnat en vacances dan les cantons suisses et sur le revers italien des Alpes, illustrés d'après les dessins de l'auteur et ornés de 15 grands dessins par M. Calame,* fourth edition (Paris: Victor Lecou, 1855), pp. 5–13, 92–95; François Arago, *Oeuvres complètes* (Paris: Gide; Leipzig: Weigel, 1857), IX, pp. 1–4; Carl Linnaeus, *Select Dissertations from the Amoenitates Academicae,* tr. F. J. Brand (New York: Arno, 1977), p. 12.

79. Nadar [Félix Tournachon], *Mémoires du Géant, avec une introduction par M. Babinet,* second edition (Paris: Dentu, 1865), pp. 76, 101–111, 148–155, 215–222, 248–263, 287–297; *Le droit au vol* (Paris: J. Hetzel, 1865), pp. 106–107; *Les ballons en 1870. Ce qu'on aurait pu faire, ce qu'on a fait* (Paris: E. Chatelain, 1870), pp. 10–11.

80. James Henry Rubin, *Realism and Social Vision in Courbet and Proudhon* (Princeton University Press, 1980), pp. 63, 72–76.

81. Jean-Claude Lebensztejn, *Zigzag. La philosophie en effet* (Paris: Flammarion, 1981), pp. 27–37, 44.

NOTES

Bibliography

The bibliography is organized as follows:

Primary Sources
    Travel Accounts
    Related Aesthetic, Philosophical, and Scientific Treatises

Secondary Sources

Primary Sources
Travel Accounts

Abel, Clarke. *Narrative of a Journey in the Interior of China, and of a Voyage to and from that Country in the Years 1816 and 1817.* London: Longman, Hurst, Rees, Orme, and Brown, 1818.

Acerbi, Joseph. *Travels through Sweden, Finland, and Lapland, to the North Cape, in the Years 1798 and 1799.* Two vols. London: Joseph Mawman, 1802. Engravings.

Adanson, Michel. *Histoire naturelle du Sénégale. Coquillages avec la relation abrégée d'un voyage fait en ce pays, pendant les années 1749, 50, 52 & 53.* Paris: Claude-Jean-Baptiste Bauche, 1757. Drawings and engravings by T. Reboul.

Alexander, William. Journal of a Voyage to Pekin in China on Board the Hindostan Which Accompanied Lord Macartney on His Embassy to the Emperor. Add. Mss. 35174, British Library, London.

Alexander, William. 870 Drawings Made during Lord Macartney's Embassy to the Emperor of China, 1792–1794. 3 vols. W.D. 959/1–70, 960/1–66, 960/1–89, India Office Library, London.

Allom, Thomas. *China in a Series of Views, Displaying the Scenery, Architecture, and Social Habits of That Ancient Empire. Drawn from Original and Authentic Sketches by . . . With Historical and Descriptive Notices by the Reverend G. N. Wright, M.A.* Four vols. in two. London and Paris: Fisher, Son, & Co., 1843. Steel engravings.

Anburey, Thomas. *Hindoostan Scenery Consisting of Twelve Select Views in India Drawn on the Spot . . . of the Corps of Engineers, Bengal during the Campaign of the Most Noble the Marquis Cornwallis Shewing the Difficulty of a March thro' the Gundecotta Pass.* London: n.p., 1799. Drawings by author, color engravings by Francis Tukes.

Annesley, George [Viscount Valentia]. *Voyages and Travels to India, Ceylon, the Red Sea, Abyssinia, and Egypt.* Three vols. London: William Miller, 1809. Drawings by Henry Salt for engravings.

Anson, George. *A Voyage round the World in the Years 1740, I, II, III, IV.* Two vols. London: John and Paul Knapton, 1744. Drawings by Piercy Brett for engravings.

Anson, George. *Voyage autour du monde fait dans les années, 1740, 1, 2, 3, 4. Drawn from the Journals and Other Papers of Richard Walter, Chaplain on the Centurion.* Amsterdam and Leipzig: Arkste'e & Merkus, 1751.

Anson, George. *Anson's Voyage: Lieutenant [Percy] Brett's Original Drawings, December 1740–July 1743.* Engraved for the narrative, 1748. National Maritime Museum, Greenwich, England.

Arago, Dominique-François-Jean. *Instructions, rapports et notices sur les questions à resoude pendant les voyages scientifiques; Mémoires scientifiques. Oeuvres complètes.* Vols. IX, X, XI. Paris: Gide; Leipzig: T. O. Weigel, 1857–1859.

Arago, Jacques-Etienne-Victor. *Narrative of a Voyage round the World, in the* Uranie *and* Physicienne *Corvettes, Commanded by Captain Freycinet, during the Years 1817, 1818, 1819, and 1820; on a Scientific Expedition Undertaken by Order of the French Government. In a Series of Letters to a Friend by . . . , Draughtsman to the Expedition.* Two vols. in one. London: Treuttel and Wurtz, 1823. Drawings by author for engravings.

Back, George. *Expedition to Complete the Coastline between Regent Inlet and C. Turnagain.* London: G. Murray, 1836. Drawings by author and F. W. Beechey for engravings.

Back, George. *Expedition to the McKenzie River, 1824–27.* London: G. Murray, 1828. Drawings by author and E. N. Kendall, engravings by E. Finden.

Baldwin, Thomas. *Airopaidia: Containing the Narrative of a Balloon Excursion from Chester, the Eighth of September, 1785, Taken from Minutes Made during the Voyage.* Chester: J. Fletcher, 1786. Drawings by author for hand-colored engravings.

Banks, Joseph. *The Endeavour Journal of . . . , 1768–1771.* Edited by J. C. Beaglehole. Two vols. Sydney: Trustees of the Public Library of New South Wales in association with August Robertson, 1962.

Banks, Joseph. *Newfoundland and Labrador, 1766. His Diary, Manuscripts and Collections.* London: Faber and Faber, 1971.

Barrow, John. *An Account of Travels into the Interior of Southern Africa, in the Years 1797 and 1798; Including Cursory Observations on the Geology and Geography of the Southern Part of That Continent; the Natural History of Such Objects as Occurred in the Animal, Vegetable, and Mineral Kingdoms; and Sketches of the Physical and Moral Characters of the Various Tribes of Inhabitants surrounding the Settlement of the Cape of Good Hope.* Two vols. London: T. Cadell, Jr., and W. Davies, 1801. Drawings by William Alexander for color aquatints.

Bashō. *The Narrow Road to the Far North and Selected Haiku.* Translated by Dorothy Britton, photographs by Dennis Stock. Tokyo, New York, and San Francisco: Kodansha, 1974.

Beaumont, Albans. *Travels through the Rhaetian Alps in the Year 1786, from Italy to Germany, through Tyrol.* London: C. Clarke, 1792. Drawings and aquatints by author.

Beaver, Philip. *African Memoranda: Relative to an Attempt to Establish a British Settlement on the Island of Bulama on the Western Coast of Africa, in the Year 1792. With a Brief Notice of the Neighbouring Tribes, Soil, Productions, etc., and Some Observations on the Facility of Colonizing That Part of Africa, with a View to Cultivation; and the Introduction of Letters and Religion to Its Inhabitants; but More Particularly, as the Means of Gradually Abolishing African Slavery.* London: C. and R. Baldwin, 1805. Drawings and engravings by author.

Beechey, F. W. *Account of Buchan's Voyage towards the North Pole, 1818.* London: n.p., 1843. Drawings by author and George Bank for engravings.

Beechey, F. W. *Narrative of a Voyage to the Pacific and Beering's Strait, to Co-Operate with the Polar Expeditions: Performed in his Majesty's Ship* Blossom, *Under the Command of . . . , in the Years 1825, 26, 27, 28, and Published by the Authority of the Lords Commissioners of the Admiralty.* London: Henry Colburn and Richard Bentley, 1831. Drawings by author for aquatints.

Beechey, H. W. *Proceedings of the Expedition to Explore the Northern Coast of Africa, from Tripoly Eastward; in MDCCCXXI and MDCCCXXII. Comprehending the Greater Syrtis and Cyrenaica; and of the Ancient Cities Composing the Pentapolis.* London: John Murray, 1828. Drawings by author for aquatints.

Beeckman, Daniel. *A Voyage to and from the Island of Borneo, in the East-Indies. With a Description of the Said Island: Giving an Account of the Inhabitants, Their Manners, Customs, Religion, Products, Chief Ports, and Trade.* London: T. Warner and J. Batley, 1718. Engravings.

Bellasis, George Hutchins, *Views of Saint Helena.* London: John Tyler, 1815. Drawings by author, color aquatints by Robert Havell.

Belzoni, Giuseppi. *Narrative of the Operations and Recent Discoveries within the Pyramids, Temples, Tombs, and Excavations in Egypt and Nubia; and of a Journey to the Coast of the Red Sea, in Search of the Ancient Berenice; and Another to the Oasis of Jupiter Ammon.* London: John Murray, 1820.

Belzoni, Giuseppi. *Plates Illustrative of the Researches and Operations of . . . in Egypt and Nubia.* London: John Murray, 1820. Drawings by author, colored etchings by A. Aglio.

Belzoni, Giuseppi. *Six New Plates Illustrative of the Researches and Operations of . . . in Egypt and Nubia.* London: John Murray, 1822. Drawings by author, hand-colored lithographs by A. Aglio.

Benucci, F. P. *Six Views of Gibraltar and Its Neighborhood.* Munich: n.p., 1825. Drawings and hand-colored lithographs by author.

Benyowsky, Mauritius Augustus, Count of. *The Memoirs and Travels of . . . , Magnate of the Kingdoms of Hungary and Poland, One of the Chiefs of the Confederation of Poland, etc., etc.* Two vols. London: G. G. and J. and J. Robinson, 1789. Engravings.

Berg, Albert. *Physiognomy of Tropical Vegetation in South America; A Series of Views Illustrating the Primeval Forests on the River Magdalena and in the Andes of New Granada, With a Fragment of a Letter from Baron Humboldt to the Author and a Preface by Frederick Klotzsch.* London: Paul and Dominic Colnaghi and Co., 1854. Drawings and lithographs by author.

Bernardin de Saint-Pierre, Jacques-Henri. *Voyage à l'Ile de France, à l'Ile de Bourbon, au Cap de Bonne-Espérance.* Two vols. Amsterdam and Paris: Merlin, 1773.

Bernardin de Saint-Pierre, Jacques-Henri. *Voyage à l'Ile de France, 1768–1771. Oeuvres complètes.* Edited by L. Aimé-Martin. Vol. I. Paris: Méquignon-Marvis, 1818. Drawings by author for engravings.

Bernier, François. *Voyage de . . . , docteur en médecine de la Faculté de Montpellier, contenant la description des états du Grand Mogol, de l'Hindoustan, du royaume de Kachemire, etc.* Two vols. Amsterdam: Paul Marret, 1699. Engravings.

Blaeu, Jean. *Nouveau théâtre d'Italie, ou description exacte de ses villes, palais, églises, etc. Et les cartes géographiques de toutes ses provinces.* Three vols. Amsterdam: Pierre Mortier, 1704. Drawings by Jan Hackaert et al. for engravings.

Blagdon, Francis William. *A Brief History of Ancient and Modern India, from the Earliest Periods of Antiquity to the Termination of the Late Mahratta War. Embellished with Color Engravings by T. Daniell, Col. [F. S.] Ward, and James Hunter.* London: Edward Orme, 1805.

Bligh, William. *A Narrative of the Mutiny on Board His Britannic Majesty's Ship* Bounty; *and the Subsequent Voyage of Part of the Crew, from Tofoa, One of the Friendly Islands, to Timor, a Dutch Settlement in the East-Indies.* Philadelphia: William Spotswood, 1790.

Blunt, James Tillyer. Thirty-One Drawings of Landscapes in Delhi, U.P., Bihar, Orissa, Madras and Mysore between 1788–1800. 156/1–29, India Office Library, London.

Boisgelin [de Kerdu], Louis. *Ancient and Modern Malta: Containing a Description of the Ports and Cities of the Islands of Malta and Goza, together with the Monuments of Antiquity Still*

Remaining, the Different Governments to Which They Have Been Subjected, Their Trade and Finances. And a History of the Knights of St. John of Jerusalem and a Particular Account of the Events Which Preceded and Attended Its Capture by the French and Conquest by the English. Three vols. in two. London: G. and J. Robinson, 1804. Engravings.

Boisgelin [de Kerdu], Louis. Travels through Denmark and Sweden, to Which is Prefixed a Journal of a Voyage Down the Elbe to Hamburgh; Including a Compendious Historical Account of the Hanseatic League . . . With Views from Drawings Taken on the Spot by Dr. Charles Parry. Two vols. London: Wilkie and George Robinson, 1810. Drawings by Charles Parry for color aquatints.

Bougainville, Louis-Antoine de. Voyage autour du monde par la frégate du roi La Boudeuse et la flûte L'Etoile, en 1766, 1768, & 1769. Two vols. Second revised edition. Paris: Saillant & Nyon, 1772. Drawings by Philibert Commerson des Humbers, engravings by Croisey.

Supplément au voyage de M. de Bougainville; ou journal d'un voyage autour du monde, fait par MM. Banks & Solander, anglois, en 1768, 1769, 1770, 1771. Traduit d'anglois, par M. de Fréville. Paris: Saillant & Nyon, 1772.

Bouguer, Pierre. La figure de la terre, déterminée par les observations de Messieurs . . . , & De La Condamine, de l'Académie Royale des Sciences, envoyés par ordre du roy au Pérou, pour observer aux environs de l'équateur. Avec une relation abrégée de ce voyage, qui contient la description du pays dans lequel les opérations ont été faites. Paris: Charles-Antoine Jombert, 1749. Engravings.

Bourrit, Marc-Théodore. Description des aspects du Mont-Blanc. Lausanne: Société Thypographique, 1776.

Bourrit, Marc-Théodore. Nouvelle description des vallées de glace et des hautes montagnes qui forment la chaîne des Alpes Pennines & Rhétiennes. Three vols. in one. Geneva: Paul Barde, 1783. Drawings by author, engravings by Moitte.

Bowdich, T. Edward. Mission from Cape Coast Castle to Ashantee, with a Statistical Account of That Kingdom, and Geographical Notices of Other Parts of the Interior of Africa. London: John Murray, 1819. Drawings by author, color aquatints by R. Havell and son.

Bowery, Thomas. Asia: Wherein Is Contained ye Scituation, Comerse, etc. of Many Provinces, Isles, etc, in India, Per., Arabia, and ye South Seas—Experienced by Me . . . in ye Aforementioned India. viz from Anno MDCLXIX to MDCLXXIX. Ms. EUR D 782, India Office Library, London. Pen-and-ink drawings by author.

Breydenbach, Bernard von. Le saint voiage et pélérinage de la cité saincte de Hierusalem. Translated by Jean de Hersin. Lyons: n.p., 1489. Woodcuts by Erhard Rervich.

Brooke, Arthur de Capell. Travels through Sweden, Norway, Finmark to the North Cape in the Summer of 1820. London: Rodwell and Martin, 1823. Drawings by author, lithographs by C. Hullmandel and J. D. Harding.

Brooke, Arthur de Capell. Winter Sketches in Lapland, or Illustrations of a Journey from Alten on the Shores of the Polar Sea in 69° 55" North Latitude through Norwegian, Russian, and Swedish Lapland to Tornea at the Extremity of the Gulf of Bothnia Intended to Exhibit a Complete View of the Mode of Travelling with Rein-Deer, the Most Striking Incidents That Occurred during the Journey, and the General Character of the Winter Scenery of Lapland. London: J. Rodwell, 1827. Drawings by Brooke and D. Dighton, lithographs by J. D. Harding and C. Hullmandel.

Brosses, Charles de. Histoire des navigations aux terres australes. Contenant de ce que l'on sçait des moeurs & des productions des contrées découvertes jusqu'à ce jour; & ou il est traité de l'utilité d'y faire de plus amples découvertes, & des moyens d'y former un établissement. Two vols. Paris: Durand, 1756.

Broughton, William Robert. A Voyage of Discovery to the North Pacific Ocean . . . Performed in His Majesty's Sloop Providence and Her Tender in the Years 1795, 1796, 1797, 1798. London: T. Cadell and W. Davies, 1804. Engravings.

Browne, W. G. Travels in Africa, Egypt, and Syria, from the Years 1792 to 1798. London: T. Cadell, Jr., and W. Davies, 1799.

Bruce, James. *Travels to Discover the Source of the Nile in the Years 1768, 1769, 1770, 1771, 1772, and 1773.* Five vols. Edinburgh: J. Ruthven for G. and G. J. and J. Robinson, 1790. Drawings by author for engravings.

Bry, Theodor de. *Dritte Buch Americae, darinn Brasilia durch Johann Staden von Homberg aus eigener Erfahrung in Teutsch beschrieben. Item Historia der Schiffart Joannis Lerii in Brasilien Welche Er selbst publiciert hat.* Frankfurt-am-Main: de Bry, 1593. Engravings by author and sons.

Bry, Theodor de. *Sammlung von Reisen nach dem Occidentalischen Indien.* Fifteen vols. Frankfurt-am-Main: de Bry, 1590. Engravings by author and sons.

Brydone, Patrick. *A Tour through Sicily and Malta, in a Series of Letters to William Beckford, Esq. of Somerly in Suffolk.* Two vols. London: W. Strahan and T. Cadell, 1773.

Buchanan, Francis. *A Journey from Madras through the Countries of Mysore, Canara, and Malabar, Performed under the Orders of the Most Noble Marquis Wellesley, Governor General of India, for the Express Purpose of Investigating the States of Agriculture, Arts, and Commerce; the Religion, Manners, and Customs; the History Natural and Civil, and Antiquities.* Three vols. London: T. Cadell and W. Davies, 1807. Engravings.

Burchell, William. *Travels in the Interior of Southern Africa.* Two vols. London: Longman, Hurst, Rees, Orme, and Brown, 1822. Drawings by author for color aquatints.

Burckhardt, John Lewis. *Travels in Arabia, Comprehending an Account of Those Territories in Hedjas [Holy Land] Which the Mohammedans Regard as Sacred by the Late . . . Published by Authority of the Association for Promoting the Discovery of the Interior of Africa.* Two vols. Edited by William Ouseley. London: Henry Colburn, 1829.

Burckhardt, John Lewis. *Travels in Nubia; by the Late. . . . Published by the Association for Promoting the Discovery of the Interior Parts of Africa. With Maps, etc.* Edited by Col. Leake. London: John Murray, 1819.

Burckhardt, John Lewis. *Travels in Smyrna and the Holy Land; by the Late. . . . Published by the Association for Promoting the Discovery of the Interior Parts of Africa.* Edited by Col. Leake. London: John Murray, 1822.

Byron, John. *The Narrative of the Honourable. . . . Commodore in a Late Expedition round the World, Containing an Account of the Great Distresses Suffered by Himself and His Companions on the Coast of Patagonia, From the Year 1740, till Their Arrival in England in 1746, With a Description of Saint Jago de Chile.* London: S. Baker and G. Leigh and T. Davies, 1768. Etchings by S. Wale and C. Grignion.

Caldcleugh, Alexander. *Travels in South America, during the Years 1819, 20, 21, Containing an Account of the Present State of Brazil, Buenos Ayres, and Chile.* Two vols. London: John Murray, 1825. Sketches by William Waldegrave, drawings by William Daniell for color aquatints by Finden.

Carne, John. *Syria, the Holy Land, Asia Minor, etc. Illustrated. In a Series of Views Drawn from Nature [by] W. H. Bartlett, William Purser, etc. With Descriptions of the Plates by . . . Author of "Letters from the East."* Two vols. in one. London: Fisher, Son, & Co., 1836. Drawings by author for steel engravings.

Carruthers's scrapbook. National Air and Space Museum, Washington, D.C.

Carver, Jonathan. *Travels through the Interior Parts of North-America, in the Years 1766, 1767, and 1768.* London: printed for the author, 1778. Drawings by author for engravings.

Cassas, Louis-François. *Voyage pittoresque et historique de l'Istrie et de la Dalmatie, rédigé d'après l'itineraire de . . . , par Joseph Lavallée, de la Société Philotechnique, de la Société Libre des Sciences, Lettres et Arts de Paris, de celle d'Agriculture du Département de Seine et Marne, etc.* Paris: Pierre Didot, 1802. Drawings by author, engravings by Levée.

Cassas, Louis-François. *Voyage pittoresque de la Syrie, de la Phénicie, de la Palestine, et de la Basse Egypte: Ouvrage divisé en trois volumes, contenant environ trois cent trente planches, gravées sur les dessins et sous la direction du . . . , peintre, l'un des artistes employés par l'auteur du voyage de la Grèce.* Text by C. F. C. Volney, J. J. G. La Porte, J. G. Legrand, and L. Langles. Paris: Imprimerie de la République, An VII [1798–99]. Drawings by author, etchings by Née.

Chappe d'Auteroche, Jean. *Voyage en Californie pour l'observation du passage de Vénus sur le disque du soleil, le 3 Juin 1769; contenant les observations de ce phénomène, & la description historique de la route de l'auteur à travers le Mexique.* Paris: Charles-Antoine Jombert, 1772.

Chappe d'Auteroche, Jean. *Voyage en Siberie, fait par ordre du roi en 1761; contenant les moeurs, les usages des russes, et l'état actuel de cette puissance; la description géographique & le nivellement de la route de Paris à Tobolsk; l'histoire naturelle de la même route; des observations astronomiques, & des expériences sur l'électricité naturelle.* Two vols. in three. Paris: Debure, Père, 1768. Drawings by J. B. Le Prince, engravings by J. B. Tilliard.

Chappell, Edward. *Narrative of a Voyage to Hudson's Bay in His Majesty's Ship* Rosamond, *Containing Some Account of the North-Eastern Coast of America and of the Tribes Inhabiting That Remote Region.* London: J. Mauman, 1817. Engravings.

Voyages de M. le Marquis de Chastellux dans l'Amerique Septentrionale dans les années 1780, 1781 & 1782. Two vols. Paris: Prault, 1786.

Choiseul-Gouffier, Marie-Gabriel-Auguste-Florent de. *Voyage pittoresque de la Grèce.* Two vols. Paris: Tilliard, De Bure, Père et Fils, and Tilliard Frères, 1782 and 1809. Drawings by J. B. Hilaire and L. F. Cassas, engravings by J. B. Tilliard.

Choris, Louis. *Voyage pittoresque autour du monde, avec des portraits de sauvages d'Amerique, d'Asie, d'Afrique, et des Iles du Grand Océan; des paysages, des vues maritimes.* Paris: Firmin-Didot, 1820. Drawings by Adelbert von Chamisso, lithographs by author and Langlumé.

Choris, Louis. *Vues et paysages des régions équinoxiales, recueillis dans un voyage autour du monde . . . avec un introduction et un texte explicatif.* Paris: Paul Renouard, 1826. Drawings and color lithographs by author.

Choris, Louis. Sketchbook, 1816. Fuller Collection, Bishop Museum, Honolulu.

Cochrane, Charles Stuart. *Journal of a Residence and Travels in Colombia, during the Years 1823 and 1824.* Two vols. London: Henry Colburn, 1825. Drawings by author for color aquatints.

Cockburn, George. *A Voyage to Cadiz and Gibraltar up the Mediterranean to Sicily and Malta, in 1810, & 11, Including a Description of Sicily and the Lipari Islands, and An Excursion in Portugal.* Two vols. London: J. Harding, 1815. Color aquatints by John Harding.

Cockburn, James Pattison. *Swiss Scenery from Drawings by. . . .* London: Rodwell and Martin, 1820. Engravings by C. Westwood et al.

Cockburn, James Pattison. *Views to Illustrate the Route of Mont Cenis.* London: Rodwell and Martin, 1822. Drawings by author, lithographs by C. Hullmandel.

Cockburn, James Pattison. *Views to Illustrate the Route of Simplon Pass.* London: Rodwell and Martin, 1822. Drawings by author, lithographs by J. Harding.

Colebrooke, R. H. *Twelve Views of Places in the Kingdom of Mysore, the Country of Tippoo Sultan, from Drawings Taken on the Spot.* London: Edward Orme, 1805. Color aquatints by J. W. Edy.

Conté, Nicolas-Jacques. Watercolors Recording Activities of the Ecole Aérostatique de Meudon. 1794. Musée de l'Air, Paris.

Cook, James. *A Voyage towards the South Pole, and Round the World. Performed in His Majesty's Ships the* Resolution *and* Adventure, *in the Years 1772, 1773, 1774, and 1775. In Which Is Included Captain Furneaux's Narrative of His Proceedings in the Adventure during the Separation of the Ships. Illustrated with Maps, Charts, a Variety of Portraits of Persons, Views of Places Drawn during the Voyage by Mr. [William] Hodges, and Engraved by the Most Eminent Masters.* Fourth edition. Two vols. and atlas. London: W. Strahan and T. Cadell, 1777.

Cook, James. *A Voyage to the Pacific Ocean, Undertaken by the Command of His Majesty, for Making Discoveries in the Northern Hemisphere. To Determine the Position and Extent of the West Side of North America; Its Distance from Asia and the Practicability of a Northern Passage to Europe. Performed under the Direction of Captains . . . , Clerke, and Gore, in His Majesty's Ships the* Resolution *and* Discovery *in the Years 1776, 1777, 1779, and 1780.* Three vols. and atlas. London: W. and A. Strahan, 1784. Drawings by John Webber, engravings by Newton, Byrne, Ellis, Heath, Middiman, et al.

Cook Collection. National Maritime Museum, Greenwich.

Cordiner, Charles. *Remarkable Ruins and Romantic Prospects of North Britain. With Ancient Monuments and Singular Subjects of Natural History.* London: Peter Mazell, 1791. Drawings by author, engravings by Peter Mazell.

Cordiner, James. *A Description of Ceylon, Containing an Account of the Country, Inhabitants and Natural Productions.* Two vols. London: Longman, Hurst, Rees, and Orme, 1807. Drawings by author for engravings.

Coxe, William. *Travels in Switzerland. In a Series of Letters to William Melmoth, Esq.* London: T. Cadell, 1789.

Crozet's [Nicolas-Thomas] Voyage to Tasmania, New Zealand, the Ladrone Islands, and the Philippines in the Years 1771–1772. Translated by H. Ling-Roth. London: Truslove & Shirley, 1791. Engravings.

Dallaway, James. *Constantinople Ancient and Modern, with Excursions to the Shores and Islands of the Archipelago and to the Troad.* London: T. Bensley for T. Cadell, Jr., & W. Davies, 1797. Color aquatints by Mereati and Stadler.

Dampier, William. *A Collection of Voyages.* Four vols. London: James and John Knapton, 1729.

Daniell, William. *Illustrations of the Island of Staffa, in a Series of Views.* London: Longman, Hurst, Rees, Orme, and Brown, 1818. Drawings and aquatints by author.

Daniell, William. *Interesting Selections from Animated Nature with Illustrative Scenery.* Two vols. London: T. Cadell and W. Davies, 1807–08. Drawings and aquatints by William and Thomas Daniell.

Daniell, William, and Hobart, Counter. *The Oriental Annual, or Scenes in India.* London: Edward Churton, 1834–1840. Drawings by Daniell and H. Warren from sketches by Capt. Meadows; engravings by John Pye, T. Jeavons, et al.

Daniell, William, and Thomas Daniell. *Antiquities of India. Twelve Views from the Drawings of . . . , in Two Parts.* London: Thomas and William Daniell, 1799.

Daniell, William, and Thomas Daniell. *Hindu Excavations in the Mountains of Ellora, Near Aurungabad, in the Decan in Twenty-Four Views from the Drawings of James Wales, Under the Direction of. . . .* London: Thomas and William Daniell, 1816.

Daniell, William, and Thomas Daniell. *Oriental Scenery.* Six vols. London: Longman, Hurst, Rees, Orme, and Brown, 1795–1815. Color aquatints.

Daniell, William, and Thomas Daniell. *A Picturesque Voyage to India by Way of China.* London: Longman, Hurst, Rees, and Orme, 1810. Color aquatints.

Daniell, William, and Thomas Daniell. Sketches and Drawings. India Office Library, London.

Dapper, d'O. *Description de l'Afrique, contenant les noms, la situation & les confins de toutes ses parties, leur rivières, leurs villes & leurs habitations, leurs plantes & leurs animaux; les moeurs, les coutumes, la langue, les richesses, la religion & le gouvernement de ses peuples.* Translated from the Flemish. Amsterdam: Wolfgang, Waesberge, Boom & Van Someren, 1686. Etchings.

BIBLIOGRAPHY

Darwin, Charles. Sketches from the Voyage of the *Beagle*. National Maritime Museum, Greenwich.

Davis, Samuel. *Views in Bootan: From the Drawings of . . . .* London: William Daniell, 1813. Color aquatints by Daniell.

Davy, John. *An Account of the Interior of Ceylon, and of Its Inhabitants, With Travels in That Island*. London: Longman, Hurst, Rees, Orme, and Brown, 1821. Drawings by William Littleton; aquatints and engravings by J. Clark, Charles Auber, et al.

Debret, Jean-Baptiste. *Voyage pittoresque et historique au Brésil depuis 1816 jusqu'à 1831. Séjour d'un artiste français au Brésil*. Three vols. Paris: Firmin-Didot, 1834. Drawings by Debret; lithographs by J. Motte and Thierry Frères.

D'Entrecasteaux, Antoine de Bruny, Chevalier. *Voyage de . . . , envoyé à la recherche de La Pérouse. Publié par ordre de sa majesté l'empereur et roi, sous le ministère de S.E. le vice-amiral Décres, comte de l'empire*. Edited by M. de Rossel. Two vols. Paris: Imprimerie Impériale, 1808.

Descourtis, Charles-Melchior, *Vues remarquables des montagnes de La Suisse*. Amsterdam: J. Yntema, 1785. Drawings by Caspar Wolf, color aquatints by author.

Dixon, George. *A Voyage Round the World, Performed in 1785, 1786, 1787, and 1788, in the* King George *and* Queen Charlotte. London: Geo. Goulding, 1789. Engravings.

D'Oyly, Charles. Scrapbook: Drawings and Lithographs. 1828–1830. India Office Library, London.

Du Camp, Maxine. *Le Nil. Egypte et Nubie*. Fourth edition. Paris: Hachette et Cie, 1877.

Du Mont, Jean. *Voyages de Mr. . . . en France, en Italie, en Allemagne, à Malthe, et en Turquie. Contenant les recherches & observations curieuses qui'il a faites en tous ces païs: Tant sur les moeurs, les coutumes des peuples, leurs différens gouvernemens & leurs religions; que sur l'histoire ancienne & moderne, la philosophie & les monumens antiques*. Four vols. The Hague: Etienne Foulque & François l'Honoré, 1699. Engravings.

Dumont D'Urville, Jules-Sébastien-César. *Voyage de la corvette l'Astrolabe, executé par ordre du roi pendant les années 1826–1829, sous le commandement de. . . .* Seven vols. and atlas. Paris: J. Tastu, 1830–1834. Drawings by Auguste de Sainson.

Duperrey, Louis Isidore. *Voyage autour du monde, executé par ordre du roi, sur la corvette de la majesté*, la Coquille, *pendant les années 1822, 1823, 1824 et 1825*. Text and Atlas. Paris: Arthus Bertrand, 1827. Drawings by Le Jeune and T. A. Chazal.

Dupré, Louis. *Voyage à Athènes et à Constantinople, ou collection de portraits, de vues et de costumes grecs et ottomans, peints sur les lieux, d'après nature, lithographiés et coloriés par . . . Accompagné d'un texte orné de vignettes*. Paris: Dondey-Dupré, 1825.

Dusaulx, Jean. *Voyage à Barège et dans les Hautes Pyrénées, fait en 1788*. Two vols. in one. Paris: Didot Jeune, 1796.

Edy, John William. *Boydell's Picturesque Scenery of Norway; with the Principal Towns from the Naze by the Route of Christiana, to the Magnificent Pass of the Swinesund; From Original Drawings Made on the Spot, and Engraved by . . . With Remarks and Observations Made in a Tour through the Country, and Revised and Corrected by William Tooke, F.R.S., Member of the Imperial Academy of Sciences, and of the Economical Society at St. Petersburgh*. Two vols. in one. London: Hurst, Robinson, and Co., 1820.

Egmont, J. Aegidius van. *Travels through Part of Europe, Asia Minor, the Islands of the Archipelago; Syria, Palestine, Egypt, Mt. Sinai, etc. Giving a Particular Account of the Most Remarkable Places, Structures, Ruins, Inscriptions, etc. in These Countries*. Two vols. Translated from the Dutch. London: L. Davis and C. Reymers, 1759. Engravings.

Elliott, Robert. *Views in the East: Comprising India, Canton, and the Shores of the Red Sea. With Historical and Descriptive Illustrations*. Two vols. in one. London: H. Fisher, Son, &

Co., 1833. Drawings by S. Prout, T. Boys, W. Purser, and D. Cox; engravings by W. Taylor, W. Higham, et al.

Ellis, Henry. *Journal of the Proceedings of the Late Embassy to China; . . . Interspersed with Observations upon the Face of the Country, the Polity, Moral Character, and Manners of the Chinese Nation.* London: John Murray, 1817. Drawings by Charles Abbot, color aquatints by J. Clark.

Erdmann, Johann Friedrich. *Beiträge zur Kentniss des Innern von Russland.* Riga: Meinshausen, 1822–1825.

Faujas de Saint-Fond, Barthélemy. *Description des experiences de la machine aérostatique de MM. de Montgolfier et de celles auxquelles cette découverte à donné lieu.* Two vols. Paris: Cuchet, 1783. Engravings by Chevalier Lorimer.

Faujas de Saint-Fond, Barthélemy. *Recherches sur les volcans éteints du Vivarais et du Vélay; avec un discours sur les volcans brûlans.* Grenoble and Paris: Chez Joseph Cuchet et Chez Nyon aîné, Née et Masquelier, 1778. Drawings by A. E. Gautier Dagoty, engravings by P. C. Le Bas.

Faujas de Saint-Fond, Barthélemy. *Voyage en Angleterre, en Ecosse et aux Iles Hébrides.* Two vols. Paris: H. J. Jansen, 1797. Drawings by author for engravings.

Wahreste und neueste Abbildung des Türchischen Hofes/ Welche nach denen Gemählden der königliche Französische Ambassadeur Monsr. de Ferriol, zeit seiner Gesandschafft in Constanipol im Jahr 1707 und 1708. Durch einen geschickten Mahler [Jean-Baptiste Vanmour] nach den Leben hat verfertigen lassen in fünff und sechzig Kupffer-Blatten gebracht worden. Nebst einer aus dem Französischens ins Teutsche übersetzen Beschreibung. Nuremberg: Adam Jonathan Felssecker, 1719. Hand-colored engravings by C. Weigel.

Fitzroy, Robert. *Narrative of the Surveying Voyages of His Majesty's Ships* Adventure *and* Beagle, *between the Years 1826 and 1836, Describing Their Examination of the Southern Shores of South America, and the Beagle's Circumnavigation of the Globe.* Three vols., appendix, and atlas. London: Henry Colburn, 1839. Drawings by Augustus Earle and Conrad Martens; etchings by S. Bull et al.

Flinders, Matthew. *A Voyage to Terra Australis; Undertaken for the Purpose of Completing the Discovery of That Vast Country, and Prosecuted in the Years 1801, 1802, and 1803, in His Majesty's Ship the* Investigator, *and Subsequently in the Armed Vessel* Porpoise *and* Cumberland *Schooner. With an Account of the Shipwreck of the* Porpoise, *Arrival of the* Cumberland *at Mauritius, and Imprisonment of the Commander during Six years and a Half in That Island.* Two vols. and atlas. London: W. Bulmer and Co., 1814. Drawings by William Westall; engravings by J. Byrne, W. Woolnoth, L. Scott, John Pye, and J. Middiman.

Forbes, James. *Oriental Memoirs, Selected and Abridged from a Series of Familiar Letters Written during Seventeen Years Residence in India: Including Observations on Parts of Africa and South America.* London: T. Bensley, 1813.

Forrest, Charles. *A Picturesque Tour along the Rivers Ganges and Jumna, in India: Consisting of Twenty-Four Highly Finished and Coloured Views, a Map, and Vignettes, from Original Drawings Made on the Spot; With Illustrations, Historical and Descriptive.* London: R. Ackermann, 1824. Drawings by author, color aquatints by G. Hunt and T. Sutherland.

Forster, Georg. *Ein Blick in das Ganze der Natur* [1794]. *Schriften zu Natur, Kunst, Politik.* Edited by Karl Otto Conrady. Reinbeck bei Hamburg: Rowohlt, 1971.

Forster, Georg. *A Voyage round the World, in His Brittanic Majesty's Sloop,* Resolution, *Commanded by Captain James Cook, during the Years 1772, 3, 4, and 5.* Two vols. London: B. White, J. Robson, P. Elmsly, G. Robinson, 1777.

Forster, Georg. *Voyage philosophique et pittoresque sur les rives du Rhin, à Liège, dans la Flandre, le Brabant, la Hollande, l'Angleterre, la France, etc, fait en 1790.* Translated by Charles Pougens. Two vols. Paris: F. Buisson and Charles Pougens, An VIII [1799–1800].

Forster, Johann Reinhold. *Observations Made during a Voyage round the World, on Physical Geography, Natural History, and Ethic Philosophy. Especially on 1) the Earth and Its Strata 2) Water and the Ocean 3) the Atmosphere 4) the Changes of the Globe 5) Organic Bodies, and 6) the Human Species.* London: G. Robinson, 1778.

Fortia de Piles, Alphonse-Toussaint-Joseph-André-Marseilles, Comte de. *Voyage de deux français en Allemagne, Danemarck, Suède, Russie et Pologne, fait en 1790–1792.* Paris: Desenne, 1796.

Franklin, John. *Narrative of a Journey to the Shores of the Polar Sea, in the Years 1819, 20, 21, and 22. With an Appendix on Various Subjects Relating to Science and Natural History. Illustrated by Numerous Plates and Maps.* London: John Murray, 1823. Drawings by Lt. Hood and Lt. Back, color aquatints by Edward Finden.

Franklin, John. *Narrative of a Second Journey to the Shores of the Polar Sea, in the Years 1825, 1826, and 1827. Including an Account of the Progress of a Detachment to the Eastward, by John Richardson, M.D., F.R.S., F.L.S. Illustrated by Numerous Plates and Maps.* London: John Murray, 1828. Drawings by Capt. Back and Lt. Kendall, engravings by Edward Finden.

Fraser, John Baillie. *Views in the Himala Mountains.* London: Rodwell & Martin, 1820. Drawings by author, color aquatints by R. Havell and son.

Freminville, Chevallier de La Poix de. *Voyage to the North Pole in the Frigate the* Syrene. Translated from the French. London: Sir Richard Phillips and Co., 1819.

Freycinet, Louis-Claude de Saulces de, and Rose-Marie de Freycinet. *Voyage de découvertes aux Terres Australes, éxecutés sur les corvettes le* Géographe, *le* Naturaliste, *et la goélette le* Casuarina, *pendant les années 1800, 1801, 1802, 1803 et 1804.* One vol. and atlas. Paris: Imprimerie Royale, 1815. Drawings by Jacques-Etienne-Victor Arago for engravings.

Frézier, A.-F. *Relation du voyage de la Mer de Sud aux côtes du chily et du Pérou fait pendant les années 1712, 1713, & 1714.* Paris: Jean-Géoffroy Nyon, Etienne Ganeau, Jacque Quillau, 1716. Etchings by N. Guerard, le fils.

Fromentin, Eugène. *Sahara & Sahel: Un été dans le Sahara (1856); Une année dans le Sahel (1858).* Third Edition. Two vols. in one. Paris: E. Plon et Cie, 1879. Drawings and etchings by author.

Fromentin, Eugène. *Voyage en Egypte (1869). Journal publié d'après le carnet manuscrit.* Edited by Jean-Marie Carré. Paris: Montaigne, 1935.

Gaimard, Paul. *Voyage en Islande et Groenland. Atlas historique.* Three vols. Paris: Arthus-Bertrand, Firmin-Didot Frères, 1838–1842. Drawings by A. Mayer, lithographs by Sabatier and Bayot.

Gaimard, Paul. *Voyages de la commission scientifique du Nord en Scandanavie, en Laponie au Spitzberg et aux Feröe pendant les années 1838, 1839, et 1840 sur la corvette la* Récherche, *commandé par M. Fabvre, lieutenant de vaisseau. Publiés par ordre du roi sous la direction de . . . , président de la commission scientifique du Nord.* Twenty vols. and seven atlases. Paris: Arthus-Bertrand, 1839–1852. Drawings by MM. Mayer, Lauvergne, Giraud, and Bevalet; lithographs by Sabatier and Ackermann.

Gardiner, Allen F. *Narrative of a Journey to the Zoolu Country in South Africa, Undertaken in 1835.* London: William Crofts, 1836. Lithographs by T. M. Baynes and C. Hullmandel.

Gautier, Theophile. *Voyage pittoresque en Algérie (1845).* Edited by Madeleine Cottin. Geneva: Droz, 1973. Etchings.

Gessner, Conrad. *On the Admiration of Mountains (1543); A Description of the Riven Mountain, Commonly Called Mount-Pilatus (1555).* Translated by H. B. D. Soule and edited by W. Dock and J. Monroe Thorington. San Francisco: Grabhorn, 1937.

Gilpin, William. *Remarks on Forest Scenery, and Other Woodland Views, Relative Chiefly to Picturesque Beauty. Illustrated by the Scenes of New Forest in Hampshire.* Third edition. Two vols. London: T. Cadell and W. Davies, 1808.

Gmelins, Samuel Georg. *Reise durch Russland zur Untersuchung der drey Natur-Reiche. Reise von St. Petersburg bis nach Ischerkask, der Hauptstadt der Donischen Kosacken in den Jahren 1768 und 1769.* Four vols. Saint Petersburg: Kayserliche Akademie der Wissenschaften, 1770. Line engravings.

Gmelins, Samuel Georg. *Reise durch Sibirien, von dem Jahr 1733 bis 1743.* Four vols. Göttingen: Abram Bandenhoecks See., Wittwe, 1751–1752. Line engravings.

Gold Charles. *Oriental Drawings: Sketched between the Years 1791 and 1793.* London: Bunney and Co., 1806. Colored aquatints.

Golovnin, Vasili. *Voyage de . . . contentant le récit de sa captivité chez les Japponais pendant les années 1811, 1812 et 1813. Traduit sur la version allemande par J. B. B. Eyries.* Two vols. Paris: n.p., 1818.

Graham, Maria. *Journal of a Voyage to Brazil, and Residence there, during Part of the Years 1821, 1822, 1823.* London: Longman, Hurst, Rees, Orme, Brown, and Green, 1824. Drawings by author, aquatints by Edward Finden.

Graham, Maria. *Journal of a Residence in Chile, during the Year 1822, and a Voyage from Chile to Brazil.* London: Longman, Hurst, Rees, Orme, Brown, and Green, 1824. Drawings by author, aquatints by Edward Finden.

Graham, Maria. *Journal of a Residence in India.* Edinburgh: George Ramsay and Company, 1812. Drawings by author, aquatints by James Storer.

Grandpré, Louis O'Hier de. *Voyage à la côte occidentale d'Afrique, fait dans les années 1786 et 1787 . . . Suivi d'un voyage fait au Cap de Bonne-Espérance; contenant la description militaire de cette colonie.* Two vols. Paris: Dentu, 1801. Drawings by author, engravings by Le Villain, Godfroi, and Michel.

Grandpré, Louis O'Hier de. *Voyage dans l'Inde et au Bengale, fait dans les années 1789 et 1790 . . . Suivi d'un voyage fait dans la Mer Rouge, contenant la description de Moka, et du commerce des arabes de l'Yemen; des détails sur leur caractère et leurs moeurs.* Two vols. Paris: Dentu, 1801. Drawings by author, engravings by Michel.

Gratet de Dolomieu, Guy Sylvain Tancrède. *Mémoires sur les Iles Ponces et catalogue raisonné des produits de l'Etna; pour servir à l'histoire des volcans.* Paris: Cuchet, 1788.

Grierson, J. *Twelve Selective Views of the Seat of War, Including Views Taken at Rangoon, Cachar, and Andaman Islands from Sketches Taken on the Spot by . . . .* Calcutta: Asiatic Lithographic Press, 1825. Lithography by E. Billon.

Grindlay, Robert Melville. *Scenery, Costumes, and Architecture, Chiefly on the Western Side of India.* Two vols. London: R. Ackermann, 1826, 1830. Drawings by author, color aquatints by R. Ackermann.

Grose, John Henry. *A Voyage to the East-Indies, with Observations on Various Parts There.* London: S. Hooper and A. Morley, 1757.

Gruner, Gottlieb Siegmund. *Histoire naturelle des glacières de Suisse.* Translated by M. de Keralio. Paris: Panckoucke, 1770. Drawings by S. H. Grim, engravings by A. Zingg.

Gruner, Gottlieb Siegmund. *Die Eisgebirge des Schweizerlandes: Beschrieben von . . . Fürsprech vor den zweyhunderten des Freystaates Bern.* Three vols. Bern: Abraham Wagner, Sohn, 1760. Engravings by A. Zingg.

Guibert, Jacques-Antoine Hippolyte de. *Journal d'un voyage en Allemagne fait en 1773.* Two vols. Paris: Treuttel et Wurtz, An XI [1802–03].

Guibert, Jacques-Antoine Hippolyte de. *Voyages de . . . dans diverses parties de la France et en Suisse. Faits en 1775, 1778, 1784 et 1785. Ouvrage posthume, publié par sa veuve.* Paris: D'Hautel, 1806.

BIBLIOGRAPHY

Hakewell, James. *A Picturesque Tour of the Island of Jamaica, from Drawings Made in the Years 1820 and 1821 by . . . , Author of the "Picturesque Tour of Italy."* London: Hurst and Robinson, 1825. Aquatints by Sutherland.

Hall, Basil. *Account of a Voyage of Discovery to the West Coast of Corea, and the Great Loo-Choo Island; with an Appendix Containing Charts, and Various Hydrographical and Scientific Notices.* London: John Murray, 1818. Drawings by author, color aquatints by Robert Havell and son.

Hamilton, Francis [formerly Buchanan]. *An Account of the Kingdom of Nepal and of the Territories Annexed to This Dominion by the House of Gorkha.* Edinburgh: Archibald Constable and Company, 1819. Engravings by J. Hawksworth.

Hamilton, William. *Campi Phlegraei; Observations on the Volcanoes of the Two Sicilies.* Two vols. Naples: n.p., 1776. Drawings by author, color aquatints by Peter Fabris.

Hardy, Joseph. *A Picturesque and Descriptive Tour in the Mountains of the High Pyrenees: Comprising Twenty-Four Views of the Most Interesting Scenes, from Original Drawings Taken on the Spot; with Some Account of the Bathing Establishments in That Department of France.* London: R. Ackermann, 1825. Color aquatints.

Hawkesworth, John. *An Account of a Voyage Round the World with a Full Account of the Voyage of the* Endeavour *in the Year 1770 along the East Coast of Australia by Lt. James Cook, Commander of His Majesty's Bark* Endeavour. *Compiled by D. Warrington Evans, Illustrated with a Variety of Cuts and Charts related to the Country Discovered (1773).* Brisbane: W. R. Smith & Paterson, 1969. [Facsimile of first edition.] Drawings by Sidney Parkinson, Andrew Sparrmann, and Alexander Buchan.

Hawkesworth, John. *Relation des voyages entrepris par ordre de sa majesté britannique, actuellement régnante, pour faire découvertes dans l'hemisphère meridional, et successivement executés par le commodore Byron, le capitaine Carteret, le capitaine Wallis & le capitaine Cook, dans les vaisseaux le* Dauphin, *le* Swallow *& l'*Endeavour. Four vols. Translated from the English journals of the commanders and from the papers of Joseph Banks. Paris: Saillant et Nyon and Panckoucke, 1774.

Hearne, Samuel. *A Journey from Prince of Wales's Fort, in Hudson's Bay to the Northern Ocean. Undertaken by Order of the Hudson's Bay Company. For the Discovery of Copper Mines, a North West Passage, etc. in the Years 1769, 1770, 1771, & 1772.* Dublin: P. Byrne. Engravings.

Heine, Heinrich. *Reisebilder.* In *Werke.* Edited by Stuart Atkins and Oswald Schonberg. Two vols. Munich: C. H. Beck, 1973.

Hentzi[y], Rodolphe. *Vues remarquables des montagnes de la Suisse, première partie.* Bern: Wagner, 1776. Preface by Albert Haller, natural-history commentary by Jac. Sam. Wyttenbach, drawings by Caspar Wolf, color aquatints by R. Hentzi.

Heriot, George. *A Picturesque Tour Made in the Years 1817 and 1820 through the Pyrenean Mountains, Auvergne, the Departments of the High and Low Alps, and in Part of Spain. The Engravings are Taken from Drawings Executed on the Spot by. . . .* London: R. Ackermann, 1824. Color aquatints by F. C. Lewis.

Heriot, George. *Travels through the Canadas, Containing a Description of the Picturesque Scenery on Some of the Rivers and Lakes; with an Account of the Productions, Commerce, and Inhabitants of Those Provinces. To Which Is Subjoined a Comparative View of the Manners and Customs of Several of the Indian Nations of North and South America.* London: Richard Phillips, 1807. Aquatints.

Herschel, Frederick William. *Altre Scoverte fatte nella Luna dal Sigr. Herschel.* Naples: n.p., 1836. Hand-colored engravings by L. Gatti e Dura and Leopoldo Galluzzo.

Hobhouse, J. C. *A Journey through Albania, and Other Provinces of Turkey in Europe and Asia, to Constantinople, during the Years 1809 and 1810.* London: James Cawthorn, 1813. Color aquatints.

Hodges, William. *Select Views in India, Drawn on the Spot in the Years 1780, 1781, 1782, and 1783, and Executed in Aquatinta.* London: J. Edwards, 1786.

Hodges, William. *Travels in India during the Years 1780, 1781, 1782, and 1783.* Second revised edition. London: J. Edwards, 1794.

Home, Robert. *Select Views in Mysore, the Country of Tipoo Sultan; from Drawings Taken on the Spot by . . . ; With Historical Descriptions.* London: Bowyer, 1794. Engravings.

Hooge, Romein de. *Les Indes Orientales et Occidentales, et autres lieux: représentés in très belles figures (1645–1708.)* New York: Abner Schram, 1980. [41 facsimile engravings]

Horsfield, Thomas. Horsfield Collection and portfolio of Javanese Drawings (1805–1817) [for Raffles' *History of Java*]. India Office Library, London.

Houel, Jean. *Voyage pittoresque des isles de Sicile, de Malte et de Lipari, ou l'on traite des antiquités qui s'y trouvent encore; des principaux phénomènes que la nature y offre; du costume des habitans, & de quelques usages.* Four vols. Paris: Imprimerie de Monsieur, 1782. Aquatints.

Hugel, Carl Freiherr von. *Kaschmir und das Reich der Siek.* Four vols. in three. Stuttgart: Halberger'sche Verlagshandlung, 1840–1842. Drawings by Prosper Marilhat, engravings.

Humboldt, Alexander von. *Aspects of Nature, in Different Lands and Different Climates.* Translated by Mrs. Sabine. Two vols. London: Longman, Brown, Green, and Longmans, 1850.

Humboldt, Alexander von. *Geographie der Pflanzen.* Tübingen: F. G. Cotta, 1807.

Humboldt, Alexander von. *Researches Concerning the Institutions and Monuments of the Ancient Inhabitants of America.* Translated by Helen Maria Williams. Two vols. London: Longman, Hurst, Rees, Orme & Brown, J. Murray, & H. Colburn, 1814.

Humboldt, Alexander von. *Voyage de Humboldt et Bonpland. Relation historique.* Paris: Librairie de Gide, 1813–1834. Three vols. and two atlases. Drawings by author; color aquatints by F. Schoell, Koch, Schick, Marchais, and Gmelin.

Humboldt, Alexander von. *Zerstreute Bemerkungen über den Basalt der ältern und neuern Schriftsteller.* n.l.: n.p. [1800].

An Historical and Descriptive Account of Iceland, Greenland, and the Faroe Islands; with Illustrations of Their Natural History. Edinburgh: Oliver & Boyd; London: Simpkin, Marshall, & Co., 1841. Engravings by Jackson and Bruce.

Irwin, Eyles. *A Series of Adventures in the Course of a Voyage up the Red-Sea on the Coasts of Arabia and Egypt; and of a Route through the Desarts of Thebais, hitherto Unknown to the European Traveller, in the year 1777.* London: J. Dodsley, 1780. Drawings and aquatints by E. Irwin.

Jackson, James Grey. *An Account of the Empire of Morocco, and the Districts of Suse and Tafilelt; Compiled from Miscellaneous Observations Made during a Long Residence in, and Various Journies through, These Countries. To Which Is Added an Account of Shipwrecks on the Western Coast of Africa and an Interesting Account of Timbuctoo, the Great Emporium of Central Africa.* Second revised edition. London: J. Bulmer and Co., 1811. Engravings.

Jackson, James Grey. *An Account of Timbuctoo and Housa, Territories in the Interior of Africa by El Hege Abd Salam Shabeeny, with Notes, Critical and Explanatory. To Which is Added Letters Descriptive of Travels through West and South Barbary, and across the Mountains of Atlas.* London: Longman, Hurst, Rees, Orme, and Brown, 1820.

Johnson, James. *The Oriental Voyager; or, Descriptive Sketches and Cursory Remarks on a Voyage to India and China in His Majesty's Ship* Caroline, *Performed in the Years 1803-4-5-6.* London: Joyce Gold for James Asperne, 1807.

Johnson, James. *No. [1] of a Series of Views in the West Indies: Engraved from Drawings Taken Recently in the Islands: With Letter Press Explanations Made from Actual Observations.* London: Underwood, 1827. Color engravings by T. Fielding.

Journal des voyages de découvertes et navigations modernes, ou archives géographiques du XIXe siècle. Paris: C. Ballard, 1819–1841.

Journal für die neuesten Land- und Seereisen und das Interessanteste aus der Volker- und Landerkunde. Berlin: Friedrich Braunes, 1808.

Kaempfer, Engelbertus. *The History of Japan, Giving an Account of the Ancient and Present State and Government of That Empire; of Its Temples, Palaces, Castles and Other Buildings; of its Metals, Minerals, Trees, Plants, Animals, Birds, and Fishes . . . Together with a Description of the Kingdom of Siam.* Translated by J. G. Scheuchzer. Two vols. London: J. G. Scheuchzer, 1727. Engravings.

Kerguelen-Trémarec, Yves-Joseph de. *Relation d'un voyage dans la mer du Nord aux côtes d'Islande, du Groenland, de Ferro, de Schettland, des Orcades & de Norwège; fait en 1767 & 1768.* Paris: Prault, 1771. Engravings.

Kershaw, J. *Description of a Series of Views in the Burman Empire. Drawn on the Spot by . . . and Engraved by William Daniell, R.A.* London: Smith, Elder, and Co., [1831?]. Color aquatints.

Kirkpatrick, William. *An Account of the Kingdom of Nepaul, Being the Substance of Observations Made during a Mission to That Country, in the Year 1793. Illustrated with a Map and Other Engravings.* London: William Miller, 1811. Drawings by A. W. Devis, engravings by J. Greig.

Kotzebue, Moritz von. *Narrative of a Journey into Persia in the Suite of the Imperial Russian Embassy in the Year 1817.* London: Longman, Hurst, Rees, Orme, Brown, 1819.

Kotzebue, Otto von. *Entdeckungs-Reise in die Süd-See und nach der Berings-Strasse zur Erforschung einer nordöstlichen Durchfahrt, unternommen in den Jahren 1815, 1816, 1817, und 1818.* Three vols. in one. Weimar: Gebrüder Hoffmann, 1821. Color engravings after drawings by Adelbert von Chamisso.

Kotzebue, Otto von. *A Voyage of Discovery into the South Sea and the Bering Straits, for the Purpose of Exploring a North-East Passage, Undertaken in the Years 1815–1818.* Translated by H. E. Lloyd. Three vols. London: Longman, Hurst, Rees, Orme, and Brown, 1821. Color engravings after drawings by Adelbert von Chamisso.

Krusenstern, A. J. von. *Voyage round the World in the Years 1803, 1804, 1805, & 1806 by Order of His Imperial Majesty Alexander the First, on Board the Ships* Nadeshda *and* Neva. Translated by Richard Belgrave Hoppner. Two vols. in one. London: John Murray, 1813. Sketches by W. Tilesius, drawings by H. Alexander Orloffsky, color engravings by J. A. Atkinson.

Labillardière, Jacques-Julien Houton de. *Relation du voyage à la recherche de La Pérouse.* Two vols. Paris: H. J. Jansen, An VIII [1799–1800].

Labillardière, Jacques-Julien Houton de. *Atlas pour servir à la relation du voyage à la recherche de La Pérouse fait par l'ordre de l'assemblée constituante pendant les années 1791, 1792, et pendant la 1ere et 2eme année de la république française.* Paris: H. J. Jansen, An VIII [1799–1800]. Drawings by Piron and Redouté for engravings.

Laborde, Alexandre-Louis Joseph de. *Description des nouveaux jardins de la France et de ses anciens châteaux.* Paris: Desmarquette, 1808–1815. Drawings by Constant Bourgeois for engravings.

Laborde, Alexandre-Louis Joseph de. *Voyage pittoresque et historique de l'Espagne.* Four vols. Paris: Pierre Didot, l'aîné, 1806–1818. Engravings.

Laborde, Jean-Benjamin de. *Description générale et particulière de la France.* Twelve vols. Paris: Imprimerie de Monsieur, 1784–1788. Etchings.

Laborde, Jean-Benjamin de. *Voyage pittoresque de la France, avec la description de toutes ses provinces.* Eight vols. Paris: Imprimerie de Monsieur, 1781–1796. Etchings.

Laborde, Jean-Benjamin de. *Tableaux topographiques, pittoresques, physiques, historiques, moraux, politiques, littéraires de la Suisse et de l'Italie, ornée de 1200 estampes . . . d'après les dessins de MM. Robert, Perignon, Fragonard, Paris, Poyet, Raymond, Le Barbier, Berthélémy, Ménageot, Le May, Houel, etc.* Three vols. Paris: Née & Masquelier, 1780–1786. Etchings.

VOYAGE INTO SUBSTANCE

Laborde, Leon-Emmanuel-Simon-Joseph de. *Voyage de l'Arabie Petrée par . . . et Linant*. Paris: Giard, 1830. Drawings by author and Linant, lithographs by Sabatier and Villeneuve.

La Follie, Louis-Guillaume. *Le philosophe sans prétention, ou l'homme rare. Ouvrage physique, chymique et moral, dedié au savans*. Paris: Clousier, 1775. Engravings by C. Boissel.

Dialogues de Monsieur le baron de Lahontan et d'un sauvage, dans l'Amerique . . . avec les voyages du même en Portugal & en Danemarc, dans lesquels on trouve des particularitez très curieuses, & qu'on n'avoit point encore remarqués. London: David Mortier; Amsterdam: Bolteman, 1704. Engravings.

Laing, John. *A Voyage to the Spitzbergen, Containing an Account of That Country*. Second revised edition. Edinburgh: Adam Black, 1818.

Lamartine, Alphonse-Marie-Louis de. *Souvenirs, impressions, pensées et paysages pendant un voyage en Orient, 1832–1833*. In *Oeuvres complètes* (Paris: author, 1861), vols. VI–VIII.

Landmann, George. *Historical, Military, and Picturesque Observations on Portugal, Illustrated by Seventy-Five Coloured Plates, Including Authentic Plans of the Sieges and Battles Fought in the Peninsula during the Late War*. Two vols. London: T. Cadell and W. Davies, 1818. Drawings by author for color aquatints.

Lang, Carl. *Gallerie der unterirdischen Schöpfungswunder und des menschlichen Kunstfleisses unter der Erde*. Two vols. Leipzig: Karl Tauchniss, 1806–1807. Drawings by author for color aquatints.

La Pérouse, Jean-François de Galaup de. *Voyage de . . . autour du monde, publié conformement au décret du 22 avril 1791, et rédigé par M.L.A. Milet-Mureau général de brigade dans le corps du génie, directeur des fortifications, ex-constituant, membre de plusieurs sociétés littéraires de Paris*. Four vols. and atlas. Paris: Imprimerie de la République, An V [1796–97]. Drawings by Duché de Vancy for engravings.

La Place, M. *Voyage autour du monde par les mers de l'Inde et de la Chine de la corvette de sa majesté la* Favorite, *exécuté pendant les années 1830, 1831, 1832*. Paris: Arthus Bertrand, 1835. *Drawings by Sainson for aquatints*.

La Rochefoucauld-Liancourt, François-Alexandre-Frédéric, Duc de. *Voyage dans les Etats-Unis d'Amerique fait en 1795, 1796, et 1797*. Eight vols. Paris: Du Pont, Buisson, Charles Pougens, An VII [1798–99].

Lear, Edward. *Journals of a Landscape Painter in Southern Calabria*. London: Richard Bentley, 1852. Lithographs.

Lear, Edward. *Views in Rome and Its Environs Drawn from Nature and on Stone*. London: C. Hullmandel for T. M'Lean, 1841. Lithographs.

Le Bruyn, Cornelius. *Travels into Muscovy, Persia, and Part of the East-Indies. Containing an Accurate Description of Whatever Is Most Remarkable in Those Countries. And Embellished with 320 Copper Plates, Representing the Finest Prospects, and Most Considerable Cities in Those Parts; the Different Habits of the People; the Singular and Extraordinary Birds, Fishes, and Plants Which Are There to Be Found: As Likewise the Antiquities of Those Countries . . . The Whole Being Delineated on the Spot, from the Respective Objects*. Two vols. Translated from the French. London: A. Bettesworth, C. Hitch, S. Birt, C. Davis, J. Clarke, S. Harding, D. Browne, A. Miller, J. Schuckburg, and T. Osborne, 1737.

Ledru, André-Pierre. *Voyage aux Iles de Ténériffe, La Trinité, Saint-Thomas, Sainte-Croix et Porto-Ricco, exécuté par ordre du gouvernement français depuis le 30 septembre 1796 jusqu'au 7 juin 1798, sous la direction du capitaine [N.] Baudin, pour faire des recherches et des collections relatives à l'histoire naturelle*. Two vols. Paris: Arthus-Bertrand, 1810.

Le Gentil, Jean-Baptiste-Joseph. *Voyage dans les mers de l'Inde fait par l'ordre du roi à l'occasion du passage du Vénus, sur le disque du soleil, le 6 juin 1761 & du même mois 1769*. Two vols. Paris: Imprimerie Royale, 1779. Engravings.

Legh, Thomas. *Narrative of a Journey in Egypt and the Country beyond the Cataracts.* London: John Murray, 1816.

Lesseps, Jean-Baptiste-Barthélemy, Baron de. *Journal historique du voyage de . . . , consul de France, employé dans l'expédition de M. le comte de La Pérouse, en qualité d'intérprète du roi. Depuis l'instant ou il a quitté les frégates françoises au Port Saint-Pierre & Saint-Paul du Kamtschatka jusqu'à son arrivée en France, le 17 octobre 1788.* Two vols. Paris: Imprimerie Royale, 1790. Engravings.

Le Vaillant, François. *Voyage de . . . dans l'intérieur de l'Afrique, par le Cap de Bonne-Espérance, dans les annés 1780, 81, 82, 83, 84, & 85.* Two vols. Paris: Chez Le Roy, 1790. Engravings.

Lewis, Meriwether, and William Clark. *History of the Expedition under the Command of Captains Lewis and Clark, to the Sources of the Missouri, thence Across the Rocky Mountains and Down the River Columbia to the Pacific Ocean. Performed during the Years 1804–5–6. By Order of the Government of the United States and Prepared for Press by Paul Allen, Esq.* Two vols. Philadelphia: Bradford and Inskeep; New York: A. H. Inskeep, 1814.

Leyden, John. *A Historical & Philosophical Sketch of the Discoveries & Settlements of the Europeans in Northern & Western Africa at the Close of the Eighteenth Century.* Edinburgh: J. Mour, 1799.

Leyden, John. *Historical Account of Discoveries and Travels in Africa, by the Late . . . , Enlarged, and Completed to the Present Time, with Illustrations of Its Geography and Natural History, as well as of the Moral and Social Condition of Its Inhabitants by Hugh Murray, Esq. F.R.S.E.* Two vols. Edinburgh: George Ramsay and Co., 1817.

Lichtenstein, Heinrich. *Reisen im Südlichen Africa in den Jahren 1803, 1804, 1805 und 1806.* Two vols. Berlin: C. Salford, 1811. Engravings.

Liddiard, Nicholas John. *Narrative of a Voyage to New Zealand, Performed in the Years 1814 and 1815.* Two vols. London: James Black and Son, 1817.

Lisiansky, Urey. *A Voyage round the World in the Years 1803, 4, 5, & 6; Performed by the Order of His Imperial Majesty Alexander the First, Emperor of Russia, in the Ship* Neva. Translated from the Russian. London: John Booth, 1814.

Lobo, Jerome. *A Voyage to Abyssinia.* Translated by M. Le Grand. London: A. Bettesworth, 1735.

Lunardi, Vincent. *An Account of the First Aerial Voyage in England. In a Series of Letters to His Guardian, Chevalier Gherardo Compagni.* London: author, 1784.

Lycett, Joseph. *Views in Australia or New South Wales, & Van Diemen's Land, Delineated in Fifty Views, with Descriptive Letter Press, Dedicated by Permission, to the Right Hon.ble Earl Bathurst, etc, by . . . , Artist to Major-General Macquarie, Late Governor of Those Colonies.* London: J. Souter, 1824. Lithographs and aquatints by author.

Lyon, G. F. *A Narrative of Travels in Northern Africa, in the Years 1818, 19, and 20; Accompanied by Geographical Notices of Soudan, and of the Course of the Niger.* London: John Murray, 1821. Drawings by author, lithographs by G. Harley.

Lyon, G. F. *The Private Journal of . . . H.M.S.* Hecla *during the Recent Voyage of Discovery under Captain Parry.* London: John Murray, 1824. Drawings by author, engravings by E. Finden.

Macartney, John. *An Account of an Embassy from the King of Great Britain to the Emperor of China.* Edited by George Staunton. Two vols. and atlas. London: W. Bulmer and Co., 1797. Drawings by William Alexander for engravings.

Macculoch, John. *A Description of the Western Islands of Scotland, Including the Isle of Man: Comprising an Account of Their Geological Structure; with Remarks on Their Agriculture, Scenery, and Antiquities.* Three vols. London: Archibald Constable and Co.; Edinburgh: Hurst, Robinson, and Co., 1819. Drawings by author, engravings by Charles Heath.

MacKenzie, Alexander. *Voyages from Montreal, on the River Saint Lawrence, through the Continent of North America to the Frozen and Pacific Oceans; in the Years 1789 and 1793. With a Preliminary Account of the Rise, Progress, and Present State of the Fur Trade of That Country.* London: T. Cadell, Jr., and W. Davies, 1801.

MacKenzie, Colin. *MacKenzie Collection, 1782–1821.* India Office Library, London.

MacKenzie, George Steuart. *Travels in the Island of Iceland, during the Summer of the Year 1810.* Edinburgh: Thomas Allan and Company, 1811. Drawings by author, color aquatints by I. Clark.

M'Leod, John. *Narrative of a Voyage in His Majesty's Late Ship* Alceste, *to the Yellow Sea, along the Coast of Corea, and through Its Numerous Hitherto Undiscovered Islands to the Island of Lewchew, with an Account of Her Shipwreck in the Straits of Gaspar.* London: John Murray, 1817. Drawings by author, color aquatints by W. H. Dwarris and I. Clark.

Magalotti, Lorenzo. *Travels of Cosmo the Third, Grand Duke of Tuscany through England, during the Reign of King Charles the Second (1664). Translated from the Italian Manuscript in the Laurentian Library at Florence.* London: J. Mauman, 1821. Aquatints.

Maillet, Benoît de. *Description de l'Egypte, contenant plusieurs remarques curieuses sur la géographie ancienne et moderne de ce païs, sur ses monuments anciennes, sur les moeurs, les coutumes & la religion des habitans, sur le gouvernement & le commerce, sur les animaux, les arbres, les plantes, etc.* Edited by M. l'Abbé Le Mascrier. Two vols. The Hague: Isaac Beauregard, 1740.

Malaspina, Alejandro. *Viaje al Rio de La Plata en el siglo XVIII.* Edited by Hector R. Ratto. Buenos Aires: Libreria y Editorial "La Facultad," 1938.

Malaspina, Alejandro. *Letters of Alexandre Malaspina (1790–1791).* Edited by William Inglis Morse and translated by Christopher M. Dawson. Boston: McIver-Johnson, 1944.

Manson, James. *Twelve Drawings of Almorah (1826) accompanying "Report of the Mineral Survey of the Himalaya Mountains Lying Between the Rivers Sutlej and Kalee."* Ms. E. 96, India Office Library, London.

Mariner, William. *Voyage aux Iles des Amis, situées dans l'Ocean Pacifique fait dans les années 1805 à 1810, avec l'histoire des habitans depuis leur découverte par le capitaine Cook.* Second edition. Two vols. Paris: J. Smith, 1819.

Marsden, William. *Views of Sumatra.* London: Andrews and Stadler, 1799. Color aquatints.

Martens, Conrad. *Watercolors from Beagle* Expedition: Survey to Southern Australia, 1837–1843. National Maritime Museum, Greenwich.

Mayer, Luigi. *Views in Egypt from the Original Drawings in the Possession of Sir Robert Ainslie, Taken during His Embassy to Constantinople by . . . ; Engraved by and Under the Direction of Thomas Milton: With Historical Observations and Incidental Illustrations of the Manners and Customs of the Natives of This Country.* London: Thomas Bensely for R. Bowyer, 1801. Color aquatints.

Mayer, Luigi. *Views in the Ottoman Empire, Chiefly in Caramania, a Part of Asia Minor hitherto Unexplored; with Some Curious Selections from the Islands of Rhodes, and Cyprus, and the Celebrated Cities of Corinth, Carthage, and Tripoli: From the Original Drawings in the Possession of Sir R. Ainslie, Taken during His Embassy to Constantinople by. . . . With Historical Observations and Incidental Illustrations of the Manners and Customs of the Natives of the Country.* London: R. Bowyer, 1803. Color aquatints.

Mayer, Luigi. *Views in Palestine, from the Original Drawings by . . . , With an Historical and Descriptive Account of the Country, and Its Remarkable Places.* London: T. Bensley for R. Bowyer, 1804. Color aquatints.

Meares, J. *Collection de cartes géographiques, vues, marines, plans et portraits, relatifs aux voyages du . . . , traduits de l'anglois par J.B.L. J. Billecocq.* Paris: F. Buisson, An III [1794–95].

Mignan, Robert. *Travels in Chaldea, Including a Journey from Bussorah to Baddad, Hillah, and Babylon, Performed on Foot in 1827*. London: Henry Colburn and Richard Bentley, 1829. Aquatints and wood engravings by R. Craggs.

Milbert, Jacques-Gérard. *Itinéraire pittoresque du fleuve Hudson et des parties latérales de l'Amerique du Nord, d'après les dessins originaux pris sur les lieux par . . . .* Two vols. in one and atlas. Paris: Henri Gaugain et Cie, 1828. Lithographs by Adam, Bichebois, Deroy, Dupressoir, Jacottet, Joly, Sabatier, Tirpenne, and Villeneuve.

Milbert, Jacques-Gérard. *Voyage pittoresque à l'Ile de France, au Cap de Bonne-Espérance et à l'Ile de Ténériffe*. Two vols. and atlas. Paris: A. Nepveu, 1812. Drawings and engravings by author.

Millin, Aubin-Louis. *Voyage dans les departémens de la France*. Five vols. Paris: Imprimerie Impériale, 1807.

Millin, Aubin-Louis. *Voyage en Savoie, en Piémont, à Nice, et à Gènes*. Two vols. Paris: C. Wasserman, 1816.

Moerenhout, J. A. *Voyages aux iles du Grand Océan* (1837). Two vols. Facsimilie of first edition. Paris: Adrien Maisonneuve, 1942.

Mollien, G. *Travels in the Interior of Africa, to the Sources of the Senegal and Gambia; Performed by Command of the French Government, in the Year 1818*. Edited by T. E. Bowdich. London: Henry Colburn & Co., 1820. Aquatints.

Rapport fait à l'académie des sciences sur la machine aérostatique inventée par MM. de Montgolfier. Paris: Moutard, 1784.

Moore, J., and Capt. Marryat. *Views of Rangoon and Combined Operations in the Birman Empire*. London: n.p., 1825–1826. Color aquatints.

Morier, James. *A Journey through Persia, Armenia, and Asia Minor, to Constantinople, in the Years 1808 and 1809; in Which is Included, Some Account of the Proceedings of His Majesty's Mission, Under Sir Hartford Jones, Bart. K.C. to the Court of the King of Persia*. London: Longman, Hurst, Rees, Orme, and Brown, 1812. Drawings by author for aqautints.

Nadar [Felix Tournachon]. *Mémoirs du Géant*. Second edition. Paris: Dentu, 1865.

Nadar [Felix Tournachon]. Ballooning material. Musée Carnavalet, Paris.

Nadar [Felix Tournachon]. *Les ballons en 1870. Ce qu'on aurait pu faire, ce qu'on a fait*. Paris: E. Chatelain, 1870.

Nadar [Felix Tournachon]. *Le droit au vol*. Paris: J. Hetzel, [1865].

Neale, Adam. *Travels through Some Parts of Germany, Poland, Moldavia and Turkey*. London: Longman, Hurst, Rees, Orme and Brown, 1818. Drawings by author, color aquatints by J. Clark.

Niebuhr, Carsten. *Description de l'Arabie d'après les observations et recherches faites dans le pays même*. Copenhagen: Nicolas Moller, 1773. Engravings.

Nieuhof, John. *An Embassy from the East-India Company of the United Provinces to the Grand Tartar Cham, Emperor of China*. Translated by John Ogilby. London: John Macock, 1669. Engravings.

Norden, Frederick Lewis. *Travels in Egypt and Nubia. Enlarged with Observations from Ancient and Modern Authors, that Have Written on the Antiquities of Egypt by Dr. Peter Templeman*. Two vols. London: Lockyer Davis and Charles Reymers, Printers to the Royal Society, 1756–1757. Engravings by Mark Tuscher.

Olivier, G. A. *Voyage dans l'Empire Othoman, l'Egypte et la Perse, fait par l'ordre du gouvernement, pendant les six premières années de la république*. Three vols. and atlas. Paris: H. Agasse, An IX [1800–1801]. Drawings by A. Caroffe, engravings by R. U. Massaud et al.

Orme, William. *Twenty-Four Views in Hindostan from the Original Pictures Painted by Mr. Daniell & Col. Ward*. London: Edward Orme, 1805. Color aquatints.

O'Reilly, Bernard. *Greenland, the Adjacent Seas, and the North-West Passage to the Pacific Ocean, Illustrated in a Voyage to Davis's Strait, during the Summer of 1817. With Charts and Numerous Plates from Drawings by the Author Taken on the Spot*. London: Baldwin, Cradock, and Joy, 1818. Drawings by S. Koenig, aquatints by F. C. Lewis.

W. F. W. Owen, *Narrative of Voyages to Explore the Shores of Africa, Arabia, and Madagascar*. Two vols. London: Richard Bentley, 1833. Lithographs.

Oxley, John. *Journals of Two Expeditions into the Interior of New South Wales, Undertaken by Order of the British Government in the Years 1817–18*. London: John Murray, 1820. Etchings by J. Clark, color aquatints by William Havell.

Pagès, Pierre-Marie-François de. *Voyages autour du monde, et vers les deux Pôles, par terre et par mer pendant les années 1767, 1768, 1769, 1770, 1771, 1773, 1774 & 1776*. Two vols. in one. Paris: Moutard, 1782.

Pallas, Pierre-Simon. *Nouveau voyage dans les gouvernements mériodionaux de l'Empire de Russie dans les années 1793 et 1794*. Translated from the German. Two vols. and atlas. Paris: Armand Koenig, 1801. Color aquatints.

Park, Mungo. *Travels in the Interior Districts of Africa: Performed under the Direction and Patronage of the African Association in the Years 1795, 1796, and 1797*. London: W. Bulmer, 1799. Sketches by author, drawings by J. C. Barrow, engravings by W. C. Wilson.

Parkinson, Sydney. *A Journal of a Voyage to the South Seas in His Majesty's Ship, the* Endeavour, *faithfully Transcribed from the papers of the Late . . . , Draughtsman to Joseph Banks, Esq., on His Late Expedition, with Dr. Solander, Round the World. Embellished with Views and Designs, Delineated by the Author, and Engraved by Capital Artists*. London: Stanfield Parkinson, 1773.

Parkinson, Sydney. A Collection of Drawings Made in the Countries Visited by Captain Cook in His First Voyage, also of Prints Published in Hawkesworth's *Voyages of Biron, Wallis and Cook* as well as Cook's Second and Third Voyages. By . . . , Alexander Buchan, etc. Add. Ms. 23921, British Library, London.

Parry, William Edward. *Journal of a Voyage for the Discovery of a North-West Passage from the Atlantic to the Pacific, Performed in the Years 1819–20*. London: John Murray, 1821. Drawings and engravings by William Westall.

Pasumont, François. *Voyages physiques dans les Pyrénées en 1788 et 1789. Histoire naturelle d'une partie de ces montagnes; particulièrement des environs de Barège, Bagnères, Cautères et Gavarnie. Avec des cartes géographiques*. Paris: Le Clere, 1797.

Pennant, Thomas. *The Journey to Snowden*. London: Henry Hughes, 1781. Drawings by Moses Griffith.

Pennant, Thomas. *A Tour in Scotland and Voyage to the Hebrides*. Chester: John Monk, 1774. Drawings and engravings by John Frederick Miller.

Pennant, Thomas. *A Tour in Wales*. London: Henry Hughes, 1778. Drawings by Moses Griffith, engravings by P. Mazell and P. C. Canot.

Pernety, A. J. *Journal historique d'un voyage fait aux Iles Malouines en 1763 & 1764*. Two vols. Berlin: Etienne de Bourdeaux, 1769.

Péron, François. *Mémoires du Capitaine . . . sur ses voyages*. Edited by Louis Freycinet. Second edition. Two vols. Paris: Brissot-Thivars, 1824. Drawings by Charles-Alexandre Lesueur.

Pertusier, Charles. *Promenades pittoresques dans Constantinople et sur les rives du Bosphore, suivies d'une notice sur la Dalmatie*. Three vols. and atlas. Paris: H. Nicolle, 1815. Drawing by Preault for engravings by B. Piringer.

Phipps, Constantine John. *A Voyage towards the North Pole Undertaken by His Majesty's Command, 1773*. London: W. Bowyer and J. Nichols, 1774. Drawings by P. d'Auvergne for engravings.

Pigafetta, Antonio. *Magellan's Voyage. A Narrative Account of the First Circumnavigation*. Translated and edited by R. A. Skelton. Two vols. in facsimile. New Haven, Conn.: Yale University Press, 1969.

Pilâtre de Rozier, J. F. *Première expérience de la montgolfière construite par l'ordre du roi*. Second edition. Paris: Imprimerie de Monsieur, 1784.

Pilâtre de Rozier, J. F. *La vie et les mémoires de . . . , écrits par lui-même, publiés par Tournon de La Chapelle*. Paris: Editor, 1786.

Pitton de Tournefort, Joseph. *Relation d'un voyage du Levant, fait par ordre du roy. Contenant l'histoire ancienne & moderne de plusieurs Isles de l'Archipel, de Constantinople, des côtes de la Mer Noire, de l'Arménie, de la Georgie, des frontiers de Perse & de l'Asie Mineure . . . Enrichie de descriptions & de figures d'un grand nombre de plantes rares, de divers animaux; et de plusieurs observations touchant l'histoire naturelle*. Two vols. Paris: Imprimerie Royale, 1717. Drawings by author and engravings.

Pococke, Richard. *A Description of the East, and Some Other Countries. Observations on Palestine or the Holy Land, Syria, Mesopotamia, Cyprus and Candia*. Two vols. in three. London: W. Bowyer, 1745.

Poivre, Pierre. *Voyage d'un philosophe, ou observations sur les moeurs & les arts des peuples de l'Afrique, de l'Asie, et de l'Amerique*. Yverdon: n.p., 1768.

Porter, Robert Ker. *Travels in Georgia, Persia, Armenia, Ancient Babylonia*. Two vols. London: Longman, Hurst, Rees, Orme, and Brown, 1822. Drawings by author, engravings by J. C. Stadler.

Porter, Robert Ker. *Travelling Sketches in Russia and Sweden during the Years 1805, 1806, 1807, 1808*. Two vols. London: John Stockdale, 1813. Drawings by author, engravings by J. C. Stadler.

Postans, Thomas. *Hints to Cadets, with a Few Observations on the Military Service of the Honourable East-India Company*. London: William H. Allen and Co., 1842.

Postans, Thomas. *Two hundred and Twelve Drawings and Twelve Lithographs Depicting Costume, Occupation, Scenery and Buildings in Sind, Cutch, and Bombay, 1830–1845*. W.D. 485/1–114, India Office Library, London.

Proceedings of the Association for Promoting the Discovery of the Interior Parts of Africa. London: C. Macral, 1790.

Proceedings of the Association for Promoting the Discovery of the Interior Parts of Africa. Two vols. London: W. Bulmer and Co., 1810.

Ramond de Carbonnières, Louis-François-Elizabeth de. *Observations faites dans les Pyrénées, pour servir de suite à des observations sur les Alpes, insérées dans une traduction des Lettres de W. Coxe, sur la Suisse*. Paris: Belin, 1789.

Raoul-Rochette, D. *Lettres sur la Suisse par H. Sazerac and G. Engelmann*. Two vols. Paris: G. Engelmann, 1823. Drawings and lithographs by Villeneuve.

Rattray, James. *Scenery, Inhabitants, & Costumes of Afghanistan. From Drawings Made on the Spot by . . . , Lieut. 2nd Grenadiers Bengal Army*. London: Hering & Remington, 1847. Chromolithographs.

Roberts, David. *The Holy Land, Syria, Idhmia, Egypt, and Arabia. With Historical Descriptions by the Rev. George Croly, L.L.D.* Two vols. London: F. G. Moon, 1842. Lithographs by Louis Haghe.

Ross, John. *A Voyage of Discovery, Made under the Orders of The Admiralty, in His Majesty's Ships* Isabella *and* Alexander, *for the Purpose of Exploring Baffin's Bay, and Inquiring into the Probability of a North-West Passage.* Second edition. London: John Murray, 1819. Color aquatints by R. and D. Havell.

Royal Society. *Directions for Seamen Bound for Far Voyages. Philosophical Transactions.* Vol. I. 1666.

Rugendas, João Mauricio. *Viagem pitoresca a traves dõ Brasil.* Edited by Rubens Borba de Morals. San Paolo: Martins, 1940.

Ruschenberger, W. S. W. *Narrative of a Voyage round the World, during the Years 1835, 36, and 37; Including a Narrative of an Embassy to the Sultan of Muscat and the King of Siam.* Two vols. London: Richard Bentley, 1838.

Saint-Non, Jean-Claude-Richard de. *Voyage pittoresque ou description des royaumes de Naples et de Sicile.* Five vols. Paris: Clousier, 1781–1786. Drawings by Chatelet; etchings by Varin, A. Guttenberg, et al.

Salchi, E. *L'optique de l'univers, ou la philosophie des voyages autour du monde.* Berne: Emmanuel Haller, 1799.

Salt, Henry. *These Twenty-Four Views Taken in Saint Helena, the Cape, India, Ceylon, Abyssinia, and Egypt.* London: William Miller, 1809. Drawings by author, color aquatints by R. Havell.

Salt, Henry. *A Voyage to Abyssinia and Travels into the Interior of That Country, Executed under the Orders of the British Government, in the Years 1809 and 1810; in Which Are Included an Account of the Portuguese Settlements on the East Coast of Africa, Visited in the Course of the Voyage.* London: F. C. and J. Rivington, 1814. Drawings by author, etchings by C. Heath.

Sauer, Martin. *An Account of a Geographical and Astronomical Expedition to the Northern Parts of Russia, for Ascertaining the Degrees of Latitude and Longitude of the Mouth of the River Kovima; of the Whole Coast of the Tshutski, to East Cape; and of the Islands in the Eastern Ocean, Stretching to the American Coast. By Command of Catherine II, by Commodore Joseph Billings in the Years 1785, etc. to 1794.* London: T. Cadell, Jr., and W. D. Davies, 1802. Engravings.

Saugnier, Raymond de. *Relations de plusieurs voyages à la côte d'Afrique, à Maroc, au Sénégal, à Gorée, à Galam, etc. Avec des détails intéressans pour ceux qui se destinent à la traite des nègres, de l'or, de l'ivoire, etc, tirées des journaux de . . . qui a été long-temps esclave des maures et de l'empereur de Maroc.* Paris: Gueffier Jeune, 1791.

Saussure, Horace-Bénédict. *Voyage dans les Alpes, précédés d'un essai sur l'histoire naturelle des environs de Génève.* Four vols. Neufchâtel: n.p., 1779. Drawings by Bourrit, engravings by Carl Hackert, et al.

Sazerac, Hilaire. *Un mois en Suisse, ou souvenirs d'un voyageur.* Paris: Sazerac & Duval, 1825. Drawings by Edouard Pingret, lithographs by Langlumé.

Scheuchzer, Johann Jacob. *Beschreibung der Natur-Geschichten des Schweizerlandes.* Three vols. in one. Zurich: author, 1706–1708. Drawings and engravings by F. Melchior Fuesli.

Scheuchzer, Johann Jacob. *Geschichte des Schweizerlandes, samt seinen Reisen über die Schweizerische Gebürge.* Two vols. Edited and revised by Johann George Sulzer. Zurich: David Gessner, 1746. Engravings.

Schmidtmeyer, Peter. *Travels into Chile, over the Andes, in the Years 1820 and 1821, With Some Sketches of the Productions and Agriculture; Mines and Metallurgy; Inhabitants, History, and Other Features of America; Particularly of Chile and Aranco.* London: Longman, Hurst, Rees, Orme, Brown, & Green, 1824. Sketches by author, lithographs by G. Scharf.

Scoresby, William. *An Account of the Arctic Regions, with a History and Description of the Northern Whale-Fishery.* Two vols. Edinburgh: Archibald Constable and Co., 1820. Sketches by author, drawings by R. K. Greville, engravings by W. & D. Lizars.

Seddon, Thomas. *Memoirs and Letters of the Late . . . , Artist. By His Brother [1854–1856]*. London: James Nisbet and Co., 1858. Drawings by author, steel engravings.

Sherwill, Markham. Fourteen Narratives Written by Those Travellers Who Have Successfully Attained the Summit of This Mountain, between the Years 1786 and 1838 . . . Accompanied by a Series of Views, Portraits, and Original Letters Collected by . . . , One of the Intrepid Adventurers. Three vols. 1840. Ub. 72, 72a, 72b, Cabinet des Estampes, Bibliothèque Nationale, Paris.

Shillibeer, James. *A Narrative of the Briton's Voyage to Pitcairn's Island*. Second edition. London: Law and Whittaker, 1817. Etchings by author.

Skjöldebrand, Anders F. *[Les cataractes et le canal de Tröllhatta en Suède.] Description des cataractes et du canal de Tröllhatta en Suède; avec un précis historique*. Stockholm: Charles Delen, 1804. Drawings and aquatints by author.

Skjöldebrand, Anders F. *A Picturesque Journey to the North Cape*. Translated from the French [1805]. London: J. M. Richardson, 1813. Drawings by author, aquatints by Arnald and Alken Senior.

Sonnerat, P. *Voyage aux Indes Orientales et à la Chine, fait par ordre de Louis XVI, depuis 1774 jusqu'en 1781; dans lequel on traite des moeurs, de la religion, des sciences et des arts des indiens, des chinois, des pégouins et des madegasses; suivi d'observations sur le Cap de Bonne-Espérance, les Iles de France et de Bourbon, les Maldines, Ceylan, Malacca, les Philippines et les Moluques, et de recherches sur l'histoire naturelle de ces pays*. Second edition. Two volumes in one. Paris: Dentu, 1806.

Sonnini, C. S. *Voyage dans le Haute et Basse Egypte fait par ordre de l'ancien gouvernement, et contenant des observations de tous genres*. Three vols. and atlas. Paris: F. Buisson, An VII [1798–99]. Drawings by J. B. P. Tardieu for etchings.

Sonnini, C. S. *Voyage en Grèce et en Turquie, fait par ordre de Louis XVI, et avec l'autorisation de la cour ottomane*. Two vols. and atlas. Paris: F. Buisson, An IX [1800–1801]. Etchings by Marechal and Tardieu l'aîné.

Sparrman, Andrew. *A Voyage to the Cape of Good Hope, towards the Antarctic Polar Circle and round the World: But Chiefly into the Country of the Hottentots and Caffres, from the Year 1772 to 1776*. Translated from the Swedish. Two vols. in one. London: G. and G. J. and J. Robinson, 1785. Engravings.

Staunton, George. *An Authentic Account of an Embassy from the King of the Great Britain to the Emperor of China; Including Cursory Observations Made, and Information obtained, in Travelling through That Ancient Empire, and a Small Part of Chinese Tartary . . . Taken Chiefly from the Papers of His Excellency, the Earl of Macartney, Knight of Bath, His Majesty's Ambassador Extraordinary and Plenipotentiary to the Emperor of China; Sir Erasmus Gower, commander of the Expedition*. Two vols. and atlas. London: W. Bulmer and Co., 1797. Drawings by William Alexander and engravings.

Stedman, J. G. *Voyage à Surinam et dans l'intérieur de la Guiane, contenant la relation des cinq années de courses et d'observations faites dans cette contrée intéressante et peu connue; avec des détails sur les indiens de la Guiane et les nègres*. Translated by P. F. Henry. Three vols. and atlas. Paris: F. Buisson, An VII [1798–99]. Drawings by author, etchings by Tardieu l'aîné.

Strabo. *The Geography*. Translated by Horace Leonard Jones. Eight vols. London: William Heinemann; New York: G. P. Putnam's Sons, 1917.

Sulzer, Johann Georg. *Tagebuch einer von Berlin nach den mittaglichen Ländern von Europa in den Jahren 1775 und 1776 gethanen Reise und Rückreise*. Leipzig: Weidmanns Erben und Reich, 1780.

Tavernier, J. B. *Recueil de plusieurs relations et traitez singuliers et curieux de . . . , Escuyer, Baron d'Aubonne, qui n'ont point esté mis dans ses six premiers voyages*. Second edition. Paris: Clouzier, Pierre Aubouyn, Pierre Emery, 1685. Etchings.

Taylor, Baron, and Charles Nodier. *Histoire pittoresque de l'Angleterre et de ses possessions dans les Indes.* Three vols. Paris: Administration de l'Histoire Pittoresque de l'Angleterre, 1835. Lithographs.

Temple, Edmond. *Travels in Various Parts of Peru, Including a Years Residence in Potosi.* Two vols. London: Henry Colburn and Richard Bentley, 1830. Drawings by W. Hornsby, aquatints by J. Clark.

Thompson, George. *Travels and Adventures in Southern Africa by . . . , Eight Years a Resident at the Cape. Comprising a View of the Present State of the Cape Colony. With Observations on the Progress and Prospects of British Emigrants.* Second edition. Two vols. in one. London: Henry Colburn, 1827. Drawings by author for aquatints.

Thorn, William. *Memoir of the Conquest of Java; With the Subsequent Operations of the British Forces in the Oriental Archipelago, to Which is Subjoined a Statistical and Historical Sketch of Java; Being the Result of Observations Made in a Tour through the Country; With an Account of its Dependencies. Illustrated by Plans, Charts, Views, etc.* London: J. Egerton, 1815. Aquatints by J. Jeakes.

Thorn, William. *Memoir of the War in India, Conducted by General Lord Lake, Commander-in-Chief and Major-General Sir Arthur Wellesley, Duke of Wellington; From Its Commencement in 1803, to Its Termination in 1806, on the Banks of the Hyphasis. With Historical Sketches, Topographical Descriptions, and Statistical Observations.* London: T. Egerton, Military Library, 1818.

Thunberg, Carl Peter. *Flora Japonica.* Facsimile of 1784 edition. New York: Oriole, 1980.

Tissandier, Gaston. *Simples notions sur les ballons et la navigation aérienne.* Paris: Librairie Illustrée, [1876].

Tissandier, Gaston. *Voyages dans les airs.* Paris: Hachette et Cie, 1898.

Tissandier, Gaston. Tissander and Landauer Collections of Early Ballooning Material. Library of Congress, Washington, D.C.

Töpffer, Rodolphe. *Nouveaux voyages en zigzag. A la grande Chartreuse, autour du Mont Blanc, dans les vallées d'Henenz, de Zermatt, au Grimsel, à Gènes et à Corniche, précédés d'une notice par Sainte-Beuve.* Paris: Victor LeCou, 1854. Drawings by author; wood engravings by Alexandre Calame, Karl Girardet, Français D'Aubigny, De Bar, Gagnet, and Forest.

Töpffer, Rodolphe. *Premières voyages en zigzag, ou excursions d'un pensionnat en vacances dans les cantons suisses et sur le revers italien des Alpes.* Fourth edition. Paris: Victor LeCou, 1855. Drawings by author, wood engravings by Plon Frères.

[Trant, Captain]. *Two Years in [J]ava. From May 1824 to May 1826. By an Officer on the Staff of the Quarter-Master-General's Department.* London: John Murray, 1827. Drawings by W. Gova after sketches by author; lithographs by G. C. Engelmann.

Trapaud, Elisha. *Twenty Views in India.* London: John Wells, 1788.

Tuckey, J. K. *Narrative of an Expedition to Explore the River Zaire, Usually Called the Congo, in South Africa, in 1816, Under the Direction of . . . , to Which Is Added the Journal of Professor Smith; Some General Observations on the Country and Its Inhabitants; and an Appendix: Containing the Natural History of that Part of the Kingdom of Congo through which the Zaire Flows.* London: John Murray, 1818. Sketches by John Hawkey; engravings by W. Finden, James Fittler, et al.

Valentia, George, Viscount. *Voyages and Travels to India, Ceylon, the Red Sea, Abyssinia, and Egypt, in the Years 1802, 1803, 1804, 1805, and 1806.* Three vols. London: William Miller, 1809. Drawings by Henry Salt for engravings.

Vancouver, George. *A Voyage of Discovery to the North Pacific Ocean and Round the World; in Which the Coast of North-West America Has Been Carefully Examined and Accurately Surveyed, Undertaken by His Majesty's Command, Principally with a View To Ascertain the Existence of*

Any Navigable Communication between the North Pacific and North Atlantic Oceans; and Performed in the Years 1790, 1791, 1792, 1793, 1794, and 1795. Three vols. London: Printed for G. G. and J. Robinson and J. Edwards, 1798. Sketches by J. Sykes; drawings by William Alexander; engravings by J. Landseer, J. Heath, J. Fittler, and T. Hedding.

Vidal, E. E. *Picturesque Illustrations of Buenos Ayres and Monte Video Consisting of Twenty-Four Views: Accompanied with Descriptions of the Scenery, and of the Costumes, Manners, etc, of the Inhabitants of Those Cities and Their Environs.* London: R. Ackermann, 1820. Drawings by author, color aquatints by T. Sutherland.

Vivant-Denon, Dominique. *Description de l'Egypte.* Second edition. Twelve vols. Paris: Panckoucke, 1820. Engravings by Baltard, Paris, Petit, et al.

Vivant-Denon, Dominique. *Voyage dans la Basse et la Haute Egypte, pendant les campagnes du Général Bonaparte.* Two vols. Paris: Didot, 1802. Drawings by author; engravings by L. Petit, Baltard, Duparc, L. Garreau, Paris, et al.

Volney, Constantin-François Chasseboeuf de. *Tableau du climat et du sol des Etats-Unis d'Amerique.* Two vols. Paris: Courcier, 1803; Dentu, 1803. Engravings.

Waddington, George. *Journal of a Visit to Some Parts of Ethiopia.* London: John Murray, 1822. Drawings by author and Linant, lithographs by A. Aglio.

Wales, James. *Hindoo Excavations in the Mountain of Ellora Near Aurungabad in the Decan in Twenty-Four Views.* London: n.p., 1803. Color aquatints by Thomas Daniell.

Wales, James. *Twelve Views of the Island of Bombay and Its Vicinity Taken in the Years 1791 and 1792.* London: R. Goodwin, 1804. Color aquatints.

Walsh, Thomas. *Journal of the Late Campaign in Egypt Including Descriptions of That Country, and of Gibraltar, Minorca, Malta, Marmorice, and Macri; With an Appendix Containing Official Papers and Documents.* London: T. Cadell, Jr., and W. Davies, 1803. Drawings by author for color aquatints.

Wathen, James. *Journal of a Voyage in 1811 and 1812, to Madras and China; Returning by the Cape of Good Hope and Saint Helena.* London: J. Nichols, Son, and Bentley, 1814.

Webber, John. *Brown and Grey Sepia Set.* Soft ground etchings. 1790. Fuller Collection, Bishop Museum, Honolulu.

Webber, John. *Drawings Made on Cook's Third Voyage.* 1776–1780. Add. Mss. 15,513, 15,514, 17,277, and 23921, British Library, London.

Webber, John. *Views in the South Seas, from the Drawings by the Late . . . , from the Year 1776 to 1780. With Letter Press Description of the Various Scenery.* London: Boydell and Co., 1808. Color aquatints.

Weddell, James. *A Voyage towards the South Pole, Performed in the Years 1822–24, Containing an Examination of the Antarctic Sea to the 74th [degree] of Latitude: and a Visit to Tierra del Fuego With a Particular Account of the Inhabitants.* London: Longman, Hurst, Rees, Orme, Brown, and Green, 1825. Sketches by author, drawings by A. Masson, aquatints by J. Clark.

Weld, Isaac. *Travels through the States of North America, and the Provinces of Upper and Lower Canada, during the Years 1795, 1796, and 1797.* London: John Stockdale, 1799. Drawings by author, etchings.

West, H. A. *Six Views of Gibraltar in Two Parts with Six Views Each.* London: R. Ackermann, 1828. Color lithographs.

Westall, William. *Views of the Coves near Ingleton, Gordale Scar, and Malham Cove in Yorkshire.* London: John Murray, 1818. Drawings and aquatints by author.

Wetzel, J. J. *Voyage pittoresque aux lacs de Zurich, Zoug, Lowerz, Eggeri et Wallenstadt.* Two vols. Zurich: Orell, Fussli et Compagnie, 1819–1820. Engravings by Franz Hegi.

Williams, H. W. *Travels in Italy, Greece, and the Ionian Islands*. Two vols. Edinburgh: Archibald Constable and Co., 1820.

Williamson, Thomas. *The East India Vademecum; or, Complete Guide to Gentlemen Intended for the Civil, Military, or Naval Service of the Honorable East India Company*. Two vols. London: Black, Parry, and Kingsbury, 1810.

Williamson, Thomas. *Oriental Field Sports; Being a Complete, Detailed, and Accurate Description of the Wild Sports of the East; and Exhibiting in a Novel and Interesting manner the Natural History of the Elephant . . . , the Whole Interspersed with a Variety of Original, Authentic, and Curious Anecdotes, Which Render the Work Replete with Information and Amusement. The Scenery Gives a Faithful Representation of that Picturesque Country, Together with the Manners and Customs of Both the Native and European Inhabitants*. London: Edward Orme, 1807. Drawings by Samuel Howett, color aquatints engraved under direction of Edward Orme.

Wilson, Henry. *An Account of the Pelew Islands, Situated in the Western Part of the Pacific Ocean. Composed from the Journals and Communications of . . . and Some of His Officers, Who, in August 1783, Were There Shipwrecked, in the* Antelope. Edited by George Keate. Third edition. London: author, 1789.

Wolf, Caspar. *Vues remarquables des montagnes de la Suisse*. Second edition. Paris: n.p., 1787–1791. Drawings by author, color aquatints by Jean-François Janinet.

Wolf, Caspar. *Vues remarquables des montagnes de la Suisse avec leur description. Première partie*. Berne: Wagner, 1778. Drawings by author, color aquatints by B. A. Dunker and M. G. Eichler.

Related Aesthetic, Philosophical, and Scientific Treatises

Adams, George. *An Essay on Electricity*. Second revised edition. London: Logographic Press, 1785.

Addison, Joseph. *The Works*. Six vols. Edited by Mr. Ticknell. London: Vernor and Hood, 1804.

Agricola, Georg. *Mineralogische Schriften*. Three vols. Translated and edited by Ernst Lehmann. Freiburg: Craz und Gerlach, 1806–1812.

Almanach des Muses. 1783–1784.

Aristotle. *On Poetry and Music*. Little Library of the Liberal Arts, No. VI. Edited by Oscar Piest, translated by S. H. Butcher. New York: Liberal Arts Press, 1948.

Armand-Gouffe, Buhan. *Gilles aéronaut; ou l'Amerique n'est pas loin*. Paris: Logerot, 1799.

Artemidorus. *The Interpretation of Dreams*. Noyes Classical Studies. Translated and edited by Robert J. White. Park Ridge, N.J.: Noyes, 1975.

Bacon, Francis. *Advancement of Learning; Novum Organum; New Atlantis*. Great Books of the Western World, vol. XXX. Chicago: Encyclopaedia Britannica, Inc., 1952.

Bailly, Jean-Sylvain. *Discours et mémoires, par l'auteur de l'Histoire de l'astronomie*. Two vols. Paris: De Bure, 1790.

Bailly, Jean-Sylvain. *Lettres sur l'origine des sciences et sur celle des peuples de l'Asie adressées à M. de Voltaire*. London: M. Elmsley; Paris: De Bure, 1777.

Baudelaire, Charles-Pierre. *Oeuvres complètes*. Bibliothèque de La Pléiade. Edited by Y.-G. Le Dantec, revised by Claude Pichois. Paris: Gallimard, 1961.

Bayle, Pierre. *Historical and Critical Dictionary. The Second Edition to Which Is Prefixed; the Life of the Author by Mr. Des Maizeaux, Fellow of the Royal Society*. Five vols. London: J. J. and P. Knapton, D. Midwinter, J. Brotherton, 1735–1738.

Beckmann, Johann. *Beyträge zur Geschichte der Erfindung*. Five vols. Leipzig: Paul Gotthelf Kummer, 1799.

Behn, Friedrich Daniel. *Das Nordlicht*. Lubeck: Christian Gottfr. Donatius, 1770.

Bentley, Richard. *Matter and Motion Cannot Think: or, A Confutation of Atheism from the Faculties of the Soul. A Sermon Preached at St. Mary-le-Bow, April 4, 1692* [Second Boyle Lecture]. London: Thomas Parkhurst, 1692.

Beroald, François. *Théâtre des instrumens mathématiques de Jacques Besson Dauphinois, docte mathématicien. Avec l'interprétation des figures d'iceluy par. . . .* Lyon: Barthélemy Vincent, 1579.

Bernardin de Saint-Pierre, Jacques-Henri. *Oeuvres complètes*. Ten vols. Edited by L. Aimé-Martin. Paris: Mequignon-Marvis, 1818.

Berthollet, C. L. *Essai de statique chimique*. Two vols. Paris: Demoiselle et Soeurs, 1803.

Bertholon, Pierre. *Des avantages que la physique, et les arts qui en dépendent, peuvent retirer des globes aérostatiques*. Montpellier: Jean Martel Aîné, 1784.

Bertholon, Pierre. *De l'électricité des météores*. Two vols. Paris: Croullebois, 1787.

Bertholon, Pierre. "De la salubrité de l'air des villes, & en particulier des moyens de la procurer." *Journal Encyclopédique* (May 1787), 407–417.

Bertrand, M. E. *Recueil de divers traités sur l'histoire naturelle de la terre et des fossiles*. Avignon: Louis Chambeau, 1766.

Biot, Jean-Baptiste. *Recherches sur les réfractions extraordinaires qui ont lieu près de l'horizon*. Paris: Bachelier, 1810.

Blair, Hugh. *A Critical Dissertation on the Poems of Ossian, the Son of Fingal*. Second edition. London: T. Becket and P. A. De Hondt, 1765.

Bonanni, Philippo. *Musaeum Kircherianum sive musaeum A.P. Athanasio Kirchero in Collegio Romano Societatis Jesu jam pridem incoeptum nuper restitutum, auctum, descriptum, & iconibus illustratum*. Rome: Typis Georgii Plachi Caelaturam Profitentis, & Characterum, 1709.

Bonnet, Charles. *Contemplation de la nature*. Second edition. Two vols. Amsterdam: Marc-Michel Rey, 1769.

Bonnet, Charles. *Essai analytique sur les facultés de l'âme*. Copenhagen: Frères Cl. & Ant. Philibert, 1760.

Borlase, William. *Antiquities, Historical and Monumental of the County of Cornwall*. Second edition. London: W. Bowyer and J. Nichols, 1769.

Borlase, William. *The Natural History of Cornwall*. Oxford: W. Jackson, 1758.

Borlase, William. *Observations on the Ancient and Present State of the Islands of Scilly and Their Importance to the Trade of Great Britain*. Oxford: W. Jackson, 1756.

Boscovich, Roger-Joseph. "Dissertation sur la lumière." *Journal de Trévoux* (July 1750), 1642–1657.

Bouhours, Dominique. *Les entretiens d'Artiste et d'Eugène*. Amsterdam: Jacques Le Jeune, 1671.

Boullée, Etienne-Louis. *Architecture, Essai sur l'art*. Edited by J.-M. Pérouse de Montclos. Paris: Hermann, 1968.

Bourguet, Louis. *Traité des pétrifications avec figures*. Paris: Briasson, 1742.

Boyle, Robert. *The Aerial Noctiluca: or Some New Phenomena, and a Process of a Facetious Self-Shining Substance*. London: T. Snowdon, 1680.

Boyle, Robert. *An Essay about the Origine & Virtue of Gems. Wherein Are Propos'd and Historically Illustrated Some Conjectures about the Consistence of the Matter of Precious Stones, and the Subjects Wherein Their Chiefest Virtues Reside*. London: William Godbid, 1672.

Bracelli, Giovanni-Battista. *Bizzarie* [1624]. Paris: Alain Brieux, 1963.

Brewster, David. *Letters on Natural Magic, Addressed to Sir Walter Scott, Bart.* London: John Murray, 1834.

Brewster, David. *A Treatise on the Kaleidoscope*. Edinburgh: Archibald Constable & Co.; London: Longman, Hurst, Rees, Orme, & Brown, 1819.

Breynius, Johannis Philippi. *Epistola de melonibus petrefactis Montis Carmel vulgo creditis*. Leipzig: Immanuelis Titii, 1722.

Breynius, Johannis Philippi. *Prodromus fasciculi rariorum plantarum, anno MDCLXXIX in hortis celeberrimis Hollandiae, praefertim incomparabili& nobilissimo illo florae pandocheo*. Gedani: David Fridericus Rhetius, 1680.

Buffon, Georges-Louis-LeClerc de. *Oeuvres complètes avec les supplémens*. Nine vols. Paris: P. Dumenil, 1835.

Burke, Edmund. *Philosophical Enquiry into the Origin of Our Ideas of the Sublime and Beautiful*. New York: Harper & Brothers, 1844.

[Burnet, Thomas]. *Remarks upon an Essay Concerning Human Understanding: In a Letter Addres'd to the Author [John Locke]*. London: M. Wotton, 1697.

Le cabinet de Courtagnon, poème, dédié à Madame la Douairière de Courtagon, avec un discours préliminaire sur l'histoire naturelle *dea Fossilea de Champagne*. Chalons: Seneuse, 1763.

Calmet, Augustin, Dom. *Traité sur les apparitions, des esprits, et sur les vampires, ou les revenans de Hongrie, de Moravie, etc.* Revised edition. Two vols. Senonnes: Joseph Pariset, 1754.

Cambry, M. *Monumens celtiques, ou recherches sur le culte des pierres*. Paris: Johanneau, 1805.

Capper, James. *Meteorological and Miscellaneous Tracts Applicable to Navigation, Gardening, and Farming, With Calendars of Flora for Greece, France, England, and Sweden*. Cardiff: J. D. Bird, [ca. 1800].

Carra, Jean-Louis. *Nouveaux principes de physique, ornés de planches; dédiés au Prince Royal de Prussie*. Three vols. Paris: Esprit, 1781.

Carus, Carl Gustave. *Neun Briefe über Landschaftsmalerei*. Leipzig: Gerhard Fleischer, 1831.

Caus, Salomon de. *Les raisons des forces mouvantes*. Paris: Hierosme Drouart, 1624.

Cavallo, Tiberius. *The History and Practice of Aerostation*. London: C. Dilly, 1785.

Champfleury [Jules Fleury]. *Histoire de la caricature antique*. Third revised edition. Paris: E. Dentu, [1879].

Champfleury [Jules Fleury]. *Histoire de la caricature moderne*. Third revised edition. Paris: Dentu, 1879.

Champfleury [Jules Fleury]. *Histoire de la caricature au moyen âge et sous la renaissance*. Second revised edition. Paris: Dentu, 1875.

Champfleury [Jules Fleury]. *Histoire des faiences patriotiques sous la révolution*. Paris: Dentu, 1867.

Champfleury [Jules Fleury]. *Histoire de l'imagerie populaire*. Revised edition. Paris: Dentu, 1886.

Champfleury [Jules Fleury]. *Le réalisme*. Collection Savoir. Edited by Géneviève and Jean Lacambre. Paris: Hermann, 1973.

Chateaubriand, François-Auguste-René de. *Génie du christianisme, ou beautés de la religion chrétienne*. Paris: Hernan, 1807.

Chateaubriand, François-Auguste-René de. *Mémoires d'outre-tombe*. Edition du Centenaire. Second revised edition. Two vols. Edited by Maurice LeVaillant. Paris: Flammarion, 1964.

Chenier, André. *L'Invention*. Edited by Paul Dimoff. Paris: Nizet, 1966.

Chenier, André. *Oeuvres poétiques*. Two vols. Edited by Louis Moland. Paris: Garnier Frères, 1884.

Colonne, François-Marie-Pompe'e [Crosset de la Haumerie]. *Histoire naturelle de l'univers, dans laquelle on rapporte des raisons physiques sur les effets les plus curieux, & les plus extraordinaires de la nature*. Four vols. Paris: André Cailleau, 1734.

Colonne, François-Marie-Pompe'e [Crosset de la Haumerie]. *Le nouveau miroir de la fortune, ou abrégé de la géomance. Pour la récréation des personnes curieuses de cette science*. Paris: André Cailleau, 1726.

Colonne, François-Marie-Pompe'e [Crosset de la Haumerie]. *Les principes de la nature, ou de la génération des choses*. Paris: André Cailleau, 1731.

Colonne, François-Marie-Pompe'e [Crosset de la Haumerie]. *Les secrets les plus cachés de la philosophie des anciens, découverts et expliqués, à la suite d'une histoire des plus curieuses*. Paris: Houry Fils, 1722.

Constable, John. *Discourses*. Edited by R. B. Beckett. Vol. XIV. Ipswich, England: Suffolk Records Society, 1970.

Cotte, Louis. *Mémoires dur la météorologie pour servir de suite & de supplément au traité de météorologie publié en 1774*. Two vols. Paris: Imprimerie Royale, 1788.

Cotte, Louis. "Rapport fait par MM. Duhamel du Monceau & Tillet, présenté à l'Académie par le Père . . . , prêtre de l'Oratoire, & correspondent de cette Académie." *Observations sur la physique, sur l'histoire naturelle et sur les arts* II (April 1772), 10–15.

Cotte, Louis. *Traité de météorologie*. Paris: Imprimerie Royale, 1774.

Court de Gebelin, Antoine. *Monde primitif, analysé et comparé avec le monde moderne, considéré dans son génie allegorique et dans les allegories auxquelles conduisit ce génie*. Nine vols. Paris: author, 1773–1782.

Cudworth, Robert. *The Intellectual System of the Universe: The First Part; Wherein All the Reason and Philosophy of Atheism is Confuted; and Its Impossibility Demonstrated*. London: Richard Royston, 1678.

Cuvier, Georges. *Histoire des progrès des sciences naturelles, depuis 1789 jusqu'à ce jour*. Four vols. Paris: Baudouin Frères, 1826–1828.

Daguerre, Louis-Jacques-Mandé. *Diorama, Regent's Park. Two Views: Ruins of Holyrood Chapel, A Moonlight Scene, Painted by . . . and the Cathedral of Chartres, Painted by M. Bouton*. London: G. Schulze, 1825.

Daguerre, Louis-Jacques-Mandé. *Historique et descripiton des procédés du daguerreotype et du diorama*. Revised edition. Paris: Alphonse Giroux et Cie, 1839.

D'Alembert, J. L., C. Bossut, and J. J. Lalande. *Dictionnaire encyclopédique des mathématiques*. Four vols. Paris: Panckoucke, 1789.

Daniel, J. Frederic. *Meteorological Essays and Observations*. London: Thomas and George Underwood, 1823.

D'Avallon, Charles-Yves-Cousin. *Linguetiana ou recueil*. Paris: Jouannet, 1801.

David d'Angers, Pierre. *Les Carnets*. Two vols. Edited by André Bruel. Paris: Plon, 1958.

De Bononiensi Scientiarum et Artum Instituto atque Academia Commentarii. Seven vols. in ten. Bologna: Laetii a Vulpe, 1748–1791.

Découvertes et inventions depuis les temps les plus anciens jusqu'à nos jours. Third revised edition. Paris: n.p., 1846.

Delacroix, Eugene. *Journal*. Three vols. Revised edition. Edited by André Joubin. 1950.

De l'Isle de Sales, Jean-Claude-Izouard. *De la philosophie de la nature, ou traité de morale pour l'espèce humaine, tiré de la philosophie et fondé sur la nature*. Six vols. Third edition. London: n.p., 1777.

De l'Isle de Sales, Jean-Claude-Izouard. *Histoire philosophique du monde primitif*. Seven vols. Fourth revised edition. Paris: Didot l'aîné, 1793.

Delius, Christoph Traugott. *Anleitung zu der Bergbaukunst nach ihrer Theorie und Ausübung, nebst einer Abhandlung von den Grundsatzen der Berg-Kammerwissenschaft*. Vienna: Joh. Thomas Edlen v. Trattnern, 1773.

Delius, Christoph Traugott. *Traité sur la science de l'exploration des mines, par théorie et pratique, avec un discours sur les principes des finances*. Translated by M. Schreiber. Two vols. Paris: Phillippe-Denys Pierres, 1778.

Deluc, J.-A. *Lettres physiques et morales sur les montagnes et sur l'histoire de la terre et de l'homme*. The Hague: Detune, 1778.

Deluc, J.-A. *Recherches sur les mondifications de l'atmosphère*. Four vols. Paris: Duchesne, 1784.

De Piles, Roger. *Cours de peinture par principes*. Paris: Barrois l'aîné, Firmin-Didot, 1791.

Dézallier D'Argenville, Antoine-Joseph. *La conchyliologie, ou histoire naturelle des coquilles de mer, d'eau douce, terrestres et fossiles; avec un traité de la zoomorphose, ou représentation des animaux qui les habitent: ouvrage dans lequel on trouve une nouvelle méthode de les diviser*. Third edition. Two vols. and atlas. Paris: Guillaume De Bure, l'aîné, 1780.

Dézallier D'Argenville, Antoine-Joseph. *L'histoire naturelle éclaircie dans une de ses parties principales, l'oryctologie, qui traite des terres, des pierres, des métaux, des minéraux, et autres fossiles*: Paris: De Bure, l'aîné, 1755.

Diderot, Denis. *Oeuvres complètes de*. Edited by J. Assezat. Vol. X. Paris: Garnier, 1876.

Diderot, Denis. *Pensées sur l'interprétation de la nature*. Paris, 1754.

Diderot, Denis. *Le rêve de D'Alembert (1769)*. Paris: Marcel Didier, 1951.

Diderot, Denis. *Salons*. Edited by Jean Seznec and Jean Adhémar. Four vols. Oxford: Clarendon, 1963–1967.

Du Bos, Jean-Baptiste. *Réflexions critiques sur la poésie et sur la peinture*. Fourth revised edition. Two vols. Paris: Pierre-Jean Mariette, 1746.

Dubuffet, Jean. *Prospectus et tous écrits suivants*. Edited by Hubert Damisch. Two vols. Paris: Gallimard, 1967.

Duff, William. *An Essay on Original Genius; and Its Various Modes of Exertion in Philosophy and the Fine Arts, particularly Poetry*. Second edition. London: Edward and Charles Dilly, 1767.

Encyclopédie, ou dictionnaire raisonné des sciences, des arts et des métiers. Vols. IV–XVI. Paris and Neufchâtel: Briasson and Samuel Faulche & Compagnie, 1754–1765.

Ercker, Lazarum. *Aula subterranea. Domina dominantium subdita subditorum. Das ist: Untererdische Ofhaltung ohne Welche weder die Herren regiren / noch die Unterthänen gehorchen konnen. Oder gründliche Beschreibung derjenigen Sachen / so in der Tiefe der Erde wachsen / als aller Ertzen der königlichen und gemeinen Metallen / auch furnehmster Mineralien / durch Welche / nachst Gott / alle Künste / Übungen und Stände der Welt gehandhabet und erhalten werden.* Frankfurt: Johann David Zunners and Johannes Haass, 1684.

Fabre D'Olivet, Antoine. *The Golden Verses of Pythagoras. Explained and Translated into French and Preceded by a Discourse upon the Essence and Form of Poetry among the Principal Peoples of the Earth* (1813). Translated by Nayan Louise Redfield. New York: G. P. Putnam's Sons, 1917.

Faujas de Saint-Fond, Barthélemy. *Essai de géologie ou mémoires pour servir à l'histoire naturelle du globe.* Three vols. Paris: Gabriel Dufour, 1803–1809.

Fergusson, James. *Rude Stone Monuments in All Countries; Their Age and Uses.* London: John Murray, 1872.

Fesc, R. P. du. "Dissertation sur la lumière septentrionale avec l'explication de ses divers phénomènes," in *Mémoires pour l'histoire des sciences et des beaux-arts [Journal de Trévoux],* July–September 1732, 1205–1233, 1574–1605.

Fischer von Erlach, Johann Bernhard. *Entwurff einer historischen Architektur.* Vienna: n.p., 1721.

Fontenelle, Bernard Bouvier de. *A Plurality of Worlds* (1686). Translated by John Glanville. London: Nonesuch, 1929.

Forster, Thomas. *Researches about Atmospheric Phaenomena.* London: Thomas Underwood, 1813.

Gautier D'Agoty, Jean-Fabien. *Histoire naturelle ou exposition générale de toutes ses parties. Gravées et imprimées en couleurs naturelles; avec des notes historiques. Première partie, Règne minéral.* Paris: author, 1781.

Gautier D'Agoty, Jean-Fabien. *Minéralogie. Recueil factice de gravures par....* Paris: n.p., ca. 1780.

Gerard, Alexander. *An Essay on Genius.* London and Edinburgh: W. Strahan, T. Cadell, and W. Creech, 1774.

Giardina, P. Domenico. *Discorso sopra la fata morgana di Messina, comparsa nell' anno 1643 al di XIV d'agosto ... della compagnia di Gesu, con alcune note dell'eruditissimo Sig. Andrea Gallo, Messinese, in Opuscoli di autori siciliani, I.* Catania: Giachimo Pulejo, 1753.

Goethe, Johann Wolfgang von. *Werke.* Edited by Erich Schmidt. Six vols. Leipzig: Insel, 1940.

Gratet de Dolomieu, Déodat-Guy-Sylvain-Tancrède de. *Sur la philosophie minéralogique et sur l'espèce minéralogique par le citoyen ... , membre de l'Insitut National et und des professeurs-administrateurs du Jardin des Plantes.* Paris: De l'Imprimerie de Bossange, An IX [1801–1802].

Grimm, Jakob. *Teutonic Mythology* (1835–1836). Transcribed by Adolf Warnstedt. Fourth edition. London: E. H. Meyer, 1875–1878.

Hamper, William. *Observations on Certain Ancient Pillars of Memorial Called Hoar-Stones.* Birmingham: William Hodgetts, 1820.

D'Hancarville [Pierre-François Hugues]. *Recherches sur l'origine, l'esprit, et le progrès, des arts de la Grèce.* Three vols. London: B. Appleyard, 1785.

Hartley, David. *Observations on Man, His Frame, His Duty, and His Expectations.* Two vols. London: S. Richardson, 1749.

Hartley, David. *Various Conjectures on the Perception, Motion, and Generation of Ideas (1746)*. Translated by Robert E. A. Palmer, edited by Martin Kallich. Los Angeles: Augustan Reprint Society, 1959.

Haüy, René-Just. *Traité de minéralogie*. Five vols. Paris: Delance, 1801.

Hazlitt, William. *The Complete Works*. Edited by P. P. Howe. Vol. XII. London and Toronto: J. M. Dent and Sons, 1931.

Heinrich, Joseph Placidus. *Die Phosphorescenz der Körper oder die im Dunkeln bemerkbaren Lichtphänomene der anorganischen Natur*. Nuremberg: Johann Leonhard Schrag, 1811.

Helvétius, Claude-Adrien. *De l'esprit, or Essays on the Mind and Its Several Faculties*. Translated from the French. New York: Burt Franklin, 1970.

Henckel, Johann Friedrich. *Flora Saturnis. Die Verwandschaft des Pflanzen mit dem Mineral-Reich*. Leipzig: Johann Christian Martini, 1722.

Henckel, Johann Friedrich. *Unterricht von der Mineralogie oder Wissenschaft von Wassern, Erdsäfften, Sältzen, Erden, Steinen und Ertsen*. Dresden: J. N. Gerlachen, 1747.

Herder, Johann Gottfried von. *Vom Erkennen und Empfinden der menschlichen Seele (Bemerkungen und Träume)*, in *Gesammelte Werke*. Vol. I. Potsdam: Rütten & Loening, 1939.

Higgins, Godfrey. *The Celtic Druids*. London: R. Hunter, 1829.

Histoire des Kosaques. Epreuve. Paris: n.p., 1813.

Hoare, Richard Colt. *The History of Modern Wiltshire*. Six vols. London: John Nichols and Son, 1825.

Hume, David. *A Treatise of Human Nature (1740)*. Edited by L. A. Selby-Bigge. Oxford: Clarendon, 1949.

James, Henry. "The Real Thing." In *Selected Short Stories*. Edited by Quentin Anderson. New York: Holt, Rinehart and Winston, 1961.

Johnson, Samuel. *The Rambler*. In *Works*. Edited by W. J. Bate and Albrecht B. Strauss. Three vols. New Haven, Conn.: Yale University Press, 1969.

Junius, Franciscus. *The Painting of the Ancients, in Three Bookes: Declaring by Historicall Observations and Examples, the Beginning, Progresse, and Consummation of That Most Noble Art*. London: Richard Hodgkinsonne, 1638.

Kames, Henry Home, Lord. *Elements of Criticism*. Fourth edition. Two vols. New York: S. Campbell & Son, E. Duyckinck, G. Long, Collins & Co., Collins of Hannay, and W. B. Gilley, 1823.

Kircher, Athanasius. *Arca Noe*. Amsterdam: Apud Joannem Janssonium a Waesberge, 1675.

Kircher, Athanasius. *China Monumentis qua sacris qua profanis*. Amsterdam: Joannem Janssonium a Waesberge & Elizeum Weyerstraet, 1667.

Kircher, Athanasius. *Mundus Subterraneus*. Two vols. in one. Amsterdam: Joannis Janssony a Waesberge and Elizaei Weyerstraet, 1665.

Kircher, Athanasius. *Oedipus Aegyptiacus*. Four vols. in one. Rome: Vitalis Mascardi, 1652–1654.

Kircher, Athanasius. *Turris Babel sive archontologia*. Amsterdam: Janssonio Waebergiana, 1679.

Kirwan, Richard. "Estimation de la temperature de différens degrés de latitude par . . . , écuyer de la société royale de Londres . . . ouvrage traduit de l'anglois par M. Adet fils, docteur-régent de la faculté de médecine de Paris." *Journal Encyclopédique*, May 1790, 196–209.

Kleist, Heinrich von. *Über das Marionettentheater*. Zurich: Flamberg, 1971.

Knight, Richard Payne. *The Landscape, a Didactic Poem, in Three Books Addressed to Uvedale Price*. London: W. Bulmer and Co., 1794.

Knight, Richard Payne. *The Progress of Civil Society, a Didactic Poem, in Six Books*. London: W. Bulmer and Co., 1796.

Knight, Richard Payne. *The Symbolical Language of Ancient Art and Mythology, an Inquiry* (1818). New York: J. W. Bouton, 1876.

Knorr, George Wolfgang. *Recueil de monumens des catastrophes que le globe de la terre a essuiées, contenant des pétrifications dessinées, gravées, et enluminées, d'après les originaux commencé par . . . , et continué par ses hérétiers avec l'histoire naturelle de ces corps par Mr. Jean Ernest Emanuel Walch, professeur d'eloquence et de poésie à l'Université de Jène*. Three vols. in four. Nuremberg: n.p., 1768–1775.

Lambert, Johann Heinrich. *Anlage zur Architectonic, oder Theorie des Einfachen und des Ersten in der philosophischen und mathematischen Erkenntniss*. Two vols. Riga: Johann Friedrich Hartknoch, 1771.

La Métherie, Jean-Claude de. *Analyse des travaux sur les sciences naturelles pendant les années 1795, 1796 & 1797*. Paris: A. J. Dugour, 1798.

La Pluche, N. A. *Le spectacle de la nature ou entretiens sur les particularités de l'histoire naturelle*. Nine vols. Paris: Estienne & Fils, 1740–1752.

Leeuwenhoek, Anthony van. *The Select Works of . . . , Containing His Microscopical Discoveries in Many of the Works of Nature*. Translated by Samuel Hoole. Two vols. London: Henry Fry, 1798.

Leibniz, Gottfried Wilhelm. *The Philosophical Works*. Second edition. Edited by George Martin Duncan. New Haven, Conn.: Tuttle, Morehouse & Taylor, 1908.

Lenglet Dufresnoy, Nicolas. *Traité historique et dogmatique sur les apparitions, les visions & les révélations particulières*. Two vols. Avignon: Jean-Noël Leloup, 1751.

Leonhard, Karl Caesar von. *Lehrbuch der Geognosie und Geologie. Naturgeschichte der drei Reiche*. Vol. III. Stuttgart: E. Schweizerbart, 1835.

Le Rouge, Georges-Louis. *Jardins anglo-chinois*. Nine vols. Paris: n.p., 1775–1788.

Linnaeus, Carl. *Reflections on the Study of Nature*. London: George Nicol, 1785.

Linnaeus, Carl. *Select Dissertations from the Amoenitates Academicae*. Translated by F. J. Brand. New York: Arno, 1977.

Locke, John. *The Works*. Vols. I and II. New, corrected edition. London: Thomas Tegg, W. Sharpe and Son, G. Offor, G. and J. Robinson, J. Evans and Co., 1823.

Lomazzo, Giovanni Paolo. *Idea del tempio della pittura*. Edited and translated by Robert Klein. Two vols. Florence: Nella Sede dell'Istituto Palazzo Strozzi, 1974.

Longinus, Cassius. *On the Sublime*. Translated by A. O. Prickard. Oxford: Clarendon, 1906.

Le Magasin Pittoresque. 1833–1841.

Maillet, Benoît de. *Description de l'Egypte, contenant plusieurs remarques curieuses sur la géographie ancienne et moderne de ce païs, sur ses monumens anciennes, sur les moeurs, les coutumes & la religion des habitans, sur le gouvernement & le commerce, sur les animaux, les arbres, les plantes, etc*. Edited by M. l'Abbé Le Mascrier. Two vols. The Hague: Isaac Beauregard, 1740.

Maillet, Benoît de. *Telliamed, ou entretiens d'un philosophe indien avec un missionnaire françois sur la diminution de la mer, la formation de la terre, l'origine de l'homme*. Two vols. Amsterdam: Chez l'Honoré et fils, 1748.

Mairan, Jean-Jacques Dortous de. *Traité physique et historique de l'aurore boréale*. Paris: Imprimerie Royale, 1733.

Malebranche, Nicolas. *De la recherche de la vérité. Ou l'on traite de la nature de l'esprit de l'homme, & de l'usage qu'il en doit faire pour éviter l'erreur dans les sciences*. Paris: André Pralard, 1678.

Mandeville, Bernard. *A Treatise of the Hypochondriac and Hysterick Diseases. In Three Dialogues*. Second revised edition. London: J. Tonson, 1730.

Maupertuis, P. L. Moreau de. *Oeuvres*. Two vols. Hildesheim: Georg Olms, 1965.

Mayer, Tobias. *Bericht von den Mondskugeln, Welche bey der kosmographischen Gesellschaft in Nurnberg, aus neuen Beobachtungen verfertigt werden durch. . . .* Nuremberg: Homannischen Officin, 1750.

Mercier, Louis-Sebastien. *Mon bonnet de nuit*. Two vols. Neufchâtel: n.p., 1785.

Millin, A. L. *Minéralogie homerique, ou essai sur les minéraux, dont il est fait mention dans les poèmes d'Homère*. Second edition. Paris: C. Wasermann, 1816.

Monge, Louis, et al. *Dictionnaire de physique*. Vol. I. Paris: Hotel de Thou, 1793.

Montgolfier, Etienne. "Discours de . . . sur l'aérostat, prononcé dans une séance de l'académie des sciences, belles-lettres & arts de la ville de Lyon, en novembre 1783." *Journal Encyclopédique*, April 1784, 10–19.

Moritz, Karl Philipp. *Schriften zur Ästhetik und Poetik. Kritische Ausgabe*. Edited by Hans Joachim Schrimpf. Tübingen: Max Neumeyer, 1962.

Muller, Adam. *Von der Idee der Schönheit. In Vorlesungen gehalten zu Dresden im Winter 1807/8*. Berlin: Julius Eduard Hitzig, 1809.

Newton, Isaac. *The Mathematical Principles of Natural Philosophy*. Third edition. Translated by Andrew Motte. Two vols. London: Benjamin Motte, 1729.

"Notices diverses concernant la machine aérostatique." *Journal Encyclopédique*, January 1784, 304–326.

Palissy, Bernard. *Oeuvres complètes*. Edited by Paul-Antoine Cap. Paris: J.-J. Dobochet et Cie., 1844.

Paracelsus [Theophrastus, Philipp of Hohenstein]. *A New Light of Alchymie: Taken Out of the Fountaine of Nature, and Manuall Experience. To Which Is Added a Treatise of Sulphur: Written by Micheel Sandivogius. . . . Also Nine Books of the Nature of Things Written. . . .* Translated by Gerardus Dorn. London: Richard Cotes, 1650.

Parcieux, Antoine de. *Dissertation sur les globes aérostatiques*. Paris: author, 1783.

Paris, M. *Le globe aérostatique, ode*. 1784.

Patrin, Eugène-Melchior. *Histoire naturelle des minéraux*. Five vols. Paris: Crapelet, An IX [1800–1801].

Perrault, Charles. *Paralèlle des anciens et des modernes, en ce qui regarde les arts et les sciences. Dialogues. Avec le poème du siècle de Louis le Grand, et une épistre en vers sur le génie*. Paris: Jean-Baptiste Coignard, 1688.

Perrault, Pierre. *On the Origin of Springs*. Translated by Aurèle La Rocque. New York and London: Hafner, 1967.

Pingré, Alexandre-Guy. "Précis du mémoire sur l'isle qui a paru en 1783, au sud-oeust de l'Islande, lu par . . . dans la séance publique de l'académie royale des sciences de Paris, tenue le 12 novembre dernier." *Journal Encyclopédique*, January 1784, 116–118.

Playfair, John. *Illustrations of the Huttonian Theory of the Earth*. London: Cadell and Davies; Edinburgh: William Creech, 1802.

Poe, Edgar Allan. *The Complete Tales and Poems*. New York: Vintage, 1975.

Porta, Giambattista della. *Phytognomonica*. Naples: Apud Horatium Saluianum, 1588.

Price, Uvedale. *On the Picturesque*. Edinburgh: Caldwell, Lloyd, and Co., 1842.

Priestley, Joseph. *A Course of Lectures on Oratory and Criticism*. London: J. Johnson, 1777.

Priestley, Joseph. *Disquisitions Relating to Matter and Spirit. To Which Is Added, the History of the Philosophical Doctrine Concerning the Origin of the Soul, and the Nature of Matter; With Its Influence on Christianity, especially with Respect to the Doctrine of the Pre-Existence of Christ*. London: J. Johnson, 1777.

Priestley, Joseph. *Experiments and Observations on Different Kinds of Air, and Other Branches of Natural Philosophy*. Three vols. Birmingham: Thomas Pearson, 1790.

Priestley, Joseph. *The History and Present State of Discoveries Relating to Vision Light, and Colours*. London: J. Johnson, 1772.

Priestley, Joseph. *The History and Present State of Electricity, with Original Experiments*. Second revised edition. London: J. Dodsley, J. Johnson, J. Payne, and T. Cadell, 1769.

Pujoulx, J. B. *Paris à la fin du XVIIIe siècle, ou esquisse historique et morale des monuments et des ruines de cette capitale; de l'état des sciences, des arts et de l'industrie à cette époque, ainsi que des moeurs et des ridicules de ses habitans*. Paris: Brigitte Mathé, 1801.

Pythagoron, The Religious, Moral and Ethical Teachings of Pythagoras. Edited by Hobart Huson. Privately published, 1947.

Quatremère de Quincy, Antoine-Chrysostôme. *Considérations sur les arts du dessin en France*. Paris: Desenne, 1794.

Quatremère de Quincy, Antoine-Chrysostôme. *Encyclopédie méthodique: Architecture*. Vols. II and III. Paris: Henri Agassé. An IX [1800–1801].

"Remarques adressés aux auteurs de ce journal, sur la cause des chaleurs excessives des brouillards, etc., de l'été dernier, & sur celle du rigoureux hiver qu'on a essuyé cette année." *Journal Encyclopédique*, May 1784, 297–306.

Reynolds, Joshua. *Discourses on Art*. Edited by Robert R. Wark. New Haven, Conn.: Yale University Press, 1975.

Richard, Jérôme. *Histoire naturelle de l'air et des météores*. Ten vols. Paris: Saillant & Nyon, 1770.

Richard, Jérôme. "La théorie des songes." *Journal de Trévoux*, June 1766, 1502–1507.

Richter, Jean-Paul. *Sämtliche Werke. Abteilung II: Jugendwerke und vermischte Schriften*. Edited by Norbert Miller. Three vols. Munich: Carl Hanser, 1974.

Richter, Jean-Paul. *Vorschule der Aesthetik nebst einigen Vorlesungen in Leipzig über die Parteien der Zeit*. Second revised edition. Three vols. in one. Stuttgart and Tübingen: J. G. Cotta, 1813.

Robinet, Jean-Baptiste. *Considérations philosophiques de la gradation naturelle des formes de l'être, ou les essais de la nature qui apprend à faire l'homme*. Second edition. Paris: Charles Saillant, 1768.

Robinet, Jean-Baptiste. *De la nature*. Four vols. Amsterdam: E. van Harrevelt, 1763–1766.

Romé de L'Isle, J. B. L. *Cristallographie, ou description des formes propres à tous les corps du règne minéral, dans l'état de combinaison saline, pierreuse ou métallique.* Second edition. Four vols. Paris: Imprimerie de Monsieur, 1783.

Romé de L'Isle, J. B. L. *Description méthodique d'une collection de minéraux du cabinet de M.D.R.D.L.* Paris: Didot-Jeune and Knapen, 1773.

Romé de L'Isle, J. B. L. *Essai de cristallographie, ou description des figures géometriques propres à différens corps du règne minéral, avec un tableau cristallographique. . . . Catalogue raisonné d'une collection de minéraux.* Paris: Didot-Jeune and Knapen, 1772.

Rouland, M. *Tableau historique des propriétés et des phénomènes de l'air.* Paris: Gueffier, 1784.

Rousseau, Jean-Jacques. *Les rêveries du promeneur solitaire.* Paris: Bibliothèque Indépendante d'Edition, 1905.

Roux, M. "Histoire naturelle, chymique & médicinale des corps des trois règnes de la nature, ou abrégé des oeuvres chymiques de M. Gaspard Neumann." *Journal de Monsieur,* February 1781, 349–355.

Ruskin, John. *The Ethics of the Dust. Ten Lectures to Little Housewives on the Elements of Crystallisation.* Second edition. New York: Wiley, 1886.

Ruskin, John. *Modern Painters.* London: Smith, elder and Co., 1851.

Ruskin, John. *The Poetry of Architecture: or the Architecture of the Nations of Europe Considered in Its Association with Natural Scenery and National Character.* Sunnyside, Orpington: George Allen, 1893.

Ruskin, John. *Praeterita. Outlines of Scenes and Thoughts perhaps Worthy of Memory in My Past Life.* Introduced by Kenneth Clark. Two vols. in one. London: Rupert Hart-Davis, 1949.

Ruskin, John. *Proserpina. Studies of Wayside Flowers while the Air was yet Pure among the Alps, and in Scotland and England Which My Father Knew.* New York: Wiley, 1888.

Ruskin, John. *Science. A Ruskin Anthology.* Compiled by William Sloane Kennedy. New York: John B. Alden, 1886.

Ruskin, John. *Selections from the Writings of. . . .* New York: Wiley, 1890.

Ruskin, John. *The Two Paths: Being Lectures on Art, and Its Application to Decoration and Manufacture, Delivered in 1858–9.* New York: Wiley, 1876.

Russell, John. *The Lunar Planispheres, Engraved by the Late . . . , Esq. R.A. From His Original Drawings. With a Description.* London: William Bulmer and Company, 1809.

Sabatier, Antoine. *Dictionnaire des origines, découvertes, inventions, et établissemens.* Three vols. Paris: Moutard, 1776.

Schäffer, Jacob Christian. *Die Blumenpolypen der sussen Wasser beschrieben und mit den Blumenpolypen der sälzigen Wasser verglichen.* Regensburg: Emanuel Adam Weiss, 1755.

Schelling, F. W. J. *The Unconditional in Human Knowledge. Four Early Essays (1794–1796).* Translated by Fritz Marti. Lewisburg, Pa.: Associated University Presses, 1980.

Schott, Gaspar. *Iter extaticum coeleste, quo mundi opificium, id est, coelestis expansi, siderung. . . .* Herbipoli: Johannis Andreae Endteri & Wolf, 1660.

Schott, Gaspar. *Physica curiosa, sive mirabilia naturae et artis.* Herbipoli: Johannis Andreae Endteri & Wolf, 1667.

Schubert, Gotthilf Heinrich. *Ansichten von der Nachtseite der Naturwissenschaft (1808).* Darmstadt: Wissenschaftliche Buchgesellschaft, 1967.

Seba, Albertus. *Locupletissimi rerum naturaliam thesauri accurata descriptio et iconibus arti-ficiosissimis expressio, per universam physices historiam.* Indexes by J. B. Robinet. Four vols. Amsterdam: Janssonio-Waesbergios & J. Wetstenium & Gul. Smith, 1734–1765.

[Serao, Francesco]. *The Natural History of Mount Vesuvius, with the Explanation of the Various Phenomena That Usually Attend the Eruptions of This Celebrated Volcano.* Translated from the Italian. London: E. Cave, 1743.

Shaftesbury, Anthony, Earl of. *Characteristics of Men, Manners, Opinions, Times (1711).* Edited by John M. Robertson. Two vols. in one. Indianapolis: Bobbs-Merrill, 1964.

Sharpe, William. *A Dissertation upon Genius (1755).* Delmar, N.Y.: Scholars' Facsimiles & Reprints, 1973.

Shelley, Mary Wollstonecraft. *Frankenstein or the Modern Prometheus* (1817). New York: Harrison Smith and Robert Haas, 1934.

Sigaud-La Fond, Joseph-Aignan. *Dictionnaire des merveilles de la nature.* Two vols. in one. Paris: Rue et Hôtel Serpente, 1781.

Sobry, J. F. *Poétique des arts, ou cours de peinture et de littérature comparées.* Paris: Delaunay, 1810.

Sprat, Thomas. *The History of the Royal Society of London, for the Improving of Natural Knowledge.* London: T.R. for F. Martyn, 1667.

Stendhal [Marie-Henri Beyle]. *De l'amour, I–II. Oeuvres complètes de Stendhal.* Vol. XII. Edited by Daniel Muller and Pierre Jourda. Paris: Librairie Ancienne Honoré Champion, 1926.

Stewart, John ["Walking"]. *The Revelation of Nature with the Prophecy of Reason.* New York: Mott & Lyon for the author, 1813[?].

Stifter, Adalbert. *Bunte Steine. Gesammelte Werke.* Vol. III. Munich: Insel, 1959.

Stukeley, William. *Abury, a Temple of the British Druids.* London: W. Innys, R. Manby, B. Dod, J. Brindley, 1743.

Stukeley, William. *Stonehenge, a Temple Restored to the British Druids.* Two vols. in one. London: W. Innys and R. Manby, 1740.

Swammerdam, Jan. *Histoire générale des insectes. Ou l'on expose clairement la manière lente & pres'qu'insensible de l'accroissement de leurs membres, & ou l'on découvre evidemment l'erreur ou l'on tombe d'ordinaire au sujet de leur prétendue transformation.* Utrecht: Guillaume de Walcheren, 1682.

Swinden, Jan Hendrik van. *Mémoire sur les observations météorologiques.* Amsterdam: Marc-Michel Rey, 1780.

Switzer, Stephen. *An Universal System of Water and Water-Works, Philosophical and Practical.* Two vols. London: Thomas Cox, 1734.

Table analytique et raisonnée du dictionnaire des science, arts et métiers. Vol. I. Paris: Panckoucke; Amsterdam: Marc-Michel Rey, 1780.

Thoreau, Henry David. *Walden or, Life in the Woods* (New York: Libra, 1960), see, especially: "The Ponds," pp. 155–178.

Torre, Giovanni Maria della. "Incendio del Vesuvio accaduto li 19 d'octobre del 1767." *Journal des Sçavans* 36 (1769): 46–59.

Turnor, Hatton Christopher. *Astra Castra. Experiments and Adventures in the Atmosphere.* London: Chapman and Hall, 1865.

Valenciennes, Pierre-Henri. *Eléments de perspective pratique à l'usage des artises. Suivis de réflexions et conseils à un éleve sur la peinture et particulièrement sur le genre du paysage.* Geneva: Minkoff Reprint, 1973.

Volta, Giuseppi. *Neueste Versuch über Galvanismus. Beschreibung eines neuen Galvanometers und andere kleine Abhandlungen über diesen Gegendstand*. Vienna: Camesinaischen Buchhandlung, 1803.

Voltaire, François-Marie-Arouet de. *Letters Concerning the English Nation*. London: C. Davis and A. Lyon, 1733.

Warburton, William. *The Divine Legation of Moses Demonstrated (1741)*. Four vols. New York and London: Garland, 1978.

Watelet, Claude-Henri. *L'art de peindre. Poème. Avec des réflexions sur les différentes parties de la peinture*. Paris: J. L. Guerin & L. F. Delatour, 1760.

Werner, Abraham Gottlob. *Axel von Kronstedts Versuch einer Mineralogie. Aufs neue und nachst verschiedenen Anmerkungen vorzüglich mit äussern Beschreibungen der Fossilien. Vermehrt von.* . . . Leipzig: Siegfried Lebrecht Crusius, 1780.

Werner, Abraham Gottlob. *On the External Characters of Minerals (1774)*. Translated by Albert V. Carozzi. Urbana: University of Illinois Press, 1962.

Whitehurst, John. *An Inquiry into the Original State and Formation of the Earth*. Second edition. London: W. Bent, 1786.

Witte, Samuel Simon. *Ueber die Bildung und den Ursprung des keilformigen Inschriften zu Persepolis. Ein philosophisch-geschichtlicher Versuch*. Rostock and Leipzig: Karl Christoph Stiller, 1799.

Witte, Samuel Simon. *Ueber den Ursprung der Pyramiden in Egypten und der Ruinen von Persepolis, ein neuer Versuch*. Leipzig: J. G. Müller, 1789.

Wright, Thomas. *An Original Theory or New Hypothesis of the Universe*. London: author, 1750.

Young, Edward. *Conjectures on Original Composition (1759)*. Leeds: Scolar, 1966.

Secondary Sources

Abbey, J. R. *Scenery of Great Britain and Ireland in Aquatint and Lithography, 1770–1860*. London: Curwen, 1952.

Abbey, J. R. *Travel in Aquatint and Lithography, 1770–1860*. Two vols. London: Curwen, 1956.

Abrams, M. H. *Natural Supernaturalism. Tradition and Revolution in Romantic Literature*. New York: Norton, 1971.

Adams, Eric. *Francis Danby: Varieties of Poetic Landscape*. New Haven, Conn.: Yale University Press, 1973.

Adams, Percy G. "The Achievements of James Cook and His Associates in Perspective." In *Exploration in Alaska: Captain Cook Commemorative Lectures, June–November 1978*. Anchorage: Cook Inlet Historical Society, 1980.

Adams, Percy G. *Travellers and Travel Liars, 1600–1800*. Berkeley and Los Angeles: University of California Press, 1962.

Adams, William Howard, ed. *The Eye of Thomas Jefferson*. Washington, D.C.: National Gallery of Art, 1976.

Adhémar, Jean. *Les joies de la nature au XVIIIᵉ siècle*. Paris: Bibliothèque Nationale, 1971.

Adhémar, Jean. "Les lithographies de paysage en France à l'époque romantique." *Archives de l'art français* 19 (1938).

Adolph, Robert. *The Rise of the Modern Prose Style*. Cambridge, Mass.: MIT Press, 1968.

Allen, David Elliston. "The Lost Limb: Geology and Natural History." *British Society for the History of Science* 1 (1979): 200–212.

Allen, John Logan. *Passage through the Garden: Lewis and Clark and the Image of the American Northwest.* Urbana: University of Illinois Press, 1975.

Alpers, Svetlana. "Describe or Narrate? A Problem in Realistic Representation." *New Literary History* 8 (autumn 1976): 15–42.

Altick, Richard D. *The Shows of London.* Cambridge, Mass.: Belknap Press of Harvard University Press, 1978.

Anamorfosen, Spel met Perspectief. Amsterdam: Rijksmuseum, 1975.

Ananoff, Alexandre. "Effets d'aquarelle et de gouache." *Connaissance des arts* 197–198 (July–August 1968): 97–103.

Anderson, Wallace E. "Immaterialism in Jonathan Edwards' Early Philosophical Notes." *Journal of the History of Ideas* 25 (April–June 1964): 182–200.

Anglesea, Martyn, and John Preston. " 'A Philosophical Landscape.' Susanna Drury and the Giant's Causeway." *Art History* 3 (September 1980): 252–273.

Anson, P. G. "Rocks and Gardens." *Landscape* 11 (winter 1961–62): 3–4.

Appareils de laboratoire. Matériel d'enseignement. Presse et documentation techniques rétrospective: Sciences et techniques au temps de la révolution et de l'empire, 1789–1815. Paris: Ecole Technique Supérieure du Laboratoire, 1959.

Appleton, Jay. *The Experience of Landscape.* New York: Wiley, 1975.

Archer, Mildred. *Artist Adventurers in Eighteenth-Century India: Thomas and William Daniell.* London: Spink & Son, 1974.

Archer, Mildred. *British Drawings in the India Office Library.* Two vols. London: Her Majesty's Stationery Office, 1969.

Archer, Mildred. *Early Views of India.* London: Thames and Hudson, 1980.

Archer, Mildred, and W. G. Archer. *Indian Painting for the British, 1770–1880.* Oxford: Oxford University Press, 1955.

Archer, Mildred, and John Bastin. *The Raffles Drawings in the India Office Library, London.* Kuala Lumpur: Oxford University Press, 1975.

Arthos, John. *The Language of Natural Description in Eighteenth-Century Poetry.* New York: Octagon, 1966.

Ashton, Mark. "Allegory, Fact and Meaning in Giambattista Tiepolo's Four Continents in Wurzburg." *Art Bulletin* 60 (March 1978): 109–125.

Ashwin, Clive. "Graphic Imagery, 1837–1901: A Victorian Revolution." *Art History* 1 (September 1978): 360–370.

Assunto, Rosario. *Il paesaggio e l'estetica. Geminae ortae.* Vol. XIV. Edited by Rafaello Franchini. Two vols. Naples: Giannini, 1973.

Assunto, Rosario. *Specchio vivente del mondo (Artisti straineri in Roma, 1600–1800.* Rome: De Luca, 1978.

Atkinson, Geoffroy. *Les relations de voyages du XVIIe siècle et l'évolution des idées.* Paris: Librairie Ancienne Edouard Champion, 1924.

Atkinson, Geoffroy. *Le sentiment de la nature et le retour à la vie simple (1690–1740).* Geneva: Droz, 1960.

Aubert, Andreas. *Caspar David Friedrich: Gott, Freiheit, Vaterland.* Berlin: Bruno Cassirer, 1915.

Aubin, Robert A. "Grottoes, Geology, and the Gothic Revival." *Studies in Philology* 31 (July 1934): 408–416.

Aubin, Robert A. *Topographical Poetry in XVIII–Century England*. New York: Modern Language Association of America, 1936.

Auden, W. H. *The Enchafèd Flood, or, the Romantic Iconography of the Sea*. New York: Random House, 1950.

Auerbach, Erich. *Mimesis. The Representation of Reality in Western Literature*. Translated by Willard R. Trask. Princeton, N.J.: Princeton University Press, 1953.

Auerbach, Erich. "*Passio* als Leidenschaft." *PMLA* 56 (1941): 1178–1196.

Ault, Donald P. *Visionary Physics, Blake's Response to Newton*. University of Chicago Press, 1974.

Babelon, Jean. "Découverte du monde et littérature." *Comparative Literature* 2 (spring 1950): 157–166.

Bache, Christopher. "Towards a Unified Theory of Metaphor." *Journal of Aesthetics and Art Criticism* 39 (winter 1980): 185–194.

Bachelard, Gaston. *L'air et les songes. Essai sur l'imagination du mouvement*. Paris: José Corti, 1943.

Bachelard, Gaston. *L'eau et les rêves. Essai sur l'imagination de la matière*. Paris: José Corti, 1942.

Bachelard, Gaston. *The Poetics of Reverie*. Translated by Daniell Russell. New York: Orion, 1969.

Bachelard, Gaston. *The Poetics of Space*. Translated by Maria Jolas. New York: Orion, 1964.

Bachelard, Gaston. *La terre et les rêveries du répos*. Paris: José Corti, 1948.

Bachelard, Gaston. *La terre et le rêveries de la volonté*. Paris: José Corti, 1948.

Bacou, Roseline. *Piranesi, Etchings and Drawings*. Boston: New York Graphic Society, 1975.

Badger, G. M., ed. *Captain Cook Navigator and Scientist*. Canberra: Australian National University Press, 1970.

Bätschmann, Oskar. "Poussins Narziss und Echo im Louvre: Die Konstruktion von Thematik und Darstellung aus den Quellen." *Zeitschrift für Kunstgeschichte* 42 (June 1979): 31–47.

Baker, Keith Michael. *Condorcet. From Natural Philosophy to Social Mathematics*. University of Chicago Press, 1975.

Baltrušaitis, Jurgis. *Anamorphoses, ou perspectives curieuses*. Paris: Olivier Perrin, 1955.

Baltrušaitis, Jurgis. *Essai sur une légende scientifique: Le miroir. Révélations, science-fiction et fallacies*. Paris: Elmayan, Le Seuil, 1978.

Baltrušaitis, Jurgis. "Lands of Illusion. China and the Eighteenth-Century Garden." *Landscape* 11 (winter 1961–62): 5–11.

Baltrušaitis, Jurgis. *Le moyen âge fantastique, antiquités et exotismes dan l'art gothique*. Paris: Armand Colin, 1955.

Baltrušaitis, Jurgis. "Un musée des miroirs." *Macula* 2 (1977): 2–16.

Bang, Marie. "Two Alpine Landscapes by C. D. Friedrich." *Burlington* 107 (November 1966): 571–575.

Banks, Oliver Talcott. *Watteau and the North: Studies in the Dutch and Flemish Baroque Influences on French Rococo Painting*. New York: Garland, 1977.

Bandmann, Günter, Hans Blumenberg, Hans Sachsse, Heinrich Vormweg, and Dieter Wellershoff, eds. *Zum Wirklichkeitsbegriff*. Mainz: Franz Steiner, 1974.

Barbier, Carl Paul. *William Gilpin, His Drawings, Teachings, and Theory of the Picturesque*. Oxford: Clarendon, 1963.

Barrell, John. *The Idea of Landscape and the Sense of Place, 1730–1840: An Approach to the Poetry of John Clare*. Cambridge University Press, 1972.

Barrell, John. *The Dark Side of the Landscape: The Rural Poor in English Painting 1730–1840*. Cambridge University Press, 1980.

Barrière, Gérard. "L'émotion que peut donner un arpent de terre quand on sait ce que signifie un jardin au Japon." *Connaissance des Arts* 270 (August 1974): 62–67.

Barthes, Roland. *The Eiffel Tower and Other Mythologies*. Translated by Richard Howard. New York: Hill and Wang, 1981.

Bate, Walter Jackson. "The Sympathetic Imagination in Eighteenth-Century Criticism." *ELH* 12 (June 1945): 144–164.

Batten, Charles L., Jr. *Pleasurable Instruction: Form and Convention in Eighteenth-Century Travel Literature*. Berkeley and Los Angeles: University of California Press, 1978.

Battisti, Eugenio. *L'antirinascimento*. Milan: Feltrinelli, 1962.

Bauer, Hermann. *Probleme der Kunstwissenschaft*. Vol. I. Berlin: Walter de Gruyter & Co., 1963.

Bauer, Hermann. *Rocaille, zur Herkunft und zum Wesen eines Ornament-Motivs*. Berlin: Walter de Gruyter & Co., 1962.

Bauer, Linda Freeman. " 'Quanto si disegna, si dipinge ancora;' Some Observations on the Development of the Oil Sketch." *Storia dell'Arte* 32 (January–April 1978): 45–58.

Baxandall, Michael. *The Limewood Sculptors of Renaissance Germany*. New Haven, Conn.: Yale University Press, 1980.

Beach, Joseph Warren. *The Concept of Nature in Nineteenth-Century English Poetry*. New York: Macmillan, 1936.

Beaglehole, J. C. *The Life of Captain James Cook*. London: Adam & Charles Black, 1975.

Beck, Hanno, ed. *Alexander von Humboldt—Werk und Werkgeltung*. Munich: R. Piper, 1969.

Béguin, Albert. *L'âme romantique et le rêve. Essai sur le romantisme allemand et la poésie française*. Two vols. Paris: Editions des Cahiers du Sud, 1937.

Benay, Jacques G. "L'hônnete homme devant la nature, ou philosophie du Chevalier de Méré." *PMLA* 79 (March 1964): 122–132.

Bendiner, Kenneth. "Thomas and William Daniell's 'Oriental Scenery': Some Major Themes." *Arts* 55 (December 1980): 98–103.

Benichou, Paul. *Le sacre de l'écrivain, 1750–1830*. Paris: José Corti, 1973.

Benjamin, Walter. *Das Kunstwerk im Zeitalter seiner technischer Reproduzierbarkeit. Drei Studien zur Kunstsoziologie*. Frankfurt-am-Main: Suhrkamp, 1963.

Benjamin, Walter. *Reflections: Essays, Aphorisms, Autobiographical Writings*. Translated by Edmund Jephcott and edited by Peter Demetz. New York: Harcourt Brace Jovanovich, 1978.

Bertrand, Alexis, *François Rude*. Paris: Librairie de l'Art, 1888.

Bessmertny, Bertha. "Les principaux ouvrages sur l'histoire des sciences parus en France pendant le XVIIIe siècle." *Archeion* 16 (1934): 325–328.

Bettex, Albert. *The Discovery of Nature*. New York: Simon and Schuster, 1965.

Bettex, Albert. L'invention du monde, une histoire des découvertes illustrés par les images du temps. French text by Armel Guerne. Paris: Delpire, 1960.

Beurdeley, Cecile, and Michel Beurdeley. *Castiglione, peintre jésuite à la cour de Chine*. Paris: Bibliothèque des Arts, 1971.

Biermann, Kurt R., and Fritz G. Lange. *Alexander von Humboldt Festschrift aus Anlass seiner 200. Geburtstages*. Berlin: Akademie-Verlag, 1969.

Biese, Alfred. *Das Naturgefühl im Wandel der Zeiten*. Leipzig: Quelle & Meyer, 1926.

Bitterli, Urs. *Die "Wilden" und die "Zivilisierten." Grundzüge einer Geistes- und Kulturgeschichte der Europaisch-überseeischen Begegnung*. Munich: C. H. Beck, 1976.

Bjurström, Per. "La gravure en Suède." *Nouvelles de l'Estampe* 51 (May–June 1980): 9–18.

Blanckenhagen, Peter Heinrich von. "The Odyssey Frieze." *Mitteilungen des Deutschen Archaelogischen Instituts Roemische Abteilung* 70 (1963): 100–146.

Blanckenhagen, Peter Heinrich von, and Christine Alexander. *The Paintings from Boscotrecase*. Heidelberg: F. H. Kerle, 1962.

Bland, David. *A History of Book Illustration: The Illuminated Manuscript and the Printed Book*. Berkeley and Los Angeles: University of California Press, 1969.

Bluche, François. *La vie quotidienne au temps de Louis XVI*. Paris: Hachette, 1980.

Boase, T. S. R. *English Art, 1800–1870*. Oxford: Clarendon, 1959.

Boase, T. S. R. *Les peintres anglais et la vallée d'Aoste*. Translated by A. P. d'Entrèves. Novara: Departement du Tourisme des Antiquités et Beaux-Arts Région Autonome Vallée d'Aoste, 1959.

Boerlin-Brödbeck, Yvonne. *Caspar Wolf (1735–1783). Landschaft im Vorfeld der Romantik*. Basel: Kunstmuseum, 1980.

Boppe, A. *Les peintres du Bosphore au dix-huitième siècle*. Paris: Hachette, 1911.

Börsch-Supan, Helmut. *Caspar David Friedrich*. Munich: Prestel, 1973.

Börsch-Supan, Helmut. "Caspar David Friedrich et Carl Friedrich Schinkel." *Revue de l'Art* 45 (1979): 9–20.

Börsch-Supan, Helmut, and K. W. Jahnig. *Caspar David Friedrich Gemälde, Druckgraphik und bildmässige Zeichnungen*. Munich: Prestel, 1973.

Bogel, Fredric V. "The Rhetoric of Substantiality: Johnson and the Later Eighteenth Century." *Eighteenth-Century Studies* 12 (summer 1979): 457–480.

Boime, Albert. *The Academy and French Painting in the Nineteenth Century*. London: Phaidon, 1971.

Boime, Albert. "Marmontel's *Belisaire* and the Pre-Revolutionary Progressivism of David." *Art History* 3 (March 1980): 81–101.

Boime, Albert. *Thomas Couture and the Eclectic Vision*. New Haven, Conn.: Yale University Press, 1980.

Bornstein, Marc H. "The Ecological Approach to Visual Perception." *Journal of Aesthetics and Art Criticism* 39 (winter 1980): 203–206.

Bosse, Heinrich. "The Marvellous in Romantic Semiotics." *Studies in Romanticism* 14 (summer 1975): 211–234.

Botting, Douglas. *Humboldt and the Cosmos*. New York: Harper & Row, 1973.

Bouthoul, Gaston. *L'invention*. Paris: Marcel Giard, 1930.

Boyce, Benjamin. "Mr. Pope in Bath Improves the Design of His Grotto." In *Restoration and Eighteenth-Century Literature*. Edited by Carroll Camden. University of Chicago Press, 1963.

Braham, Allan. *The Architecture of the French Enlightenment*. Berkeley and Los Angeles: University of California Press, 1980.

Branca, Vittore, ed. *Rappresentazione artistica e rapresentazione scientifica nel "Secolo dei Lumi."* Venice: Sansoni, 1970.

Branca, Vittore, ed. *Sensibilità e razionalità nel settecento*. Venice: Sansoni, 1967.

Braunburg, Rudolf. *Leichter als Luft. Aus der Geschichte der Ballonluftfahrt*. Hamburg: Marion von Schoder, 1963.

Bredvold, Louis I. "The Tendency toward Platonism in Neo-Classical Esthetics." *ELH* 1 (September 1934): 91–119.

Briganti, Giuliano. *I pittori dell'immaginazio. Arte e rivoluzione psicologica*. Milan: Electa, 1977.

Briganti, Giuliano. *I vedutisti*. Milan: Electa, 1970.

Broc, Numa. *La géographie des philosophes. Géographes et voyageurs français au XVIIIe siècle*. Paris: Ophrys, 1975.

Broc, Numa. *Les montagnes vues par les géographes et les naturalistes de langue française au XVIIIe siècle*. Paris: Bibliothèque Nationale, 1969.

Brombert, Victor. "Pascal's Happy Dungeon." In *The Classical Line: Essays in Honor of Henri Peyre. Yale French Studies*, 38 (1967).

Brooks, Peter. "The Aesthetics of Astonishment." *Georgia Review* 30 (fall 1976): 615–639.

Brooks, Peter. "Godlike Science/Unhallowed Arts: Language and Monstrosity in *Frankenstein*." *New Literary History* 9 (spring 1978): 591–606.

Brossard, C.-A. *Kerguelen le découvreur et ses îles*. Two vols. Paris: Gallimard, 1970.

Brown, Harcourt. *Science and the Creative Spirit: Essays on the Humanistic Aspect of Science*. University of Toronto Press, 1958.

Brown, Harcourt. *Science and the Human Comedy: Natural Philosophy in French Literature from Rabelais to Maupertuis*. University of Toronto Press, 1976.

Bruel, François. *Histoire aéronautique par les monuments peints, sculptés, dessinés et gravés des origines à 1830*. Paris: André Marty, Imprimerie de Frazier-Soye, 1909.

Bryson, Norman. *Word and Image: French Painting of the Ancien Régime*. Cambridge University Press, 1981.

Bucher, Bernadette. *Icon and Conquest: A Structural Analysis of de Bry's Great Voyages*. Translated by Basia Miller Gulati. University of Chicago Press, 1981.

Bukdahl, Else Marie. *Diderot Critique d'Art*. Translated from the Danish by Jean-Paul Faucher. Two vols. Copenhagen: Rosenkilde et Bagger, 1980.

Bundy, Murray Wright. *The Theory of the Imagination in Classical and Mediaeval Thought.* Urbana: University of Illinois Press, 1927.

Bunn, James H. "The Aesthetics of British Mercantilism." *New Literary History* 11 (winter 1980): 303–321.

Burda, Hubert. *Die Ruine in den Bildern Hubert Roberts.* Munich: Wilhelm Fink, 1969.

Burkert, Walter. *Lore and Science in Ancient Pythagoreanism.* Translated by Edwin L. Minar, Jr. Cambridge, Mass.: Harvard University Press, 1972.

Burnell, Devin. "The Good, the True and the Comical: Problems Occasioned by Hogarth's *The Bench." Art Quarterly,* N.S., 2 (spring 1978): 17–46.

Burns, Sarah. "Girodet-Trioson's *Ossian*: The Role of Theatrical Illusionism in a Pictorial Evocation of Otherworldly Beings." *Gazette des Beaux-Arts* 95 (January 1980): 13–24.

Bush, Virginia. *Colossal Sculpture of the Cinquecento.* New York: Garland, 1976.

Busiri Vici, Andrea. *Trittico paesistico romano del '700. Paolo Anesi-Paolo Monaldi-Alessio de Marchis.* Rome: Ugo Bozzi, 1976.

Butor, Michel. "Monet, or the World Turned Upside Down." *Art News Annual* 34 (1968).

Cahn, Walter. *Masterpieces: Chapters on the History of an Idea.* Princeton, N.J.: Princeton University Press, 1979.

Callender, Geoffrey. " 'Capetown' by William Hodges, R.A." *Burlington* 79 (September 1941): 93–94.

Calvesi, Maurizio. "Il Sacro Bosco di Bomarzo. "*Scritti di Storia dell'Arte in Onore di Lionello Venturi.* Rome: De Luca, 1956.

Cantor, G. N. "Revelation and the Cyclical Cosmos of John Hutchinson." *British Society for the History of Science* 1 (1979): 3–22.

Carnahan, D. H. "The Romantic Debate in the French Daily Press of 1809." *PMLA* 53 (June 1938): 475–488.

Carnochan, W. B. *Confinement and Flight: An Essay on English Literature of the Eighteenth Century.* Berkeley and Los Angeles: University of California Press, 1977.

Carpenter, Richard Bruce. The Dutch Sources of the Art of J.-H. Fragonard. Ph.D. diss., Harvard University, 1955.

Carr, J. L. "Pygmalion and the *philosophes.* The Animated Statue in Eighteenth-Century France." *Journal of the Warburg and Courtauld Institutes* 23 (1960): 239–255.

Celant, Germano, ed. *Art Povera, Conceptual, Actual or Impossible Art?* London: Studio Vista, 1969.

Cherpack, Clifton. "Warburton and Some Aspects of the Search for the Primitive in Eighteenth-Century France." *Philological Quarterly* 36 (April 1957): 221–233.

Chinard, Gilbert. *L'Amerique et le rêve exotique dans la littérature française au XVIIe et au XVIIIe siècle.* Paris: Droz, 1934.

Chouillet-Roche, Anne-Marie. "Le clavecin-oculaire du Père Castel." *Dix-Huitième Siècle* 8 (1976): 141–166.

Christ, Carol T. *The Finer Optic: The Aesthetic of Particularity in Victorian Poetry.* New Haven, Conn.: Yale University Press, 1975.

Christ, Yvan. *Projets et divagations de Claude-Nicolas Ledoux, architecte du roi.* Paris: Minotaure, 1961.

Chu, Petra ten Doesschate. *French Realism and the Dutch Masters. The Influence of Dutch Seventeenth Century Painting on the Development of French Painting between 1830 and 1870.* Utrecht: Haentjens Dekker & Gumbert, 1974.

Cikovsky, Nikolai, Jr. " 'The Ravages of the Axe': The Meaning of the Tree Stump in Nineteenth-Century American Art." *Art Bulletin* 61 (December 1979): 611–626.

Cioranescu, Alexandre. "La découverte de l'Amerique et l'art de la description." *Revue des Sciences Humaines* 29 (April–June 1962): 161–168.

Clark, H. F. "Eighteenth-Century Elysiums. The Role of 'Association' in the Landscape Movement." *Journal of the Warburg and Courtauld Institutes* 6 (1943): 165–189.

Clark, Kenneth. *Landscape into Art.* New edition. London: John Murray, 1976.

Clark, T. J. *The Absolute Bourgeois: Artists and Politics in France, 1848–1851.* London: Thames and Hudson, 1973.

Clark, T. J. *Image of the People: Gustave Courbet and the 1848 Revolution.* London: Thames and Hudson, 1973.

Clasen, Wolfgang. "Piranesi und die Architektur-Phantasie." In *Aspekte zur Kunstgeschichte von Mittelalter und Neuzeit.* Weimar: Hermann Böhlaus Nachfolger, 1971.

Clifford, Derek. *A History of Garden Design.* New York: Praeger, 1963.

Coffin, David R., ed. *The Italian Garden.* Washington, D.C.: Dumbarton Oaks, 1972.

Coffin, David R., ed. *The Villa d'Este at Tivoli.* Princeton, N.J.: Princeton University Press, 1960.

Cohen, I. Bernard. *The Newtonian Revolution. With Illustrations of the Transformation of Scientific Ideas.* Cambridge University Press, 1980.

Cohen, Murray. *Sensible Words: Linguistic Practice in England, 1640–1785.* Baltimore: Johns Hopkins University Press, 1977.

Cohen, Ralph. "Association of Ideas and Poetic Unity." *Philological Quarterly* 36 (October 1957): 465–474.

Coleman, Francis X. J. *The Aesthetic Thought of the French Enlightenment.* University of Pittsburgh Press, 1971.

Coleman, Patrick. "The Idea of Character in the *Encyclopédie*." *Eighteenth-Century Studies* 13 (fall 1979): 21–47.

Collier, Katharine Brownell. *Cosmogonies of Our Forefathers: Some Theories of the Seventeenth and Eighteenth Centuries.* New York: Octagon, 1968.

Collingwood, R. G. *The Idea of Nature.* New York: Oxford University Press, 1960.

Colton, Judith. *The Parnasse François: Titon du Tillet and the Origins of the Monument to Genius.* New Haven, Conn.: Yale University Press, 1979.

Conisbee, Philip. "French Landscapes in London." *Burlington* 116 (January 1978): 43–44.

Conner, Patrick. "China and the Landscape Garden: Reports, Engravings and Misconceptions." *Art History* 2 (December 1979): 429–440.

Captain Cook in the South Seas. London: British Museum and British Library, 1979.

Captain James Cook: His Artists and Draughtsmen. Auckland City Art Gallery, 1964.

Corboz, André. *Peinture militante et architecture révolutionnaire. A propos du thème du tunnel chez Hubert Robert.* Basel and Stuttgart: Birkhäuser, 1978.

Cottom, Daniel. "Taste and the Cultivated Imagination." *Journal of Aesthetics and Art Criticism* 34 (summer 1981): 367–380.

Crary, Douglas. "A Geographer Looks at the Landscape." *Landscape* 9 (autumn 1959): 22–25.

Crocker, Lester G. *Diderot's Chaotic Order: Approach to Synthesis.* Princeton, N.J.: Princeton University Press, 1974.

Croll, Morris William. *"Attic" and Baroque Prose Style; the Anti-Ciceronian Movement.* Edited by J. Max Patrick, Robert O. Evans, and John M. Wallace. Princeton, N.J.: Princeton University Press, 1969.

Croll, Morris William. *Style, Rhetoric, and Rhythm: Essays.* Edited by J. Max Patrick. Princeton, N.J.: Princeton University Press, 1966.

Crow, Thomas. "The *Oath of the Horatii* in 1785. Painting and Pre-Revolutionary Radicalism in France." *Art History* 1 (December 1978): 424–471.

Curtis, Melinda. *Search for Innocence: Primitive and Primitivistic Art of the Nineteenth Century.* College Park: University of Maryland Art Gallery, 1975.

Daemmrich, Ingrid G. "The Ruins Motif as Artistic Device in French Literture." *Journal of Aesthetics and Art Criticism* 30 (summer 1972): 449–457; 31 (fall 1972): 31–41.

Dahl, Curtis. "The American School of Catastrophe." *American Quarterly* 11 (fall 1959): 380–390.

Dahl, Curtis. "Bulwer-Lytton and the School of Catastrophe." *Philological Quarterly* 32 (October 1953): 428–442.

Damisch, Hubert. *Théorie du nuage. Pour une histoire de la peinture.* Paris: Seuil, 1972.

Dance, Peter S. *The Art of Natural History.* Woodstock, N.Y.: Overlook, 1978.

Dance, Peter S. *Shell Collecting: A History.* Berkeley and Los Angeles: University of California Press, 1966.

Darnton, Robert. *Mesmerism and the End of the Enlightenment in France.* Cambridge, Mass.: Harvard University Press, 1968.

Darnton, Robert. *The Widening Circle: Essays on the Circulation of Literature in Eighteenth-Century Europe.* Philadelphia: University of Pennsylvania Press, 1976.

D'Aubarade, Gabriel. *André Chenier.* Paris: Hachette, 1970.

De David à Delacroix, la peinture française de 1774 à 1830. Paris: Grand Palais, 1975.

Deane, C. V. *Aspects of Eighteenth Century Nature Poetry.* Oxford: Blackwell, 1935.

Dedeyan, Charles. *Le cosmopolitanisme éuropéen sous la révolution et l'empire.* Paris: Société d'Edition d'Enseignement Supérieur, 1976.

Delange, Henri. *Monographie de l'oeuvre de Bernard Palissy, suivie d'un choix de ses continuateurs ou imitateurs.* Paris: Quai Voltaire, 1862.

De Laura, David J. "The Context of Browning's Painter Poems: Aesthetics, Polemics, Historics." *PMLA* 95 (May 1980): 367–388.

Dempsey, Charles. *Annibale Carracci and the Beginnings of Baroque Style.* Gluckstadt: J. J. Augustin, 1977.

Deprun, Jean. "Mystique, Lumières, Romantisme: Jalons pour une histoire des 'miroirs vivants.'" In *Approaches des Lumières: Mélanges offerts à Jean Fabre.* Paris: Klincksieck, 1974.

Derrida, Jacques. *L'archéologie du frivole.* Paris: Galilée, 1973.

Derrida, Jacques. *De la grammatologie*. Collection "Critique." Paris: Minuit, 1967.

Dobai, Johannes. *Die Kunstliteratur des Klassizismus und der Romantik in England*. Vol. I. Berne: Bentelli, 1974.

Dorival, Bernard. "Ukiyo-e and European Painting." In *Dialogue in Art: Japan and the West*. Tokyo: Kodansha International, 1976.

Duchet, Michele. "*L'histoire des voyages*: Originalité et influence." In *L'Abbé Prevost. Actes du Colloque d'Aix-en-Provence*, 1963. Aix-en-Provence: Ophrys, 1965.

Duncan, Carol Greene. The Persistence and Re-Emergence of the Rococo in French Painting. Ph.D. diss., Columbia University, 1969.

Dunmore, John. *French Explorers in the Pacific*. Two vols. Oxford: Clarendon, 1965.

Du Prey, Pierre. "Eighteenth-Century English Sources for a History of Swiss Wooden Bridges." *Zeitschrift für Schweizerische Archaologie und Kunstgeschichte* 36, no. 1 (1979): 51–63.

Durler, Josef. *Die Bedeutung des Bergbaus bei Goethe und in der Deutschen Romantik*. Edited by Emil Ermatinger, Frauenfeld and Leipzig: Huber, 1936.

Durliat, Marcel. "Alexandre du Mège, ou les mythes archéologiques à Toulouse dans le premier tiers du XIXe siècle." *Revue de l'Art* 23 (1974): 30–41.

Eather, Robert H. *Majestic Lights. The Aurora in Science, History, and the Arts*. Washington, D.C.: American Geophysical Union, 1980.

Earth, Air, Fire, Water: Elements of Art. Two vols. Boston: Museum of Fine Arts, 1971.

Eddelmann, William Smiley, III. Landscape on the Seventeenth and Eighteenth-Century Italian Stage. Ph.D. diss., Stanford University, 1972.

Eddy, John A. "The Maunder Minimum." *Science* 192 (June 18, 1976): 1189–1202.

Egan, Rose Frances. "The Genesis of the Theory of 'Art for Art's Sake' in Germany and in England." *Smith College Studies in Modern Language* 2 (July 1921): 34–37.

Ehrard, Jean. *L'idée de la nature en France dans la première moitié du XVIIIe siècle*. Two vols. Paris: S.E.U.P.E.N., 1963.

Eichler, Inge. "Die Cervarafeste der Deutschen Künstler in Rom." *Zeitschrift des Deutschen Vereins für Kunstwissenschaft* 31, no. 1 (1977): 81–114.

Einem, Herbert von. *Deutsche Malerei des Klassizismus und der Romantik 1760 bis 1840*. Munich: C. H. Beck, 1978.

Einem, Herbert von. *Festschrift für . . . zum 16. Februar, 1965*. Edited by Gert von der Osten. Berlin: Gebr. Mann, 1965.

Einem, Herbert von. *Goethe-Studien*. Munich: Wilhelm Fink, 1972.

Eisenstein, Elizabeth L. *The Printing Press as an Agent of Change. Communications and Cultural Transformations in Early-Modern Europe*. Two vols. Cambridge University Press, 1979.

Elledge, Scott. "The Background and Development in English Criticism of the Theories of Generality and Particularity." *PMLA* 62, no. 3 (1947): 147–182.

Eliade, Mircea. *Cosmos and History, the Myth of the Eternal Return*. New York: Harper & Row, 1959.

Engelhardt, Wolf von. "Schonheit im Reiche der Mineralien." *Jahrbuch für Asthetik und Allgemeine Kunstwissenschaft* 4 (1958–59): 55–72.

Engell, James. *The Creative Imagination: Enlightenment to Romanticism*. Cambridge, Mass.: Harvard University Press, 1981.

Etlin, Richard A. *The Architecture of Death: The Transformation of the Cemetery in Eighteenth-Century Paris.* Cambridge, Mass.: MIT Press, 1983.

Etlin, Richard A. The Cemetery and the City: Paris, 1744–1804. Ph.D. diss., Princeton University, 1978.

Fabre, Jean. *Chenier.* Connaissance des Lettres. Paris: Hatier, 1966.

Fabre, Jean. *Approches des Lumières: Mélanges offerts à. . . .* Paris: Klincksieck, 1974.

Fabricant, Carole. *Swift's Landscape.* Baltimore: Johns Hopkins University Press, 1982.

Farber, Marvin, ed. *Philosophical Essays in Memory of Edmund Husserl.* New York: Greenwood, 1968.

Faré, Michel. "De quelques termes designant la peinture d'objet." *Etudes d'Art français offertes à Charles Sterling.* Edited by Albert Chatelet and Nicole Reynaud. Paris: Presses Universitaires de France, 1975.

Feaver, William. *The Art of John Martin.* Oxford: Clarendon, 1975.

Fidell-Beaufort, Janine, and Jean Bailly-Herzberg. *Charles-François Daubigny.* Translated by Judith Schub. Paris: Geoffroy-Dechaume, 1975.

Field, Crosby. *Invention through the Ages.* Cleveland: National Association of Manufacturers, 1948.

Finley, Gerald. "The Genesis of Turner's 'Landscape Sublime.'" *Zeitschrift für Kunstgeschichte* 42, no. 2/3 (1979): 141–165.

Fisch, Harold. "The Scientist as Priest: A Note on Robert Boyle's Natural Theology." *Isis* 44 (September 1953): 252–265.

Fletcher, Angus, ed. *The Literature of Fact: Selected Papers from the English Institute.* New York: Columbia University Press, 1976.

Fletcher, Ian, ed. *Romantic Mythologies.* New York: Barnes & Noble, 1967.

Focillon, Henri. *The Life of Forms in Art.* New York: Wittenborn, Schultz, 1948.

Forbes, Vernon S. *Pioneer Travellers of South Africa: A Geographical Commentary upon Routes, Records, Observations and Opinions of Travellers at the Cape, 1750–1800.* Capetown and Amsterdam: A. A. Balkema, 1965.

Force, Roland W., and Maryanne Force. *Art and Artifacts of the Eighteenth Century.* Honolulu: Bishop Museum Press, 1968.

Forest, H. U. "Théodore Jouffroy et le problème de l'imitation dans les arts." *PMLA* 56 (1941): 1095–1102.

Forssman, Erik. *Dorisch, Jonisch, Korinthisch. Studien über den Gebrauch der Säulenordnungen in der Architektur des 16.–18. Jahrhunderts.* Stockholm: Almquist & Wiksell, 1961.

Forssman, Erik. *Säule und Ornament. Studien zum Problem des Manierismus in der Nordischen Säulenbüchern und Vorlageblättern des 16. und 17. Jahrhunderts.* Stockholm: Almquist & Wiksell, 1956.

Foster, William, "William Hodges, R.A., in India." *Bengal Past & Present* 30 (July–September 1925): 1–8.

Foucault, Michel. *The Archaeology of Knowledge.* Translated by A. M. Sheridan Smith. London: Tavistock, 1972.

Foucault, Michel. *The Birth of the Clinic: An Archaeology of Medical Perception.* Translated by A. M. Sheridan Smith. New York: Pantheon, 1973.

Foucault, Michel. *Folie et déraison. Histoire de la folie à l'âge classique.* Paris: Plon, 1961.

Foucault, Michel. *Les mots et les choses. Une archéologie des sciences humaines.* Paris: Gallimard, 1966.

Fox, Christopher. "Locke and the Scriblerians: The Discussion of Identity in Early Eighteenth Century England." *Eighteenth-Century Studies* 16 (fall 1982): 1–25.

Frank, Robert G., Jr. *Harvey and the Oxford Physiologists: A Study of Scientific Ideas.* Berkeley and Los Angeles: University of California Press, 1980.

Franz, Heinrich Gerhard. "Meister der Spätmanieristischen Landschaftsmalerei in den Niederlanden." *Jahrbuch des Kunsthistorischen Institutes der Universitäts Graz,* no. 3/4 (1968–69): 19–72.

Franz, Heinrich Gerhard. "Niederlandische Landschaftsmaler im Künstlerkreis Rudolf II." *Uměni* 18 (1970): 224–244.

Franz, Heinrich Gerhard. *Niederlandische Landschaftsmalerei im Zeitalter des Manierismus.* Graz: Akademische Druck und Verlagsanstalt, 1969.

Fried, Michael. *Absorption and Theatricality: Painting and Beholder in the Age of Diderot.* Berkeley and Los Angeles: University of California Press, 1980.

Fried, Michael. "The Beholder in Courbet: His Early Self-Portraits and Their Place in His Art." *Glyph* 4 (1978): 85–129.

Friedlander, Max J. *Landscape, Portrait, Still-Life.* Oxford: Bruno Cassirer, 1949.

Fritz, Paul, and David Williams, eds. *City & Society in the Eighteenth-Century.* Toronto: Hakkert, 1973.

Fritz, Paul, and David Williams, eds. *The Triumph of Culture: Eighteenth-Century Perspectives.* Toronto: Hakkert, 1972.

Fromer-Im-Obersteg, Liselotte. *Die Entwicklung der Schweizerischen Landschaftsmalerei im 18. und fruhen 19. Jahrhundert.* Basel: Birkhauser, 1945.

Fry, Edward F. Projects in Nature: Eleven Environmental Works Executed at Merriewold West, Far Hills, New Jersey (1975).

Frye, Northrop. *Fables of Identity: Studies in Poetic Mythology.* New York: Harcourt, Brace & World, 1963.

Frye, Northrop. *A Study of English Romanticism.* New York: Random House, 1968.

Furstenberg, Jean. *La gravure originale dans l'illustration du livre français du dix-huitième siècle.* Hamburg: Hauswedell, 1975.

Fussell, Paul, Jr., ed. *Literature as a Mode of Travel: Five Essays and a Postscript.* New York Public Library, 1963.

Gage, John. "Turner and the Picturesque." *Burlington* 107 (February 1965): 75–81.

Gage, John. *Turner on Colour.* London: Oxford University Press, 1969.

Ganay, E. de. "Les rochers et les eaux dans les jardins à l'anglaise." *Revue de l'Art Ancien et Moderne* 66 (July 1934): 63–80.

Garai, Pierre. "Le cartesianisme et le classicisme anglais." *Revue de Littérature Comparée* 31 (July–September 1957): 373–387.

Garms, Jörg. "Machine, Composition, und Histoire in der Französischen Kritik un 1750." *Zeitschrift für Asthetik und Allgemeine Kunstwissenschaft* 16, no. 1 (1971): 27–42.

Gaston, Marguerite. *Images romantiques des Pyrénées. Les Pyrénées dans la peinture et dans l'estampe à l'époque romantique.* Pau: Amis du Musée Pyrénéen, 1975.

Gay, Peter. *Art and Act. On Causes in History—Manet, Gropius, Mondrian.* New York: Harper & Row, 1976.

Georgel, Pierre, "Le romantisme des années 1860 et correspondance Victor Hugo-Philippe Burty." *Revue de l'Art* 20 (1973): 8–64.

Gerszi, Terez. "Brueghels Nachwirkung auf die Niederländischen Landschaftmaler um 1600." *Oud Holland* 90, no. 4 (1976): 201–229.

Giehlow, Karl. "Die Hieroglyphenkunde des Humanismus in der Allegorie der Renaissance besonders der Ehrenspforte Kaisers Maximilian I; mit einem Nachwort von Arpad Weixlgartner." *Jahrbuch der Kunsthistorischen Sammlungen der Allerhöchsten Kaiserhauses, Wien,* 32, no. 1 (1915): 1–232.

Gilbert, Sandra M., and Susan Gubar. *The Madwoman in the Attic: The Woman Writer and the Nineteenth-Century Literary Imagination.* New Haven, Conn.: Yale University Press, 1979.

Gille, Bertrand. *Exposition internationale de l'industrie minérale, 18 juin–3 juillet 1955: Les mines, les forges, et les arts.* Paris: P. Fournie et Cie, 1955.

Ginsberg, Robert. "The Aesthetics of Ruins." *Bucknell Review* 18 (winter 1970): 89–102.

Giraud, Raymond. "Winckelmann's Role in Gautier's Conception of Classical Beauty." In *The Classical Line. Essays in Honor of Henri Peyre. Yale French Studies* 38 (1967): 172–182.

Girdlestone, Cuthbert. *Poésie, politique, Pyrénées. Louis-François Ramond (1755–1827). Sa vie, son oeuvre littéraire et politique.* Paris: Lettres Modernes Minard, 1968.

Glacken, Clarence. "On Chateaubriand's Journey from Paris to Jerusalem, 1806–07." In *The Terraqueous Globe: The History of Geography and Cartography.* Los Angeles: William Andrews Clark Memorial Library, 1969.

Glacken, Clarence. *Traces on the Rhodian Shore: Nature and Culture in Western Thought from Ancient Times to the End of the Eighteenth Century.* Berkeley and Los Angeles: University of California Press, 1967.

Godechot, Jacques. "L'aérostation militaire sous le Directoire." *Annales de la Révolution Française* 8 (1931): 213–228.

Goldstein, Thomas. "The Role of the Italian Merchant Class in Renaissance and Discoveries." *Terrae Incognitae* 8 (1976): 19–28.

Golson, Lucile M. "Serlio, Primaticcio and the Architectural Grotto." *Gazette des Beaux-Arts* 77 (February 1971): 95–108.

Gombrich, E. H. *The Heritage of Apelles: Studies in the Art of the Renaissance.* Ithaca, N.Y.: Cornell University Press, 1976.

Gombrich, E. H. *Meditations on a Hobby Horse.* London: Phaidon, 1968.

Gombrich, E. H. "Renaissance Artistic Theory and the Development of Landscape Painting." *Gazette des Beaux-Arts* 41 (May–June 1953).

Gombrich, E. H. *The Sense of Order. A Study in the Psychology of Decorative Art.* Wrightsman Lectures. Ithaca, N.Y.: Cornell University Press, 1979.

Grand-Carteret, Jean, and Leo Delteil. *La conquête de l'air vue par l'image (1495–1909).* Paris: Libraires des Annales, 1909.

Grand-Carteret, Jean, and Leo Delteil. *La montagne à travers les âges. Rôle joué par elle. Façon dont elle a été vue.* Two vols. Grenoble: H. Falque et F. Perrin Librairie Dauphinoise, 1903–04.

Grandjean, Serge. *Bernard Palissy et son école*. Paris: Au Pont des Arts, 1952.

Grant, R. "Hutton's Theory of the Earth." *British Society for the History of Science* 1 (1979): 23–38.

Green, Richard. "John Martin Reconsidered." *Connoisseur* 181 (December 1972): 247–252.

Greenbaum, Louis S. "The Humanitarianism of Antoine-Laurent Lavoisier." *Studies on Voltaire and the Eighteenth Century* 88 (1972): 651–675.

Grigson, Geoffrey. "Fingal's Cave." *Architectural Review* 104 (August 1948): 51–54.

Gruber, Alain-Charles. *Les grandes fêtes et leurs décors à l'époque de Louis XVI*. Histoire des idées et critique littéraire, XXII. Geneva and Paris: Droz, 1972.

Gruber, Alain-Charles, and Dominique Keller. "Chinoiserie-China als Utopie." *Du* 4 (April 1975): 18–55.

Grundmann, Gunther. *Das Riesengebirge in der Malerei der Romantik*. Third revised edition. Munich-Pasing: Bergstadtverlag Wilh. Gottl. Korn, 1965.

Gudiol Jose. *Goya, 1746–1828: Biography, Analytical Study and Catalogue of His Paintings*. Translated by Kenneth Lyons. Four vols. Barcelona: Poligrafa, 1971.

Guerlac, Henry. "An Augustan Monument: The Optics of Isaac Newton." In *The Varied Pattern: Studies in the Eighteenth Century*. Edited by Peter Hughes. Toronto: Hakkert, 1971.

Guillén, Glaudio. *Literature as System: Essays toward the Theory of Literary History*. Princeton, N.J.: Princeton University Press, 1971.

Guillerme, Jacques. "Lequeu, entre l'irregulier et l'éclectique." *Dix-Huitième Siècle* 6 (1974): 167–180.

Guillerme, Jacques. "Lequeu et l'invention du mauvais gôut." *Gazette des Beaux-Arts* 66 (September 1968): 153–166.

Guillerme, Jacques. "Le malsain et l'économie de la nature." *Dixhuitieme Siècle* 9 (1977): 61–72.

Guitton, Edouard. *Jacques Delille (1738–1813), et le poème de la nature en France de 1750 à 1830*. Paris: Klincksieck, 1974.

Guitton, Edouard. "Un theme 'philosophique': 'l'invention' des poètes de Louis Racine à Népomucène Lemercier." *Studies on Voltaire and the Eighteenth Century* 88 (1972): 677–709.

Guldan, Ernst. "Das Monster-Portal am Palazzo Zuccari in Rom." *Zeitschrift für Kunstgeschichte* 32, no. 3/4 (1969): 229–261.

Guyenot, Emile. *Les sciences de la vie au XVIIᵉ et XVIIIᵉ siècles. L'idée d'évolution*. Paris: Albin Michel, 1941.

Hadfield, Miles. *Topiary and Ornamental Hedges: Their History and Cultivation*. London: A. and C. Black, 1971.

Hagen, Victor Wolfgang von. *F. Catherwood, Architect-Explorer of Two Worlds*. Barre, Mass.: Barre, 1968.

Hahn, Roger. *The Anatomy of a Scientific Institution*. Berkeley and Los Angeles: University of California Press, 1971.

Haigh, Elizabeth. "The Roots of the Vitalism of Xavier Bichat." *Bulletin of the History of Medicine* 79 (spring 1975): 72–86.

Haigh, Elizabeth. "The Vital Principle of Paul Joseph Barthez: The Clash between Monism and Dualism." *Medical History [Great Britain]* 21, no. 1 (1977): 1–14.

Hall, A. Rupert. *The Scientific Revolution, 1500–1800: The Formation of the Modern Scientific Attitude*. Second edition. Boston: Beacon, 1962.

Hall, Richard. "The Wilder Shores of Art." *Connoisseur* 188 (July 1980): 194–201.

Hammel-Haider, Gabriele. "Bemerkungen zu Meryons Stadtlandschaften." *Zeitschrift für Kunstgeschichte* 40, no. 3–4 (1977): 245–264.

Hammond, L. Davis, ed. *News from New Cythera: A Report of Bougainville's Voyage, 1766–1769*. Minneapolis: University of Minnesota Press, 1970.

Hans, James S. "Gaston Bachelard and the Phenomenology of the Reading Consciousness." *Journal of Aesthetics and Art Criticism* 35 (spring 1977): 315–327.

Hardie, Martin. *Watercolour Painting in Britain*. Three vols. New York: Barnes & Noble, 1967.

Hardie, Martin, and Muriel Clayton. "Thomas Daniell, R.A. (1749–1840), William Daniell, R.A. (1769–1837)." *Walker's Quarterly* 35/36 (1932): 70–75.

Harris, Eileen. "Burke and Chambers on the Sublime and the Beautiful." In *Essays in the History of Architecture Presented to Rudolf Wittkower*. London: Phaidon, 1967.

Harris, Eileen. *Thomas Wright, Arbours & Grottos. Facsimile*. New York: Scolar, 1979.

Hart, Clive. "Flight in the Renaissance." *Explorations in Renaissance Culture* 5 (1979): 20–32.

Hartman, Geoffrey H. *Beyond Formalism: Literary Essays 1958–1970*. New Haven, Conn.: Yale University Press, 1970.

Hartman, Geoffrey H. *Wordsworth's Poetry: 1787–1814*. New Haven, Conn.: Yale University Press, 1964.

Hauterive, Ernest. *Le merveilleux au XVIIIe siècle*. Geneva: Slatkine Reprints, 1973.

Hawes, Louis. *Constable's Stonehenge*. London: Victoria and Albert Museum, 1975.

Haydn, Ira. "Il Controrinascimento e la natura della natura." In *Problemi del Manierismo*. Edited by Amadeo Quondam. Naples: Guida, 1975.

Heidegger, Martin. *Der Ursprung des Kunstwerkes*. Stuttgart: Reclam, 1960.

Heilbron, J. L. *Electricity in the 17th and 18th Centuries: A Study of Early Modern Physics*. Berkeley and Los Angeles: University of California Press, 1979.

Heimann, P. M., and J. E. McGuire. "Newtonian Forces and Lockean Powers: Concepts of Matter in Eighteenth-Century Thought." In *Historical Studies in the Physical Sciences*, III. Edited by Russell McCormmach. Philadelphia: University of Pennsylvania Press, 1971.

Hellebranth, Robert. *Charles-François Daubigny (1817–1878)*. Morges: Matute, 1976.

Heller, Erich. *The Artist's Journey into the Interior, and Other Essays*. New York: Random House, 1965.

Heller, Erich. *The Disinherited Mind: Essays in Modern German Literature and Thought*. Cambridge: Bowes & Bowes, 1952.

Heller, Erich. "The Dismantling of a Marionette Theatre; or, Psychology and the Misinterpretation of Literature." *Critical Inquiry* 4 (spring 1978): 417–432.

Helsinger, Elizabeth K. *Ruskin and the Art of the Beholder*. Cambridge, Mass.: Harvard University Press, 1982.

Hemmings, F. W. J. "The Origins of the Terms *naturalisme, naturaliste*." *French Studies* 8 (April 1954): 109–121.

Hemphill, Marie-Louise. "Le carnet de croquis du séjour en Angleterre en 1815 de Charles-Alexandre Lesueur (1778–1846)." *Bulletin de la Société de l'Histoire de l'Art Français, 1975* (1976): 237–244.

Hennebo, Dieter, and Alfred Hoffmann. *Geschichte der Deutschen Gartenkunst.* Vol. III. Hamburg: Broschek, 1963.

Hercenberg, Bernard. *Nicolas Vleughels peintre et directeur de l'Académie de France à Rome, 1668–1737.* Paris: Léonce Laget, 1975.

Herget, Elisabeth. *Die Sala Terrena im Deutschen Barock.* Frankfurt-am-Main: n.p., 1954.

Herrmann, Luke. *British Landscape Painting of the Eighteenth-Century.* New York: Oxford University Press, 1974.

Hermann, Wolfgang. *Laugier and Eighteenth-Century French Theory.* London: A. Zwemmer, 1962.

Hewison, Robert. *John Ruskin: The Argument of the Eye.* Princeton, N.J.: Princeton University Press, 1976.

Hilles, Frederick W., and Harold Bloom, eds. *From Sensibility to Romanticism: Essays Presented to Frederick A. Pottle.* New York: Oxford University Press, 1965.

Hobson, Marian. *The Object of Art. The Theory of Illusion in Eighteenth-Century France.* Cambridge University Press, 1982.

Hocke, Gustav René. *Die Welt als Labyrinth. Manier und Manie in der Europäischer Kunst.* Hamburg: Rowohlt, 1957.

Hofmann, Werner. *Caspar David Friedrich, 1774–1840.* Hamburg: Kunsthalle, 1974.

Hofmann, Werner. *Caspar David Friedrich und die Deutsche Nachwelt.* Frankfurt-am-Main: Suhrkamp, 1977.

Hofmann, Werner. "Les écrivains-dessinateurs." *Revue de l'Art* 44 (1979): 7–18.

Holcomb, Adele M. "The Bridge in the Middle Distance: Symbolic Elements in Romantic Landscape." *Art Quarterly* 37 (spring 1974): 31–58.

Holcomb, Adele M. "Devil's Den: An Early Drawing by John Sell Cotmann." *Master Drawings* 2, no. 4 (1973): 393–398.

Honour, Hugh. *The European Vision of America.* Kent, Ohio: Kent State University Press, 1975.

Honour, Hugh. *Romanticism.* New York: Harper & Row, 1979.

Hourticq, Louis. "L'exposition du paysage français de Poussin à Corot." *La Revue de l'Art Ancien et Moderne* 48 (July–August 1925): 101–114.

Howell, Wilbur Samuel. *Poetics, Rhetoric, and Logic: Studies in the Basic Disciplines of Criticism.* Ithaca, N.Y.: Cornell University Press, 1975.

Huard, P., and M. Wong. "Les enquêtes scientifiques françaises et l'exploration du monde exotique aux XVIIᵉ et XVIIIᵉ siècles." *Bulletin de l'Ecole Française d'Extrême Orient* 52, no. 1 (1964): 143–156.

Huisman, Philippe. *French Watercolors of the Eighteenth Century.* Translated by Diane Imber. New York: Viking, 1969.

Huizinga, Jan. *Parerga.* Basel: Burg, 1945.

Humbert, Jean. "Les obélisques de Paris—projets et réalisations." *Revue de l'Art* 23 (1974): 9–29.

Hunt, John Dixon, ed. *Encounters: Essays on Literature and the Visual Arts.* London: Studio Vista, 1971.

Hunt, John Dixon, ed. *The Figure in the Landscape: Poetry, Painting, and Gardening during the Eighteenth Century.* Baltimore: Johns Hopkins University Press, 1976.

Hunt, John Dixon. "Wondrous Deep and Dark: Turner and the Sublime." *Georgia Review* 30 (spring 1976): 139–164.

Hunt, John Dixon, and Peter Willis, eds. *The Genius of the Place. The English Landscape Garden 1620–1820.* London: Paul Elek, 1975.

Husserl, Edmund. *Ideas: General Introduction to Pure Phenomenology.* Translated by W. R. Boyce Gibson. London: Allen & Unwin, 1931.

Hussey, Christopher. *English Gardens and Landscapes, 1700–1750.* New York: Funk & Wagnalls, 1967.

Hussey, Christopher. *The Picturesque: Studies in a Point of View.* New York: G. P. Putnam's Sons, 1927.

Ilg, Albert. *Die Fischer von Erlach.* Two vols. Vienna: Carl Konegen, 1895.

Irwin, David. "Jacob More, Neo-Classical Landscape Painter." *Burlington* 114 (November 1972): 775–778.

Irwin, David, and Francina Irwin. *Scottish Painters at Home and Abroad, 1700–1900.* London: Faber and Faber, 1975.

Irwin, John T. *American Hieroglyphics: The Symbol of the Egyptian Hieroglyphics in the American Renaissance.* New Haven, Conn.: Yale University Press, 1980.

Iseninger, Gary. "The Work of Art as Artifact." *British Journal of Aesthetics* 13 (winter 1973): 3–16.

Ivins, William M., Jr. *Prints and Books. Informal Papers.* Edited by A. Hyatt Mayor. New York: Da Capo, 1969.

Ivins, William M., Jr. *Prints and Visual Communication.* Cambridge, Mass.: Harvard University Press, 1953.

Jackson, J. B. *The Necessity for Ruins and Other Topics.* Amherst: University of Massachusetts Press, 1980.

Jackson, Wallace. *Immediacy: The Development of a Critical Concept from Addison to Coleridge.* Amsterdam: Rodopi, 1973.

Jammer, Max. *Concepts of Force: A Study in the Foundations of Dynamics.* Cambridge, Mass.: Harvard University Press, 1957.

Janeck, Axel. "Naturalismus und Realismus. Untersuchungen zur Darstellung der Natur bei Pieter van Laer und Claude Lorraine." *Storia dell'Arte* 28 (1976): 285–307.

Janson, H. W. "The 'Image Made by Chance' in Renaissance Thought." In *De Artibus Opuscula, XL, Essays in Honor of Erwin Panofsky.* Edited by Millard Meiss. Zurich: Buehler, 1960.

Jauss, H. R., ed. *Nachahmung und Illusion, Colloquium, Giessen, Juni 1963.* Munich: Wilhelm Fink, 1965.

Jauss, H. R., ed. *Literaturgeschichte als Provokation.* Frankfurt-am-Main: Suhrkamp, 1970.

Johnson, Lee McKay. *The Metaphor of Painting. Essays on Baudelaire, Ruskin, Proust, and Pater.* Ann Arbor, Mich.: UMI Research Press, 1980.

Jones, Howard Mumford. *Revolution and Romanticism.* Cambridge, Mass.: Belknap Press of Harvard University Press, 1974.

Jones, Richard Foster. *Ancients and Moderns: A Study of the Rise of the Scientific Movement in Seventeenth-Century England.* Second revised edition. St Louis: Washington University, 1961.

Jones, Richard Foster. "The Background of the Attack on Science in the Age of Pope." In *Pope and His Contemporaries: Essays Presented to George Sherburn.* Oxford: Clarendon, 1949.

Jones, William Powell. *The Rhetoric of Science: A Study of Scientific Ideas and Imagery in Eighteenth-Century Poetry.* Berkeley and Los Angeles: University of California Press, 1966.

Joppien, Rüdiger. "Etude de quelques portraits ethnologiques dans l'oeuvre d'André Thévet." *Gazette des Beaux-Arts* 89 (April 1978): 125–136.

Joppien, Rüdiger. *Philippe Jacques de Loutherbourg, R.A.* Kenwood, Iveagh Bequest: Greater London Council, 1973.

Jullian, Philippe. *Les orientalistes. La vision de l'Orient par les peintres européens au XIXᵉ siècle.* Fribourg: Office du Livre, 1977.

Kaeppler, Adrienne L. *"Artificial Curiosities": An Exposition of Native Manufactures Collected on the Three Pacific Voyages of Captain James Cook, R.N.* Honolulu: Bishop Museum Press, 1978.

Kallich, Martin. "The Association of Ideas and Critical Theory: Hobbes, Locke, and Addison." *ELH* 12 (December 1945): 290–315.

Kammerer, Friedrich. *Zur Geschichte des Landschaftsgefühls im frühen achthzehnten Jahrhundert.* Berlin: S. Calvary, 1909.

Kaufmann, Emil. *Architecture in the Age of Reason.* Cambridge, Mass.: Archon, 1966.

Kaufmann, Thomas Da Costa. "Arcimboldo's Imperial Allegories." *Zeitschrift für Kunstgeschichte* 39, no. 4 (1976): 275–296.

Kayser, Wolfgang. *The Grotesque in Art and Literature.* Translated by Ulrich Weisstein. New York: McGraw-Hill, 1963.

Keast, William R., ed. *Seventeenth-Century English Poetry: Modern Essays in Criticism.* New York: Oxford University Press, 1962.

Keith, W. J. *The Rural Tradition: A Study of the Non-Fiction Prose Writers of the English Countryside.* University of Toronto Press, 1974.

Kemp, Martin. "A Date for Chardin's 'Lady Taking Tea.' " *Burlington* 120 (January 1978): 22–25.

Kemp, Martin. *Leonardo da Vinci: The Marvellous Works of Nature and Man.* Cambridge, Mass.: Harvard University Press, 1981.

Kemp, Wolfgang. "Die Höhle der Ewigkeit." *Zeitschrift für Kunstgeschichte* 32, no. 2 (1969): 133–155.

Kendrick, T. D. *The Lisbon Earthquake.* London: Methuen, 1956.

Kermal, Salim. "The Significance of Natural Beauty." *British Journal of Aesthetics* 19 (spring 1979): 147–166.

Keyes, George S. "Pieter Mulier the Elder." *Oud Holland* 90, no. 4 (1976): 230–261.

Kiernan, Colm. *"Science and the Enlightenment in Eighteenth-Century France." Studies on Voltaire and the Eighteenth Century* 59 (1968).

King-Hele, Desmond. *Erasmus Darwin*. New York: Charles Scribner's Sons, 1963.

Kitson, Michael. "Painting from Nature." *Burlington* 123 (February 1981): 112–115.

Kitson, Michael. *Salvator Rosa*. London: Arts Council of Great Britain, 1973.

Klein, Robert. *La forme et l'intelligible. Ecrits sur la renaissance et l'art moderne*. Edited by André Chastel. Paris: Gallimard, 1970.

Klein, Robert, and Henry Zerner. *Italian Art 1500–1600*. Edited by H. W. Janson. New York: Prentice-Hall, 1966.

Knight, G. Wilson. *The Starlit Dome. Studies in the Poetry of Vision*. London: Oxford University Press, 1941.

Knoepflmacher, U. C., and G. B. Tennyson, eds. *Nature and the Victorian Imagination*. Berkeley and Los Angeles: University of California Press, 1977.

Koch, Robert A. *Joachim Patinir*. Princeton, N.J.: Princeton University Press, 1968.

Körte, Werner. "Deinocrates und die Barocke Phantasie." *Die Antike* 13 (1937): 289–312.

Koester, Olaf. "Joos de Momper the Younger. Prolegomena to the Study of His Paintings." *Artes* 2 (1966): 5–69.

Koopmann, Helmut, and Schmoll, J. Adolf, gen. Eisenwerth, eds. *Beiträge zur Theorie der Künste im 19. Jahrhundert*. Two vols. Frankfurt-am-Main: Vittorio Klostermann, 1971.

Korsmeyer, Carolyn. "The Two Beauties: A Perspective on Hutcheson's Aesthetics." *Journal of Aesthetics and Art Criticism* 38 (winter 1979): 145–151.

Kortum, Hans. *Charles Perrault und Nicolas Boileau. Der Antike-Streit im Zeitalter der Klassischen Französichen Literatur*. Berlin: Rütten & Loening, 1966.

Koyré, Alexandre. *From the Closed World to the Infinite Universe*. Baltimore: Johns Hopkins University Press, 1957.

Koyré, Alexandre. *Newtonian Studies*. Phoenix Books of University of Chicago Press, 1965.

Kris, Ernst. "Der Stil 'rustique,' die Verwendung des Naturabgusses bei Wenzel Jamnitzer und Bernard Palissy." *Jahrbuch der Kunsthistorischen Sammlungen in Wien* N.F. 1 (1926): 137–208.

Kristeller, Paul. *Andrea Mantegna*. Berlin and Leipzig: Cosmos Verlag fur Kunst und Wissenschaft, 1902.

Kroeber, Karl, and William Walling, eds. *Images of Romanticism: Verbal and Visual Affinities*. New Haven, Conn.: Yale University Press, 1978.

Kuhn, Thomas S. *The Structure of Scientific Revolutions*. University of Chicago Press, 1962.

Lacambre, Géneviève. "Pierre-Henri de Valenciennes en Italie: Un journal de voyage inédit." *Bulletin de Société de l'Histoire de l'Art Français*, 1978 (1980): 139–172.

Lamb, Carl. *Die Villa d'Este in Tivoli, ein Beitrag zur Geschichte der Gartenkunst*. Munich: Prestel, 1966.

Lamb, H. H. *Climate: Present, Past and Future*. Two vols. London: Methuen, 1972.

Lamb, Jonathan. "Language and Hartleian Associationism in *A Sentimental Journey*." *Eighteenth-Century Studies* 13 (spring 1980): 285–312.

Landow, George P. *The Aesthetic and Critical Theories of John Ruskin*. Princeton, N.J.: Princeton University Press, 1971.

Langner, Johannes. "Architecture pastorale sous Louis XVI." *Art de France* 3 (1963): 171–186.

Lanham, Richard A. *The Motives of Eloquence: Literary Rhetoric in the Renaissance.* New Haven, Conn.: Yale University Press, 1976.

Lankheit, Klaus. *Der Tempel der Vernunft. Unveröffenliche Zeichnungen von Etienne-Louis Boullée.* Basel and Stuttgart: Birkhäuser, 1968.

La Vaissière, Pascal de. "Paysagistes et paysages voyageurs. Philibert-Bénôit Delarue et L'Encyclopédie." *Nouvelles de l'Estampe* 29 (September–October 1976): 13–17.

La Vaissière, Pascal de. "Un regain d'activité graphique de Philibert-Bénôit Delarue. Une recherche d'absolu." *Gazette des Beaux-Arts* 90 (October 1977): 113–123.

Lazzaro-Bruno, Claudia. The Villa Lante at Bagnaia. Ph.D. diss., Princeton University, 1974.

Lebensztejn, Jean-Claude. "En blanc et noir." *Macula* 1 (1977): 4–13.

Lee, Rensselaer W. *Names on Trees: Ariosto into Art.* Princeton, N.J.: Princeton University Press, 1977.

Leeuw, Hendrik de. *From Flying Horse to Man in the Moon.* New York: Saint Martin's, 1963.

Le Flamanc, Auguste. *Les utopies prérévolutionnaires et la philosophie du 18ᵉ siècle.* Paris: Librairie Philosophique J. Vrin, 1934.

Leichter als Luft. Zur Geschichte der Ballonfahrt. Edited by Peter Berghaus and Bernard Korzus. Münster: Westfälisches Landesmuseum für Kunst und Kulturgeschichte, 1978.

Le Roy Ladurie, Emmanuel. *Histoire du climat depuis l'an mil.* Paris: Flammarion, 1967.

Levine, George. *The Realistic Imagination: English Fiction from Frankenstein to Lady Chatterly.* University of Chicago Press, 1981.

Levine, Joseph M. "Ancients and Moderns Reconsidered." *Eighteenth-Century Studies* 15 (fall 1981): 72–89.

Levine, Steven Z. *Monet and His Critics.* New York: Garland, 1976.

Levitine, George. *The Dawn of Bohemianism: The Barbu Rebellion and Primitivism in Neoclassical France.* University Park: Pennsylvania State University Press, 1977.

Levitine, George. "The Influence of Lavater and Girodet's *Expression des sentiments de l'âme.*" *Art Bulletin* 36 (March 1954): 32–44.

Levitine, George. "Quelques aspects peu connus de Girodet." *Gazette des Beaux-Arts* 65 (April 1965): 230–246.

Levitine, George. *The Sculpture of Falconet. With Translations of Eda Mezer Levitine of the Réflexions sur la sculpture.* Greenwich, Conn.: New York Graphic Society, 1971.

Licht, Fred. *Sculpture 19th and 20th Centuries. A History of Western Sculpture.* Edited by Fred Licht. Greenwich, Conn.: New York Graphic Society, 1967.

Lindsay, Jack. *J. M. W. Turner, His Life and Work, a Critical Biography.* Greenwich, Conn.: New York Graphic Society, 1966.

Lindsay, Lionel. *Conrad Martens: The Man and His Art.* Revised by Douglas Dundas. Sydney: Angus and Robertson, 1968.

Lippky, Gerhard. "Eduard Hildebrandt: der Maler des Kosmos aus Danzig." *Westpreussen Jahrbuch* 19 (1969): 78–84.

Litz, Francis Edwards. "Richard Bentley on Beauty, Irregularity, and Mountains." *ELH* 12 (December 1945): 327–332.

Löschner, Renate. *Deutsche Künstler in Latein Amerika. Maler und Naturforscher des 19. Jahrhunderts illustrieren einen Kontinent.* Berlin: Dietrich Reimer, 1978.

Lonchamp, F. C. *J.-L. Aberli (1723–1786), son temps, sa vie et son oeuvre.* Paris and Lausanne: Librairie des Bibliophiles, 1927.

Lonchamp, F. C. *Un siècle d'art suisse (1730–1830). L'estampe et le livre à gravures. Guide de l'amateur.* Lausanne: Librairie des Bibliophiles, 1920.

Lovejoy, Arthur O. "The Chinese Origin of Romanticism." *Journal of English and Germanic Philology* 32 (January 1933): 1–20.

Lovejoy, Arthur O., and George Boas. *Primitivism and Related Ideas in Antiquity.* Vol. I. Baltimore: Johns Hopkins University Press, 1935.

Lowenthal, David, and Hugh C. Prince. "The English Landscape." *Geographical Review* 54 (July 1964): 309–346.

Lukács, Georg. *Studies in European Realism: A Sociological Survey of the Writings of Balzac, Stendhal, Zola, Tolstoy, Gorki and Others.* Translated by Edith Bowe. London: Hillway, 1950.

Lunsingh Scheurleer, D. F. *Chinese Export Porcelain. Chine de commande.* Salem, N.H.: Faber and Faber, 1974.

McCarthy, Michael. "Sir Roger Newdigate: Some Piranesian Drawings." *Burlington* 120 (October 1978): 671–674.

Macaulay, Rose. *Pleasure of Ruins.* New York: Walker, 1966.

Mack, Maynard. *The Garden and the City: Retirement and Politics in the Later Poetry of Pope, 1731–1743.* University of Toronto Press, 1969.

McFarland, Thomas. *Romanticism and the Forms of Ruin: Wordsworth, Coleridge, and Modalities of Fragmentation.* Princeton, N.J.: Princeton University Press, 1981.

McKay, Helen M., ed. *The South African Drawings of William J. Burchell.* Two vols. Johannesburg: Witwatersrand University Press, 1952.

McMordie, Colin. "Louis-François Cassas: The Formation of a Neo-Classical Landscapist." *Apollo* 103 (March 1976): 228–230.

McMullin, Ernan. *Newton on Matter and Activity.* Notre Dame, Indiana: University of Notre Dame Press, 1978.

Majewski, Henry F. "Mercier and the Preromantic Myth of the End of the World." *Studies in Romanticism* 7 (autumn 1967): 16–29.

The Malaspina Expedition: "In the Pursuit of Knowledge." Santa Fe: Museum of New Mexico Press, 1977.

Malek, James. "Charles Lamotte's 'An Essay upon Poetry and Painting' and Eighteenth-Century British Aesthetics." *Journal of Aesthetics and Art Criticism* 29 (summer 1971): 467–473.

Malins, Edward. *English Landscaping and Literature, 1660–1840.* London: Oxford University Press, 1966.

Manley, Lawrence. *Convention, 1500–1700.* Cambridge, Mass.: Harvard University Press, 1980.

Manwaring, Elizabeth. *Italian Landscape in Eighteenth-Century England.* New York: Oxford University Press, 1925.

Marandel, Jean Patrice. "Pittori stranieri a Napoli." *Civiltà del '700 a Napoli, 1734–1799.* Vol. I. Naples: Centro Di, 1979.

Margolis, Joseph. "Aesthetic Appreciation and the Imperceptible." *British Journal of Aesthetics* 16 (August 1976): 305–312.

Marlier, Georges. "Pourquoi ces rochers à visages humains?" *Connaissances des Arts* 129 (June 1962): 82–91.

Martienssen, Heather. "Madame Tussaud and the Limits of Likeness." *British Journal of Aesthetics* 20 (spring 1980): 128–134.

Marty-L'Herme, Jean-Jacques. "Les cas de Jean-Jacques Lequeu." *Macula* 5/6 (1979): 138–149.

Mauner, George. *Manet, peintre-philosophe.* University Park: Pennsylvania State University Press, 1975.

Maury, Fernand. *Etude sur la vie et les oeuvres de Bernardin de Saint-Pierre.* Geneva: Slatkine Reprints, 1971.

Mazzeo, J. A., ed. *Reason and the Imagination: Studies in the History of Ideas 1600–1800.* New York: Columbia University Press, 1962.

Megaw, J. V. S., ed. *Employ'd as a Discoverer: Papers Presented at the Captain Cook Bi-Centenary Symposium.* Sydney: A. H. & A. W. Reed, 1971.

Méjanès, J.-F. "A Spontaneous Feeling for Nature. French Eighteenth-Century Landscape Drawings." *Apollo* 104 (November 1976): 396–404.

Mercier, Roger. "La théorie des climats des 'Réflections critiques' à 'l'Esprit des lois.' " *Revue d'Histoire Littéraire de la France* 53 (1953): part I, 17–37.

Methken, Günter. "Jean-Jacques Lequeu ou l'architecture rêvée." *Gazette des Beaux-Arts* 65 (April 1965): 213–230.

Metzger, Hélène. "La littérature scientifique française au XVIIIᵉ siècle." *Archeion* 16 (1934): 1–17.

Miller, Craig W. "Coleridge's Concept of Nature." *Journal of the History of Ideas* 25 (January–March 1964): 77–96.

Miller, Naomi. *Heavenly Caves: Reflections on the Garden Grotto.* New York: Braziller, 1982.

Miller, Norbert. *Archäologie des Traums.* Munich and Vienna: Hanser, 1978.

Mitchell, T. C. *Captain Cook and the South Pacific.* British Museum Yearbook 3 London: British Museum Publications, 1979.

Mittig, Hans-Ernst, and Völker Plagemann. *Denkmaler im 19. Jahrhundert, Deutung und Kritik.* Studien zur Kunst des 19. Jahrhunderts, vol. 20. Munich: Prestel, 1972.

Monglond, André. *Le préromantise français.* Two vols. Grenoble: B. Arthaud, 1930.

Moore, Cecil Albert. *Backgrounds of English Literature, 1700–1760.* New York: Octagon, 1969.

Mornet, Daniel. *Le romantisme en France au XVIIIᵉ siècle.* Geneva: Slatkine Reprints, 1970.

Mornet, Daniel. *Les sciences de la nature en France au XVIIIᵉ siècle. Un châpitre de l'histoire des idées.* Paris: Armand Colin, 1911.

Mornet, Daniel. *Le sentiment de la nature en France de J.-J. Rousseau à Bernardin de Saint-Pierre.* Paris: Hachette, 1907.

Mortier, Roland. " 'Sensibility,' 'Neoclassicism,' or 'Preromanticism.' " In *Eighteenth-Century Studies Presented to Arthur M. Wilson.* Edited by Peter Gay. Hanover, N.H.: University Press of New England, 1972.

Moss, Roger B. "Sterne's Punctuation." *Eighteenth-Century Studies* 15 (winter 1981–82): 179–200.

Mosser, Monique. *Jardins en France, 1760–1820. Pays d'illusion, terre d'expériences*. Paris: Hôtel de Sully, 1977.

Mrazek, Wilhelm. "Metaphorische Denkform und ikonologische Stilform. Zur Grammatik und Syntax bildlicher Formelelemente der Barockkunst." *Alte und Moderne Kunst* 9 (March–April 1964): 15–23.

Muller-Hofstede, Annedore. *Der Landschaftsmaler Pascha Johann Friedrich Weitsch (1723–1803)*. Braunschweig: Waisenhaus, 1973.

Murphy, Alexandra R. *Visions of Vesuvius*. Boston: Museum of Fine Arts, 1978.

Naef, Weston J., and James N. Wood. *Era of Exploration. The Rise of Landscape Photography in the American West, 1860–1885*. Boston: New York Graphic Society, 1975.

National Maritime Museum: Catalogue of the Library. Voyages and Travels. Vol. I. London: Her Majesty's Stationery Office, 1968.

The Natural Paradise: Painting in America 1800–1950. Edited by Kynaston McShine. New York: Museum of Modern Art, 1976.

Néagu, Philippe. "Meryon: Le voyage en Océanie. Lettres de Meryon à l'administration des beaux-arts concernant la publication de son *Voyage en Océanie*." *Nouvelles de l'Estampe* 58–59 (July–October 1981): 12–23.

Nelkin, Halina. *Alexander von Humboldt. His Portraits and Their Artists: A Documentary Iconography*. Berlin: Dietrich Reimer, 1980.

Nelkin, Halina. *Humboldtiana at Harvard*. Cambridge, Mass.: Harvard University Press, 1976.

Nemitz, Fritz. *Caspar David Friedrich, die unendliche Landschaft*. Munich: F. Bruckmann, 1940.

Nerdinger, Winfried. "Zur Entstehung des Realismus-Begriffs in Frankreich und zu seiner Anwendung im Bereich der ungegendständlichen Kunst." *Städel-Jahrbuch*, N.F., 5 (1975): 227–246.

Nicolson, Marjorie Hope. *The Breaking of the Circle: Studies in the Effect of the "New Science" upon Seventeenth-Century Poetry*. New York: Columbia University Press, 1960.

Nicolson, Marjorie Hope. *Mountain Gloom and Mountain Glory: The Development of the Aesthetics of the Infinite*. Ithaca, N.Y.: Cornell University Press, 1959.

Nicolson, Marjorie Hope. *Newton Demands the Muse. Newton's "Opticks" and the Eighteenth-Century Poets*. London: Archon, 1963.

Nicolson, Marjorie Hope. *Science and the Imagination*. Hamden, Conn.: Archon, 1976.

Nicolson, Marjorie Hope, and G. S. Rousseau. *"This Long Disease, My Life." Alexander Pope and the Sciences*. Princeton, N.J.: Princeton University Press, 1968.

Noël, Martha. "Le thème de l'eau chez Senancour." *Revue des Sciences Humaines* 29 (July–September 1962): 357–365.

Nørgaard, Eric. *The Book of Balloons*. Translated and revised by Eric Hildesheim. New York: Crown, 1971.

Novak, Barbara. *American Painting of the Nineteenth Century: Realism, Idealism, and the American Experience*. New York: Harper & Row, 1979.

Novak, Barbara. *Nature and Culture: American Landscape Painting 1825–1875*. New York: Oxford University Press, 1980.

Novotny, Fritz. *Adalbert Stifter als Maler*. Vienna: A. Schroll, 1941.

Noyes, Russell. *Wordsworth and the Art of Landscape*. Bloomington: Indiana University Press, 1968.

Nyberg, Dorothea. *Meissonnier, an Eighteenth-Century Maverick*. New York: Benjamin Blom, 1969.

Oechslin, Werner. "Pyramide et sphère. Notes sur l'architecture révolutionnaire du XVIIIe siècle et ses sources italiennes." *Gazette des Beaux-Arts* 77 (April 1971): 200–238.

O'Gorman, Edmundo. *The Invention of America*. Bloomington: University of Indiana Press, 1961.

Okun, Henry. "Ossian in Painting." *Journal of the Warburg and Courtauld Institutes* 30 (1967): 327–356.

Ong, Walter J. *Rhetoric, Romance, and Technology*. Ithaca, N.Y.: Cornell University Press, 1971.

Opper, Jacob. *Science and the Arts: A Study in Relationships from 1600–1900*. Rutherford, N.J.: Fairleigh Dickinson University Press, 1973.

Orgel, Stephen. *The Illusion of Power: Political Theater in the English Renaissance*. Berkeley and Los Angeles: University of California Press, 1975.

Orgel, Stephen, and Roy Strong. *Inigo Jones: The Theatre of the Stuart Court*. Two vols. Berkeley and Los Angeles: University of California Press, 1973.

Orian, Alfred. *La vie et l'oeuvre de Philibert Commerson des Humbers*. Mauritius: Mauritius Printing Co., 1973.

Osbourne, Harold. "Concepts of Order in the Natural Sciences and the Visual Fine Arts." *Leonardo* 14 (autumn 1981): 290–294.

Ossian und die Kunst um 1800. Hamburg: Kunsthalle, 1974.

Ozouf, Mona. *La fête révolutionnaire 1789–1799*. Paris: Gallimard, 1976.

Panofsky, Erwin. " 'Nebulae in Pariete': Notes on Erasmus' Eulogy on Dürer." *Journal of the Warburg and Courtauld Institutes* 14 (1951): 34–39.

Parks, George P. "The Turn to the Romantic in the Travel Literature of the Eighteenth Century." *Modern Language Quarterly* 25 (March 1964): 22–23.

Parris, Leslie, Ian Fleming-Williams, and Conal Shields. *Constable: Paintings, Watercolours & Drawings*. London: Tate Gallery, 1976.

Patterson, Helen Temple. "Poetic Genesis: Sebastien Mercier into Victor Hugo." *Studies on Voltaire and the Eighteenth Century* (1960).

Paulson, Ronald. *Emblem and Expression. Meaning in English Art of the Eighteenth-Century*. London: Thames and Hudson, 1975.

Pearce, Roy Harvey. "The Eighteenth-Century Scottish Primitivists: Some Reconsiderations." *ELH* 12 (September 1945): 203–220.

Penny, Nicholas. "Ruskin's Ideas on Growth in Architecture and Ornament." *British Journal of Aesthetics* 13 (summer 1973): 276–286.

Percy, Ann. *Giovanni Benedetto Castiglione (1616–1670)*. Philadelphia: Museum of Art, 1971.

Pérouse de Montclos, J.-M. *Etienne-Louis Boullée (1728–1799) de l'architecture classique à l'architecture révolutionnaire*. Paris: Arts et Métiers, 1969.

Pérouse de Montclos, J.-M. "Le sixième ordre d'architecture, ou la pratique des ordres suivants les nations." *Journal of the Society of Architectural Historians* 36 (December 1977): 223–240.

Pevsner, Nikolaus, ed. *The Picturesque Garden and Its Influence outside the British Isles.* Washington, D.C.: Dumbarton Oaks, 1974.

Pevsner, Nikolaus, ed. *Studies in Art, Architecture and Design.* Two vols. London: Thames and Hudson, 1968.

Piechotta, Hans Joachim, ed. *Reise und Utopie. Zur Literatur der Spätaufklarung.* Frankfurt-am-Main: Suhrkamp, 1976.

Piel, Friedrich. *Das Ornament-Groteske in der Italienischen Renaissance; zu Ihrer kategorialen Struktur und Entstehung.* Berlin: de Gruyter, 1962.

Piel, Friedrich, and Jörg Traeger, eds. *Festschrift Wolfgang Braunfels.* Tübingen: Ernst Wasmuth, 1977.

Piggott, Stuart. *The Druids.* New York: Praeger, 1975.

Piper, H. W. *The Active Universe: Pantheism and the Concept of Imagination in the English Romantic Poets.* London: Athlone, 1962.

Piper, H. W. "The Pantheistic Sources of Coleridge's Early Poetry." *Journal of the History of Ideas* 20 (January 1959): 47–59.

Piranèse et les français, 1740–1790. Rome: Edizione dell'Elefante, 1976.

Pochat, Götz. *Der Exotismus des Mittelalters und der Renaissance.* Stockholm: Almquist & Wiksell, 1970.

Pointon, Marcia. "Geology and Landscape Painting in Nineteenth-Century England." *British Society for the History of Science* 1 (1979): 84–108.

Pomeau, René. "La Pérouse philosophe." *Approches des Lumières. Mélanges offerts à Jean Fabre.* Paris: Klincksieck, 1974.

Popyzecka, Maria. "Le paysage industriel vers 1600." *Bulletin du Musée National de Varsovie* 14 (1973): 42–51.

Possin, Hans-Joachim. *Natur und Landschaft bei Addison.* Edited by Gerhard Müller-Schwefe and Friedrich Schubel. Tübingen: Max Niemeyer, 1965.

Possin, Hans-Joachim. *Reisen und Literatur. Das Thema des Reisens in der Englischen Literatur des 18. Jahrhunderts.* Tübingen: Max Niemeyer, 1972.

Poulet, Georges. *The Metamorphoses of the Circle.* Translated by Carley Dawson and Elliott Coleman. Baltimore: Johns Hopkins University Press, 1966.

Poulet, Georges. *Trois essais de mythologie romantique.* Paris: José Corti, 1966.

Prause, Marianne. *Carl Gustav Carus, Leben und Werke.* Berlin: Deutscher Verlag für Kunstwissenschaft, 1968.

Price, Martin. *To the Palace of Wisdom. Studies in Order and Energy from Dryden to Blake.* Garden City, N.Y.: Doubleday, 1964.

Prince, Hugh C. "The Geographical Imagination." *Landscape* 11 (winter 1961–62): 22–25.

Proust, Jacques. *L'Encyclopédie.* Paris: Armand Colin, 1965.

Raeber, Willi. *Caspar Wolf, 1735–1783, sein Leben und sein Werk. Ein Beitrag zur Geschichte der Schweizer Malerei des 18. Jahrhunderts.* Munich: Sauerländer, Prestel, 1979.

Raines, Robert. "Watteaus and 'Watteaus' in England before 1760." *Gazette des Beaux-Arts* 88 (February 1977): 51–64.

Rappaport, Rhoda. "Geology and Orthodoxy: The Case of Noah's Flood in Eighteenth-Century Thought." *British Journal of the History of Science* 11 (1978): 1–18.

Raval, R. L. "The Picturesque: Knight, Turner and Hipple." *British Journal of Aesthetics* 18 (summer 1978): 249–260.

Ray, N. R. *A Descriptive Catalogue of the Daniells' Work in the Victoria Memorial.* Calcutta: M. R. Mitra, n.d.

Rehder, Helmut. *Die Philosophie der unendlichen Landschaft. Ein Beitrag zur Geschichte der Romantischen Weltanschauung.* Halle and Saale: Max Niemeyer, 1932.

Reudenbach, Bruno. *G. B. Piranesi. Architektur als Bild.* Munich: Prestel, 1979.

Reutersvärd, Oscar. "De 'sjunkande' cenotafierna hos Moreau, Fontaine, Boullée och Gay." *Könsthistorisk Tidskrift* 28 (1959): 110–126.

Revello, Jose Torre. *Los artistas pintores de la expedicion Malaspina.* Buenos Aires: Jacobo Pevser, 1944.

Rheims, Maurice. *La sculpture au XIXe siècle.* Paris: Arts et Métiers Graphiques, 1972.

Richert, Gertrud. *Johann Moritz Rugendas. Ein Deutscher Maler im Ibero-Amerika.* Munich: Filser, 1952.

Ritterbush, Philip C. *Overtures to Biology: The Speculations of Eighteenth-Century Naturalists.* New Haven, Conn.: Yale University Press, 1964.

Robson-Scott, W. D. *The Literary Background of the Gothic Revival in Germany.* Oxford: Clarendon, 1965.

Robson-Scott, W. D. *The Younger Goethe and the Visual Arts.* Cambridge University Press, 1981.

Røstvig, Maren-Sofie. *The Happy Man: Studies in the Metamorphoses of a Classical Ideal.* Two vols. New York: Humanities Press, 1971.

Röttigen, Steffi. "Mengs, Alessandro Albani und Winckelmann—Idee und Gestalt des Parnass in der Villa Albani." *Storia dell'Arte* 30/31 (1977): 87–156.

Role, A. *Vie adventureuse d'un savant: Philibert Commerson, martyr de la botanique, 1727–1773.* Saint Denis: Cazal, 1973.

Rose, Mary Carmen. "Nature as Aesthetic Object: An Essay in Meta-Aesthetics." *British Journal of Aesthetics* 16 (winter 1976): 3–12.

Rosenau, Helen. *The Ideal City, Its Architectural Evolution.* New York: Harper & Row, 1972.

Rosenberg, Albert. "Bishop Sprat on Science and Imagery." *Isis* 43 (September 1952): 220–222.

Rosenberg, Pierre, and Isabelle Compin. "Quatre nouveaux Fragonard au Louvre." *Revue du Louvre* 2, no. 4–5 (1974): 263–278.

Rosenblum, Robert. *Modern Painting and the Northern Romantic Tradition: Friedrich to Rothko.* New York: Harper & Row, 1975.

Rosenthal, Bernard. *City of Nature: Journeys to Nature in the Age of American Romanticism.* East Brunswick, N.J.: University of Delaware Press, 1980.

Rossi, Paolo. *Francis Bacon: From Magic to Science.* Translated by Sacha Rabinovitch. London: Routledge & Kegan Paul, 1968.

Roth, Alfred G. *Die Gestirne in der Landschaftsmalerei des Abendlandes.* Edited by Hans R. Hahnloser. Bern-Bümplitz: Benteli, 1945.

Rothgeb, John Reese. The Scenographic Expression of Nature (1545–1845): The Development of Style. Ph.D. diss., Case Western Reserve University, 1971.

Rothstein, Eric. " 'Ideal Presence' and the 'Non Finito' in Eighteenth-Century Aesthetics." *Eighteenth-Century Studies* 9 (spring 1976): 307–332.

Roule, Louis. *Bernardin de Saint-Pierre et Harmonie de la nature.* Paris: Flammarion, 1930.

Rubin, James Henry. "Endymion's Dream as a Myth of Romantic Inspiration." *Art Quarterly,* N.S., 2 (spring 1978): 47–84.

Rubin, James Henry. "Gros and Girodet." *Burlington* 121 (November 1979): 716–721.

Rubin, James Henry. *Realism and Social Vision in Courbet and Proudhon.* Princeton, N.J.: Princeton University Press, 1980.

Rudwick, M. J. S. "The Emergence of a Visual Language for Geological Science, 1760–1840." *History of Science* 14 (1976): 149–195.

Rudwick, M. J. S. "Transposed Concepts from the Human Sciences in the Early Work of Charles Lyell." *British Society for the History of Science* 1 (1979): 67–83.

Russell, H. Diane. *Jacques Callot: Prints & Related Drawings.* Washington, D.C.: National Gallery of Art, 1975.

Russell, John, and Andrew Wilton. *Turner in der Schweiz.* Dubendorf: De Clivo, 1976.

Said, Edward W. *Orientalism.* New York: Pantheon, 1978.

Saisselin, Remy G. "Neoclassicisme, discours et temps." *Gazette des Beaux-Arts* 94 (July–August 1979): 18–24.

Saisselin, Remy G. *Taste in Eighteenth-Century France: Critical Reflections on the Origins of Aesthetics.* Syracuse, N.Y.: Syracuse University Press, 1965.

Salerno, Luigi, "La pittura di paesaggio." *Storia dell'Arte* 34/35 (1975): 111–124.

Sarton, George. *Six Wings. Men of Science in the Renaissance.* Bloomington: Indiana University Press, 1957.

Saunders, Jason Lewis. *Justus Lipsius, the Philosophy of Renaissance Stoicism.* New York: Liberal Arts Press, 1955.

Schapiro, Meyer. *Words and Pictures: On the Literal and the Symbolic in the Illustrations of a Text.* Edited by Thomas A. Sebeok. The Hague and Paris: Mouton, 1973.

Schenck, Eva-Maria. *Das Bilderrätsel.* Cologne: Walter Kleikamp, 1968.

Schinkel, Karl Friedrich. Werke und Wirkungen. Berlin: Martin-Gropius-Bau, 1981.

Schlosser, Julius von. *Die Kunst und Wunderkammern der Spätrenaissance. Ein Beitrag zur Geschichte des Sammelwesens.* Edited by Jean-Louis Spousel. Leipzig: Klinkhardt & Biermann, 1908.

Schlumberger, Eveline. "La foi artistique de Chateaubriand." *Connaissance des Arts* 197/ 198 (July–August 1968): 129–135.

Schmid, Walter. *Romantic Switzerland, Mirrored in the Literature and Graphic Art of the Eighteenth and Nineteenth Centuries.* Bern: Hallwag, 1965.

Schmitt, Otto. "Ein Skizzenbuchblatt C.D. Friedrich im Wallraf-Richartz-Museum." *Wallraf-Richartz Jahrbuch* 11 (1939): 290–295.

Schmoll, J. A., gen. Eisenwerth. "Naturalismus und Realismus: Versuch zur Formulierung verbindlicher Begriffe." *Städel-Jahrbuch*, N.F., 5 (1975): 247 ff.

Schofield, Robert E. *The Lunar Society of Birmingham, A Social History of Provincial Science and Industry in Eighteenth-Century England.* Oxford: Clarendon, 1963.

Schofield, Robert E. *Mechanism and Materialism: British Natural Philosophy in an Age of Reason.* Princeton, N.J.: Princeton University Press, 1970.

Schofield, Robert E. "John Wesley and Science in Eighteenth-Century England." *Isis* 49 (December 1953): 331–340.

Schon, Donald A. *Invention and the Evolution of Ideas.* London: Tavistock, 1963.

Schreiber-Favre, Alfred. *La lithographie artistique en Suisse au XIXᵉ siècle: Alexandre Calame: le paysage.* Neuchâtel: A la Baconnière, 1967.

Schwartz, Richard B. *Samuel Johnson and the New Science.* Madison: University of Wisconsin Press, 1971.

Schweiger, Peter. "The Masculine Mode." *Critical Inquiry* 5 (summer 1979): 621–633.

Schweizer, W. R. "The Swiss Print." *Connoisseur* 130 (November 1952): 85–89.

Scott, Jonathan. *Piranesi.* New York: Saint Martin's, 1975.

Scott, Wilson L. "The Significance of 'Hard Bodies' in the History of Scientific Thought." *Isis* 50 (June 1959): 199–210.

Scully, Vincent. *The Earth, the Temple, and the Gods: Greek Sacred Architecture.* New Haven, Conn.: Yale University Press, 1962.

Sergel, Johan Tobias, 1740–1814. Hamburg: Kunsthalle, 1975.

Serullaz, Arlette, and Nathalie Volle. "Dessins inédits de Fragonard, David et Drouais." *Revue du Louvre* 2 (1974): 77–81.

Sewell, Elizabeth. *The Orphic Voice: Poetry and Natural History.* New Haven, Conn.: Yale University Press, 1960.

Seznec, Jean. *Essais sur Diderot et l'antiquité.* Oxford: Clarendon, 1957.

Shapiro, Gary. "Intention and Interpretation in Art: A Semiotic Analysis." *Journal of Aesthetics and Art Criticism* 33 (fall 1974): 33–42.

Shearman, John. *Mannerism.* Harmondsworth: Penguin, 1967.

Shellim, Maurice. *The Daniells in India and the Waterfall at Papanasam.* Calcutta: The Statesman Ltd., 1970.

Shephard, Paul, Jr. "The Cross Valley Syndrome." *Landscape* 10 (spring 1961): 4–8.

Sircello, Guy. *Mind and Art.* Princeton, N.J.: Princeton University Press, 1972.

Siren, Osvald. *China and Gardens of Europe of the Eighteenth Century.* New York: Ronald, 1950.

Siren, Osvald. *Gardens of China.* New York: Ronald, 1949.

Sjögren, Christine Oertel. *The Marble Statue as Idea: Collected Essays on Adelbert Stifter's Der Nachsommer.* Chapel Hill: University of North Carolina Press, 1972.

Skultans, Vieda. *English Madness: Ideas on Insanity 1580–1890.* London: Routledge & Kegan Paul, 1980.

Smith, Anthony D. "The 'Historical Revival' in Late Eighteenth-Century England and France." *Art History* 2 (June 1979): 156–178.

Smith, Bernard. *The Antipodean Manifesto: Essays in Art and History.* Melbourne: Oxford University Press, 1976.

Smith, Bernard. *Art as Information: Reflections on the Art from Captain Cook's Voyages.* Sydney University Press, 1978.

Smith, Bernard. *Australian Painting, 1788–1960.* Melbourne: Oxford University Press, 1962.

Smith, Bernard. *European Vision and the South Pacific, 1768–1850. A Study in the History of Art and Ideas.* Oxford: Clarendon, 1960.

Snelders, H. A. M. "Romanticism and Naturphilosophie and the Inorganic Natural Sciences, 1797–1840." *Studies in Romanticism* 9 (summer 1970).

Snyder, Joel. "Picturing Vision." In *The Language of Images.* Edited by W. J. T. Mitchell. University of Chicago Press, 1980.

Snyder, Joel, and Doug Munson. *The Documentary Photograph as a Work of Art: American Photographs, 1860–1876.* Chicago: David and Alfred Smart Gallery, 1976.

Soboul, Albert. *La civilisation et la révolution française.* Collections les grandes civilisations. Edited by Raymond Bloch. Vol. I. Paris: Arthaud, 1970.

Solar, Gustav, and Jost Hösli. *Hans Conrad Escher von der Linth. Ansichten und Panoramen der Schweiz. Die Ansichten 1780–1822.* Zurich: Atlantis, 1974.

Sommervogel, Carlos. *Table méthodique des Mémoires de Trévoux.* Geneva: Slatkine Reprints, 1969.

Spector, Jack J. *Delacroix: The Death of Sardanapalus.* London: Allen Lane, 1974.

Stafford, Barbara Maria. "Beauty of the Invisible: Winckelmann and the Aesthetics of Imperceptibility." *Zeitschrift für Kunstgeschichte*, Sonderdruck, 43 (1980): 65–78.

Stafford, Barbara Maria. "Endymion's Moonbath: Art and Science in Girodet's Early Masterpiece." *Leonardo* 15, no. 3 (1982): 193–198.

Stafford, Barbara Maria. "Les météores de Girodet." *Revue de l'Art* 46 (1979): 46–51.

Stafford, Barbara Maria. "Rude Sublime: The Taste for Nature's Colossi in the Late Eighteenth and Early Nineteenth Centuries." *Gazette des Beaux-Arts* 97 (April 1976): 113–126.

Stafford, Barbara Maria. "Toward Romantic Landscape Perception: Illustrated Travel Accounts and the Rise of 'Singularity' as an Aesthetic Category." *Art Quarterly*, N.S., 1 (autumn 1977): 89–124.

Stafford, Barbara Maria. *Symbol and Myth. Humbert de Superville's Essay on Absolute Signs in Art.* Cranbury, N.J.: Associated University Presses, 1979.

Staley, Allen. *The Pre-Raphaelite Landscape.* Oxford: Clarendon, 1973.

Starobinski, Jean. "Rousseau's Happy Days." *New Literary History* 11 (autumn 1979): 147–166.

Starobinski, Jean. *1789, Les emblèmes de la raison.* Paris: Flammarion, 1973.

Stavenhagen, Lee. "Narrative Illustration and the Mute Books of Alchemy." *Explorations in Renaissance Culture* 5 (1979): 56–69.

Stechow, Wolfgang. *Peter Brueghel, the Elder.* London: Thames and Hudson, 1970.

Stechow, Wolfgang. *Dutch Landscape Painting of the Seventeenth Century.* London: Phaidon, 1966.

Steiner, George. *After Babel: Aspects of Language and Translation.* New York: Oxford University Press, 1975.

Steiner, Wendy. *The Colors of Rhetoric: Problems in the Relation between Modern Literature and Painting.* University of Chicago Press, 1982.

Stempel, Daniel. "Revelation on Mount Snowdon: Wordsworth, Coleridge, and the Fichtean Imagination." *Journal of Aesthetics and Art Criticism* 29 (spring 1971): 371–384.

Stilgoe, John R. *Common Landscape of America, 1580 to 1845.* New Haven, Conn.: Yale University Press, 1982.

Stuebe, Isabel Combs. *The Life and Works of William Hodges.* New York: Garland, 1979.

Stuebe, Isabel Combs. "William Hodges and Warren Hastings: A Study in Eighteenth-Century Patronage." *Burlington* 115 (October 1973): 659–666.

Sullivan, Michael. "Pictorial Art and the Attitude toward Nature in Ancient China." *Art Bulletin* 36 (March 1954): 1–20.

Summers, David. "Contrapposto: Style and Meaning in Renaissance Art." *Art Bulletin* 59 (September 1977): 336–361.

Summers, David. *Michelangelo and the Language of Art.* Princeton, N.J.: Princeton University Press, 1980.

Summers, Joseph H. "The Poem as Hieroglyph." In *Seventeenth-Century English Poetry.* Edited by William R. Keast. Revised edition. London: Oxford University Press, 1971.

Summerson, John. "Le tombeau de Sir John Soane." *Revue de l'Art* 30 (1975): 51–54.

Sumowski, Werner. *Caspar David Friedrich-Studien.* Wiesbaden: Franz Steiner, 1970.

Sutton, Thomas. *The Daniells, Artists and Travellers.* London: Bodley Head, 1954.

Taillemite, Etienne. *Bougainville et ses compagnons autour du monde, 1766–1769.* Two vols. Paris: Imprimerie Nationale, 1977.

Takeuchi, Toshio. "Die Schönheit des Unbelebten." In *Proceedings of the VIth International Congress of Aesthetics,* 1968. Edited by Rudolf Zeitler. Uppsala: Almquist and Wiksell, 1972.

Teyssèdre, Bernard. *Roger de Piles et les débats sur le coloris au siècle de Louis XIX.* Paris: Bibliothèque des Arts, 1957.

Thackray, Arnold. *Atoms and Powers: An Essay on Newtonian Matter-Theory and the Development of Chemistry.* Cambridge, Mass.: Harvard University Press, 1970.

Thalmann, Marianne. *Zeichensprache der Romantik.* Heidelberg: Stiehm, 1967.

Theurillat, Jacquelline. *Les mystères de Bomarzo et des jardins symboliques de la renaissance.* Geneva: Trois Anneaux, 1973.

Thielemann, Leland. "Diderot and Hobbes." *Diderot Studies* 2 (1952): 221–278.

Thompson, H. R. "The Geographical and Geological Observations of Bernard Palissy the Potter." *Annals of Science* 10 (June 1954): 149–165.

Thornes, John. "Constable's Clouds." *Burlington* 121 (November 1979): 697–704.

Todorov, Tzvetan. *The Fantastic: A Structural Approach to a Literary Genre.* Translated by Richard Howard. Cleveland: Press of Case Western Reserve University, 1973.

Tombo, Rudolf. *Ossian in Germany.* New York: AMS, 1966.

Toulmin, Stephen, and June Goodfield. *The Architecture of Matter.* New York: Harper & Row, 1962.

Trachtenberg, Marvin. "The Statue of Liberty: Transparent Banality or Avant-Garde Conundrum." *Art in America* 62 (May–June 1974): 36–42.

Traeger, Jörg. *Philipp Otto Runge und sein Werk. Monographie und kritischer Katalog.* Munich: Prestel, 1975.

Trimpi, Wesley. *Ben Jonson's Poems, A Study of the Plain Style.* Stanford, Calif.: Stanford University Press, 1962.

Trimpi, Wesley. "The Meaning of Horace's *ut pictura poesis.*" *Journal of the Warburg and Courtauld Institutes* 36 (1973): 1–34.

Trousson, Raymond. *Le thème de Prométhée dans la littérature éuropéene.* Two vols. in one. Geneva: Droz, 1964.

Tuan, Yi-Fu. *Topophilia. A Study of Environmental Perception, Attitudes, and Values.* Englewood Cliffs, N.J.: Prentice-Hall, 1974.

Tucker, Susie I. *Enthusiasm, A Study in Semantic Change.* Cambridge University Press, 1972.

Turner, A. Richard. *The Vision of Landscape in Renaissance Italy.* Princeton, N.J.: Princeton University Press, 1966.

Turner, James. "Landscape and the 'Art Prospective' in England, 1584–1660." *Journal of the Warburg and Courtauld Institutes* 42 (1979): 290–293.

Tuveson, Ernest Lee. *The Imagination as a Means of Grace. Locke and the Aesthetics of Romanticism.* Berkeley and Los Angeles: University of California Press, 1960.

Tuveson, Ernest Lee. "Space, Deity, and the 'Natural Sublime.' " *Modern Language Quarterly* 12 (1951): 20–38.

Twyman, Michael. *Lithography, 1800–1850.* London: Oxford University Press, 1970.

Van Gennep, Arnold. *The Rites of Passage.* Translated by Monika B. Vizedom and Gabrielle L. Caffee. University of Chicago Press, 1960.

Van Leeuwen, Henry G. *The Problem of Certainty in English Thought.* Second edition. The Hague: Martinus Nijhoff, 1970.

Van Luttervelt, R. *De "Turkse" Schilderijen van J. B. Vanmour en zijn School. De Verzameling van Cornelis Calkoen, Ambassadeur bij de Hoge Porte, 1725–1743.* Istanbul: Nederlands Historisch-Archaeologisch Instituut in het Nabije Oosten, 1958.

Van Tieghem, Paul. *L'Année Littéraire (1754–1790) comme intermediare en France des littératures étrangères.* Geneva: Slatkine Reprints, 1969.

Van Tieghem, Paul. *Le sentiment de la nature dans le préromantisme éuropéen.* Paris: A. G. Nizet, 1960.

Van Zanten, Ann Lorenz. "The Palace and the Temple: Two Utopian Architectural Visions of the 1830's." *Art History* 2 (June 1979): 179–200.

Vartanian, Aram. *Diderot and Descartes. A Study of Scientific Naturalism in the Enlightenment.* Princeton, N.J.: Princeton University Press, 1953.

Vartanian, Aram. "Trembley's Polyp, La Mettrie, and Eighteenth-Century French Materialism." In *Roots of Scientific Thought, A Cultural Perspective.* Edited by Philip P. Wiener and Aaron Noland. New York: Basic, 1957.

Viallaneix, Paul. "Chateaubriand voyageur." *Approches des Lumières. Mélanges offerts à Jean Fabre*. Paris: Klincksieck, 1974.

Viellard-Baron, J.-L. "Hemsterhuis, platonicien, 1721–1790." *Dix-Huitième Siècle* 7 (1975): 130–146.

Vietor, Karl. "De Sublimitate." *Harvard Studies and Notes in Philology and Literature* 19 (1937): 255–289.

Vinge, Louise. *The Narcissus Theme in Western European Literature up to the Early Nineteenth Century*. Lund: Gleerups, 1967.

Vogt, Adolf Max. *Boullées Newton-Denkmal. Sakralbau und Kugelidee*. Basel and Stuttgart: Birkhäuser, 1969.

Volkmann, Ludwig. "Die Hieroglyphen der Deutschen Romantiker." *Münchner Jahrbuch der Bildenden Kunst*, N.F., 3, no. 1 (1926).

Les Voyageurs naturalistes français de la Renaissance à la fin de l'ancien régime. XXI Semaine du laboratoire. Présentation philatelique. Paris: Ecole Technique Superieure du Laboratoire, 1966.

Voyages et découvertes au XVIIIᵉ siècle. Lille: Bibliothèque Municipale, 1973.

Walsh, Dorothy. "Some Functions of Pictorial Representation." *British Journal of Aesthetics* 21 (winter 1981): 32–38.

Wartofsky, Marx W. "Diderot and the Development of Materialistic Monism." *Diderot Studies* 2 (1952): 279–329.

Wasserman, Earl R. "Nature Moralized: The Divine Analogy in the Eighteenth Century." *ELH* 20 (March 1953): 39–76.

Watkin, David. *Thomas Hope (1769–1831) and the Neo-Classical Idea*. London: Murray, 1968.

Weber, Bruno. "Die Figur des Zeichners in der Landschaft." *Zeitschrift für Schweizerische Archaologie und Kunstgeschichte* 34, no. 1 (1977): 44–82.

Webster, Charles. *The Great Instauration. Science, Medicine and Reform, 1626–1660*. London: Duckworth, 1975.

Weisberg, Gabriel P. *The Realist Tradition: French Painting and Drawing 1830–1900*. Bloomington: University of Indiana Press, 1980.

Weise, Georg. "Vitalismo, animismo e panpsichismo e la decorazione nel cinquecento e nel seicento." *Critica d'Arte* 6 (November–December 1959): 375–398; 7 (March–April 1960): 85–96.

Weiskel, Thomas. *The Romantic Sublime: Studies in the Structure and Psychology of Transcendence*. Baltimore: Johns Hopkins University Press, 1976.

Wellek, Rene. *Concepts of Criticism*. Edited by Stephen G. Nichols, Jr. New Haven, Conn.: Yale University Press, 1963.

Werner, Abraham Gottlob, Gedenkschrift. Leipzig: UEB Deutscher Verlag für Grundstoffindustrie, 1967.

Werner, Thomas. "Zeichner der Admiralität." *Die Kunst* 93 (July 1981): 464–468.

West, Hugh Allen. From Tahiti to Terror: Georg Forster, the Literature of Travel, and Social Thought in the Late Eighteenth Century. Ph.D. diss., Stanford University, 1980.

Weydt, Günter. *Naturschilderung bei Annette von Dröste-Hulshoff und Adalbert Stifter*. Berlin: Emil Ebering, 1930.

Wheelock, Arthur K., Jr. *Perspective, Optics, and Delft Artists around 1650.* New York: Garland, 1977.

White, Hayden. *Metahistory: The Historical Imagination in Nineteenth-Century Europe.* Baltimore: Johns Hopkins University Press, 1973.

White, Hayden. *Tropics of Discourse: Essays in Cultural Criticism.* Baltimore: Johns Hopkins University Press, 1978.

Whiteley, J. J. L. "Light and Shade in French Neo-Classicism." *Burlington* 117 (December 1975): 768–773.

Whitfield, Clovis. "Nicolas Poussin's 'l'Orage' and 'Temps calme.' " *Burlington* 119 (January 1977): 4–12.

Wiebenson, Dora. " 'l'Architecture terrible' and the 'Jardin anglo-chinois.' " *Journal of the Society of Architectural Historians* 27 (May 1968): 136–139.

Wiebenson, Dora. *The Picturesque Garden in France.* Princeton, N.J.: Princeton University Press, 1978.

Wiebenson, Dora. *Sources of Greek Revival Architecture.* University Park: Pennsylvania State University Press, 1969.

Wiener, Philip P., and Aaron Noland, eds. *Roots of Scientific Thought: A Cultural Perspective.* New York: Basic, 1957.

Wiles, Bertha Harris. *The Fountains of Florentine Sculptors and Their Followers from Donatello to Bernini.* Cambridge, Mass.: Harvard University Press, 1933.

Wilhelmy, Herbert. *Geographische Forschungen in Südamerika. Ausgewählte Beiträge.* Edited by Hanno Beck. Berlin: Dietrich Riemer, 1979.

Willey, Basil. *Samuel Taylor Coleridge.* New York: Norton, 1977.

Williams, Iolo A. *Early English Watercolours and Some Cognate Drawings by Artists Born Not Later than 1785.* London: The Connoisseur, 1952.

Williams, L. Pearce. "Science, Education and the French Revolution." *Isis* 44 (December 1953): 311–330.

Williams, Raymond. *The Country and the City.* London: Chatto & Windus, 1973.

Williamson, George. *The Senecan Amble: A Study in Prose Form from Bacon to Collier.* University of Chicago Press, 1951.

Williamson, George. " 'Strong Lines.' " *English Studies* 18 (August 1936): 152–159.

Wilmerding, John. *American Light: The Luminist Movement, 1850–1875. Paintings, Drawings, Photographs.* New York: Harper & Row, 1980

Wilson, Harold S. "Some Meanings of 'Nature' in Renaissance Literary Theory." *Journal of the History of Ideas* 2 (October 1941): 430–438.

Wilton, Andrew. *Turner and the Sublime.* London: British Museum, 1980.

Wilton-Ely, John. *The Mind and Art of Giovanni Battista Piranesi.* London: Thames and Hudson, 1978.

Wimsatt, W. K. *The Verbal Icon: Studies in the Meaning of Poetry.* Lexington: University of Kentucky Press, 1954.

Winkelmann, Heinrich. *Der Bergbau in der Kunst.* Essen: Gluckauf, 1958.

Wirth, Alberto. "Kandinsky and the Science of Art." *British Journal of Aesthetics* 19 (autumn 1979): 361–365.

Wittkower, Rudolph. *Allegory and the Migration of Symbols.* London: Thames and Hudson, 1977.

Woodbridge, Kenneth. *Landscape and Antiquity, Aspects of English Culture at Stourhead 1718 to 1838.* Oxford: Clarendon, 1970.

Woodfield, Richard. "Thomas Hobbes and the Formation of Aesthetics in England." *British Journal of Aesthetics* 20 (spring 1980): 146–152.

Woolfe, Harry. *The Transits of Venus: A Study of Eighteenth-Century Science.* Princeton, N.J.: Princeton University Press, 1959.

Worrall, David. "Blake's Derbyshire: A Visionary Locale in *Jerusalem.*" *Blake* 9 (summer 1977): 34–35.

Wright, C. J. "The 'Spectre' of Science. The Study of Optical Phenomena and the Romantic Imagination." *Journal of the Warburg and Courtauld Institutes* 43 (1980): 186–200.

Yolton, John W. "As in a Looking Glass: Perceptual Acquaintance in Eighteenth-Century Britain." *Journal of the History of Ideas* 40 (April–June 1979): 207–234.

Yolton, John W. " Locke and Malebranche: Two Concepts of Ideas." *John Locke Symposium, Wolfenbüttel.* Edited by Reinhard Brandt. Berlin and New York: Walter de Gruyter, 1981.

Zobel, M. *Les naturalistes voyageurs et les grands voyages maritimes au XVIIIe et XIXe siècles.* Paris: Presses Universitaires, 1961.

Zucker, Paul. *Fascination of Decay: Ruins: Relic-Symbol-Ornament.* Ridgewood, N.J.: Gregg, n.d.

Zucker, Paul. "Ruins—An Aesthetic Hybrid." *Journal of Aesthetics and Art Criticism* 20 (winter 1961): 119–130.

Zweig, Paul. *The Adventurer.* London: J. M. Dent & Sons, 1974.

Index

Abel, Clark, 69
Aberli, Johann Ludwig, 265
Académie des Sciences, 36, 41, 63–64, 132, 325, 447, 484, 485
Acerbi, Joseph, 46, 83, 147, 360
Adams, George, 11, 331
Adanson, Michel, 46, 125, 274–278
Addison, Joseph, 4, 361, 408, 413, 414
  on art versus nature, 8
  on primary and secondary pleasures, 33, 39
  Spectator, 33, 154, 201–202, 391
Africa, exploration of, 156–162, 327, 333–336
Agrippa, Cornelius, 194, 288
Air, theories of, 190–194, 196–197, 205, 351–352, 360–361. *See also* Vapors
Alberti, Leon Battista, 8, 191, 301, 424
Alchemy, 16, 53, 194, 361
Alexander the Great, 15, 173
Alexander, William, 80–83, 105–109, 128, 237, 368, 430
Allan, Sir Alexander, 96
Almanach des Muses, 390–391
Alps, 46, 54, 89–91, 93, 226, 242, 272, 300, 315, 360, 362, 368, 449, 460, 478, 480, 481
Altdorfer, Albrecht, 13
Altmann, Johann Georg, 89
Ammanati, Bartolommeo, 13
Anamorphic games, 287, 424
Anburey, Thomas, 116
Andes, 92–93, 109–112, 151–154, 327, 386, 407
Annesley, George, 162
Anson, George, Baron, 69, 80, 336–338, 422
Antiparos, Grotto of, 116, 294, 354
Apelles, 16, 203, 204
Aphorism, 307–310
Apocalyptics, 462
Apuleius, 292
Arago, François, 483
Arago, J. E. V., 46, 133, 338, 350, 378, 381, 422–423

Architecture. *See also* Ruins
  colossal, 10, 59
  nature versus, 9, 10, 12, 15
  Ruskin on, 479–481
  Schopenhauer on, 457
  Utopian, 459
Aristotle, 31, 40, 293
  literary theory of, 45–47, 425
  on matter, 65, 206
Arndt, Ernst Moritz, 215
Arnold, Matthew, 44
Artemidorus, 312
Associationism, 2–5, 8–9, 38, 409
Atlantis, 255
Auerbach, Erich, 34, 352
Augustans, 8, 12, 37, 44, 425
Augustine, Saint, 240, 284, 402
Auroras, 40–41, 223, 226–231, 367, 410–412, 461
Ausonius, 203–204
Avalanches, 197, 242, 265–272, 462

Baader, Franz von, 450
Bachelard, Gaston, 401
Back, George, 226–227, 331
Bacon, Francis, 59, 185, 381–384, 386–387, 402, 423, 439, 443, 445, 471
  Advancement of Learning, 37, 307, 310, 438
  and discovery, 22
  and language, 51, 307, 310, 446
  method of, 31–32, 37–55 passim, 283–285, 395
  Novum organum, 31, 37, 437
Bailly, Jean-Sylvain, 28, 321, 326, 386–387, 402
Baldwin, Thomas, 149, 222–223, 363, 369, 394, 405, 418, 423, 434
Balloon voyages, 53, 385
  and discovery, 22–25
  and fugitive effect, 190, 219–223, 463, 464
  instruments used in, 426–428
  land viewed in, 149
  and "new Icarus," 390–394

Gaimard, Paul, 262, 368
Galileo, 387
Gama, Vasco da, 24–25, 105
Gardiner, Allen, 163
Garnerin, Jacques, 230, 328, 406, 435, 466
Gautier, Théophile, 452
Gay-Lussac, Jean-Louis, 24, 222, 391
Genius, idea of, 20, 36, 41–42, 381–384, 402, 413, 450
George III of England, 20, 52, 385
Gerard, Alexander, 321, 402
Gérôme, Jean-Léon, 475–476
Geysers, 237–240, 329, 377, 406
Ghauts, 96–101
Ghosts, 200–203
Gian da Bologna, 13
Giant's Causeway, 72, 151, 285
Giardina, Domenico, 280
Gibbon, Edward, 54, 442
Gibraltar, 112
Gilpin, William, 3, 5
Girodet-Trioson, Anne-Louis, 464–466
Girtin, Thomas, 460
Glaciers, 197, 264–272, 368, 375, 404, 406, 420
Gmelins, Samuel Georg, 318, 367
Goethe, Johann Wolfgang von, 10, 33, 34, 53, 139, 200, 212, 254, 290, 314, 322, 452–453, 455
  and balloon flight, 385, 394
  empiricism of, 31, 46
  and mountains, 46, 360
Gold, Charles, 96, 163, 173–174, 416
Gordale Scar, 418
Graham, Maria, 150, 176, 207, 407
Grandpré, Louis O'Hier de, 167, 235, 335
Grand Tour, 4, 12, 28, 387, 482
Gravitation, 62, 186, 188, 189, 195, 203, 287, 394
Great Barrier Reef, 151
Great Dismal Swamp, 172
Great Geyser, 237, 377, 406
Greece, 8, 15, 16, 31, 311, 473
Grimm, Jakob, 138
Grindelwald Glacier, 315, 404

Grindlay, Robert, 96, 116, 210, 236, 407, 412
Grose, John Henry, 80, 215
Grottos. *See* Caves and caverns
Gruner, Gottlieb Siegmund, 89, 264, 375
Guardi, Francesco, 200, 204, 427
Guardi, Giovanni Antonio, 16
Guibert, Jacques-Antoine Hippolyte de, 360
Guilbert de Pixérécourt, René-Charles, 461

Hakewell, James, 322–324, 433
Hall, Basil, 241
Haller, Albrecht von, 89, 242, 362, 432
Halley, Edmund, 331
Hamilton, Francis, 150, 336
Hamilton, Sir William, 9, 60, 105, 139, 245, 249–254, 305, 329–330, 403, 407, 415, 421, 428
Hardy, Joseph, 3
Hartley, David, 195, 474
Hausmann, Johann Friedrich Ludwig, 215
Havell, Robert, 101
Havell, William, 241
Hawkesworth, John, 20, 381
Haze. *See* Vapors
Hazlitt, William, 453, 466–467
Heade, Martin, 470
Hearne, Samuel, 25, 338
Hearne, Thomas, 460
Heine, Heinrich, 452–453
Heinse, Johann Jakob Wilhelm, 10
Helvétius, Claude-Adrien, 381–384
Hemsterhuis, François, 194
Henckel, Johann Friedrich, 293, 341
Hennepin, Louis, 244
Heraclitus, 188, 194, 197, 401
Herder, Johann Gottfried von, 61, 195, 321, 457
Heriot, George, 45, 176, 244, 374, 375, 386, 390, 420
Herodotus, 28
Herschel, William, 226, 231, 240, 321, 428
Hesiod, 289
Hieroglyphs and heiroglyphics
  curiologic, 311–313

Egyptian, 49, 310–312
  natural, 284–286, 305, 321
Higgins, Godfrey, 139
Hildebrandt, Eduard, 167
Hilleström, Pehr, 124
Himalayas, 101–105, 241
Hippocrates, 191, 201
Hirschfeld, C. C. L., 362
History
  Aristotle on, 45
  use of term, 53–54
Hobbes, Thomas, 4, 31, 185, 196, 201–202
  Leviathan, 438
Hobhouse, J. C., 150, 418
Hodges, William, 52, 72, 96, 116, 162, 167–173, 218–219, 241, 264, 274, 385, 416, 463
Hogarth, William, 315
Homer, 34
  Odyssey, 384
Horace, 8, 28, 425, 426
Hornemann, Friedrich, 160
Houel, Jean, 10, 73, 124, 176, 215, 254, 330, 333, 341, 403, 412, 431
Howard, Luke, 466
Hugh of Saint Victor, 37, 284
Hugo, Victor, 93, 395, 454
Humanism, 29–35, 37, 352
Humboldt, Alexander von, 43, 73, 80, 92–93, 109, 116, 132, 147, 151–154, 162, 182, 207, 255, 290, 305, 327, 362, 366, 389–390, 394, 455
  Geographie der Pflanzen, 167
  on language, 49
  Relation historique, 93
Hume, David, 54, 185, 284, 347, 409, 439
  Treatise of Human Nature, 348
Humoral theory, 201–202, 401
Hutcheson, Francis, 4, 321–322, 408
Hutton, James, 286–287, 301
Hylozoism, 60–65, 186, 190, 194–195, 338–339, 357, 438, 456

Icebergs, 272–274, 330–331, 406
Idealism, 60, 65, 188

Schelling, Friedrich, 450, 452
Scheuchzer, Johann Jacob, 89, 292–293, 432
Schiller, Friedrich von, 361
Schlegel, A. W., 314
Schmidtmeyer, Peter, 237
Schopenhauer, Arthur, 402, 457
Schubert, Gotthilf Heinrich, 314, 318, 454–455
Scientific gaze, defined, 31–34, 40
Scientific method, 31, 34, 426, 448, 473, 475
Scoresby, William, 207, 218, 272, 375–377, 404
Sea, 176, 182–183, 240–242, 318, 331–333, 344, 355–356, 375, 405–406, 433, 463
Senancour, Étienne Pivert de, 242, 400–401
Seneca, 289, 292, 357
Sergel, Tobias, 202
Sexual imagery, 357–361
Shaftesbury, Anthony Ashley Cooper, Earl of, 1, 9–10, 62, 189, 290, 361, 390, 408
Shakespeare, William, 285, 352
Sharpe, William, 384
Shelley, Mary, 320, 347, 453
Shelley, Percy, 462, 467
  Defence of Poetry, 450
Sherwill, Markham, 375
Shintoism, 7
Signatures, doctrine of, 287–288
Silence, in travel accounts, 367–379
Simultaneity, in experiencing, 413–421
Sismonde de Sismondi, L. C. L., 400
Skepticism, 38, 284, 348, 438–439, 442
Skjöldebrand, Anders, 231, 242, 380, 420
Smith, Robert, 83
Soane, Joan, 460, 462
Social Darwinians, 471
Solander, Daniel, 43–44
Solitude, in travel accounts, 361–367, 378–379
Sonnini, C. S., 443
Sophists, 188
Space

absolute, and Newton, 186
contiguity in, 403, 421–423
metaphors of, 353
penetration in, 318–321
perspective in, 399, 423–435
social replacing physical, 471–472
Sparrman, Andrew, 21, 33–34, 43–44, 47, 56, 255, 332, 336, 380
Spinoza, Benedict de, 39, 61, 62, 194, 451
Spon, Jacob, 28
Spöring, H. D., 43–44, 73
Sports of nature (ludi), 9, 12, 15, 292, 294–299, 301, 306
Sprat, Thomas, 35–37, 283, 307, 447
Stahl, Georg Ernst, 191
Stanyon, Abraham, 89
Staubbach waterfall, 210–214, 242, 329, 374
Staunton, George, 83
Stedman, J. G., 378
Stendhal, 449–450, 459
Sterne, Lawrence, 305
Stevens, Peter, 13
Stewart, John ("Walking"), 187, 189
Stifter, Adalbert, 476–478
Stoics, 60, 89, 290, 292, 423
Stolberg, Graf, 46
Stonehenge, 59, 129
Storms, 241
Strabo, 28, 154, 194, 425
Strato Lampsacenus, 60
Stromboli, 191, 254, 403
Stukeley, William, 139, 460
Sublime, idea of, 348, 353, 360
Sudden, apprehension of, 408–413
Suffering, in travel accounts, 387–390
Suger of Saint-Denis, 65
Sulzer, Johann Georg, 272, 292–293
Swammerdam, Jan, 295
Swamps, 172
Swinburne, Henry, 249

Table Mountain, 109, 218–219, 377, 380, 415
Tahiti, 129, 132, 166, 235, 326, 337, 355, 408, 412

Taine, Hippolyte, 473
Talbot, William Henry Fox, 440
Taoism, 7, 64, 68, 210
Taylor, Isidore-Justin-Séverin, Baron, 92
Tedium, in travel accounts, 350
Telescope, 36, 226, 231, 424, 426–430, 432, 433, 434
Temple, Edmond, 150, 416
Teneriffe, Peak of, 105, 218, 255
Terni cataract, 210
Testu-Brissy, Pierre, 369–374
Thales, 7–8, 61, 293
Theophrastus, 294
Thompson, George, 380
Thomson, James, 46, 200
Thoreau, Henry David, 470
Thorn, William, 42, 223, 236, 404
Tiepolo, Giovanni Battista, 200
Time, 400–421
Toeput, Lodewijk, 6
Topiary, 4
Topography, 16–17
Töppfer, Rodolfe, 457–458, 482–484
Torelli, Giacomo, 6
Torre, Giovanni Maria della, 215
Tournefort, Joseph Pitton de, 33, 112, 294, 325–327, 353–354, 366
Tramentum, 198
Trembley, Abraham, 299
Trimpi, Wesley, 425
Tuckey, J. K., 72, 335, 380, 386, 413
Turner, James Mallord William, 391, 427, 454, 460, 462, 464, 466–470
Turner, Samuel, 101, 338
Tussaud, Madame, 470
Twickenham grotto, 3, 6, 112

Universal character, 35, 307–314, 448

Valckenborch, Lucas van, 13
Valenciennes, Pierre-Henri, 5, 46, 205, 240, 244, 249, 385, 421–422, 449
  Elements de perspective, 196–197
Valentia, George, Viscount, 96, 109, 245, 336, 374–375

VOYAGE INTO SUBSTANCE